HANDBOOK OF RESEARCH ON COMPETITIVE STRATEGY

Handbook of Research on Competitive Strategy

Edited by

Giovanni Battista Dagnino

University of Catania, Italy

Edward Elgar
Cheltenham, UK • Northampton, MA, USA

Published by
Edward Elgar Publishing Limited
The Lypiatts
15 Lansdown Road
Cheltenham
Glos GL50 2JA
UK

Edward Elgar Publishing, Inc.
William Pratt House
9 Dewey Court
Northampton
Massachusetts 01060
USA

A catalogue record for this book
is available from the British Library

Library of Congress Control Number: 2011934958

MIX
Paper from
responsible sources
FSC
www.fsc.org
FSC® C018575

ISBN 978 1 84720 044 0 (cased)

Typeset by Servis Filmsetting Ltd, Stockport, Cheshire
Printed and bound by MPG Books Group, UK

Contents

Contributors

Asli Arikan
Visiting Assistant Professor of Management and Human Resources, Max
M. Fisher College of Business
Ohio State University
arikan_1@fisher.osu.edu

Africa Ariño
Professor of General Management and Academic Director of Anselmo
Rubiralta Research Center on Globalization and Strategy
IESE Business School
afarino@iese.edu

Jay B. Barney
Professor of Management and Chase Chair for Excellence in Corporate
Strategy, Max M. Fisher College of Business
Ohio State University
barney_8@cob.osu.edu

Joel A.C. Baum
Professor of Strategy and Organization and Canadian National Chair in
Strategic Management, Rotman School of Business
University of Toronto
baum@rotman.utoronto.ca

Arturo Capasso
Professor of Corporate Governance
Director of the Economics and Management Program
University of Sannio at Benevento
capasso@unisannio.it

Ramon Casadesus-Masanell
Professor of Business Administration
Harvard Business School
rmasanell@hbs.edu

Bruno Cassiman
Professor of Economics and Strategy, IESE Business School
Senior Researcher at the Center for R&D and Innovation Policy

University of Leuven
bcassiman@iese.edu

Sandro Castaldo
Professor of Marketing Management
Bocconi University
sandro.castaldo@sda-bocconi.it

Asda Chintakananda
Assistant Professor
Nanyang Technological University, Singapore
ASDA@ntu.edu.sg

Maria Cristina Cinici
Assistant Professor of Management
University of Messina
mcinici@unime.it

Giorgia M. D'Allura
Assistant Professor of Business Economics and Management
University of Catania
gdallura@unict.it

Giovanni Battista Dagnino
Deputy Chair and Professor, Department of Business Economics and Management
University of Catania
dagnino@unict.it

Elena Dalpiaz
Assistant Professor in Strategy
Imperial College Business School
e.dalpiaz@imperial.ac.uk

Valentina Della Corte
Associate Professor of Business Economics and Management
University of Naples
vdellaco@unina.it

Maria Chiara Di Guardo
Associate Professor of Management and Organization
University of Cagliari
cdguardo@unica.it

Roger L.M. Dunbar
Professor of Management
New York University
rdunbar@stern.nyu.edu

Rosario Faraci
Professor of Business Economics and Management
University of Catania
faraci@unict.it

Simone Ferriani
Associate Professor of Business Economics and Management
University of Bologna
Fellow, Cambridge University
ferriani@economia.unibo.it

Igor Filatotchev
Professor of Corporate Governance and Strategy
City University London
Igor.filatotchev@city.ac.uk

Nicolai J. Foss
Professor of Strategy and Head of Department of Strategic Management
and Globalization
Copenhagen Business School
Professor of Knowledge-based Value Creation, Department of Strategy
and Leadership
Norwegian School of Economics
njf.smg@cbs.dk; nicolai.foss@nhh.no

Esteban García-Canal
Professor of Organization and Management
University of Oviedo
egarcia@uniovi.es

Francesco Garraffo
Associate Professor of Business Economics and Management
University of Catania
garraffo@unict.it

Antonio Giuliani
Assistant Professor in Entrepreneurship
University of Illinois at Chicago
agiulia2@uic.edu

Henrich R. Greve
Professor of Entrepreneurship and Organizational Behaviour
The INSEAD Chaired Professor of Organization and Management
Theory
INSEAD
henrich.greve@bi.no

J. Richard Harrison
Associate Professor of Organizations, Strategy and International
Management
University of Texas at Dallas
harrison@utdallas.edu

Michael A. Hitt
Distinguished Professor and Joe B. Foster Chair in Business Leadership,
C.W. and Dorothy Conn Chair in New Ventures
Texas A&M University
mhitt@cgsb.tamu.edu

Elvira Tiziana La Rocca
Assistant Professor of Business Economics and Management
University of Messina
tlarocca@unime.it

Maurizio La Rocca
Associate Professor of Business Economics and Management
University of Calabria
m.larocca@unical.it

Gwendolyn Lee
William R. Hough Faculty Fellow
University of Florida
gwendolyn.lee@warrington.ufl.edu

Constantinos Markides
Robert P. Bauman Chair in Strategic Leadership
Professor, Strategy and Entrepreneurship
London Business School
cmarkides@london.edu

Olimpia Meglio
Assistant Professor of Management
University of Sannio at Benevento
meglio@unisannio.it

Alessandro Minichilli
Assistant Professor of Management
Bocconi University
alessandro.minichilli@unibocconi.it

Giovanna Padula
Associate Professor of Management
Bocconi University
giovanna.padula@uni-bocconi.it

Vincenzo Pisano
Assistant Professor of Business Economics and Management
University of Catania
vpisano@unict.it

Katia Premazzi
Assistant Professor of Management
Bocconi University
katia.premazzi@unibocconi.it

Roberto Ragozzino
Assistant Professor
University of Texas at Dallas
rragozzino@utdallas.edu

Rhonda K. Reger
Associate Professor and Co-chair Management and
Organization Department
University of Maryland
rreger@rhsmith.umd.edu

Patrick Regnér
Associate Professor of Management
Stockholm School of Economics
patrick.regner@hhs.se

Jeffrey J. Reuer
Blake Family Endowed Chair in Strategic Management and Governance
Purdue University
jreuer@purdue.edu

Joan E. Ricart
Carl Schroeder Professor of Strategic Management
Chairman, Strategic Management Department
IESE Business School
ricart@iese.edu

Violina P. Rindova
Ralph B. Thomas Professor in Business
University of Texas at Austin
violina.rindova@mccombs.utexas.edu

Grazia D. Santangelo
Professor of Economics
University of Catania
grsanta@unict.it

Mauro Sciarelli
Professor of Management
University of Naples
msciarel@unina.it

Wei Shen
Associate Professor of Management
Arizona State University
wei.shen@cba.ufl.edu

Mario Sorrentino
Professor of Entrepreneurship and Business Planning
Second University of Naples
mario.sorrentino@unina2.it

Christian Stadler
Associate Professor of Strategic Management
Warwick Business School
christian.stadler@wbs.ac.at

Gordon Walker
Professor and Chair of the Department of Strategy and Entrepreneurship
Southern Methodist University
gwalker@mail.cox.smu.edu

Acknowledgements

At the end of this almost quadrennial editorial endeavor, I wish to thank all the contributors. They have generously devoted their scholarship and wisdom to detect the conceptual and empirical advancements and assess the promises and practical relevance of the competitive strategy domain. I feel extremely grateful to all of them because, after enthusiastically accepting to contribute to the *Handbook of Research on Competitive Strategy*, they responded rapidly and effectively when I requested multiple changes in and additions to the successive drafts of their chapters so as to turn this book's editorial endeavor into a reality. I owe them a lot for this reason, and because they have indulgently waited for the editor to complete his editorial task.

Anna Minà and Massimo Picone have kindly helped me out with the task of collecting and formatting a few chapters to turn out the full manuscript. My gratitude goes to a few people at Edward Elgar Publishing in Cheltenham who have assisted me in navigating the rough waters of turning this book from a lovely idea into a project and eventually into a real solid physical object. Francine O'Sullivan who, as early as 2007, took the initiative and advanced the proposal to take care of assembling the *Handbook* to the present editor who, at that time, was pretty reluctant to take on a novel editorial challenge that evidently required significant time and energy. Jo Betteridge and Jenny Wilcox, who have accompanied the successive preparation steps of the *Handbook* with care, grace and patience, deserve particular mention.

I wish to express special appreciation to all my colleagues in the Department of Business Economics and Management at the University of Catania, who have always given the greatest importance to the elaboration of this book, escorting it since its inception and along its formation and developmental process. In a way, now that the *Handbook* has finally managed to surface and see the light, I honestly recognize that much of it is due to the affection and dedication that the management faculty and PhDs of the University of Catania have decided to confer to it. Six of them have constantly granted their support to the advancement of this endeavor: Carmelo Buttà, the Dean of the School of Economics and Business, Maria Cristina Cinici (now at Messina), Giorgia D'Allura, Rosario Faraci, Francesco Garraffo and Vincenzo Pisano. My home institution, the University of Catania, also deserves recognition for providing generous support for my travel around conferences, workshops and seminars across Europe, South America, and the US, where the *Handbook* was envisaged and carefully cultivated. I also wish to thank Rich D'Aveni, Bob Hansen and their colleagues at the Tuck School of Business at Dartmouth, who have kindly provided me with a good cocktail of the requisite psychological and financial support in the pleasant autumnal New England atmosphere. I am grateful to Roberto Vassolo and the other faculty members at IAE Business School, Universidad Austral, who supplied, in a relaxing wintertime Buenos Aires, the critical encouragement required for finalizing the demanding editorial tasks related to this book.

Last but not least, I owe so much to Arabella, my other half, for buttressing me, sympathetically and constantly, in all of the *Handbook*'s preparatory stages. For these reasons, this volume is lovingly dedicated to her.

Giovanni Battista Dagnino

1 Introduction: why a handbook of research on competitive strategy?
Giovanni Battista Dagnino

In this introductory essay, I first wish to draw the reader's attention to the four most relevant reasons that have initially inspired the publisher, Edward Elgar, and the present editor to take steps towards assembling and publishing a *Handbook of Research on Competitive Strategy*. Second, I shall explain how and why the competitive strategy approach has rapidly become a subfield of strategy and the different theories that currently exist on the subject. Third, I shall speculate on the emergence, persistence and shortcomings of a so-called 'competitive strategy mindset' and finally outline the structure of the handbook. As the reader may expect, any handbook is an opportunity to encapsulate in one comprehensive volume the state of a research field and ruminate on its current development. As it may be read in Wikipedia:[1]

> A handbook is a type of reference work, small manual, or other collection of instructions, that is intended to provide ready reference. A vade mecum (Lat. 'go with me') or pocket reference is intended to be carried at all times. Handbooks may deal with any topic, and are generally compendiums of information in a particular field or about a particular technique. They are designed to be easily consulted and provide quick answers in a certain area.

For this reason, handbooks are usually published when a research field has grown too large to master easily through the study of journals and books, so they appear when the contributors of the field are ready to celebrate progress. In this view, a handbook is nothing but a last-ditch commemorative monument erected in memory of the efforts already made by others. In a way this handbook is no exception, because competitive strategy is a subfield of the strategy arena that has grown quickly and accumulated several strong branches of research organized around specific theories and applications, as many of the chapters in this collection will show. Uniquely, this handbook also summarizes the state of the art in the field, and thus some of its most established research traditions. However, this handbook also follows a different strategy since it also tries to uncover and shed light on a variety of smaller branches and twigs that are hidden among the major branches of competitive strategy research and that claim larger relevance in strategy inquiry. That is why I chose to baptize the fifth and last part of the volume 'Competitive Strategy at the Intersection between Research and Practice: A Look into the Future'. This is perhaps the most remarkable contribution that, collectively, the authors of this book have chosen to make towards strategic management investigation and the broad business community. Because, by doing so, they have supplied the reader with a number of signposts and tips that need to be developed, matured and turned into conceptual approaches and managerial advice in the years to come.

This handbook appears inspiring and thought-provoking to those who are genuinely interested in fast-developing strategy dynamics since it marshals a notable assortment of conceptual lenses (i.e. the resource-based theory, the network perspective, the social-cognitive perspective, the competitive dynamics view and the strategy-as-practice view), fresh themes (i.e. governance, entrepreneurship, family business, multinational enterprises, strategic alliances, innovation and technology management and M&As), cutting-edge methodological perspectives (i.e. quantitative methods, semiotic analysis and computer simulation modeling), and eventually looks at new strategic intersections (i.e. business-model competition, trust-based strategies, the bridge between finance and strategy, the relationship between ownership structure and strategy, coopetition strategy and impact on business practice) that prove to be increasingly important to today's informed students, managers and thriving companies.

The handbook is the outcome of the collective effort of 47 scholars who operate in the strategy domain. We are pleased to proclaim that some of the best-minded and much-acclaimed thought gurus of strategic management have kindly accepted to contribute to the volume. This, however, is not the topical feature of this endeavor. Since in crafting and delivering their chapters our most authoritative intellectual leaders have, in many cases, decided to interact with more greenhorn and ascending scholars, overall the volume is the product of a set of contributions from an excellent mix of senior, mid-career and junior researchers. For its breadth and depth and for its 25 original contributions (other than this introductory essay), the book aims to provide executives, entrepreneurs, students and scholars in management a myriad of lively and captivating insights on the nature and process of strategy formation, configuration and development.

COMPETITIVE STRATEGY AS A RESEARCH FIELD IN STRATEGIC MANAGEMENT

In recent years, competitive strategy has taken center stage in discussions of strategic management. This contention is corroborated, on one hand by the extensive and increasing number of articles, books, and textbooks on this theme that have cumulated (and are cumulating) over time and, on the other, by the upspring of a large quantity of courses and cases dedicated to competitive strategy in universities and business schools throughout the world. This is also testified by the inauguration, in 2004, of a highly attended Interest Group, labeled 'Competition Strategy', within the sphere of the Strategic Management Society, currently the world's major congregation of academics and practitioners in strategic management. In addition, when asked to position themselves, many strategy scholars and researchers would have no doubt identifying themselves immediately as scholars of competitive strategy. This state of affairs becomes apparent by reading a number of researchers' curricula vitae in which it is possible to find the major research interests they cover. Finally, in some universities and business schools, the academic group or faculty area concerned with strategic management is usually named 'competitive strategy'. The condition that reveals the soundest recognition of competitive strategy as a subfield of study within strategic management, and the concurrent identification of a competitive strategy scientific community, is consistent with sociology of science predicaments that science proceeds by the succession of generations of scientists. Kuhn's (1970) point was that 'community assent', rather than 'canons of reason', is often the final arbiter in whether a new paradigm or a theory affirms over the old one.

To be sure, the circumstance that competitive strategy is connected today to the very heart of strategic management, intended as an academic discipline as well as a practitioner domain, comes as no surprise. First, competitive strategy constitutes the foundational nucleus around which strategic management has developed in the last decades since its inception in the early 1980s.[2] In fact, absent of a strategy curriculum at the PhD level, the majority of early strategic management scholars had academic backgrounds in industrial organization and applied economics. Given their background, they were almost naturally driven to bring post-Marshallian economics, competition research and the Mason-Bain Structure-Conduct Performance paradigm industry analysis into the newly-born field of strategic management (Porter, 1981; Rumelt, Schendel and Teece, 1991; Foss, 1996). Second, when anyone interested in management and strategy (e.g. an MBA student, a business executive, a consultant or an entrepreneur) hears or reads of 'competitive strategy', he or she immediately credits a connotation to it, since he or she has a rather mechanical and lucid idea of what it is. This condition is the result of a pathway that the phrase's use has traced across time and space and in standard textbooks (e.g. Porter, 1980; Kay, 1993; Ghemawat and Rivkin, 1999; Saloner, Shepard and Podolny, 2001; Barney, 2002; Thompson et al., 2011; Hitt, Ireland and Hoskisson,

2011) since the early 1980s. In fact, in order to activate the process of *path recognition*, the recognizer is to be equipped ex ante for the recognition of the word's significance and its significance path (Dagnino and Rocco, 2009). Third, professional consultants in strategy have contributed by generating, adopting, and widely applying an entire kit of rough-and-ready analytical tools (such as the SWOT analysis, the BCG and GE-McKinsey matrixes, the five forces framework, and the value chain model) that are today the familiar paraphernalia and, hence, the consultant standard equipment in competitive strategy practical breakdown. Fourth, for the reasons above, starting in the early 1990s – roughly speaking from the publication of Porter's third book *The Competitive Advantage of Nations* (1990) – the use of competitive strategy has also managed to trespass the original realm of strategic management to affect other fields of inquiry, such as marketing, industrial and regional economics, economic geography, business and economic history and international affairs. Based on these considerations, it is possible to confirm that competitive strategy is nowadays one of the essential components of the inner circle or mainstream in strategic management.

Competitive Strategy Definition

Notwithstanding these evolutions, we still lack a definite unambiguous understanding of the meaning of 'competitive strategy'. Statements about competitive strategy abound, ranging from strategy, to marketing, to regional economics and economic geography to international affairs, but a precise definition is elusive.[3]

In reviewing the use of the term competitive strategy in the literature, the common theme is how to achieve a *competitive advantage* in a typical and unique way. In Michael Porter's (1980) initial view, competitive strategy refers to how a company competes in a particular business. Competitive strategy is concerned with how a company can gain a competitive advantage through a distinctive way of competing. In his landmark book, *Competitive Strategy* (1980), Porter identifies four fundamental competitive strategies (cost leadership, differentiation, focus on cost and focus on differentiation, eventually developed in a more sophisticated way in his 1985 book on *Competitive Advantage*) and lays out the required skills and assets, organizational elements and risks associated with each strategy.

Competitive advantage results from a firm's ability to perform the required activities at a collectively lower cost than rivals or to perform the same activities in unique ways that create greater value for buyers and hence allow the firm to command a premium price. Pursuing one of these advantages will make a firm's product or service unique, and is strongly

Source: Adaptation from Porter, 1980; 1985.

Figure 1.1 Five generic strategies

suggested so that the firm is not "stuck in the middle" (Porter, 1980: 40); a position where, by pursuing both competitive advantages, neither one is achieved.

More recently, some authors (Flynn and Flynn, 1996; D'Aveni, 2010; Grant, 2010) have criticized the idea that cost and differentiation strategies are actually self-excluding by purporting that they are all but incompatible.[4] An *integrated* cost leadership-differentiation strategy is a *hybrid* strategy chasing the lower or lowest cost and product differentiation concurrently. Various benefits may be associated with effectively pursuing cost leadership and differentiation strategies simultaneously. While differentiation allows a firm to charge a premium price, cost leadership makes it possible to charge the lowest price. Hence, the firm may be capable of achieving a competitive advantage by delivering value to customers based on both product features and low price. In this way, the classic generic strategies become five instead of four (see Figure 1.1).[5]

We second Porter's basic idea that an economic organization's competitive strategy is tightly related to the accomplishment of a 'competitive advantage'. However, as we have observed in the case of competitive strategy, there is not yet much agreement on the issue of to whom and when comparative advantage accrues. Consequently, in the two following subsections we shall discuss first the 'elusive' nature of the competitive advantage concept and then the essence of dynamic competitive advantages.

Competitive Advantage

Since there is no unanimous consensus on the meaning of the concept, scholarly views of competitive advantage have proliferated in the last three

Table 1.1   Competitive advantage definitions

---

1. Competitive advantage is created by favorable terms of trade in product markets (Dierickx and Cool, 1989). That is, sales in which revenues exceed costs.
2. Competitive advantage is revealed by 'super-normal' returns (Barney, 2002; Peteraf, 1993).
3. Competitive advantage is revealed by superior stock market performance stemming from surprising increases in expectations (financial economics view).
4. Competitive advantage is manifested in terms of shareholders' returns.

Source: Our elaboration from Rumelt, 2003.

decades. Richard Rumelt (2003) emphasized that there are four schools of thought in defining competitive advantage. According to the first, competitive advantage is created by favorable terms of trade in product markets (Porter, 1980; Dierickx and Cool, 1989). That is, sales in which revenues exceed costs. A second school of thought maintains that advantage is revealed by 'super-normal' returns (Barney, 2002; Peteraf, 1993). A third school of thought eventually ties advantage to stock market performance. According to financial economics, in fact, superior stock market performance stems from surprising increases in expectations (that is, the financial economics view). A fourth idea, that is more tightly tied to measurement, essentially refers to those strategy consulting firms that measure competitive advantage in terms of shareholder returns (see Table 1.1).

There are some intriguing areas of confusion here. We will focus on one of these areas that we consider the most stimulating for current competitive advantage investigation: does competitive advantage mean winning the game or having sufficient distinctive resources to maintain a position in the game (Rumelt, 2003)? This resembles the deep-seated story that is often told in strategy and leadership classes in universities and business schools. Is it worthwhile to stay in business and keep on competing only when one is the first or the second in the industry, as purported in the 1980s by Jack Welch, the commanding CEO of GE at the time? Or, more simply, when one is able to barely stay in business or to survive the competitive arena?

In this regard, two rather influential and countervailing streams of thought exist in strategic management. The former argues that sustainable competitive advantage (SCA) actually does exist (Porter, 1980; 1991; Barney, 2002; Saloner, Shepard and Podolny, 2001) as an organization can gain and sustain an advantage over time. The latter supports instead the apparently opposite contention that, in today's technology-driven, volatile, and unstable hypercompetitive environments, sustained competitive advantage does not exist. According to this view, since we actually live in the age of temporary advantage (D'Aveni, Dagnino and Smith, 2010) epitomized by a series of frequent endogenous and exogenous competence-destroying disruptions and discontinuities, competitive advantage can be achieved only for a concatenation of limited time periods (D'Aveni, 1994). This contention drives us inescapably to dedicate space to the concept of dynamic competitive advantage.

Dynamic Competitive Advantage

Since we have come to recognize that the achievement of a stable competitive position at all times is impossible, it is high time to turn to dynamic competitive advantages; i.e. to understand the dynamic processes by which firms perceive and attain superior competitive positions. This is a theme that Porter (1991) had pioneered two decades ago, when he rightly acknowledged that, till that date, strategy had fallen short in explaining the true origin of advantage. Porter also emphasized that this origin rests in strategic dynamic processes viewed not as static symbols but as moving targets. Nonetheless, Porter's (1991) immediate response was the proposition of his 'diamond', intended – in his own words – as "a dynamic system" and a way to detect and respond to the environmental influences on the dynamics of competitive advantage.

Two decades after that early contribution, the study of the detection of the antecedents of the dynamics of competitive advantage has become key in strategy research, and for the inauguration and rapid affirmation of at least four significant streams of study. The literature on high-velocity, hyperturbulent, and chaotic environments inaugurated by the intuition regarding hypercompetition (D'Aveni, 1994; Wiggins and Ruefli, 2005), the studies on competitive dynamics that specifically focus on the speed and aggressiveness of firm actions that may undermine the effectiveness of a firm's position and movements (Ferrier, Smith and Grimm, 1999; Smith, Ferrier and Grimm, 2001), the dynamic resource-based view of the firm (Helfat and Peteraf, 2003), and finally the dynamic capability approach (Teece, Pisano and Shuen, 1997; Eisenhardt and Martin, 2000; Teece, 2007; Helfat et al., 2007). In sum, to respond to ever-changing environmental pressures (e.g. competitive, social and technological), the continuous reconfiguration and deployment of new resources and capabilities have become the essential seeds from which the dynamics of organizational competitive advantage are grown. In a nutshell, the Rosetta stone of today's dynamics of competitive strategy is firmly engraved with an inscription on the ability to relentlessly re-align the firm's resource and capability base to the varying environmental opportunities or to the creation of new ones (see Alvarez and Barney, 2007, for an introduction to the idea of 'creation opportunities').

THE COMPETITIVE STRATEGY MINDSET

As we have attempted to show, bearing a competitive strategy mindset is no doubt relevant in the strategic management field, since it has allowed substantial conceptual and practical advancements. Nonetheless, looking beyond popular perception, it is important to examine what a competitive mindset is really about. Therefore, I ask: what does having a competitive strategy mindset mean? What is the logic underlying a competitive strategy mindset? Does the competitive strategy mindset evolve?

Interestingly enough, if we wish to understand a competitive strategy mindset, it may be helpful to leverage the etymologies of the three related words that compose the phrase. Actually this specific mindset is based concurrently on 'competition' and on 'strategy'. While the Latin etymology of the word 'competition' recalls the issue that brings us to 'the act to ask or request together' with some other party, the ancient Greek word 'strategy' (the *'strategòs'* – from *stratòs* = army and *egos* derivation of *agein* = to lead – was the one who was designated as commander-in-chief of the army) drives us to recognize the inner interdependence of two or more actors within the same game. Accordingly, we can confirm that, etymologically speaking, a competitive strategy refers to a game in which the actors involved request the same object or aim at the same target in a specifically interdependent setting. If we pass from the actor level to the organization or firm level, we can purport that competitive strategy is related to a game in which two or more firms aim at the same target in a strategically interdependent setting.

Finally, we can introduce the third ingredient: mindset. A mindset is a set of assumptions, methods, or notations held by one or more people or groups of people, which is so established that it creates a powerful incentive within these people or groups to continue to adopt or accept prior behaviors, choices, or tools (see Hutchins, 1995). According to this definition, a competitive strategy mindset involves the full acceptance of "a game in which two or more firms aim at the same target while operating in strategically interdependent settings" (see Table 1.2).

In this sense, since the late 1980s and early 1990s the competitive strategy mindset has revolved around concepts such as, respectively, 'competitive organization' and 'competitiveness'. A competitive organization entails, in this view, an organization that vis-à-vis its competitors, in a defined time period and setting, can temporarily be more cost efficient (pure economic

Table 1.2   Etymology and definition of the competitive strategy mindset

	Competition	Strategy	Mindset
Etymology Original Meaning	Latin *Cum-petere* i.e., "the act to ask or request together"	Ancient Greek *Strategos* commander-in-chief of the army (etym: *stratòs* = army + *egos* derivation of *agein* = to lead)	Anglo-Saxon A set of assumptions, methods, or notations held by one or more people or groups of people, which is so established that it creates a powerful incentive within these people or groups to continue to adopt or accept prior behaviors, choices, or tools
Current Meaning	"A game in which the actors involved request together the same object or aim at the same target in a specifically interdependent setting" and, *by extension,* "a game in which two or more firms aim at the same target in a strategically interdependent setting"		
Definition	Full acceptance of "a game in which two or more firms aim at the same target while operating in strategically interdependent settings"		

perspective), or more able to differentiate, or both (pure competitive perspective), or more transaction efficient (transaction cost perspective), or more able to learn (behavioral perspective), or more able to manage agency relationships (agency theory view), or more able to play with selective pressures (evolutionary perspective) (see Pearson, 1992; Pucik, Tichy and Barnett, 1993). Competitiveness is in turn the comparative ability and performance of a firm, sub-sector or even country to sell and supply goods and/or services in a given market. A good degree of competitiveness is believed paramount for achieving corporate success (Hitt, Ireland and Hoskisson, 2011).

The one depicted earlier was roughly the situation of the competitive strategy mindset especially following the launch of Michael Porter's two books, respectively, on competitive strategy (1980) and competitive advantage (1985), and the mild influx that game theory has exerted in the development of strategic management in that age (Camerer, 1991; Saloner, 1994). In the course of the 1990s, fueled by the dramatically shifting realities of business phenomena in the new decade, the issue of interfirm cooperation and cooperative strategy (Contractor and Lorange, 1988; Dussauge and Garrette, 1999; Faulkner and de Rond, 2002) has emerged and progressively managed to find burgeoning room in the competitive strategy domain. By extension, cooperative strategy has joined the vast, flexible and expanding domain of competitive strategy and has been incorporated into it.

As illustrated earlier, the inauguration and development of the research field related to competitive strategy has marked several steps forward in strategy and management. Nonetheless, the competitive strategy mindset has been henceforth guided by a pure Aristotelian logic that is fundamentally binary or dual. A two-valued logic reasons by extremes, excluding any degrees of variation in a continuum. For the 'law of excluded middle', which has long dominated the thought of the Western world, any other solution is deemed paradoxical and therefore simply unacceptable (Chen, 2008). Competitive strategy has relied on and only admitted two opposite and supposedly irreconcilable behaviors: competitive behavior and cooperative behavior. Accordingly, the possibility of admitting a multi-valued logical reasoning was denied and the simultaneous coexistence of a mix of competition and cooperation, trustworthy and opportunistic behaviors, multiple business models, ownership problems and conflicts, and so forth, has been completely neglected.

To moderate this initial condition in the beam of some recent developments in strategy research, the last section of this volume hosts a handful of essays in which the pure competitive mindset is actually blended with the pure cooperative mindset and trust and opportunism are reputed concomitant items, so as to allow a seemingly paradoxical 'coopetition mindset', the strategic management of trust, multiple business models interaction and, finally, an in-depth discussion of the value of the ownership issue. According to these multi-valued perspectives, the volume is also home to other contributions that dig out, respectively, the impact that competitive strategy investigation has had (and currently has) on practice and the elucidation of how strategy research has started to study not only how firms and their competitors perceive and respond to each other, but also how stakeholders make sense of firms at the collective level; and the consequences of collective cognitive and interpretative processes and structures on performance. A complementary contribution in this vein pinpoints that micro-foundations – such as activities and beliefs – are crucial in the inspection of how novel competitive positions materialize, frequently amalgamating with the macro-conditions – or practices and meanings. In the next and final section of this essay, we provide a full account of the structure and content of the handbook.

Table 1.3 Synopsis of the Handbook of Research on Competitive Strategy

Part 1: Origins and developments	Part 2: Theoretical approaches	Part 3: Advanced topics	Part 4: Methodological issues	Part 5: Look into the future at the intersection between research and practice
2. *Origins and developments* Vincenzo Pisano and Michael Hitt	6. *Resource-based theory and managerial implications* Jay Barney, Valentina Della Corte, Mauro Sciarelli and Asli Arikan	11. *Role of mergers and acquisitions* Olimpia Meglio and Arturo Capasso	18. *Use of quantitative methodologies* Roberto Ragozzino, Asda Chintakananda and Jeffrey Reuer	21. *Management of trust* Sandro Castaldo and Katia Premazzi
3. *The genesis: a historian's view* Christian Stadler	7. *Socio-cognitive perspective* Violina Rindova, Rhonda Reger and Elena Dalpiaz	12. *Strategic implications of alliance formation and dynamics* Africa Ariño and Esteban García-Canal	19. *Semiotic methods and the meaning of strategy in firm annual reports* Maria Cristina Cinici and Roger Dunbar	22. *Competing through business models* Ramon Casadesus-Masanell and Joan Ricart
4. *Theory of science perspectives: debates and a novel view* Nicolai Foss	8. *Management of growth strategies in firm networks* Simone Ferriani and Antonio Giuliani	13. *Innovation and technology management* Bruno Cassiman and Maria Chiara Di Guardo	20. *Role and impact of computer simulation modeling* J. Richard Harrison and Gordon Walker	23. *Coopetition: nature, challenges, and implications* Giovanni Battista Dagnino, Maria Chiara Di Guardo and Giovanna Padula

Table 1.3 (continued)

Part 1: Origins and developments	Part 2: Theoretical approaches	Part 3: Advanced topics	Part 4: Methodological issues	Part 5: Look into the future at the intersection between research and practice
5. *Young and growing research directions* Joel Baum and Henrich Greve	9. *Strategy-as-practice* Patrick Regnér	14. *Governance issues* Igor Filatotchev		24. *Crossing boundaries between research in strategy and finance: the firm's financial structure and competitive strategy* Maurizio La Rocca and Elvira Tiziana La Rocca
	10. *Competitive dynamics stimulated by pioneers' technological innovation* Francesco Garraffo and Gwendolyn Lee	15. *Entrepreneurial issues* Mario Sorrentino		25. *Investors, corporate governance and strategic competitiveness in privately-held firms* Rosario Faraci and Wei Shen
		16. *Family business* Giorgia D'Allura and Alessandro Minichilli		26. *Competitive strategy research's impact on practice* Constantinos Markides
		17. *Multinational firms* Grazia D. Santangelo		

STRUCTURE AND CONTENT OF THE HANDBOOK

Though some handbooks may dedicate a great deal of room to recapitulating the book's content in an analytical fashion, we have chosen to make the content synopsis as handy and small as possible. Table 1.3 gathers the general synoptic summary of the contributions to this handbook.

The handbook is divided into five basic parts, which respond to a compelling organizational logic. In the following paragraphs, we will display the main features of the focal parts of the book, pinpointing some glimpses on each of the 25 relevant chapters. The five parts are asymmetric in length, responding to a rationale given by the themes sheltered within them.

As it may be straightforward to anticipate, the first part regards, broadly speaking, the origin and developments of research in competitive strategy. It presents four unique chapters. Chapter 2 by Vincenzo Pisano and Mike Hitt speculates on the internal and external factors that are posited at the origins and developments of competitive strategy considered as a relevant research area in strategic management, while Chapter 3 by Christian Stadler offers an interesting historian's view on the genesis of competitive strategy, supplying a few historical examples that span from ancient times to medieval Greenland and nineteenth century Hong Kong, and dissecting the view of military strategy. Chapter 4 by Nicolai Foss deepens the influx of theory of science perspectives in competitive strategy research, by casting original light on the recent methodological debate on the matter and the swinging strategic management pendulum oscillating between the micro and the macro. Last but not least, Chapter 5 by Henrich Greve and Joel Baum summons a number of captivating hints for discussing a set of young and growing research directions in competitive strategy research (e.g. multiunit rivalry, geographic location and spatial structure, ecological dynamics).

The second part of the book is dedicated to the discussion of the main conceptual approaches that inform today's competitive strategy research. It consists of five chapters. Although it has proved unfeasible to gather all the approaches in competitive strategy research, we are confident to say that we have managed to pull together some of the most important and promising ones. Chapter 6 by Jay Barney, Valentina Della Corte, Mauro Sciarelli and Asli Arikan provides a thorough discussion of one of today's mainstream theories in competitive strategy – the resource-based theory – and examines its relevant managerial implications. Chapter 7 by Violina Rindova, Rhonda Reger and Elena Dalpiaz covers the advent of the socio-cognitive perspective in strategy research, clearly extricating the inception of collective cognitions and sensemaking in markets and organizational fields. Chapter 8 by Simone Ferriani and Antonio Giuliani addresses the issue of management growth strategies in firm networks, proposing a stylized model of opportunity discovery via network ties. Chapter 9 by Patrick Regnér illustrates another appealing theoretical perspective in today's competitive strategy landscape that is labeled strategy as practice, especially as concerns the emergence of organizational competitive positions. Finally, in Chapter 10 Francesco Garraffo and Gwendolyn Lee supply a tempting discussion of the antecedents of firms' competitive dynamics stimulated by the introduction of pioneers' technological innovation.

By offering an issue-based rather than theory-oriented view of competitive strategy, the third part considers an ample array of significant topics in competitive strategy research. This is the largest part of the book, featuring seven original chapters. Chapter 11, by Arturo Capasso and Olimpia Meglio, is concerned with the relevant evolving role that M&A research increasingly plays in the competitive strategy subfield of investigation. Chapter 12, by Africa Ariño and Esteban Garcia-Canal, gives a notable portrait of the consequences of alliance formation and dynamics for competitive strategy formulation and implementation. Chapter 13 by Bruno Cassiman and Chiara Di Guardo clearly depicts the fundamental position in competitive strategy of studies in innovation and technology management. In Chapter 14, Igor Filatochev discusses in detail the current emergence of important governance issues in competitive strategy (e.g. board characteristics, strategic decisions and performance and the roles of block-holders and shareholder activism). Chapter 15 by Mario Sorrentino carefully reviews and discusses the role of entrepreneurial issues and wealth creation through new ventures in competitive strategy research. In Chapter 16, Giorgia D'Allura and Alessandro Menichilli give a sound picture of what undoubtedly is a rising and promising subject in competitive strategy research: that related to the dissection of family business and family enterprises. In Chapter 17 Grazia Santangelo argues about the central importance of the conversation on multinational firms in competitive strategy research (this stream has recently witnessed the launch of the *Global Strategy Journal*).

The fourth part of the volume is devoted to discussing thoroughly what is today a fundamental requirement for the scholarship of any researcher working in a university, research center, or a business school, or in industry and consulting practice: the role of methodological issues in competitive strategy research. It comprises three unique chapters. Chapter 18 by Roberto Ragozzino, Jeff Reuer and Asda Chintakananda looks at the comparative use of quantitative methodologies in competitive strategy research. Taking a rather different but in many ways complementary perspective, which makes use of a series of annual reports, Chapter 19 by

Roger Dunbar and Cristina Cinici provides an original extrication of how semiotic methods can shed light on the meaning of competitive strategy. Chapter 20 by Richard Harrison and Gordon Walker shows the role and impact of computer simulation modeling in competitive strategy research.

The fifth and final part of the volume harbors an array of contributions for taking a (hopefully smart and foresightful!) look at the future of competitive strategy. As briefly anticipated in the prior section, the contributors to this section have collectively attempted to look ahead, by excavating the grounds and boundaries of a particular frontier area, which lies at the interface between current research in strategy, other disciplines and professional practice. This part comprises six intriguing chapters. Chapter 21 by Sandro Castaldo and Katia Premazzi is devoted to meticulously detecting and extracting new important additions that the management of trust may offer today to competitive strategy research. Chapter 22 by Ramon Casadesus-Masanell and Joan Enric Ricart lays down a suite of compellingly rigorous insights to firms that wish to compete through business models. Chapter 23 by Giovanni Battista Dagnino, Chiara Di Guardo and Giovanna Padula is committed to the study of the strategy mid-way between competition and cooperation strategies, which has been named coopetition strategy. In the process, the authors provide some clues on the nature, challenges, and implications of this novel managerial mindset for firms' strategy. Since it vigorously connects the dots between the firm's financial structure and competitive strategy, Chapter 24 by Maurizio La Rocca and Elvira Tiziana La Rocca is a true boundary-spanning piece, which intersects research in the realms of strategy and finance. In Chapter 25 Rosario Faraci and Wei Shen investigate whether and to what extent ownership matters. In so doing, they hook up the expanding roles of investors, corporate governance, and strategic competitiveness as specifically concerns privately-held firms. In the final chapter of the handbook, Chapter 26, Costas Markides explores the impact on practice that competitive strategy research has had in the last couple of decades.

As a final tip, we are confident that the reader may appreciate the collective effort of the contributors to this volume and, therefore, that the publication and dissemination of this handbook will have the best of fortune among students, researchers and practitioners. We are also confident that the volume will more than satisfy the reader interested in the strategy and management domain, to actually reach thinkers and practitioners in disciplines and fields that are germane to it, and with which there has been (and there is) good trade. Scholars and professionals in such topical areas as regional and applied economics, economic geography, business history, political science and international affairs may actually find it (or at least some part of it) helpful to their daily thinking and practice. I look forward to receiving any kind of constructive and critical feedback from all these communities.

NOTES

1. I am conscious that, for its open source design, Wikipedia may not be considered a reliable source of information. Nonetheless, in this very case, among the three that I have detected in my research, it appears to provide the most comprehensive and accountable discussion of the word at hand. In fact, at the entry "handbook," the *Oxford Dictionary* online reports "*a book giving information such as facts on a particular subject or instructions for operating a machine*", while the *Merriam-Webster Online Dictionary* conveys "*a book capable of being conveniently carried as a ready reference*: MANUAL; *a concise reference book covering a particular subject*".
2. Actually, I am perfectly aware that, according to some authors (Porter, 1991; Rumelt, Schendel and Teece, 1994), the birth of strategy (or better business policy, as it was called at that time) as a research field conventionally dates back to the early 1960s. The steep signpost of this dating is given by appearance of the works of the triad of founding fathers, Alfred Chandler, Igor Ansoff and Kenneth Andrews, who supplied as many classical contributions in the vein in those years. For our purpose, we have taken into account the initial daylight of 'strategic management' as a scientific discipline by making unequivocal reference to both: (a) the launch of the *Strategic Management Journal* (1980) and (b) the establishment of the Strategic Management Society (1981). In a way, we could perhaps contend that the strategy field presents us with an unexpected two-step dawn: (1) the primeval one in the early 1960s, as reported by the foundational writers upsurge, and (2) the contemporary one at the onset of the 1980s.
3. While we recognize that the accrual of various discord definitions in the competitive strategy vein may cause confusion, we do not support the contention, originating from some scholars, that, in order to achieve cumulativeness, we must reach a shared consensus on a single distinctive definition. For instance, *The American Heritage Dictionary of Business Terms* (2010) defines competitive strategy as "A plan for how a firm will compete, formulated after evaluating how its strengths and weaknesses compare to those of its competitors", while *BusinessDictionary.com* (www.businessdictionary.com/definition/competitive-strategy.html) reports that competitive strategy is a "Long-term action plan that is devised to help a company gain a competitive advantage over its rivals." Finally, taking a marketing view, the *Barron's Business Dictionary* (www.answers.com/topic/competitive-strategy) says that it is "A promotional strategy used in an advertising campaign that is designed to compete with rival brands. For example: A competitive strategy may try to discredit another brand or undercut another brand in terms of price, or may point out qualities and consumer benefits that are not present in another brand".
4. According to Michael Porter cost and differentiation strategies are not incompatible, but a hybrid cost-differentiation strategy is indeed very unusual and sporadic. Porter (1985) stated that, in the rare occasions when firms were successful at simultaneously pursuing both competitive advantages, they reaped even greater benefits than firms which pursued only one competitive advantage: "If a firm can achieve cost leadership and differentiation simultaneously, the rewards are great as the benefits are additive – differentiation leach to premium prices when cost leadership implies lower costs" (1985: 18).
5. Similarly, low cost, and low price, alone do not sell products and services. The products must possess qualities that are perceived as desirable and of value (Stonehouse and Snowdon, 2007: 258). Furthermore, Mintzberg et al. (1995) argue that price – together with image, after sales support, quality and design – can be used as the traction for product differentiation.

REFERENCES

Alvarez, S. and J.B. Barney (2007), 'Discovery and creation: alternative theories of entrepreneurial action', *Strategic Entrepreneurship Journal*, **1**(1–2), 11–26.

Barney, J.B. (1991), 'Firm resources and sustained competitive advantage', *Journal of Management*, **17**(1), 99–120.

Barney, J.B. (2002), *Gaining and Sustaining Competitive Advantage*, 2nd edn, Reading, MA: Addison-Wesley.

Barron's Business Dictionary (2011), 'Entry: Competitive strategy', available at: www.answers.com/topic/competitive-strategy (accessed 7 July 2011).

Besanko, D., D. Dranove and M. Shanley (2000), *Economics of Strategy*, 2nd edn, New York: John Wiley & Sons.

BusinessDictionary.com (2011), 'Entry: Competitive strategy', available at: www.businessdictionary.com/definition/competitive-strategy.html (accessed 7 July 2011).

Camerer, C.F. (1991), 'Does strategy research need game theory?', *Strategic Management Journal*, **12**, 137–152.

Chen, M.J. (2008), 'Reconceptualising the competition – cooperation relationship: a trans-paradox perspective', *Journal of Management Inquiry*, **17**(4), 288–304.

Contractor, F. and P. Lorange (1988), *Cooperative Strategies in International Business*, Lexington, MA: Lexington Books.

D'Aveni, R.A. (1994), *Hypercompetition: Managing the Dynamics of Strategic Manoeuvering*, New York: The Free Press.

D'Aveni, R.A. (2010), *Beating the Commodity Trap: How to Maximize Your Competitive Position and Improve Your Pricing Power*, Boston: Harvard Business Press.

D'Aveni, R.A., G.B. Dagnino and K.G. Smith (2010), 'The age of temporary advantage', *Strategic Management Journal*, **31**(special issue 13), 1371–1385.

Dagnino, G.B. and E. Rocco (2009), *Coopetition Strategy: Theory, Experiments and Cases*, London: Routledge.

Dierickx, I. and K. Cool (1989), 'Asset stock accumulation and sustainability of competitive advantage', *Management Science*, **35**, 1504–1511.

Dussauge, P. and B. Garrette (1999), *Cooperative Strategies: Competing Successfully through Strategic Alliances*, Chichester, UK: John Wiley & Sons.

Eishenhart, K.M. and J.A. Martin (2000), 'Dynamic capabilities: what are they?', *Strategic Management Journal*, **21**(special issue 10–11), 1105–1121.

Falkner, D. and M. de Rond (2002), *Cooperative Strategy: Economic, Business, and Organizational Issues*, New York: Oxford University Press.

Ferrier, W.J., K.G. Smith and C.M. Grimm (1999), 'The role of competitive action in market share erosion and industry dethronement: a study of industry leaders and challengers', *Academy of Management Journal*, **42**, 372–388.

Flynn, E.J. and B.F. Flynn (1996), 'Achieving simultaneous cost and differentiation competitive advantages through continuous improvement: world class manufacturing as a competitive strategy', *Journal of Managerial Issues*, **8**(3), 360–379.

Foss, N.J. (1996), 'Research in strategy, economics, and Michael Porter', *Journal of Management Studies*, **33**(1), 1–24.

Ghemawat, P. and J. Rivkin (1999), *Strategy and the Business Landscape*, Reading, PA: Addison-Wesley.

Grant, R.M. (2010), *Contemporary Strategy Analysis: Concepts, Techniques and Applications*, 7th edn, New York: Wiley.

Helfat, C.E. and M.A. Peteraf (2003), 'The dynamic resource-based view: capability life-cycles', *Strategic Management Journal*, **24**(10), 997–1010.

Helfat, C.E., S. Finkelstein, W. Mitchell, M.A. Peteraf, H. Singh, D.J. Teece and S.G. Winter (2007), *Dynamic Capabilities: Understanding Strategic Change in Organizations*, Malden, MA: Blackwell.

Hitt, M.A., D. Ireland and R.E. Hoskisson (2011), *Strategic Management: Competitiveness and Globalization*, 9th edn, Cincinnati, OH: South-Western College.

Hutchins, E. (1995), *Cognition in the Wild*, Cambridge, MA: MIT Press.
Kay, J. (1993), *Foundations of Corporate Success*, Oxford: Oxford University Press.
Kuhn, T.S. (1970), *The Structure of Scientific Revolutions*, Chicago: Chicago University Press.
Merriam-Webster Online Dictionary (2011), 'Entry: Handbook', available at www.merriam-webster.com/dictionary/handbook (accessed 10 July 2011).
Mintzberg, H., J.B. Quinn and S. Ghoshal (1995), *The Strategy Process: Concepts, Contexts and Cases* (European edn), Englewood Cliffs, NJ: Prentice Hall.
Oxford Dictionaries Online (2011), 'Entry: Handbook', available at http://oxforddictionaries.com/definition/handbook?region=us (accessed 10 July 2011).
Pearson, G.J. (1992), *The Competitive Organization*, Maidenhead: McGraw-Hill.
Peteraf, M.A. (1993), 'The cornerstones of competitive advantage: a resource-based view', *Strategic Management Journal*, **14**, 179–191.
Porter, M.E. (1980), *Competitive Strategy*, New York: The Free Press.
Porter, M.E. (1981), 'The contribution of industrial organization to strategic management', *Academy of Management Review*, **6**(4), 609–620.
Porter, M.E. (1985), *Competitive Advantage*, New York: The Free Press.
Porter, M.E. (1990), *The Competitive Advantage of Nations*, New York: The Free Press.
Porter, M.E. (1991), 'Towards a dynamic theory of strategy', *Strategic Management Journal*, **12**(S2), 95–117.
Pucik, V., N.M. Tichy and C.K. Barnett (eds) (1993), *Globalizing Management: Creating and Leading the Competitive Organization*, New York: Wiley.
Rumelt, R.P. (2003), 'What in the world is competitive advantage?', policy working paper, 2003–15 Anderson School, UCLA, available at: www.anderson.ucla.edu/faculty/dick.rumelt/Docs/Papers/WhatisCA_03.pdf (accessed November 15, 2010).
Rumelt, R.P., D. Schendel and D.J. Teece (1991), 'Strategic management and economics', *Strategic Management Journal*, **12**(S2), 5–29.
Rumelt, R.P., D. Schendel and D.J. Teece (eds) (1994), *Fundamental Issues in Strategy: A Research Agenda*, Boston: Harvard Business School Press.
Saloner, G. (1994), 'Game theory and strategic management: contributions, applications, and limitations', in Rumelt, R.P., D. Schendel and D.J. Teece (eds), *Fundamental Issues in Strategy: A Research Agenda*, Boston: Harvard Business School Press.
Saloner, G., A. Shepard and J. Podolny (2001), *Strategic Management*, New York: John Wiley & Sons.
Scott, D.L. (2010), *American Heritage Dictionary of Business Terms*, Boston: Houghton Mifflin.
Smith, K.G., W.J. Ferrier and C.M. Grimm (2001), 'King of the hill: dethroning the industry leader', *Academy of Management Executive*, **15**(2), 59–70.
Stonehouse, G. and Brian Snowdon (2007), 'Competitive advantage revisited: Michael Porter on strategy and competitiveness', *Journal of Management Inquiry*, **16**, 256–273.
Teece, D.J. (2007), 'Explicating dynamic capabilities: the nature and microfoundations of (sustainable) enterprise performance', *Strategic Management Journal*, **28**(13), 1319–1350.
Teece, D.J., G. Pisano and A. Shuen (1997), 'Dynamic capabilities and strategic management', *Strategic Management Journal*, **18**(7), 509–533.
Thompson, A., M.A. Peteraf, J. Gamble and A.J. Strickland III (2011), *Crafting and Executing Strategy: The Quest for Competitive Advantage*, 18th edn, New York: McGraw-Hill/Irwin.
Wiggins, R.R. and T.W. Ruefli (2005), 'Schumpeter's ghost: is hypercompetition making the best of times shorter?', *Strategic Management Journal*, **26**(10), 887–911.
Wikipedia (2010), 'Entry: Handbook', available at: http://en.wikipedia.org/wiki/Handbook (accessed 20 October 2010).

PART 1

COMPETITIVE STRATEGY RESEARCH: ORIGINS AND DEVELOPMENTS

2 What is competitive strategy? Origins and developments of a relevant research area in strategic management

Vincenzo Pisano and Michael A. Hitt

INTRODUCTION

Strategy matters because it provides precise directions to a firm. A competitive strategy is a set of decisions necessary to support organizational goals within a specific business. By implementing a certain competitive strategy, a firm defines its position relative to its rivals, which in turn contributes to a competitive advantage. The necessity to embark upon a work on competitive strategy is justified by the huge evolution that has characterized firms' competitive environments since Michael Porter elaborated one of the first and most well-known business strategies' classifications.[1]

Today's industries may be viewed as complex adaptive systems that evolve through several life stages (birth, growth, maturity and death). The rate of change from one stage to the next can be slowed or amplified because of the impact of a series of factors influencing each industry's life cycle, such as technological change, environmental uncertainty, competitive dynamics, changes in consumer preferences and so on. These factors – which we examine later in this chapter – need to be analyzed by each firm in order to organize and establish the most effective competitive behavior to adopt in their industry. Having knowledge of these factors is required for all firms because their impact can reshape the nature of the industry (i.e. the industry structure) very rapidly in today's environment. These changes (sometimes sudden and unpredictable, sometimes slower but incontrovertible) may force firms to readapt their strategies, for instance adopting a different technology or trying to create new sources of competitive advantage.

For these reasons, we view current industries and competitive environments as adaptive systems: in such systems, products and production methods evolve following new patterns that are often completely different from the ones adopted in the past. Nonetheless, evolving systems must be seen not just from a negative perspective. Whereas change can represent a threat for a firm's competitiveness, it may represent an opportunity to exploit for its rivals.

Thus, one of the main goals of modern organizations should be to constantly scan their environment so that they can understand the possible changes that might influence their future survival and competitiveness.

In this chapter, we present an introductory analysis of the competitive strategy concept, guiding the reader from the origins of this important research topic for the management field to the present and its possible future developments. We also outline a conceptual model that helps to visualize the development of a modern competitive strategy together with the main factors affecting the process.

The work is divided in two parts. In the first part, we introduce the construct of competitive strategy at a general level, providing a definition and including the constructs of core competences and competitive advantage. Then, in the following sections, we analyze the intriguing debate between strategy content and strategy process.

In the second part of the chapter, following a review of the literature, we present our model of factors affecting the performance of current competitive strategy. This part is divided into four subsections dedicating attention to each group of factors characterizing the model. Therefore, in the first and second subsection, we analyze the external and internal factors affecting competitive strategy. Then, in the third subsection, we briefly focus on the strategic actions that a firm can implement in order to improve or defend its knowledge base. Finally, we consider the construct of business model innovation as a possible solution for the sustainability of today's competitive advantages.

WHAT IS COMPETITIVE STRATEGY? AN INTRODUCTORY OVERVIEW OF THE MAIN POINTS OF ANALYSIS

The competitive strategy construct has been debated in strategic management since its inception almost 30 years ago. Several diverse definitions occur in today's literature, but no agreement exists among scholars regarding several aspects of the strategy construct. For instance, what are the main issues managers need to consider in strategy formulation (the debate on strategy content) and what kind of path should be followed in the formation and implementation of a strategy (the debate on strategy process)? In order to define competitive strategy today, we start by offering the following definition of strategy taken from a prominent scholar: strategy is a set of objectives, policies and plans that, taken together, define the scope of an enterprise and its approach to survival and success (Rumelt, 1991). In our opinion, this is a general definition of strategy that resembles the concept of corporate strategy. For this reason, we feel that the same author would agree that, in order to cope with a complex and dynamic competitive environment, some of those objectives, policies and plans should be developed in the firm's business strategy.[2]

Business-level strategy is about the choices a firm makes when deciding 'how to compete' in individual product markets.[3] Thus, it can be defined more specifically as 'an integrated and coordinated set of commitments and actions the firm uses to gain a competitive advantage by exploiting core competences in specific product markets' (Rindova and Fombrun, 1999). Before defining the two constructs of competitive advantage and core competences used in this latter definition, we first need to clarify what we mean by 'choices about how to compete'.

After three decades of debates, management scholars tend to agree on the assumption that competitive strategy content cannot avoid considering three important dimensions: the *who*, the *what* and the *how*. Basically, these dimensions represent the three main questions that each manager should ask him or herself in the process of building a business strategy.

The first question (who?) refers to choosing the customer segment(s) the firm wants to serve. This decision is relevant for the consequent choices that must be made (i.e. marketing choices) in terms of positioning the products or services.

The second question (what?) relates to the features of the product or service the firm decides to offer. The firm should consider the needs it expects to satisfy through that product or service. In this regard, the choice will be between two options: a) satisfying a need in a different manner from competitors; b) identifying a need that has never been satisfied before by any other firm.

The third question (how?) refers to the way the firm provides its product (i.e. how to produce and distribute it) and differentiates itself from its rivals. For example, the firm might offer a variety of choices in technology and production systems to adopt, or the channel typology that would be more profitable or viable to choose.

Therefore, creating an effective competitive strategy means being able to answer the following questions: 1) who are my targeted customers and what are their unsatisfied needs? 2) What kind of products or services should I offer them? 3) How should I present my current products or services to customers while simultaneously being efficient and innovative relative to competitors?

If these are the main components of its content, the essence of a business strategy should mirror the peculiarities that differentiate each firm from its competitors in the way it performs activities differently (or it performs different activities compared to its rivals).

As mentioned, Rindova and Fombrun's (1999) definition of business strategy includes two constructs (competitive advantage and core competences) that require clarification. We assume that a competitive advantage is the final outcome of the competitive strategy a firm develops through the exploitation of its core competences. Prahalad and Hamel (1990) were the first scholars to use the concept of core competences (or distinctive competences).[4] In this concept, they incorporated the capability of managers to develop a peculiar set of skills distinguishing their firm from all competitors, giving them a competitive advantage. More specifically, core competences develop through experience. Managers learn how to compete in a certain field and, through a process of trial and error (Eisenhardt and Tabrizi, 1995), they are able to improve their professional capabilities transferring such knowledge to the overall organization. Organizations, at the same time, try to take advantage of their industry experience (in terms of consumer behavior, competitive environment, endowed resources and so on), developing internal systems to translate such managers' knowledge into organizational knowledge and routines. This learning approach with continuous improvement is the basis for developing the firm's competitive advantage.

The concept of competitive advantage was first developed by Porter (1980), who identified three main typologies of advantage (cost leadership, differentiation and focalization). The following subsection will highlight the origins of the competitive strategy construct.

The Origins of the Debate: the Strategy Content

Research on business strategy derives from Industrial Organization (IO) scholars such as Mason (1939) and Bain (1956). These studies were originally focused on the industry and, therefore, not firms themselves. This choice implied a lack of relevance of managerial decisions, since managerial actions were conceived as mostly unable to influence a firm's performance. Moving from these roots, scholars looked at the content of strategy in different ways. Today, overall, we can identify three main schools of thought.[5]

The first school – whose roots can be traced back to Porter's works on competitive strategy (1980) and competitive advantage (1985) – views competitive strategy as a 'positioning strategy' (D'Aveni, 2007). More specifically, in Porter's view, firms can capture a competitive advantage after analyzing existing markets and identifying new opportunities. This analysis can be performed through the implementation of the five forces model (Porter, 1980). Thus, the role of competitive strategy requires aligning the firm with the identified environmental opportunities. Basically, Porter views strategy as mainly industry-driven. Thus, a firm must adapt to the competitive context inside an industry by choosing the most suitable position in order to contrast with its rivals.[6]

Positioning is determined by this choice of the most suitable competitive advantage over rivals. Competitive advantage is based on the capability to produce at lower costs than rivals (competitive advantage based on cost leadership) or to offer a 'somehow unique' product that is different from those offered by competitors (competitive advantage based on differentiation). In addition, such generic competitive strategies may be related to different market scopes. Market scope can be wide or restricted to a niche of customers (focused strategy). In the latter case, competitive strategies will be 'differentiation focused' or 'cost leadership focused'.[7]

Barney and other resource-based scholars (Peteraf, 1993) concentrated their main critiques on the assessment of firms' conduct and behavior. These authors offered a different perspective (an endogenous one) in which every firm distinguishes itself from all competitors by accumulating a unique bundle of resources. Heterogeneity and imperfect mobility of resources lie at the basis of this view. Each firm must prove its ability to develop strategies and competitive advantages based on heterogeneous resources and capabilities that maximize its returns (Barney, 1986, 1991; Dierickx and Cool, 1989; Reed and DeFilippi, 1990). Therefore, according to this second school of thought, competitive advantage is not the result of market positioning, but is created through the distinctive, unique and valuable firm resources that competitors are unable to replicate (Makhija, 2003).

The third school of thought considers the previous two views as static and, therefore, emphasizes a more dynamic view of strategy. More specifically, the first approach was developed in a stable and predictable environment. As we will show later in our model, today's environmental context is in fact different from the one originally developed. The second approach has been criticized for not attributing importance to market analysis, but concentrating more on the internal aspects of a firm. Another criticism concerned the static nature of core competences and the risk of imitation from competitors.

In contrast, by following the third school's approach, a firm's competitive advantage can be defended and sustained through the development of dynamic capabilities and competences peculiar to that company. We will expand our analysis on dynamic capabilities later, in the subsection dedicated to the internal factors affecting competitive strategy.

The Origins of the Debate: the Strategy Process

Markides (2001) states that the two main areas of the strategy process debate include planning a strategy (debate between design and emergent school) (Mintzberg and Waters, 1985; Ansoff, 1991, 1994; Mintzberg,

1990, 1991, 1994) and an analytical approach to building a strategy (debate between internal/resource- and external/market-oriented approach).

We agree with scholars who view the process of strategy creation as composed of both elements.[8] While strategy should not be left entirely to improvisation, it is important to ensure that excessive planning and determination do not result in core rigidities. In fact, a lack of sufficient flexibility might hinder the capability of a firm to react to any possible external change.

On the contrary, an excess of attention to flexibility and creativity might hinder the capability of a firm to follow a precise and united direction. The lack of a predetermined direction could cause chaos in the entire organization and workforce.

In the second area of the debate, we believe it is necessary to adopt both perspectives, the internal and the external approach. For example, it is impractical to look at the main resources and capabilities of a firm without considering the kind of market in which the firm would like to operate. On the other hand, a firm should not look exclusively at the market without considering the resources needed to succeed in that market.

COMPETITIVE STRATEGY TODAY: A REPRESENTATIVE MODEL FOR FUTURE DEVELOPMENTS

Modern organizations must constantly scan the environment in order to predict any possible change that might influence their future survival and competitiveness. This necessity is determined by the complex competitive landscape that has evolved over the last three decades.

Today's decision makers need to develop ways of interpreting competitive strategy by integrating the formulation process with a more complete analysis of the variables influencing the internal and external context of competition. Our aim here is to provide a comprehensive overview of the major variables.

Over time, management literature has produced a consistent analysis stressing the comparison between the traditional strategy context versus today's context, as pictured in Table 2.1. As shown, today's external environments are increasingly dynamic and characterized by a continuous change in products and markets. In addition, rapidly escalating competition demands an increasing flexibility and innovation capability of organizations, transforming the environment in a hypercompetitive context (D'Aveni, 1994).

In order to assist our reasoning, we have developed a conceptual model, as shown in Figure 2.1. This model suggests three groups of factors affecting the process of strategy formulation that decision makers should

Table 2.1   Traditional strategy context versus today's context[9]

	Traditional context	Today's context
Rate of change	Static	Dynamic
Environment	Stable	Turbulent and volatile
Production context	Mass production	Customized
Competing context	Competitive or cooperative	Hypercompetitive and co-opetitive
Structure	Enterprise-specific	Networked
Transformation	Physical assets	Information and knowledge
Strategy process	Top-down	Top-down and bottom-up
Corporation	Multinational corporation	Global corporation
Competitive advantage	Cost leadership or differentiation	Integrated cost leadership and differentiation
Technological regime	Moderate	Very fast

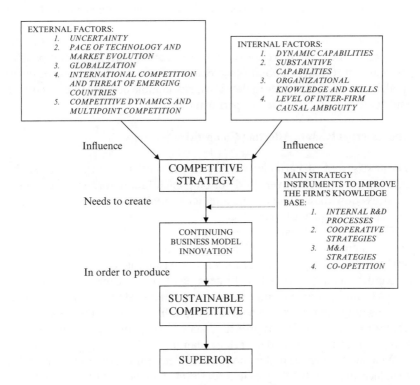

Figure 2.1   The new competitive strategy model and the factors affecting its path to reach superior levels of performance

consider when creating a highly competitive modern organization. Such an approach to competitive strategy should help the firm ensure the sustainability of its competitive advantage and, thus, achieve a superior performance for the benefit of its stakeholders.

Next, we analyze these three groups of factors that influence strategy formulation. The first group of external factors decision makers must learn to cope with includes: a general level of uncertainty, the pace of technology and market evolution, the phenomenon of globalization, the competition at international level and the additional threat represented by emerging countries, the dynamics of competition and the concept of multipoint or multi-market competition.

The second group of factors is internal to the firm. They need to be analyzed by decision makers to reinforce their firm's competitiveness. Dynamic and substantive capabilities, organizational knowledge and skills, and the level of inter-firm causal ambiguity represent the internal factors considered in our model.

Finally, a third group is represented by the main strategic actions a firm can implement to improve its knowledge base. Such actions can be R&D processes, cooperative or acquisitive strategies, and co-opetition. The analysis of these three groups of factors should impact upon competitive strategy and the firm's ability to create a culture of continuous business model innovation in order to develop a sustainable competitive advantage and achieve a superior level of performance.

The External Factors Affecting Competitive Strategy

The first group of variables we find in the model is represented by the external factors. However, in describing each factor forming the model, we stress how these components interact reciprocally thereby widening or reducing the impact of each other.[10]

The first external factor represented in our model is the construct of environmental uncertainty. Uncertainty means that a firm cannot foresee any possible change in the future with a reasonable degree of reliability. Therefore, its survival is strictly dependent on its capability to rapidly adapt to any possible change as soon as it manifests itself. Such capability is usually favored by the degree of flexibility of its organization and its ability to determine the appropriate actions (i.e. contingency plans) that favor adaptation during the strategy planning.

What are the factors that managers consider particularly relevant in trying to reduce uncertainty? They include: the level of predictability of financial and capital markets, government regulations and intervention, possible actions of competitors or suppliers, and general conditions facing the organization.

In the process of strategy building, decision makers should consider the risk of uncertainty regarding their future decisions. This might imply, for instance, the necessity to consider some contingency plans in order to have a certain number of alternative solutions for the worst possible scenarios, or the need to hedge the risk of their future strategic choices by resorting to financial products (Hrebiniak and Snow, 1980).

The uncertainty factor is strictly linked to the second group of external factors presented in the model: the pace of technology and market evolution. In order to define these two constructs, we adopted the definition that Suarez and Lanzolla (2007) proposed and that fits with our view of today's industries evolving through life cycles' states. Suarez and Lanzolla define both constructs with reference to the period spanning from the first introduction to the onset of maturity. More specifically, they define: a) the pace of technology as the average change in the level of technology performance up to the onset of maturity; and b) the pace of market evolution as the average market change up to the onset of maturity.[11]

The reason for interest in this construct is the possibility of technology innovation to render a firm's knowledge obsolete (even for a market leader), and destroy existing competences or inhibit possible experience curve advantages. Such uncertainty in technology trajectories may represent a threat for any organization. Thus, in considering how to develop their competitive strategy, firms must evaluate the technological pace as a critical component of their analysis independent of whether the firm is a technology leader or follower. In the case of technological leadership, decision makers should create an organizational structure able to monitor technological trends that could potentially develop in the external environment. Such monitoring activity should allow the leader to prevent any possible threat to its leading technology. When the firm is a follower, its objective will be monitoring the external environment with the intent to discover an alternative (cheaper or superior) to the leading technology. Therefore, in this case, the firm may adopt or buy the leading technology, while financing research projects aiming to achieve developments in that specific technological area.

Consequently, even though the pace of technology evolution may represent a threat for certain organizations, it may signify an opportunity for those firms outside (or at the edge of) the market trying to attack incumbents to subvert their dominance. It is from the perspective of these latter firms that the pace of technology development may represent a crucial threat to their competitive strategy.

In addition, the pace of market evolution may be influenced by some variables' dynamics. For example, these dynamics may include a change in the customers' preferences or the emergence of new external regulations.

Such variables may affect the pace of market evolution representing a threat to firms' future competitiveness, and managers must cautiously consider these factors when implementing their competitive strategy. For example, when implementing an international strategy, decision makers should take into consideration the different tastes, regulations and culture of the countries they wish to enter.

Literature on internationalization illustrates the influence of this strategic choice on the likelihood of success of the investing firm. For example, studies have analyzed 1) the problem of double-layered acculturation faced by firms trying to enter a new market through a cross-border acquisition (Barkema, Bell and Pennings, 1996), 2) the importance of a different institutional context in trying to succeed in a foreign market (Calori, Lubatkin, Véry and Veiga, 1997), 3) the risk of different and severe regulations whose impact can be crucial to the firm's expansion and success (Harris and Ravenscraft, 1991; Kissin and Herrera, 1990), and 4) the risk of an international customer's preference being too different from that of the domestic client (Hitt and Pisano, 2002).

Furthermore, the pace of market evolution can be interpreted as the evolution in customers' needs and tastes. From this perspective, decision makers should consider their competitive strategy focusing on the loyalty of their clients. The loyalty construct is a crucial issue in the marketing literature. It is through a faithful and loyal client that a firm can monitor market evolution trying to influence any new trend for its own advantage.

A third critical factor outlined in the model is represented by the concept of globalization. Globalization has been variously treated in the literature and its complex definition is beyond the aim of this work.[12] What we mean here by globalization is an economy in which goods, services, people, skills and ideas move freely across geographic borders (Hitt, Ireland and Hoskisson, 2007). It is a feature that significantly expands and complicates a firm's competitive environment.[13]

The peculiar nature of the global economy reflects the realities of today's hypercompetitive business environment, challenging firms to think carefully about the markets in which they will compete tomorrow.

Therefore, a global view of competition drives firms to look at each market as a unique world market. This view of competition implies a new approach to business strategy in which decision makers need to rethink their approach to competition. In fact, the globalization of economies creates both opportunities and threats for modern organizations. By virtue of such opportunities, firms can, for example, have their headquarters in one country, produce in another, obtain the necessary resources from several countries, and sell the final product in another one. This situation may represent an obvious advantage for those organizations capable of exploiting potential cost advantages (i.e. cheap workforce, low-cost production sites, outsourcing decisions). And, at the same time, a disadvantage represented by the threat of new competitors that, even though physically distant, are still capable of attacking what once was a secure market position.

Thus, the globally competitive landscape increasingly requires firms to build high quality and unique products of value and to do so with an efficient cost structure. It is for this reason that we previously mentioned the integrated differentiation-cost leadership strategy. This is a strategy that involves a set of actions designed to differentiate the product in the marketplace while simultaneously maintaining a low-cost position relative to competitors (Hitt et al., 2007; D'Aveni, 2007). This strategy is difficult to develop and implement effectively because some of the objectives of both strategies often conflict.[14] Michael Porter once recommended against such a strategy, referring to it as 'stuck in the middle' – firms trying to achieve both are likely to do neither.

In some industries, firms are unable to survive without rethinking their competitive strategy relative to the changed context. Having access to global markets and using sophisticated information technology help firms to achieve economies and to recoup major investments in R&D[15] (Franko, 1989).

Finally, looking at our model and its variables' interrelations, globalization is another factor that increases the level of uncertainty. In fact, critical new trends and market or technology changes may be overlooked or simply not detected by strategists. Therefore, when formulating their competitive strategy, decision makers need to monitor their external environment in global perspective. This might mean that a potential opportunity or threat to their company could arise in a very distant international context. A fourth factor presented in the model that is strictly connected to globalization is the growth of internationalization strategy and the emergence of new competitors coming from developing countries.

Even though management scholars typically classify international strategy as a corporate level strategy, we can look at internationalization from a competitive strategy perspective. Trying to capture potential new customers and economies by adopting a business strategy perspective offers the possibility to extend products' life cycles with sales of the same product in new geographical locations.

In this situation, the most complex aspects of the expansion process regard the firm's ability to cope with a diverse context (Johanson and Vahlne, 1977) characterized by a series of components such as a different culture, institutional context, and regulations (Vermeulen and Barkema, 2002). A new context implies the necessity for the firm to build new relationships with suppliers, customers, competitors, governments and so on. Moreover, the firm must be capable of organizing operations in the new location (Davidson, 1983), purchasing new structures or building partnerships with local firms, and adapting its systems and processes (Bettis and Prahalad, 1995) to the new and different international context (Barkema and Vermeulen, 1998; Stopford and Wells, 1972; Bartlett and Ghoshal, 1989).[16]

In addition, foreign markets not only represent a possible extension for products' life cycles; but also, with regard to those firms particularly active in innovation capabilities, international markets represent an opportunity to increase innovations sales. More specifically, the higher the number of foreign markets in which a firm decides to expand, the higher the likelihood that the firm will earn a better return on its innovations. Furthermore, the possibility to interact with new markets gives the expanding firm the opportunity to learn from such markets and improve its efficiency through new experiences (Ghoshal, 1987; Kim, Hwang and Burgers, 1993; Almeida, 1996).

However, even if both internationalization and globalization may represent an opportunity for modern firms, they may also represent a risk because of the diverse institutional and socio-cultural environments of each country. The inability to understand such differences can be lethal for the survival of multinational firms. For this reason, decision makers must consider the different peculiarities of international markets when formulating an international business strategy.

The combination of a global economy and the trend towards internalization has created a new important factor: competition represented by firms located in fast developing countries (e.g. China, India, Korea and Brazil). Management literature has typically analyzed the context of developing countries from a different perspective. In fact, scholars have always looked at emerging countries as locations for a potential profitable expansion of 'western' (developed) firms. One of the most debated issues has been the possibility to exploit a first-mover advantage or to enter through an alliance with a local partner, trying to exploit its local connections at both the political and institutional levels. In our model, we look at this same issue from an opposite perspective, mostly overlooked by the theory: the competitive threat of firms located in developing countries trying to sell their product to 'western' markets.

This type of firm often suffers a technology gap with competitors from more developed countries (Svetlicic and Rojec, 1994). Such a gap forces them to compete on different products' peculiarities rather than quality.[17] However, the possibility to sell at considerably lower prices – being at the same time able to reproduce a sufficient quality level – represents a serious threat to developed firms' profitability.[18] For instance, China and India (like many others) have moved in a common direction. If, in the past, they attracted developed firms' requests for opening their market borders for growth, today's situation is very much changed. In fact, today, some of these same firms have developed their own competences with knowledge gained from their network of partnerships with more technology-advanced firms.[19] Many of these firms are now able to offer their own products to more advanced and developed markets, allowing these firms to develop their own international strategies. Moreover, many of these products are no longer inferior in quality and today's consumer behavior is changing in their favor.

Thus, decision makers from more developed countries must consider this potential threat when formulating their competitive strategy. For example, these firms may focus on patent protection and apply pressure on international institutions (e.g. WTO) to expose different forms of illegal (or unfair) competition. However, this is not always the solution to the situation. In fact, there are cases in which this competition is not illegal, but represents a potential alternative to 'western' products.[20]

Therefore, possible choices for decision makers to consider when reacting to the threat originating from emerging countries include:

1) monitoring the possibility of an imminent attack from competitors located in emerging countries;
2) setting policies to defend domestic production;
3) repositioning the activity in the same industry, but with a further differentiation of the products in order to exclude them from the risk of price competition;
4) planning a progressive retirement from the activity under imminent attack;
5) abandoning the activity and moving to a radical diversification.

One of the main goals of the literature on competitive dynamics (the last external factor considered in our model) is evaluating the possible responses that each move may elicit from rivals.[21] When these competitive interactions involve two or more firms that are rivals in more than one product category or market at a time, we name it 'multipoint competition'. A multipoint competition strategy involves competing with firms across markets by using strengths in one market to overcome weaknesses in another (Fuentelsaz and Gomez, 2006). The competition can occur across product markets, geographic markets or both.[22]

The choices about the moves or countermoves necessary to surpass competitors are strictly interrelated with the concept of strategic positioning expressed by Porter. However, the competitive dynamics perspective substantially differs from Porter's view. First, it is a dynamic, not a static, view of competition. Second, it considers the internal resources and capabilities that each firm possesses (or should possess) in order to choose the right move (or countermove) and the right positioning. Thus, it is not a mere exogenous view.

As we have shown in this subsection, there is a considerable number of external factors affecting a firm's competitive strategy. Some have gained more importance in the last two decades (after Porter's work on competitive strategy). In the following subsection, we will try to examine some of the main internal factors affecting today's business strategy for decision makers' consideration.

The Internal Factors Affecting Competitive Strategy

The second group of variables analyzed in the model is represented by the internal factors influencing business strategy. The internal factors we included in our model should help a firm to exploit the opportunities or to protect itself from the threats proceeding from the external environment.

Because it is valuable in helping a firm change its business strategy, dynamic capability is the first internal factor considered in the model (Teece et al., 1997; Eisenhardt and Martin, 2000; Zahra, Sapienza and Davidsson, 2006). In fact, in order to protect their competing skills, firms need to continuously reconfigure their strategic resources (Sirmon and Hitt, 2003; Sirmon, Hitt and Ireland, 2006). This ability is ensured by the firms' dynamic capabilities. It is necessary to protect competing skills because of the pressure exerted by environmental dynamics and uncertainty (as stated in the first part of the model). Thus, these external factors (environmental dynamics and uncertainty) challenge firms to revise their routines and restructure their organization (March, 1991). Dynamic capabilities ensure the firm's ability to revise and restructure.

In this work, we define dynamic capabilities as the ability to reconfigure a firm's resources and routines as envisioned and considered appropriate by its main decision makers (Zahra et al., 2006).

Although much of the literature focuses on the benefits of possessing dynamic capabilities, herein we primarily refer to dynamic capabilities as the ability to change or reconfigure existing substantive capabilities (the second internal factor in our model). Thus, we start by determining the difference between substantive and dynamic capabilities.

An existing substantive capability is an organization's ability to produce a desired output (Winter, 2003). Such capabilities are the result of firms' experience, knowledge base and learning. A firm's knowledge base (the third internal factor of our model) includes all factors known by an organization and their continuous interaction with its substantive capabilities. Together, they represent the firm's skills and its ability to be particularly competitive in a certain area.

How can this interaction be kept constant for the benefit of a firm's competitiveness? Such continuous interaction is affected by dynamic capabilities, such that, in a situation of external change, firms need to reshape and reconfigure their skills. Their reshaping and reconfiguring abilities will depend on the dynamic capabilities they possess.[23] Dynamic capabilities should help firms develop new strategic advantages. As a response to a relevant external change, they should intervene in order to avoid internal rigidities and maintain organizational flexibility.

The necessity to use dynamic capabilities will be related to the decision makers' perceived need for a change. For example, when the environment appears volatile, a firm's substantive capabilities may be inadequate. Thus, in an industry characterized by rapid technological innovativeness, firms will need to frequently reconfigure their existing capabilities. The same holds true if the market evolution should rapidly change (like the emergence of new customer preferences). Therefore, decision makers should constantly invest in the development of dynamic capabilities to facilitate the formulation of a competitive business strategy.

However, as asserted by Eisenhardt and Martin (2000), dynamic capabilities are a necessary but not sufficient condition to achieve a superior performance. If the existing substantive capabilities upon which they operate are mediocre and remain so even after having been reconfigured, no competitive advantage will accrue. On the contrary, the positive impact of dynamic capabilities on performance and competitive advantage will depend on the quality of the existing knowledge base and substantive capabilities.[24]

The construct of causal ambiguity (the fourth internal factor in our model) is strictly linked to the literature on dynamic capabilities (Kogut and Zander, 1992; Teece et al., 1997; Zollo and Winter, 2002). As asserted by Lippman and Rumelt (1982), causal ambiguity is a construct that describes to what degree decision makers are able to explain the relationship between a competency and its organizational outcome. In our model, causal ambiguity represents an internal factor decision makers need to reinforce in their competitive strategy in order to prevent imitation from competitors. The literature identifies the three main sources of ambiguity as: a) complexity, b) tacitness, and c) asset specificity (Reed and DeFilippi, 1990).

Tacitness, the first antecedent, can be defined as a non-codifiable accumulation of knowledge and skills typically accrued through experience.

The higher the degree of tacitness, the higher the levels of ambiguity competitors face in understanding the link between a competency and its outcome.

Complexity, the second antecedent of causal ambiguity, can be defined as the number of interrelated technologies, resources and individuals involved in a specific competency. Complexity also plays a relevant part in complicating competitors' capability to understand the link between a competency and its outcome.

Finally, the level of asset specificity – the third antecedent of causal ambiguity – can be defined as the uniqueness of a certain investment made by a firm. Ultimately, it increases the level of ambiguity faced by competitors in determining the relationship between a competency and its outcome. Therefore, in order to strengthen their competitiveness and avoid external attacks, decision makers need to focus on the improvement of causal ambiguity. However, as stressed by the recent work of King (2007), it is important to make a distinction between the concept of inter-firm and intra-firm causal ambiguity. In fact, even though the first creates continuous barriers to competitors' imitation, the causal ambiguity within a firm weakens its competitive capability (King and Zeithaml, 2001). More specifically, intra-firm causal ambiguity prevents a firm from successfully reinvesting in a competency as new opportunities develop. This occurs when managers are unable to understand the link between an internal competency and the resulting performance. Thus, in our model, we exclusively use inter-firm causal ambiguity, trying to stress the weight of such an internal factor on the sustainability of a firm's competitive advantage.

In the last two subsections, we have stressed the relevance of a firm's knowledge base in the improvement of its skills and degree of competitiveness. The following subsection is dedicated to the strategic instruments each firm can use in order to extend and improve its knowledge base.

STRATEGIC ACTIONS TO IMPROVE A FIRM'S KNOWLEDGE BASE

As illustrated in our model, the relationship between a firm's competitive strategy and its performance is moderated by a series of actions each firm can use in order to ensure its process of continuous business model innovation. Therefore, all these actions support a firm when trying to maintain a sustainable competitive advantage.[25]

The first action is investing in internal research and development. Of course, there is a strong correlation between internal R&D investments and investing in the creation of dynamic capabilities in order to ensure either innovation, or a sufficient level of flexibility to respond to external changes.

Strategic alliances (as well as acquisitions) are typically adopted by firms in order to improve their knowledge base and learn from another firm. More specifically, a business-level cooperative strategy is a strategic action used by a firm to help it improve its performance in an individual product market (Hitt et al., 2007). A firm uses a cooperative strategy when it believes that combining its resources and capabilities with those of one or more partners will create competitive advantages that it cannot create on its own and that will help it to succeed in a specific product market.

We would like to stress the interrelation between strategic actions (such as cooperation strategies) and external factors influencing business strategy (such as the level of uncertainty). In fact, the management literature shows four different types of business-level cooperative strategies (Hitt et al., 2007); however, here we briefly focus our attention on cooperative strategies that reduce the level of uncertainty.

As we previously mentioned, uncertainty represents a serious threat to modern firms. This threat is especially strong in a situation of high technological pace or high market pace. Thus, in order to reduce or hedge the risk of uncertainty, firms may decide to form business-level strategic alliances. An interesting characteristic of strategic alliances pointed out by some authors (Gomes-Casseres, 1996; Harbison and Pekar, 1998; Brandenburger and Nalebuff, 1996) is that there has been a proliferation of cooperative agreements among competitors (the so-called co-opetition phenomenon, the last action considered in our model). Of course, being part of a cooperative network influences these firms' competitive behavior. We define co-opetition as a situation in which competitors simultaneously cooperate and compete with each other.[26] Co-opetition represents a new category in strategic analysis (Dagnino, 2007). In fact, while competitive models mainly focus on rent appropriation strategies and cooperation frameworks mainly focus on collective strategies for rent generation, co-opetition encourages firms to learn new ways to both strategically interact and seek for rents.

Strategists need to consider the use of one or more of these actions when developing their competitive strategy. Research has shown the importance of being part of a network in order to improve competitiveness, particularly when operating in the global competitive landscape. This is why we chose to include strategic actions as moderators of the success of a firm.

CREATING CONTINUOUS BUSINESS MODEL INNOVATION TO ACHIEVE SUSTAINABLE COMPETITIVE ADVANTAGE

The construct of business strategy introduced by Porter (1980) seems to be inadequate for today's competitive landscape. Today, most firms are trying to achieve a combination of the two original typologies: the so-called integrated differentiation-cost leadership strategy. As we previously mentioned, an integrated differentiation-cost leadership strategy involves a set of actions designed to differentiate the product in the marketplace, while simultaneously maintaining a low-cost position relative to competitors.

In developing our model, we linked competitive advantage sustainability with continuous business model innovation to ensure competitiveness. A recent study by IBM (2006) shows how managers from several industries are being proactive in renewing their business models to improve their ability to create value. In fact, if a firm concentrates on continuous business model improvement, its competitors are likely to be uncertain about how to respond in an effective manner. We believe that this is the best way to avoid imitation and thereby to maintain a competitive advantage and achieve superior performance.

Even though there are several definitions of a business model (Shafer, Smith and Linder, 2005), we define it as a firm's plan or diagram for how it competes, uses its resources, structures its relationships, interfaces with customers, and creates value to sustain itself on the basis of the profits it earns (Barringer and Ireland, 2008).[27] In order to ensure their competitive advantage sustainability, business models need to be modified over time. Eventually competitors will learn how to replicate their benefits. Continuous business model innovation implies a series of initiatives that are undertaken to revolutionize how a particular product or service is produced, sold, and supported after the sale. Therefore, firms need a perennial change whose focus is a continuous improvement on the three main dimensions of competitive strategy: the *who*, the *what*, and the *how* dimensions.

Today's most successful firms must be able to combine effective strategies with powerful business model innovations on a regular basis (Mitchell and Coles, 2003). Continuous business model improvement means changing or recombining the three dimensions of competitive strategy. When a firm makes a change in its business model by offering something that was not previously available, this is a business model innovation. For example, being able to change the who dimension by creating or entering a new customer segment (before competitors do) is a way to improve a firm's business model. The same applies if a firm is able to discover a new way to provide its products (the how) or to improve its features (the what), anticipating its rivals' action. Moreover, to stay ahead of its rivals, a firm must adopt the innovation process with a reasonable degree of continuity; otherwise, competitors would have enough time to reduce or eliminate the firm's competitive advantage. Therefore, when a firm pursues an ongoing process of developing and installing business model improvements, replacements and innovations, we refer to this process as 'continuous business model innovation'.

One of the major changes that has occurred during the last decade is that business model innovation used to be a peculiarity of outsiders' attacks: new entrants were able to break into an industry through the implementation of a new successful business model (e.g. Dell or Starbucks) exploiting incumbents' weaknesses due to their myopia and rigidities. On the contrary, only in the last few years, some incumbent firms (typically leading firms) have started to adopt continuing business model innovation as a strategy to maintain their future competitiveness.

NOTES

1. Other famous classifications have been elaborated in the strategy literature immediately before and after Porter's framework. One of the most famous, for instance, was developed by Miles and Snow (1978) who viewed strategy as an agglomeration of decisions regarding the alignment of business units' managerial processes with the environment. Their framework is known as the Prospector-Analyzer-Defender-Reactor (P-A-D-R) framework.
2. In this work, we use the term 'business' and 'competitive' strategy interchangeably.
3. On the other hand, the choice about how many individual product markets have to shape the scope of the firm (determining the number of businesses in which it has to compete) is an issue regarding corporate-level strategy. In this regard, there will be a coincidence of the two strategy levels only for those firms competing in a single-product market area within a single geographic location.
4. Actually, the first author to talk about distinctive competences was Selznick (1957), whose work gave inspiration to Prahalad and Hamel (1990) who talked about core competences. Since, the concept has evolved through the definition of dynamic core competences (Lei et al., 1996) and dynamic capabilities (Teece et al., 1997).
5. With regard to the process of strategy formation and to the amount of different schools of thought on this issue, Mintzberg, Ahlstrand and Lampel (1998) individuate ten different schools or approaches. In particular, they provide a thorough critique of the limitations and contributions of each school (the design, planning, positioning, entrepreneurial, cognitive, learning, power, cultural, environmental, and configurational school) trying to combine them in a unique coherent school (Mintzberg et al., 1998).
6. A few years later, he assigned a central role to management conduct in deciding a firm's positioning, thus in influencing its performance (Porter, 1991).
7. Today, as we will see later on in this chapter, firms tend to use a combination of differentiation and cost leadership strategy: it is named 'integrated differentiation-cost leadership strategy'.
8. It is impossible to assert the supremacy of the adaptive (Mintzberg) or rationalist (Ansoff) school.

9. Adapted from Brown and Blackmon (2005).
10. For instance, just to mention one of these interrelations, there is a strong correlation between the level of environmental uncertainty and the pace of technology evolution.
11. Of course, different products may experience different paces of technology evolution up to the onset of maturity. The literature on innovation typically represents technology's life cycle through an 'S-curve' whose length obviously depends on the technological progress and consequently worthy investments in that specific product (Abernathy and Utterback, 1978).
12. Pankaj Ghemawat, for example, believes that differences between countries are larger than generally acknowledged. Therefore, he speaks about semi-globalization (Ghemawat, 2007).
13. In explaining the difference between a multinational and a global corporation, Ted Levitt once said that the multinational corporation operates in a number of countries and adjusts its products and processes at high relative cost; the global corporation, on the contrary, operates with resolute constancy selling the same things in the same way everywhere (Levitt, 1983).
14. For example, achieving differentiation may require substantial investments in R&D to develop innovative products and in advertising to inform the market of the benefits of new products. It is difficult to achieve economies of scale when continuously introducing new products to the market. Additionally, a cost leadership strategy often emphasizes efficient manufacturing, making retooling to produce new products a challenge.
15. For example, Target stores use this strategy by building a strong, distinctive brand for quality goods while competing with other Department stores who focus on low costs (e.g. Wal-Mart).
16. Vermeulen and Barkema (2002) assert that the process of internationalization can be profitable only if the growing strategy is well balanced in relation to some determinants like the speed (Eisenhardt and Martin, 2000), scope and regularity of the expansion process.
17. Usually, this kind of firm tries to enter strategic alliances with 'western' firms in order to learn new capabilities from its partners.
18. A typical example is represented by Chinese firms, able to reproduce high quality look-alike products in the fashion or in the leather industry threatening the most celebrated Italian brands.
19. Michael Porter, in *Competitive Advantage of Nations* (1990), tries to apply the concepts and theories of strategic management to international economics with the aim of explaining why certain countries are more successful than others. He affirms that a nation is a home base in which each firm develops its competitive advantage, in which a strategy is set and its core product and technology are defined. According to this view, a nation is a set of contextual variables that influences the competitive performance of firms and industries.
20. When not considering such a threat (likely to become serious especially in productions with a high degree of intensive but not qualified labor), firms are accused of marketing myopia.
21. A central goal of strategic management is to reveal how precise competitive moves can help firms achieve a long-term (sustainable) competitive advantage while improving their level of performance (Hitt, Boyd and Li, 2004). These moves may include – for instance – the choice of developing an innovative product or collaborating with a rival firm within a foreign market.
22. For example, at one time UPS was the market leader in ground shipping and delivery whereas FedEx was the market leader in overnight delivery. However, UPS entered the overnight delivery market and FedEx bought trucks and other ground shipping assets to compete in that market. Thus, they compete with each other in both markets and also compete in many geographic markets: domestic and international. In recent times, they have been engaging in fierce competition in China in both service markets. Recently, UPS has been gaining market share by becoming a logistics company and

making value chain activities, particularly for small and medium sized businesses operating in foreign markets (Friedman, 2005).
23. For a deeper analysis, we suggest to refer to Zahra et al.'s (2006) model on dynamic capabilities.
24. For a review of the literature about the potential value of dynamic capabilities in creating and sustaining competitive advantage please refer to Lee et al. (2002).
25. However, deepening the analysis of these instruments is beyond the aim of this chapter. Therefore, we will just mention them in order to render more organic the presentation of our model.
26. The term co-opetition was first introduced to strategy research by Brandenburger and Stuart (1996), and by Brandenburger and Nalebuff (1996).
27. Hamel (2000) believes that a business model consists of four components: 1) the firm's core strategy (how it competes), 2) its strategic resources (thus, how the firm acquires and uses them), 3) its network of partnerships (thus, the way the firm organizes and nurtures its partnerships), and 4) the customer interface (so, how the firm interacts with its clients).

REFERENCES

Abernathy, W.J. and J.M. Utterback (1978), 'Patterns of industrial innovation', *Technology Review*, **80**, 97–107.
Almeida, P. (1996), 'Knowledge sourcing by foreign multinationals: patent citation analysis in the U.S. semiconductor industry', *Strategic Management Journal*, **17** (winter special issue), 155–165.
Ansoff, I. (1991), 'Critique to Henry Mintzberg's The Design School: reconsidering the basic premises of strategic planning', *Strategic Management Journal*, **12** (6), 449–461.
Ansoff, I. (1994), 'Comment on Henry Mintzberg rethinking strategic planning', *Long Range Planning*, **27** (3), 31–32.
Bain, J.S. (ed.) (1956), *Barriers to New Competition*, Cambridge, MA: Harvard University Press.
Barkema, H.G. and F. Vermeulen (1998), 'International expansion through start-up or acquisition: a learning perspective', *Academy of Management Journal*, **41** (1), 7–26.
Barkema, H.G., J.H.J. Bell and J.M. Pennings (1996), 'Foreign entry, cultural barriers, and learning', *Strategic Management Journal*, **17**, 151–166.
Barney, J.B. (1986), 'Organizational culture: can it be a source of competitive advantage?', *Academy of Management Review*, **11**, 656–665.
Barney, J.B. (1991), 'Firm resources and sustained competitive advantage', *Journal of Management*, **17**, 99–120.
Barringer, B.R. and R.D. Ireland (2008), *Entrepreneurship: Successfully Launching New Ventures*, Upper Saddle River, New Jersey: Pearson Education.
Bartlett, C. and S. Ghoshal (eds) (1989), *Beyond Global Management: The Transnational Solution*, Boston, MA: Harvard Business School Press.
Bettis, R.A. and C.K. Prahalad (1995), 'The dominant logic: a retrospective and extension', *Strategic Management Journal*, **16**, 5–14.
Brandenburger, A.M. and B.J. Nalebuff (eds) (1996), *Co-opetition*, New York: Doubleday.
Brandenburger, A.M. and S. Stuart (1996), 'Value-based business strategy', *Journal of Economics and Management Strategy*, **5** (1), 5–14.
Brown, S. and K. Blackmon (2005), 'Aligning manufacturing strategy and business-level competitive strategy in new competitive environments: the case for strategic resonance', *Journal of Management Studies*, **42** (4), 793–815.
Calori, R., M. Lubatkin, P. Véry and J.F. Veiga (1997), 'Modeling the origins of nationally-bound administrative heritages: a historical institutional analysis of French and British firms', *Organization Science*, **8**, 681–696.

D'Aveni, R.A. (ed.) (1994), *Hypercompetition: Managing the Dynamics of Strategic Maneuvering*, New York: Free Press.

D'Aveni, R.A. (2007), 'Mapping your competitive position', *Harvard Business Review*, November, 110–120.

Dagnino, G.B. (2007), 'Coopetition strategy: toward a new kind of interfirm dynamics?', *International Studies of Management & Organization*, **37** (2), 3–10.

Davidson, W.H. (1983), 'Market similarity and market selection: implications of international marketing strategy', *Journal of Business Research*, **11**, 439–456.

Dierickx, I. and K. Cool (1989), 'Asset stock accumulation and sustainability of competitive advantage', *Management Science*, **35**, 1504–1512.

Eisenhardt, K.M. and M. Martin (2000), 'Dynamic capabilities: what are they?', *Strategic Management Journal*, **21**, 1105–1121.

Eisenhardt, K.M. and B.N. Tabrizi (1995), 'Accelerating adaptive processes: product innovation in the global computer industry', *Administrative Science Quarterly*, **40**, 84–110.

Franko, L.G. (1989), 'Global corporate competition: who's winning, who's losing and the R&D factor as one reason why', *Strategic Management Journal*, **10**, 449–474.

Friedman, T.L. (ed.) (2005), *The World Is Flat: A Brief History of the Twenty-first Century*, New York: Farrar, Straus & Giroux.

Fuentelsaz, L. and J. Gomez (2006), 'Multipoint competition, strategic similarity and entry into geographic markets', *Strategic Management Journal*, **27**, 477–499.

Ghemawat, P. (2007), *Redefining Global Strategy: Crossing Borders in a World Where Differences Still Matter*, Boston: Harvard Business School Press.

Ghoshal, S. (1987), 'Global strategy: an organizing framework', *Strategic Management Journal*, **8**, 425–440.

Gomes-Casseres, B. (ed.) (1996), *The Alliance Revolution: The New Shape of Business Rivalry*, Cambridge, MA: Harvard University Press.

Hamel, G. (ed.) (2000), *Leading the Revolution*, Boston: Harvard Business School Press.

Harbison, J.R. and P. Pekar (eds) (1998), *Smart Alliances: A Practical Guide to Repeatable Success*, San Francisco: Jossey-Bass.

Harris, R.S. and D. Ravenscraft (1991), 'The role of acquisitions in foreign direct investment: evidence from the U.S. stock market', *The Journal of Finance*, **46**, 825–844.

Hitt, M.A. and V. Pisano (2003), 'The cross-border merger and acquisition strategy: a research perspective', *Management Research*, April, **1** (2), Spring (2003), 133–144.

Hitt, M.A., B. Boyd and D. Li (2004), 'The state of strategic management research and vision of the future', in D.J. Ketchen and D.D. Bergh (eds), *Research Methodology in Strategy and Management*, Greenwich, CT: JAI Press.

Hitt, M.A., R.D. Ireland and R.E. Hoskisson (eds) (2007), *Strategic Management*, Mason, OH: Thomson South-Western.

Hrebiniak, L.G. and C.C. Snow (1980), 'Industry differences in environmental uncertainty and organizational characteristics related to uncertainty', *Academy of Management Journal*, **23** (4), 750–759.

IBM Global Business Services (eds) (2006), *Expanding the Innovation Horizon: The Global CEO Study 2006*, IBM Corporation.

Johanson, J. and J.-E. Vahlne (1977), 'The internationalization process of the firm: a model of knowledge development and increasing foreign market commitments', *Journal of International Business Studies*, **8**, 23–32.

Kim, W.C., P. Hwang and W.P. Burgers (1993), 'Multinationals' diversification and the risk-return trade-off', *Strategic Management Journal*, **14**, 275–286.

King, A.W. (2007), 'Disentangling interfirm and intrafirm causal ambiguity: a conceptual model of causal ambiguity and sustainable competitive advantage', *Academy of Management Review*, **32** (1), 156–178.

King, A.W. and C.P. Zeithaml (2001), 'Competencies and firm performance: examining the causal ambiguity paradox', *Strategic Management Journal*, **22**, 75–99.

Kissin, W.D. and J. Herrera (1990), 'International mergers and acquisitions', *Journal of Business Strategy*, **11**, 51–55.

Kogut, B. and U. Zander (1992), 'Knowledge of the firm, combinative capabilities, and the replication of technology', *Organization Science*, **3** (3), 383–397.

Lee, J., K. Lee and S. Rho (2002), 'An evolutionary perspective on strategic group emergence: a genetic algorithm-based model', *Strategic Management Journal*, **23** (8), 727–747.

Lei, D., M.A. Hitt and R. Bettis (1996), 'Dynamic core competences through meta-learning and strategic context', *Journal of Management*, **22**, 549–569.

Levitt, T. (1983), 'The globalization of markets', *Harvard Business Review*, **61** (3), 92–102.

Lippman, S.A. and R.P. Rumelt (1982), 'Uncertain imitability: an analysis of interfirm differences in efficiency under competition', *Bell Journal of Economics*, **13**, 418–438.

Makhija, M. (2003), 'Comparing the resource-based and market-based views of the firm: empirical evidence by Czech privatization', *Strategic Management Journal*, **24**, 433–451.

March, J.G. (1991), 'Exploration and exploitation in organizational learning', *Organization Science*, **2**, 71–78.

Markides, C. (2001), 'Strategy as balance: from "either-or" to "and"', *Business Strategy Review*, **12** (3), 1–10.

Mason, E.S. (1939), 'Price and production policies of large scale enterprises', *American Economic Review*, **29**, 61–74.

Miles, R. and C. Snow (eds) (1978), *Organizational Strategy, Structure, and Process*, New York: McGraw-Hill.

Mintzberg, H. (1990), 'The design school: reconsidering the basic premises of strategic planning', *Strategic Management Journal*, **11** (3), 171–195.

Mintzberg, H. (1991), 'Learning 1, planning 0: reply to Igor Ansoff', *Strategic Management Journal*, **12** (6), 463–466.

Mintzberg, H. (1994), 'Rethinking strategic planning', *Long Range Planning*, **27** (3), 12–30.

Mintzberg, H. and J.A. Waters (1985), 'Of strategies, deliberate and emergent', *Strategic Management Journal*, **6** (3), 257–272.

Mintzberg, H., B. Ahlstrand and J. Lampel (eds) (1998), *Strategy Safari: A Guided Tour through the Wilds of Strategic Management*, New York: The Free Press.

Mitchell, D. and C. Coles (2003), 'The ultimate competitive advantage of continuing business model innovation', *Journal of Business Strategy*, **24** (5), 15–21.

Peteraf, M.A. (1993), 'The cornerstone of competitive advantage', *Strategic Management Journal*, **14**, 179–191.

Porter, M.E. (ed.) (1980), *Competitive Strategy*, New York: The Free Press.

Porter, M.E. (ed.) (1985), *Competitive Advantage: Creating and Sustaining Superior Performance*, New York: The Free Press.

Porter, M.E. (ed.) (1990), *Competitive Advantage of Nations*, New York: The Free Press.

Porter, M.E. (1991), 'Towards a dynamic theory of strategy', *Strategic Management Journal*, **12** (1), 95–117.

Prahalad, C.K. and G. Hamel (1990), 'The core competence of the corporation', *Harvard Business Review*, **68** (3), 79–91.

Reed, R. and R.J. DeFilippi (1990), 'Causal ambiguity, barriers to imitation, and sustainable competitive advantage', *Academy of Management Review*, **15**, 88–102.

Rindova, V. and C. Fombrun (1999), 'Constructing competitive advantage: the role of firm-constituent interactions', *Strategic Management Journal*, **20**, 691–710.

Rumelt, R.P. (1991), 'The evaluation of business strategy', in H. Mintzberg (ed.), *The Strategy Process: Concepts, Contexts and Cases*, New York: Englewood Cliffs, Prentice Hall, pp. 52–59.

Selznick, P. (ed.) (1957), *Leadership in Administration: A Sociological Interpretation*, Evanston, IL: Pew, Peterson, and Co.

Shafer, S.M., H.J. Smith and J.C. Linder (2005), 'The power of business models', *Business Horizons*, **48**, 199–207.

Sirmon, D.G. and M.A. Hitt (2003), 'Managing resources: linking unique resources, management and wealth creation in family firms', *Entrepreneurship: Theory and Practice*, **27** (4), 339–358.

Sirmon, D.G., M.A. Hitt and R.D. Ireland (2007), 'Managing firm resources in dynamic environments to create value: looking inside the black box', *Academy of Management Review*, **32** (1), 273–292.

Stopford, J.M. and L.T. Wells (eds) (1972), *Managing the Multinational Enterprise*, New York: Basic Books.

Suarez, F.F. and G. Lanzolla (2007), 'The role of environmental dynamics in building a first mover advantage', *Academy of Management Review*, **32** (2), 377–392.

Svetlicic, M. and M. Rojec (1994), 'Foreign direct investment and the transformation of Central European economies', *Management International Review*, **34**, 293–312.

Teece, D.J., G.P. Pisano and A. Shuen (1997), 'Dynamic capabilities and strategic management', *Strategic Management Journal*, **18**, 509–533.

Vermeulen, F. and H.G. Barkema (2002), 'Pace, rhythm, and scope: process dependence in building a profitable multinational corporation', *Strategic Management Journal*, **23**, 637–653.

Winter, S.G. (2003), 'Understanding dynamic capabilities', *Strategic Management Journal*, **24** (10), 991–995.

Zahra, S.A., H.J. Sapienza and P. Davidsson (2006), 'Entrepreneurship and dynamic capabilities: a review, model and research agenda', *Journal of Management Studies*, **43** (4), 917–955.

Zollo, M. and S.G. Winter (2002), 'Deliberate learning and the evolution of dynamic capabilities', *Organization Science*, **13**, 339–351.

3 The genesis of competitive strategy: a historian's view
Christian Stadler

STRATEGY IN HISTORICAL TIMES

Around 980 AD 25 Viking ships landed in Greenland and started a permanent settlement (Diamond, 2005). For the next 500 years a population of around 5000 Vikings was able to withstand the harshness of the North. Essentially though, they were always bound to struggle in an environment which was not suited to a European pastoral society. By cutting trees, stripping turf and overgrazing they caused soil erosion and a slow depletion of their resources. The Vikings failed to comply with the notion of strategic fit. A strategy can only be successful if it is consistent with the characteristics of the external environment. Goals and values, resources and capabilities, structures and systems need to be aligned. While the Vikings never fully achieved such an alignment with their external environment the situation became truly dramatic when the climate started to cool around 1300 resulting in the so-called Little Ice Age in the early 1400s. Hay harvests declined to a point where animals and people starved to death. Icebergs blocked the fjords and ended both trade with Europe and the regular trips to obtain timber from Labrador. The consequences were fatal considering the lack of iron and wood. At the same time the survival of the Inuit – who arrived in Greenland shortly after the Vikings – shows that it would have been possible to achieve strategic fit even under the changing circumstances. Unlike the Vikings, the Inuit concentrated on the exploitation of natural resources that were readily available in Greenland: fish and whales. To extend their resource base and capabilities they also picked up useful technologies from the Vikings. In essence the Viking society in Greenland collapsed due to their unwillingness or inability to adapt to a changing environment.

A little over 500 years after the collapse of the Viking society in Greenland the experiences of the Hongkong and Shanghai Banking Corporation Limited (HSBC) and the Chartered Bank in nineteenth century China were somehow similar to those of the Vikings and Inuit in Greenland. HSBC achieved a better fit of strategy implementation and environment and as a consequence gained advantages over the Chartered

Bank. Like other specialized British banks the pair intended to finance trade between China, India and Great Britain (Jones, 1993) but chose a distinctly different approach. While HSBC set up shop in Hong Kong and developed structures that enabled them to take advantage of the entrepreneurial spirit in China (King, 1983, 1991, 1996, 2000, 2004; King et al., 1987, 1988a, 1988b), the Chartered Bank was managed from London, taking a more centralized approach (Mackenzie, 1954). This was not entirely in vain. The London base allowed top management to be close to the world's most important financial market at the time and therefore to find opportunities to raise capital for its business in the Far East relatively easily. At the same time the removal from the banks' core business created a coordination problem and a failure to engage in some of the most lucrative opportunities.

This became obvious during a discussion that occupied the exchange business concerning the period of time permitted to pay for finance and trade bills in the mid 1860s (King et al., 1987; King, 1936). London- and Paris-based banks such as the Chartered Bank shortened the periods and lost considerable business to HSBC. Customers who joined because of the trade bills arrangement stayed with the bank subsequently. As a contemporary observed:

> The bank rapidly improved its position in China and Japan – it had then no branches in India – and gained the favor of the mercantile communities. While the agreement among the other banks lasted, a lucrative part of the business of the Hongkong [bank] was to purchase six months' paper, and sell its own drafts on London at four months' sight to its competitors at a good profit which was sometimes the only way in which they could obtain remittances. This action on the part of the Hongkong Bank immensely strengthened the Hongkong [bank].
>
> (Maclellan, 1891)

Although Vikings and Inuit living in medieval Greenland seem to have little in common with two British overseas banks which started business 500 years later and almost 10 000 kilometres away, the two stories demonstrate the importance of strategic fit regardless of where and when you compete. Fundamental insights into competitive strategy are the same today as they were 1000 years ago. While this indicates that strategy scholars can benefit from the analysis of historic case studies it also draws our attention to early work on strategy. My intention is to discuss the work of military scholars in ancient China and nineteenth century Germany. Linking their work with more recent research in competitive strategy done by business scholars should help us question some of our current assumptions and find new insights. Considering the criticism some scholars direct towards the resource-based view and the difficulties in taking the managerial aspects fully into account (Foss, 1997), the historical contributions are certainly helpful. On the one hand they see a vital role for leadership but at the same time they also emphasize its limitations and pay attention to the strategy process, i.e. the role of the sovereign. In addition the historical perspective will show how some ideas prevailed over time.

STRATEGY IN ANCIENT TIMES

The original concepts of strategy are not rooted in business but military operations. A general is faced with similar challenges to those of a top manager: to provide direction and purpose for the troops, to deploy resources in the most effective manner, and to coordinate the various actions and decisions made by soldiers. The word strategy derives from ancient Greek: 'stratos' means army and 'ago' to lead, guide, or move to. 'Strategia' therefore means generalship. The oldest text on strategy does not originate in ancient Greece though, but in 500 BC China, when Sun Tzu wrote his classic *The Art of War*. Sun Tzu was a member of the landless Chinese aristocracy who worked as a military consultant. He drew on an existing body of ideas and practices. After the completion of his military treatise Sun Tzu apparently was hired by the King of Wu. With the help of Sun Tzu the kingdom conquered Chu and became the most powerful state in ancient China. In *The Art of War*, Sun Tzu does not focus on the battle itself but wants to disable the enemy before the actual battle starts. "Hence to fight and conquer in all your battles is not supreme excellence; supreme excellence consists in breaking the enemy's resistance without fighting." Careful and meticulous preparation to possibly avoid battle unless you are sure of victory, accumulation of resources, the use of time to wear down an invader, strong leadership and motivation are at the center of his work. Five essentials for victory are:

(1) He will win who knows when to fight and when not to fight.
(2) He will win who knows how to handle both superior and inferior forces.
(3) He will win whose army is animated by the same spirit throughout all its ranks.
(4) He will win who, prepared himself, waits to take the enemy unprepared.
(5) He will win who has military capacity and is not interfered with by the sovereign.

Hence the saying: If you know the enemy and know yourself, you need not fear the result of a hundred battles. If you know yourself but not the enemy, for every victory gained you will also suffer a defeat. If you know neither the enemy nor yourself, you will succumb in every battle.

In essence his work stresses the importance of positioning yourself correctly, an idea which was highly influential with business scholars in more recent times. Authors like Michael Porter can be interpreted in the tradition of Sun Tzu. A well-known passage that demonstrates this approach explains when you should attack and when you should defend: "To be certain to take what you attack, attack where the enemy cannot defend. To be certain of safety when defending, defend where the enemy cannot attack." This strategy was successfully applied in the Vietnam war by the North facing the combined US and South Vietnamese forces. In terms of logistics and tactics the US succeeded in everything they set out to do and, in battle after battle, they threw back the North Vietnamese causing them heavy losses (Summer, 1982). The one superior resource the communists had was their will to fight. North Vietnam's Prime Minister Pham Van Dong explained it the following way: "The United States is the most powerful nation on earth. But Americans do not like long, inconclusive wars... We can outlast them and we can win in the end" (Cameron, 1966). According to Grant (2005) the USA's military response was affected by an uncertainty about their goals and whom they were actually fighting. The communists exploited this weakness, building on the unpopularity of the war in the USA, and eventually won due to consistency and strength of their strategy.

For a strategy scholar, Sun Tzu's work raises two particularly interesting questions:

(1) Is it possible in today's business environment to succeed without engaging in actual competition? Løwendahl and Revang (1998) argue that in the postindustrial era firms are facing increasing complexity due to knowledge and technology dissemination. Conventional assumptions and frameworks might no longer be helpful for scholars and managers trying to understand how firms achieve competitive advantage. As the boundaries of the firm are disintegrating, new organizational forms might be called for. Coopetition (Brandenburger and Nalebuff, 1996; Contractor and Lorange, 1988; Hakansson and Snehota, 1995; Powell, Koput and Smith-Doerr, 1996; Padula and Dagnino, 2007) and blue ocean strategies (Kim and Mauborgne, 2005) could be a possible approach in line with an extended interpretation of Sun Tzu's idea that you can succeed without engaging in battle.

(2) Should strategy scholars focus on the firm or process level? Sun Tzu provides a comprehensive approach to strategy, taking structural and organizational elements into account. His research goes beyond the 'firm level', taking society as a whole into account. In strategy research a recent

trend has been to focus on one particular process in a chosen industry (Ray et al., 2004). The compelling logic is that as scientists we have to concentrate on areas where we can control all the variables affecting the outcome. Broader questions are deemed to be more art than science and therefore the playground for managers. Sun Tzu's work however shows that we should not shy away from the broad and fundamental questions to create durable contributions, able to withstand the test of time.

NINETEENTH CENTURY MILITARY STRATEGY

The Prussian general Carl von Clausewitz (1780–1831) and the French-Swiss general Antoine-Henri de Jomini (1779–1869) both studied Napoleon's successes. At the time de Jomini's work was more influential. He developed scientific principles of military strategy. Considering the rise of Napoleon this presented an attractive proposition for military men across Europe. What was the original attraction of de Jomini's work was also its major weakness though. The specificity of the principles made them obsolete once new technology changed the nature of battle. For example he proposed massive frontal attacks which worked well in the era of muskets. Already questionable when repeating rifles were available, this approach certainly did not work in the age of machine guns. More than a million casualties in the battles of Somme and Verdun during World War I proved that frontal attacks were outdated. De Jomini's work was eventually almost forgotten.

Clausewitz's writing, however, proved to be more enduring. Rather than taking a prescriptive approach he took a descriptive one. His main contribution was the explanation of the relationship between theory and practice rooted in an understanding of war as a dynamic process. He spent considerable time explaining how a commander must minimize the uncertainty – or "friction" as he calls it – that appears in the "fog of war". In some aspects Clausewitz took opposing views to Sun Tzu. Most importantly Clausewitz focused on combat, while Sun Tzu described the avoidance of battles as a vital element of his strategy (Keegan, 1993). Essentially though, there is agreement on most fundamental issues. Both see history as a dynamic process. Both emphasize political over military considerations. Both go beyond sheer physical combat, stressing the destruction of the enemy's will instead. Even a distinction in terms of battle avoidance is incomplete in the sense that Sun Tzu also discusses combat in great detail.

Clausewitz used a dialectic method, leading to frequent misinterpretations of his work. As Bassford (1994) explains, his famous line that "war is merely a continuation of politics," is not a factual statement but the antithesis to "war is nothing but a duel on a large scale." The synthesis lies in the dynamic interaction of violent emotion, chance, and rational calculation. This way the flaws of thesis and antithesis are compensated for. Neither brute force nor rational politics and policies alone would be sufficient.

A self-confessed disciple of Clausewitz who showed that his approach was beneficial in a military campaign was the German general Helmuth Moltke (1800–1891). Moltke was perhaps the greatest strategist of all time (Hinterhuber and Popp, 1992). He was the chief of the Prussian general staff from 1838 to 1888, who "engineered the strategy behind the military victories that allowed Otto von Bismarck to assemble a loose league of German states into a powerful empire" (Hinterhuber and Popp, 1992). He had the ability to understand the significance of events without being influenced by changing attitudes and took swift decisions without being deterred by a perceived danger. He also broke with the Prussian tradition of sending out specific orders. Prior to his leadership, military commanders were entangled in the detailed operations. Moltke – being convinced that "no battle plan survives contact with the enemy" – saw this as a considerable flaw and issued 'directives' instead, guidelines which allowed individual initiative in the context of a changing battle. This does not imply that Moltke was not an avid planner. He took multiple variables into consideration when he planned his war with Austria and later France. In particular the logistics such as movement of troops via the railway were carefully thought through.

Once again the work done by nineteenth century military strategists raises interesting questions for scholars today. One area which was hotly debated in recent years concerned strategy formulation. While some scholars advocate systematic, rational analysis (Ansoff, 1991; Goold, 1992) others emphasize the empirical validity and normative merits of emergent processes (Mintzberg, 1991; Mintzberg, 1994). The evidence from Moltke suggests that neither of the two schools can proclaim victory. In the real world both aspects play a role. In a recent study of the planning process of oil majors, Grant takes a similar direction when he explains that "much of the debate between the 'strategy-as-rational design' and 'strategy-as-emergent-process' schools has been based upon a misconception of how strategic planning works in the real world. The process of 'planned emergence' evident in the companies' strategic planning systems is consistent with management principles derived from complexity theory and observations of complex adaptive systems, and offers insights into the design principles of the multidivisional firm" (Grant, 2003).

EMERGENCE AND DEVELOPMENT OF STRATEGY RESEARCH IN BUSINESS

After World War II strategy also emerged as an independent discipline in business studies. Early competitive advantage studies in business were rooted in historical analyses and careful qualitative research (Andrews, 1971; Ansoff, 1965; Chandler, 1962; Selznick, 1957). They basically argue that it is simply a question of putting the right manager in charge of a company. For example Chandler's early work can be interpreted as an argument that those companies which adopted the new management form before their competitors would gain a strategic advantage. The fact that they did so was a reflection of the structure and leadership qualities of the top management. In the 1980s a new school of thought emerged when Porter (1985) published his widely acknowledged book *Competitive Advantage*. He shifted the focus of strategy outwards by transforming the study of 'imperfect competition' into the analysis of 'competitive advantage'. A simplistic interpretation of Porter's work implies that using strategy was about choosing good industries or rebuilding industry structure. In other words a company will gain competitive advantage if the management understands the implications of structural analysis and makes the commitments that it requires (Ghemawat, 1991; Shapiro and Varian, 1998).

More recently the study of the origins of competitive advantage has been enriched by the debate that followed the birth of the so-called resource-based view (RBV) of the firm (Wernerfelt, 1984). This school of thought sees the resources available to a firm at a given moment as the key to trying to understand competitive advantage. Rather than identifying the most attractive markets the RBV shifts attention to the firm itself. Such a shift has profound implications for a firm's strategy formulation. While the emphasis of positioning a firm in an attractive market has a tendency to result in similar strategies, the concentration on firm-specific resources points to the importance of exploiting differences. In other words competitive advantage is primarily a result of uniqueness. As Barney (1991) explains, "sustained competitive advantage derives from the resources and capabilities a firm controls that are valuable, rare, imperfectly imitable, and not substitutable." A resource needs to display each of these characteristics to add to competitive advantage.

Despite the emphasis of markets in the case of the market-based view and of resources in the RBV the two schools are complementary rather than contradictory. For example, barriers to enter a market – one element in Porter's Five Forces framework – can also be explained as an incumbent firm's bundle of resources such as patents, brands, distribution channels, or learning.

Since Wernerfelt's (1984) original explanation that the assets available to a firm at a given moment are crucial in the creation of competitive advantage, a large number of theoretical studies have appeared that have clarified the content of the firm resources and, more specifically, the features they have to possess in order to generate and sustain rent (Barney, 1986; Dierickx and Cool, 1989; Lippman and Rumelt, 1982; Peteraf, 1993). Other schools of thought have used a resource-based logic to provide a more detailed explanation of how to create and sustain competitive advantage. Among them: the dynamic capability view (Eisenhardt and Martin, 2000; Teece et al., 1997; Helfat, 2007) and the knowledge-based view of the firm (Conner and Prahalad, 1996; Grant, 1996; Kogut and Zander, 1992).

The dynamic capability (DC) perspective in particular has emerged as a promising attempt to unravel the ultimate roots of competitive advantage creation in contexts that are rapidly changing. As Helfat (2007) explains, "a dynamic capability is the capacity of an organization to purposefully create, extend, or modify its resources base." In a similar vein, Eisenhardt and Martin (2000: 1107) defined DC as "the processes that use resources – specifically the processes to integrate, reconfigure, gain, and release resources – to match and even create market change." The rationale of a DC is that firms build a string of temporary advantages by adding, integrating and reconfiguring resources, which amount to sustained advantage once the entire pattern is taken into account (Blyler and Coff, 2003). For this reason DC is especially useful in contexts of high uncertainty and technological instability. In contrast to traditional capabilities, they are usually considered of a higher order (Collis, 1994) because they build, integrate, and reconfigure existing resources and capabilities (Helfat and Peteraf, 2003; Zollo and Winter, 2002). In this sense DCs are different from ordinary capabilities (sometimes named operational capabilities) by being concerned with change. Lavie (2006) for example presented a model recently which integrates the Schumpeterian perspective on technological discontinuities with the dynamic capabilities literature to explain the responses of incumbents to technological change.

Referring back to the insights provided by military strategists in ancient China and nineteenth century Germany highlights some of the issues facing resource-based scholars. Most notably the RBV and DC contributions paid limited attention to the managerial aspects of competitive advantage, an area of great interest in the past. Both Sun Tzu and Clausewitz drew considerable attention to the managerial aspect of strategy by focusing on the role of generals. In fact some of the fundamental criticism that rests on the logic of the resource-based view and its incompleteness today points in that direction too (Collis, 1994; Foss, 1997; McGahan and Porter, 1997; Priem and Butler, 2000). According to this critique, resource-based studies give priority to the content aspect of strategy (Mahoney, 1995) and leave the managerial aspect that underlies the creation and management of resource-based strategies in second place.

Fortunately a number of recent resource-based studies such as Rosenbloom's (2000) study of NCR, Tripsas and Gavetti's (2000) work about Polaroid, and Adner and Helfat's (2003) observation of the oil industry, started to take this challenge seriously. Their works show that top management has a strong influence on how firms respond to external change. Adner and Helfat (2003) for example identify three important aspects of dynamic managerial capabilities: managerial human capital (Castanias and Helfat, 1991; Castanias and Helfat, 2001), managerial social capital (Burt, 1992; Gelatkanycz et al., 2001) and managerial cognition (Tripsas and Gavetti, 2000). Linking the literature on leadership more closely to these observations on competitive advantage should further enhance our understanding of the managerial aspects of strategy (Stadler, 2007). The essentially holistic approach adopted by Sun Tzu and Clausewitz might be a promising path to take.

REVISITING MEDIEVAL GREENLAND AND NINETEENTH CENTURY HONG KONG

Before concluding this chapter I want to return once again to its original intention: providing a historian's view of competitive strategy. History can aid the quest to understand competition in two separate ways. Firstly the rich material provided by history provides scholars with vast amounts of data to test their theories. As Helfat (2000) suggests, ". . . those who ignore history are doomed to repeat it. Thus, if we look only at a cross-section of resources and capabilities, we may draw incorrect inferences about why some firms have better resources than other firms. We also may draw the wrong lessons for the future. Retrospective understanding of competitive success and failures therefore can help to provide a firmer foundation for prospective advice."

Secondly, the concepts developed by theorists in the past offer many valuable lessons for scholars and practitioners today. While the contributions of modern management thinkers are most relevant in today's context, an occasional glimpse into the work of military strategies in ancient China and nineteenth century Germany is not in vain. Many of the issues they faced, e.g. fierce competition, are the same as those that managers battle with today.

To demonstrate the value of both historical data and ideas I want to conclude this chapter by returning once more to the stories of the Vikings and British overseas banking which I introduced in the beginning. Sun Tzu said that you have to know both your enemy and yourself to succeed. Both the Vikings and the Chartered Bank would have benefited greatly from this ancient wisdom. In the Vikings' case the cooling climate presented their greatest enemy. Had they been able to interpret the signs such as longer winters accurately and adapted their behavior accordingly, there is no reason why they could not have continued to prosper in Greenland in the same way the Inuit did. In the Chartered Bank's case its main enemy was the top management's cognition of the China business. Had the bank taken another message from Sun Tzu – "he will win who . . . is not interfered with by the sovereign" – to heart, the firm would have relied on local management and consequently been in a better position.

In sum, the works of Sun Tzu, Moltke, and Clausewitz present an interesting read that reminds us of the important role of managers. Their style and research do not fit the rigorous standards of today's strategy scholars but time has proved the relevance of their work, a test which modern strategists still have to pass.

REFERENCES

Adler, P., B. Goldoftas and D. Levine (1999), 'Flexibility versus efficiency? A case study of model changeovers in the Toyota production system', *Organization Science,* **10**, 43–68.
Adner, R. and C.E. Helfat (2003), 'Corporate effects and dynamic managerial capabilities', *Strategic Management Journal*, **24**, 1011–1025.
Andrews, K.R. (ed.) (1971), *The Concept of Corporate Strategy,* Homewood, IL: Dow-Jones Irwin.
Ansoff, H.I. (ed.) (1965), *Corporate Strategy: An Analytic Approach to Business Policy for Growth and Expansion,* New York: McGraw-Hill.
Ansoff, H.I. (1991), 'Critique of Henry Mintzberg's "The design school: reconsidering the basic premises of strategic management"', *Strategic Management Journal*, **12**, 449–462.
Barney, J.B. (1986), 'Strategic factor markets: expectations, luck, and business strategy', *Management Science*, **32**, 1231–1241.
Barney, J.B. (1991), 'Firm resources and sustained competitive advantage', *Journal of Management,* **17**, 99–120.
Bassford, C. (ed.) (1994), *Clausewitz in English: The Reception of Clausewitz in Britain and America,* New York: Oxford University Press.
Blyler, M. and R. Coff (2003), 'Dynamic capabilities, social capital, and rent appropriation: ties that split pies', *Strategic Management Journal*, **24**, 677–687.
Brandenbueger, A. and B.J. Nalebuff (eds) (1996), *Co-opetition,* New York: Doubleday.
Burt, R.S. (ed.) (1992), *Structural Holes: The Social Structure of Competition,* Cambridge, MA: Harvard University Press.

Cameron, J. (ed.) (1966), *Here Is Your Enemy,* New York: Holt, Rinehart, Winston.

Castanias, R.P. and C. Helfat (1991), 'Managerial resources and rents', *Journal of Management,* **17**, 155–171.

Castanias, R.P. and C. Helfat (2001), 'The managerial rents model: theory and empirical analysis', *Journal of Management,* **27**, 661–678.

Chandler, A. (ed.) (1962), *Strategy and Structure,* Cambridge, MA: MIT Press.

Collis, D.J. (1994), 'How valuable are organizational capabilities?', *Strategic Management Journal,* **15**, 143–152.

Conner, K.R. and C.K. Prahalad (1996), 'A resource-based theory of the firm: knowledge versus opportunism', *Organization Science,* **7**, 478–496.

Contractor, F.J. and P. Lorange (eds) (1988), *Cooperative Strategies in International Business,* Boston, MA: Lexington Books.

Diamond, J. (ed.) (2005), *Collapse: How Societies Choose to Fail or Succeed,* New York: Penguin Books.

Dierickx, I. and K. Cool (1989), 'Asset stock accumulation and sustainability of competitive advantage', *Management Science,* **35**, 1504–1511.

Druker, P. (ed.) (1985), *Innovation and Entrepreneurship: Practice and Principles,* New York: Harper & Row.

Eisenhardt, K.M. and R.A. Martin (2000), 'Dynamic capabilities: what are they?', *Strategic Management Journal,* **21**, 1105–1121.

Foss, N.J. (1997), 'Resources and strategy: problems, open issues, and ways ahead' in N.J. Foss (ed.), *Resources, Firms, and Strategies: A Reader in the Resource-based Perspective,* New York: Oxford University Press.

Galbraith, J. (2002), 'Organizing to deliver solutions', *Organizational Dynamics,* **31**, 194–206.

Gelatkanycz, M.A., B.K. Boyd and S. Finkelstein (2001), 'The strategic value of CEO external directorate networks: implications for CEO compensation', *Strategic Management Journal,* **22**, 889–898.

Ghemawat, P. (ed.) (1991), *Commitment: The Dynamics of Strategy,* New York: Free Press.

Gibson, C.B. and J. Birkinshaw (2004), 'The antecedents, consequences, and mediating role of organizational ambidexterity', *Academy of Management Journal,* **47**, 209–226.

Goold, M. (1992), 'Design, learning and planning: a further observation on the design school debate', *Strategic Management Journal,* **13**, 169–170.

Grant, R.M. (1996), 'Prospering in dynamically-competitive environments: organizational capability as knowledge creation', *Organization Science,* **7**, 375–387.

Grant, R.M. (2003), 'Strategic planning in a turbulent environment: evidence from the oil majors', *Strategic Management Journal,* **24**(6), 491–517.

Grant, R.M. (ed.) (2005), *Contemporary Strategy Analysis,* Oxford: Blackwell Publishing.

Hakansson, H. and I. Snehota (eds) (1995), *Developing Relationships in Business Networks,* London: Routledge.

Hedlund, G. and J. Ridderstrale (1997), 'Toward a theory of the self-renewing MNC', in B. Toyne and D. Nigh (eds), *International Business: An Emerging Vision*, Columbia: University of South Carolina Press.

Helfat, C. (2000), 'Guest editor's introduction to the special issue: the evolution of firm capabilities', *Strategic Management Journal,* **21**, 955–959.

Helfat, C. (ed.) (2007), *Dynamic Capabilities: Understanding Strategic Change in Organizations,* Malden, MA: Blackwell Publishing.

Helfat, C. and M. Peteraf (2003), 'The dynamic resource-based view: capability lifecycles', *Strategic Management Journal,* **24**, 997–1010.

Hinterhuber, H.H. and W. Popp (1992), 'Are you a strategist or just a manager?', *Harvard Business Review,* January–February, 105–113.

Holland, J.H. (ed.) (1975), *Adaptation in Natural and Artificial Systems,* Ann Arbor, MI: University of Michigan Press.

Joner, G. (ed.) (1993), *British Multinational Banking 1830–1990,* Oxford: Oxford University Press.

Keegan, J. (ed.) (1993), *A History of Warfare,* New York: Knopf.

Kim, W.C. and R. Mauborgne (eds) (2005), *Blue Ocean Strategy*, Boston: Harvard Business School Press.

King, F.H.H. (ed.) (1983), *Eastern Banking: Essays in the History of the Hong Kong and Shanghai Banking Corporation,* London: Athlone Press.

King, F.H.H. (ed.) (1991), *The Hong Kong Bank in the Period of Development and Nationalism, 1941–1984: From Regional Bank to Multinational Group,* New York: Cambridge University Press.

King, F.H.H. (1996), 'Does the corporation's history matter? Hong Kong Bank/HSBC Holdings, a case study', in A. Godley and O.M. Westall (eds), *Business History and Business Culture,* Manchester: Manchester University Press.

King, F.H.H. (2000), 'The transmission of corporate cultures: international officers in the HSBC Group', in A.J.H. Latham and H. Kawakatsu (eds), *Asia Pacific Dynamism, 1550–2000,* London: Routledge.

King, F.H.H. (2004), 'New political realities and the postwar re-establishment of foreign banks in East and South-East Asia' in E. Green, J. Lampe and F. Stiblar (eds), *Crisis and Renewal in Twentieth Century Banking,* Aldershot: Ashgate.

King, F.H.H., C.E. King and D.S.J. King (eds) (1987), *The Hong Kong Bank in Late Imperial China 1864–1902: On an Even Keel,* New York: Cambridge University Press.

King, F.H.H., C.E. King and D.J.S. King (eds) (1988a), *The Hong Kong Bank Between the Wars and the Bank Interned, 1919–1945: Return from Grandeur,* New York: Cambridge University Press.

King, F.H.H., C.E. King and D.J.S. King (eds) (1988b), *The Hong Kong Bank in the Period of Imperialism and War, 1895–1918: Wayfoong, the Focus of Wealth,* New York: Cambridge University Press.

King, W.T.C. (ed.) (1936), *A History of the London Discount Market,* London.

Kogut, B. and U. Zander (1992), 'Knowledge of the firm, combinative capabilities, and the replication of technology', *Organization Science,* **3**, 383–397.

Kuran, T. (1988), 'The tenacious past: theories of personal and collective conservatism', *Journal of Economic Behavior and Organization,* **10**, 143–171.

Lavie, D. (2006), 'Capability reconfiguration: an analysis of incumbent responses to technological change', *Academy of Management Review,* **31**, 153–174.

Lippman, S.A. and R.P. Rumelt (1982), 'Uncertain imitability: an analysis of interfirm differences in efficiency under competition', *The Bell Journal of Economics,* **13**, 418–438.

Lovendahl, B. and O. Revang (1998), 'Challenges to existing strategy theory in a postindustrial society', *Strategic Management Journal,* **19**, 755–773.

Mackenzie, C. (ed.) (1954), *Realms of Silver: One Hundred Years of Banking in the East,* London: Routledge & Kegan Paul.

Maclellan, J.W. (1891), 'Banking in India and China', *Bankers' Magazine,* **55**.

Mahoney, J. (1995), 'The management of resources and resource of management', *Journal of Business Research,* **33**, 91–101.

March, J. and H. Simon (eds) (1958), *Organizations,* New York: Wiley.

McDonough, E. and R. Leifer (1983), 'Using simultaneous structures to cope with uncertainty', *Academy of Management Journal,* **26**, 727–735.

McGahan, A.M. and M.E. Porter (1997), 'Adaptation on rugged landscapes', *Management Science,* **43**, 934–950.

Mintzberg, H. (1991), 'Learning 1, planning 0: reply to Igor Ansoff', *Strategic Management Journal,* **12**, 463–466.

Mintzerg, H. (ed.) (1994), *The Rise and Fall of Strategic Planning,* New York: Free Press.

Padula, G. and G.B. Dagnino (2007), 'Untangling the rise of coopetition: the intrusion of competition in a cooperative game structure', *International Studies of Management & Organization,* **37**, 32–53.

Peteraf, M.A. (1993), 'The cornerstones of competitive advantage: a resource-based view', *Strategic Management Journal,* **14**(3), 179–191.

Porter, M.E. (ed.) (1985), *Competitive Advantage: Creating and Sustaining Superior Performance,* New York: Free Press.

Powell, W.W., K.W. Koput and L. Smith-Doerr (1996), 'Inter-organizational collaboration and the locus of innovation: networks of learning in biotechnology', *Administrative Science Quarterly*, **41**, 116–145.
Priem, R.L. and J.E. Butler (2000), 'Is the resource-based "view" a useful perspective for strategic management research?', *Academy of Management Review*, **26**(1), 22–40.
Ray, G., J.B. Barney and W.A. Muhanna (2004), 'Capabilities, business processes, and competitive advantage: choosing the dependent variable in empirical tests of the resource-based view', *Strategic Management Journal*, **25**, 23–39.
Rosenbloom, R.S. (2000), 'Leadership, capabilities, and technological change: the transformation of NCR in the electronic era', *Strategic Management Journal*, **21**, 1083–1103.
Schumpeter, J. (ed.) (1934), *The Theory of Economic Development*, Cambridge, MA: Harvard University Press.
Selznick, P. (ed.) (1957), *Leadership in Administration: A Sociological Interpretation*, New York: Harper & Row.
Shapiro, C. and H. Varian (eds) (1998), *Information Rules*, Boston: Harvard Business School Press.
Stadler, C. (2007), 'Managing for enduring success – a historic view of dynamic capabilities in large European firms', paper presented at the Strategic Management Society Annual Conference, San Diego.
Summer, H.G. (ed.) (1982), *On Strategy*, Novato, CA: Presidio Press.
Teece, D.J., G. Pisano and A. Shuen (1997), 'Dynamic capabilities and strategic management', *Strategic Management Journal*, **18**, 509–533.
Tripsas, M. and G. Gavetti (2000), 'Capabilities, cognition, and inertia: evidence from digital imaging', *Strategic Management Journal*, **21**, 1147–1161.
Tushman, M.L. and C.A. O'Reilly (1996), 'Managing evolutionary and revolutionary change', *California Management Review*, **11**, 8–30.
Wenerfelt, B. (1984), 'A resource-based view of the firm', *Strategic Management Journal*, **5**, 171–180.
Zollo, M. and S. Winter (2002), 'Deliberate learning and the evolution of dynamic capabilities', *Organization Studies*, **13**, 339–351.

4 Theory of science perspectives on strategic management research: debates and a novel view
Nicolai J. Foss[1]

INTRODUCTION

Strategic management researchers are, as a rule, practically oriented folks who typically do not have much patience with lofty debates in the theory of science. Say the word 'ontology' and you will have eyes rolling in the audience (yes, I have tried it!). Still, treating strategic management in a theory of science perspective actually goes back at least to Bowman (1974), and quite a number of papers on essentially philosophical issues in strategic management have been published in top journals, notably the *Strategic Management Journal*, over the last two decades. Quite often – in fact, usually – these contributions mirror and apply established arguments in the theory of science literature, for example work on the growth of knowledge (Camerer, 1985; Balakrishnan et al., 1989), constructivism versus realism (Smircich and Stubbard, 1985), the role of unobservables (Godfrey and Hill, 1995), the rhetorical practice of strategic management scholars (Mahoney, 1993), so-called 'critical theory' (Knights and Morgan, 1991; Alvesson and Willmott, 1995), and even 'deconstruction' (Whipp, 1996).

Moreover, strategic management scholars are sometimes called 'implicit theorists of science'. For example, they are intensely occupied with theoretical *change* in their field and with the reasons for such change (Hoskisson et al., 1999), essentially methodological undertakings. In fact, the purpose of the highly influential bi-annual special issues of the *Strategic Management Journal* is not only to take stock of existing developments, but more importantly to signal major changes in the field. Scholars actively debate those changes, and often do so in what is essentially a philosophy of science mode. For example, they may debate whether the adoption by the strategic management community of certain core ideas (e.g., the RBV approach to competitive advantage) leads to a "loss of content" (Kuhn, 1970) (i.e. other ideas are forgotten – such as notions of positioning). They may debate the relations between old and new strategy theories (e.g. rival or complementary; Mahoney and Pandian, 1992; Oliver, 1997; Foss,

1999). Or they may issue the charge of tautology, a widespread practice in debate on the RBV (Porter, 1991; Black and Boal, 1994; Priem and Butler, 2001; Powell, 2001).

Clearly, all such discussions fundamentally touch on theory of science issues, as a traditional key concern of the theory of science has been the criteria that practising scientists apply for the evaluation of theories and choice among rival theories. In this chapter I shall make reference to, and briefly review and discuss, a subset of these discussions. However, the aim of the chapter goes further than reviewing existing contributions.

Thus, I also discuss and draw attention to some more neglected (in the strategic management field) theory of science aspects of strategic management, notably mechanism-oriented explanation and the need for micro-foundations. These belong to the theory of science proper, because they touch on issues of how we grapple with social ontology through the modes of explanation we apply (see also Tsoukas and Knudsen, 2002). Moreover, I shall argue that issues that relate to mechanisms and levels of analysis are among the reasons that scientists give and legitimately can give for rejecting or accepting theories. In fact, one can hold the view that scientific progress *is* the theoretical and empirical uncovering of the workings of the causal mechanisms that produce observable events (cf. Elster, 1989). One can go even further, and hold that such uncovering and theorizing of generative mechanisms usually entails reduction, that is, moving down the ladder of levels of analysis. In this view, which I shall state and defend, reduction is not simply a matter of explanation, but a distinct criterion for scientific progress. Whether strategic management has made scientific progress on this criterion is debatable. Specifically, I develop a variant of the 'swinging pendulum' thesis of Hoskisson et al. (1999), and argue that strategic management research has oscillated between giving explanatory primacy to collective entities, or to micro-entities and their interaction. The latter is, I argue, preferable.

THE THEORY OF SCIENCE AND STRATEGIC MANAGEMENT

The Theory of Science

As a branch of epistemology, the theory of science has historically had a number of aims, although the priorities have changed quite dramatically, perhaps particularly over the last 20 years. A traditional aim has been to characterize science as a distinct field of inquiry, to describe the procedures that secure (if indeed they do) scientists' privileged access to

Nature's Secrets, and to identify the criteria – such as potential falsifiability (Popper, 1934) – that may distinguish scientific from non-scientific arguments (i.e. the 'demarcation problem'). A closely related activity has been the search for criteria of scientific progress. Other traditional (that is, at least within the last hundred years) theory of science concerns have centered on the objectivity vs theory-laden'ness of observations; the indeterminacy of theory under empirical testing (the Duhem-Quine thesis); induction versus falsification; the clash between scientific realism and instrumentalism; foundationalism vs skepticism; and, more recently, constructivism, issues of scientific openness, and the sociology and anthropology of science.

As indicated in the Introduction, virtually all of these themes can be found – whether implicitly or explicitly – in the theory of science literature in strategic management. Overall, however, the theory of science themes that have made the most frequent appearances in the strategic management journals are those associated with the so-called growth of knowledge literature (Popper, 1934; Kuhn, 1970; Lakatos, 1970; Feyerabend, 1974; Laudan, 1977). These have also been the most important inputs into theory of science discussion in economics, perhaps the most important foundational discipline of the strategic management field. A brief review may therefore be in order.

The Growth of Knowledge Literature

The growth of knowledge literature is conventionally taken to begin with Popper (1934) and continue in his development of what he came to refer to as critical rationalism, an approach that fundamentally involved the idea that all knowledge is inherently conjectural (fallibilism) and cannot be verified by testing, only falsified. The growth of (scientific) knowledge entered the picture in Popper's thinking from his wrestling with the problem of aligning fallibilism with the observed growth of knowledge. Popper's solution to the problem was evolutionary epistemology, that is, the idea that the growth of knowledge may be explained making use of such fundamental evolutionary mechanisms as the variation-heredity-selection triad, corresponding to competing conjectures, background knowledge (problem situations arise against background knowledge; conjectures that have withstood falsification attempts become part of background knowledge), and falsification leading to error elimination, respectively. Popper seems to have thought of this as a descriptive model of the growth of knowledge, although he was aware that his emphasis on bold conjectures (the variation mechanism in his evolutionary epistemology) was more normative than strictly descriptive.

In terms of the mechanisms underlying Popper's evolutionary episte-mology, Kuhn and Lakatos can be understood as de-emphasizing the vari-ation and selection part in favor of strongly emphasizing the heredity part. Thus, both argued that individual theories are embedded in larger cogni-tive structures, the famous "paradigms" (Kuhn, 1970), that supplied large parts of the theoretical components of those individual theories. In fact, Kuhn rejected the idea that scientists pursue bold conjectures and attempt to falsify their theories. Lakatos is often portrayed as a sort of halfway house between Popper and Kuhn: while he adopted the paradigm idea, substantially refining it, he clearly admitted that falsification played a role.

The important organizing category in Lakatos' model is 'the scien-tific research program', which is clearly a more elaborate version of Kuhn's concept of paradigm (and minus ideas on incommensurability). Specifically, it should be thought of as a series of theories that comprise a continuous whole because they share some so-called hard core proposi-tions and are constructed according to heuristics that are specific to the scientific research program. The research program changes by modifying propositions in the 'protective belt' (the positive heuristic informs the researcher about how this should legitimately be done, and the negative heuristic informs him about what cannot legitimately be done), while keeping intact the hard core. As such, this is a descriptive model of sci-entific activity. However, Lakatos adds a normative dimension by intro-ducing notions of progression and degeneration. In his scheme, scientific progress obtains if a new theory within a research program has 'excess empirical content' in the sense that it puts forward some novel fact, some hitherto unnoticed prediction, which apparently (Lakatos is far from forthcoming here) should be understood as predicting novel phenomena. Degenerating research programs are those that fail to develop novel facts and/or where theories belonging to the program repeatedly are falsified.

The Theory of Science in Economics

In the social sciences, the growth of knowledge literature became par-ticularly influential in economics, arguably the discipline that overall has influenced strategic management the most. Specifically, a watered down version of Popperian falsificationism in the guise of Friedman's (1953) brand of instrumentalism became hugely influential in economics. The growth of knowledge literature became relatively influential in econom-ics in the 1970s and 1980s. In particular, Lakatos' methodology of the scientific research program proved influential.

Thus, a cottage industry – now very much a sunset industry – that explored various changes in economic theory in analytical terms from the growth of knowledge literature developed in the 1980s (see Backhouse, 1994 for a post mortem). Economic methodologists gradually realized that economists were not terribly scrupulous with respect to practising the falsificationism they hailed in their rhetorical practice. Whereas Blaug (1980) saw this as a problem for economists, increasingly it came to be seen as a problem for Popperian falsificationism. Similarly, it was found that it was quite hard to come up with convincing examples of Kuhnian revolutions or Lakatosian novel facts in economics (DeMarchi and Blaug, 1991; Backhouse, 1994; Foss, 1998).

As a consequence, the focus began to shift to examining the actual practice of economists, that is, to those criteria that may be inferred through the actual choices that are being made in theory-building, and away from abstract and context-independent criteria for theory choice (Mäki, 1992). The wish to pass judgment on actual theory choice was also downplayed. Partly in parallel with this, the economics profession had a brief flirtation with rhetorical analysis, that is, the actual acts of persuasion that practising economists employ to convince their peers of the soundness of their arguments (McCloskey, 1983). And some of the reorientation away from the growth of knowledge literature took place in tandem with and to some extent inspired by currents in the sociology of science, notably the various ('strong', 'weak') programs in the sociology of science (Bloor, 1976).[2]

Theory of Science Debates in Strategic Management: Overall

Strategic management is in a number of ways reminiscent of economics, not only because economics is an important foundational input in strategic management research, or because many strategic management scholars have an economics background, but also because strategic management seems to have gone through rather similar waves of methodological discussion and opinion. Thus, some of the first theory of science-based statements in strategic management were informed by arguments from the growth of knowledge literature. Such statements were forcefully put forward by Camerer (1985) and Balakrishnan, Montgomery and Wernerfelt (1989), that is, strategy scholars strongly influenced by economics. In particular, these scholars criticized the lack of falsifiable analytical content in strategy content research. Growth of knowledge arguments continue to be invoked in methodological discourse in strategic management (Bogner et al., 1998; Powell, 2001: 876).

However, as is the case in the theory of science in general as well as in economics, initial enthusiasm with growth of knowledge philosophers has given way to more 'pluralistic' positions (Bowman, 1990). For example, the 'rhetorical' approach of economic historian Donald (now Deirdre)

MacCloskey (1983) was forcefully applied by Mahoney in a string of papers in the beginning of the 1990s (Mahoney and Pandian, 1992; Mahoney, 1993).

It is not difficult to see why strategic management scholars initially interested in growth of knowledge arguments may gradually have become somewhat uncomfortable with them. On the one hand, strategic management is a very strongly empirical field. Almost from the takeoff of strategic management as a scientific field (circa 1980 – the launch of the *Strategic Management Journal* and the publication of Porter, 1980), the majority of researchers in their scientific practice conformed to the covering law approach to explanation and prediction (Hempel, 1965) and expressed a clear preference for the variable-centered (large-N) 'variance approach' of empirical research practice rather than other (rigorous) approaches (Abell, 2001, 2004). Hypothesis formulation and testing in the context of large-N samples was, and is, the order of the day, and the vast majority of papers published in the leading journals that publish strategic management research take this approach. On the other hand, it also seems clear that most strategic management researchers do not follow falsificationism in the form espoused by Popper, but rather the "statistical view of testing that accepts that neither refutation nor confirmation can ever be final, and that all we can hope to do is to discover on the basis of finite amounts of imperfect knowledge what is the balance of probabilities among existing hypotheses" (Lipsey, 1966: 184). Thus, strategic management research practice may not conform to at least strict falsificationism.

Moreover, the Kuhnian and Lakatosian schema seem difficult to apply to a field that does not go back more than 50 years as even a practical field, and perhaps only about 30 years (or less) as a scientific field. It is not clear that there are in any meaningful sense Kuhnian paradigms or Lakatosian scientific research programs in strategic management. In addition, it is unclear what are the Lakatosian 'novel facts' in strategic management research (perhaps depending on how exactly that enigmatic concept is defined). To be sure, competitive advantage, whether sustained or not, hardly qualifies as a novel fact, as the recognition that some firms are more successful than others on a sustained basis certainly characterizes any strategy content approach, and indeed may be seen as the defining overall research question of the field.

Recent Methodological Debate in Strategic Management

What is here interpreted as a rejection of traditional growth of knowledge arguments should by no means imply that strategic management scholars have given up on discourse that applies theory of science arguments.

Strategic management scholars continue to vigorously debate methodological issues and the subject seems to have increased in popularity recently, as witnessed by the spate of methodological work that has appeared in the pages of the *Strategic Management Journal* over the last decade.

Relative to earlier methodological pronouncements which tended to be relatively abstract and aloof, and mainly related to existing research practice in a highly critical manner (the high point of this is surely Camerer, 1985), recent methodological work tends to more explicitly relate to existing problems in strategic management research. For example, the advent and eventual dominance of the resource-based view raised a traditional problem in the theory of science – what is the explanatory role of unobservables? – as that view often emphasizes knowledge resources, and particularly tacit ones. Godfrey and Hill (1995) applied traditional philosophy positions (positivism and realism) to the debate, ultimately siding with the realist view that unobservables may be defended in terms of inference to the best explanation (i.e., abduction), in other words a better performing (predicting) theory that involves unobservables is preferred on account of its superior performance (Lipton, 2004).

Also reflecting the increased dominance of the resource-based view, Powell (2001) explored the philosophical aspects of the link between sustained competitive advantage and sustained financial performance that is foundational to the strategic management field. He provocatively argued that 1) sustained competitive advantage is neither sufficient nor necessary to sustained financial superiority; 2) there is no contemporary falsifiable, unfalsified theory of sustained competitive advantage; and 3) discussion of competitive advantage is really a Wittgensteinian language game, which may be defended on pragmatist grounds for its usefulness to the strategic management field. Powell's paper gave rise to two responses. Durand (2002: 868) took particular issue with Powell's point 1) and constructed an argument that "competitive advantage is a sufficient but not-necessary condition requiring a conjunctive factor, which is presumably organization." Arend (2003: 281) admitted Powell's point 2), but argued that even tautological and analytical propositions may be useful, because they supply "measures and laundry lists of possible manifestations of the elements of such propositions such as bargaining power, contracting costs, inimitability, and the like" that provide decision-makers with helpful categories with which to classify and arrange real phenomena.[3]

On the whole, it is characteristic of recent theory of science-based discourse in strategic management that scholars, in contrast to earlier ambitious statements by Camerer (1985) and Balakrishnan et al. (1988), seem to have given up on putting forward strong recommendations for research practice, such as generally condemning research practice for its failure to cast reasoning in sufficiently analytical terms or to honor Popperian ideals of falsification. Instead, they are taken up with such issues as the logical structure of specific arguments in strategic management (Brønn, 1998; Powell, 2001) or whether the evolution of the field can be characterized as a move towards embracing more 'organic' conceptions (Farjoun, 2002).

There is a stronger descriptive than normative stance in recent contributions, and often a strong attempt to relate to actual research practice. To illustrate how far this can go, in a discussion of whether Kuhn's paradigm development model applies to strategic management, Boyd et al. (2005) actually develop concrete measures that may allow for an assessment of the maturity of the strategic management field.[4] This increased orientation to the actual research practice of the field may reflect the corresponding development of the theory of the science over the last decades. However, it may also reflect that strategic management is now more established in terms of research heuristics, and agreement on what are the key problems, the key variables and the key findings than it was in the 1980s (but see Mintzberg et al., 1998); accordingly, there may simply be less to criticize from a theory of science perspective.

Still, there may be things left for the methodologist to normatively relate to. I propose in the following that *one* important way (certainly not the only one) in which strategic management progresses as a scientific field is by means of performing analytical reduction, that is, showing how phenomena on a given level of analysis are really constituted by the action and interaction of entities, ultimately human beings, at levels lower down. On this basis, it is possible, I argue, to pass (cautious) methodological judgment on the evolution of the field.

A DIFFERENT VIEW: REDUCTION AS PROGRESS

Of Reduction and Reductionism

The notions of reduction and reductionism are highly context-dependent. Historically, these notions have been associated with more or less controversial positions such as mechanism, physicalism, and methodological individualism (Dupree, 1993; Jones, 2000). While the notions of reduction and reductionism, as they are used here, are closely related to methodological individualism, they have nothing to do with mechanism or physicalism. The aim is not to pursue the kind of caricature reductionism well known from debates in natural science.

An extreme and classical kind of reductionism holds that "all laws governing the behaviour of complex objects should be deducible from the laws of lower-level science and thus, ultimately, the laws of all sciences should be deducible from those of particle physics" (Dupré, 2001: 309). Applied to strategic management such a view would imply that competitive advantage be reduced to the genetic endowment of firm founders (and, indeed, ultimately to the laws of particle physics); most likely a pointless exercise.

By reduction, then, we mean the process of explaining a particular phenomenon in terms of more fundamental phenomena. Reductionism here means the explanatory position that the best understanding of a complex, and in social science, collective-level, phenomenon "should be sought at the level of structure, behaviour and laws of its component parts plus their relations" (Silberstein, 2002: 81). It entails a search for the deep structure underneath aggregate phenomena (Williamson, 1996). While reduction is a description of an analytical operation, reductionism is a normative stance; it asserts that reduction is something worth striving for, and that science progresses when reductions are performed.

Reductionism and Scientific Progress

The argument here is that reduction is more than an analytical operation; it may constitute a criterion of scientific progress. On this criterion, a body of knowledge (whether a theory, research program, paradigm, research tradition, etc.) makes progress when a novel analytical reduction is performed. Such a 'novel analytical reduction' takes place when one or more explanatory mechanisms, constructs, etc. that were hitherto treated in a blackbox manner are opened up and addressed in terms that are congenial to the other elements of the body of knowledge.

Reductionism is a close ally of philosophical realism because it entails a sustained attempt to identify and theorize the real causal mechanisms – the "cogs and wheels" (Elster, 1989: 3) – that generate and explain observed associations between observed events (Harré, 1970; Bhaskar, 1978).[5] It is, however, different from the covering-law model of explanation of Hempel and others, because the covering-law model does not imply an insistence on identifying causality.

Now, whereas reductionism is naturally associated with philosophical realism, the reverse is not necessarily true: one can be a realist and hold that understanding real causal mechanisms requires doing the opposite of reduction. Some structuralist sociologists may take this position. In contrast, the reductionist position holds that the real causal mechanisms are usually located at the same or lower levels of analysis than the *explanandum* phenomenon, and that identifying and theorizing such mechanisms *means* scientific progress.[6] There is a pragmatic dimension to this, because a better understanding of real generative mechanisms usually translates into better control (cf. Coleman, 1990: chapter 1).

Reductionism in this sense is not an extraneous criterion for scientific progress; it seems to be something that many practising social scientists subscribe to. This is particularly the case of economists (cfr. also Mäki, 2001), and sociologists and political scientists who work from a rational choice basis. Thus, a massive research effort in economics over the last three decades has sought to understand aggregate phenomena, whether macro-economic outcomes or institutions, as the (possibly unintended) result of the interaction of rational individuals. The new institutional economics, contract theory, political economy, and a number of approaches in macro-economics (new classical as well as new Keynesian) are instances of this overall effort, exemplifying how strong the drive towards reduction is in economics. While reduction is by no means the only criterion that economists apply to theory evaluation, it is surely an important one and one shared by most economists. And while strategic management scholars are by no means similarly uniform with respect to reduction and reductionism, a number of strategic management scholars may, as I argue later, be seen as reductionists (e.g. Barney, 2001; Coff, 1999; Lippman and Rumelt, 2003).[7]

What Reductionism Is Not

Reductionism has generated much heated controversy (Dupree, 1993; Jones, 2000), including controversy in strategic management. For example, Bourgeois (1984: 586) argued that "reductionism eliminates much of the richness that characterizes the strategic management process" (the basis for this assertion remains, however, unclear). As the position here is the exact opposite – we need more reductionism in strategic management research to increase the richness of the field – it is advisable to be explicit about what reductionism does and does not entail. It may be easiest to start with the latter.

Reductionism is occasionally taken to imply a denial of the phenomenon of emergence. Whatever that may be in a broader disciplinary context, such a denial is not characteristic of reductionism in social science, including strategic management. Reductionism is fully compatible with acknowledging that unintended consequences take place, for example. Furthermore, reductionism in social science is sometimes taken to mean that the analyst must always make reference to the full set of concrete actions, preferences, beliefs, etc. of concrete agents when trying to explain a phenomenon on the social domain. Obviously, this is usually not feasible, first because of the sheer number of interacting agents and the complexity of their interaction – a problem that is occasionally referred to as 'Cournot's Problem' (e.g. in Davis, 2003) – , and, second, because of limited access to the preferences and beliefs of the relevant agents. Whatever that may be,[8] no such extreme reductionism is advocated here.

Reductionism, Black Boxes, and Structures

Although reductionism seeks to eschew explanatory black boxes in principle, sometimes a case can be made for some degree of black box explanation. Apart from obvious disciplinary reasons,[9] the reason for allowing some black boxes to enter explanation is explanatory parsimony. As Lewis (1986: 214) explains,

> [a]ny particular event that we might wish to explain stands at the end of a long and complicated causal history. We might imagine a world where causal histories are short and simple; but in the world as we know it, the only question is whether they are infinite or merely enormous.

Luckily, it is simply not always necessary to seek and perform 'rock-bottom explanation' for an explanation to be valid. For example, the strategic management scholar who is cognizant of economics knows that under competitive conditions, decision-makers in firms only have a very limited feasible behavioral repertoire. If they do not choose an element of this set, they will not survive. Thus, although there is no break with the ontological position that only individuals can choose, our strategic management scholar pragmatically recognizes that a structure (i.e. competitive conditions) can substitute in an explanatory sense for a much more complicated explanation involving individual action and interaction.[10] However, being a proper reductionist, he knows that such a structural story is at best a reduced-form explanation, that is, shorthand for something much more complicated. Economists and strategic management scholars perform somewhat related explanatory operations when they construct firm-level arguments. Thus, to involve the argument in an explanation that a firm has a strategy or acts in a certain way is, of course, shorthand for a complex set of underlying individual actions and interactions.

Reductionism and Methodological Individualism

In a social science context, reduction and reductionism are intimately associated with methodological individualism.[11] Reductionism in social science implies methodological individualism. Methodological individualism defines, as it were, the limits to reduction in social science, because it implies that social science explanation can stop at the level of individuals. There is no need to proceed further down the explanatory ladder.[12]

In its strongest form, methodological individualism asserts that in explanations of social phenomena reference is allowed *only* to individuals, their properties and their actions and interactions. Thus, at no point in the explanation can reference be made to supra-individual entities as in any way acting as causal agents. On this program, explaining, for example, the strategy of a firm must always involve making reference to the mental states of all relevant organizational stakeholders.[13] Many (in fact, most) methodological individualists do not espouse this strong form. For example, Agassi (1960) argues that reference to institutions, clearly a collective concept, can be permitted in social science explanation, and many methodological individualists would argue that reference to collective concepts is permissible, and sometimes necessary as a sort of explanatory shorthand. In the context of strategic management, the collective concept of (firm-level) capabilities may be invoked as a handy explanatory shorthand. However, all methodological individualists insist that *ultimately* collective phenomena must be reduced to and explained in terms of individuals, that is, individual endowments, intentions, desires, expectations, and goals (cf. Hayek, 1955; Elster, 1989). Thus, the methodological individualist strategy scholar will be skeptical of the use of the notion of capabilities until the individual-level foundations of this concept have been clarified.[14]

In contrast, methodological collectivism starts from the assumption that collectives are somehow independent from individuals and can therefore be taken as 'primitives' in social science explanation. That is, collectives such as organizations, and social facts such as institutions, culture and capabilities, serve as the primary independent variables determining individual and collective behavior and outcomes (DiMaggio and Powell, 1991: 8). The argument is that structure and institutions are prior to individuals in influencing (and even determining) choice sets and behavior. In general, individual-level explanation is rejected in favor of collective explanation.

In terms of the earlier emphasis on opening up black boxes and uncovering causal mechanisms, it is clear that methodological individualists and methodological collectivists differ strongly with respect to which boxes need to be opened and which mechanisms deserve emphasis, and perhaps even which mechanisms exist. In other words, ontological positions are very likely to accompany methodological positions. Thus, a hardcore methodological individualist (if such exist) will deny any top-down causation and insist that all that matters is bottom-up causation (i.e. from individuals to collectives). A moderate methodological individualist may accept that at least metaphorically (cf. the earlier notion of explanatory shorthand) institutions exert influence on individual behavior, for example, in the sense that they structure incentives and therefore affect behavior (Boudon, 1998). Hardcore collectivists (if such exist) may argue that causal relations that operate wholly on the collective level have real existence and are not just explanatory shorthand.

THE EVOLUTION OF STRATEGIC MANAGEMENT: OSCILLATING BETWEEN MICRO AND MACRO

The Swinging Strategic Management Pendulum

In a magisterial paper Hoskisson et al. (1999) surveyed two decades of research in strategic management and likened the evolution of the field to a swinging pendulum. Whereas early work emphasized rich case description of individual firms and individual managers' behaviors, around 1980 there was a move away from this inside perspective towards more of an outside perspective, based on industrial economics and strongly emphasizing cross-sectional work and a general quest for generalization. Without dropping these ambitions, work on strategic groups, competitive dynamics, and boundary relationships between firms began to swing the pendulum back towards an internal focus as the 1980s progressed. The strong emphasis on transaction costs economics (Williamson, 1985) in the mid- to late-1980s signified an intermediate position of the pendulum. The rise of the resource-based view towards the end of the 1980s swung the pendulum fully back towards an emphasis on the internal aspects of firms, and arguably a more eclectic approach to empirical research.

The swinging pendulum thesis is not a normative device; it is purely constructed for the purpose of historical reconstruction, and for demonstrating how changing theories imply different empirical research methods. To the extent that a view on progress in strategic management is present in the Hoskisson et al. (1999) piece, progress is a matter of being better able to cope with problems, old and new (e.g. globalization), integration of diverse perspectives, and more rigorous empirical techniques (see also Hitt et al., 1998). In fact, the issue of scientific progress is seldom addressed in the strategic management field, although some early papers highlighted it (Camerer, 1985; Balakrishnan et al., 1989). In contrast, the issue is directly confronted in the following, making use of a variation on the swinging pendulum thesis.

Scientific Progress in the Strategic Management Field

So, has the strategic management field made scientific progress? Obviously, how that question is answered depends on which criteria are applied and even on how these criteria are interpreted. On the basis of criteria essentially borrowed from economics and the growth of knowledge literature, Camerer (1985) concluded that strategic management research had not made any substantial theoretical progress. In developing prescriptions for research, he stressed conventionalist criteria such as the coherence of the theoretical structure, and in general put forward a strong advocacy for the position that "deductive use of mathematics and economic concepts is the best way to answer (and ask) corporate strategy questions" (1985: 1). Mahoney (1993) argued that the alleged coherence may effectively translate into suppressing (necessary) diversity. On the basis of what seems to be an instrumentalist criterion, Arend (2003: 283) argued that "If . . . a science is defined by an ability to predict and control the dependent variables of interest then strategy research cannot ultimately fare well. Perhaps a new definition is needed to provide a fairer measure of progress in strategy research." While Arend may pass unnecessarily harsh judgment, the argument here is that his call for new criteria for assessing scientific progress in the strategic management field is well taken. One such new criterion is analytical reduction, as has just been suggested.

Levels of Analysis

As Hackman (2003: 905) notes, "[r]egardless of the level of analysis at which we begin, we like to move to the next level for our explanations." For the practising social scientist that level, Hackman explains by means of examples, typically lies lower down, not further up.[15] However, it is not the case that the strategic management field has exhibited a natural tendency to adopt increasingly reductionist or micro-oriented explanations. On the contrary, the field has, taken as a whole, demonstrated a preference for supra-individual levels of analysis, whether capabilities, competencies, core competencies, dynamic capabilities, firm, group, or industry levels. Of course, there is nothing surprising in this, given that the key dependent variables in strategic management research have typically been located at the firm level. However, to work at levels of analysis that are higher than that of the individual does not, of course, rule out the need for establishing micro-foundations for such aggregate work (i.e. the analytical convenience or necessity of supra-individual levels of analysis does not preclude micro-foundations). However, the efforts to build explicit micro-foundations have been very few. Therefore, there have also been very few attempts to seriously reconcile micro- and macro-levels,[16] in spite of much recent attention being paid to levels issues, multiple-level analysis and the like in management in general (e.g. Klein et al., 1994; Felin and Hesterly, 2007).

There are various reasons why this sort of inquiry has so far been largely absent from strategic management. At the most basic level, strategic management is still a young field: no or few fields begin in a multi-level mode and in social science micro-foundations do not necessarily come first.[17] Another reason is that in an inherently applied and practical discipline, implicit consensus may arise that issues of micro-foundations and of bridging levels are best left at the level of the base disciplines (e.g. psychology, economics, sociology inquiry). A third possible reason is that strategic management may be inherently pluralistic (Mahoney, 1993; Mahoney and Pandian, 1993) and this precludes building specific micro-foundations (Felin and Foss, 2005). Whatever all that may be, strategic management has usually been characterized by collective-level theorizing (see also Felin and Hesterly, 2005), as will be discussed next.

Strategic Management in the Aggregate Mode

Hoskisson et al. (1998) note – correctly – that strategy thinking began with case studies of single firms and an emphasis on the general manager. However, as an analytical enterprise, strategic management rather began in a more aggregate mode. Early thinking (beginning of the 1970s) coming out of the Boston Consulting Group stressed firm-level learning-curve advantages with no attention being paid to the underlying intra-organizational generative processes of individual action and interaction that are ultimately responsible for the learning-curve phenomenon. Research inspired by the Profit Impact of Market Strategy project begun in the mid-1960s at General Electric and expanded upon by the Management Institute at Harvard from the beginning of the 1970s entailed a search for reduced-form correlations between profit variables and various potential independent variables that defined an aggregative style of theorizing that is still very much present in the field. The focus of the PIMS project arguably also helped to pave the way for the field's perhaps first serious analytical breakthrough, namely Porter's (1980) industry analysis/positioning approach.

Transferring industrial organization economics to the strategy field, Porter's approach placed all of the explanatory burden on the aggregate characteristics of the environment, as captured in the famous 'five forces'.

The firm, as has so often been observed, is completely blackboxed in this approach. Managers are mentioned, but only as the agents that have to carry out the analysis of industries and position the firm in the chosen industries. Their skills at doing this are presumably the main source of competitive advantage. Of course, as a practising economist, Porter cannot be expected to have any particular sympathy for methodological collectivism. And his industry analysis does not harbor any ontological pretensions with respect to the existence of industries as anything other but producers that recognize that their products are close or relatively close substitutes. Indeed, as Porter (1980) himself stresses, the five forces approach used as a strategic tool is first and foremost a first cut at organizing information of relevance to the firm. While starting from this cut, more sophisticated strategic analysis must deal with strategic groups and mobility barriers, with pricing tactics and the like.

In fact, later strategic management work that builds from industrial organization economics has typically dealt with exactly these kinds of more fine-grained issues. As a result, some of the somewhat fuzzy collective categories that loom so large in Porter's early work disappear. Thus, instead of anonymous 'forces' now come well-specified cooperative and non-cooperative games with (respectively) buyers, suppliers, complementors and competitors (Ghemawat, 1998; Brandenburger and Nalebuff, 1996) where the players are clearly identified, and – at least in the case of non-cooperative games – their interaction is explicitly modeled. The case of the Porter approach nicely illustrates how an aggregative approach that places all of the informational burden on the analytical level immediately above the focal firm sacrifices informational content. Thus, the industry analysis/positioning has nothing in itself to say about firm-level competitive advantage.

Towards Micro – and Back to Collectives and Collectivism

The RBV has very often been portrayed as an approach that supplied the missing pieces, specifically the analysis of (firm-level) competitive advantage,[18] by taking an explicit focus on the resources that firms control. It is often informally seen as an instance of scientific progress because it treated a hitherto untheorized set of mechanisms, that is, the links from resources to competitive advantage and in turn to performance. The other side of that coin is that the RBV was reductionist in the sense that it dug deeper than rival perspectives by placing the primary explanatory burden on the resources controlled by a firm rather than on industry structure and competitive interaction. The individual resource would, at least on first inspection, seem to lie on a substantially lower level of analysis than the industry, the group or the firm. Thus, the RBV would seem to be well suited to exploring, for example, how individual employees contribute to value creation and how created value is distributed as a result of bargaining processes among the various stakeholders whose cooperation takes place under the legal shell represented by the firm (Wernerfelt, 1989). This potential for micro-analysis was, however, sidetracked for a long time, until the important recent work of Coff (1999) and Lippman and Rumelt (2003a and b).

It is quite arguable that one of the reasons why the RBV succeeded is exactly the feature of digging deeper. Not only should this be recognized as an independent achievement, but it also had the advantage of bringing the view into contact with organizational theory (in a broad sense, including organizational economics and organizational behavior), human resource management, research on ICT and much other strategically relevant research that was hard to link to the more aggregative Porter approach.

However, as time unfolded, several things happened that implied that strategic management did not fully release the potential for micro-analysis that the advent of the RBV signaled. First, standard definitions of a 'resource' did not take an explicit micro-perspective. Thus, Barney (1991) defined a resource in a rather inclusive manner as "anything that may be thought of as an advantage to a firm." Clearly, this might conceivably encompass organization-level, collective resources, such as capabilities, culture and the like. Dierickx and Cool's (1989) extremely influential analysis was widely interpreted as implying that 'stand-alone' resources acquired on strategic factor markets could not in general be expected to give rise to competitive advantage simply because they were traded. Whatever we may think of the soundness of this conclusion (and for the contrary view, see Barney, 1986 and Denrell, Fang and Winter, 2003), the perceived force of its logic directed attention to socially complex, collectively held resources, such as the core competencies or capabilities that were gaining currency at the beginning of the 1990s.[19]

There was a move back to the collective level, as strategy scholars increasingly converged on organizational capabilities as a key construct (Eisenhardt and Martin, 1999; Winter, 2003). Indeed, the organizational capabilities approach may now be the predominant way of thinking about heterogeneity in strategic management. Sustained competitive advantage, a firm-level phenomenon, is now directly explained in terms of capabilities, competencies, etc., that is, in terms of other firm-level phenomena. This is methodological collectivism (Felin and Foss, 2005; Felin and Hesterly, 2007).

CONCLUDING DISCUSSION: WHERE IS STRATEGY HEADING?

Contribution

Although it has been claimed that the degree of reflexivity in strategic management is low (Pettigrew et al., 2002: 9, 11), methodological reflection has actually been part of the field almost since its inception (Bowman, 1974). A theory of science chapter was part of the seminal Schendel and Hofer (1979) collection of essays (Spender, 1979). Methodology papers have continuously appeared in the *Strategic Management Journal*. In addition, strategic management scholars are (as is the case of most practising scientists) active implicit theorists of science, making essentially methodological comments and observations on existing work in the field. In terms of the trends of methodological discourse in strategic management, early work was clearly under the influence of the growth of knowledge literature (particularly Balakrishnan et al., 1989), but current methodological work makes a rather pluralistic impression, ranging from constructivism to the application of formal logic.

Whereas the normative aspect of the methodological enterprise has been somewhat toned down in recent writings, this chapter has introduced a perspective that 1) is common-sense, 2) is novel, 3) may capture important aspects of the practice of strategic management research, and 4) is unabashedly normative. Thus, the argument has been that reduction may instantiate scientific progress, and that important parts of the evolution of the strategic management field can be understood as a quest for identifying the deep structure of competitive advantage. This obviously raises the issue of where strategic management is heading in the future, specifically whether we can expect future progress on the dimension of 'digging deeper' in the determinants of competitive advantage.

Future Developments

Although the pendulum has shifted back and forth between macro and micro perspectives, and currently is staying on the macro side (the capabilities perspective) there are signs that more micro-oriented perspectives are increasingly making themselves felt, and that we may be witnessing a swing back to micro. Here are some indications.

In a string of contributions, Coff (e.g. 1997, 1999) has developed a micro perspective on appropriation. Whereas in strategic management, one routinely postulates that firms appropriate, in actuality appropriation is undertaken by factor owners. Accordingly, more attention should be paid to internal processes of bargaining between key stakeholders in the firm, and Coff takes important steps towards a conceptualization of this. Lippman and Rumelt (2003b) exploit economic bargaining theory in order to comprehend the bargaining process between stakeholders.

The importance of understanding appropriation lies not just in understanding the phenomenon itself, but also in understanding how appropriation feeds back on value creation, a key point in organizational economics (e.g. Hart, 1995), but one that is presently neglected in strategic management. However, the emphasis on an aggregate entity as the appropriating agent obscures these micro-processes, and therefore risks misconstruing not only appropriation but also value creation. In fact, Lippman and Rumelt (2003a) argue that taking appropriation seriously has important implications for many of the most dearly held notions in strategic management. Among other things, they point out that there is no entity called 'the firm' that appropriates a residual known as 'profit' – all revenues are paid to factors.

Other instances of obtaining increased insight as a result of digging deeper may be cited. Thus, Makadok and Barney (2001) carefully model information acquisition strategies in an attempt to understand the micro-dynamics of strategic factor markets. Foss and Foss (2005) take an even more micro-oriented approach that focuses not on resources, but on property rights to attributes of resources (e.g. uses and functionalities of individual resources). They show that this gives considerable added insight into resource value, in addition to establishing a direct link to transaction cost economics. Abell, Felin and Foss (2007) take a modeling approach to the issue of how routines, capabilities and firm performance are linked, and explicitly incorporate individual-level factors in their approach.

That strategic management in general, and the RBV in particular, is likely to make progress by an increasing micro-focus has been explicitly emphasized by Barney (2001: 52–54). He singles out a number of areas where the RBV is currently deficient, specifically 'strategic alternatives', 'rent appropriation' and 'strategy implementation'. The first area calls for increased understanding on entrepreneurship and creativity, an undertaking unavoidable involving the level of the individual. The second area, Barney notes, has been advanced by the work of Coff (1999) and others (cf. the above), but there are still many unresolved issues, such as how different stakeholders come to enjoy different bargaining positions, why the value of such positions is not absorbed in the investments needed to create them, and so on – issues that would seem to call for making very explicit assumptions about individual agents. Thirdly, strategy implementation raises micro-level issues of the kind treated in agency and organizational behavior theory. Thus, all of the three primary pressing issues in the RBV intimately involve micro-foundations.

In closing, I submit that we are witnessing a number of manifestations of Barney's program for more micro-oriented strategy research. In addition to the examples provided above, I offer the example of the recent very strong emphasis on entrepreneurship in the strategy field, as manifested recently in the founding of the *Strategic Entrepreneurship Journal.* Entrepreneurship research must of necessity deal in a detailed manner with the actions and interaction of individuals.

NOTES

1. Parts of this chapter draw on Nicolai J. Foss, 'Scientific Progress in Strategic Management: The Case of the Resource-based View,' Center for Strategic Management and Globalization, Copenhagen Business School, WP-2005-11.
2. However, unlike the situation in many other social sciences, very few economists and economic methodologists have bought into the more extreme positions associated with the strong program in the sociology of science.
3. Another millennium debate was sparked by Mir and Watson (2000) arguing in favor of a constructivist approach (partially against the realism of Godfrey and Hill, 1995) to understanding the evolution of the strategic management field. Among other things, they took issue with the dominance of cross-sectional research methods in the field. Kwan and Tsang (2001) argued that Mir and Watson had misconstrued realism. A reply by Mir and Watson (2001) upheld the constructivism/realism distinction. In contrast to the debate initiated by Powell (2001) the debate initiated by Mir and Watson touched more on philosophy than strategic management.
4. Specifically, Boyd et al. "conduct two studies. The first is a cross-discipline comparison of productivity norms for university faculty. The second study examines longitudinal research outcomes for a sample of 945 strategy faculty. Our results indicate that strategy has the attributes of both an early stage and mature field: while overall research norms are low relative to other fields, they are driven far more by merit-based than non-merit factors" (2005: 841).
5. On the role of mechanisms in explanation, see the essays in Hedström and Swedberg (1998).
6. Although Elster's (1989: 74) dictum that "[r]eduction is at the heart of progress in science," would likely be accepted by many scientists and philosophers, I am not aware of any sustained theory of science discussions of reduction(ism) as (a) progress (strategy).
7. It is very likely that disciplinary background plays an important role here, strategic management scholars with more of an economics background arguably being more disposed towards reductionism for disciplinary reasons than strategic management scholars with more of a sociology background.
8. As an objection to reductionism, the argument is a red herring: Cournot's problem does not rule out the possibility of explaining in terms of tractable models.
9. For example, most economists *want* to treat tastes as black boxes, because not doing so would take them into entirely unfamiliar psychological territory.
10. For related arguments, see Koppl and Langlois (1991) and Satz and Ferejohn (1994). Koppl and Langlois argue that the argument originates with the economist Fritz Machlup.
11. See Udehn (2001) for a recent overview, or O'Neill (1973) for a compilation of key readings.

12. Methodological individualists are often charged with the claim that their emphasis on the individual is arbitrary as one might as well take, for example, the selfish gene as the fundamental unit. However, this argument commits the 'driver's seat fallacy', to wit, "[g]enes build bodies. Once the body is built, the genes have no control or influence on what those bodies do. It makes no more sense to say that genes drive our thoughts and emotions than it does to say that genes pump our blood. Our heart pumps our blood and our brain drives our thoughts and emotions Our genes are not in the driver's seat, we are" (Markoczy and Goldberg, 1998: 390).
13. Clearly, this program will often not be completely practicable for empirical reasons: it is usually impossible to obtain the necessary empirical information necessary to perform such a fine-grained explanation.
14. Will the scholar accept that capabilities *exist*? As I see it, the methodological individualist strategic management scholar may admit ontological status to capabilities in the sense that acknowledging that capabilities describe patterns of specialization and co-specialization of firm members' knowledge and actions that are specific to a given firm. As Felin and Hesterly (2007) note, such an argument is espoused in, for example, the view that organizations are "strong situations" (Davis-Blake and Pfeffer, 1989).
15. Hackman, however, comes out in favor of a strategy of temporarily 'bracketing' the focal level of analysis and focusing attention on the levels immediately below and immediately above this to gain increased understanding.
16. Usually, the industry and the firm levels are aligned through application of the SWOT framework, the SW representing the firm level and the OT the industry level. For a forceful critique of the soundness of this, see Makadok (2005).
17. Even economics began in the aggregate mode. Explicit microeconomics only really arrived with the marginalist revolution(s) of the 1870s, that is, about a hundred years after Adam Smith's classic (and two hundred years after William Petty).
18. Such a reading stresses (positive) complementarity between the Porter approach and the RBV. That this reading may be inconsistent is forcefully argued by Makadok (2005).
19. At the AoM meetings in 2004 at which Felin and Foss (2005) was presented, several attendants argued that micro-foundations were not relevant to strategic analysis, because all sustainable heterogeneity was located at the collective level.

REFERENCES

Abell, P. (2001), 'Causality and low-frequency complex events', *Sociological Methods and Research*, **30**, 57–80.
Abell, P. (2004), 'Narrative explanation: an alternative to variable-centered explanation,' *Annual Review of Sociology*, **30**, 287–310.
Abell, Peter, Teppo Felin and Nicolai J. Foss (2008), 'Building microfoundations for the routines, capabilities and performance link,' *Managerial and Decision Economics*, **29**, 489–502.
Agassi, J. (1960), 'Methodological individualism', *British Journal of Sociology*, **11**, 244–270.
Alvesson, M. and H. Wilmott (1995), 'Strategic management and domination and emancipation: from planning and process to communication and praxis,' in P. Shrivastava and C. Stubbart (eds), *Advances in Strategic Management: Challenges from Outside the Mainstream*, Greenwich, Conn.: JAI Press, pp. 85–112.
Arend, Richard J. (2003), 'Revisiting the logical and research considerations of competitive advantage,' *Strategic Management Journal*, **24**, 279–284.
Arrow, Kenneth J. (1951), *Social Choice and Individual Values*, New York: Wiley & Sons.
Backhouse, Roger A. (ed.) (1994), *New Directions in Economic Methodology*, London: Routledge.
Balakrishnan, Srinivasan, C.A. Montgomery and B. Wernerfelt (1989), 'Strategy content and the research process: a critique and commentary,' *Strategic Management Journal*, **10**, 189–197.

Barney, J.B. (1986), 'Strategic factor markets,' *Management Science*, **32**, 1231–1241.
Barney, J.B. (1991), 'Firm resources and sustained competitive advantage,' *Journal of Management*, **17**, 99–120.
Barney, J.B. (2001), 'Is the resource-based "view" a useful perspective for strategic management research? Yes,' *Academy of Management Review*, **26**, 41–57.
Bhaskar, R. (ed.) (1978), *A Realist Theory of Science*, 2nd edn, Brighton: Harvester.
Black, J. and K. Boal (1994), 'Strategic resources: traits, configurations, and paths to sustainable competitive advantage,' *Strategic Management Journal*, **15**, 131–148.
Blaug, M. (ed.) (1980), *The Methodology of Economics*, Cambridge: Cambridge University Press.
Bloor, D. (1976), *Knowledge and Social Imagery*, London: Routledge.
Bogner, W.C., J.T. Mahoney and T. Howard (1998), 'Paradigm shift: the parallel origin, evolution and function of strategic group analysis with the resource-based view,' *Advances in Strategic Management*, **15**, 63–102.
Boudon, R. (1998), 'Social mechanisms without black boxes,' in P. Hedström and R. Swedberg (eds), *Social Mechanisms: An Analytical Approach to Social Theory*, Cambridge: Cambridge University Press.
Bourgeois, L.J. (1984), 'Strategic management and determinism,' *Academy of Management Review*, **9**, 586–596.
Bowman, E.H. (1974), 'Epistemology, corporate strategy and academia,' *Sloan Management Review*, **15**, 35–50.
Bowman, E.H. (1990), 'Strategy changes: possible worlds and actual minds,' in J.F. Frederickson (ed.), *Perspectives on Strategic Management*, New York: Harper.
Bowman, E.H., H. Singh and H. Thomas (2002), 'The domain of strategic management: history and evolution,' in H. Thomas and A. Pettigrew (eds), *Handbook of Strategy and Management*, London: Sage.
Boyd, B.K., S. Finkelstein and S. Gove (2005), 'How advanced is the strategy paradigm? The role of particularism and universalism in shaping research outcomes,' *Strategic Management Journal*, **26**, 841–854.
Brandenburger, A. and B. Nalebuff (eds) (1996), *Co-Opetition*, New York: Currency-Doubleday.
Brønn, C. (1998), 'Applying epistemic logic and evidential theory to strategic arguments,' *Strategic Management Journal*, **19**, 81–95.
Camerer, C. (1985), 'Redirecting research in business policy and strategy,' *Strategic Management Journal*, **6**, 1–15.
Coff, R. (1997), 'Human assets and management dilemmas: coping with hazards on the road to resource-based theory,' *Academy of Management Review*, **22**, 374–402.
Coff, R. (1999), 'When competitive advantage doesn't lead to performance: resource-based theory and stakeholder bargaining power,' *Organization Science*, **10**, 119–133.
Coleman, J.S. (ed.) (1990), *Foundations of Social Theory*, Cambridge (Mass.)/London: The Belknap Press of Harvard University Press.
Davis, J.B. (ed.) (2003), *The Theory of the Individual in Economics: Identity and Value*, London: Taylor and Francis.
Davis-Blake, A. and J. Pfeffer (1989), 'Just a mirage: the search for dispositional effects in organizational research,' *Academy of Management Review*, **14**, 385–400.
Denrell, J., C. Fang and S.G. Winter (2003), 'The economics of strategic opportunity,' *Strategic Management Journal*, **24**, 977–990.
Dierickx, I. and K. Cool (1989), 'Asset stock accumulation and the sustainability of competitive advantage,' *Management Science*, **35**, 1504–1511.
Dosi, G. (1995), 'Hierarchies, markets and power: some foundational issues on the nature of contemporary economic organizations,' *Industrial and Corporate Change*, **4**, 1–19.
Dupré, J. (2001), 'Economics without mechanism,' in U. Mäki (ed.), *The Economic World View*, Cambridge: Cambridge University Press.
Dupree, J. (ed.) (1993), *The Disorder of Things*, Boston: Harvard University Press.
Durand, R. (2002), 'Competitive advantages exist: a critique of Powell,' *Strategic Management Journal*, **23**, 867–872.

Elster, J. (ed.) (1989), *Nuts and Bolts for the Social Sciences*, Cambridge: Cambridge University Press.

Farjoun, M. (2002), 'Towards an organic perspective on strategy,' *Strategic Management Journal*, **23**, 561–594.

Felin, Teppo and Nicolai J. Foss (2005), 'Strategic organization: a field in search of micro-foundations,' *Strategic Organization*, **3**, 441–455.

Felin, T. and W.S. Hesterly (2007), 'The knowledge-based view, heterogeneity, and the individual: philosophical considerations on the locus of knowledge,' *Academy of Management Review*, **32**, 118–134.

Ferejohn, J. and D. Satz (1994), 'Rational choice and social theory,' *Journal of Philosophy*, **91**, 71–87.

Foss, K. and N.J. Foss (2005), 'Value and transaction costs: how property rights economics furthers the resource-based view,' *Strategic Management Journal*, **26**, 541–553.

Foss, N.J. (1998), 'The new growth theory: some intellectual growth accounting,' *Journal of Economic Methodology*.

Foss, N.J. (2000), 'Equilibrium and evolution: the conflicting legacies of Demsetz and Penrose,' in N.J. Foss and P.L. Robertson (eds), *Resources, Technology, and Strategy*, London: Routledge.

Friedman, M. (1953), 'The methodology of positive economics,' in M. Friedman (ed.), *Essays in Positive Economics*, Chicago: University of Chicago Press.

Ghemawat, P. (ed.), *Games Businesses Play*, Cambridge: MIT Press.

Godfrey, P.C. and C.W.L. Hill (1995), 'The problem of unobservables in strategic management research,' *Strategic Management Journal*, **16**, 519–533.

Hackman, J.R. (2003), 'Learning more by crossing levels: evidence from airplanes, hospitals and orchestras,' *Journal of Organizational Behavior*, **24**, 905–922.

Hands, D.W. (1991), 'The problem of excess content: economics, novelty, and a long popperian tale,' in N. de Marchi and M. Blaug (eds), *Appraising Economic Theories: Studies in the Methodology of Research Programs*, Aldershot: Edward Elgar.

Harré, Rom (ed.) (1970), *The Principles of Scientific Thinking*, London: Macmillan.

Hedström, P. and R. Swedberg (eds) (1998), *Social Mechanisms: An Analytical Approach to Social Theory*, Cambridge: Cambridge University Press.

Hitt, M.A., J. Gimeno and R.E. Hoskisson (1998), 'Current and future research methods in strategic management,' *Organizational Research Methods*, **1**, 6–44.

Hoskisson, R.E., M.A. Hitt, W.P. Wan and D. Yiu (1999), 'Theory and research in strategic management: swings of a pendulum,' *Journal of Management*, **25**, 417–456.

Jones, R. (ed.) (2000), *Reductionism: Analysis and the Fullness of Reality*, Lewisburg, PA: Bucknell University Press.

Kincaid, H. (ed.) (1997), *Individualism and the Unity of Science: Essays on Reduction, Explanation and the Special Sciences*, Oxford: Rowman and Littlefield Publishers, Inc.

Klein, K.J., F. Dansereau and R.J. Hall (1994), 'Levels issues in theory development, data collection, and analysis,' *Academy of Management Review*, **19**, 195–229.

Knights, D. and G. Morgan (1991), 'Strategic discourse and subjectivity: towards a critical analysis of corporate strategy in organizations,' *Organization Studies*, **12**, 251–273.

Koppl, R. and R.N. Langlois (1991), 'Fritz Machlup and marginalism: a reevaluation,' *Methodus*, **3**, 86–102.

Kuhn, T. (ed.) (1970), *The Structure of Scientific Revolutions*, Chicago: University of Chicago Press.

Kwan, K.M. and E. Tsang (2001), 'Realism and constructivism in strategy research: a critical realist response to Mir and Watson,' *Strategic Management Journal*, **22**, 1163–1168.

Lakatos, I. (1970), 'Falsification and the methodology of scientific research programmes,' in I. Lakatos and A. Musgrave (eds), *Criticism and the Growth of Knowledge*, Cambridge: Cambridge University Press, pp. 91–196.

Laudan, L. (ed.) (1977), *Progress and its Problems: Toward a Theory of Scientific Growth*, London: Routledge.

Lazarsfeld, P.F. and P. Menzel (1960), 'On the relation between individual and collective properties,' in A. Etzioni (ed.), *Complex Organizations: A Sociological Reader*, New York: Holt, Rinehart and Winston.

Lewis, D. (ed.) (1986), *Philosophical Papers*, Oxford: Oxford University Press.

Lippman, S.A. and R.P. Rumelt (1982), 'Uncertain imitability: an analysis of interfirm differences under competition,' *Bell Journal of Economics*, **13**, 418–438.

Lippman, S.A. and R.P. Rumelt (2003a), 'A bargaining perspective on resource advantage,' *Strategic Management Journal*, **24**, 1069–1086.

Lippman, S.A. and R.P. Rumelt (2003b), 'The payments perspective,' *Strategic Management Journal*, **24**, 903–927.

Lipsey, R. (ed.) (1966), *An Introduction to Positive Economics*, London: Weidenfeld and Nicolson.

Lipton, P. (ed.) (2004), *Inference to the Best Explanation*, London: Routledge.

MacCloskey, D. (1983), 'The rhetorics of economics,' *Journal of Economic Literature*, **21**, 481–517.

Mahoney, J.T. (1993), 'Strategic management and determinism: sustaining the conversation,' *Journal of Management Studies*, **30**, 173–191.

Mahoney, J.T. and J.R. Pandian (1992), 'The resource-based view within the conversation of strategic management,' *Strategic Management Journal*, **13**, 363–380.

Makadok, R. (2005), 'The competence-collusion puzzle and the four theories of profit: why good resources go to bad industries,' working paper.

Makadok, R. and J.B. Barney (2001), 'Strategic factor market intelligence: an application of information economics to strategy formulation and competitor intelligence,' *Management Science*, **47**, 1621–1638.

Mäki, U. (1992), 'On the method of isolation in economics,' *Poznan Studies in the Philosophy of the Sciences and the Humanities*, **38**, 147–168.

Mäki, U. (2001), 'The way the world works (www): towards an ontology of theory choice,' in U. Mäki (ed.), *The Economic World View*, Cambridge: Cambridge University Press.

Marchi, N. and M. Blaug (eds) (1991), *Appraising Economic Theories: Studies in the Methodology of Research Programs*, Aldershot: Edward Elgar.

Markóczy, L. and J. Goldberg (1998), 'Management, organization, and human nature: an introduction,' *Managerial and Decision Economics*, **19**, 387–409.

Menger, C. (1983), 'Investigations into the method of the social sciences with special reference to economics,' reprinted in L. Schneider (ed.) (1985), New York: New York University Press.

Milgrom, P.J. and J.D. Roberts (eds) (1992), *Economics, Organization, and Management*, New York: Prentice Hall.

Mintzberg, H., J. Lampel and B. Ahlstrand (eds) (1998), *Strategy Safari*, New York: Free Press.

Mir, R. and A. Watson (2000), 'Strategic management and the philosophy of science: the case for a constructivist methodology,' *Strategic Management Journal*, **21**, 941–953.

Mir, R. and A. Watson (2001), 'Critical realism and constructivism in strategy research: toward a synthesis,' *Strategic Management Journal*, **22**, 1169–1173.

Oliver, C. (1997), 'Sustainable competitive advantage: combining institutional and resource-based views,' *Strategic Management Journal*, **18**, 697–713.

O'Neill, J. (ed.) (1973), *Modes of Individualism and Collectivism*, London: Heinemann.

Peteraf, M.A. (1993), 'The cornerstones of competitive advantage: a resource-based view,' *Strategic Management Journal*, **14**, 179–191.

Popper, K.R. (ed.) (1934), *The Logic of Scientific Discovery*, Vienna: Springer.

Popper, K.R. (ed.) (1957), *The Poverty of Historicism* (reprint 1999), London: Routledge.

Porter, M.E. (ed.) (1980), *Competitive Strategy*, New York: Free Press.

Porter, M.E. (1991), 'Towards a dynamic theory of strategy,' *Strategic Management Journal*, **12**, 95–117.

Powell, T. (2001), 'Competitive advantage: logical and philosophical considerations,' *Strategic Management Journal*, **22**, 875–888.

Powell, T. (2003), 'Strategy without ontology,' *Strategic Management Journal*, **24**, 285–291.

Priem, R.L. and J.E. Butler (2001), 'Tautology in the resource-based view and the implications of externally determined value: further comments,' *Academy of Management Review*, **26**, 57–65.
Salmon, W. (ed.) (1997), *Causality and Explanation*, Oxford: Oxford University Press.
Schendel, D. and C. Hofer (eds) (1979), *Strategic Management: A New View of Business Policy and Planning*, Boston, MA: Little, Brown.
Silberstein, M. (2002), 'Reduction, emergence and explanation,' in P. Machamer and M. Silberstein (eds), *The Blackwell Guide to the Philosophy of Science*, Oxford: Blackwell Publishers.
Smircich, L. and C. Stubbard (1985), 'Strategic management in an enacted world,' *Academy of Management Review*, **10**, 724–736.
Spender, J.C. (1979), 'Theory building and theory testing in strategic management,' in D. Schendel and C. Hofer (eds), *Strategic Management: A New View of Business Policy and Planning*, Boston, MA: Little, Brown.
Tsoukas, H. and C. Knudsen (2002), 'The conduct of strategy research,' in T. Howard and A. Pettigrew (eds), *Handbook of Strategy and Management*, London: Sage.
Udehn, L. (ed.) (2001), *Methodological Individualism: Background, History and Meaning*, London/New York: Routledge.
von Hayek, F.A. (ed.) (1955), *The Counter Revolution of Science*, Chicago: University of Chicago Press.
Wernerfelt, B. (1984), 'A resource-based view of the firm,' *Strategic Management Journal*, **5**, 171–180.
Wernerfelt, B. (1989), 'From critical resources to corporate strategy,' *Journal of General Management*.
Whipp, R. (1996), 'Creative deconstruction: strategy and organization,' in S.R. Clegg, C. Hardy and W.R. Nord (eds), *Handbook of Organization Studies*, London: Sage.
Williamson, O.E. (ed.) (1985), *The Economic Institutions of Capitalism*, New York: Free Press.
Williamson, O.E. (1996), 'Economic organization: the case for candor,' *Academy of Management Review*, **21**, 48–57.
Winter, S.G. (2003), 'Understanding dynamic capabilities,' *Strategic Management Journal*, **24**, 991–995.

5 Young and growing research directions in competitive strategy
Joel A. C. Baum and Henrich R. Greve

BRANCHES AND TWIGS IN STRATEGY

A handbook is an opportunity to summarize the state of a research field and reflect on its development. Many handbooks are published when a research field has grown too large to master easily through study of journals and books, so they appear when the participants of the field are ready to celebrate progress. This handbook is no exception, because competitive strategy is a field that has grown quickly and accumulated several strong branches of research organized around specific theories and applications, as later chapters will show. This handbook is typical also in giving most attention to the task of summarizing the state of the field, and thus on its most established research traditions. However, we will follow a different strategy. Hidden among the major branches of competitive strategy research there are some smaller branches and twigs – young and (still) small research traditions. While they have not played a major role in the past growth of the field, some of them will become important for its future growth. We do not know which ones. We are willing to make some guesses, however, based on observing their recent growth and assessing the strengths of their evidence and potential for generating new work. These judgments are obviously affected by our exposure to and participation in competitive strategy research, and are thus a subjective reading of the field.

We think there are three reasons that these research traditions are growing and may become important in strategy. First, all have high levels of paradigm development in spite of their young age, so there is broad agreement on the research questions and approaches to providing answers. As a result, there is little uncertainty about the type of research needed to make a contribution. Second, they are cross-disciplinary traditions that include researchers working in organization theory, economics, and sociology. This broadens the impact of research done in these traditions. Third, all have good fit with the field of competitive strategy. They emphasize the interaction between competitive structure and rivalry that is so important to competitive strategy research, and contribute new ways of looking at competitive structures. The result is that work done in these research traditions has clear implications for competitive strategy research more generally, and will contribute significantly to progress in our knowledge of strategic management.

We organize the research by the predictions made regarding structures and behaviors. This delineation is somewhat artificial because they are highly interdependent, but it offers a useful analytical framework. It is tied to the origins of the field of competitive strategy, because the structure-conduct-performance paradigm encouraged thinking about how different industry structures rewarded different behaviors, and hence how the structure-behavior match affected performance. Modern strategy research has benefited from this framework, while moving beyond it to also examine how firm rivalry determines industry structure.

MULTIUNIT ORGANIZATIONS

Strategy scholars have long been interested in whether specific organizational structures affect competitive actions and performance, exemplary among them. Organizational structures influence competitive strategy by facilitating certain kinds of communication and coordination, and encumbering others. The interest in organizational structures is currently expanding most vigorously in work on multiunit organizations (Greve and Baum, 2001). Multiunit organizations operate multiple establishments with similar activities, such as retail branch systems or multi-plant manufacturing firms. They seek to balance standardization across units against customization of each unit, and build their competitive strategy around activities that have proven effective overall and adaptable to local conditions. As a result, their competitive advantage and forms of rivalry are strongly dependent on the organizational structure and the diversity of environmental conditions in which they operate.

Multiunit Structure

The competitive advantage of multiunit organizational structure has been argued from many theoretical perspectives. Because units of multiunit firms conduct similar activities, learning among them is an important mechanism for gaining competitive advantage. Multiple units allow an organization to combine exploitation of activities known to be effective and exploration of new activities within a single organization, and thus to improve while limiting the costs of experimentation (March, 1991; Sorenson and Sørensen, 2001). Multiunit organizations that have discovered effective practices in one unit can spread it to others (Greve, 1996; Winter and Szulanski, 2001). These advantages require that the practice can be made equally effective in different units and environments, however, either as is or through modification. This argument leads to a potential drawback of multiunit organizations. Because it is often difficult for managers to assess the extent to which practices are transferable, learning transferred from units facing different competitive conditions can lower performance (Ingram and Baum, 1997; Greve, 1999).

Although the ability of multiunit organizations to make units more homogeneous and (often) robust competitors is well documented, recent work has studied the learning processes that make this happen. One approach has been to examine what happens when multiunit organizations acquire previously independent organizations. In such cases, the newly acquired units' service quality temporarily dips as a result of change process, but then moves towards that of the acquiring organization (Banaszak-Holl et al., 2002). The range of services offered in acquired units also changes, but it does so less readily, and is more dependent on having other components with similar tenure in the system (Banaszak-Holl et al., 2006).

Another approach has been to examine newly founded units. Overall survival rates are higher when the multiunit organization has local experience obtained before founding of the unit, showing a learning effect, but experience from distant markets has no effect (Kalnins and Mayer, 2004) or detrimental effects (Ingram and Baum, 1997). Hence the learning has to be from a relevant context to be effective. Survival rates are also higher when units of a multiunit organization observe turnover by other organizations in its markets (Kalnins et al., 2006). However, multiunit firms also have an ability to maintain and improve effective practices that exceeds that of independent organizations. As a result, units leaving a multiunit organization experience a downward drift in performance and have a lower rate of adopting innovations (Knott, 2001).

Multiunit Rivalry

The structural advantages of the multiunit organizational form are reflected in its competitive strategy. Multiunit organizations generally give higher priority to standardization across units than to local adaptation, and have in place systems to curtail variation in local units (Azoulay and Shane, 2001; Chuang and Baum, 2003; Knott, 2003). When acquiring units or implementing innovations, they seek to ensure accurate replication across units (Winter and Szulanski, 2001). Although multiunit organizations often make adaptations to the local environment, they trade this compromise off against the strategy of learning across units. Such learning is made more effective by intraorganizational networks and similar capabilities across units (Hansen, 2002), which results in unit homogeneity. However, in order to have sufficient variation to learn from, some units also need to make local experiments (Sorenson and Sørensen, 2001).

The learning advantages of the multiunit organizations imply that their most profitable acquisition targets will be single-unit firms that have low performance, and indeed there is evidence that they pursue such acquisitions (Banaszak-Holl et al., 2002; Baum, 1999). Multiunit organizations also have distinct market entry strategies. Newly founded units have low prices that are later increased, and become especially high when the organization paces entries to allow the lessons from each prior entry to influence the next (Mitsuhashi and Yamaga, 2006). Franchising structures is one option for multiunit organizations with a highly formalized set of practices. The relative independence of franchisors over company-owned outlets is an additional mechanism for learning among units, so some franchise systems use the mix of franchised versus owned units to increase learning (Shane, 1998; Sorenson and Sørensen, 2001) and to encourage intrasystem competition (Kalnins, 2004).

MULTIMARKET STRATEGY

Strategy scholars have inherited an interest in the effects of market structure on competitive strategy from the field of industrial organization, with an emphasis on market structures with imperfections such as few incumbent firms and barriers to entry. Work on multimarket strategy has extended this interest to market imperfections that occur when the same firms meet each other in multiple markets and coordinate their competitive actions. The theory predicts that firms meeting in multiple markets will mutually forbear from competitive attack as a result of their ability to retaliate broadly across many markets or selectively in markets where they can harm rivals' interests at a low cost to themselves.

Multimarket Structure

The structural source of competitive advantage in multimarket contexts has been argued from a learning perspective and a game theoretic one. The learning perspective argues that competitors meeting each other in multiple markets have frequent competitive interactions and will learn to take actions that weaken competition through such devices as niche formation and shifts from price to quality or features (Scott, 1993). Imitation of multimarket competitors may also soften the competition (Korn and Baum, 1999; Lieberman and Asaba, 2006). The game theoretic perspective argues that footholds in markets valuable to another firm can serve as punishment devices that usually compete softly, but can switch to aggressive competition if the other firm should compete aggressively (Bernheim and Whinston, 1990). These perspectives are complementary because learning without a punishment capability is fragile, while a punishment capability without knowledge of the other firm's responses can trigger costly competitive battles.

The general, and well supported, prediction is that multimarket contact leads to weaker competition and higher prices and profits (Greve and Baum, 2001). However, there are three areas of potential theory development. One is the entry prediction, where multimarket competitors face conflicting incentives between the wish to seek additional entry to bolster their capability to retaliate and the fear that such entries may be seen as aggressive and lead to retaliation (Baum and Korn, 1999). The second is the prediction regarding post-entry competition, where there is a question of whether firms enter into multimarket contact in order to mutually forbear, and thus immediately forbear, or whether some entry is coincidental and only leads to forbearance after a learning period (Korn and Baum, 1999). The final point is the predicted effect of single-market firms, where it is not clear whether such firms will participate in the weaker competition caused by multimarket firms in the market, or whether they will compete fully.

Multimarket Rivalry

The mixed motives of seeking contact to enable mutual forbearance and avoiding entry that will provoke retaliation have been investigated in recent studies. Consistent with theory of conflicting incentives, a common finding is an inverted-U relation between multimarket contact and entry rates (e.g. in Baum and Korn, 1999), which in some cases is moderated by similarity of firm resources (Fuentelhaz and Gomez, 2006) or CEO experience (Stephan et al., 2003). However, others have found that entry is likely when firms have a high extent of multimarket contact through meeting each other in a high proportion of their markets (Greve, 2006). Interestingly, the fear of entry causing retaliation is not well supported by actual reactions to entry, as firms often ignore or accommodate entrants (Smith and Wilson, 2001).

The evidence of multimarket effects on pricing behavior is strong. Prices of hotel rooms increase when multimarket contact is high (Mitsuhashi and Yamaga, 2006); as do unsecured loans rates (Feinberg, 2003) and newspaper advertising rates (while newspaper circulation falls) (Fu, 2003). Banks with high multimarket contact offer deposit interest rates that are lower and more uniform (Hannan and Prager, 2006), and charge higher fees (Hannan, 2006). Multimarket price levels spread to single-market firms, as single-market banks give lower deposit interest rates when multimarket banks are present in a market (Hannan and Prager, 2006). These findings suggest a level of price coordination that would seem difficult to maintain in markets with complex pricing. However, multimarket contact also simplifies price structures, as the cellular phone industry has more uniform pricing across markets when multimarket contact is high, suggesting that price scheme simplicity is a coordination device used to increase price levels (Busse, 2000).

INTERFIRM NETWORKS

Strategy researchers have been interested in how organizations gain competitive advantage from their external relations, starting with dyadic relations like supplier-buyer relations and alliances for research and development, production, or marketing. Alliance research is covered elsewhere in this volume, so we emphasize theory and evidence that instead examine the broader network configuration. Network theory of competitive strategy is similar to theory of how groups of organizations come to have (partially) shared interests with each other and interest conflicts with other groups. Such situations are stable provided firms have private incentives to act in ways that insulate the group against competition. Network theory treats relations that firms establish and terminate relatively easily, so two key topics of research become the movements of firms within such networks and the effect of network location on competitive strategies.

NETWORK STRUCTURE

The interfirm network literature conceptualizes structure as enduring patterns of relationships (ties) among firms. These relationships are conduits for a wide array of tangible resources like capital, or intangibles like information, social support, or status. Network positions offer competitive advantages in accessing and controlling information, knowledge, status, and other resources (Podolny, 1993; Powell et al., 1996). The creation and persistence of ties are also affected by interpersonal or institutionalized trust and by experience in managing network relations (Brass et al., 2004). An important theme in network research has been tensions between network structures that promote trust in collaboration and exchange and network structures that give information access and power over other firms (Burt, 1992; Rowley et al., 2000).

Extending Coleman's (1988) ideas on cohesive interpersonal ties, researchers theorized that firms benefit from being surrounded by dense relations among their partners and their partners' partners that perform a governance role, constraining opportunism, and encouraging cooperation (Rowley, 1997; Walker et al., 1997; Ahuja, 2000; Rowley et al., 2000). Such closed interfirm networks have established norms of behavior and efficient communication that afford firms confidence that partners will behave cooperatively and deviant behavior will be sanctioned. For example, telecom firms profited from alliances with powerful partners when these alliances were embedded in a dense network, allowing better control than sparse networks do (Bae and Gargiulo, 2004). Similarly, investment banks achieved higher performance when they were embedded within cliques with an efficient division of labor and with balance of power among participants (Rowley et al., 2004), although the benefits may be contingent on firm strategy (Shipilov, 2006).

Burt (1992), in contrast, theorizes that superior firm performance is achieved not by being embedded within dense subnetworks, but by establishing bridging ties between firms that are not connected to one another. Firms in bridging positions enjoy timely access to diverse information, referrals, and resources, and gain control over disconnected firms that rely on them to facilitate exchange. For biotech startups, networks with diverse partners and with connections to innovative and broad-scoped firms increased the rate of innovations and firm growth (Baum et al., 2000). Collaborations between Broadway musical creators were also more innovative when the network was sparsely connected (Uzzi and Spiro, 2005).

Network Rivalry

The interfirm network literature is dominated by the idea that firms' network positions can be a powerful source of competitive advantage. To date, however, research has not focused on firms' strategic use of collaborative arrangements to compete for network positions, but rather on their strategies for establishing ties to create dyadic advantages. This research emphasizes how uncertainty about the reliability, trustworthiness and capabilities of potential collaborators makes selection of more familiar past partners and partners' partners more likely (Chung et al., 2000; Gulati and Gargiulo, 1999; Li and Rowley, 2002). As a byproduct of this local search for trustworthy and reliable collaborators, dense substructures emerge within the network as pairs of firms with one or more common partners become linked themselves, generating collective benefits of closure as a side effect (Baum and Ingram, 2002). In contrast to such local search, seeking bridging ties requires firms to forego the comfort of familiarity to reach out to new, untested contacts that create brokerage opportunities (Baum et al., 2005) in order to create firm-specific network advantages (Burt, 1992; Walker et al., 1997; Madhavan et al., 1998).

Several recent studies have examined how firms' partner choices affect their network positions and advantages over time. These studies ask whether firms' network positions and advantages are shaped deliberately by partner choices or emerge coincidentally from myopic local search for reliable partners. Findings indicate that firms pursue network ties that give access to information, power, and resources, and are quite flexible in selecting which type of advantage to pursue. Firms extend their network when experiencing firm-specific uncertainty and performance deficits and strengthen existing ties when experiencing market uncertainty and acceptable performance (Baum et al., 2005; Beckman et al., 2004). Firms facing rapid technological change and significant uncertainty seek to gain centrality in the information flow by attaching to other firms that have many ties and diverse ties (Powell et al., 2005).

Firms also seek to control economic dependence through relations. Suppliers that rely on a powerful buyer establish ties with peers that have the same relation or overlay the exchange tie with social ties (Lomi and Patterson, 2006), thus making networks interdependent through the use of social relations to control exchange relations. The effectiveness of such control has been demonstrated in work on law firms, for which ongoing client relations result in a discount, while board memberships or high-status clients increase prices (Uzzi and Lancaster, 2004). Family and friendship ties reduced the failure rates of shipbuilders, but only for family-owned firms, not corporations (Ingram and Lifschitz, 2006). Friendship networks arose among competing hotels' managers, reducing price competition (Ingram and Roberts, 2001), while telecom firms were more likely to cooperate when the market was concentrated and growth opportunities were limited (Fjeldstad et al., 2004).

Network ties for resource assembly and co-production have seen much study recently. Rowley and Baum (2004) examined whether Canadian investment banks used underwriting syndicate partner selection as an opportunity to span structural holes, and whether banks differentiated between constrained and unconstrained structural holes when selecting partners, the latter of which provide superior returns. They found that, despite a strong tendency to reconstitute past syndicate ties, these banks also formed underwriting syndicates that increased the number of structural holes they spanned. The banks did not, however, discriminate between more or less constrained structural holes. Thus, the limits of bank managers' cognitive abilities appeared to fall somewhere between the identification of structural holes and the more difficult task of differentiating among them, which requires more subtle network understanding (Krackhardt, 1990).

Although a firm's own partnering decisions are vital to its pursuit of network advantage, their effect is interdependent on the choices made by other firms. When firms view their network positions strategically, advantages will be temporary as firms jockey for advantageous positions, fostering interfirm rivalry for scarce network resources. Brokerage positions, for example, can be lost through the actions of the firms that are brokered or through other firms seeking to broker the same relationship. As firms maneuver to secure these positions, network density increases and structural holes disappear along with the network advantage (Burt, 1992). Thus, the ability to improve network positions through bridging appears to depend on the willingness of others to forego such positions.

GROUPS

Firms increasingly compete within and as part of larger groups that blur organizational boundaries and transform competition fundamentally from firm-versus-firm to group-versus-group (Gomes-Casseres, 1996; Doz and Hamel, 1998). Firms comprising these groups are linked by alliances for a common purpose, though not all firms need be linked directly (Baum and Ingram, 2002; Das and Teng, 2002). The groups may have formal multilateral agreements that apply to all members, or be the informal results of bilateral agreements between firms (Nohria and Garcia-Pont, 1991; Lazzarini, 2004).

Examples are found in the computer industry, where firms pool resources to sponsor competing technologies and standards (Vanhaverbeke and Noorderhaven, 2001), and in telecommunications, where firms develop links with multiple partners to expand the reach of their networks, expand product offerings, and lower costs (Fjeldstad et al., 2004). Biotechnology firms build links to other biotechnology firms, as well as chemical and pharmaceutical firms, hospitals, universities, and marketing firms (Powell et al., 1996). Airlines have formed groups competing for international traffic (Lazzarini, 2004), as have automobile manufacturers to achieve geographic scope and share the cost and risk of R&D projects (Nohria and Garcia-Pont, 1991), investment banks to smooth execution of complex financial transactions (Rowley et al., 2004), and financial exchanges to offer distinct contract and negotiation platforms (Domowitz, 1995). These groups, referred to variously as 'coalitions' (Axelrod et al., 1995), 'constellations' (Gomes and Casseres, 1996), 'alliance blocks' (Vanhaverbeke and Noorderhaven, 2001), or 'interfirms' (Baum and Ingram, 2002), are an important organizational form for carrying out economic activity.

Group Structure

Interfirms represent an alternative to the firm as a way of governing capabilities. As with firm-based advantages, interfirm-based advantages derive from the relative value created by the resources they control. The interfirm creates advantages by assembling member resources critical for success in its industry, and by combining and governing them effectively (Zeng and Chen, 2003). Thus, as with strategic alliances, the potential of a group to create value depends on how it is structured and managed, and the members must need each other for the group to create value for them.

A unifying purpose is vital to bringing potentially diverse partners together. Although similarity and frequent interaction enhance cohesion and mutual understanding, differentiation lowers the potential for competition and conflict by creating opportunities for cooperation among firms with the complementary know-how to accomplish complex tasks. To a point, internal competition can increase flexibility and foster innovation, but it can also derail cooperation. Size also matters. As an interfirm grows, it faces a tradeoff between the value of resources from new members and the challenge of managing more members. Leadership is thus important to collective decision making and discipline. The emergence of one or a few powerful firms creates a pseudo-governance mechanism that can facilitate coordination and control of the interfirm's activities and the distribution of rewards among its members (Rowley et al., 2004, 2005).

Recent studies demonstrate the significance of these structural features. Vanhaverbeke and Noorderhaven (2001) examined a technological standards battle in the RISC (reduced instruction-set computing) microprocessor field. They showed how interfirms emerged around the competing designs, each comprising firms with all the complementary capabilities necessary to compete in the market. Group coordination was achieved through centralization when a powerful central firm emerged within the group, and through dense connections when no powerful central firm emerged.

Lazzarini (2004) reinforces these findings in his study of how networks of bilateral ties between airlines evolve into multilateral alliances (e.g. Star Alliance). He showed that multilateral alliances are more likely to form when firms possess diverse, complementary resources, and when the network of bilateral ties is centralized and moderately densely linked.

These results suggest that formal governance mechanisms help attenuate problems of cooperation and coordination among differentiated firms, that central firms in alliance networks act as leaders in the process of multilateral alliance formation, and that the need of formal governance mechanisms is partially mitigated when firms have extensive ties with one another.

GROUP RIVALRY

The emergence of interfirms has led some to propose that the locus of competition has shifted from firms to groups of firms that collaborate with one another (Gomes-Casseres, 1996; Powell and Smith-Doerr, 1994; Rowley et al., 2004, 2005). To the extent that interfirms increase members' interdependence as well as their capabilities, members' success depends increasingly on the competitive strength that groups of firms build collectively, and competition surfaces among groups. Such group competition does not lessen the importance of firm competition, but it does alter the nature of competition in a way that increases the competitive significance of firms' alliances. This suggests the importance of recasting competitive analysis at the interfirm level, as well as developing measures designed to capture the collective competitive strength of interfirms.

In group competition, industry structure can be conceived as an oligopoly of interfirms that differentiate by assembling distinct combinations of firms and by their structure and alliance management. Interfirms whose composition and social organization are group-beneficial will outcompete those with less adaptive constitutions, making a social organization that promotes a synergetic pattern of interaction within the network organization essential for the interfirm (Baum and Rao, 2004). Strong resources and group-beneficial interaction strengthen an interfirm and impose stronger competition on its rivals. This creates pressure to engage in alliance races to quickly secure the best resource-complementary partners, foreclosing rivals' partner opportunities (Gomes-Casseres, 1996).

Recent work has examined the competitive consequences of interfirms. Ingram and Simons' (2002) study of kibbutz agriculture illustrates how groups of organizations create benefits for their members, and competition for each other. Group membership facilitates transfer of experience among members, causing kibbutzim to become more profitable as the experience of their group accumulates, but less profitable as other groups' accumulate experience. Silverman and Baum (2002) examine the effects of a firm's rivals' alliances for its survival in a study of Canadian biotechnology firms, finding that they are often harmful. Rivals' downstream alliances are less harmful to a firm's survival chances than their upstream alliances, which in turn are less harmful than their horizontal alliances, suggesting that rivals' alliances that foreclose opportunities are most harmful, while alliances that increase the carrying capacity of the industry are least harmful. They also find that a firm can reduce the effect of its rivals' horizontal alliances, or even benefit from them, by collaborating with the rivals.

Group-based competition thus renders the alliance a competitive device with which to counter rivals' partnerships by connecting into their strategic networks and/or building countervailing alliances. Gimeno (2004) examined the conditions under which airlines respond to their rivals' alliance strategies by allying with their rivals' partners or by forming countervailing alliances with their rivals' rivals, or their rivals' partners' rivals. He found that allying with rivals' partners is favored when alliances involve low co-specialization, while creating countervailing alliances against common rivals is more likely when alliances are highly co-specialized.

The reality of interfirms is complex, but their implications for strategy and competition are great. If we are to understand these changes, we must think about competition and collaboration together – how they are blended and mixed to create groups of firms (interfirms) – that compete together. And we must broaden our conception of competitors and competition to include these collectives in our strategic thinking.

GEOGRAPHIC LOCATION

The last few years have witnessed a rapid rise in academic interest in location, and in particular, the advantages that co-location may offer firms (Sorenson and Baum, 2003). The starting point is research on how industrial clusters – related firms located in a confined geographic area – benefit member firms by becoming focal points of demand and reservoirs of trained labor, specialized inputs, and information. Current interest centers on knowledge spillovers that enhance firms' innovative performance and growth. Because geographic proximity helps observation, interaction, collaboration, and inquiry, certain locations enhance firm productivity through localized knowledge externalities or spillovers that provide positive economic value.

SPATIAL STRUCTURE

In contrast to labor markets and specialized inputs that operate at a regional level, knowledge spillovers tend to be highly localized (Rosenthal and Strange, 2003). Information flows slowly from its source geographically because the informal social and professional networks through which it moves tend to cluster within regions (Gordon and McCann, 2000; Staber, 2001; Sorenson, 2003). The density of social and professional ties declines rapidly with distance as the likelihood of interaction diminishes and the costs of maintaining established ties rises (Sorenson and Stuart, 2001; Owen-Smith and Powell, 2004). Although weak ties may be sufficient for knowledge transfer, movement of tacit knowledge requires empathy and familiarity between parties, so an ongoing relationship helps preserve the nature and value of knowledge (Nonaka and Takeuchi, 1995).

The cumulative nature of innovation manifests itself not just at firm and industry levels but also at the geographic level, as areas of concentrated knowledge-intensive resources become the locus of knowledge spillovers, creating advantages for firms locating within them (Audretsch and Feldman, 1996). Spatial concentration of firms with the same technological focus produces the greatest knowledge spillover benefits by generating more ideas for local diffusion and facilitating the realization of ideas, attracting new entrants and further enhancing the attractiveness of the cluster. Research confirms that broadly defined industrial clusters attract a disproportionate number of startups and produce a disproportionate share of innovative output. Moreover, compared to more isolated firms, firms located in clusters concentrated in their own industry grow faster and produce more innovations than those located in clusters concentrated in other industries (Baptista and Swann, 1998, 1999; Beaudry and Breschi, 2003).

Spatial Rivalry

Between-cluster
When locally clustered firms share resources (whether intentionally or not), they may operate at an advantage relative to rivals located outside the cluster. Thus in the same way that the emergence of interfirms can lead to competition between groups of firms that collaborate with one another, the emergence of industrial clusters can foster competition between groups of firms co-located with one another (Porter, 1990). As with interfirms, when multiple clusters compete, those whose composition and social organization are most group-beneficial will tend to outcompete those with less adaptive constitutions (Baum and Rao, 2004).

For example, Saxenian (1994) attributes differences in the success of Silicon Valley and Route 128 to the greater cooperation promoted by the Silicon Valley industrial organization culture, which enhanced the operation of social and professional networks through which information and ideas were exchanged. Likewise, Suchman and Cahill (1996) link the culture of Silicon Valley to the behavior of its law firms, which acted more like consultants – advising and connecting clients – than enforcers. Legal and institutional infrastructure also played a role in shaping the disparate business climates of these two regions (Gilson, 1999). California law precludes the enforcement of non-compete covenants (contract preventing past employees from working for a rival firm or founding a competing company), whereas Massachusetts allows such clauses. More generally, variation in legal regimes may influence firm behavior, with strong intellectual property regimes encouraging firms to invest more in internal research and development (Hall and Ziedonis, 2001).

Recent studies provide support for additional industrial organization effects. Rosenthal and Strange (2003) conjectured that small firms are more likely to be entrepreneurial and open to interacting with neighbors, which produces a greater agglomeration effect. Consistent with their premise, locations where small incumbents concentrated attracted more new entrants. Aharonson et al. (2006) suggested that younger (as well as smaller) biotech firms would be more entrepreneurial and, lacking the resources, experience and local network connections of more established firms, more open to interaction to access external resources and knowledge. They found that concentrations of adolescent incumbents with university ties were most attractive to new entrants, but did not replicate Rosenthal and Strange's (2003) small firm effect.

With varying degrees of success, regions around the world have attempted to replicate the industrial organization of Silicon Valley. Though limited systematic evidence considers whether these regions actually stimulate growth, their prominence in the media certainly creates the impression that they do. Regardless, research evidence suggests that policymakers interested in stimulating economic growth should focus centrally on elements of organizational, institutional and cultural infrastructure.

Within-cluster
Opportunities for firms to benefit from spillovers depend on the spatial distribution of R&D activity, with more concentrated areas of activity representing more promising opportunities. But knowledge spillovers are not unidirectional: firms that benefit from knowledge spillovers also find that others learn from them (Shaver and Flyer, 2000; Flyer and Shaver, 2003). Once knowledge is created it is often difficult to contain and to prevent others from benefiting from or expropriating its value. In this regard, Yoffie (1993) observed that semiconductor firms, concerned that their technology might spill over, were often wary of locating close to competitors.

Consideration of such strategic interactions complicates location decisions, suggesting that spillover-seeking may be tempered by a fear of expropriation. A key strategic issue is thus to balance potential costs of expropriation against likely gains from knowledge spillovers. If entrants locate too far from similar firms they limit access to knowledge spillovers and other specialized resources. Too close, and they risk expropriation of the firm's R&D. This challenge appears particularly acute for entrants, since incumbents are better positioned to exploit the entrant's knowledge (Aharonson et al., 2006). As a result, contemporary research on industrial clustering seeks not only to identify when and where spillovers occur, but also how the seepage of knowledge outside the firm influences its location choice.

As Shaver and Flyer (2000) point out, because firms both contribute to and benefit from spillovers, those with the best technologies, human capital, training programs, suppliers, or distributors will gain little from co-location and suffer most from spillovers to weaker competitors. Consequently, superior firms have little motivation to cluster despite the existence of agglomeration economies, while the weakest firms have little to lose and much to gain. Their analysis of location choice and survival of foreign greenfield investments in US manufacturing yields findings consistent with their predictions. They conclude that when firms are heterogeneous, agglomeration will be characterized by adverse selection.

A similar dynamic operates on the demand side. In a study of the Texas lodging industry, Chung and Kalnins (2001) find that agglomeration of chain-affiliated and larger hotels heightens demand, particularly in rural markets where these firms' actions are more likely to reduce consumers' search costs. Chain affiliation signals unobservable quality, which draws more consumers, while larger hotels advertise more and spread this cost across more units. Notably, chain presence not only heightened demand, it also raised independent hotels' revenues per room, while lowering chains' revenues. Reinforcing Baum and Haveman's (1997) finding that firms trade off competition losses for agglomeration gains when choosing locations, rural Texas hotels thus gain from the heightened demand created by dissimilar hotels.

Taken together, these results suggest that firms should choose locations with care. Optimal location choice is not only a function of a location's traits, but also of the firm's own traits vis-à-vis incumbents.

ECOLOGICAL PROCESSES

The question of how a firm's market position affects interfirm rivalry is central to strategy research. Firms position themselves horizontally through selection of product and service features and vertically through selection of quality and reputation, and the interrelationship between firms competing in the same or nearby positions constitutes an ecology of competition. When firms enter and leave the market, change positions within it, or develop entirely new positions, the ecology evolves. Ecological models addressing these interactions through an evolutionary lens have recently made significant progress.

Ecological Structure

As in the research on groups, the key insight in ecological theory is that similar firms pursuing their own interests act in ways that benefit each other, and thus obtain a mutualistic relationship, as well as compete. The basis for mutualism is that firms in a given niche increase the niche's prominence with respect to transaction partners such as customers and suppliers, and thus institutionalize the niche. Institutionalization increases the total resources available in the niche, and the firms then compete over these resources. Because institutionalization is bounded but competition is not, the result is a U-shaped relationship between the number of organizations in the niche (its density) and net competitive pressure. This relationship has been documented numerous times (Carroll and Hannan, 2000; Baum and Amburgey, 2002; and Baum and Shipilov, 2006 provide reviews), and recent research has also examined the more detailed rivalry behaviors as firms enter and leave market niches.

Resource partitioning theory describes the effect of market concentration on rivalry. Concentration results from economies of scale in serving the market center, which leads to a market structure with a center dominated by a few large firms, and a periphery that these firms do not serve well because their focus on scale makes them poorly suited to compete in the periphery. Concentration in the market center leaves an opening for smaller firms to operate on the market periphery through niche strategies. This overcomes diseconomies of small scale by providing a product of high value in their niche (Carroll, 1985). It is well established that concentration increases entry into peripheral positions (Carroll et al., 2002). Also, as the theory predicts, the market center is larger when demand is more homogenous (Boone et al., 2002), and firms serving the fringe have higher growth and survival rates when the market center is more concentrated (Boone et al., 2004). Through these dynamics, the market niche structure and the life chances of firms are simultaneously determined.

Ecological Rivalry

Niche overlap increases failure rates, especially for generalist firms (Baum and Singh, 1994; Dobrev et al., 2001). To avoid this fate, firms with high niche overlap reposition themselves in less crowded niches (Baum and Singh, 1996; Kim et al., 2003), but in the short term the survival benefit of the improved position is counteracted by the process costs of change (Barnett and Carroll, 1995; Dobrev et al., 2001; Dobrev et al., 2003). Structural inertia imposes costs on organizations seeking to change their market or technology, leading to an increased risk of failure for organizations that introduce new products too rapidly (Barnett and Freeman, 2001), and conferring a competitive advantage through R&D on experienced, early entrants (Klepper, 1996, 2002). Moreover, many niche changes fail to reduce the competition experienced by an organization (Baum and Singh, 1996; Ruef, 1997).

Some generalist firms also change niche, and are able to compete on the periphery by using multi-branding strategies to increase their own market share and beat back the specialists (Swaminathan, 2001). This strategy is costly because entering such positions requires high rates of product entry with costs that counteract the survival benefits of occupying such a niche. Moreover, broad-niche firms continue to develop more products and more risky products than would be optimal, and thus reduce their own performance (Sorenson et al., 2006). The specialists' response to incursions by generalists is to strengthen their position by developing distinct identities and forging close ties with their customers (Carroll and Swaminathan, 2000; Greve et al., 2006).

Along with the macro adaptation that occurs when firms choose niche positions, micro adaptation occurs as firms respond to competition within niches by adjusting competitive behavior. Red Queen theory describes how competing firms learn from each other's competitive moves (or fail as a result of them). One implication of the theory is that as firms adapt to their most similar competitors, they gain the ability to withstand their competition, but lose the ability to compete with dissimilar competitors, making them vulnerable to markets with a high diversity of competitors (Barnett and Hansen, 1996). Organizations appear to be weakest when meeting competitors that they rarely face (Barnett et al., 1994; Barnett and McKendrick, 2004).

CONCLUSION

The young and growing research traditions discussed here share one feature. They emphasize competition among interdependent firms, and are concerned not just with how a firm chooses a position in a landscape of competitors, but also how the landscape changes as the competitors, in turn, respond to the firm's move. They differ in how they conceptualize the competitive landscape, as these perspectives consider market contacts, network contacts, or spatial contacts among firms. They also differ in the processes considered, as some perspectives emphasize competitive interactions while others emphasize information flows and learning. Hence, each perspective offers insight into a different slice of the dynamic competitive interdependencies faced by firms.

These concerns are not new to strategy, as they have previously been addressed in work such as competitive groups research. They are concerns that the field keeps returning to because they are important and difficult to study. Although the topics are revisited, there is real and rapid progress because each turn brings in researchers with stronger conceptual ideas and methods. The branches and twigs we have covered here still look thin and green, but they are flexible and grow quickly. We think they will be thicker the next time a review of competitive strategy is written.

REFERENCES

Aharonson, B.S., J.A.C. Baum and M.P. Feldman (2006), 'Desperately seeking spillovers? Increasing returns, social cohesion and the location of new entrants in geographic and technological space', *Industrial and Corporate Change*, **16**, 89–130.
Ahuja, G. (2000), 'Collaboration networks, structural holes, and innovation: a longitudinal study', *Administrative Science Quarterly*, **45**, 425–455.
Audretsch, D.B. and M.P. Feldman (1996), 'R&D spillovers and the geography of innovation and production', *American Economic Review*, **86**, 630–640.
Axelrod, R., W. Mitchell, R.E. Thomas, D.S. Bennett and E. Bruderer (1995), 'Coalition formation in standard-setting alliances', *Management Science*, **41**, 1493–1508.
Bae, J. and M. Gargiulo (2004), 'Partner substitutability, alliance network structure, and firm profitability in the telecommunications industry', *Academy of Management Journal*, **47**, 843–859.
Banaszak-Holl, J., W.B. Berta, D.M. Bowman, J.A.C. Baum and W. Mitchell (2002), 'Antecedents to acquisitions and their effects on the quality of care in US nursing homes', *Managerial and Decision Economics*, **23**, 261–282.
Banaszak-Holl, J., W. Mitchell, J.A.C. Baum and W.B. Berta (2006), 'Transfer learning in ongoing and newly acquired components of multiunit chains: US nursing homes 1991–1997', *Industrial & Corporate Change*, **15**, 41–75.
Baptista, R. and P. Swann (1998), 'Do firms in clusters innovate more?', *Research Policy*, **27**, 525–540.
Baptista, R. and P. Swann (1999), 'The dynamics of firm growth and entry in industrial cluster: a comparison of the US and UK computer industries', *Journal of Evolutionary Economics*, **9**, 73–399.
Barnett, W.P. and G.R. Carroll (1995), 'Modeling internal organizational change', in J. Hagan and K.S. Cook (eds), *Annual Review of Sociology*, Greenwich, CT: JAI Press.
Barnett, W.P. and J. Freeman (2001), 'Too much of a good thing? Product proliferation and organizational failure', *Organization Science*, **12**, 539–558.

Barnett, W.P., H.R. Greve and D.Y. Park (1994), 'An evolutionary model of organizational performance', *Strategic Management Journal*, **15**, 11–28.

Barnett, W.P. and M. Hansen (1996), 'The red queen in organizational evolution', *Strategic Management Journal*, **17**, 139–157.

Barnett, W.P. and D.G. McKendrick (2004), 'Why are some organizations more competitive than others? Evidence from a changing global market', *Administrative Science Quarterly*, **49**, 535–571.

Baum, J.A.C. (1999), 'The rise of chain nursing homes in Ontario 1971–1996', *Social Forces*, **78**, 543–584.

Baum, J.A.C. and T.L. Amburgey (2002), 'Organizational ecology', in Joel A.C. Baum (ed.), *Companion to Organizations*, Oxford, UK: Blackwell.

Baum, J.A.C., T. Calabrese and B.S. Silverman (2000), 'Don't go it alone: alliance network composition and startups' performance in Canadian biotechnology', *Strategic Management Journal*, **21**, 267–294.

Baum, J.A.C. and R. Hayagreeva (2004), 'Dynamics of organizational populations and communities', in M.S. Poole and A.H. Van de Ven (eds), *Handbook of Organizational Change and Innovation*, New York: Oxford University Press.

Baum, J.A.C. and P. Ingram (2002), 'Interorganizational learning and network organization: toward a behavioral theory of the interfirm', in M. Augier and J.G. March (eds), *The Economics of Choice, Change and Organization: Essays in Memory of Richard M. Cyert*, Cheltenham, UK: Elsevier.

Baum, J.A.C, T.J. Rowley, A.V. Shipilov and Y.T. Chuang (2005), 'Dancing with strangers: aspiration performance and the search for underwriting syndicate partners', *Administrative Science Quarterly*, **50**, 536–575.

Baum, J.A.C. and A.V. Shipilov (2006), 'Ecological approaches to organizations', in S.R. Clegg, C.H.T. Lawrence and W. Nord (eds), *Handbook of Organizations Studies* (2nd edn), London: Sage Publications.

Baum, J.A.C., A.V. Shipilov and T.J. Rowley (2003), 'Where do small worlds come from?', *Industrial and Corporate Change*, **12**, 697–725.

Baum, J.A.C. and J.V. Singh (1994), 'Organizational niches and the dynamics of organizational founding', *Organization Science*, **5**, 483–501.

Baum, J.A.C. and J.V. Singh (1996), 'Dynamics of organizational responses to competition', *Social Forces*, **74**, 1261–1297.

Beaudry, C. and S. Breschi (2003), 'Are firms in clusters really more innovative?', *Economics of Innovation and New Technology*, **12**, 325–342.

Beckman, C.M., P.R. Haunschild and D.J. Phillips (2004), 'Friends or strangers? Firm-specific uncertainty, market uncertainty, and network partner selection', *Organization Science*, **15**, 259–275.

Bernheim, B.D. and M.D. Whinston (1990), 'Multimarket contact and collusive behavior', *RAND Journal of Economics*, **21**, 1–26.

Boone, C., G.R. Carroll and A. van Witteloostuijn (2002), 'Resource distributions and market partitioning: Dutch daily newspapers 1968 to 1994', *American Sociological Review*, **67**, 408–431.

Boone, C., G.R. Carroll and A. van Witteloostuijn (2004), 'Size, differentiation and the performance of Dutch daily newspapers', *Industrial and Corporate Change*, **13** (1), 117–148.

Burt, R.S. (ed.) (1992), *Structural Holes: The Social Structure of Competition*, Cambridge, MA: Harvard University Press.

Busse, M.R. (2000), 'Multimarket contact and price coordination in the cellular telephone industry', *Journal of Economics & Management Strategy*, **9**, 287–320.

Carroll, G.R. (1985), 'Concentration and specialization: dynamics of niche width in populations of organizations', *American Journal of Sociology*, **90**, 1262–1283.

Carroll, G.R. and M.T. Hannan (eds) (2000), .*The Demography of Corporations and Industries*, Princeton, NJ: Princeton University Press.

Chuang, Y.T. and J.A.C. Baum (2003), 'It's all in the name: failure-induced learning by multiunit chains', *Administrative Science Quarterly*, **48**, 33–59.

Chung, S.A., H. Singh and K. Lee (2000), 'Complementarity, status similarity and social capital as drivers of alliance formation', *Strategic Management Journal*, **21**, 1–22.

Chung, W. and A. Kalnins (2001), 'Agglomeration effects and performance: a test of the Texas lodging industry', *Strategic Management Journal*, **22**, 969–988.

Coleman, J.S. (1988), 'Social capital in the creation of human capital', *American Journal of Sociology*, **94**, S95–S120.

Das, T.K. and B.S. Teng (2002), 'Alliance constellations: a social exchange perspective', *Academy of Management Review*, **27**, 445–456.

Dobrev, S.D., K. Tai-Young and G.R. Carroll (2003), 'Shifting gears, shifting niches: organizational inertia and change in the evolution of the US automobile industry, 1885–1981', *Organization Science*, **14**, 264–282.

Dobrev, S.D., K. Tai-Young and M.T. Hannan (2001), 'Dynamics of niche width and resource partitioning', *American Journal of Sociology*, **106**, 1299–1337.

Domowitz, I. (1995), 'Electronic derivatives exchanges: implicit mergers, network externalities, and standardization', *The Quarterly Review of Economics and Finance*, **35**, 163–175.

Doz, Y.L. and G. Hamel (eds) (1998), *Alliance Advantage: The Art of Creating Value through Partnering*, Boston, MA: Harvard Business School Press.

Feinberg, R.M. (2003), 'The determinants of bank rates in local consumer lending markets: comparing market- and institution-level results', *Southern Economic Journal*, **70**, 144–156.

Fjeldstad, Ø.D., M. Becerra and S. Narayanan (2004), 'Strategic action in network industries: an empirical analysis of the European mobile phone industry', *Scandinavian Journal of Management*, **20**, 173–196.

Fu, W.W. (2003), 'Multimarket contact of US newspaper chains: circulation competition and market coordination', *Information Economics and Policy*, **15**, 501–519.

Fuentelsaz, L. and J. Gomez (2006), 'Multipoint competition, strategic similarity and entry into geographic markets', *Strategic Management Journal*, **27**, 477–499.

Gilson, R.J. (1999), 'The legal infrastructure of high technology districts: Silicon Valley, Route 128, and covenants not to compete', *New York University Law Review*, **74**, 575–629.

Gimeno, J. (2004), 'Competition within and between networks: the contingent effect of competitive embeddedness on alliance formation', *Academy of Management Journal*, **47**, 820–842.

Gomes-Casseres, B. (ed.) (1996), *The Alliance Revolution: The New Shape of Business Rivalry*, Cambridge, MA: Harvard University Press.

Gordon, I.R. and P. McCann (2000), 'Industrial clusters: complexes, agglomeration, and/or social networks?', *Urban Studies*, **37**, 513–532.

Greve, H.R. (1996), 'Patterns of competition: the diffusion of a market position in radio broadcasting', *Administrative Science Quarterly*, **41**, 29–60.

Greve, H.R. (1999), 'Branch systems and nonlocal learning in populations', in A. Miner and P. Anderson (eds), *Advances in Strategic Management*, vol. 16, Greenwich, CT: JAI Press.

Greve, H.R. (2006), 'The intent and extent of multimarket contact', *Strategic Organization*, **4**, 249–274.

Greve, H.R. and J.A.C. Baum (2001), 'A multiunit, multimarket world', in J.A.C. Baum and H.R. Greve (eds), *Multiunit Organization and Multimarket Strategy*, Oxford, UK: Elsevier.

Greve, H.R., J.E. Pozner and H. Rao (2006), 'Vox populi: resource partitioning, organizational proliferation, and the cultural impact of the insurgent micro-radio movement', *American Journal of Sociology*, **105**, 802–837.

Guidice, R.M., A. Vasudevan and G.M. Duysters (2003), 'From "me against you", to "us against them": alliance formation based on inter-alliance rivalry', *Scandinavian Journal of Management*, **19**, 135–152.

Gulati, R. and M. Gargiulo (1999), 'Where do interorganizational networks come from?', *American Journal of Sociology*, **104**, 1439–1494.

Hall, B.H. and R.H. Ziedonis (2001), 'The patent paradox revisited: an empirical study of patenting in the US semiconductor industry 1979–1995', *RAND Journal of Economics*, **32**, 101–128.

Hannan, T.H. (2006), 'Retail deposit fees and multimarket banking', *Journal of Banking & Finance*, **30**, 2561–2578.

Hannan, T.H.T. and R.A.R. Prager (2006), 'Multimarket bank pricing: an empirical investigation of deposit interest rates', *Journal of Economics & Business*, **58**, 256–272.

Hansen, M.T. (2002), 'Knowledge networks: explaining effective knowledge sharing in multiunit companies', *Organization Science*, **13**, 232–248.

Ingram, P. and J.A.C. Baum (1997), 'Chain affiliation and the failure of Manhattan hotels, 1898–1980', *Administrative Science Quarterly*, **42**, 68–102.

Ingram, P. and A. Lifschitz (2006), 'Kinship in the shadow of the corporation: the interbuilder network in Clyde River shipbuilding 1711–1990', *American Sociological Review*, **71**, 334–352.

Ingram, P. and P.W. Roberts (2001), 'Friendships among competitors in the Sydney hotel industry', *American Journal of Sociology*, **106**, 387–423.

Ingram, P. and T. Simons (2002), 'The transfer of experience in groups of organizations: implications for performance and competition', *Management Science*, **48**, 1517–1533.

Kalnins, A. (2004), 'Divisional multimarket contact within and between multiunit organizations', *Academy of Management Journal*, **47**, 117–128.

Kalnins, A. and K.J. Mayer (2004), 'Franchising, ownership, and experience: a study of pizza restaurant survival', *Management Science*, **50**, 1716–1728.

Kalnins, A., A. Swaminathan and W. Mitchell (2006), 'Turnover events, vicarious information, and the reduced likelihood of outlet-level exit among small multiunit organizations', *Organization Science*, **17**, 118–131.

Klepper, S. (1996), 'Entry, exit, growth, and innovation over the product life cycle', *American Economic Review*, **86**, 562–583.

Klepper, S. (2002), 'Firm survival and the evolution of oligopoly', *RAND Journal of Economics*, **33**, 37–61.

Knott, A.M. (2001), 'The dynamic value of hierarchy', *Management Science*, **47**, 430–448.

Knott, A.M. (2003), 'The organizational routines factor market paradox', *Strategic Management Journal*, **24**, 929–943.

Korn, H.J. and J.A.C. Baum (1999), 'Chance, imitative, and strategic antecedents of multimarket contact', *Academy of Management Journal*, **42**, 171–193.

Krackhardt, D. (1990), 'Assessing the political landscape: structure, cognition, and power in organizations', *Administrative Science Quarterly*, **35**, 342–369.

Lazzarini, S.G. (2004), 'From alliance networks to multilateral alliances: understanding the organization of multiple-firm linkages in the context of the global airline industry', paper presented at the Academy of Management, New Orleans, August 6–11.

Lazzarini, S.G. (2007), 'The impact of membership in competing alliance constellations: evidence on the operational performance of global airlines', *Strategic Management Journal*, **28**, forthcoming.

Li, S.X. and T.J. Rowley (2002), 'Inertia and evaluation mechanisms in interorganizational partner selection', *Academy of Management Journal*, **45**, 1104–1119.

Lieberman, M.B. and S. Asaba (2006), 'Why do firms imitate each other?', *Academy of Management Review*, **31**, 366–385.

Lomi, A. and P. Pattison (2006), 'Manufacturing relations: an empirical study of the organization of production across multiple networks', *Organization Science*, **17**, 313–332.

Madhavan, R., R.K. Balaji and E.P. John (1998), 'Networks in transition: how industry events (re)shape interfirm relationships', *Strategic Management Journal*, **19**, 439–459.

March, J.G. (1991), 'Exploration and exploitation in organizational learning', *Organization Science*, **2**, 71–87.

McKendrick, D.G. (2001), 'Global strategy and population-level learning: the case of hard disk drives', *Strategic Management Journal*, **22**, 307–334.

Mitsuhashi, H. and H. Yamaga (2006), 'Market and learning structures for gaining competitive advantage: an empirical study of two perspectives on multiunit-multimarket organizations', *Asian Business & Management*, **5**, 225–247.

Nohria, N. and C. Garcia-Pont (1991), 'Global strategic alliances and industry structure', *Strategic Management Journal*, **12**, 105–124.

Owen-Smith, J. and W.W. Powell (2004), 'Knowledge networks as channels and conduits: the effects of spillovers in the Boston biotechnology community', *Organization Science*, **15**, 5–21.

Porter, M.E. (ed.) (1990), *The Competitive Advantage of Nations*, New York: Free Press.

Powell, W.W., W.K. Koput and L. Smith-Doerr (1996), 'Interorganizational collaboration and the locus of innovation: networks of learning in biotechnology', *Administrative Science Quarterly*, **41**, 116–145.

Powell, W.W., D.R. White, K.W. Koput and J. Owen-Smith (2005), 'Network dynamics and field evolution: the growth of interorganizational collaboration in the life sciences', *American Journal of Sociology*, **110**, 1132–1205.

Rowley, T.J. and J.A.C. Baum (2004), 'Sophistication of interfirm network strategies in the Canadian investment banking industry', *Scandinavian Journal of Management*, **20**, 103–124.

Rowley, T.J., J.A.C. Baum, A.V. Shipilov, H.R. Greve and H. Rao (2004), 'Competing in groups', *Managerial and Decision Economics*, **25** (6–7), 453–471.

Rowley, T.J., D. Behrens and D. Krackhardt (2000), 'Redundant governance structures: an analysis of structural and relational embeddedness in the steel and semiconductor industries', *Strategic Management Journal*, **21**, 369–386.

Rowley, T.J., H.R. Greve, H. Rao, J.A.C. Baum and A.V. Shipilov (2005), 'Time to break up: the social and instrumental antecedents of exit from interfirm exchange cliques', *Academy of Management Journal*, **48**, 499–520.

Ruef, M. (1997), 'Assessing organizational fit on a dynamic landscape: an empirical test of the relative inertia thesis', *Strategic Management Journal*, **18**, 837–853.

Saxenien, A. (ed.) (1994), *Regional Advantage*, Cambridge, MA: Harvard University Press.

Scott, J.T. (ed.) (1993), *Purposive Diversification and Economic Performance*, Cambridge, UK: Cambridge University Press.

Shane, S. (1998), 'Explaining the distribution of franchised and company-owned outlets in franchise systems', *Journal of Management*, **24**, 717–739.

Shaver, J.M. and F. Flyer (2000), 'Agglomeration economies, firm heterogeneity, and foreign direct investment in the United States', *Strategic Management Journal*, **21**, 1175–1193.

Shipilov, A.V. (2006), 'Network strategies and performance of Canadian investment banks', *Academy of Management Journal*, **49**, 590–604.

Silverman, B.S. and J.A.C. Baum (2002), 'Alliance-based competitive dynamics', *Academy of Management Journal*, **45** (4), 791–806.

Smith, F.L. and R.L. Wilson (2001), 'The predictive validity of the Karnani and Wernerfelt model of multipoint competition', *Strategic Management Journal*, **16**, 143–160.

Sorenson, O. (2003), 'Social networks and industrial geography', *Journal of Evolutionary Economics*, **13**, 513–527.

Sorenson, O. and P.G. Audia (2000), 'The social structure of entrepreneurial activity: geographic concentration of footwear production in the United States 1940–1989', *American Journal of Sociology*, **106**, 424–462.

Sorenson, O. and J.A.C. Baum (2003), 'Geography and strategy: the strategic management of space and place', *Geography and Strategy – Advances in Strategic Management*, **20**, 1–19.

Sorenson, O., S. McEvily, C.R. Ren and R. Roy (2006), 'Niche width revisited: organizational scope, behavior, and performance', *Strategic Management Journal*, **27**, 915–936.

Sorenson, O. and J.B. Sørensen (2001), 'Finding the right mix: franchising, organizational learning, and chain performance', *Strategic Management Journal*, **22**, 713–724.

Sorenson, O. and T.E. Stuart (2001), 'Syndication networks and the spatial diffusion of venture capital investments', *American Journal of Sociology*, **106**, 1546–1588.

Staber, U. (2001), 'The structure of networks in industrial districts', *International Journal of Urban and Regional Research*, **25**, 537–552.

Stephan, J., J.P. Murmann, W. Boeker and J. Goodstein (2003), 'Bringing managers into theories of multimarket competition: CEOs and the determinants of market entry', *Organization Science*, **14**, 403–421.

Stuart, T.E., Ha Hoang and R.C. Hybels (1999), 'Interorganizational endorsements and the performance of entrepreneurial ventures', *Administrative Science Quarterly*, **44**, 315–349.

Stuart, T.E. and O. Sorenson (2003), 'The geography of opportunity: spatial heterogeneity in founding rates and the performance of biotechnology firms', *Research Policy*, **32**, 29–53.

Suchman, M.C. and M.L. Cahill (1996), 'The hired gun as facilitator: lawyers and the suppression of business disputes in Silicon Valley', *Law and Social Inquiry*, **21**, 679–712.

Uzzi, B. and R. Lancaster (2004), 'Embeddedness and price formation in the corporate law market', *American Sociological Review*, **69**, 319–344.

Uzzi, B. and J. Spiro (2005), 'Collaboration and creativity: the small world problem', *American Journal of Sociology*, **111**, 447–504.

Vanhaverbeke, W. and N.G. Noorderhaven (2001), 'Competition between alliance blocks: the case of the RISC microprocessor technology', *Organization Studies*, **22**, 1–30.

Walker, G., B. Kogut and W. Shan (1997), 'Social capital, structural holes and the formation of industry networks', *Organization Science*, **8**, 109–125.

Winter, S.G. and G. Szulanski (2001), 'Replication as strategy', *Organization Science*, **12**, 730–743.

Yoffie, D. (1993), 'Foreign direct investment in semiconductors', in Kenneth Froot (ed.), *Foreign Direct Investment*, Chicago: University of Chicago Press.

Zeng, M. and X. Chen (2003), 'Achieving cooperation in multiparty alliances: a social dilemma approach to partnership management', *Academy of Management Review*, **28**, 587–605.

PART 2

THEORETICAL APPROACHES INFORMING COMPETITIVE STRATEGY RESEARCH

6 The role of resource-based theory in strategic management studies: managerial implications and hints for research
Jay B. Barney, Valentina Della Corte, Mauro Sciarelli and Asli Arikan

A BROAD VIEW OF THE MAIN APPROACHES IN STRATEGIC MANAGEMENT

A long debate has been developed on resource-based theory (RBT) since the 1980s. When the new assumptions of this theory were explicated, deep and strong reactions came out.

The main theoretical questions that have been constantly posed in international debate are essentially two:

1) how can firms gain their competitive success, that is to say their sustainable competitive advantage?
2) why do firms exist?

In the last decades, different theories have been developed trying to answer these questions. Among them, some can be regarded as 'strategic'. Their main questions are in fact posed from a typically strategic point of view (more attention is paid to the first one of the above questions): in this category, industrial organization contributions have to be considered (Porter, 1980, 1985), as well as the strategic side of evolutionary theory (Nelson and Winter, 1982) and resource-based theory.

Other theories can be considered as non-strategic (Figure 6.1). These are, in particular, transaction cost economics, agency theory and options theory: they are all based on the assumption that in equilibrium situations or in the long run firms may make the same choices, that is they can arrive at equal results. Besides, they mainly try to answer the question: why do firms exist? They try to examine under which situations companies prefer to invest internally rather than outsource (the traditional 'make or buy' decision) and what can be the most suitable corporate governance choices.

Transaction cost economics, or TCE as it is known (Coase, 1937; Williamson, 1971, 1975, 1985), mainly considers the firm as a bundle of

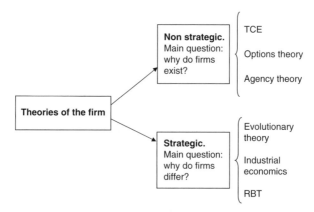

Figure 6.1   Main theories in strategic management studies

contracts. The choices refer, in particular, to the risk of opportunism in parts' behavior and the economic efficiency principle as a driving factor in governance choices. The main topic, therefore, is not strategic but rather refers to the existence of the firm and its boundaries.

Options theory focuses, in particular, on the analysis and evaluation of uncertainty risk and the implications of this factor on a firm's flexibility/rigidity in facing an uncertain context. The results reached by this theory differ a lot from those of TCE, because it often happens that opportunism and uncertainty do not coincide and can even lead to different decision solutions (Della Corte, 2004, chapter 3).

Agency theory (Alchian and Demstez, 1972; Jensen and Meckling, 1976; Eisenhardt, 1989; Barney and Hesterly, 1996; Barney and Ouchi, 1986), in particular, tries to understand the causes and consequences of goals' disagreements among the main actors involved in a firm, analyzing whether they agree about how it should be managed. This means, first of all, between managers and owners: it refers to the possibility of opportunistic behavior on the agent's part that works on behalf of the principal (owner). Agency theory's main assumptions are bounded rationality, self-interest and opportunism, information asymmetric problems in transactions and efficiency (in terms of costs to protect the principal interests to reduce the possibility that managers could misbehave). The agency problem has been widely extended to the relationships among stakeholders (with stakeholders' theory: Rhenmann, 1968; Pfeffer and Salancik, 1978; Freeman, 1984, 1989; Donaldson and Preston, 1995; Mitchell et al, 1997) and to the social responsibility concept (Davis, 1975; Frederick, 1960; Carroll, 1979, 1991; Sethi, 1975). The former tries to examine stakeholders' main different goals and objectives, in order to verify the possibility of reaching a sort of equilibrium among them. The latter tries to examine the value creation process not just for the firm itself but for the whole stakeholders' system, community and the environment. The main aspect is the firm's social success within its context.[1]

Compared to these theories, that are mainly focused on the question: 'why do firms exist?', there are those that can be defined as 'strategic', in the sense that they try to analyze why some firms outperform others. The main 'strategic approaches' are: Porter's theory (within industrial organization studies); evolutionary theory (Nelson and Winter, 1982, 2002); and resource-based theory.

Industrial organization studies are mainly concentrated on firms' product positioning within markets, taking into account, first of all, the influence of market competition driving forces on firms' performance (the five competitive forces – Porter, 1980). According to Porter, market dynamics with a firm's main forces determine its attractiveness. Therefore each firm decides whether or not to enter a market according to its resulting attractiveness and consequent profit making. Besides, a firm's competitiveness is analyzed through its main activities and types of strategic choices (cost leadership rather than differentiation choices), that are of course bound to market competitive forces. This approach is more macro-economic; it focuses the attention outside the firm and mainly regards the influence of external competitive context on firms' strategic choices (Barney, 2001).

On the other end, modern evolutionary theory (Winter, 2000, 2003, 2005) considers the roots of a firm's performance in terms of the firm's evolution over time, in a context of highly uncertain expectation formations.

For Nelson and Winter (1982: 14), organizational routines are 'all regular and predictable behavioral patterns of firms. They are a persistent feature of the organism and determine its possible behavior. . . they are heritable. . . and they are selectable. . .'. Indeed, this common emphasis on intangible assets within a firm's boundaries as a primary determinant of firm behavior/strategy has suggested to some authors an important link between resource-based theory and evolutionary theories of the firm (Barney, 2001).

However, the so-called *'clean state' opportunity set situation* (that is, a situation with no previous influences of any kind) rarely happens: in this optic, decision making is deeply embedded in specific temporal contexts that have been shaped by previous decisions. One important result, determined by evolutionary theory, is that it makes clear how the heterogeneity of firms' performances is therefore consistent with the strategy issue. The attention to firms' routines, to their capabilities of learning over time and developing different processes, more or less explicit, makes the firm unique, in the sense that it becomes extremely difficult for competitors to get to the

Table 6.1   Main characteristics of strategic management theories

Theory	Main concept	Governance choices vs strategic choices
Transaction cost economics	*Opportunism*: firm as a bundle of contracts; risk analysis in counterparts' behavior; governance choices in terms of costs and efficiency	Governance choices
Options theory	*Uncertainty*: analysis of the risk of uncertainty and of its implications in terms of strategic and operational flexibility	Governance choices
Agency theory	*Principal/agent relationship*: analysis of the risk of opportunism between property and management	Governance and management
Industrial organization (IO)	*Industry attractiveness*: competitive forces in the market determine its attractiveness and firms' chances of good performance	Strategy
Evolutionary theory (ET)	Firms' performance as the result of its *evolution* over time, in a context of uncertain expectations	Strategy
Resource-based theory (RBT)	Firm's *strategic resources* are the roots to gain sustainable competitive advantage	Strategy

same results because of the difficulty of imitation. Evolutionary theory's main implications can be associated, in particular, to two concepts, that are typical of the resource-based approach: the concept of 'causal ambiguity', which is linked to the intrinsic difficulty in explaining the modes and motivations that led to a specific use of resources and competences that brought some performance results, and the concept of 'path dependence', that refers to the specific history of the firm, its 'lived experiences', both good and bad, that can have a significant impact on the development of its capabilities over time (Barney, 2002, 2006).

It is our opinion that, even if helpful for strategic studies, evolutionary theory still shows a difficult prescription, with results inconsistent with strategy. Even if admitting the relevance and somehow complementarity among the different approaches, both strategic and non-strategic, in this chapter, we will try to underline why RBT can really add support to strategic management decisions and what is its relationship (and its main differences) with other strategic management approaches.

In Table 6.1 we synthesize the role of some different theoretical approaches, their main concepts, and their main cut (whether based on governance choices rather than strategic choices).

It is clear that some of these theories concentrate on the issue of corporate governance choices and make or buy decisions, while others focus on competitive strategy. It is our opinion that competitive advantage is the basic, first step to take forward in a firm's path toward success and even corporate strategy choices rather than governance decisions are strictly bound to this main objective. However, among the strategic theories what changes is, as known, the unit of analysis: market for IO studies, evolution for ET, the firm and its bundle of strategic resources for RBT.

RBT KEY DEFINITIONS AND BASIC CONCEPTS

In strategic management studies and applications, several definitions have been given to some important terms, with different implications. In our opinion, in order to develop a theory that is worth being applied by managers and entrepreneurs, two important definitions have to be taken into account: strategy and resources.

Since the 1950s, different definitions have been put forward: from a vision of strategy (Barney, 1986a; Drucker, 1994) as a consequence of market driving forces interactions (Porter, 1980, 1985), to the decision-making process and its main steps, like 'strategic planning' (Ansoff, 1980; Lorange, 1980).

Our definition of strategy is the following: strategy is a firm's theory of how it can gain superior performance in the markets within which it operates (Barney, 2001).

This definition includes both emergent and intended strategies (Mintzberg, 1990), can be applied at both business and corporate level, introduces firm performance explicitly into the discussion, and suggests that, before a strategy is actually implemented, it represents a 'prediction' made by a firm about the economic processes that exist in a particular market or markets and how those processes can be used to gain superior performance. This definition can even be applied to firms that have no strategy – at least as defined in a traditional way. Some other firms may appear not to have it, because it is not sufficiently explicit. In any case, a firm's theory of how to gain superior performance in the markets within which it operates is to not make explicit predictions about how those markets operate.

Connected with the strategy concept, there are some additional terms that require definition. In particular, *superior performance* requires careful definition. It has already been suggested that resource-based logic can be used to understand the sources of a firm's economic rents and its competitive advantages. *Economic rents* exist when firms generate more value with the resources they have acquired or developed than was expected by the owners of those resources (Smith, 1776; Schoemaker, 1990); *competitive advantages* exist when a firm is implementing value-creating strategies not currently being implemented by competing firms.

These ways of characterizing a firm's performance can also be temporary or persistent. Economic rents are *temporary* when expectations of owners adjust to incorporate the higher than expected level of value created by a firm. Economic rents are *persistent* when a firm is able to consistently generate higher than expected value from the resources it controls. Competitive advantages are *temporary* when they are duplicated by competing firms. Competitive advantages are *persistent* when competing firms have ceased efforts to duplicate the advantages of a particular firm.

Taken together, these concepts – *resources, strategic factor markets, strategy, superior performance, temporary* and *sustained economic rents, and temporary* and *sustained competitive advantages* – are fundamental in resource-based theory.

As emphasized, our vision of strategy concentrates on strategic decisions' contents rather than on decision-making processes and considers a firm's strategy to gain sustainable competitive advantage as generated by its specific strategic resources. This view has progressively brought to the development of resource-based theory.

Beginning in the 1980s, and continuing through the 1990s, resource-based theory has been developed through the publication of numerous papers in a wide variety of journals and books. Some of the key definitions, assumptions, assertions, and predictions of this body of literature are presented here.[2]

Starting with its key concepts and definitions, it is important to specify the meaning of the term *resources*. While this term has been defined elsewhere (e.g. Wernerfelt, 1984; Rumelt, 1984; Barney, 1991a, 2001), current use of the term suggests the following definition: *resources* are the tangible and intangible assets firms use to conceive of and implement their strategies (Barney, 2001).

Of course, the tangibility of firm resources is a matter of degree. Resources that are typically more tangible include, but are not limited to, a firm's financial capital (e.g. equity capital, debt capital, retained earnings, leverage potential) and physical capital (e.g. the machines and buildings it owns). Resources that are typically less tangible include, but are not limited to, a firm's human capital (e.g. the training, experience, judgment, intelligence, relationships, and insights of individual managers and workers in a firm) and organizational capital (e.g. attributes of collections of individuals associated with a firm, including a firm's culture, its formal reporting structure, its reputation in the market place, and so forth).

Through the 1990s, different conceptualizations of both tangible and intangible resources were developed. Wernerfelt (1984) and Barney (1991b) simply called these assets resources and made no effort to divide them into any finer categories. Hamel and Prahalad (1990) developed the concept of 'core competencies' and, building on Selznick (1957) and others, added the term competence to the resource-based lexicon. Stalk et al. (1992) argued that there was a difference between competencies and capabilities, and thus this term (capabilities) was added to the terminological fray. Teece et al. (1997) emphasized the importance of the ability of firms to develop new capabilities, a perspective emphasized by their choice of the term 'dynamic capabilities.' Most recently, several authors have suggested that knowledge is the most important resource that can be controlled by a firm and have developed what they call a 'knowledge-based theory' of sustained superior firm performance (see, for example, Grant, 1996; Liebeskind, 1996; Spender 1996).

In principle, distinctions among terms like resources, competencies, capabilities, dynamic capabilities and knowledge can be drawn. For example, Hill and Jones (1992) and Harrison et al. (2001) distinguish between resources and capabilities by suggesting that resources are a firm's fundamental financial, physical, individual, and organizational capital attributes, while capabilities are those attributes of a firm that enable it to exploit its resources in implementing strategies. Teece et al.'s (1997) concept of dynamic capabilities tends to focus on the ability of firms to learn and evolve (Lei et al., 1996). General practice suggests that the concept of competencies is most often applied in the context of a firm's corporate diversification strategy. Knowledge is clearly a special case – albeit an important one – of some of these other terms.

However, while these distinctions between types of resources can be drawn and can be helpful in understanding the full range of resources a firm may possess, the effort to make these distinctions has had at least one unfortunate side effect: those who have developed new ways to describe a firm's resources have often labeled their work as a 'new' theory of persistent superior performance. Thus, the strategic management literature currently has proponents of resource-based theories of superior performance, capability theories of superior firm performance, dynamic capability theories of superior performance, competence theories of superior performance, and knowledge-based theories of superior performance.

While each of these 'theories' has a slightly different way of characterizing firm attributes, they share the same underlying theoretical structure. All focus on similar kinds of firm attributes as critical independent variables, specify about the same conditions under which these firm attributes will generate persistent superior performance, and lead to largely inter-changeable empirically testable assertions. Battles over the label of this common theoretical framework are an extreme example of a classic academic tempest in a tea pot – full of sound and fury but signifying nothing.'[3]

What the label of this framework should be is actually not very important. In this chapter, the first label, developed by Wernerfelt (1984), has been adopted. However, the content would not change at all if it had focused on the 'capabilities view,' the 'dynamic capabilities view,' the 'competence view,' or the 'knowledge-based view.' While work should continue expanding our understanding of the different kinds of firm attributes that can have an impact on firm performance, labeling each of these insights as a new theory of firm performance is, in our opinion, counterproductive.

RESOURCE-BASED THEORY'S MAIN ASSUMPTIONS

Resource-based theory, like all theories, is based on several assumptions. Some of these assumptions are mainly linked to persistent superior firm performance theories. In particular, they focus on how to measure superior performance in order to evaluate a firm's competitiveness. Resource-based logic, for instance, adopts the assumption that firms are profit-maximizing entities[4] and that managers in firms are boundedly rational (Simon, 1945). Over and above these basic assumptions, resource-based logic makes two additional issues that distinguish it from other strategic management theories: the concept of *resource heterogeneity* and that of *resource immobility* (Barney, 1991b). These assumptions are:

- *Resource heterogeneity*: competing firms may possess different bundles of resources.
- *Resource immobility*: these resource differences may persist.

One critical aspect is that these two assumptions *may* exist. This means that some firms may have or control resources that can enable them to more effectively conceive and implement more successful strategies than other firms over time. Besides, as will be further explained, these resources can be either possessed or controlled by the firm: this implies they do not necessarily have to be owned within the firm's physical boundaries.

The heterogeneity issue also incorporates two attributes of firm resources: scarcity and non-substitutability (Barney, 1991b). A firm resource is considered to be *scarce* when the demand for that resource is greater than its supply. A resource is *non-substitutable* when no other resources can enable a firm to conceive of and implement the same strategies as efficiently or effectively as the original resource. The concept of immobility mainly refers to the issue of *inelasticity in supply*, that is, more of a particular resource is not forthcoming even though demand for that resource is greater than its supply. Firm resources may vary significantly in the extent to which they are scarce, non-substitutable, and inelastic in supply.

In recent contributions, however, some further and important implications have been considered, with reference to the inelasticity question and to the fact that through capabilities' use and organization factors some resources that are imitable in principle are, however, not copied or duplicated in practice. This aspect will be explained further in this chapter.

RESOURCE-BASED THEORY'S MAIN PROPOSITIONS

Related to these definitions and assumptions, RBT develops a series of propositions. While numerous propositions have been developed, four are particularly important to resource-based logic (Peteraf, 1993). These propositions show the relationship between factor market competition and the possible situations of competitiveness. These can be imagined along a continuous line, which extends from temporary rents to sustained competitive advantage (Barney and Arikan, 2001):

1) *Factor market competition and temporary rents.* This proposition refers to the relationship between the competitiveness of the market within which a firm acquires or develops a resource and the ability of that resource to generate at least a temporary economic rent:

> *Firms that acquire or develop valuable resources in imperfectly competitive strategic factor markets can gain at least temporary economic rents by using them to develop and implement strategies.*

As suggested in Barney (1986c), when strategic factor markets are perfectly competitive, the cost of acquiring or developing a resource will equal the value of that resource in enabling a firm to conceive of and implement a strategy. Since the cost of acquiring or developing a resource equals its value in conceiving of or implementing a strategy, these resources will not be a source of economic rent. However, to the extent that these factor markets are imperfectly competitive, a rent can be generated by acquiring or developing a resource and implementing a strategy in the short term. In other words, the economic rent will just be temporary, since expectations about a firm's performance will adjust over time, and "any unanticipated value creation will be anticipated whenever a firm acquires or develops additional resources to implement the same strategies in the future" (Barney and Arikan, 2001: 29).

2) *Factor market competition and sustained economic rents.* In general, expectations about the value of a resource to enable a firm to develop and implement strategies will adjust to reflect previously unanticipated levels of value. However, to the extent that a firm can continue to find ways of generating value with the resources it controls that were not anticipated, based on previous levels of performance, a firm can continue to generate economic rents.

> *Firms that continue to use valuable resources to develop and implement strategies in ways others cannot anticipate can gain sustained economic rents.*

3) *Resource heterogeneity and temporary competitive advantages.* Proposition three focuses on the relationship between heterogeneous firm resources and temporary competitive advantages:

> *Firms that control valuable and scarce resources can gain temporary competitive advantages by using them to develop and implement strategies.*

This proposition is a straightforward application of the Ricardian economic logic presented earlier but refers to situations where just a few firms have those valuable resources. It is however not so difficult for other companies to imitate those resources. That's why the competitive advantage can just be temporary.

4) *Resource heterogeneity and immobility and sustainable competitive advantages.* In this situation, the scarce resources are also difficult or costly to imitate. This makes it possible to generate sustained competitive advantage.

> *"Firms that control valuable, scarce, and non-substitutable resources that are inelastic in supply can gain persistent competitive advantages by using them to develop and implement strategies" (Barney and Arikan, 2001: 29).*

When resources that are a source of temporary competitive advantage (i.e. resources that are scarce) are also inelastic in supply or difficult or costly to replicate, the superior performance they generate does not lead to competitive imitation, since this becomes a much more difficult process. The roots of this inimitability can be found either in path dependence, social complexity, causal ambiguity or patents rights.[5]

DEVELOPING TESTABLE HYPOTHESES

Taking into account the propositions outlined here, it is possible to develop a series of testable hypotheses from resource-based logic, according to which pointing out the issue that it is worth parameterizing. The interesting thing is that the following hypotheses show how resource-based logic has progressively moved from a more static to a dynamic view of competitive advantage. Examples of these hypotheses include:[6]

Hypothesis one: Firms that acquire or develop valuable resources under conditions of high uncertainty may gain temporary economic rents.

Hypothesis two: Firms that acquire or develop rare resources or, rather, valuable resources in ways that exploit rare resources they already control *will* gain temporary economic rents.

Hypothesis three: Firms that continue to acquire or develop valuable resources in consistently uncertain settings *can* gain temporary economic rents.

Hypothesis four: Firms that exploit valuable, rare, and non-substitutable resources in choosing and implementing strategies, where those resources are also path dependent, causally ambiguous, or socially complex will gain sustainable competitive advantages.

Hypothesis five: Firms that continue to acquire or develop valuable resources in ways that exploit rare and non-substitutable resources they already control, where those resources are also path dependent, causally ambiguous, or socially complex will gain persistent economic rents.

Hypothesis six: Firms that continue to acquire or develop valuable and rare resources in ways that exploit rare and non-substitutable resources they already control, where those resources are also path dependent, causally ambiguous, or socially complex will gain persistent economic rents.

Hypothesis seven: Some strategy implementation skills that are in principle imitable can have important competitive implications.

These hypotheses regard the competitive implications of the use of strategic resources, also in uncertain contexts. The last one is extremely important and needs some further reflection. The point is: if these resources are imitable in principle, why are they not copied/duplicated?

They can be someway bound to organizational factors that are so efficient to become strategic resources themselves and therefore make it difficult to replicate or substitute those resources (a sort of implementation capability) or entrepreneurial capabilities in exemplifying the implementation phase, or in deciding in advance and soon passing to action (these could be defined as 'proactive resources'). They can also depend on some specific managerial competences, in organizing and implementing strategies in an apparently easy way, beyond which there is very hard work, know-how and expertise.

On this topic, further research and empirical tests are still necessary for a continuous and constant progression in the theory. Investigation on managerial practice on this aspect can add a real value to RBT further advances.

RESOURCE-BASED THEORY APPLICATIONS

VRIO Framework

In order to understand RBT's concrete applications not only as a theory but also in managerial practice, it is necessary to proceed, even with empirical tests, through the parameterizing process. The first stage of this process uses RBT's theoretical framework to analyze the firm's competitiveness. This framework is aimed at evaluating a resource's capability of generating superior performance and, therefore, sustainable competitive advantage. The variables used are:

1) the question of value;
2) the question of rareness;
3) the question of imitability;
4) the question of organization.

The RBT theoretical framework is the so-called VRIO framework (Table 6.2), according to which if a firm that controls strategic resources (that are valuable, rare, difficult or costly to imitate, and used by the organization) it can gain above normal results and sustainable competitive advantage. If a firm has non-valuable assets, this means it has no sources of competitive advantage at all. Even worse, companies may operate in competitive disadvantage and show below normal performance. As regards the possible perspectives, it depends on what the 'non-valuable' assets are. If, for example, the problem is management (bad management in this case), the options could be different. The firm could plunge over

Table 6.2   The VRIO framework

RESOURCES				Competitive implications	Performance
Value	Rareness	Imitability	Organization		
NO	–	–	NO	Competitive disadvantage	Below normal
YES	NO	–	YES	Competitive parity	Normal
YES	YES	NO	YES	Temporary competitive advantage	Above normal
YES	YES	YES	YES	Sustainable competitive advantage	Above normal

time into a crisis situation, or recover itself by being acquired by another firm with valuable management or giving way to a management change, through the development or acquisition of new resources (new good management).

If resources are just valuable and rare, this can lead to competitive parity, since almost all firms can control it. A typical example can be financial resources, in rather developed financial markets.

If resources are also rare, this means they are controlled by a small number of firms and can lead to temporary competitive advantage, since the imitation process is not widespread; if they are rare and difficult and/ or costly to imitate, they are 'strategic' and can generate sustainable competitive advantage. Therefore, companies do have to invest constantly in strategic resources, in order to assure competitive advantage sustainability.

Of course, if resources are not adequately used in organizational terms, they run the risk of remaining just potential without being implemented.

In order to point out the concrete possibilities of application of the VRIO framework, we attempt to parameterize its main variables.

The Question of Value

This variable refers to a resource's ability to implement successful strategies. The value of resources can also be determined by their ability to enable firms to conceive of and implement strategies that are appropriate to the market within which a firm operates, so strategies should be able to:

- in strategic terms, allow the firm to catch external opportunities and/ or avoid or reduce menaces;
- in economic terms, increase the firm's revenues and/or reduce its costs.

A firm that possesses valuable resources does not necessarily show superior performance: valuable resources can only lead to competitive parity. For example, if competing firms in an industry possess the same resources and use them to conceive of and implement the same strategies, these resources will not be a source of superior performance, even if the costs of all these firms are lower and revenues higher than what would have been the case if these resources had not been used. In this sense, setting aside the role of luck, possessing valuable resources is a necessary, but not sufficient, condition for firms to obtain superior performance.

A firm attribute, whether tangible or intangible, is valuable when it enables a firm to develop and implement a strategy that someway generates value (both in economic and strategic terms, as previously emphasized). In respect to this issue, the point is to find out a way of appraising firms' attributes, in order to verify whether they are valuable.

If resources allow a firm to develop and implement strategies that have the effect of reducing a firm's net costs or increasing its net revenues compared to what would have been the case had those resources not been used, then they can be thought of as valuable.

It is possible to describe the market structure within which a firm operates, as a consequence of firms' strategic choices. This also makes the difference between RBT and IO studies. While for the latter in traditionally monopolistically competitive markets (Chamberlain, 1933), product differentiation is almost seen as a source of superior performance, according to RBT logic it is the creativity and innovativeness of a firm in developing new products or processes that can have an important impact on its ability to conceive of and implement differentiation strategies and, therefore, product differentiation. To the extent that a firm's creativity and innovativeness allow it to catch outside opportunities, reduce external threats, increase its revenues and/or reduce its costs, they can be conceived of as valuable resources.

In addition, the value of these resources can vary significantly according to the specific industry/market: their impact on increasing revenues or reducing cost may be connected to some structural aspects of a firm's organization (economies of scale, of scope, learning curves). This does not mean, however, that value depends on the external environment but rather that the firm's specific activities, due to its business, someway characterize the overall cost-revenues structure. For example, in a very uncertain market setting, the ability of a firm to remain flexible and rapidly change strategies may be valuable (Kogut, 1991; Trigeorgis, 1996). The point is, however, to see which of these resources are able to generate competitive advantage. Some scholars (Brush et al., 2001) underlined, on this subject, the significant role of external context on the value variable; this is true for the above discussed reasons but it is important to notice the subjective aspect of the question, since within the same market even resources' value can vary from firm to firm (Barney, 2001).

In conclusion, firm attributes are objectively neither good nor bad, neither valuable nor non-valuable. Rather, their value depends entirely on their ability to enable firms to conceive of and implement strategies that satisfy both the strategic and economic dimension previously pointed out. In this optic the 'SWOT' (strengths, weaknesses, opportunities and threats) analysis still remains an important tool in strategic decision making but its results are different among firms.

The question of the parameterization of the value variable has been much discussed. However, there are some interesting contributions that test this variable (Barney and Arikan, 2001). Industrial organization contributions mainly refer to the ability of different strategies to create economic value. According to Michael Porter's approach a cost leadership strategy creates value if it enables a firm to reduce its costs below those of its main competitors; product differentiation if it allows a firm to practice higher prices for its more differentiated products (Porter, 1980). Further studies, applying resource-based logic, have analyzed the ability of some specific resources to create and implement the above-mentioned strategies. The attention is much more focused on strategic contents rather than 'types' of strategy and external environment, as this can vary substantially from firm to firm. The work developed up to the present favors an approach aimed at studying the ability of those resources to create and implement strategies. Examples of this attempt are Henderson and Cockburn's article (1994), in which they try to verify why some pharmaceutical firms are more effective than others in developing new patents. Provided that it has been shown that patents are a source of economic value in the industry (Mansfield et al., 1981), Henderson and Cockburn identified 'architectural competence' (that is the capability of favoring cooperation among different disciplines in research and development) as a source of economic value. Ray et al. (2004) examined the relationship between customer service and information technology functions within a sample of insurance companies in North America. Specifically, they found that the careful use of information can help the quality of customer service and that customer satisfaction, in turn, is related to important economic values, such as customer retention. They developed a measure of the cooperation between customer service and IT functions (a socially complex resource), showing how this relationship can create economic value (Barney et al., 2005).

Della Corte et al. (2007) applied resource-based theory to a sample of companies operating in the tourism industry in Southern Italy, comparing them with other samples analyzed in different areas of the country. In their study, important network competences came out for a tourism destination success. Interfirm non-formal relationships, trust and sharing of common goals are considered to be the most relevant aspects to create value for tourists and therefore for tourism business companies.

The examples mentioned above show some important implications for managerial practice:

1) *To apply resource-based theory it is necessary to go deeply into the firm through more appropriate methods:* the strategic resources that are identified as a source of economic value can vary significantly from firm to firm. In research, a qualitative case study approach is often more appropriate: the mere elaboration of statistical data does not help concrete understanding.

2) *Analyses and results are often referred to firms operating in the same industry:* that is, results are mainly generalizable within the specific industry context. This does not mean that successive comparisons between industries (e.g. service industry) cannot be made, but if the level of specificity of strategic resources is high between companies, this approach can work.

3) *In the firm's analysis, strategic resources often refer to some sub-firm sections* (e.g. specific functions), rather than to the firm as a whole, so the unit of analysis changes significantly.

4) *As regards firms operating within strategic networks and interfirm aggregations (e.g. business districts), some sources of value are to be found at the network/aggregation level:* those resources, however, become valuable and increase the single firm's value significantly.

The Question of Rareness and Imitability

When a firm develops a certain strategy, this can soon become known: it can take a very short time for other firms to understand that strategy. What is less known are the strategic resources that a firm uses to implement its successful strategy. According to resource-based theory, strategy using resources that are widely controlled or easy to imitate cannot bring sustained competitive advantage (Barney, 2001).

The imitability variable refers to situations in which resource duplication and/or substitution is difficult. In this case, there are roots for sustainable competitive advantage.

The parameterization of these two fundamental aspects is difficult for several reasons, as will be explained further.

The question of scarcity
As known, the 'rareness' variable refers to the scarcity of resources: as far as a resource is controlled by a number of firms which is lower than that in a perfect competition setting, it can be considered rare. Therefore, resources are scarce to the extent that demand for them outstrips supply. When there is this condition, there is also the potential for competitive advantage and, therefore, superior performance. More precisely, companies operate in a situation of competitive advantage up to other firms in the industry imitate those rare resources. For this reason, rareness can favor temporary advantage.

There is one other aspect that determines a situation that is close to resource rareness: the role of strategic factor markets on competitiveness.

Strategic factor markets
Barney (1986c) suggests that strategic factor markets can be imperfectly competitive when:

− commonly held expectations about the future value of resources enabling a firm to develop and implement a strategy underestimate the actual value of those resources;
− some firms have more accurate expectations about the future value of those resources than others.

In other words, with respect to the first situation, in a strategic factor market significant uncertainty about the actual future value of a resource can lead to imperfect competition. In this sense, the level of uncertainty that exists in a strategic factor market can indicate the extent to which that market is imperfectly competitive. It depends, however, even if in the difficult context, on the low 'insight' capacity of many firms.

The second situation, that refers to different expectations about the future value of a resource, reveals a different ability in the evaluation process and implies that the future level of a resource can differ according to the overall bundle of resources a firm already has (Barney, 1991b; Dierickx and Cool, 1989). Thus, for example, the value of an acquisition, as a resource a firm needs to conceive of and implement a corporate diversification strategy, depends on the resources that a firm already possesses and the relationship between those resources and the firm it is going to acquire (Barney, 1988).

Because heterogeneous expectations in strategic factor markets are derived from prior heterogeneously distributed firm resources, the parameterization of this form of imperfect competition in a strategic factor market is actually a special case of parameterizing the concept of firm resource heterogeneity – through the parameterization of scarcity and non-substitutability.

The question of resource immobility
Resources are immobile or non-substitutable when they can be uniquely used to help conceive of and implement a strategy. As far as such a one-to-one correspondence exists between a resource and a strategy, strategy itself may be non-substitutable.

This one-to-one correspondence approach to parameterizing non-substitutability can be complicated by two factors. First, it may not be single resources that enable a firm to develop and implement a strategy, but rather bundles of such resources. Isolating bundles of resources and characterizing the extent to which they uniquely enable a firm to develop and implement a strategy can complicate this parameterization effort (Barney and Arikan, 2001: 33).

Second, it is also important to analyze not only the single resource but its combination with others, which can make it non-substitutable. In this context, the task of parameterizing non-substitutability is to isolate all those resources that, separately and/or in combination, can enable a firm to develop and implement a strategy.

It has been argued that the non-substitutability aspect has to be considered with reference to both supply inelasticity and capabilities' use. Some scholars (Makadok, 2001) tend to distinguish between 'resource picking' (referring to the resources' selecting process) and 'capability building' (termed as the process of 'resource development'). The former derives from the Ricardian perspective in the creation of economic rent (Ricardo, 1817) and mainly implies cognitive and informational factors (supply inelasticity); the latter is more bound to the Schumpeterian dynamic capability view, closed to entrepreneurship and implies structural factors. In this direction, a capability is defined as a special type of resource (non-transferable, firm-specific and organizationally embedded), whose aim is to improve the productivity of the firms' resources. This aspect explains why some resources, apparently not so rare or imitable, can generate competitiveness and superior performance: it is because they are involved in a 'profitable' bundle of resources and competencies.

This distinction can be relevant in situations, like strategic network in the tourism industry, where tourism destination success is connected with local resources, as well as with firms' capabilities and network competencies developed by the network itself (Della Corte and Sciarelli, in Barney, 2006).

Parameterizing supply inelasticity

Several authors have parameterized the Smithian concept of supply inelasticity. For example, Dierickx and Cool (1989) suggest that resources are inelastic in supply when they are subject to time compression diseconomies, are causally ambiguous, are characterized by high interconnectedness among asset stocks, or subject to asset mass efficiencies or asset erosion. Barney (1991b) suggests that resources are inelastic in supply when they are path dependent, causally ambiguous, or socially complex. Itami (1987) suggests they are inelastic in supply when they are invisible.

While these different ways of parameterizing the extent to which resources are inelastic in supply vary somewhat in detail, they also overlap. Clearly, resource-based logic suggests that resources tend to be inelastic if they are developed or acquired over long periods of time, link numerous individuals and technologies, and are based on often taken-for-granted intangible relationships within a firm and between a firm and its stakeholders. Barney (2001) applies these concepts in evaluating when different sources of cost leadership, product differentiation, vertical integration, corporate diversification, and other strategies are more or less likely to be sources of persistent superior performance.

Parameterizing capabilities' use

According to some scholars a capability succeeds in augmenting the firm's profits by enhancing the productivity of the other resources that are acquired (Makadok, 2001). This approach has pushed some scholars to talk about knowledge management and so on (Kogut and Zander, 1992; Grant, 1996). For example, Helfat and Peteraf (2003) tried to analyze the capability lifecycle in order to explain the main sources of a firm's heterogeneity. This is a way of thinking about capacities' evolution, arriving at a more dynamic approach to resource-based theory. This, however, does not give way to new theories but rather, since dynamic capabilities can be strategic resources themselves, proves that the RBT framework is in truth dynamic.

Parameterizing imitable resources is not an easy endeavor. Barnett et al. (1994) show that in a difficult market situation for commercial banks in Illinois, some succeeded in outperforming others, thanks to some difficult resources to imitate, connected with their path-dependent nature

(Barney and Mackey, 2005: 7). However, they did not measure directly the resources that enabled this outperformance.

In the identification process of the main sources of firms' competitiveness, one important consideration has to be made. As shown before, it is important to isolate, at a further sub-level, the identifications of strategic resources: this is as much harder as the combinations of a firm's resources can be determinant to outperform competitors. In this case, it is important to single out those specific capabilities and competences that make it possible to better combine other resources; this process is important both at the firm level and at the network level of analysis.

The Organization Variable

The organization variable refers to complementary resources (Barney, 2001), such as an organization's structure, management control and information systems, compensation policies that are not sources of competitive advantage by themselves but are useful to convert potential resources into real ones, able to generate competitive advantage.

Three main considerations have to be made on this topic.

1) Through a qualitative study, Miller (2003) shows how firms can develop asymmetries into valuable assets. Attention is paid to how design can influence the process of resource allocation, control and motivation both through more formal levels, such as structure and systems and informal variables, like culture and networks (Galbraith, 2000). According to this approach organizational design can be used to discover asymmetries, easier more common than fully expressed resources and easier to defend than imitable assets. "Careful probing of the strategic advantages of unique weaknesses" (Miller, 2003: 973) can be extremely useful.

2) There are important competitive implications on strategy implementation skills that are in principle imitable. This, however, does not mean that they will be widely imitated. Why, then, do companies in competitive disadvantage not imitate those resources that create value for other companies?

3) It is necessary to evaluate resources and capabilities' combinations in order to find out the real roots of competitive advantage.

In some sense, some organizational resources, such as managers' design or architectural skills allow better identification of the business's weaknesses, to single out valuable resources even in non-profitable business, in order to use and combine them differently to create value for the company.

Considering not only competitive opportunities but also competitive threats and firms' weaknesses surely broadens the mindset of managers and entrepreneurs that make strategic decisions. *In these cases, however, it is not just the organizational variable but rather the organization itself that becomes a strategic resource.*

Parameterizing the Link Between Strategic Resources and Firm Performance

In general, it is very difficult to define satisfactory measures for firm performance, let alone to parameterize the connection between strategic resources and firm performance.

It is necessary to single out some specific variables of the firm's performance to which to connect resources, in order to verify their specific contribution to the company's success.

First, firms can gain competitive advantages from different businesses, can earn from some businesses and lose from others: therefore, linking resources to the overall performance of the firm can be misleading. From this point of view, Ray et al. (2004) propose a test where the single business of the firm becomes the unit of analysis and the performance of the business process the dependent variable. For example, in analyzing the competitiveness of a sample of insurance companies, they refer to the performance of customer service, through a list of different variables. When analyzing destinations' competitiveness within the tourism business firms' networks, Della Corte et al. (2007) refer to some specific variables to measure the impact of single resources and competences (perceptions of the services provided during the stay in the destination, analyzed through qualitative approaches) on destination performance.

Second, resources and capabilities that cannot be translated into activities, routines and business processes cannot have a positive impact on firm performance. This is very important with reference to managerial implications, because a firm may have limited possibilities of changing its own endowment of resources in the short and medium term but managers can show the ability to redesign some activities and businesses and routines more efficiently and effectively in order to better exploit, in organizational terms, those specific resources.

EMPIRICAL TESTS OF RESOURCE-BASED LOGIC

These, and other hypotheses, have been examined both in strategic management studies and other literatures. In Table 6.3 the main research

Table 6.3   RBT managerial implications: main areas

Strategic management
Human resources
Marketing
Entrepreneurship
Management information systems
Operations management
Information and communication technology management
Other disciplines

---

applications are pointed out, connecting to a previous elaboration started by Barney and Arikan (2001), completed and updated.

The major trends and findings in each of these areas of work will be briefly described.

Strategic Management Research

Not surprisingly, strategic management scholars have conducted the most empirical tests of resource-based logic. These tests examine several important assertions derived from the theory, including:

1) firm effects should be more important than industry effects in determining firm performance;
2) valuable, rare, and costly-to-imitate resources should have a more positive impact on firm performance than other kinds of resources;
3) corporate strategies (including mergers, acquisitions, and diversification) that exploit valuable, rare, and costly-to-imitate resources should generate greater returns than corporate strategies that exploit other kinds of resources;
4) international strategies that exploit valuable, rare, and costly-to-imitate resources will outperform international strategies that exploit other kinds of resources;
5) strategic alliances that exploit valuable, rare, and costly-to-imitate resources will outperform other kinds of alliances;
6) there cannot be a 'rule for riches' derived from strategic management theory;
7) strategic networks and interfirm systems can develop network competences that can be a source of sustained competitive advantage and even favor the single firms' performances.

All these aspects are summarized in Figure 6.2.

Strategic mgmt	{	Firm vs industry effects
		Impact of resources and capabilities on firms' performance
		Corporate strategy and corporate governance
		International strategies
		Strategic alliances
		Rules of riches
		Strategic networks and interfirm systems

Figure 6.2   RBT implications for strategic management: main areas

Industry vs. firm effects on firm performance

Initial work developed, respectively, by Porter (1980) and Schmalensee (1985) on industry versus firm effects in explaining variance in firm performance was inconsistent with resource-based expectations. In particular, this work suggested that industry effects were more important than firm effects. However, in 1991 Rumelt published an article that contradicted these earlier findings. Rumelt (1991) argued that previous work had applied the wrong methods or had used inadequate data to evaluate the relative impact of industry and firm effects on firm performance. After solving these problems, Richard Rumelt's results were consistent with resource-based expectations. Several authors have tried to replicate these results (McGahan and Porter, 1997; Mauri and Michaels, 1998; Brush and Bromiley, 1997). Some of these are critical of Rumelt's findings, but primarily in terms of the small corporate effect that Rumelt (1991) identified (Brush and Bromiley, 1997). However, all these replications continue to document that firm effects are a more important determinant of firm performance than industry effects, although the relative size of these effects can vary according to the industry.

Resources and firm performance

The bulk of empirical resource-based work in the field of strategic management has focused on identifying resources that have the attributes that resource-based theory predicts will be important for firm performance and then examining whether or not the predicted performance effects exist. The performance effects of a wide variety of types of firm resources have been examined, including a firm's history (Collis, 1991; Barnett et al., 1994; Rao, 1994), employees' know-how (Hall, 1992), integrative capabilities (e.g. Henderson and Cockburn, 1994), innovativeness (McGrath et al., 1996), culture (Moingeon et al., 1998), network belonging and relative position (McEvily and Zaheer, 1999; Gulati, 1998; Della Corte, 2004), to name a few. A wide variety of methods have been used to examine the performance effects of firm resources including large sample surveys, small sample surveys, case studies, and simulations. Overall, results are consistent with resource-based expectations.

There are, however, a few studies that generate results that are inconsistent with resource-based expectations. For example, Poppo and Zenger's (1995) analysis of vertical integration is more consistent with transactions cost economics than resource-based theory. Also, Sherer et al. (1998) suggest that compensation policy can have an effect on cooperation among a firm's employees, but that environmental conditions are a more important determinant of this cooperation. These and similar results suggest that the conditions under which different resources are and are not valuable requires further development in resource-based theory (Priem and Butler, 2001).

Resources and corporate strategy
The impact of resources on corporate strategies has also been examined empirically. One of the most important findings in this area is that SIC-code-based measures of strategic relatedness must be augmented by resource-based measures to capture the full performance effects of diversification strategies (Robins and Wiersema, 1995). Moreover, only when the basis of a diversification strategy is valuable, rare, and costly to imitate can firms expect such a strategy to generate superior firm performance (Markides and Williamson, 1996). While finance scholars have identified an important discount in the value of firms when they begin to diversify (Lang and Stulz, 1994), resource-based theorists have shown that this discount either does not exist or is consistent with shareholders' interests when the characteristics of the resources on which a firm's diversification strategies are based are accounted for (Miller, 2000, 2003). Similar results have been found in studies on the return to mergers and acquisitions (Coff, 1999).

International strategies
Resource-based work on international strategies is a logical extension of the work on diversification strategies cited earlier. However, some attributes of resource-based arguments are highlighted in an international context. For example, this work shows that a firm's resources reflect its country of origin, and that these country differences are long lasting (Karnoe, 1995). This work also examines the role of different forms of governance in realizing cross-border economies of scope and suggests that the tacitness of the resources used to realize these economies is an important determinant of governance choices (Zou and Ozsomer, 1999).

Resources and strategic alliances
Closely related to resource-based international research is work that focuses on the impact of resources of strategic alliances. In particular, this

work focuses on how firms can use alliances to either exploit their preexisting resources or to develop new resources. This latter work integrates insights from research on learning with resource-based logic (Shenkar and Li, 1999; Dussauge et al., 2000).

Rules for riches
Finally and connected with previous remarks, resource-based logic suggests that it is not possible to deduce 'rules for riches' from strategic management theories. 'Rules for riches' are rules that any firm can apply to gain sustained competitive advantages and economic rents. In empirical work, the difficulty in deriving 'rules for riches' from strategic management theory is examined in the context of the difficulty of sustaining competitive advantages through the application of well-known, widely understood managerial practices. These include the use of re-engineering, learning curve logic, the structure of training programs, formal long range planning, and patenting procedures (Schankerman, 1998).

Resources and strategic networks (systems)
The wide research internationally conducted has proved that, in some contexts, like Europe, where small and medium enterprises prevail in many industries, strategic alliances often evolve towards strategic networks. These involve entire groups of companies, physically close or strictly bound by client-supplier relationships, and are characterized by high specialization and complementarity of firms' activities and products. This is also called the 'business districts' configuration, based on the activities and production of more firms, which compete together in the face of big companies or other networks. This scheme regards not only manufacturing industries but also service industries, like the tourism industry, where destinations' competitiveness almost depends on the single firms' and the networks' strategic resources, able to generate sustainable competitive advantage for a whole destination. The results of the scheme are particularly relevant with reference to resource-based theory advances in its applications. While in fact, in the application of RBT, it can be sometimes necessary or at least adequate to go deep into the analysis at a sub-unit level, and to measure the resources' capacity of generating competitive advantage through more specific (even if perhaps more partial) performance results, in this case it is absolutely necessary to conduct the analysis not only at the single firm level, but also at the network or system level, in order to verify:

– the network or system's performance as a whole (e.g. a business district rather than a tourism destination);

–   whether a single company performance can be influenced and ameliorated by the fact that it operates within a group or network of firms, each of them characterized by specific resources and competences. This is a serious implication because a network's strategic resources are important for single firms' performances. Therefore, the parameterization issue becomes even more complex.

Considering business districts based on network configurations or tourism destinations, for example, their competitiveness depends on:

1)   local strategic resources (resources of the territory; in tourism, both historical and natural, rather than just natural, etc.);
2)   individual firms' capabilities in providing their own specific products or services (hotels' competences in managing hospitality, restaurants in cooking, serving and creating atmosphere, local authorities in creating events and expositions, etc.);
3)   network competences in developing strategic plans for the network or destination, in formulating innovative marketing ideas and communication patterns, deciding where to address the main investments locally speaking, carrying out efficient infrastructures and so on.

This also has important implications in respect of the outsourcing question, which, in some cases, may depend on the necessity or strategic opportunity to use firms' specialization and specific resources. This is a typical scheme of strategic networks.
We think this aspect undoubtedly opens up new horizons and opportunities for progress in the vein of resource-based theory, which represents a fundamentally new way of thinking strategically, outside the ordinary schemes and matrixes, which are often no longer useful for decision makers.

Human Resource Management Research

While the bulk of empirical research on the resource-based view of the firm focuses on strategic management implications of the theory, RBT has had implications in related fields as well. Among the most important of these is human resource management. Resource-based logic suggests that socially complex resources and capabilities should be among the most important sources of sustained competitive advantages for firms. Human resources are examples of socially complex resources and thus it is not surprising that human resource theorists have drawn heavily on resource-based logic to examine the impact of human resources and human resource policies on firm performance (Wright and MacMahan, 1992; Barney and Wright, 1998).

Some of the earliest work in this area focused on the impact of human resources on cost and quality in manufacturing (Womack et al., 1990; MacDuffie, 1995). More recently, this work has focused on various bundles of human resource practices that can have the effect of creating significant firm-specific human capital investments (Huselid and Becker, 1997). While some of this work has been criticized (Becker and Gerhart, 1996), there is little doubt that resource-based logic has had an important impact on human resources research as well as on the interactions between human resource management and strategy and marketing studies (Della Corte et al., 2011).

Other Disciplines

Several other disciplines have begun to explore the empirical implications of resource-based logic. These include marketing, entrepreneurship, management information systems, operations management, and technology and innovation management.

As regards marketing, interesting contributions examine the link between market knowledge competence and product market performance (Li and Calantone, 1998); and the impact of market-oriented and humanistic culture on employees' commitment (Maignan et al., 1999), and the connection between market-driven management and resource-based theory (Sciarelli, 2008) to cite only a few.

Another incredibly important field of research application is that of entrepreneurship (entrepreneurial behavior – Grebel et al., 2003; entrepreneurial intent – Chrisman, 1999; entrepreneurial recognition and resources combination – Alvarez and Busenitz, 2001; proactive capacity – Della Corte, 2004; innovativeness as a dynamic capability – Foss and Foss, 2006).

While research approaches vary by discipline, in all these different settings, research examines how various kinds of functional resources affect firm performance in ways that are consistent with resource-based logic.

MANAGERIAL IMPLICATIONS OF THE RESOURCE-BASED VIEW

The resource-based view has generated empirically testable hypotheses. Many of these hypotheses have, in fact, been tested. However, consistent with the tradition of strategic management as a field of application, resource-based logic can also have important implications for management practice (Mosakowski, 1998).

For example, this logic can be used to help managers in firms that are experiencing strategic disadvantages to gain strategic parity by identifying those valuable and rare resources their firm currently does not possess and pointing out that the value of these resources can be duplicated either through imitation or substitution. In this sense, resource-based logic can be used to provide a theoretical underpinning to the process of benchmarking in which many firms engage (Fuld, 1995).

Resource-based logic can also be used to help managers in firms that have the potential for gaining sustained competitive advantages, but where that potential is not being fully realized, to more fully express this potential. This is done by helping managers more completely understand the kinds of resources that can generate sustained competitive advantages, using this understanding to evaluate the full range of resources a firm may possess, and then exploiting those resources a firm possesses that have the potential to generate sustained competitive advantage more completely. Resource-based logic can help identify what the most critical resources controlled by a firm are and thereby increase the likelihood that they will be used to gain sustained competitive advantages.

RBT also allows managers and entrepreneurs to ensure that they nurture and maintain those resources that are sources of a firm's current competitive advantages. Competitive advantages for firms are often based on bundles of related resources. Some of these resources are likely to be valuable, but not rare, or not imperfectly imitable, or not non-substitutable. Others of these resources are likely to have these competitively important attributes. Nurturing and protecting this second class of resources are important if a firm is to maintain its sustained competitive advantage. For example, suppose a firm possesses a nurturing organizational culture. In some settings, such a culture may be valuable (Barney, 1986b). If only one competing firm possesses this culture, it is rare, and thus perfect competition dynamics around this culture are not likely to develop. Moreover, because an organizational culture develops over long periods of time (the role of history) and is socially complex, it is likely to be inelastic in supply. Finally, there are few obvious close strategic substitutes for an organizational culture. In this situation, it is likely that a firm's culture will be a source of sustained competitive advantage. However, even if it takes many decades for an organizational culture with these specific attributes to develop, that culture can be destroyed very quickly by senior managers in a firm making decisions that are inconsistent with that culture. Resource-based logic identifies this kind of culture as a potentially important source of sustained competitive advantage. Armed with this understanding, managers may be less inclined to make decisions that have the effect of destroying the very resource that is generating a sustained competitive advantage for their firm.

However, while it is clear that resource-based logic can have very important managerial implications, this logic also suggests that there are important prescriptive limits associated with resource-based theories of competitive advantage. First, to the extent that a firm's competitive advantage is based on causally ambiguous resources, managers in that firm cannot know, with certainty, which of their resources actually generates that competitive advantage. This can significantly limit the prescriptions derived from the theory.

Second, no theories of sustained competitive advantage can be used by managers in firms without the potential for generating sustained competitive advantages to create these advantages. That is, resource-based logic cannot be used to create sustained competitive advantages when the potential for these advantages does not already exist. Any theory that purports to be able to accomplish this is proposing a 'rule for riches.' However, it can give very useful hints concerning invaluable assets. It can also happen that a firm with much hidden potential cannot express it through its organization, but, if acquired by another firm with a different and more efficient organization or even with organizational resources, can significantly change the situation.

In any case, as is well known, there cannot be a 'rule for riches.' If the application of a theory to a firm without any special resources can be used to create competitive advantages for that firm, then it could be used to create competitive advantages for any firm, and the actions undertaken by any one of these firms would not be a source of sustained competitive advantage. Even if a 'rule for riches' created economic value, that value would be fully appropriated by those that invented and marketed this rule.

Thus, while the resources identified by resource-based logic as being most likely to generate sustained competitive advantages are frequently not amenable to managerial manipulation, it certainly does not follow that there are no prescriptive implications of that resource-based logic. Indeed, that resource-based logic is consistent with causal ambiguity and 'rules for riches' constraints on theory-derived prescription provides an important external validity check on this logic.

Generating Strategic Alternatives

Resource-based theory has a very simple view about how resources are connected to the strategies that a firm pursues. It is almost as if, once a firm becomes aware of the valuable, rare, costly-to-imitate, and non-substitutable resources it controls, the actions it should take to exploit these resources will be self-evident. That certainly may be true some of the time. For example, if a firm possesses valuable, rare, costly-to-imitate, and non-substitutable economies of scale, learning curve economies, access to low-cost factors of production, and technological resources, it seems clear that it should pursue a cost leadership strategy (Barney, 2001). However, it may often be the case that the link between resources and the strategies a firm should pursue will not be so obvious.

For example, sometimes it might be the case that a firm's resources will be consistent with several different strategies, all with the ability to create the same level of competitive advantage. In this situation, how should a firm decide which of these strategies it should pursue?

Even more importantly, there may be times when choosing a strategy consistent with the resources a firm controls is a creative and even entrepreneurial act. This could occur, for example, when a firm possesses valuable, rare, costly-to-imitate, and non-substitutable resources most agree are consistent with one strategy, and the firm is able to conceive of and implement a very different strategy that exploits these same resources, but in very different ways.

To the extent that developing strategic alternatives that a firm can use to exploit the resources it controls is a creative and entrepreneurial process, resource-based models of competitive advantage may need to be augmented by theories of the creative and entrepreneurial process. The application of these theories could then be used to understand the strategic alternatives a firm might be able to pursue, given the resources it controls. While we are currently unaware of such a highly developed theory, these observations suggest a very close relationship between theories of competitive advantage and theories of creativity and entrepreneurship.[7]

Rent Appropriation

As has already been suggested, resource-based theory can be used to evaluate the competitive potential of different strategic alternatives facing firms. However, this logic, as it was developed in the 1991 article, and as it has evolved since, does not address how the economic rents that a strategy might create are appropriated by a firm's stakeholders. It might be the case, for example, that implementing a particular strategy generates real economic rents for a firm, but that those rents are fully appropriated by a firm's employees, its customers, or even its suppliers. Some work has begun to examine this rent appropriation process (Coff, 1999). This work focuses on the relative bargaining power of a firm's stakeholders and the role of team production (Alchian and Demsetz, 1972) in determining how rents are distributed among a firm's stakeholders. While this work is promising, it still does not constitute a complete theory of the rent appropriation process. For example, how do different stakeholders come to enjoy different bargaining positions? Why is the value of a stakeholder's bargaining position not reflected in the cost of the investments necessary to create that position? Under what conditions will team production reduce the ability of employees to appropriate rents created by a firm's strategies? Why would employees agree to employment conditions that significantly reduce their ability to appropriate the rents that are created when a firm implements its strategies?

Strategy Implementation

Finally, in the 1991 paper, issues of strategy implementation do not receive sufficient attention. This chapter seems to adopt the remarkably naive view that, once a firm understands how to use its resources to implement strategies that can be sources of sustained competitive advantage, that implementation follows, almost automatically. This view is inconsistent both with agency theory arguments taken from organizational economics (Jensen and Meckling, 1976) and a huge organizational behavior literature on motivation, cooperation, and managerial decision making.

Of course, that issues of strategy implementation are not emphasized in the 1991 paper does not imply that these issues are unimportant. It only implies that other issues received more attention in that paper than implementation issues. However, more work is needed before the full range of strategy implementation issues not included in the 1991 paper are integrated with a resource-based theory of competitive advantage.

In general, there have been two approaches to addressing strategy implementation issues in the context of resource-based theory. First, some have suggested that the ability to implement strategies is, itself, a resource that can be a source of sustained competitive advantage. Work on the role of 'cooperative capabilities' in implementing strategic alliance strategies (e.g. Hansen et al., 2000) and the impact of 'trustworthiness' on exchange opportunities for a firm (Barney and Hansen, 1994) is consistent with this first approach, not only at the single firm's level, but also at the network or system's level.

Second, it has also been suggested that implementation depends on resources that are not themselves sources of sustained advantage, but rather are strategic complements to the other valuable, rare, costly-to-imitate, and non-substitutable resources controlled by a firm (Barney, 1995, 2001).

Which of these approaches ultimately is most fruitful in bringing the analysis of strategy implementation into resource-based logic is an open question. However, it is clear that additional work is required here.

CONCLUSIONS

According to what has previously been explained, some main conclusions can be drawn:

1) the resource immobility/substitution issue has to be faced considering not only sustainability conditions of competitive advantage but also its attainment;
2) resource scarcity has to be considered as strictly connected to its functionality in terms of business processes rather than to its specific nature;
3) some resources that are imitable in principle are not copied or duplicated: this can be due to implementation capabilities (that refers to the case when organization factors become strategic resources) or to entrepreneurial competences (heuristics, rather than proactive capabilities – Busenitz and Lau, 1996; Alvarez and Busenitz, 2001; Wright et al., 2000; Della Corte, 2004). This topic still needs further research but opens up research advances in the direction of resources and capabilities' use;
4) in order to evaluate the contribution of firms' strategic resources to performance it is sometimes necessary to go deep into a sub-unit level of analysis and to consider some performance measures that are different from the overall performance;
5) on the other hand, it is sometimes difficult, in parameterizing the RBT's main propositions, to isolate each specific resource's contribution to a company's performance results;
6) when a firm is part of a network, it is important to point out also resources and competences at the network level and to verify whether these can have an impact on a firm's performance as well.

In the analysis, we have not considered the wider effects of RBT as concerning relations rather than knowledge, that referred to specific views, but we have just focused on the more direct effects of this approach in management.

These are the main aspects to take into account in resource-based logic and we believe that further research and applications in this direction will confirm its validity in strategic management studies and in managers' and entrepreneurs' decision making.

NOTES

1. From social success theory other important concepts have been developed, such as corporate ethics (Frederick, 1992; Wood, 1991).
2. For further reading on this topic, see Barney (2002) and Barney (2006).
3. We recognize that the state of the theory summarized in this section will reflect the tastes and biases of the current authors. Thus, there may be some scholars that label themselves as resource-based researchers who will disagree with this characterization. We have made an effort to incorporate as many different perspectives as possible, but we also acknowledge that there may still be some disagreements with the way the theory is here summarized.
4. Imagine, for example, if every application of the law of gravity was labeled as a 'new' theory, e.g., the theory of the earth's rotation around the sun, the theory of the moon's rotation around the earth, the theory of the solar system's rotation around the galaxy. While each of these 'theories' would vary with respect to details in calculation and application, they would all be applying the same underlying theoretical framework. Such 'theoretical proliferation' currently exists in the field of strategic management.
5. This assumption sets aside important agency problems that are discussed later in the paper.
6. For expositional convenience, these hypotheses temporarily set aside issues about the effectiveness with which firms implement their strategies. These organizational issues are discussed later in the paper.
7. Recent work on real options (McGrath and MacMillan, 2000) and innovation management (Brown and Eisenhardt, 1998; Christensen, 2000; McGrath et al., 1995).

REFERENCES

Alchian, A. and H. Demsetz (1972). "Production, information costs, and economic organization." *American Economic Review*, 62, pp. 777–795.

Alvarez, S. A. and L. W. Busenitz (2001). "The entrepreneurship of resource-based theory." *Journal of Management*, 27, pp. 755–775.

Barnett, W. P., H. R. Greve and D. Y. Park (1994). "An evolutionary model of organizational performance." *Strategic Management Journal*, 15, pp. 11–28.

Barney, J. B. (1986a). "Types of competition and the theory of strategy: toward an integrative framework." *Academy of Management Review*, 11, pp. 791–800.

Barney, J. B. (1986b). "Organizational culture: can it be a source of sustained competitive advantage?" *Academy of Management Review*, 11, pp. 656–665.

Barney, J. B. (1986c). "Strategic factor markets: expectations, luck and business strategy." *Management Science*, 32, pp. 1512–1514.

Barney, J. B. (1988). "Returns to bidding firms in mergers and acquisitions: reconsidering the relatedness hypothesis." *Strategic Management Journal*, 9, pp. 71–78.

Barney, J. B. (1991a). "The resource based view of strategy: origins, implications, and prospects." Editor of Special Theory Forum in *Journal of Management*, 17, pp. 97–211.

Barney, J. B. (1991b). "Firm resources and sustained competitive advantage." *Journal of Management*, 17, pp. 99–120.

Barney, J. B. (1995). "Looking inside for competitive advantage." *Academy of Management Executive*, 9, pp. 49–61.

Barney, J. B. (2001). "Is the resource-based 'view' a useful perspective for strategic management research? Yes." *Academy of Management Review*, 26(1), pp. 41–56.

Barney, J. B. (2002). *Gaining and Sustaining Competitive Advantage*. Second edition, NJ: Prentice-Hall.

Barney J. B. (2006). *Risorse, Competenze e Vantaggi Competitivi*. Edizione Italiana a cura di Della Corte V. e M. Sciarelli, Carocci Editore.

Barney, J. B. and A. M. Arikan (2001). "The resource-based view: origins and implications," in M. A. Hitt, R. E. Freeman and J.S. Harrison (eds), *Handbook of Strategic Management*. Oxford: Blackwell Publishing, pp. 124–188.

Barney, J. B., V. Della Corte and M. Sciarelli (2005). "Digital economy and sustained competitive advantage in the tourism industry", in A. Capasso, G.B. Dagnino and A. Lanza (eds), *Strategic Capabilities and Knowledge Transfer Within and Between Organizations*. Northampton: Edward Elgar Publishing, pp. 35–55.

Barney, J. B. and M. Hansen (1994). "Trustworthiness as a source of competitive advantage." *Strategic Management Journal*, 15, pp. 175–190.

Barney, J. B. and W. S. Hesterly (1996). "Organizational economics: understanding the relationship between organizations and economic analysis," in S. Clegg, C. Hardy and W. R. Nord (eds), *Handbook of Organization Studies*. London: Sage Publications.

Barney, J. B. and T. B. Mackey (2005). "Testing resource-based theory," in D. J. Ketchen and D. D. Bergh (eds), *Research Methodology in Strategy and Management*, Vol. 2, New York: Elsevier, pp. 1–13.

Barney, J. B. and W. Ouchi (eds) (1986). *Organizational Economics*. San Francisco: Jossey-Bass.

Barney, J. B. and P. Wright (1998). "On becoming a strategic partner: the role of human resources in gaining competitive advantage." *Human Resource Management*, 37, pp. 31–46.

Becker, B. and B. Gerhart (1996). "The impact of human resource management on organizational performance: progress and prospects." *Academy of Management Journal*, 39(4), pp. 779–801.

Black, F. and M. Scholes (1973). "The pricing of options and corporate liabilities." *The Journal of Political Economy*, 81, pp. 637–654.

Brown, S. L. and K. M. Eisenhardt (1998). *Competing on the Edge: Strategy as Structured Chaos*. Boston: Harvard Business School Press.

Brush, C. G., P. G. Greene and M. H. Hart (2001). "From initial idea to unique advantage: the entrepreneurial challenge of constructing a resource base." *Academy of Management Executive*, 15(1), pp. 64–78.

Brush, T. H. and P. Bromiley (1997). "What does a small corporate effect mean? A variance components simulation of corporate and business effects." *Strategic Management Journal*, 18, pp. 325–835.

Busenitz, L. and C. Lau (1996). "A cross-cultural cognitive model of new venture creation." *Entrepreneurship Theory and Practice*, 20(4), pp. 25–39

Carroll, A. B. (1979). "A three-dimensional model of corporate social performance." *Academy of Management Review*, 4, pp. 497–505.

Carroll, A. B. (1991). "The pyramid of corporate social responsibility: toward the moral management of organizational stakeholders." *Business Horizons*, 34, pp. 39–48.

Chamberlin, E. H. (1933). *The Theory of Monopolistic Competition*. Cambridge, MA: Harvard University Press.

Chrisman, J. J. (1999). "The influence of outsider-generated knowledge resources on venture creation." *Journal of Small Business Management*, 37, pp. 42–58.

Christensen, C.M. (2000). *The Innovator's Dilemma*. New York, NY: HarperCollins.

Coase, R. H. (1937). "The nature of the firm." *Economica*, n.s., pp. 386–405.

Coff, R. (1999). "How buyers cope with uncertainty when acquiring firms in knowledge-intensive industries: Caveat emptor." *Organization Science*, 10(2), March-April, pp. 144–161.

Collis, D. J. (1991). "A resource-based analysis of global competition: the case of the bearings industry." *Strategic Management Journal*, 12, Summer, pp. 49–68.

Davis, K. (1975). "Five propositions for social responsibility." *Business Horizons*, 18, pp. 19–24.

Della Corte, V. (2004). *La gestione strategica e le scelte di governo di un'impresa tour operator*. CEDAM, Padova.

Della Corte, V., G. Mangia, R. Micera and G. Zamparelli (2011). "Strategic employer branding: the brand and image management as attractiveness for talented capital" in *International Marketing Trends Conference*, January.

Della Corte, V., M. Migliaccio and M. Sciarelli (2007). "I sistemi turistici locali: lo stato dell'arte e le prospettive." in Sciarelli, S. (eds), *Il management dei sistemi turistici locali*, Torino: Giappichelli, pp. 127–161.
Della Corte V. and M. Sciarelli (2006), "I percorsi di sviluppo aggregativo: dall'impresa al sistema". In Barney J.B., *Risorse, Competenze e Vantaggi Competitivi*, Roma: Carocci.
Dierickx, I. and K. Cool (1989). "Asset stock accumulation and sustainability of competitive advantage." *Management Science*, 35, pp. 1504–1511.
Donaldson, T. and L. E. Preston (1995). "The stakeholder theory of the corporation: concepts, evidence, and implications." *Academy of Management Review*, 20, pp. 65–91.
Drucker, P. (1994). "The theory of business." *Harvard Business Review*, 75, pp. 95–105.
Dussauge, P., B. Garrette and W. Mitchell (2000). "Learning from competing partners: outcomes and durations of scale and link alliances in Europe, North America and Asia." *Strategic Management Journal*, 21(2), pp. 9–126.
Eisenhardt. K. M. (1989). "Agency theory: an assessment and review." *Academy of Management Review*, 14, pp. 57–74.
Foss, K. and N. Foss (2006). "Entrepreneurship, transaction costs, and resource attributes." *International Journal of Strategic Change Management*, 1, pp. 53–60.
Frederick, W. C. (1960). "The growing concern over business responsibility.", *California Management Review*, 2, pp. 54–61.
Frederick, W. C. (1992). "Anchoring values in nature: toward a theory of business values." *Business Ethics Quarterly*, 2, pp. 283–303.
Freeman, R. E. (1984). *Strategic Management: a Stakeholder Approach*. London: Pitman.
Freeman, R. E. (1989). "Divergent stakeholder theory." *Academy of Management Review*, 24, pp. 233–236.
Fuld, L. M. (1995). *The New Competitor Intelligence: The Complete Resource for Finding, Analyzing, and Using Information About Your Competitors*. New York: John Wiley.
Galbraith, J. R. (2000). *Designing the Global Corporation*. San Francisco: Jossey-Bass Inc. Publishers.
Grant, R. M. (1996). "Toward a knowledge-based theory of the firm." *Strategic Management Journal*, 17, Winter Special Issue, pp. 109–122.
Grebel, T., A. Pyka and H. Hanusch (2003). "An evolutionary approach to the theory of entrepreneurship." *Industry & Innovation*, 10, pp. 493–514.
Gulati, R. (1998). "Alliances and networks." *Strategic Management Journal*, 19, pp.293–317
Hall, R. (1992). "The strategic analysis of intangible resources." *Strategic Management Journal*, 13, pp. 35–144.
Hamel, G. and C. K. Prahalad (1990). "The core competence of the corporation." *Harvard Business Review*, 68, pp. 79–91.
Hansen, M., R. Hoskisson, and J. B. Barney (2000). "Resolving the opportunism minimization-opportunity maximization paradox." Presented at the Annual Meeting of Academy of Management, 1999.
Harrison, J. S., M. A. Hitt, R. E. Hoskisson and R. D. Ireland (2001). "Resource complementarity in business combinations: extending the logic to organizational alliances." *Journal Of Management*, 27, pp. 679–690.
Helfat, C. E. and M. A. Peteraf (2003). "The dynamic resource-based view: capability lifecycles." *Strategic Management Journal*, 24, pp. 997–1010.
Henderson, R. and I. Cockburn (1994). "Measuring competence? Exploring firm effects in pharmaceutical research." *Strategic Management Journal*, 15, pp. 63–84.
Hill, C. W. L. and G. R. Jones (1992). *Strategic Management Theory: An Integrated Approach*. Boston: Houghton Mifflin.
Huselid, M. A. and B. E. Becker (1997). "The impact of high performance work systems, implementation effectiveness, and alignment with strategy on shareholder wealth." *Academy of Management Proceedings '97*, pp. 144–148.
Itami, H. (1987). *Mobilizing Invisible Assets*. Cambridge: Harvard University Press.
Jensen, M. C. and W. H. Meckling (1976). "Theory of the firm: managerial behavior, agency costs, and ownership structure." *Journal of Financial Economics*, 3, pp. 305–360.

Karnoe, P. (1995). "Competence as process and the social embeddedness of competence building." *Academy of Management Journal*, pp. 427–431.

Kogut, B. (1991). "Joint ventures and the option to expand and acquire." *Management Science*, 37, pp. 19–33.

Kogut, B. and U. Zander (1992). "Knowledge of the firm. Combinative capabilities, and the replication of technology." *Organization Science*, 3 pp. 383–397.

Lang, L. H. P. and R. M. Stulz (1994). "Tobin's q, corporate diversification, and firm performance." *Journal of Political Economy*, 102, pp. 1248–1280.

Lei, D., M. A. Hitt and R. A. Bettis, (1996). "Dynamic core competences through meta-learning and strategic context." *Journal of Management*, 22, pp. 549–569.

Li, T. and R. J. Calantone (1998). "The impact of market knowledge competence on new product advantage: Conceptualization and empirical examination." *Journal of Marketing*, 62, pp. 3–29.

Liebeskind, J. P. (1996). "Knowledge, strategy, and the theory of the firm." *Strategic Management Journal*, Winter Special Issue, v. 17, pp. 93–107.

Lorange, P. (1980). *Corporate Planning: An Executive Viewpoint*. Prentice-Hall, Englewood Cliffs, N.J.

MacDuffie, J. (1995). "Human resource bundles and manufacturing performance: Organizational logic and flexible production systems in the world auto industry." *Industrial and Labor Relations Review*, 49, pp. 197–221.

Maignan, I., O. C. Ferrell and G. T. M. Hult (1999). "Corporate citizenship: Cultural antecedents and business benefits." *Journal of the Academy of Marketing Science*, 27, pp. 455–469.

Makadok, R. (2001). "Toward a synthesis of the resource-based and dynamic-capability views of rent creation." *Strategic Management Journal*, 22, pp. 387–401.

Mansfield, E., M. Schwartz and S. Wagner (1981). "Imitation costs and patents: an empirical study." *Economic Journal*, 91, pp. 907–918.

Markides, C. C. and P. J. Williamson (1996). "Corporate diversification and organizational structure: a resource-based view." *Academy of Management Journal*, 39, pp. 340–367.

Mauri, A. J. and Michaels, M. P. (1998). "Firm and industry effects within strategic management: an empirical examination." *Strategic Management Journal*, 19, pp. 211–219.

McEvily, B. and A. Zaheer (1999). "Bridging ties: a source of firm heterogeneity in competitive capabilities." *Strategic Management Journal*, 20, pp. 1133–1156.

McGahan, A. M. and Porter, M. E. (1997). "How much does industry matter, really?" *Strategic Management Journal*, 18(Special Issue), pp. 15–30.

McGrath, R. G. and I. C. MacMillan (2000). *The Entrepreneurial Mindset: Strategies for Continuously Creating Opportunity in an Age of Uncertainty*. Boston: Harvard Business School Press.

McGrath, R. G., I. C. MacMillan and S. Venkataraman (1995). "Defining and developing a competence: a strategic process paradigm." *Strategic Management Journal*, 16, pp. 251–275.

McGrath, R. G., M-H. Tsui, S. Venkataraman and I. C. MacMillan (1996). "Innovation, competitive advantage and rent: a model and test." *Management Science*, 42(3), pp. 389–403.

Miller, D. J. (2000). *Corporate Diversification, Relatedness, and Performance.* Unpublished dissertation, The Ohio State University.

Miller, D. J. (2003). "An asymmetry-based view of advantage: towards an attainable sustainability." *Strategic Management Journal*, 24, pp. 961–976.

Mintzberg, H. (1990). "The design school: reconsidering the basic premises of strategic management." *Strategic Management Journal*, 113, pp. 171–195.

Mitchell, R. K., B. R. Agle and D. J. Wood (1997) "Toward a theory of stakeholder identification and salience: defining the principle of who and what really counts." *Academy of Management Review*, 22, pp. 853–886.

Moingeon, B., B. Ramanantsoa, E. Metais and J. D. Orton (1998). "Another look at strategy-structure relationships: the resource-based view." *European Management Journal*, 16, pp. 297–305.

Mosakowski, E. (1998). "Managerial prescriptions under the resource-based view of strategy: the example of motivational techniques." *Strategic Management Journal*, 19, pp. 1169–1182.

Nelson, R. and S. Winter (1982). *An Evolutionary Theory of Economic Change*. Cambridge, MA: Belknap Press.

Nelson, R. and S. Winter (2002). "Evolutionary theorizing in economics." *Journal of Economic Perpectives*, 16, pp. 23–46.

Peteraf, M. A. (1993). "The cornerstones of competitive advantage: A resource-based view." *Strategic Management Journal*, 14, pp. 179–191.

Pfeffer, C. and G. Salancik (1978). *The External Control of Organization*. New York: Harper & Row.

Poppo, L. and T. Zenger (1995). "Opportunism, routines, and boundary choices: A comparative test of transaction cost and resource-based explanations for make-or-buy decisions." *Academy of Management Journal*, 38, pp. 42–46.

Porter, M. E. (1980). *Competitive Strategy*. New York: Free Press.

Porter, M. E. (1985). *Competitive Advantage*. New York: Free Press.

Priem, R. L. and J. E. Butler (2001). "Is the resource-based view a useful perspective for strategic management research?" *Academy of Management Review*, 26, pp. 22–40.

Rao, H. (1994). "The social construction of reputation – certification contests, legitimation, and the survival of organizations in the American automobile-industry – 1895–1912." *Strategic Management Journal*, 15 (Special Winter Issue), pp. 29–44.

Ray, G., J. B. Barney and W. A. Muhanna (2004). "Capabilities, business processes, and competitive advantage: choosing the dependent variable in empirical tests of the resource-based view." *Strategic Management Journal*, 25, pp. 27–37.

Rhenman, E. (1968). *Industrial Democracy and Industrial Management: A Critical Essay on the Possible Meanings and Implications of Industrial Democracy*. London and Assen: Tavistock.

Ricardo, D. (1817). *Principles of Political Economy and Taxation*. London: J. Murray.

Robins, J. and M. F. Wiersema (1995). "A resource-based approach to the multibusiness firm: Empirical analysis of portfolio interrelationships and corporate financial performance." *Strategic Management Journal*, 16, 277–299.

Rumelt, R. (1984). "Toward a strategic theory of the firm." In R. Lamb (ed.), *Competitive Strategic Management*. Englewood Cliffs, NJ: Prentice-Hall.

Rumelt, R. (1991). "How much does industry matter?" *Strategic Management Journal*, 12, pp. 167–185.

Schankerman, M. (1998). "How valuable is patent protection? Estimates by technology field." *The Rand Journal of Economics*, 29, pp. 77–107.

Schmalensee, R. (1985). "Do markets differ much?" *American Economic Review*, 75, pp. 341–351.

Schoemaker, P. J. H. (1990). "Strategy, complexity and economic rent." *Management Science*, 36, pp. 1178–1192.

Sciarelli, M. (2008). "Resource-based theory and market-driven management", *Symphonya. Emerging Issues in Management* (www.unimib.it/symphonya), 2, pp. 73–86.

Selznick, P. (1957). *Leadership in Administration*. New York: Harper and Row.

Sethi, P. (1975). "Dimensions of corporate social responsibility.", *California Management Review*, 17, pp. 58–64.

Shenkar, O. and J. T. Li (1999). "Knowledge search in international cooperative ventures." *Organizational Science*, 10, pp. 134–143.

Sherer, P. D., N. Rogovsky and N. Wright, N. (1998). "What drives employment relationships in taxicab organizations? Linking agency to firm capabilities and strategic opportunities." *Organization Science*, 9, pp. 34–48.

Simon, H. A. (1945). *Administrative Behavior*. New York: Free Press.

Smith, A. (1776). *An Inquiry into the Nature And Causes of the Wealth of Nations*. Public Domain.

Spender, J. C. (1996). "Making knowledge the basis of a dynamic theory of the firm." *Strategic Management Journal*, 17, Winter Special Issue, pp. 45–62.

Stalk, G., P. Evans and L. Shulman (1992). "Competing on capabilities: the new rules of corporate strategy." *Harvard Business Review*, 70, pp. 57–69.

Teece, D. J, G. Pisano and A. Shuen (1997). "Dynamic capabilities and strategic management." *Strategic Management Journal*, 18, pp. 509–533.

Trigeorgis, L. (1996). *Real Options: Managerial Flexibility and Strategy in Resource Allocation*. Cambridge, MA: MIT Press.

Wernerfelt, B. (1984). "A resource-based view of the firm." *Strategic Management Journal*, 5, pp. 171–180.

Williamson, O. E. (1971). "The vertical integration of production: market failure considerations." *American Economic Review*, 61, pp. 112–123.

Williamson, O. E. (1975). *Markets and Hierarchies: Analysis and Antitrust Implication*. New York: Free Press.

Williamson, O. E. (1985). *The Economic Institutions of Capitalism*. New York: Free Press.

Winter, S. G. (2000). "The satisficing principle in capability learning." *Strategic Management Journal*, 21, pp. 981–997.

Winter, S. G. (2003). "Understanding dynamic capabilities." *Strategic Management Journal*, 24, pp. 991–995.

Winter, S. G. (2005). "Developing evolutionary theory." in K. G. Smith and M. A. Hitt (eds), *Great Minds in Management*. Oxford: Oxford University Press, pp. 509–546.

Womack, J. P., D. I. Jones and D. Roos (1990). *The Machine That Changed the World*. New York: Rawson.

Wood, D. J. (1991). "Corporate social performance revisited." *The Academy of Management Review*, 16(4), pp. 691–718.

Wright, M., R. E. Hoskisson, L. W. Busenitz and J. Dial (2000). "Entrepreneurial growth through privatization: the upside of management buyouts." *Academy of Management Review*, 25(3), pp. 591–601.

Wright, P. M. and G. C. McMahan (1992). "Theoretical perspectives for strategic human resource management." *Journal of Management*, 18(2), pp. 295–320.

Zou, S. and A. Ozsomer (1999). "Global product R&D and the firm's strategic position." *Journal of International Marketing*, 7(1), pp. 57–76.

7 The mind of the strategist and the eye of the beholder: the socio-cognitive perspective in strategy research
Violina P. Rindova, Rhonda K. Reger and Elena Dalpiaz

INTRODUCTION

This chapter provides an overview of strategy research that concerns itself with the effects of socio-cognitive processes and structures on the strategic behavior of firms and on the environments in which firms operate. Our overview highlights how the socio-cognitive perspective contributes to the central question of theoretical interest in strategy research: how do firms make strategic choices and how do these choices affect their performance? We show how socio-cognitive researchers address this central question by reviewing two main streams of works: the work on the decision-making processes and cognitive structures of managers (Starbuck and Milliken, 1988; Thomas et al., 1993; Gioia and Chittipeddi, 1991; Porac and Thomas, 1990; Porac et al., 1989; Reger and Huff, 1993) and the work on the processes of collective sensemaking by stakeholders and various organizational observers in markets and organizational fields (Rindova and Fombrun, 1999; Hargadon and Douglas, 2001; Hoffman and Ocasio, 2001; Rindova et al., 2004; Rindova et al., 2005). We refer to the first stream of work as studying the mind of the strategist and to the second as studying the eye of the beholder.

We discuss the accomplishments in each stream of strategic socio-cognitive research and the contributions that they have made to specific areas of strategy research. In particular, we highlight that a) the research on managerial cognitive processes has contributed to the development of a more fine-grained understanding of strategic change and organizational adaptation; b) the research on managerial cognitive structures has provided an alternative conceptualization of the origins and effects of industry structures and competitive interactions; and c) the research on collective sensemaking among stakeholders has articulated the processes through which market-based intangible assets are generated and sustained. We further identify areas where our understanding of the economic exchanges that firms engage in can be enhanced by further research that examines the interplay between actors' cognition – perceptions, ideas and beliefs – and their actions in organizations and markets.

THE SOCIO-COGNITIVE PERSPECTIVE IN THE FIELD OF STRATEGY

The fundamental question for strategic research is why some firms perform better than others and how strategic choices enable firms to achieve superior performance (Porter, 1991). A central issue in strategy research then is to understand how firms choose strategic actions and what the performance consequences of their actions are. This question has been answered from two different perspectives that have dominated the conversation in the field of strategy through the 1980s and the 1990s. The proponents of the 'structure-conduct-performance' paradigm (Porter, 1980) place the origins of superior firm performance in the structural characteristics of the industry; the proponents of the resource-based view of the firm (Wernerfelt, 1984; Dierickx and Cool, 1989; Barney, 1991; Peteraf, 1993) attribute superior firm performance to firms' heterogeneous endowment of resources, and the specific characteristics of these resources. Examining the cross citation patterns from 1980 to 2000, a bibliometric study of the intellectual structure of the field (Ramos-Rodriguez and Ruiz-Navarro, 2004) shows that contributions from these perspectives have become some of the most influential works in the strategy field.

Interestingly, both perspectives emphasize various socio-cognitive phenomena as important sources of superior performance. For example, in their discussion of mobility barriers, Caves and Porter (1977) suggested that managers' capabilities of screening and evaluating information from the external environment are important in reducing the cost and the uncertainty of decisions of entry in other industries or strategic groups. Later, Porter (1980) argued that crucial for competitive analysis is the identification of competitors' assumptions about themselves, the industry and other players and that those assumptions are shaped by "blind spots" (p. 59) that bias the perceptions of significance of events. From a resource-based perspective, Barney (1991) argued that causal ambiguity may hamper competitors' ability to imitate a firm's resource as they cannot interpret the causal links through which the resource is related to competitive advantage. He further suggested that culture and reputation are imperfectly imitable resources because they represent complex social phenomena that competitors cannot readily disentangle, understand and reproduce. Adner and Helfat (2003) argued that heterogeneity in managerial dynamic capabilities underpins the variance of business performance and that managerial cognitive structures are an important determinant of those heterogeneous capabilities.

Yet, despite the fact that cognitive phenomena such as capabilities, blind spots and causal ambiguity are recognized in both perspectives as important to the generation and sustainability of competitive advantage, the socio-cognitive nature of competitive interactions, market exchanges, resource acquisition and deployment is seldom recognized and made a focal point of enquiry in these perspectives.

In our view, the reticence of strategy research in adopting a socio-cognitive approach more broadly stems from the fundamental differences in the assumptions about human information processing in neoclassical economic theory, on the one hand, and in behavioral decision theory and cognitive and social psychology on the other hand. Since economic theories have been proposed to provide the primary disciplinary back-bone for much of strategy content research because of their equilibrium assumptions and econometric instruments for interpreting data on firms' performance differentials (Rumelt et al., 1991), their view of human information processing has also become predominant in the strategy field. Yet, the rational information-processing view, which assumes a homo economicus that knows all relevant information and has unlimited computational capabilities allowing him or her to choose the course of action that optimizes his or her preferences, stands in stark contrast with findings of decision (Tversky and Kahneman, 1974) and socio-cognitive research (Fiske and Taylor, 1991). This research has shown that a) human rationality is bounded by the possibility to access only a limited set of alternatives and by limited computational capabilities that lead actors to choose actions that satisfice rather than optimize performance outcomes; b) human judgment is biased by the use of heuristics under conditions of uncertainty; c) social contexts and social interactions influence and color judgments.

The socio-cognitive perspective in strategy is therefore rooted in a bounded rationality view of strategic decision makers who satisfy rather than optimize performance outcomes, as they rely on heuristics and cognitive simplifications to cope with uncertainty and cognitive overload. It is distinct from the psychological perspectives it draws on in its focus on managerial, organizational, and stakeholders' sensemaking (Meindl et al., 1994). Yet, it does not represent a unified paradigm with consistent theoretical assumptions and methodological approaches. Scholars working in the area differ along several dimensions. First, they may be grounded theoretically in cognitive psychology, social psychology or, more recently, neoinstitutional theory. In neoinstitutionalism, schemas and scripts are collectively established, institutionalized logics of action (DiMaggio and Powell, 1991). Second, the level of analysis may be the individual, the group, the organization or the industry (see Walsh, 1995 for a comprehensive review of these issues). Third, scholars differ in their emphasis of cognitive structures versus cognitive processes and in their beliefs about the relationship between cognitive structures and processes, and performance outcomes.

Despite this theoretical and methodological diversity, and potentially because of it, the socio-cognitive approach has made important contributions to central areas of strategy research. By examining the variety in the processes through which key strategic decisions and variables emerge as a result of the differences in the ways in which decision makers process, interpret and use information stimuli, the socio-cognitive approach brings strategy research closer to the complex realities of organizational and market environments. In these environments, information overload and diversity of interests and experiences coupled with the need to think while acting, or to convey meaning to others in the face of pervasive uncertainty, accord primary importance to understanding, perceiving, sensemaking, and sensegiving – the core phenomena that define the agenda of the socio-cognitive approach in strategy. These phenomena are foundational to understanding both why firms do what they do: why they take certain strategic actions, and why stakeholders respond in the ways they do by increasing or decreasing their willingness to exchange resources with firms and to pay for their product offerings.

More specifically, the socio-cognitive approach offers important insights into how individuals and collectives gather and interpret information from complex data environments such as industries (Porac and Thomas, 1990; Reger and Huff, 1993; Rindova et al., 2004) and organizational fields (Rindova and Fombrun, 1999; Hoffman and Ocasio, 2001), and how knowledge and perceptions develop at the collective level and influence the performance of firms (Porac et al., 1989; Barr et al., 1992; Clark and Montgomery, 1998; Rindova and Fombrun, 1999; Rindova et al., 2004). Thus, the socio-cognitive approach expands and elaborates on the understanding of both the processes through which firms make strategic choices and the mechanisms that link strategic actions to firm performance. As noted earlier, one stream of socio-cognitive research focuses on the cognitive processes and mental models of decision makers that shape the strategic course of action of firms, thereby studying what we term 'the mind of the strategist'. Another major stream of research focuses on the impact of firms' strategic decisions and actions on the perceptions and actions of stakeholders, thereby studying what we term 'the eye of the beholder'. Together both streams of work contribute to strategic management

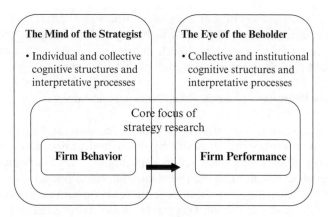

Figure 7.1   Main theories in strategic management studies

research's understanding of the unique effects of human cognition on the actions that firms take, and on the perceptions, interpretations, and responses that these actions evoke among diverse stakeholder audiences (Rindova and Fombrun, 1999). Figure 7.1 positions the contribution of socio-cognitive strategy research to the fundamental questions of strategy.

THE MIND OF THE STRATEGIST: PROCESSES AND STRUCTURES

We broadly categorize as studying the mind of the strategist researchers who focus on two general areas of interest: cognitive processes, which describe how information is noticed and interpreted (Fiske and Taylor, 1991), and cognitive structures that describe how knowledge is organized and how, once organized, it provides filters through which new information is interpreted and used.

Process researchers study how firm strategists attend to stimuli in their environments (Starbuck and Milliken, 1988; Thomas et al., 1993), frame environmental stimuli (as opportunities or threats, for example see Jackson and Dutton, 1988) and ultimately take action and instigate strategic change (see Rajagopalan and Spreitzer, 1996, for a review). Conversely, structures researchers study the sediments of cognition and perception, the knowledge structure and the cognitive maps that organize and represent the information gathered and the experiences and views that the strategists of a given firm hold (Barr et al., 1992; Reger and Huff, 1993). Cognitive structures have been shown to affect managers' perceptions of strategic group membership (Reger and Huff, 1993), of an industry and transaction network boundaries (Porac et al., 1989; Porac and Thomas, 1990) and of the 'competitive recipes' through which they seek to compete and create value in an industry (Spender, 1989). In this section, we summarize some important contributions made in each of these two areas.

Cognitive Processes of Sensemaking: Noticing and Interpreting

In order to take actions, managers must make sense of the information that surrounds them: they must first be able to notice information and then to interpret it as having some action implications (Daft and Weick, 1984; Weick et al., 2005). Because managers have limited information-processing capabilities, when they scan the information environment they notice only a subset of the available stimuli. They tend to notice more recent and dramatic events and larger changes in the current situation (Mezias and Starbuck, 2003) and to ignore both the really unfamiliar, which is likely to appear irrelevant, and the extremely familiar, which becomes taken for granted and ignored (Starbuck and Milliken, 1988). However, Porac and Rosa (1996) argue that despite their inaccuracy, managerial perceptions can effectively guide firms' subsequent actions and even lead to competitive advantage if firms are able to impose their interpretive frameworks on their environments. This is because, as we discuss later, the socio-cognitive perspective emphasizes that environments are not objective and given, but are instead enacted through the processes of perception, interpretation and action.

Depending on the different assumptions about the analyzability of environment and the type of organizational intrusiveness, firms differ in the nature of the 'inquiry systems' they develop to scan the environment systematically and to select stimuli for further processing conscientiously (Daft and Weick, 1984). Ocasio (1997) advanced an attentional theory of the firm, where he theorizes about the nature of organizational attributes such as organizational structures, rules, and vocabularies that systematically channel organizational attention. These ideas from organizational theory suggest interesting possibilities for strategy researchers to recognize that attention is neither completely free and unbound, nor completely automatic and pre-programmed by structures and routines, but a resource that can be managed strategically by developing a better understanding of the factors that influence its allocation at the organizational and market level of analysis. Further, psychological research that distinguishes between automatic and mindful attention (Bargh and Ferguson, 2000) holds significant promise for strategy researchers to begin to understand more systematically the underlying differences in organizational capabilities for search and dynamic discovery of opportunities (Teece et al., 1997). For instance, Reger and Palmer (1996) found significant differences in the automatic and mindful cognitive maps of managers in three financial services markets. These differences were especially interesting as the mindful cognitive maps tracked relatively well with the regulatory and competitive changes occurring in the financial services industry. However, the automatic maps continued to map the old economic and regulatory environments. Since theorists have postulated that much of strategic decision making relies on automatic processing and automatic maps, these results show that decision errors are likely in rapidly changing environments, even if the decision makers are mindfully aware of the changes.

The process of managerial interpretation of (noticed) stimuli has been mainly explored within the studies of strategic change, where the process of ascribing meanings to information affects what strategic action is undertaken. Barr et al. (1992) show that the effectiveness of organizational renewal is influenced not so much by the ability of noticing significant changes in the environment but rather by the ability of making sense of them and changing the strategists' mental models accordingly. Dutton and Jackson (1987) also observe that, although relevant information is recognized, managers may not categorize and, thus, interpret it appropriately as requiring strategic renewal. Related to their findings are the findings of Lant and Milliken (1992) that internal factors are more likely than external ones to be interpreted as requiring strategic actions. Similarly, Gioia and Chittipeddi (1991) observed that the initiation of strategic change in a large university involved ascribing meanings to environmental stimuli and construing a future image for the university that makes sense of the revised mental models of organizational members.

Only a few studies have examined explicitly the link between the processes of noticing and interpreting, and firm performance (Rajagopalan and Spreitzer, 1996). For example, Barr et al. (1992) suggest that frequent changes in strategists' mental models improve firms' survival. Thomas et al. (1993) found that attending to more information led to interpreting it as favorable, and that interpreting issues as controllable enhanced the likelihood of change and, ultimately, improvement in firms' performance.

Collectively, the studies on the managerial processes of noticing and interpreting information shed light on the individual and group level processes that underpin firms' strategic actions and adaptation to environmental changes.

Cognitive Structures

The processes of interpretation discussed so far depend on fitting incoming stimuli into the pre-existing cognitive structures, or schemas (Fiske and Taylor, 1991). Individuals and collectives rely upon these pre-existing knowledge structures to organize information environments that are vast, complex, and uncertain, and to take action in them (Daft and Weick, 1984). The research on cognitive structures has two important messages for strategy research. First, the environments in which managers operate are not necessarily objective, but are instead enacted: created through processes of interpretation and social interaction (Smircich and Stubbart, 1985; Porac et al., 1989). The concept of 'enacted environments' was introduced by Weick (1969), who argued that actors do not act in objective environments, but in those captured and reflected in their knowledge structures. Second, the cognitive structures of strategists – as individuals and groups – create heterogeneity in firms' ability to identify attractive positions and resources that enable their firms to generate rents. We return to this point in our discussion of future directions suggested to the resource-based view from a socio-cognitive perspective.

In terms of enacted environments, cognitive strategy research has made important contributions to our understanding of how managers structure competitive environments. In an extensive field study of the Scottish knitwear industry, Porac et al. (1989) observed that competitors in an industry develop consensual beliefs about how to manage their task environments, and in the process, define the industry's boundaries and structure. In contrast to the popular concept of strategic groups, the competitive groups observed in this study were not an analytical abstraction determined by SIC or other external classifications, but were based on the actual managers' experience of their industry and competitive dynamics. Reger and her colleagues (Reger and Huff, 1993; Reger and Palmer, 1996) elaborated these concepts further by building on personal construct theory (Kelly, 1955) and showed that banking industry participants shared perceptions of strategic similarities among members that led them to cognitively group their competitors in fairly homogeneous clusters (strategic groups). The core contribution of these studies is that both industry structure and competitive rivalry are subjective as much as objective phenomena.

In sum, this body of work shows that managerial cognitive structures make industries and competitive dynamics 'enacted' rather than objectively determined by the nature of products or technology (Schmalensee, 1989). This perspective then provides a set of theoretical lenses through which some of the fundamental issues in strategy research about explaining heterogeneity in firms' actions and performance can be addressed.

Within the work on interpretative structures, a special note should be made of the concept of organizational identity and its links to strategic decision making and organizational performance. Among the various conceptualizations that students in the field have developed (Gioia et al., 2000) from the original definition of Albert and Whetten (1985), organizational identity may be conceived as the organizational members' cognitive schema about the collectively shared beliefs and meanings of central and enduring features of the organization (Elsbach and Kramer, 1996; Ravasi and Schultz, 2006). In a theoretical paper, Fiol (1991) argued that identity represents the cognitive link between behaviors and organizational culture because it guides members in making sense of their behaviors in relation to a firm's general system of rules and values. In a longitudinal study of the events and actions of the Port Authority of New York and New Jersey toward the issue of homelessness, Dutton and Dukerich (1991) suggested that organizational identity informs and triggers members' interpretation of a strategic issue by serving as a reference point for assessing its relevance. They found that identity affects not only the motivation for acting, but also the choices of specific courses of action that are seen as feasible and appropriate. Reger et al. (1994) offered a complementary view on the role of organizational identity in the interpretation of changes by developing a conceptual framework for understanding cognitive impediments to implementing changes in organizations. They argued that organizational identity may lead to failure in the implementation of strategic change when a new initiative does not fit the set of beliefs that constitute the organizational identity. Ravasi and Schultz (2006), similarly, found that responses to environmental changes must account for the preservation of the identity. Finally, Martins (2005) found that the discrepancy between organizational identity and external perceptions reflected in reputational rankings triggered strategic actions from top managers. At the same time, a strong sense of identity guided top managers toward more autonomous managerial action and provided the impetus to uphold organizational distinctiveness and uniqueness. Together, the work on cognitive structures and organizational identity identifies key sources of firm heterogeneity and uniqueness, which are central to the development of a successful competitive strategy (Porter, 1996).

THE EYE OF THE BEHOLDER: COLLECTIVE COGNITIONS AND SENSEMAKING IN MARKETS AND ORGANIZATIONAL FIELDS

More recently, strategy researchers have begun to expand their interest in socio-cognitive processes and structures beyond organizational boundaries. They have begun to study not only how firms and their competitors perceive and respond to each other, but also how stakeholders make sense of firms at the collective level; and what consequences these collective cognitive and interpretative processes and structures have for performance. We refer to this second major stream of socio-cognitive strategy research as studying 'the eye of the beholder' because it focuses primarily on the perceptions of various external stakeholders. This research is consistent with strategic stakeholder theories that seek to understand the effects of stakeholders' perceptions on the ability of firms to acquire resources and achieve desired outcomes (Rindova and Fombrun, 1999; Fombrun, 1996; Scott and Lane, 2000). Work on the dynamics of stakeholders' perceptions has also increasingly incorporated research done from an institutional theory perspective (Suchman, 1995; Elsbach, 1994; Pollock and Rindova, 2003), which follows DiMaggio and Powell's (1991) suggestion that the microfoundations of institutions can be understood at the socio-cognitive level.

Rooted in the organizational tradition according to which competition happens among systems of beliefs (Pfeffer, 1981), strategy scholars hold that stakeholders' collective perceptions of legitimacy (Suchman, 1995), status (Podolny, 1994) and reputation (Rindova et al., 2005) may constitute intangible assets for firms because they influence stakeholders' willingness to exchange resources with them (Rindova and Fombrun, 1999). There are two important implications of the socio-cognitive and sociological research in this area for strategy research. First, such perceptions embody reactions of a collectivity of stakeholders to firms' past actions. Second, because these perceptions vary in cognitive content, they have different effects on firms' performance. The first important attribute of collective stakeholders' perceptions of firms is that they constitute a generalized, umbrella evaluation, which transcends both specific actions of firms and perceptions of particular stakeholders. As Suchman (1995) aptly points out, these collective perceptions are resilient to particular occurrences, yet dependent upon the past pattern of occurrences. They are also dependent upon a collective public, yet independent of particular observers. In other words, they are not aggregations of individual perceptions but are socially constructed through dynamic processes of social influence and information exchange (Pollock et al., 2008).

A second important attribute of these collective perceptions that are all viewed as intangible assets for firms, is that they have different cognitive content and therefore influence to a different degree and in different ways the decisions and choices of a large number of different stakeholders (Rindova and Fombrun, 1999). Because different perceptions accrue for different types of firms' behaviors, they do not have the same performance consequences (Rindova et al., 2005) and therefore their value as intangible assets varies. Legitimacy represents a collectively perceived fit of firms' activities with social values and norms (Suchman, 1995) and ensures basic firm survival. It can be built through external validation granted by structural conformity with established norms (Meyer and Rowan, 1977), institutional certifications (Rao, 1994) and endorsement by intermediaries (Zuckerman, 1999; Pollock and Rindova, 2003). Status increases the confidence of stakeholders in the potential of firms to provide quality products and is gauged from the observed relative centrality of the firm in the network of market exchanges (Podolny, 1994). Reputation refers to the collective perception of stakeholders that a firm will be able to deliver value along key dimensions of performance (Rindova and Fombrun, 1999). Thus, like status, it focuses on firms' strategic choices and performance outcomes rather than on the degree of congruence with societal expectations as in the case of legitimacy. Reputation is inferred from firms' resource allocations (Dierickx and Cool, 1989; Rindova et al., 2005) and financial performance (Fombrun and Shanley, 1990). Finally, celebrity captures the market popularity that some firms gain for their identities and perceived strategic importance in their industry (Rindova et al., 2006). Collectively this work highlights two central socio-cognitive processes through which stakeholders select firms to exchange resources with, thereby influencing performance differences among firms. First, due to cognitive constraints, stakeholders focus their attention on a subset of firms; second, they evaluate the relative merits of the offerings of those included in the subset (Zuckerman, 1999; Rindova et al., 2005). These observations suggest that an important question for strategy research is to understand the factors that enable firms to enter this selected set and to enhance their positions in it. An interesting set of answers to this question comes from a promising body of work that examines how prior collective choices shape subsequent collective choices in the form of information and availability cascades (see Pollock et al., 2008 for a review). The key insight from this work is that social perception is both inertial and fragile, continuously stretched between the power of collective inertia and the quest for information advantages that can confer economic pay-offs.

To conclude, there is wide agreement among management scholars that intangible resources are important competitive resources for firms (Dierickx and Cool, 1989; Barney, 1991; Rindova et al., 2005). A socio-cognitive perspective offers valuable insights regarding how firms build these assets by managing their information exchanges with stakeholders and institutional intermediaries and by attending to the varied collective dynamics through which different types of intangible assets, such as legitimacy, status, reputation and celebrity, are formed. As such, the socio-cognitive perspective has contributed greatly to the study of competitive resources, which, given their intangible nature, have proved to be difficult to analyze through the conventional strategy research lens (see Barney, 1991).

THE FUTURE IS IN THE INTERACTIONS

The contributions of socio-cognitive work described in this paper can provide exciting, invigorating, and complementary ways of thinking about all major areas that constitute the primary domains of strategic management research. Below we articulate some of the possibilities that we believe offer considerable promise for invigorating core areas of strategy research with novel and exciting perspectives on the interactions of actors' cognition and their actions in the markets: research on industry structure and competitive interactions, on the resource-based view and dynamic capabilities, and on value creation.

Industry Structures and Competitive Interactions

Socio-cognitive research has made some of its most important contributions to the work on industry structure and competitive interaction. This progress can be attributed both to the long-standing reliance of strategy research on industrial organization economics as an underlying theoretical paradigm, and to the well developed theory of categorization in both cognitive and social psychology (Porac and Thomas, 1990; Reger and Huff, 1993).

This research, however, can be further enriched and extended in two key directions. First, greater attention should be paid to the dynamic features of industries, such as the socio-cognitive influences on competitive dynamics. Rindova et al. (2004), for example, linked the economic view of rivalry with a more socially informed one by focusing on the 'language games' surrounding competitive rivalry. They emphasized that several important socio-cognitive processes including allocation of attention and interpretation of actions take place within the context of a specific language game. The second promising new direction in this area is to focus greater attention on the influences of non-market forces and players on managers' and stockholders' cognitions and sensemaking. To date, a very small amount of work has begun to look at the role of non-market actors such as standard setting, governmental and quasi-governmental bodies, the media and other third-party actors who influence the socio-cognitive construction of markets, but who are non-market participants (Deephouse, 2000; Rao, 1994; Pollock and Rindova, 2003; Fleming and

Waguespack, 2007). We applaud this work, and encourage more explicit attention to the micro-processes of cognition to complement the focus on institutional pressures emanating from non-market players. Focus on this broader set of organizations and players that define an organizational field as opposed to a narrower focus on industry per se, opens up questions as to how managers allocate attention and balance competing demands from both market and non-market sources. As more forces are recognized as important to managerial decision making, it becomes clear that a greater focus on the mind of the strategist (including the strategic team) is needed as this becomes an increasingly taxed and constraining resource.

The Resource-based View from a Socio-cognitive Perspective

The socio-cognitive perspective holds a great deal of potential for enriching the resource-based view of the firm. This is because the value of resources and the possibility of creating value through them are a function of the knowledge and imagination of top management teams (TMTs). Thus, the cognitive structures TMTs develop individually and as a group and how they apply them to think about strategic actions and environments become a prime area for study under an RBV of the firm.

Despite this observation and the hints to the importance of managerial and organizational cognitive resources contained in some of the works on organizational learning (Lant and Mezias, 1992), absorptive capacity (Cohen and Levinthal, 1990), and dynamic capabilities (Adner and Helfat, 2003), research on the managerial interpretative capabilities remains surprisingly limited. Ginsberg (1994), for example, uses a cognitive perspective to argue that both environmental attributes (such as uncertainty, complexity and ambiguity) and individual cognitive limitations (such as decision-making heuristics and biases) impede firms' performance. He proposes that firms stand to gain from honing specific socio-cognitive capabilities such as comprehension, creativity, and consensus building. In the case study of the evolution of the cognitive maps of the top management teams of two railroad companies over 50 years, Barr et al. (1992) find that the top management team of the surviving firm had more dynamic cognitive structures, which changed frequently as new concepts were added and obsolete concepts dropped; in contrast, the top management team of the failing firm maintained stable cognitive maps over long periods of time, followed by a dramatic overhaul and 're-freezing'. Hargadon and his collaborators emphasize the role played by the cognitive resources and capabilities of organizational members in enhancing innovation and creativity. For example, Hargadon and Fanelli (2002) highlight how the cognitive knowledge of members enhances the innovative activity when it complements the empirical knowledge that resides in the organization. Hargadon and Bechky (2006) find that the individual and collective cognitive ability of bridging previously unconnected ideas and of making new ideas accepted in the organizational context enhances creativity. These emerging works on cognitive capabilities enrich strategy research by showing not only that prior knowledge structures shape and constrain managerial decisions and actions, but also that information-processing capacities and abilities can vary in quality and can be built specifically in order to take successful actions in complex, ambiguous environments.

The Social Construction of 'Value'

The final broad area in which greater incorporation of socio-cognitive research can significantly enhance strategic research is the understanding of value creation. Specifically, socio-cognitive research has shown that the usefulness and value of innovations are subject to considerable social negotiation and construction (e.g. Rosa et al., 1999; Hargadon and Douglas, 2001; Lounsbury and Rao, 2004; Rindova and Petkova, 2007). An emerging body of work has begun to examine the formation of cognitive structures at the institutional level, such as product categories that define the legitimate value-creating attributes of products and producers. For example, Rosa et al. (1999) show that new product markets (or new markets for old products) emerge from the socio-cognitive interaction of producers and potential consumers, through which they define and stabilize the conceptual system that surrounds a given product. They describe the process as consisting of both reciprocal adaptation of behaviors in response to environmental stimuli, such as specific product design or consumption habits, and interpretation of respective responses contained in the producers' and consumers' narratives in the media. In a similar vein, Lounsbury and Rao (2004) characterize industry media as editors of product categories and find that the change of existing product categories depends mainly on producers' political power of influencing media discretion. More recently, Rindova and Petkova (2007) theorized about how innovating firms use product form design to influence the perceived value of new products. They argue that the perception of value is determined by a cognitive and an emotional response to the incongruity of the novelty elements of the product that rest on design choices along functional, symbolic and aesthetic dimensions.

This work has begun to show that the success of innovation strategies depends on keen understanding of the socio-cultural meanings and emotional processes that consumers bring to the process of engaging with the products that firms create. Yet most strategy research continues to adhere to a narrowly defined view of value creation from a supply-side cost-driven perspective (see Priem, 2007, for a compelling critique), largely overlooking the creative constructive interactions that take place (or must take place) between firms and their customers. We believe that the area of value creation is where strategy research can be enriched from a variety of disciplinary perspectives, as questions of value are rooted in philosophy and art (aesthetics), psychology (human values), and sociology (the social construction of value).

In conclusion, we propose that as strategy research becomes increasingly enriched by the insights of research conducted from a socio-cognitive perspective, it will also become increasingly aware that its fundamental questions about firms' choices and performances are in fact fundamental questions of human choice and human preferences, which are ultimately questions of the mind and the eye of the beholder.

REFERENCES

Adner, R. and C.E. Helfat (2003), 'Corporate effects and dynamic managerial capabilities', *Strategic Management Journal*, **24** (10), 1011–1025.
Albert, S. and D.A. Whetten (1985), 'Organizational identity', in L.L. Cummings and B.M. Staw (eds), *Research in Organizational Behavior*, vol. 7, Greenwich, US and London, UK: JAI Press.
Bargh, J.A. and M.J. Ferguson (2000), 'Beyond behaviorism: on the automaticity of higher mental processes', *Psychological Bulletin*, **126** (6), 925–945.
Barney, J.B. (1991), 'Firm resources and sustained competitive advantage', *Journal of Management*, **17** (1), 99–120.
Barr, P.S., J.L. Stimpert and A.S. Huff (1992), 'Cognitive change, strategic action, and organizational renewal', *Strategic Management Journal*, **13**, 15–36.
Caves, R.E. and M.E. Porter (1977), 'From entry barriers to mobility barriers: conjectural decisions and contrived deterrence to new competition', *Quarterly Journal of Economics*, 241–261.
Clark, B. and D. Montgomery (1998), 'Deterrence, reputation, and competitive cognition', *Management Science*, **44** (1), 62–82.
Cohen, W.M. and D.A. Levinthal (1990), 'Absorptive capacity: a new perspective on learning and innovation', *Administrative Science Quarterly*, **35** (1), 128–152.
Daft, R.L. and K.E. Weick (1984), 'Toward a model of organizations as interpretation systems', *Academy of Management Review*, **9** (2), 284–295.
Deephouse, D. (2000), 'Media reputation as a strategic resource: an integration of mass communication and resource-based theories', *Journal of Management*, **26** (6), 1091–1112.
Dierickx, I. and K.O. Cool (1989), 'Asset stock accumulation and sustainability of competitive advantage', *Management Science*, **35**, 1504–1511.
DiMaggio, P.J. and W.W. Powell (1991), 'Introduction', in W.W. Powell and P.J. DiMaggio (eds), *The New Institutionalism in Organizational Analysis*, Chicago, US: The University of Chicago Press, pp. 1–40.
Dutton, J.E. and J.M. Dukerich (1991), 'Keeping an eye on the mirror: image and identity in organizational adaptation', *Academy of Management Journal*, **34** (3), 517–554.

Dutton, J.E. and S.E. Jackson (1987), 'Categorizing strategic issues', *Academy of Management Review*, **12** (1), 76–90.

Elsbach, K.D. (1994), 'Managing organizational legitimacy in the California cattle industry: the construction and effectiveness of verbal accounts', *Administrative Science Quarterly*, **39** (1), 57–88.

Elsbach, K.D. and R.M. Kramer (1996), 'Members' responses to organizational identity threats: encountering and countering the *Business Week* rankings', *Administrative Science Quarterly*, **41** (3), 442–476.

Fiol, M.C. (1991), 'Managing culture as a competitive resource: an identity-based view of sustainable competitive advantage', *Journal of Management*, **17** (1), 191–211.

Fiske, S.T. and S.E. Taylor (1991), *Social Cognition*, New York: McGraw-Hill.

Fleming, L. and D.M. Waguespack (2007), 'Brokerage, boundary spanning, and leadership in open innovation communities', *Organization Science*, **18** (2), 165–180.

Fombrun, Charles J. (ed.) (1996), *Reputation: Realizing Value from the Corporate Image*, Boston, MA: Harvard Business School Press.

Fombrun, C.J. and M. Shanley (1990), 'What's in a name? Reputation-building and corporate strategy', *Academy of Management Journal*, **33** (2), 233–258.

Ginsberg, A. (1994), 'Minding the competition: from mapping to mastery', *Strategic Management Journal*, **15** (8), 153–174.

Gioia, D.A. and K. Chittipeddi (1991), 'Sensemaking and sensegiving in strategic change initiation', *Strategic Management Journal*, **12** (6), 433–448.

Gioia, D.A., M. Schultz and K. Corley (2000), 'Organizational identity, image and adaptive instability', *Academy of Management Review*, **25** (1), 63–82.

Hargadon, A.B. and B.A. Bechky (2006), 'When collection of creatives become creative collectives: a field study of problem solving at work', *Organization Science*, **17** (4), 484–500.

Hargadon, A.B. and Y. Douglas (2001), 'When innovations meet institutions: Edison and the design of the electric light', *Administrative Science Quarterly*, **46** (3), 476–503.

Hargadon, A.B. and A. Fanelli (2002), 'Action and possibility: reconciling dual perspectives of knowledge in organizations', *Organization Science*, **13** (3), 290–302.

Hoffman, A.J. and W. Ocasio (2001), 'Not all events are attended equally: toward a middle-range theory of industry attention of external events', *Organization Science*, **12** (4), 414–434.

Jackson, S.E. and J.E. Dutton (1988), 'Discerning threats and opportunities', *Administrative Science Quarterly*, **33** (3), 370–388.

Kelly, G.A. (ed.) (1955), *The Psychology of Personal Constructs*, vols 1 and 2, New York, NY: Norton.

Lant, T.K. and S.J. Mezias (1992), 'An organizational learning model of convergence and reorientation', *Organization Science*, **3**, 47–71.

Lant, T.K. and F.T. Milliken (1992), 'The role of managerial learning and interpretation in strategic persistence and reorientation: an empirical exploration', *Strategic Management Journal*, **13** (8), 585–608.

Lounsbury, M. and H. Rao (2004), 'Sources of durability and change in market classifications: a study of the reconstitution of product categories in the American mutual fund industry, 1944–1985', *Social Forces*, **82** (3), 969–999.

Martins, L.L. (2005), 'A model of the effects of reputational rankings on organizational change', *Organization Science*, **16** (6), 701–720.

Meindl, J.R., C. Stubbart and J.F. Porac (1994), 'Cognition within and between organizations: five key questions', *Organization Science*, **5** (3), 289–293.

Meyer, J.W. and B. Rowan (1977), 'Institutionalized organizations: formal structure as myth creation', *American Journal of Sociology*, **83** (2), 340–363.

Mezias, J.M. and W.H. Starbuck (2003), 'Studying the accuracy of managers' perceptions: a research odyssey', *British Journal of Management*, **14** (3), 3–17.

Ocasio, W. (1997), 'Towards an attention-based view of the firm', *Strategic Management Journal*, **18**, 187–206.

Peteraf, M.A. (1993), 'The cornerstones of competitive advantage: a resource-based view', *Strategic Management Journal*, **14** (3), 179–191.

Pfeffer, J. (1981), 'Management as symbolic action. The creation and maintenance of organizational paradigms', in L.L. Cummings and B.M. Staw (eds), *Research in Organizational Behaviour*, vol. 13, Greenwich, CT: JAI Press, pp. 1–52.
Podolny, J. (1994), 'Market uncertainty and the social character of economic exchange', *Administrative Science Quarterly*, **39** (3), 458–483.
Pollock, T.G. and V.P. Rindova (2003), 'Media legitimation effects in the market for initial public offerings', *Academy of Management Journal*, **46** (5), 631–642.
Pollock, T.G., V.P. Rindova and P.G. Maggitti (2008), 'Market watch: information and availability cascades among the media and investors in the US IPO market', *Academy of Management Journal*, **51** (12), 335–358.
Porac, J.F. and J.A. Rosa (1996), 'In praise of managerial narrow mindedness', *Journal of Management Inquiry*, **5** (1), 35–42.
Porac, J.F. and H. Thomas (1990), 'Taxonomic mental models of competitive definition', *Academy of Management Review*, **15** (2), 224–240.
Porac, J.F., H. Thomas and C. Baden-Fuller (1989), 'Competitive groups as cognitive communities: the case of the Scottish knitwear industry', *Journal of Management Studies*, **26** (4), 397–416.
Porter, Michael E. (ed.) (1980), *Competitive Strategy*, New York, NY: Free Press.
Porter, M.E. (1991), 'Towards a dynamic theory of strategy', *Strategic Management Journal*, **12** (8), 95–117.
Porter, M.E. (1996), 'What is strategy?', *Harvard Business Review*, **74** (6), 61–78.
Priem, R.L. (2007), 'A consumer perspective on value creation', *Academy of Management Review*, **32** (1), 219–235.
Rajagopalan, N. and G.M. Spreitzer (1996), 'Towards a theory of strategic change', *Academy of Management Review*, **22** (1), 48–79.
Ramos-Rodriguez, A.R. and J. Ruiz-Navarro (2004), 'Changes in the intellectual structure of strategic management research: a bibliometric study of the Strategic Management Journal, 1980–2000', *Strategic Management Journal*, **25** (10), 981–1004.
Rao, H. (1994), 'The social construction of reputation: certification contests, legitimation, and the survival of organizations in the American automobile industry: 1895–1912', *Strategic Management Journal*, **15**, 29–44.
Ravasi, D. and M. Schultz (2006), 'Responding to organizational identity threats: exploring the role of organizational culture', *Academy of Management Journal*, **49** (3), 433–458.
Reger, R.K., L.T. Gustafson, S.M. Demarie and J.V. Mullane (1994), 'Reframing the organization: why implementing total quality is easier said than done', *Academy of Management Review*, **19** (3), 565–584.
Reger, R.K. and A.S. Huff (1993), 'Strategic groups: a cognitive perspective', *Strategic Management Journal*, **14**, 103–124.
Reger, R.K. and T.B. Palmer (1996), 'Managerial categorization of competitors: using old maps to navigate new environments', *Organization Science*, **7** (1), 22–39.
Rindova, V.P., M. Becerra and I. Contardo (2004), 'Enacting competitive wars: competitive activity, language games, and market consequences', *Academy of Management Review*, **29** (4), 670–686.
Rindova, V.P. and C.J. Fombrun (1999), 'Constructing competitive advantage: the role of firm-constituent interactions', *Strategic Management Journal*, **20** (8), 691–710.
Rindova, V.P. and A.P. Petkova (2007), 'When is a new thing a good thing? Technological change, product form design, and perception of value for product innovations', *Organization Science*, **18** (2), 217–232.
Rindova, V.P., T.G. Pollock and M.L.A. Hayward (2006), 'Celebrity firms: the social construction of market popularity', *Academy of Management Review*, **31** (1), 50–71.
Rindova, V.P., I.O. Williamson, A.P. Petkova and J.M. Sever (2005), 'Being good or being known: an empirical examination of the dimensions, antecedents, and consequences of organizational reputation', *Academy of Management Journal*, **48** (6), 1033–1049.
Rosa, J.A., J.F. Porac, J. Runser-Spanjol and M.S. Saxon (1999), 'Sociocognitive dynamics in a product market', *Journal of Marketing*, **63**, 64–77.

Rumelt, R.P., D. Schendel and D.J. Teece (1991), 'Strategic management and economics', *Strategic Management Journal*, **12**, 5–29.

Schmalensee, R. (1989), 'Inter-industry studies of structure and performance', in R. Schmalensee and R.D. Willig (eds), *Handbook of Industrial Organization*, vol. 2, Amsterdam: Elsevier Science Publishers.

Scott, S.G. and V.R. Lane (2000), 'A stakeholder approach to organizational identity', *Academy of Management Review*, **25** (1), 43–62.

Smircich, L. and C. Stubbart (1985), 'Strategic management in an enacted world', *Academy of Management Review*, **10** (4), 724–736.

Spender, J.C. (1989), *Industry Recipes: The Nature and Sources of Managerial Judgment*, Cambridge, MA: Blackwell.

Starbuck, William H. and France J. Milliken (1988), 'Executive perceptual filters', in Donald C. Hambrick (ed.), *The Executive Effect: Concepts and Methods for Studying Top Managers*, Greenwich, CT: JAI Press.

Suchman, M.C. (1995), 'Managing legitimacy: strategic and institutional approaches', *Academy of Management Review*, **20** (3), 571–610.

Teece, D.J., G. Pisano and A. Shuen (1997), 'Dynamic capabilities and strategic management', *Strategic Management Journal*, **18** (7), 509–533.

Thomas, J.B., S.M. Clark and D.A. Gioia (1993), 'Strategic sensemaking and organizational performance', *Academy of Management Journal*, **36** (2), 239–270.

Tversky, A. and D. Kahneman (1974), 'Judgment under uncertainty: heuristics and biases', *Science*, **185** (4157), 1124–1131.

Walsh, J.P. (1995), 'Managerial and organizational cognition: notes from a trip down memory lane', *Organization Science*, **6** (3), 280–322.

Weick, Karl E. (ed.) (1969), *The Social Psychology of Organizing*, Reading, MA: Addison-Wesley.

Weick, K.E., K.M. Sutcliff and D. Obstfeld (2005), 'Organizing and the process of sensemaking', *Organization Science*, **16** (4), 409–421.

Wernerfelt, B. (1984), 'A resource-based view of the firm', *Strategic Management Journal*, **5** (2), 171–180.

Zuckerman, E.W. (1999), 'The categorical imperative: securities analysts and the illegitimacy discount', *American Journal of Sociology*, **104** (5), 1389–1438.

8 The management of growth strategies in firm networks: a stylized model of opportunity discovery via network ties
Simone Ferriani and Antonio Giuliani

INTRODUCTION

The model hereafter proposed elaborates on the informational value of network ties to set the stage for a network-based approach to firm growth. Drawing on Austrian economics, growth is modeled as the outcome of an opportunity discovery-recognition process, which in turn is molded by the availability of information to the firm. Asymmetries in growth potential arise because firms engage in multirelational networks that imply heterogeneous access to information and, consequently, a different positioning within the space of opportunities. This process is moderated by the firm's ultimate ability to recognize and absorb the commercial value of the information conveyed by its ties (i.e. the firm's absorptive capacity).

Although abundant empirical evidence already exists that points to the important role of networks as drivers of firm growth (Zaho and Aram, 1995; Powell et al., 1996; Lee and Tsang, 2001), the literature is less clear in elucidating the theoretical mechanisms that govern this effect. Either because the 'networking metaphor' is endorsed with a taken-for-granted facilitator role (Burt, 2000), or because it is credited with a multiplicity of overlapping benefits (resource, power, status, information, legitimacy, etc.), with no explanation of the basic underlying mechanisms linking networks and firm growth. To address this shortcoming we suggest an original framework where network ties can be understood as enablers of firm growth via information-based processes of opportunity discovery and recognition. In essence, we argue that because the discovery of economic opportunities is profoundly shaped by the availability and distribution of information in society, and since "information can be acquired by use of social relations maintained for various purposes" (Coleman, 1988: 104), firm networks represent a crucial interface between the information space and the opportunity space, and thus they may play a critical role in the process of firm growth.

Our causal logic is premised on two key considerations. First, building on the observation that firms are immersed not in one but in many types of networks, we advance the notion of multirelational embeddedness to account for the fact that the information-based influence process may operate at multiple levels of analysis and through different network channels. Second, building on the observation that accrued information needs to be absorbed in order to be commercialized (Cohen and Levinthal, 1990), we suggest the importance of looking at network effects in the light of cognitive arguments. In fact, while it is customary in empirical research on networks and performance to apply extensive statistical controls to rule out spurious, firm-level determinants from the influence processes of interest, less attention has been paid to how cognitive features at the firm level may moderate the network effect. Thus, building on these arguments, we develop an empirically testable conceptual model of how firms' structural features and absorptive capacity jointly affect the likelihood of firm growth by influencing the chances to access and recognize valuable opportunities.

After formalizing these ideas into a set of testable propositions, in the final section we conclude by discussing the contribution of the paper to the rich debate on networks as enablers of organizational outcomes, and we suggest a few guidelines for extending the model.

CONCEPTUAL FRAMEWORK

Why are social networks central to the process of firm growth? What is the relationship between networks and growth? To answer this question we first establish three interlinked arguments that serve as the starting point for our model: (1) the concept of firm growth as opportunity discovery and exploitation; (2) the idea of network resources as devices through which firms tap the information space; and (3) the role of absorptive capacity as an interface between the information and the opportunity space.

Opportunity Discovery and Firm Growth

Growth is a complex, multifaceted phenomenon whose organizational manifestation has been addressed and conceptualized in several ways (Davidsson et al., 2003). Not only do firms grow in many different ways but also these patterns of growth, over time, can vary significantly (Delmar et al., 2003). Firstly, growth is a process of change: it may refer to change in size or magnitude from one time period to another; it may entail the expansion of existing entities and/or their multiplication; or it may imply an improved ability in solving problems. The wide variety of measures, indicators and operationalization criteria that have been proposed to gauge firms' growth (Evans, 1987; Weinzimmer et al., 1998) provide a pretty clear image of the difficulties in establishing whether and how an organization is growing. All the same, while there are certainly several ways in which the outcome of this process may unfold and reify, the antecedents of firm growth are typically to be found in the discovery and recognition of one or more economic opportunities. These include opportunities to expand the business, enhance current activities, enter new product domains, learn new practices, improve the current skills or capitalize on existing resources. Various scholars support this idea by viewing the process of opportunity discovery and recognition as a crucial feature of firm growth (Timmons et al., 1987; Venkataraman, 1997; Companys and McMullen, 2007). Indeed, the relationship between opportunity recognition and firm growth has been empirically proved (Corbett and Koberg, 2001) and is at the core of the Penrosian idea of growth as discovery of productive opportunities (Penrose, 1959). As Edith Penrose stated: "A theory of the growth of the firm is essentially an examination of the changing productive opportunity of firms. . . It is clear that this opportunity will be restricted to the extent to which a firm does not *see opportunities* for expansion. . ." (1959: 31).

Opportunities may be located within the boundaries of the firm, among its skills and resources, or they may appear externally, between the interstices of the environment (Powell, 1990). Regardless of their ultimate location, however, they will remain in a latent state until their discovery. This is basically the key argument of Austrian economics (Hayek, 1945; Kirzner, 1973 and 1997): opportunities exist because different people access and control different information. People do not discover business opportunities through deliberate search (because, as Kirzner (1997) posits, the searcher will be unaware of it until discovery), but through recognition of the value of information that they happen to receive through other means (Shane, 2000). Stated differently, the possession of idiosyncratic information allows people to occupy differential positions within the opportunity space (Mariani and Dagnino, 2007). Once an opportunity is spotted (which implies it is valuable to the firm), it can be exploited and this process is likely to lead to growth potential.

The next two sections illustrate the crucial role of networks in molding this process. It is suggested that, by influencing the conditions of information access, network resources provide firms with idiosyncratic informational endowments, which, in turn, contribute to shape the unique positioning of each firm within the space of economic opportunities.

Networks and Information Transfer

The informational value of network ties is a prominent and well-established idea among network theorists (Stephenson and Zelen, 1989; Burt, 1992;

Wassermann and Faust, 1994), and represents a core assumption in a variety of studies that have investigated the relational foundations of organizational outcomes. The transfer of information takes place because people in different firms linked to each other have the possibility to meet and talk; consequently information and knowledge diffuse through the network (Gulati, 1999; Koka and Prescott, 2002). Accordingly, networks can be thought of as an information-gathering device or as a search and monitoring mechanism (Burt, 1992).

Gulati (1999), for example, refers to the notion of network resources as resources that firms accrue from the networks in which they are embedded and whose value revolves around the information that circulates within this network. Following this approach, McEvily and Zaheer (1999) assume network resources to represent the informational advantages associated with a firm's network of ties. Obviously there are many types of networks that embed firms in their environment. Recognizing this multiplicity allows a broader understanding of how the social context may be exploited by firms in order to obtain resources (Gulati, 1999) and reflects the different analytical levels that are spanned by network resources.

- *Organizational level*: First of all, firms are bound to other organizations that contribute to the firm's *interorganizational field* via prescribed relations (Nohria, 1992). According to DiMaggio and Powell (1983: 148) the key 'alters' of this field are to be identified in four categories of actors: customers, suppliers, institutions and other organizations that provide similar or related products or services. Each of these actors contributes to the structuration of the field and may crucially add to the focal firm's inflow of information. Yili-Renko et al. (2001), for example, illustrated the critical transfer of information occurring between a sample of tech-based firms and their customers. The transfer of strategic information was a salient feature of the relation between the Japanese automobile producers studied by Cusumano (1985) and their US suppliers. Likewise, the exchange of valuable information between Toyota and its Japanese suppliers has been a crucial determinant in Toyota's competitive growth (Dyer and Nobeoka, 2000). The transmission of information is portrayed as a driving force of the alliance patterns widely investigated by Gulati (1995, 1999) and Gulati and Gargiulo (1999). By serving as 'go-betweens' for actors located in different parts of the social system, local governmental institutions have been shown to provide firms with a repository of information critical in the development of their capabilities (McEvily and Zaheer, 1999). Finally, several studies have illustrated the rich movement of interorganizational information that may be directed via interlocking directorates (Useem, 1984; Mizruchi, 1996; Davis and Greve, 1997).

- *Individual level*: The previous networks do not entirely capture the web of external relations that may contribute to the information exposure of the firm, as stated by Gulati and Gargiulo (1999: 1445): "Beneath the formalities of contractual agreements, multiple informal interpersonal relationships emerge across organizational boundaries, which facilitate the active exchange of information". These informal ties may be based, among other things, on friendship, advice, acquaintance, or other sorts of link that cross formal organizational boundaries (Nohria, 1992: 5). The literature on entrepreneurial networking, for instance, has widely illustrated the importance of personal ties in getting strategic information (Borch and Huse, 1993; Ostgaard and Birley, 1996). Furthermore, individuals who move between firms typically offer their social networks to a hiring firm (Dokko and Rosenkopf, 2002). Although some studies seem to suggest that the importance of informal ties in acquiring information relevant for the performance of the firm tends to decrease with the size and age of the firm (Butler and Hansen, 1988; Mohan-Neill, 1995), personal networks do have a part in this process and require specific consideration.

The above arguments suggest that firms may act upon multiple relational levels to enhance their exposure to valuable information. Sources of information are to be found in the interstices between firms, customers, universities, suppliers and in the wider social context in which every firm is embedded (Powell, 1990). By helping the firm to fill these interstices, network resources nurture a fertile ground of opportunities. As a result, the degree to which firms may learn about new opportunities can be regarded as a function of the extent of their participation in such space of relations. We refer to this multiplicity of ties as multirelational embeddedness.

The Moderating Role of Absorptive Capacity

There may be a great chasm between having growth potential and realizing it. In fact, an opportunity-rich position is likely to remain confined in the realm of perceptions and possibilities until active understanding and appreciation of the opportunity value is reached. One way to discriminate among firms that may take this further step and firms that, in this regard, are in a more disadvantageous stance, is to focus on their knowledge base.

This idea has been convincingly formalized by Cohen and Levinthal's (1990) absorptive capacity construct, that is: "the ability to recognize the value of new information, assimilate it, and apply it to commercial use" (p. 128). By assimilating and combining bits and pieces of different information a firm is able to make up or discover an opportunity and exploit its previously accumulated knowledge in order to turn it into a feasible business idea.

Regardless of the steps that one will eventually take to gauge this multifaceted knowledge construct, the key insight here is that in order to assess firms' network-enabled process of growth it may prove useful to account for the moderating effect of absorptive capacity. This expectation is consistent with Tsai's (2001) recent finding that business units with high levels of absorptive capacity are more likely to benefit from their interorganizational network centrality in terms of innovation and performance. In abstract, the absorptive capacity construct may be imagined as the point of junction between the information space and the opportunity space (Dagnino and Mariani, 2007): the higher the exposition and accessibility of the firm to external knowledge and information, the higher the need for absorptive capacity in order to benefit from such knowledge.

In summary, our conceptual model builds on five interlinked arguments as follows:

- Firms are embedded in multirelational networks that determine their 'overall network configuration';
- Diverse configurations cause the firms to have diverse abilities and chances to access relevant information;
- These differences, in turn, contribute to shaping the unique positioning of each firm within the space of economic opportunities;
- The result of this heterogeneous positioning is a diversely distributed growth potential: the better the positioning within this space, the higher likelihood that the firm will come across valuable opportunities;
- Finally, the ultimate ability to recognize these opportunities will vary according to the firms' absorptive capacity. Firms with a high degree of absorptive capacity will be more likely to translate their network-based informational endowment into exploitable growth opportunities.

As network ties convey new and diverse information, new opportunities are discovered and a process of change is enabled. Accordingly, the firm's networks act as a bridge between the information and the opportunity space (Figure 8.1).

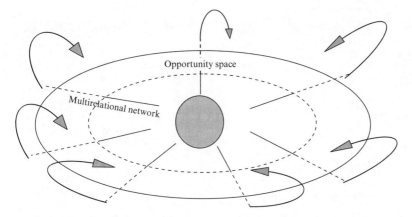

Opportunity space

Multirelational network

Figure 8.1   *Firm's multirelational network as a bridge between the information space and the opportunity space*

CAUSAL MODEL

Assumptions

In order to set up a plausible causal model it is crucial to define neat boundary conditions under which conjectures may hold. We have drawn this boundary around five assumptions which, taken together, constitute the substantive grounds in which the model is rooted:

1) The firm assumed by the model is an organization already in existence and in operation. This firm is conceptualized as an open system interacting with other organizations in its environment, where inducements as well as constraints to growth are located[1] (Penrose, 1959; Garnsey, 1998).
2) In line with Penrose (1959), while the unpredictability of specific growth paths is recognized, it is assumed that firm growth involves certain common processes that may be uncovered. The focus here is on a subclass of these processes that may generally be defined as information-based inducements to growth.
3) Consistently with a network perspective, the environment in which the firm operates is portrayed as a field[2] of relationships that bind organizations together (Nohria, 1992). This 'interorganizational field' includes a variety of organizational actors like key suppliers, resource and product consumers, regulatory agencies, and other organizations

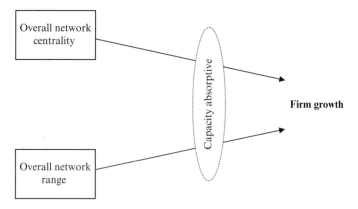

*Figure 8.2   Multirelational embeddedness, information access and firm
growth: a conceptual model*

whose linkages give rise to the relational fabric of this field (DiMaggio
and Powell, 1983: 148).

4) An embedded based conception of market functioning looms in the
    background of the model. Although arm's-length relations are not
    disregarded from this conception, the key assumption here is that
    valuable information is less likely to circulate via purely market-based
    transactions. Instead, organization networks operate on the logic of
    embedded exchange, where ongoing social ties imbue relationships
    with information which has not been impoverished by the competitive
    pressures operating in the market. It is this information that may cru-
    cially enlighten the opportunity space available to the firm (Uzzi, 1996).

5) While embedded networks are more likely to channel valuable infor-
    mation, the diffusion of this information across types of network ties
    is conceived as a stochastic process. Or, in less restrictive terms, it is
    extremely difficult to anticipate what embedded ties will be sources of
    critical information. This assumption builds upon two basic tenets: (a)
    the discovery of economic opportunities is not a result of optimizing
    choices; rather it is more a matter of 'serendipity', where the effort
    was not initially directed to the specific end realized (Denrell et al.,
    2003); (b) accordingly, the information that may trigger the discovery
    process is not a deliberately searchable good; instead it tends to befall
    the firm via unintended, if not unexpected, means.[3] The discovery of
    economic opportunities is not entirely governed by chance or fortui-
    tous forces, though. Strategy plays a focal role in creating favorable
    conditions which may enable the discovery itself and thus lead to a
    better positioning within the opportunity space.

PROPOSITIONS

Drawing on existing research, we suggest two primary ways in which an actor's network position may impact his information access conditions: First, the structure of the network may affect the volume of information accessed, which can be expressed as a function of the actor's centrality within the system; second, it can affect the variety of information accessed, which is interpretable as a function of the range (or diversity) of the actor's ties (Koka and Prescott, 2002). Further, in order to account for the multirelational nature of firms' embeddedness, we introduce the notion of 'overall network position', that is, the focal firm's network position as resulting from the observation of its overall set of network ties with the key constituents of its multirelational cluster environment.

Overall Network Centrality and Firm Growth

Centrality, which refers to the position of an actor in the network, is a structural attribute indicating the extent to which the actor occupies a strategic position by virtue of being involved in many significant ties (Wasserman and Faust, 1994). Drawing on the conceptualization provided above, we argue that a high centrality enhances the informational values of network resources along two dimensions: access and control. Being at the point of convergence of multiple sources of information conveyed by their ties, central actors are more likely to discover relevant business information (Valente, 1995) and thus to have timely access to promising new ventures (Powell et al., 1996). Furthermore, firms that are more centrally located enjoy status and power benefits since central connectedness shapes a firm's reputation and generates visibility (Brass and Burkhardt, 1992); the status improvement, in turn, may greatly strengthen a firm's tendency to take initiatives and thus enhance its proactivity before emerging opportunities (Freeman, 1979; Powell et al., 1996). We summarize these ideas in the following proposition:

Proposition 1: Other things being equal, an increase in the firm's overall network centrality will positively affect its growth probability.

Overall Network Range and Firm Growth

Because firms embedded in the network may operate in different segments, utilize different technologies and belong to different (but related) industries, they are also likely to be sources of heterogeneous information. Burt (1982) defines the concept of network range as the extent to which an actor's network links it to diverse other units. Thus, while central-ity emphasizes the volume dimension of information access, range has mainly to do with the variety of the information. Our idea is that a firm's overall network range has a positive impact on its growth probability via leveraging information diversity. There are several ways in which network range may enhance information benefits: first, diversity of contacts across parties reduces access redundancy, that is, tapping information that is superfluous and/or obsolete. On the contrary, the likelihood of entering novel niches of information is enhanced, and the overall flow of information enjoyed by the focal actor tends to be more effective.

Second, whereas networks with a narrow range of contacts are likely to confirm one's beliefs and mental models, networks with higher range allow a finer and more mindful understanding of the system, which may then convert into a higher awareness of original developments, innovations and potential opportunities as they emerge in the surrounding environment (Powell et al., 1996). Further, when the actors tap heterogeneous domains of knowledge and information they are more likely to enjoy advantages in the shape of information asymmetries and control since the probability that the other parties of the relation know each other, on average, tends to be low. Hence we posit:

Proposition 2: Other things being equal, an increase in the firm's overall network range will positively affect its growth probability.

Preexisting Knowledge Structure as Moderating Variable

According to Cohen and Levinthal, the absorptive capacity level of an organization heavily depends on the "richness of its preexisting knowledge structure" (p. 131). Whether developed from work experience, education, or other means, the preexisting knowledge structure influences the firm's ability to comprehend, extrapolate, interpret, and apply new informa-tion in ways that those lacking such prior information cannot replicate (Roberts, 1991). For instance, consistent with this idea, Shane (2000) con-nects the level of prior knowledge to the entrepreneur's ability to recognize new opportunities. We contend that, when a firm plays a pivotal role in terms of access to diverse information (i.e. it has both high overall network centrality and overall network range), it has a higher growth probability when it can tap into a rich preexisting knowledge structure. Accordingly we suggest the following summary propositions:

Proposition 3: Other things being equal, an increase in a firm's overall network centrality is more likely to be positively related to the firm's growth when the firm has a rich preexisting knowledge structure rather than when the firm has a poor preexisting knowledge structure.

Proposition 3b: Other things being equal, an increase in a firm's overall network range is more likely to be positively related to the firm's growth when the firm has a rich preexisting knowledge structure rather than when the firm has a poor preexisting knowledge structure.

DISCUSSION

This chapter offers a valuable contribution to the competitive strategy and organizational field by advancing an original conceptual linkage between two important strands of literature: interorganizational networks and firm growth. Although numerous studies have already empirically approached the firm growth through the lenses provided by the network perspective, to the best of our knowledge, this work represents one of the first attempts to formalize our understanding of firm growth based on a conceptual framework that brings together social network arguments with the theoretical stream on the economics of opportunities (De Carolis and Saparito, 2006).

First, we sought to provide a theoretically grounded conceptualization of relational ties as enablers of firm growth. In spite of the copious empirical indications that networks play an important role in shaping the process of firm growth, the driving forces of this relational influence appear often vague or loosely specified; either because the 'networking metaphor' is endorsed with a taken-for-granted facilitator role, or because it is credited with a multiplicity of overlapping benefits (resource, power, status, information, legitimacy, etc.), with no clear explanation as to the basic underlying mechanism linking these elements to the process of firm growth. We have taken two steps forward in order to address this issue: first, building on a well-established stream of network literature we provided an information-based conceptualization of network ties.

Second, drawing on some key ideas dating back to the work of Penrose, but mainly established within the Austrian economics framework, we have further elaborated on the concept of firm growth deemed as a process of entrepreneurial discovery and of recognition of economic opportunities. Opportunities exist because different firms access and control different information, rather than being an intended outcome of a deliberate search process (e.g. Honda's success in entering the US market with an emerging and unintended strategy, based on heuristics and lacking a coherent and linear strategic planning; Pascale, 1984; Rumelt, 1996), they are serendipitously discovered through the recognition of the value of information that firms happen to receive through other means. By way of this heterogeneous exposition to information, firms wind up occupying diverse positions within the space of economic opportunities. These two arguments allowed us to stretch out a more transparent line of causal reasoning between firm networks and firm growth. Because the discovery of economic opportunities is profoundly shaped by the availability and distribution of information in society, and since "information can be acquired by use of social relations maintained for various purposes" (Coleman, 1988: 104), networks represent a natural bridge between the information space and the opportunity space, and thus play a critical role in the process of firm growth.

Third, we sought to highlight and criss-cross a conceptual gap that appears to characterize the majority of the organizational approaches that have adhered to the structural embeddedness perspective. As stated in the introduction, such approaches are premised on the basic assumption that the firm is embedded in multiple interfirm networks, yet they typically focus on just one network dimension (Ahuja, 2000; Dyer, 1996; Dyer and Nobeoka, 2000; Davis and Greve, 1997; Zaheer and Bell, 2005). In drawing inferences from such mono-dimensional research, however, one should carefully discount the fact that other relational dimensions have been disregarded from the analysis. As an antidote to the perils of this inherent myopia we encouraged the adoption of multirelational lenses, providing an initial step for a multidimensional approach to the study of network effects on firm growth. By introducing the idea of overall network position (overall network centrality and overall network range), as the result of the full relational configuration of the firm within the whole set of networks in which it is embedded, we hope that we paved the way for a conceptually more consistent network approach to the study of firm-level and network-based outcomes.

Fourth, while the assumption that the relations represent information conduits has led much research to focus on the identification of high conductivity network configurations, the literature has shown little concern for the effective capability of the firm to recognize and absorb the value of the information distributed within the network. Building on this argument we have suggested the possibility to integrate the analysis of network properties with the concept of absorptive capacity (Cohen and Levinthal, 1990), as a filter between the firm and its network environment. Bits and pieces of information are gathered and recollected via sense making informed by a firm's absorptive capacity and its prior knowledge. Within the Austrian view the role of prior knowledge is an implicit, but concurrently a very important one. By describing the opportunity recognition process as a continuous trial and error effort, Austrian economics scholars suggest that the recognition of opportunities is enabled by a state of alertness which, in turn, is informed by the lessons firms may learn from previous experiences (both own and foreign). By analyzing the causes of successes and failures and combining these rationales with the information they receive through their ties (information that is idiosyncratic to the specific position the firm occupies as a result of being suspended in a set of networks), firms are able to discover opportunities that were in a latent state until then. As Blau et al. (1982) once noted, an actor's network position and attributes offer complementary insights that taken together offer a fuller explanation of the actor's action. Absorptive capacity represents a powerful conceptual tool to improve our understanding of network-based influences on firm behavior, yet there have been only sporadic attempts to incorporate this construct into interorganizational research designs (Powell et al., 1996; Tsai, 2001).

The structural location the firm occupies within different networks, the set of information it is able to tap, the firm's absorptive capacity, its set of resources: they all contribute to determine the position of the firm within the opportunity space, thereby influencing its stance with respect to the ability of recognizing and exploiting business opportunities. Once a firm spots an opportunity it can seize it in order to exploit it (thus implying the opportunity being recognized as valuable to the firm). This process is likely to lead to growth potential. We emphasize that the assumption here lies in the fact that recognition implies that the firm values the opportunity (in both a strategic and an economic sense) and it has access to the resources and capabilities needed to exploit the business opportunity it recognizes.

SUMMARY AND CONCLUSION

To conclude this chapter, we note a few avenues for extending our model further. First, the model implicitly attributes and assumes an equal weight for all networks' ties as concerns their information-channeling ability and capacity. However, different actors may (and usually) have different relationships with firm ties imbued with various degrees of richness and depth of informational value. A more refined approach could take into account these differences and propose a weighting scheme of ties based, for example, on their content and/or origin. Another fruitful extension of our model along this line might also consist in developing more fine-grained hypotheses, where the firm's growth likelihood is related not just to the change in its network properties over time, but also on the alleged informational value of the alters it is connected to.

Second, in an effort to maintain conceptual clarity and parsimony, the influence model was built on a basic, implicit assumption of environmental stationariness, that is, we did not elaborate on the possibility that different environments may entail different levels of uncertainty, and thus imply different information requirements (Galbraith, 1977). Based on the exploration/exploitation dualism the model could be enhanced by taking into account the structural features of the networks in response to the existence of specific environmental conditions. The environmental conditions are just one of the several contingencies that could be incorporated in our model. Another viable direction would be to investigate how the firm range and centrality compare to each other relative to the outcome variable, given the diverse emphasis on diversity and volume that different network types are likely to entail. Each of these issues points toward additional inquiry that can possibly enhance the framework and add to its practical applicability.

By explicitly modeling the process of firm growth as embedded in a network of multiple ties shaping, together with the firm's absorptive capacity, the interplay between information space and opportunity space, we hope we have made a step forward in enriching our understanding of some of the mechanisms that operate at the interface between the firm and its environment. Obviously we do not mean to imply that firms' overall network position and absorptive capacity entirely explain differences in growth potential, which is undoubtedly the outcome of numerous other individual and firm-level variables. We argue, however, that the adoption of a multirelational embeddedness perspective may help illuminate in new and innovative ways such complex, multifaceted phenomenon as the process of firm growth.

NOTES

1. While inducements may obviously be both internal and external to the firm, the focus here is on the external side, by way of the information-based growth incentives that the firm accrues from its network environment.
2. With the term field we refer to a community of organizations that engage in common activities and are subject to similar reputational and regulatory pressures (DiMaggio and Powell, 1983). Such fields have been defined as "a network, or a configuration, of relations between positions" (Bourdieu, 1992). Fields emerge when social, technological, or economic changes exert pressure on existing relations, and reconfigure both models of action and the structure of interaction (see also Powell et al., 2005).
3. These ideas are consistent with a key behavioral consequence of embeddedness: the relationship becomes separate from the narrow economic goal that initially constituted the exchange and generates outcomes that are independent from the original expectations of the parties (Uzzi, 1996).

REFERENCES

Ahuja, G. (2000), 'Collaboration networks, structural holes, and innovation: a longitudinal study', *Administrative Science Quarterly*, **45**, 425–455.

Baum, J.A.C. and J.E. Dutton (1996), 'The embeddedness of strategy', in J.A.C. Baum and J.E. Dutton (eds), *The Embeddedness of Strategy (Advances in Strategic Management)*, vol. 13, Stamford, CT: JAI Press, pp. 1–15.

Blau, P. (1982), 'Structural sociology and network analysis: an overview', in P.V. Mardsen and N. Lin (eds), *Social Structure and Network Analysis*, Beverly Hills, CA: Sage, pp. 273–279.

Borch, O.J. and M. Huse (1993), 'Informal strategic networks and boards of directors', *Entrepreneurship: Theory & Practice*, **18** (1), 23–36.

Brass, D.J. and M.E. Burkhardt (1992), 'Centrality and power in organizations', in N. Nohria and R. Eccles (eds), *Networks and Organizations*, Boston: HBS Press.

Burt, R. (2000), 'The network structure of social capital', in B.M. Staw (ed.), *Research in Organizational Behavior*, **22**, 345–423.

Burt, R. (ed.) (1992), *Structural Holes: The Social Structure of Competition*, Cambridge, MA: Harvard University Press.

Burt, R. (ed.) (1982), *Toward a Structural Theory of Action*, New York: Academic Press.

Butler, J. and G. Hansen (1988), 'Managing social network evolution and entrepreneurial benefits', *Frontiers of Entrepreneurship Research*, Proceedings of the Eighth Annual Babson College Entrepreneurship Research Conference, Wellesley, MA.

Cohen, W. and D. Levinthal (1990), 'Absorptive capacity: a new perspective on learning and innovation', *Administrative Science Quarterly*, **35**, 128–152.

Coleman, J.S. (1988), 'Social capital in the creation of human capital', *American Journal of Sociology*, **94**, S95–S120.

Companys, Y. and J. McMullen (2007), 'Strategic entrepreneurs at work: the nature, discovery, and exploitation of entrepreneurial opportunities', *Small Business Economics*, **28** (4).

Corbett, A. and C. Koberg (2001), 'Patterns of opportunity recognition and growth in technology firms', paper presented at the Babson College Conference on Entrepreneurship.

Cusumano, M. (1985), 'The Japanese automobile industry: technology and management at Nissan and Toyota', *Harvard Business Press*.

Davidsson, P., F. Delmar and J. Wiklund (2003), 'Entrepreneurship as growth; growth as entrepreneurship', working paper, Jönköping International Business School.

Davis, G. and G. Greve (1997), 'Corporate elite networks and governance changes in the 1980s', *American Journal of Sociology*, **103** (1), 1–37.

De Carolis, D.M. and P. Saparito (2006), 'Social capital, cognition, and entrepreneurial opportunities: a theoretical framework', *Entrepreneurship Theory and Practice*, **30** (1), 41–56.

Delmar, F., P. Davidsson and W.B. Gartner (2003), 'Arriving at the high growth firm', *Journal of Business Venturing*, **18** (2), 189–216.

Denrell, J., C. Fang and S. Winter (2003), 'The economics of strategic opportunity', *Strategic Management Journal*, **24** (10).

Dhanaraj, C. and A. Parkhe (2006), 'Orchestrating innovation networks', *Academy of Management Review*, **31** (3), 659–669.

DiMaggio, P. and W. Powell (1983), 'The iron cage revisited: institutional isomorphism and collective rationality in organizational fields', *American Sociological Review*, **48**, 147–160.

Dokko, G. and L. Rosenkopf (2002), 'Mobility of technical professionals and firm influence in wireless standards committees', The Wharton School Working Paper.

Dyer, J.H. (1996), 'Specialized supplier networks as a source of competitive advantage: evidence from the auto industry', *Strategic Management Journal*, **17**, 271–291.

Dyer, J.H. and Nobeoka (2000), 'Creating knowledge and managing a high performance knowledge-sharing network: the Toyota case', *Strategic Management Journal*, **21**, 345–367.

Dyer, J.H. and H. Singh (1998), 'The relational view: cooperative strategy and sources of interorganizational competitive advantage', *Academy of Management Review*, **23**, 660–679.

Evans, D. (1987), 'Test of alternative theories of firm growth', *Journal of Political Economy*, **95** (41).

Freeman, L. (1979), 'Centrality in social networks: conceptual clarification', *Social Networks*, **1**, 215–239.

Galbraith, J. (ed.) (1977), *Organization Design*, Reading, MA: Addison-Wesley.

Garnsey, E. (1998), 'A theory of the early growth of the firm', *Industrial and Corporate Change*, **7** (3).

Gnyawali, D.R. and R. Madhavan (2001), 'Network structure and competitive dynamics: a structural embeddedness perspective', *Academy of Management Review*, **26** (3), 431–445.

Granovetter, M. (1985), 'Economic action and social structure: the problem of embeddedness', *American Journal of Sociology*, **91**, 481–510.

Gulati, R. (1999), 'Network location and learning: the influence of network resources and firm capabilities on alliance formation', *Strategic Management Journal*, **20** (5), 397–420.

Gulati, R. (1995), 'Social structure and alliance formation patterns: a longitudinal analysis', *Administrative Science Quarterly*, **40**, 619–650.

Gulati, R. and M. Gargiulo (1999), 'Where do interorganizational networks come from?', *American Journal of Sociology*, **104** (5), 1439–1493.

Hayek, F.A. (1945), 'The use of knowledge in society', *American Economic Review*, **15** (4), 519–530.

Kirzner, I. (1997), 'Entrepreneurial discovery and the competitive market process: an Austrian approach', *Journal of Economic Literature*, **35**, 60–85.

Kirzner, I. (ed.) (1973), *Competition and Entrepreneurship*, Chicago and London: The University of Chicago Press.

Koka, B.R. and J.E. Prescott (2002), 'Strategic alliances as social capital: a multidimensional view', *Strategic Management Journal*, **23** (9), 795–816.

Lee, D. and E. Tsang (2001), 'The effects of entrepreneurial personality, background and network activities on venture growth', *Journal of Management Studies*, **38** (4), 583–602.

Mariani, M. and G.B. Dagnino (2007), 'Unveiling the modal capability lifecycle: the coevolutionary foundations of the firm's effectiveness in capturing strategic opportunities', *International Journal of Learning and Intellectual Capital*, **4** (1–2), 132–145.

McEvily, B. and A. Zaheer (1999), 'Bridging ties: a source of firm heterogeneity in competitive capabilities', *Strategic Management Journal*, **20**, 1133–1156.

Mizruchi, M. (1996), 'What do interlocks do? An analysis, critique and assessment of research on interlocking directorates', *Annual Review of Sociology*, **22**, 271–302.

Mohan-Neill, S. (1995), 'The influence of firm's age and size on its environmental scanning activities', *Journal of Small Business Management*, **33** (4), 10–22.

Nohria, N. (1992), 'Is a network perspective a useful way of studying organizations?', in N. Nohria and R. Eccles (eds), *Networks and Organizations*, Boston, MA: Harvard Business School Press, pp. 1–22.

Ostgaard, A. and S. Birley (1996), 'New venture growth and personal networks', *Journal of Business Research*, **36**, 37–50.

Pascale, R. (1984), 'Perspectives on strategy: the real story behind Honda's success', *California Management Review*, **26** (3), 47–73.

Penrose, E. (ed.) (1959), *The Theory of the Growth of the Firm*, Oxford: Oxford University Press.

Powell, W. (1990), 'Neither market nor hierarchy: network forms of organization', in B. Staw and L.L. Cummings (eds), *Research in Organizational Behavior*, Greenwich, CT: JAI Press.

Powell, W., K.W. Koput and L. Smith-Doerr (1996), 'Interorganizational collaboration and the locus of innovation: networks of learning in biotechnology', *Administrative Science Quarterly*, **41**, 116–145.

Roberts, E. (1991), *Entrepreneurs in High Technology*, Oxford: Oxford University Press.

Rumelt, D. (1996), 'The many faces of Honda', *California Management Review*, **38** (4), 103–111.

Shane, S. (2000), 'Prior knowledge and the discovery of entrepreneurial opportunities', *Organization Science*, **11**, 448–469.

Stephenson, K.A. and M. Zelen (1989), 'Rethinking centrality: methods and examples', *Social Networks*, **11**, 1–37.

Timmons, J.A., D.F. Muzyka, H.A. Stevenson and W.D. Bygrave (1987), 'Opportunity recognition: the core of entrepreneurship', in N. Churchill et al. (eds), *Frontiers of Entrepreneurship Research*, Wellesley, MA: Babson College, pp. 118–129.

Tsai, W. (2001), 'Knowledge transfer in intra-organizational networks: effects of network position and absorptive capacity on business unit innovation and performance', *Academy of Management Journal*, **44**, 996–1004.

Useem, M. (ed.) (1984), *The Inner Circle*, Oxford: Oxford University Press.

Uzzi, B. (1996), 'The sources and consequences of embeddedness for the economic performance of organizations: the network effect', *American Sociological Review*, **61**, 674–698.

Valente, T. (ed.) (1995), *Network Models of the Diffusion of Innovations*, Cresskill: Hampton Press.

Venkataraman, S. (1997), 'The distinctive domain of entrepreneurship research: an editor's perspective', in J. Katz and R. Brockhaus (eds), *Advances in Entrepreneurship, Firm Emergence, and Growth*, vol. 3, Greenwich, CT: JAI Press, pp. 119–138.

Wasserman, S. and K. Faust (1994), *Social Network Analysis: Methods and Applications*, Cambridge: Cambridge University Press.

Weinzimmer, L., P. Nystrom and S. Freeman (1998), 'Measuring organizational growth: issues, consequences and guidelines', *Journal of Management*, **24** (2).

Yili-Renko, H., E. Autio and H.J. Sapienza (2001), 'Social capital, knowledge acquisition, and knowledge exploitations in young technology-based firms', *Strategic Management Journal*, **23**, 587–613.

Zaheer, A. and G. Bell (2005), 'Benefiting from network position: firm capabilities, structural holes, and performance', *Strategic Management Journal*, **26** (9), 809–825.

Zaheer, A. and N. Venkatraman (1995), 'Relational governance as an interorganizational strategy: an empirical test of the role of trust in economic change', *Strategic Management Journal*, **16**, 373–392.

Zhao, L. and J.D. Aram (1995), 'Networking and growth of young technology-intensive ventures in China', *Journal of Business Venturing*, **10**, 349–370.

9   Strategy-as-practice: untangling the emergence of competitive positions
Patrick Regnér

INTRODUCTION

Even though great achievements have been made in explaining the basis of competitive advantage it is rather surprising that we still do not know more about the fundamental mechanisms involved in the emergence of competitive advantage and new competitive positions in terms of new resource and capability and/or industry positions. Whether competitive advantage is explained in terms of imperfectly imitable resources (Barney, 1986 and 1991; Wernerfelt, 1984) or by competitive forces (Porter, 1980 and 1981) our understanding of how these competitive positions emerge still remains limited. While general processes have been described (e.g. Teece et al., 1997) they often represent aggregate firm-level outcomes. These are however preceded by micro-foundations including individual beliefs and activities as well as macro-conditions involving institutionalized meanings and practices. The aim of this chapter is to analyze and clarify the characteristics of these antecedents to new competitive positions.

Although research in strategic management has addressed individual beliefs (Huff, 1982; Porac and Thomas, 1990) and managerial activities (Mintzberg, 1973) on the one hand and institutionalized meanings and practices (Oliver, 1991 and 1997) on the other, the full implication of them for the emergence of new competitive positions has not been examined. Since the former micro-foundations are embedded in the latter macro-conditions it is critical to analyze these two levels of analysis collectively. Moreover, given that beliefs and meanings are embodied in activities and practices respectively (Weick, 1995; Giddens, 1984; Mohr, 2005) they too need to be analyzed jointly. This suggests a two-level understanding of strategy emergence including micro-foundations and macro-conditions and their embodied beliefs and activities, and meanings and practices respectively. These intertwined antecedents have received less attention in strategic management research and are thus the focus of this chapter. While strategy process research has made great progress and there is an increased interest generally in evolutionary explanations, we are still far away from a more processual theory of strategy. Resource-based (Barney,

1986 and 1991) and competitive force (Porter, 1980 and 1981) views have not primarily focused on developmental processes and consequently have less to say regarding how competitive positions emerge, develop and change over time (Cockburn et al., 2000; Regnér, 1999; Tsoukas and Knudsen, 2002). The dynamic capabilities view (Teece et al., 1997; Eisenhardt and Martin, 2000) specifically addresses capability development, but has largely avoided examinations of the detailed mechanisms and activities underlying capabilities and has instead concentrated on the use and exploitation of dynamic capabilities on the firm-level. Strategy process research, on the other hand (Bower and Doz, 1979; Burgelman, 1983; Mintzberg, 1978; Johnson, 1987; Pettigrew, 1985), has provided rich descriptions, overviews and typologies to build on, but less in terms of theoretical constructs and mechanisms related to strategy outcome and competitive advantage. Nevertheless, a new perspective of strategic management, the strategy-as-practice approach (Johnson et al., 2007; Johnson et al., 2003; Whittington, 2006) may be able to assist in untangling some of the processes and mechanisms involved. With its focus on micro-foundations and their relationship with macro-conditions it promises to uncover some pieces in the puzzle of how new competitive positions develop.

The challenges in examining the mechanisms of how micro-foundations and macro-conditions interact to produce new competitive positions are vast. An examination of strategy processes involves numerous complexity dimensions including inter-connectedness and inter-temporality between different units of analysis and interrelationships between many diverse actors (Peteraf and Shanley, 2006). This may explain why strategy process has not received more attention despite its centrality and why many have found it necessary to ignore or black box process.

Scholars have, however, recently made calls for causal explanations and mechanisms in social science generally (Coleman, 1990; Elster, 1989; Swedberg and Hedström, 1998) and in strategic management specifically (Bromiley, 2005; Felin and Foss, 2005; Tsoukas and Knudsen, 2002). The basic argument is that we need explanations of how a set of prior conditions interact to determine (strategic) outcome in terms of mechanisms and not merely correlations between variables. Micro-foundations of strategy outcomes from behavioral (Bromiley, 2005) as well as rational choice points of view (Felin and Foss, 2006) have been suggested. Likewise their history in a social context has been emphasized (Tsoukas and Knudsen, 2002), as have their institutional foundations (Jonsson and Regnér, 2009; Oliver, 1997). At this point it seems premature to ascertain the primacy of one or the other of these potential influences. Hence, behavioral as well as individual micro-level and socio-cultural macro-level influences need to be considered. This makes the strategy-as-practice approach particularly useful at this stage since it is specifically focused on bridging micro-levels involving individual and groups of managers' activities and beliefs, and macro-levels including organizational and institutionalized practices and meanings.

The purpose of this chapter is to examine how the strategy-as-practice approach linked with cognitive and institutional perspectives may grasp complex processes and mechanisms involved in the emergence of new competitive positions. Given that it is a fairly new research area and that we still have limited knowledge concerning strategy emergence the objective here is modest and naturally only a tentative response to questions concerning how new competitive positions may emerge and how this can be examined. The aim is to try out some alternative views of what conditions may provide for new competitive positions and some general mechanisms that may operate on those. The argument presented emphasizes the importance of examining the mutual interdependence between beliefs/ meanings and activities/practices on various levels of analysis.

THE STRATEGY-AS-PRACTICE APPROACH

The strategy-as-practice approach (Johnson et al., 2003; Whittington, 2006) builds on social theory generally (Bourdieu, 1990; Giddens, 1984; Sztompka, 1991) and its practice-turn particularly (Schatzki et al., 2001). This direction in social theory aims to move beyond the dualism between an exaggerated focus on social structures and systems (societism) on the one hand and individual actions and positions (individualism) on the other (Schatzki, 2005). The strategy-as-practice approach is characterized by three key interrelated standpoints. First, it sees strategy as an ongoing activity and accomplishment, something people and firms do rather than have (Jarzabkowski, 2004). This corresponds to the change in focus in organization theory from what an organization is to its accomplishment in terms of organizing (Weick, 1979). Second, the approach emphasizes the day-to-day activities of people on multiple organizational levels (Johnson et al., 2003), what individual and groups of managers actually do in practice (Mintzberg, 1973). A third and related emphasis concerns practices and routines of organizations and organizational outcomes (cf. Cyert and March, 1963; Nelson and Winter, 1982) and practices that have become institutionalized among groups of organizations (Oliver, 1997; Spender, 1989). The approach emphasizes the ongoing interrelationships between these organizational and institutionalized practices and individual managerial activities (Whittington, 2006).

In sum, the strategy-as-practice approach is concerned with "what people do in relation to strategy and how this is influenced by and influences their organizational and institutional context" (Johnson et al., 2007: 7). Much of the research has so far focused on specific strategic planning and analysis practices, but the approach stays open to any activities and practices that may have a strategic outcome. Even though the area is fairly new it has started to contribute both conceptually (Hendry, 2000; Hendry and Seidl, 2003; Johnson et al., 2007; Whittington, 2006 and 2003) and empirically (Johnson and Balogun, 2004; Mantere, 2005; Jarzabkowski, 2005; Regnér, 2003; Rouleau, 2005). Since some useful overviews of the area have been provided recently (Jarzabkowski et al., 2007; Johnson et al., 2003 and 2007; Whittington, 2006), there is no need to provide yet another one here. Instead the continued focus will be on its potential value in examining the emergence of new competitive positions.

Three key elements in the strategy-as-practice approach stand out as particularly valuable when evaluating the generation of new competitive positions. First, it focuses on diverse actors' actual activities on multiple levels, which allows for explorations of 'micro-foundations' of new competitive position build-up. Second, it emphasizes that industry- and societal-level fields and systems may influence firm-level practices, which provide for examinations of the 'macro-conditions' under which new competitive positions emerge. Third, the approach emphasizes interrelationships between actors and interactions between micro- and macro-levels. This provides for examinations not only of how relationships between internal actors and between them and external actors may shape new competitive positions, but how broader socio-cultural contexts may influence the development of them. In brief, the emergence of new competitive positions can be conceived in terms of managerial activities (individual or group) and institutionalized (industry and societal) practices that together shape firm-level practices, which in turn determine new competitive positions that may potentially generate competitive advantage (Figure 9.1). The focus on practices clearly has a commonality with

Figure 9.1   Emergence of competitive positions: micro-foundations and macro-conditions

contemporary strategic management research that emphasizes organizational capabilities (Eisenhardt and Martin, 2000; Winter, 2003), but the practice approach emphasizes social embeddedness (macro-conditions) and individual activities (micro-foundations) to a larger degree.

As illustrated, the strategy-as-practice approach has the potential to attack some of the challenges that lie ahead in examining mechanisms that generate certain competitive positions and, in the end, competitive advantage. The space here does not allow for a complete analysis of its potentials and the focus will therefore not be on the general relationship between micro-foundations and macro-conditions, but more on their sub-parts: activities/beliefs and practices/meanings relationships respectively. Some words and concepts that will be used are defined before moving into the discussion; they are partly based on useful distinctions made earlier (Johnson et al., 2007; Whittington, 2006). Activities refers to what individual actors and groups of actors do (e.g. planning, gathering intelligence, doing scenarios) and practices refers to institutionalized and organizational routines or practices with which actors engage (e.g. strategic planning, intelligence gathering, scenario planning). Similarly, beliefs refers to what individual actors think (e.g. individual cognition and perception) and meanings to collective-level cognitive frameworks (e.g. shared cognitive maps, dominant logic) in which actors are embedded. As indicated earlier, competitive positions refers to resource and capability and/or industry positions that provide for competitive advantage.

In brief, there are micro-foundations in terms of individual actors' activities and beliefs and macro-conditions in terms of institutionalized and organizational practices and meanings. The difference made between the two pairs (activities/beliefs and practices/meanings) relates to the distinction between performative routines and ostensive routines respectively. The former refers to particular activities in specific places and times and the latter is the ideal, schematic or principle form of a routine or practice (Feldman and Pentland, 2003: 101). In the following, we discuss how the practice turn of strategy with its focus on activities and practices together with cognitive and institutional perspectives that examine cognitions and meanings respectively may untangle the emergence of new competitive positions.

IMPORTANT STEPS IN UNTANGLING COMPETITIVE POSITION EMERGENCE

As indicated earlier, the strategy-as-practice approach may draw on cognitive (Huff, 1982; Porac and Thomas, 1990; Reger and Huff, 1993) as well as institutional perspectives (Oliver, 1991 and 1997; Jonsson and Regnér, 2007) when analyzing the emergence of competitive positions, but there are some issues that need to be addressed before they can be fully exploited for this purpose. First, there has so far not been sufficient focus on interactions between activities/practices and beliefs/meanings respectively and, second, there has been a tendency to overlook possible heterogeneity in these on different levels of analysis. Finally, individual actors and agency have often been undervalued in previous perspectives. Each one of these fundamental ingredients in explicating the emergence of competitive positions is discussed below.

Interactions Between Activities/Practices and Beliefs/Meanings

The full implication of the intimate linkage between activities/practices and beliefs/meanings, although emphasized in early (March and Simon, 1958) as well as later organizational theory work (Weick, 1979 and 1995) has yet to be fully incorporated into strategic management. Beliefs/meanings have been identified as particularly central in an analysis of economic development and change generally (North, 2005), and something that needs particular attention in examinations of markets, industries and resources. Hence, Mohr (2005) argues that any analysis of organizational competition requires recognition of the mutual constitution between practices and meanings; an adequate study of one requires the other.

Examinations of activities/practices and beliefs/meanings have tended to accentuate one or the other, primarily emphasizing either beliefs/meanings (Lyles and Schwenk, 1992) or activities/practices (Jarzabkowski, 2004). The relationship between them and, in particular, their interaction mechanisms in the development of new competitive positions has been less commonly evaluated. While the cognitive approach to strategy (Huff et al., 1992; Walsh, 1995) has contributed significantly to our understanding of managerial cognition and collective-level meanings it has often been separated from or at least not explicitly related to activities or practices. Much work has focused on information processing and calculation by humans (primarily individual or groups of top managers) and on various biases associated with these procedures (Hogarth and Makridakis, 1981; Schwenk, 1984). Social context is incorporated in these examinations to the extent that they investigate social thought, but social action and behavior are often left out. The mapping of, interaction between, and development of collective beliefs/meanings become the prime interest while often leaving out how they may develop from activities/practices in interaction with elements in the environment. What traditionally has been examined is in a sense the move forward from the environment and activities/practices towards beliefs/meanings, but less attention has been given to the move backwards from beliefs/meanings towards activities/ practices and environment (when beliefs/meanings are applied in action). The latter process is of vital importance when examining the emergence of new competitive positions since it may capture imagination and creativity. There are, however, important exceptions where activities/practices and perceptions or beliefs/meanings have been analyzed jointly (Porac et al., 1989) and later work has been more concerned with management as a social endeavor, avoiding a mere focus on individual and group cognitions or cognitive filters (e.g. Meindl et al., 1996; Weick, 1995). Similarly, institutional approaches to strategy, even though more rare, have started to underline the link between norms or meanings and practices, emphasizing the need for firms to respond to institutional pressures in terms of changed strategic directions and practices (Ingram et al., 1995; Jonsson and Regnér, 2009; Oliver, 1991).

The relationship between practices and meanings is central in the structuration theories (Bourdieu, 1977; Giddens, 1984; Sewell, 1992) that the strategy-as-practice approach builds on. Practice theory defines practices as arrays of human activity centrally organized around shared understandings (Schatzki et al., 2001). Accordingly, the strategy-as-practice approach has started to explore this, showing how social interaction influences managerial schema and organizational change (Balogun and Johnson, 2004), how meanings change in interaction with external stakeholders (Roleau, 2003) and, moreover, how managerial activities/practices are closely linked to beliefs/meanings in the emergence of new competitive positions (Regnér, 2003). These studies demonstrate the importance of beliefs/meanings and activities/practices interrelationships and more importantly that firms may build new activities (or capabilities) through new beliefs/meanings and vice versa. This has significant implications in an analysis of how new competitive positions emerge since these may be generated through social constructs that develop over time in interaction among members on different organizational levels.

In sum, while the cognitive approach to strategy has focused on one primary aspect of social actors, belief systems, and institutional theory on another, norm systems, the strategy-as-practice approach has started to penetrate a closely related aspect: practices. With the advent of studies in the strategy-as-practice approach that analyzes the intersection of these factors the dynamics in strategy emergence may be uncovered. To capture the development of new competitive positions the focus thus needs to be more explicitly on the social interplay between activities/practices and beliefs/meanings.

Heterogeneous Activities/Practices and Beliefs/Meanings

The homogeneous character of activities/practices and beliefs/meanings has often been overemphasized in prior examinations. While the individual has been central in examinations of cognitive biases, much of cognitive research that relates to strategy process has rather focused on shared meanings on the collective level. The focal point has most often been on descriptions of homogeneous meanings on different levels of analysis such as top management group interpretations (Hambrick, 1981), firms' dominant logics (Prahalad and Bettis, 1986) and industry recipes (Spender, 1989). The common characteristic is that past experiences guide present information processing, making meanings more homogeneous in these entities. Similarly, examinations on the institutional level underline the importance of homogeneous norms or meanings (DiMaggio and Powell, 1991; Scott, 1995).

In contrast, empirical research within the cognitive strategy approach has recently demonstrated large disagreements among actors of how they interpret the common business context in which they operate (e.g. Hodgkinson and Johnson, 1994; Porac and Thomas, 2002). While common meanings may force individuals and firms to adapt on the one hand, they may provide opportunities for strategizing around them and exploitation of competitors' inertia in following them on the other. Hence, while firms generally conform to common meanings and practices they sometimes also deviate from them (Deephouse, 1999). Departure from meanings or norms may thus create certain abilities and new competitive positions that provide for competitive advantage (Oliver, 1997).

When the focus is turned to the strategy-as-practice approach, homogeneity is still often central since the approach builds on ideas about shared understandings and a common character of meanings (Schatzki et al., 2001), but there is a clear recognition of individual- and group-level beliefs and activities. Hence, there is openness to a plurality of actors involving strategy work at the top, middle and lower management levels as well as including external groups (Whittington, 2004), which provides for heterogeneity and possible variation in the emergence of new competitive positions. Accordingly, the approach with its dual focus on micro- and macro-levels (Johnson et al., 2007) allows for an analysis of macro-level conditions in terms of homogeneous meanings and practices, but also for an examination of the micro-level beliefs and activities that may exploit and potentially change institutionalized meanings and practices. Indeed, when the emergence of new competitive positions has been examined empirically there appear to be significant differences regarding both activities/practices and beliefs/meanings on various organizational levels (Burgelman, 1983 and 1991; Regnér, 1999). Accordingly, the importance of beliefs and activities other than those of top management has been examined in strategy as practice research (Balogun and Johnson, 2004; Regnér, 2003).

It is evident that a careful examination of both commonalities and differences regarding activities/practices and beliefs/meanings on multiple levels and their interplay would be rewarding when analyzing the strategy processes involved in the emergence of new competitive positions. Observed homogeneity concerning meanings and practices on various levels of analysis (societal, industry, strategic group) may provide important macro-level conditions in the examination of competitive position build-up, but they must not exclude a scrutiny of micro-level foundational beliefs and activities that may provide for exploitation of them or, in fact, possibilities to change them altogether. Hence, macro-level conditions in terms of common meanings and norms may provide for strategizing opportunities by individual firms and actors via beliefs and activities that deviate from these on the micro-level (Jonsson and Regnér, 2009). Opportunities for this may be especially evident under unstable circumstances when technologies and/or customer preferences and maybe industry borders change. Under these circumstances individual or groups of managers (and firms) thus have the opportunity to challenge and change institutionalized meanings and practices on the firm- (or industry-) level. This leads us to the discussion below about agency.

Managerial Intentionality

The limited attention paid to interactions between activities/practices and beliefs/meanings in strategic management together with their homogeneity assumptions relates to a third important issue that needs to be taken into consideration in an examination of strategy emergence: the role of managerial intentionality and agency. Examinations of practices and meanings (and activities and beliefs) in organizational theory and strategic management, and more broadly in social theory, show that they are notoriously difficult to change and manage. Both cognitive and institutional approaches emphasize the stability and often rigidity of collective beliefs/ meanings (and of related activities/practices).

However, as indicated above there are conflicting findings that point to major differences among actors' cognitive maps or collective meanings (Hodgkinson and Johnson, 1994; Porac and Thomas, 2002) and thus possibilities of deviating from them (Deephouse, 1999; Jonsson and Regnér, 2007; Regnér, 2003). This allows for an investigation of individual- and group-level interest and agency in relation to firm- and industry-level homogeneous meanings and practices and, thus, of mechanisms involved in the emergence of new competitive positions. Differences in individual- and group-level beliefs and activities may provide for endogenous change of firm-level meanings and practices (cf. Feldman and Pentland, 2003) that shape new competitive positions. Similarly, differences in firm-level meanings and practices may provide for endogenous change of industry-level meanings and practices.

When the strategy-as-practice approach is analyzed regarding intentionality its foundation, the structuration view, could be attacked for reducing the individual influence from managers since it tends to allow structure primacy over agency (Archer, 1995). This is of course quite challenging in an analysis of how new competitive positions emerge; if managers have a diminutive function this would be in sharp contrast to basic premises in strategic management. This brings matters to a head in analyzing the emergence of new strategic positions. Do macro-conditions and contextual factors or micro-foundations and individual elements play the primary role?

The aim of this chapter is certainly not to untangle this extremely intriguing question, but a pragmatic answer of the strategy-as-practice approach at this stage would be: both! In fact, new conceptualizations of agency in sociology and social theory[1] pave the road for an integration of these diverse forces (Emirbayer and Mische, 1998; Sewell, 1992). The historical social context of practices and meanings provides a raw material which the current interplay between beliefs and activities can draw on with the potential to change future views and competitive positions. Thus, while practices reproduce meanings individual- and group-level activities and beliefs have the ability to change them, indicating a duality of agency (Zafirovski, 1999). Recent work on routines has, in line with this reasoning, challenged traditional conceptions of them in organizational theory and strategy and has emphasized routines' agentic qualities including individual actors that cognitively reflect over and have the potential to change them (Feldman, 2000; Feldman and Pentland, 2003; Pentland and Rueter, 1994).

Besides the above there is an agentic quality of firm-level practices (and meanings) where individuals and groups of individuals employ combinations of past strategy practices in new ways or use practices from other sources to deal with current situations. In addition, prevailing meanings can be applied in new or changed competitive environments. Hence, actors have a capacity to reinterpret and activate practices in new ways in environments outside the ones in which they were initially generated. Agency, hence, involves the capacity to transpose or transfer understandings to new environments (Sewell, 1992). The traditional conceptualization of meanings in terms of social thought and as constraining at the expense of social action severely restricts the role of agency in earlier cognitive approaches. In contrast, to be an agent implies some degree of control over beliefs/meanings and social actions and relations (Sewell, 1992).

The reasoning above is in accordance with writings in sociology that focus on social and relational qualities of agency and interplay between it and structure (Emirbayer and Mische, 1998). In brief, the analysis of agency from a strategy-as-practice perspective is not solely based on an understanding of meanings and practices as mutually constitutive (Giddens, 1984), but rather as a dynamic interplay between the two more focused on the interaction as the unit of analysis (Archer, 1982; Emirbayer and Mische, 1998).

UNTANGLING THE EMERGENCE OF NEW COMPETITIVE POSITIONS

The discussion above illustrates that examinations of beliefs/meanings and activities/practices in strategic management often have kept away from their inherent mutual dynamics and, hence, blocked assessments of how new competitive positions emerge in terms of this interaction. It was further suggested that alternative assumptions that recognize the possibility to deviate from institutional- and firm-level practices and institutionalized meanings and norms may provide for explanations. In particular, this includes possibilities of heterogeneity between diverse organizational levels' activities/practices and beliefs/meanings and, thus, possible endogenous changes. This difference requires an increased role for micro-level agency in relation to established institutional and organizational meanings and practices.

It is imperative to observe that this portrayal of strategy emergence in terms of activities/practices and beliefs/meanings does not include an exclusion of their core assumptions in social and organizational theory; stability and regularity, and unconsciousness and isomorphism respectively. However, compared to structuration theory it emphasizes new developments in social theory and sociology that recognize that practices and meanings may differ between levels and units and that exogenous or endogenous change might trigger change in them. This view is grounded in practice views of social theory and their aim to transcend an overemphasis on social structure and systems on the one hand and individual actions and status on the other.

Based on the discussion above it may be suggested that the emergence of new competitive positions is influenced by macro-conditions in terms of institutionalized meanings and practices as well as micro-foundations in terms of individual (and group) beliefs and activities and that these are

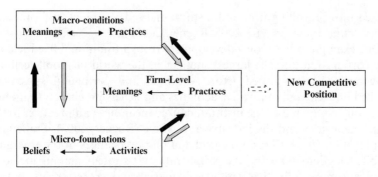

*Figure 9.2   The interplay between beliefs/meanings and activities/
practices: history- and future-dependent processes*

mutually constitutive on each level of analysis; macro, micro and firm (see Figure 9.2). The generation of change and new competitive positions may involve exogenous as well as endogenous change. First, exogenous forces including technology and market changes that make prior practices obsolete may provide for change in them (e.g. Barley, 1986; Orlikowski, 1992; Tushman and Romanelli, 1985). In this history-dependent process, practices are changed based on experience (grey thick arrows in Figure 9.2). This process forms the basis in experiential learning where routines or practices capture the past (March, 1994). Second, change may be endogenously generated; on the micro-level managers actively engage in the firm-level practice or routine itself and form new beliefs and activities towards an anticipated future (cf. Feldman, 2000; Feldman and Pentland, 2003) and/or firms engage in and change industry-level practices. Hence, in this future-dependent process, individual or groups of managers (or firms) may change their conception and understanding of firm-level (and/or industry-level) practices based on beliefs/meanings and activities/practices towards the future (black thick arrows in Figure 9.2). In brief, the emergence of new competitive positions may be history dependent in that it is a re-elaboration of prior firm-level practices and/or it may be future dependent involving imagination and exploration of new activities/practices.

There are many examples where micro- and/or macro-level social embeddedness and their interplay have been of importance in the emergence of competitive positions. At the micro-level, middle- and lower-level managers close to technological and market developments may provide for endogenous change via the introduction and application of new beliefs and activities that may change not only firm-level practices and meanings, but industry-level ones. In contrast, upper echelons appear to be more locked into prevailing firm and institutionalized meanings and practices (Burgelman, 1983; Gavetti, 2005; Regnér, 2003).

One example is Ericsson's development from a traditional fixed telephony corporation into the largest supplier in the world of mobile/cellular telecommunication infrastructure. A small and peripheral subsidiary applied unusual and innovative activities and beliefs in relation to mobile telephony compared to the institutionalized meanings and practices in the corporate center and the industry as a whole (Regnér, 2003). Embedded in a location closer to technological and market changes in the emerging mobile telephony industry, the peripheral unit's strategy making included relatively more inductive activities like trial and error, experimenting and informal noticing compared to the center's more institutionalized deductive practices including planning, business intelligence gathering, etc. Similarly, the activities in the peripheral unit interacted with alternative and innovative beliefs regarding the competitive circumstances compared to the traditional institutionalized meanings in the center. This is an example of how both micro-foundational and macro-conditional antecedents may be vital in untangling the emergence of new competitive positions. In brief, the example shows that micro-foundational activities and beliefs in the periphery interacted and that they helped change macro-conditions in the form of institutionalized firm-level meanings and practices and thus, in the end, Ericsson's corporate strategy.

Other examples can illustrate the huge importance of macro-conditions in the emergence of new competitive positions. Institutionalized meanings and practices at the macro-level and the lock-in and inertia that this provides may be at least as important in the emergence of new competitive positions as the micro-foundational innovativeness that provides for them (Rumelt, 1995). An example of this is the development of the world's first smoking cessation drug, Nicorette, and its subsequent dominance in the global market (Regnér, 1999). The development of the first nicotine chewing gum in the world by a small innovative unit in the pharmaceutical company Pharmacia (later merged with Pfizer) was in sharp conflict not only to the corporate center, but even more so with institutionalized and deeply rooted meanings and practices in the pharmaceutical industry. Nicotine was considered a poison that clearly was off limits in the drug industry and the practice of medication distribution via chewing gum was at least as awkward as was the sales and revenue logic compared to that in traditional drugs. Once accepted internally the resistance from the industry provided Pharmacia with a considerable lead ahead of competitors. The emergence of low-cost carriers in the airline industry (e.g. Southwest Airlines, Ryanair) can be seen in this light as well. The lock-in of incumbents into institutionalized and recursive meanings and practices has been at least as important as the innovativeness in the activities and beliefs of the new entrants.

The emergence of Wal-Mart's and IKEA's competitive positions provides two interesting examples in the retailing industry that both included micro-foundational innovativeness including strong linkages between certain beliefs (including organizational cultures) and innovative activities in the presence of macro-conditions involving institutionalized meanings and practices among incumbents that provided for their inertia. Another classical example is Honda's success in the US market, involving quite diverse activities and beliefs compared to the established meanings and practices in the motorcycle industry (Pascale, 1984). Inertia in terms of institutionalized meanings may thus provide for active strategizing around them. An additional example of this is the introduction of index and socially responsible investment funds by a few independent players in the Swedish mutual fund industry. Since these types of product were notoriously regarded as improper and illegitimate by the established industry competitors, the introduction of these funds created a normative (meanings) barrier to imitation (Jonsson and Regnér, 2009).

These brief examples demonstrate that micro-foundations (activities and beliefs) are essential in an examination of how new competitive positions emerge and often in combination with the macro-conditions (practices and meanings) under which they evolve. Careful examinations of these two fundamental mechanisms may reveal important details in the emergence of new competitive positions. They both include complex social contexts that may influence the development of new competitive positions. In sum, social interactions between activities/beliefs and practices/meanings on the individual, group, firm and institutional levels respectively may have important implications for the creation of new competitive positions.

CONCLUSIONS AND IMPLICATIONS

This paper has demonstrated that the strategy-as-practice approach based on the 'practice turn' in social theory, which emphasizes a balanced view between individual activities and structural influences, may be a fruitful basis when exploring micro-foundations and macro-conditions in the emergence of new competitive positions. Hence, the recently developed strategy-as-practice approach provides a fertile foundation in an investigation of the dynamic interplay between micro-foundational activities/beliefs and macro-conditional meanings/practices. While cognitive and institutional perspectives have contributed to the analysis of micro and macro considerations of strategy emergence respectively, the strategy-as-practice approach may be able to bridge these perspectives by bringing in a focus on activities and practices. In particular, the approach's emphasis on inter-actions between, and heterogeneity among, activities/practices and beliefs/meanings on different levels of analysis may, together with a recognition of both agency and structure, contribute to new explorations and explica-tions. In brief, it may be proposed that the emergence of new competitive positions is influenced by micro-foundations in terms of individual (and group) beliefs and activities as well as macro-conditions in terms of insti-tutionalized meanings and practices and their interplay. Moreover, the beliefs/activities and meanings/practices respectively that these two levels of analysis involve are mutually constitutive.

Following from the above, the emergence of new competitive positions may involve history-dependent processes where firm-level meanings and practices capture the past in experiential learning and/or future-dependent processes where managers engage in firm-level meanings and practices and form new beliefs and activities towards an anticipated future. A provi-sional proposal based on this reasoning is that history-dependent interac-tions between meanings and practices would play a relatively larger role in stable situations while the reverse future-dependent interactions involving activities and beliefs towards the future might be of more importance in ambiguous and novel situations. In the former, experiential learning based on prior practices can potentially upgrade meanings and subsequently appropriate adjustments in practices can be made. In the latter, more crea-tive and imaginary learning based on new combinations of old practices, the application of them in new contexts or more fundamental change of them through new activities may be included. The emergence of new com-petitive positions would thus involve a combination of backward-looking experiential learning and forward-looking analysis of future consequences with the latter providing for more radical change (Gavetti and Levinthal, 2000; March, 1994). Indeed, it might be suggested that the former is more related to exploitation and what has been labeled adaptive strategy logics, and the latter is more related to exploration, labeled creative strategy logics (Regnér, 2005). In sum, it seems as if the dynamic interplay between and within the institutional- and firm-level practices/meanings and indi-vidual- and group-level activities/beliefs pairs may be fruitful arenas for strategic management research.

What might the managerial implications be from this two-level under-standing of competitive position emergence? It is clearly premature to draw any distinct conclusions, but some provisional recommendations might be tentatively suggested. First, managers should be reflexive around practices and meanings; question them and allow for other internal and external actors to do the same. Second, they should make sure that there are alternative activities/practices and beliefs/meanings available in the firm or in its immediate surroundings for easy access since changes in the competitive environment require alternative practices and meanings (Miller, 2003). Third, managers need to act and penetrate changes in the competitive environment rather than simply try to analyze and understand them, that is, to apply their strategic meanings as well as strategy practices in practice. The latter will generate possible insights, knowledge and changes that the former cannot.

Future research should examine the detailed interplay between micro-foundations and macro-conditions and within the activities/beliefs and meanings/practices pairs. While cognitive and institutional approaches to strategic management have started to address beliefs and meanings respectively, it is now time for the strategy-as-practice approach to add activities and practices and the interplay. Detailed empirical investigations of strategy development processes in terms of beliefs/meanings and activities/practices and their interaction are encouraged. This naturally calls for ethnographic approaches, but there are also possibilities of more formal methods of investigation (Mohr, 2005).

NOTE

1. The concept 'social theory' is primarily used here rather than 'sociology', but the differences between the concepts are not obvious. 'Social theory' relates to issues concerning human action, acting and interaction and their relation to institutions (Giddens, 1984: xvii). While these factors are part of sociology as well, humans need not be pivotal in social theory; events and configurations of the material and non-human are as important in an acknowledgment of the fact that activity and these latter factors are closely intertwined (Schatzki, 2002: 110–111). Moreover, 'social theory' is employed rather than 'sociology' since it is used in the intellectual roots of the practice approach (e.g. Giddens, 1984) and it is also the term it has hitherto employed (Jarzabkowski, 2004). Often 'social theory' is used as a broader interdisciplinary term compared to 'sociology' since ideas from a broad range of disciplines are considered and theorized about. In addition, it "involves the analysis of issues which spill over into philosophy" (Giddens, 1984: xvii), although not being primarily philosophical.

REFERENCES

Archer, M.S. (1982), 'Morphogenesis versus structuration: on combining structure and action', *British Journal of Sociology*, **33**, 455–483.
Balogun, J. and G. Johnson (2004), 'Organizational restructuring and middle manager sense-making', *Academy of Management Journal*, **47**, 523–549.
Barley, S.R. (1986), 'Technology as an occasion for structuring: evidence from observations of CT scanners and the social order of radiology departments', *Administrative Science Quarterly*, **28**, 78–108.

Barney, J. (1986), 'Strategic factor markets: expectations, luck, and business strategy', *Management Science*, **32**, 1231–1241.
Barney, J.B. (1991), 'Firm resources and sustained competitive advantage', *Journal of Management*, **17**, 99–120.
Barr, P.S., J.L. Stimpert and A.S. Huff (1992), 'Cognitive change, strategic action and organizational renewal', *Strategic Management Journal*, **13**, 15–36.
Bettis, R.A. and C.K. Prahalad (1995), 'The dominant logic: retrospective and extension', *Strategic Management Journal*, **16**, 5–14.
Bower, J.L. and Y. Doz (1979), 'Strategy formulation: a social and political process', in D.E. Schendel and C.W. Hofer (eds), *Strategic Management*, Boston: Little, Brown, pp. 152–166.
Bromiley, P. (ed.) (2005), *The Behavioral Foundation of Strategic Management*, Malden, MA, USA: Blackwell.
Burgelman, R.A. (1983), 'A process model of internal corporate venturing in the diversified major firm', *Administrative Science Quarterly*, **28**, 223–244.
Burgelman, R.A. (1991), 'Intraorganizational ecology of strategy making and organizational adaptation: theory and field research', *Organization Science*, **2** and **3**, 239–262.
Cockburn, I.M, R.M. Henderson and S. Stern (2000), 'Untangling the origins of competitive advantage', *Strategic Management Journal*, **21**, 1123–1145.
Cyert, R. and J.G. March (eds) (1963), *A Behavioral Theory of the Firm*, Englewood Cliffs, NJ: Prentice-Hall.
Deephouse, D.L. (1999), 'To be different, or to be the same? It's a question (and theory) of strategic balance', *Strategic Management Journal*, **20**, 147–166.
DiMaggio, P.J. and W.W. Powell (1983), 'The iron cage revisited: institutional isomorphism and collective rationality in organizational fields', *American Sociological Review*, **35**, 147–160.
Eisenhardt, K.M. and J.A. Martin (2000), 'Dynamic capabilities: what are they?', *Strategic Management Journal*, **21**, 1105–1121.
Emirbayer, M. and A. Mische (1998), 'What is agency?', *American Journal of Sociology*, 962–1023.
Feldman, M.S. (2000), 'Organizational routines as a source of continuous change', *Organization Science*, **11** (6), 611–629.
Feldman, M.S. and B.T. Pentland (2003), 'Reconceptualizing organizational routines as a source of flexibility and change', *Administrative Science Quarterly*, **39**, 484–510.
Felin, T. and N.J. Foss (2005), 'Strategic organization: a field in search of microfoundations', *Strategic Organization*, **3**, 441–455.
Gavetti, G. (2005), 'Cognition and hierarchy: rethinking microfoundations of capabilities development', *Organization Science*, **16**, 599–617.
Gavetti, G. and D. Levinthal (2000), 'Looking forward and looking backward: cognitive and experiential search', *Administrative Science Quarterly*, **45**, 113–137.
Giddens, A. (ed.) (1984), *The Constitution of Society*, Berkeley, CA: University of California Press.
Hambrick, D.C. (1981), 'Environment, strategy, and power within top management teams', *Administrative Science Quarterly*, **26**, 253–276.
Hendry, J. and D. Seidl (2003), 'The structure and significance of strategic episodes: social systems theory and the routine practices of strategic change', *Journal of Management Studies*, **40** (1).
Hogarth, R.M. and S. Makridakis (1981), 'Forecasting and planning: an evaluation', *Management Science*, **27**, 115–138.
Huff, A.S. (1982), 'Industry influence on strategy reformulation', *Strategic Management Journal*, **4**, 119–131.
Ingram, P. and B.S. Silverman (eds) (2002), *The New Institutionalism in Strategic Management*, Boston: JAI.
Jarzabkowski, P. (2004), 'Strategy as practice: recursiveness, adaptation, and practices-in-use', *Organization Studies*, **25**, 529–560.

Jarzabkowski, P. (ed.) (2005), *Strategy as Practice – an Activity Based View*, London: Sage.

Johnson, G. (ed.) (1987), *Strategic Change and the Management Process*, Oxford: Basil Blackwell.

Johnson, G., A. Langley, L. Melin and R. Whittington (eds) (2007), *The Practice of Strategy: Research Directions and Resources*, Cambridge, UK: Cambridge University Press.

Johnson, G., L. Melin and R. Whittington (2003), 'Micro strategy and strategizing: towards an activity-based view', *Journal of Management Studies*, **40** (1), 3–22.

Jonsson, S. and P. Regnér (2009), 'Normative barriers to imitation: social complexity of core competences in a mutual fund industry', *Strategic Management Journal*, **30** (5), 517–536.

Lyles, M.A. and C.R. Schwenk (1992), 'Top management, strategy and organizational knowledge structures', *Journal of Management Studies*, **29** (2).

March, J.G. (ed.) (1994), *A Primer on Decision Making – How Decisions Happen*, New York: The Free Press.

Miller, D. (2003), 'An asymmetry-based view of advantage – overcoming the sustainability-attainability dilemma', *Strategic Management Journal*, **24**, 961–975.

Mintzberg, H. (1978), 'Patterns in strategy formation', *Management Science*, **24**, 934–948.

Mohr, J.W. (2005), 'Implicit terrains: meaning, measurement, and spatial metaphors in organizational theory', in J.F. Porac and M. Ventresca (eds), *Constructing Industries and Markets*, New York: Elsevier, pp. 1–38.

Nelson, R. and S. Winter (eds) (1982), *An Evolutionary Theory of Economic Change*, London: The Belknap Press of Harvard University Press.

Oliver, C. (1991), 'Strategic responses to institutional processes', *Academy of Management Journal*, **16**, 145–179.

Oliver, C. (1997), 'Sustainable competitive advantage: combining institutional and resource based views', *Strategic Management Journal*, **18**, 697–713.

Orlikowski, W.J. (1992), 'The duality of technology: rethinking the concept of technology in organizations', *Organization Studies*, **3**, 398–427.

Pascale, R. (1984), 'Perspectives on strategy: the real story behind Honda's success', *California Management Review*, **26** (3), 47–72.

Pentland, B.T. and H.H. Rueter (1994), 'Organizational routines as grammars of action', *Administrative Science Quarterly*, **39**, 484–510.

Peteraf, M. and M. Shanley (2006), 'The centrality of process', *International Journal of Strategic Change Management*, **1**, 5–19.

Pettigrew, A.M. (ed.) (1985), *The Awakening Giant – Continuity and Change in Imperial Chemical Industries*, Oxford: Basil Blackwell.

Porac, J.F. and H. Thomas (1990), 'Taxonomic mental models in competitor definition', *Academy of Management Review*, **15**, 224–240.

Porac, J.F. and H. Thomas (2002), 'Managing cognition and strategy: issues, trends and future directions', in A. Pettigrew, H. Thomas and R. Whittington (eds), *Handbook of Strategy and Management*, London: Sage.

Porac, J.F., H. Thomas and C. Baden-Fuller (1989), 'Competitive groups as cognitive communities: the case of Scottish knitwear manufacturers', *Journal of Management Studies*, **26**, 397–416.

Porter, M.E. (ed.) (1980), *Competitive Strategy*, New York: The Free Press.

Porter, M.E. (ed.) (1981), 'The contributions of industrial organization to strategic management', *Academy of Management Review*, **6** (4), 609–620.

Pozzebon, M. (2004), 'The influence of a structurationist view on strategic management research', *Journal of Management Studies*, **41**, 247–272.

Reger, R.K. and A.S. Huff (1993), 'Strategic groups: a cognitive perspective', *Strategic Management Journal*, **14**, 103–124.

Regnér, P. (1999), *Strategy Creation and Change in Complexity – Adaptive and Creative Learning Dynamics in the Firm*, published doctoral dissertation, Institute of International Business, Stockholm, Sweden: Stockholm School of Economics.

Regnér, P. (2003), 'Strategy creation in the periphery: inductive versus deductive strategy making', *Journal of Management Studies*, **40** (1), 57–82.

Regnér, P. (2005), 'Adaptive and creative strategy logics in strategy processes', *Advances in Strategic Management*, **22**, 189–211.

Schatzki, T.R. (ed.) (2002), *The Site of the Social – a Philosophical Account of the Constitution of Social Life and Change*, Philadelphia: Pennsylvania University Press.

Schatzki, T.R., K. Knorr Certina and E. von Savigny (2001), *The Practice Turn in Contemporary Theory*, London: Routledge.

Schwenk, C.R. (1984), 'Cognitive simplification processes in strategic decision-making', *Strategic Management Journal*, **5**, 111–128.

Sewell, W.H.J. (1992), 'A theory of structure: duality, agency and transformation', *American Journal of Sociology*, **98** (1), 1–29.

Spender, J.C. (ed.) (1989), *Industry Recipes: The Nature and Sources of Managerial Judgement*, Oxford: Blackwell.

Tsoukas, H. and C. Knudsen (2002), 'The conduct of strategy research', in A. Pettigrew, H. Thomas and R. Whittington, *Handbook of Strategy and Management*, London: Sage.

Walsh, J. (1995), 'Managerial and organizational cognition: notes from a trip down memory lane', *Organizational Science*, **6** (3), 280–321.

Weick, K.E. (1979), *The Social Psychology of Organizing* (2nd edn), New York: Random House.

Weick, K.E. (ed.) (1995), *Sensemaking in Organizations*, Thousand Oaks, CA: Sage.

Whittington, R. (2003), 'The work of strategizing and organizing: for a practice perspective', *Strategic Organization*, **1** (1), 117–125.

Whittington, R. (2006), 'Completing the practice turn in strategy research', *Organization Studies*, **27**, 613–634.

Winter, S.G. (2003), 'Understanding dynamic capabilities', *Strategic Management Journal*, **24**, 991–995.

Zafirovski, M. (1999), 'Unification of sociological theory by the rational choice model: conceiving the relationships between economics and sociology', *Sociology*, **33** (3), 495–514.

10 Competitive dynamics stimulated by pioneers' technological innovation: a theoretical framework

Francesco Garraffo and Gwendolyn Lee

INTRODUCTION

This chapter provides a theoretical framework for the factors that influence the competitive dynamics stimulated by pioneers' technological innovation. The issues of competitive dynamics analyzed are: a) the speed and number of competitors' responses, and b) the nature of responses undertaken against the pioneer's innovation, in terms of imitation versus differentiation.

Adding to the literature on pioneers' market (dis)advantages and interfirm rivalry, this chapter provides some initial insights to the following fundamental question related to the competitive dynamics stimulated by pioneers' technological innovation:

What variables affect the speed and number of competitors' responses and the nature of their responses? Our answer to this question explains how the competitive dynamics stimulated by pioneers begins, and how it evolves over time. The theoretical bases of the analysis come from the literature on pioneers' market advantages and interfirm rivalry. The joint consideration of these two complementary research streams provides an explanation for the evolution of competition between the pioneer and its competitors.

Studies of pioneers' market (dis)advantages (Adner, 2002; Cooper and Schendel, 1976; Foster, 1986; Golder and Tellis, 1993; Lieberman and Montgomery, 1988 and 1998; Robinson and Fornell, 1985; Urban et al., 1986) and interfirm rivalry (Baum and Korn, 1996; Bettis and Weeks, 1987; Cooper and Smith, 1992; Cusumano et al., 1992; Gatignon et al., 1989; Karnany and Wernerfelt, 1985; Mylonadis and Rosenbloom, 1982; D'Aveni, 1994; Hill and Rothaermel, 2003; Peteraf, 1993; Porter, 1980 and 1985; Smith and Wilson, 1995) occupy a central position in strategy.

The literature on pioneers' market advantages includes investigations of sources of first movers' advantages (Lieberman and Montgomery, 1988) and disadvantages (Lieberman and Montgomery, 1998). Some studies have focused on the elements (industry characteristics, resource asymmetries, network externalities, managerial orientation, and so on) that influence pioneers' competitive and market advantages (Lambkin, 1988; Robinson and Fornell, 1985; Schilling, 2002; Sull, 1999; Urban et al., 1986), while others have examined competitors' ability to retaliate and seize pioneers' advantages (Cooper and Smith, 1992; Schnaars, 1994). Although these studies are well recognized and individually well developed, there have been few systematic attempts to integrate them into a framework that focuses on the speed and number of responses as well as on the choice between imitation and differentiation as competitive responses, where the responses are stimulated by the pioneer.

The theoretical framework developed in this chapter adds to the literature on pioneers' market advantages by analyzing the factors that affect competitors' response behaviors and performance outcomes. Specifically, this chapter focuses on competitive factors that affect the speed and number of competitors' responses. In addition, it integrates the literature on pioneers' market advantage with that on interfirm rivalry, highlighting the factors that affect the nature of competitors' response behaviors.

This chapter also contributes to managerial practice. The framework provides insights on variables (pioneers' market impact, competitors' information filter, pioneers' licensing policy, competitors' strength in internal and external complementary resources related to the old technology, and so on) that affect the competitive dynamics related to technological innovations. It also yields important implications for competitive factors that affect an incumbent's competitive advantage over time. For instance, the framework explains which elements affect the market advantage during the competition stimulated by pioneers' innovation.

The chapter begins with definitions of the concepts considered in the study, continues with the literature review, and presents a framework on factors that drive competitive dynamics stimulated by pioneers' technological innovation.

DEFINITIONS

The following are the key concepts used in this chapter:

Pioneer is a first mover introducing a technological innovation in the market.

Competitors are incumbents whose competitive position is threatened by pioneers' innovation.

Competitors' response behavior concerns any kind of differentiating or imitating action undertaken by incumbents against the pioneer (improvements in old technology, increases in marketing expenditure, innovation in products and processes, and so on).

Technological innovation considered covers only radical innovations, such as the iPhone, iTunes, iPod and iPad. Incremental innovations are excluded because competitors can generally easily imitate them. Instead, radical innovation can strongly affect an incumbent's competitive advantage because this innovation does not share any significant technology or component with previous products and requires vastly different manufacturing activities, organizational routines, and managerial competencies.

LITERATURE REVIEW

The literature review provided in this section on pioneers' market advantages and interfirm rivalry allows the identification of the main factors that researchers have already classified as drivers of competitive dynamics stimulated by pioneers' innovation.

According to the literature on pioneers' market advantages, first movers gain market share and profits when they are able to innovate in technology and the market, change customer preferences, and create switching costs (Lieberman and Montgomery, 1988; McGrath et al., 1996; Nehrt, 1998). The leverage on a specific set of resources (Lieberman and Montgomery, 1998; Teece, 1986), which are helpful for being a pioneer in technological innovation (Georghiou et al., 1986) and in the market (Robinson and Fornell, 1985), is a source (see Table 10.1).

In addition, some literature on the standard setting process (Abernathy and Utterback, 1978; Anderson and Tushman, 1990; David, 1985; Katz and Shapiro, 1992) is helpful in analyzing the competitive dynamics stimulated by pioneers' technological innovation because it highlights the specific factors that affect firms' behavior during the process in which the technological innovation competes against a standard. In industries characterized by network externalities (Schilling, 2002), timing, investments in core capabilities and absorptive capacities (Rosenbloom and Cumumano, 1987), imitation barriers, and complementary goods are factors affecting the competition between pioneers and competitors in a market (Schilling, 1998) (see Table 10.2).

Finally, the literature on interfirm rivalry is useful in highlighting competitive outcomes in terms of success or failure in competition against the pioneer (Henderson and Clark, 1990; Henderson, 1993). Although studies on interfirm rivalry vary on the type of incumbent behavior studied, the literature on interfirm rivalry in general reveals elements of

Table 10.1 Literature on first-mover (dis)advantages

Author and title	Issue/research question	Industry/market	Main findings
Lieberman, M.B. and D.B. Montgomery (1988), 'First-mover advantages', *Strategic Management Journal*, vol.9, Special Issue: Strategy Content Research, pp. 41–58.	What are first-mover's advantages? What conditions allow for the creation of these advantages? Do first movers earn extra profits? When is it convenient to pursue first-mover opportunities and when is it best to leave these to competitors?	Several high-tech and low-tech examples	The conclusions are based upon the following considerations: 1. Definition of the first-mover advantage generation process 2. Potential advantages of the first mover, related to: product or process technology leadership, the development of customer switching costs 3. Potential first-mover disadvantages (which represent advantages for the late movers) are related to: free riding, technological discontinuity which proved opportunities for new entries 4. Fundamental conceptual and measurement aspects (for example, the definition of 'first mover', the measurement of first-mover advantages in terms of profits, market share and probability of survival).

| Teece, D.J. (1986), 'Profiting from technological innovation: implications for integration, collaboration, licensing and public policy', *Research Policy*, **15**, pp. 285–305. | The article seeks to explain the reason as to why innovative firms are not always capable of acquiring economic advantages from introducing an innovation, while consumers, imitators, and other market operators are able to obtain benefits. The primary role of 'complementary assets' is highlighted. | Electric musical instruments, chemical industry, computer science | The article underlines how, in markets in which imitative processes occur, it is probable that economic benefits derived from innovation are acquired by firms which detain 'complementary assets' rather than those that develop the innovation. The author underlines how innovating firms must have access to 'relevant specialized and co-specialized assets' by means of collaborative relations with firms which produce them, in order to limit imitation processes. |
| Georghiou, L., M. Gibbons and J.S. Metcalfe (1986), 'Staying the distance – technological development and competition', *International Journal of Technology Management*, **1**, (3–4), pp. 425–439. | Evaluation of competitive processes with regards to incremental innovations. | 35 innovators in high-tech and low-tech industries | In the case of sequential innovations, a firm may be both a follower and a leader throughout the technology development cycle. The first mover, in order to maintain economic advantages, must be capable of rapidly imagining and implementing a sequence of incremental improvements to the new technology, coherent with consumer expectations. |

Table 10.1 (continued)

Author and title	Issue/research question	Industry/market	Main findings
McGrath, R.G., M.H. Tsai, S. Venkataraman and I.C. MacMillan (1996), 'Innovation, competitive advantage and rent: a model and test', *Management Science*, **42** (3), pp. 389–403.	Which factors allow an innovating firm to acquire sustainable competitive advantages?	58 projects regarding innovation under-taken by 40 firms operating in 8 countries	The possibility that a firm has to extract value from an innovation is related to the possibility to acquire, through the innovation itself, sustainable competitive advantages. The creation of these advantages depends on the capability of the firms to create distinctive innovations (distinctive efficiency), judged positively by the market.
Lieberman, M.B. and D.B. Montgomery (1998), 'First-mover (dis)advantages: retrospective and link with the resource-based view', *Strategic Management Journal*, **19** (12), pp. 1111–1125.	The authors examine the relation between empirical results and research conducted with regards to first-mover advantages, on the one hand, and the developments of the resource-based view on the other.	None	The authors underline the importance of uniting the first-mover advantage doctrine with the resource-based view and identify potential synergies between the two. In particular, the first may provide the empirical anchorage that the second is in need of. The resource-based view, on the other hand, is capable of providing a substantial theoretical framework which may be useful in projecting a more detailed analysis on the timing of entry.

Nehr, C. (1998), 'Maintainability of first mover advantages when environmental regulations differ between countries', *The Academy of Management Review*, **23** (1), pp. 77–98.	1. Are first-mover advantages maintainable when a firm competes with a rival that operates in a market regulated in a less restricted manner? 2. What factors determine this maintainability?	Anti-pollution technologies	First-mover advantages may exist even when confronting firms which operate in markets that are regulated in a less restrictive manner. It is the management's responsibility to study the market's specific conditions in order to verify ways in which the firm can acquire first-mover advantages regardless of non favourable regulations.
Robinson, W.T. and C. Fornell (1985), 'Sources of market pioneer advantages in consumer goods industries', **XXII**.	What is the relation between order of entry and market share?	371 consumer good markets	Order of entry is a major determinant of market share for a broad cross section of consumer goods businesses. Specifically, firm-based superiority as well as consumer information advantages result in long-term market share advantages for pioneers relative to late entrants.

Table 10.2 Literature on standard setting processes

Author and title	Issue/research question	Industry/market	Main findings
Abernathy, W.J. and J.M. Utterback (1978), 'Patterns of industrial innovation', *Technology Review*, **80** (7).	The combined evolution of process and product innovation following the introduction of a new technology.	Semiconductors, aeronautics, lamps, automobiles, food industry	Abernathy and Utterback propose a model which reconstructs the combined evolution of process and product innovation that take place following the introduction of new technologies. The three phases of the model are as follows: 1. Fluid Pattern; 2. Transitional Pattern; 3. Specific Pattern.
David, P. (1985), 'Clio and the economics of QWERTY', *American Economic Review*, **75** (2), pp. 332–337.	What conditions provoke an industry to consolidate an 'inefficient' technology?	Computer industry	Network externalities and the attempt to maintain compatibility among diverse technologies are among the elements that favor the premature decision of an industry to consolidate an 'inefficient technology'.
Rosenbloom, R.S. and M.A. Cusumano (1987), 'Technological pioneering and competitive advantage: the birth of the VCR industry', *California Management Review*, **29** (4), pp. 51–76.	Analysis of firms' success in relation to the development process of new technologies that favor new industry creation.	Historiographic analysis of the birth, development and affirmation of a new technology	Firms which are successful in developing new technological standards are those which possess the ability to: 1. correctly and constantly identify new market opportunities 2. maintain an elevated productivity of technical divisions 3. implement, in an efficient manner and through learning processes, the development of different technological components.

Reference	Focus	Examples	Summary
Anderson, P. and M.L. Tushman (1990), 'Technological discontinuities and dominant designs: a cyclical model of technological change', *Administrative Science Quarterly*, **35** (4), pp. 604–633.	If and when technological discontinuity generates the affirmation of a dominant design.	Cement; glass; minicomputer	Technological change is comprised of a series of phases. Technological discontinuity is followed by a period of instability, which concludes with the creation of a dominant design. Successively, a period begins in which incremental technological change takes place. This period continues until technological discontinuation does not take place again. Summary: 1. Discontinuity; 2. Period of instability; 3. Dominant design; 4. Period of incremental change; 5. New discontinuity.
Katz, M.L. and C. Shapiro (1992), 'Product introduction with network externalities', *Journal of Industrial Economics*, **40** (1), pp. 55–83.	Analysis of product introduction onto markets characterized by network externalities.	None	The authors reveal how, in a market characterized by network externalities, the development of technologies which are compatible with those existing is conditioned by the nature of property rights and by the availability of license contracts.

Table 10.2   (continued)

Author and title	Issue/research question	Industry/market	Main findings
Schilling, M.A. (1998), 'Technological lockout: an integrative model of the economic and strategic factors driving technology success and failure', *The Academy of Management Review*, **23** (2), pp. 267–284.	Following a technological innovation, which factors favour market exclusion?	Software, semiconductors, microprocessors, video	Research propositions explain the exclusion of firms from the market provoked by the decision to utilize a standard which the market refuses or by the incapability of accessing an existing technological standard. The propositions address the following factors: timing, network externalities, failures regarding investments in the accumulation of core capabilities and absorptive capabilities, imitation barriers, complementary goods.
Schilling, M.A. (2002), 'Technology success and failure in winner-take-all-market: the impact of learning orientation, timing, and network externalities', *Academy of Management Journal*, **45** (2), pp. 387–398.	Which factors reduce a technological standard's probability of failure?	89 cases regarding various sectors (bicycles, computers, word processors, etc.) in the USA	In industries characterized by network externalities, competitive factors that reduce the probability of failure of a new technological standard are represented by: the number of users, the availability of complementary technologies, the orientation of a leader company towards continuous learning, and timing.

competitors' behavioral homogeneity in the circumstance of a pioneer's technological innovation (Cooper and Schendel, 1976). The timing of response and the number of competitors' responses are affected by a pioneer's market strategy (Chen, 1996), as well as incumbents' managerial cognition (Tripsas and Gavetti, 2000), which retards competitors' response (Christensen and Bower, 1996). Moreover, the competitors' response behavior, in spite of patent protection systems (Mansfield and Schwartz, 1981), and more generally pioneer's isolating barriers (Reed and De Filippi, 1990), can vary between two extremes of imitating (Banbury and Mitchell, 1995) and differentiating behavior according to the effect of economic, strategic, and organizational factors (Hill and Rothaermel, 2003) (see Table 10.3).

THEORETICAL FRAMEWORK

On the basis of the literature review, we find that the evolution of competition between the pioneer and the incumbents is affected by several factors that drive the speed, number, and nature of competitors' responses. In this section, we will characterize the dynamics of competition as a two-step sequence in analyzing the incumbents' competitive responses. The analysis of how competitive responses change in two steps will lead to a better understanding of if, when, and how incumbents respond to pioneers' technological innovation. The two steps in our analysis are:

1) the factors that affect the speed and number of competitors' responses to a pioneer's innovation, and
2) the factors that affect the nature of competitors' response behavior to a pioneer's innovation.

THE FACTORS THAT AFFECT THE SPEED AND NUMBER OF COMPETITORS' RESPONSES

The speed and number of responses depend on each competitor's awareness and motivation to respond to a pioneer's innovation. According to the literature on first-mover (dis)advantages and interfirm rivalry, two groups of variables affect the dynamics of a competitor's response: characteristics of the pioneer's market strategy (Chen, 1996; Chen et al., 1992) and filters affecting the competitors' decision-making processes (Ansoff, 1984; Bower and Christensen, 1995; Christensen, 1997; Tripsas and Gavetti, 2000).

Table 10.3 Literature on interfirm rivalry and incumbents' behavior

Author and title	Issue/research question	Industry/market	Main findings
Cooper, A.C. and D. Schendel (1976), 'Strategic responses to technological threats', *Business Horizons*, **19** (1), pp. 61–69.	Decision processes that are at the base of incumbents' responses to radical technological innovation.	Locomotive, stenographic pens, razors, leather goods, carbon heaters	When facing radical technological innovation, incumbents' behavior varies, from case to case. However, research carried out by Cooper and Schendel reveals elements of incumbents' behavioral homogeneity in the circumstance of a pioneer's technological innovation. Firms threatened by innovation often adopt a cautious 'wait and see' posture. A strong commitment towards improving existing technology is observed among firms during and after the introduction of the innovation.
Mansfield, E., M. Schwartz and S. Wagner (1981), 'Imitation costs and patents: an empirical study', *The Economic Journal*, **91** (364), pp. 907–918.	Analysis of the role and costs of imitative processes and the evaluation of the effects of those processes on firms' inclination towards introducing new technologies.	Chemical, pharmaceutical, electric and machinery sectors	In spite of patent protection systems, the imitative process is not easily controllable. In fact, this process greatly reduces firms' inclination towards developing new technologies.
Henderson, R.M. and K.B. Clark (1990), 'Architectural innovation: the reconfiguration of existing product	The traditional distinction between incremental and radical innovations is incomplete and potentially misleading. In particular, it is not useful	Photolithographic equipment	The concept of 'architectural innovation' is defined. This concept does not stem from a change in product components, but from a change in the relations among those same components. This type of innovation may have very significant effects such as the destruction

technologies and the failure of established firms', *Administrative Science Quarterly*, **35** (1), pp. 9–30.	in explaining the disastrous consequences that apparently marginal technological improvements may have with regards to incumbents belonging to a specific sector.		of an affirmed organization's patrimony of productive knowledge. The destruction process is both difficult to identify and stop.
Reed, R. and **R.J. De Filippi** (1990), 'Causal ambiguity, barriers to imitation and sustainable competitive advantage', *The Academy of Management Review*, **15** (1), pp. 88–102.	The role of a firm's resources and competences in the creation of imitation barriers that favor the sustainability of competitive advantages.	None	The authors propose a thesis which states that continuous investments in causally ambiguous competencies which favor tacitness, complexity and specificity create imitation barriers and therefore allow for the creation of a sustainable competitive advantage. Reed and De Filippi's work concludes with regard the relation between: a. Ambiguity and tacitness with regards to core competencies and the interaction among competencies. b. The creation of imitation barriers and the interaction among tacitness, complexity and specificity. c. The sustainability of the competitive advantage based upon distinctive competencies and the re-investment in competencies characterized by tacitness, complexity and specificity.

Table 10.3 (continued)

Author and title	Issue/research question	Industry/market	Main findings
Henderson, R. (1993), 'Underinvestment and incompetence as responses to radical innovation: evidence from the photolithographic alignment equipment industry', *RAND Journal of Economics*, **24** (2), pp. 248–270.	The causes of firms' failure when attempting to respond to threats provoked by technological innovation.	Photolithographic equipment industry	Henderson concludes that it is possible to comprehend why existing firms fail to respond to technological innovation by taking into consideration neoclassic theories and those resulting from research regarding capability accumulation and development processes. In fact, failure is caused by the firms' incapability of undertaking investments regarding technological innovation and accumulating competences that allow for the improvement and development of technology performance.
Banbury, C.M. and W. Mitchell (1995), 'The effect of introducing important incremental innovations on market share and business survival', *Strategic Management Journal*, **16**, pp. 161–182.	The authors analyze the effects that the introduction of incremental innovation or the adoption of incremental innovation introduced by competitors have on market share and survival of an incumbent.	Pacemakers	If an incumbent is among one of the first firms to introduce a significant incremental innovation, its market share will grow significantly. The adoption of an incremental innovation launched by a competitor will also have a positive, yet weaker, effect on the firm's market share. The market share increase generated by the introduction of an incremental innovation significantly contributes towards firm survival.

| Christensen, C.M. and J.L. Bower (1996), 'Customer power, strategic investment, and the failure of leading firms', *Strategic Management Journal*, **17** (3), pp. 197–218. | Why do well-managed companies often lose their leadership when faced with technological change? | Disk drives | The failure of solid firms that face technological changes is not a matter of competences. Rather, it is a question of investment policies. The authors analyze a series of cases in which successful companies developed a series of innovations in order to satisfy customer needs. Those same companies did not develop other technologies that (initially) seemed effective only with regards to emerging markets. The firms' projects were therefore characterized by a lack of resources and motivation. Technologies which initially appear only to be effective with regards to emerging markets may, however, invade principal markets and therefore determine the success of new entrants. |
| Tripsas, M. and G. Gavetti (2000), 'Capabilities, cognition, and inertia: evidence from digital imaging', *Strategic Management Journal*, **21** (10–11), pp. 1147–1161. | The influence of managerial cognition on the evolution of firm capability and, therefore, organizational inertia. | Digital imaging | Managerial cognition greatly influences the development of new capabilities through decisions regarding activities connected to technology development. The analysis of the inertial forces associated with the development of new capabilities and the impact that managerial cognition has on those same processes allows for an understanding of organization change processes. |

Table 10.3 (continued)

Author and title	Issue/research question	Industry/market	Main findings
Chen, M.J. (1996), 'Competitor analysis and interfirm rivalry: toward a theoretical integration', *The Academy of Management Review*, **21** (1), pp. 100–134.	The examination of factors which allow one to foresee the probability that a firm will react to attacks deriving from its competitors.	Air transportation	In order to foresee the probability that a firm will react to attacks from competitors, the author creates the concept of market commodity based on 'multiple-point competition' and the concept of resource similarity based on the resource-based view. Chen's reflections are followed by a series of research propositions that take into consideration: a. The relation between probability of attack and market commonality b. The relation between probability of attack and resource similarity c. The possibility that market commonality represents a stronger indicator rather than resource similarity.
Hill, C.W.L. and F.T. Rothaermel (2003), 'The performance of incumbent firms in the face of radical technological innovation', *The Academy of Management Review*, **28** (2), pp. 257–274.	Which factors moderate the decline of economic performance of companies that take on a radical technological innovation?	X-rays, computers, DNA	The authors propose a series of research propositions which take into consideration the nature of economic, strategic, and organizational factors. These factors explain the way in which existing companies acquire benefits generated by radical technological innovation.

Characteristics of a Pioneer's Market Strategy

As is largely considered in theory and practice, a new technology increases uncertainty about market opportunities and technology evolution. In this perspective, characteristics of a pioneer's market strategy provide meaningful information for the competitors in assessing the level of uncertainty and deciding whether and when to respond.

We introduce market impact, competitive pressure, and attack intensity as three stimulus factors that capture the characteristics of a pioneer's market strategy:

(a) market impact, which concerns the number of competitors' businesses threatened by the pioneer
(b) competitive pressure, which concerns the competitors' market share threatened by the pioneer
(c) attack intensity, which concerns the competitors' profits threatened by the pioneer.

Depending on the degrees of competitors' businesses, market share, and profits threatened, the characteristics of a pioneer's market strategy affect, positively or negatively, the speed and number of competitors' responses.

Filters of Competitors' Decision-making Process

Competitors' responses are a consequence of a decision-making process that affects the speed and the number of responses. During the decision-making process a group of filters affects the competitor's final decision. A filter captures the competitor's awareness of the threat/opportunity and motivation to respond. We introduce information, cognition, and power filters as three response factors that may characterize competitors' behavior:

(a) information filter: competitors' perception of threats/opportunities coming from the environment
(b) cognition filter: competitors' resource allocation process patterns
(c) power filter: competitors' managerial skills and power threatened by the innovation.

Depending on the effect of information, cognition, and power filters, the competitors' decision-making process affects, positively or negatively, the speed and number of competitors responding to a pioneer's innovation.

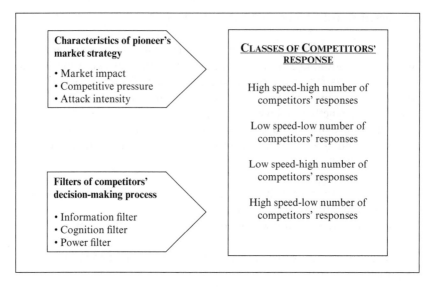

*Figure 10.1   A theoretical framework: factors affecting classes of
competitors' response*

How the characteristics of a pioneer's market strategy and filters of competitors' decision-making processes affect the speed and number of competitors' responses can be organized into four classes (See Figure 10.1):

I – high speed and high number of responses
II – low speed and low number of responses
III – low speed but high number of responses
IV – high speed but low number of responses.

In this perspective, the class of competitive dynamics following a pioneer's innovation depends on how the filters of competitors' decision-making process affect the way they consider as a threat/opportunity the pioneer's innovation and market strategy.

FACTORS THAT AFFECT THE NATURE OF COMPETITORS' RESPONSE BEHAVIOR

During the process with which competitors become aware of a pioneer's innovation and are motivated to respond, separate factors affect the decision of whether to imitate the pioneer or differentiate from it. According to the literature on pioneers' market advantages and interfirm rivalry,

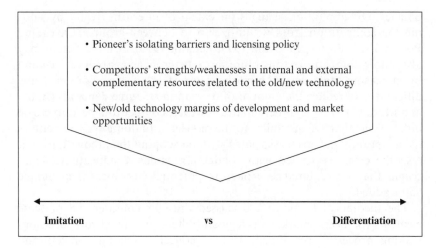

Figure 10.2   A theoretical framework: factors affecting the nature of competitors' response behavior

the nature of a competitor's response is dependent on: the pioneer's decision to make higher or lower costs of imitation (Reed and De Filippi, 1990; MacMillan, 1983; Mansfield et al., 1981), the competitor's stock of complementary resources related to the old technology compared to that associated with the new one (Teece, 1986; Robinson and Fornell, 1985; Robinson et al., 1992), and the evolution of market opportunities and technology developments concerning the new technology compared to the old one (Abernathy and Utterback, 1978; Anderson and Tushman, 1990; David, 1985; Katz and Shapiro, 1992).

In summary, competitors' response behavior depends on (see Figure 10.2):

(a) a pioneer's isolating barriers and licensing policy
(b) competitors' strengths and weaknesses in internal and external complementary resources related to the old technology compared to those associated with the new one
(c) the difference between the new and old technology in terms of the margins of development and market opportunities.

These factors affect a competitor's choice of whether to imitate or differentiate from the pioneer. Competitors may decide to imitate because factors listed above reduce the costs and risks of market entry. However, instead of imitating a pioneer's innovation, competitors may decide to differentiate from it. They may develop a rival technology and/or promote responses based on new competitive strategies and marketing policies. Differentiation changes the extent of interfirm rivalry by shifting the competition from within-group to between-groups (Caves and Porter, 1977; Porter, 1976 and 1979; Peteraf, 1993). Being different may also allow competitors to capture more heterogeneous market demand by increasing the size of the market (Porter, 1980). In addition, being different may reduce the amount of overlap in resource demands (Baum and Mezias, 1992). To differentiate, however, competitors need to create innovations that are dissimilar to the pioneer's. In doing so, competitors incur not only the costs associated with developing the innovations, but also the costs associated with conducting extensive educational campaigns that are required to explain to potential customers their unique value added.

The theoretical framework discussed thus far considers all of these elements (pioneers' market strategy and filters of competitors' decision-making process – see Figure 10.1 – pioneer's isolating barriers and licensing policy, competitors' strengths and weaknesses in internal and external complementary resources, and margins of development and market opportunities of new and old technology – see Figure 10.2) working as a blueprint of factors affecting the competitive dynamics stimulated by a pioneer's technological innovation. The following discussion will further explain, with illustrative examples, each group of factors that affect the speed and number of competitors' responses and the nature of their response behavior.

THE FACTORS THAT AFFECT THE SPEED AND NUMBER OF COMPETITORS' RESPONSES

Characteristics of a Pioneer's Market Strategy

The pioneer's market strategy aims at gaining competitive advantage but, at the same time, affects the competitors' awareness of the threat or opportunity and motivation to respond. Specifically, characteristics of a pioneer's market strategy provide useful information for competitors' analysis of uncertainty and decision of whether and when to respond.

The main characteristics of a pioneer's market strategy that affect the competitors' awareness and motivation to respond are: (a) the market impact, in terms of the number of competitors' businesses threatened by the pioneer, (b) the competitive pressure, in terms of the competitors' market share threatened by the pioneer, and (c) the attack intensity, in terms of the competitors' profits threatened by the pioneer (Chen, 1996; Chen et al., 1992).

Some pioneers' market strategies involve few businesses and affect only a handful of competitors (low market impact), while others are more pervasive (high market impact). Moreover, the competitors' market share threatened by the pioneer can be significant in certain cases because competitors are leaders or co-leaders (high competitive pressure). Finally, the competitors' profits threatened by the pioneer can be substantial (high attack intensity).

A pervasive and intense pioneer's market strategy makes competitors more likely to react. Although competitors may initially be uncertain of the threat and/or opportunities generated by the new technology, the high pervasiveness and intensity of a pioneer's strategy will tend to impel them to react.

Once a few competitors respond, others will tend to follow (soon after), creating a snowball effect (Chen et al., 1992; Farrell and Saloner, 1985). This effect enhances the likelihood that other competitors will react because each reaction represents, by itself, a new threat in the market.

The snowball effect in terms of growing number and speed of reactions is frequent in several industries both for consumer products (electronics, computers, software, and video games) (Cusumano et al., 1992) and industrial products (medical, office automation, telecommunications, wireless, networking, automotive, and industrial equipment) (Schnaars, 1994).

Market impact

The pioneer's decision about the number of businesses targeted has a positive effect on the speed and number of competitors' reactions. First, the decision affects the number of competitors that react because, in general, the more businesses targeted, the higher the likelihood that more competitors are threatened. If the pioneer applies its technological innovation in only one business, as opposed to two, three, or more, it competes against a smaller number of rivals.

The decision to apply its innovation across a larger number of businesses also increases the likelihood that more multi-market-contact competitors become threatened. When the pioneer threatens a larger number of competitors which compete against the pioneer across multiple businesses, the speed of response increases with the pervasiveness of the threat (multipoint competition) (Gimeno and Woo, 1996; Karnani and Wernerfelt, 1985).

When EMI pioneered the CAT scanner in the US market, the market impact of its strategy was really high because EMI simultaneously targeted the three main groups of US customers: small hospitals and specialists, medium hospitals, and big hospitals. The pervasiveness of EMI's competitive strategy stimulated, after one year, reactions from four competitors, ten reactions after two years, and 15 reactions after three years (Abell, 1978). The Bowmar Instrument Corporation of Fort Wayne pioneered the pocket calculator in the US market in the early 1970s. In only one year, 12 new entrants followed Bowmar's instant success in the most attractive market in the world (Schnaars, 1994). Amazon opened its website in 1995, Barnes & Noble inaugurated its first wide-range website in 1996, and other competitors followed in 1997 (Borders, Ingram, and Simon & Schuster).

Competitive pressure
Whereas the market impact concerns the pervasiveness of the pioneer's competitive strategy, the competitive pressure and attack intensity focus on how strongly the pioneer's competitive strategy affects each competitor's market position.

The pioneer's threat to the competitors' market share may increase the speed of competitors' responses and, by this effect, the number of reactions. When customers' switching costs are low, they can easily switch to a pioneer's new technology if competitors do not have it (Lieberman and Montgomery, 1988). In these circumstances, the pioneer can seize or seriously threaten the competitors' market share, and the likelihood of a speedy response is high due to the risk of their survival in the market.

This phenomenon occurs faster when the pioneer attacks the leader. If the leader reacts, other competitors will soon follow in a chain reaction triggered by the pioneer and fed by the leader. The chain reaction affects the number of competitors that react as well. Whenever the pioneer stimulates a speedy counteraction, this reaction alone impels other competitors to react. However, it is important to recognize that, in several circumstances, competitors' sales and market share do not decline immediately and can continue to grow for a relatively long time. In many cases, competitive advantages that come from a new technology are not immediate and self-moving. Initially, the new technology has typical low performances that appeal to particular customers (Utterback and Kim, 1986). The length of time in which the new technology becomes adopted can vary widely. In some cases, the new technology immediately penetrates the entire market. In other cases, it needs some improvements before it becomes appealing to the mass market. In the latter case, the pioneer imposes a lower competitive pressure. As such, the competitive dynamics would belong to the class of low speed and low number of competitors' responses.

ENIAC/UNIVAC pioneered the mainframe computer in the American market and its computers sought to replace punch card machines, sorters, mechanical tabulators, and printers, all businesses dominated by IBM. Although ENIAC/UNIVAC had a relative market success, IBM did not take any significant countermeasures for several years and reacted after seven years because the pioneer did not threaten its market share in the old businesses for a long time (Schnaars, 1994).

Attack intensity

Finally, the competitors' profits threatened or seized by the pioneer can increase the speed and number of responses. The attack intensity reflects the degree to which the current and future profitability of a given competitor is threatened by the pioneer. The level of threat depends on whether competitors are mono- or multi-business. When competitors are mono-business, the level of threat tends to be higher due to the 'mono-source' of profits; hence, the threat stimulates more and speedier responses. Moreover, the number of responses can be enhanced by the reaction of other competitors. In these circumstances, the competitive dynamics stimulated by the pioneer would belong to the class of high speed and high number of competitors' responses.

If competitors are multi-business, the level of threat depends on the importance of the strategic business unit (SBU) threatened by the pioneer. When the SBU is less important, the competitors' reaction tends to be slower. In these circumstances, the competitive dynamics stimulated by the pioneer would belong to the class of low speed and low number of competitors' responses.

Within two years of Michelin selling its radial tire in the US market all the US tire makers (Goodyear, Firestone, Uniroyal, BF Goodrich, and General), all mono-business firms, reacted to the French manufacturer's innovation. In this case, the threat of Michelin's radial tires impelled the largest mono-business US manufacturers to place a speedy counteraction against this radical innovation (Sull, 1999).

Filters that Affect Competitors' Decision-making Processes

The fact that a pioneer innovates does not automatically mean that the competitors become aware of the threat or opportunity and are then motivated to react (Schelling, 1960). Even if the characteristics of a pioneer's market strategy should lead to a specific class of dynamics of response, it is also possible that a competitor might decide not to respond for specific reasons such as strategic redirection, major resource commitments, or portfolio position (MacMillan, 1988). If a competitor decides to respond, the following three types of filter attenuate the decision-making process with which the competitor considers whether the new technology is a threat or opportunity, becomes motivated to react, and decides when to respond: (a) information filters; (b) cognition filters; and (c) power filters.

Information filters

An effective response requires a clear perception of the competitive environment. This perception comes from the methods for evaluating the environment. Competitors can adopt different evaluation methods: (a) business, economic, or technological forecasting (extrapolation, multiple regression, curve fitting, scenarios, competitive analysis, Delphi, asymptotic analysis, threats and opportunities analysis); (b) models of the environment (input-output, econometric, cybernetic, and stochastic); and (c) estimation of impact (impact analysis, cross impact analysis, deductive analysis, and force field analysis). The effectiveness of each method depends on the type of forecast. In particular, some methods may misrepresent the environmental conditions when the environment changes. As Ansoff says: "the environmental surveillance and analysis techniques can be viewed as a filter through which the environmental information must pass on its way into the firm" (Ansoff, 1984).

The effect of information filters can be summarized in this example that Cooper and Schendel refer to:

> In 1934, when General Motors introduced the first mainline diesel-electric locomotive, the producers of steam locomotives could look back upon two earlier threats which they had survived: the electric locomotive, and, in the 1920s, passenger cars with individual gasoline-powered engines. Both of these prior threats captured only small segments of the American locomotive market. According to the methods used by the producers of steam locomotives in the control of competitive conditions, there was no indication that the next threat, the diesel-electric, would destroy the industry within fifteen years.
>
> (Cooper & Schendel, 1976)

Managers of steam locomotive firms were not aware of the threat because the environment changed and increased the effect of the information filter.

Cognition filter

Even if the methods for evaluating the environment give meaningful information on a threat or opportunity, managers of threatened firms can reject this information or consider it to be irrelevant (Tripsas and Gavetti, 2000). Sociological and psychological literatures explain this behavior with the concept of 'mindset'. Managers who experience successes and failures cumulate convictions about 'things that do work' and 'things that do not'. These convictions represent a cognition filter that becomes critical whenever from the competitive environment brings a threat that changes the 'things that do work'.

In several articles, Bower and Christensen tell how Seagate lost its market after a disruptive technology came into the disk drive industry.

They discuss how senior managers quite rationally decided that the 3.5-inch drive would not provide the sales volume and profit margins that Seagate needed from a new product. As a former Seagate marketing executive recalled, "we needed a new model that could become the next ST412. At the time, the entire market for 3.5-inch drivers was less than $50 million. The 3.5-inch drive just didn't fit the bill – for sale or profits" (Bower and Christensen, 1995). The 'things that do work' for Seagate's managers were markets that fit the bill – for sale or profits. Even though Seagate's revenues of 5.25-inch drives had grown to more than $700 million by 1986, sales of 8 and 5.25-inch products had largely evaporated by 1987.

Sometimes, the well-established patterns of resource allocation (in strategic planning, budgeting, and marketing or manufacturing planning (Bower, 1970)) among competitors that have been effective in the past become unexpectedly ineffective. As Sull states in his analysis of the rubber industry after the advent of radials, "Firestone had in place a bottom-up capital budgeting process that excelled in adding new production capacity in response to growing demand." After the advent of radials, "Firestone's bottom-up capital budgeting process, which promoted investment so smoothly, unfortunately stalled in reverse and therefore hindered the company from closing unnecessary factories" (Sull, 1999). Bower and Christensen have described the same situation when Seagate's management was deciding whether to produce the 3.5-inch drives:

> According to manufacturing and financial executives' analysis, the new drives would never be competitive with the 5.25-inch architecture on a cost-per-megabyte basis . . . . Senior managers quite rationally decided that the 3.5-inch drive would not provide the sales volume and profit margins that Seagate needed from a new product.
>
> (Bower and Christensen, 1995)

Power filter

Finally, technological discontinuities have major implications for the power of managers. As Ansoff states, "it's natural for managers and departments, whose power base is threatened by a discontinuity, to minimize or even refuse to recognize the impact of the discontinuity on the firm" (Ansoff, 1984). Moreover, even if a technological innovation is not a threat to the power structure, the management can refuse to recognize the innovation because it represents a threat to employees and host communities. These phenomena work as a power filter.

As Cooper and Schendel discussed in their study of seven industries threatened by new technologies, it was common for the spokespersons of traditional firms to emphasize the shortcomings of new technology with comments such as "It is no wonder the public feels that the steam locomotive is about to lay down and play dead" and "It is certain that substantially all airplanes which operate at speeds of 550 mph or less will use propeller propulsion" (Cooper and Schendel, 1976). The managers of these industries were conditioned not only by their involvement with old technology, but also by their skills and positions of influence inside the threatened firms. For these reasons, they minimized the threat and initially acted as if nothing had happened.

The effect of these two groups of factors (characteristics of a pioneer's market strategy and filters of competitors' decision-making process) explain the timing and number of early movers, followers, and late movers.

While the characteristics of a pioneer's market strategy affect the likelihood of a specific class of competitors' response, the filters of competitors' decision-making process influence the timing of each competitor's response as well as the specific response undertaken. The managerial power structure can lead to a specific response that fits with the managers' power or with stakeholder or local community interests, but is inconsistent with the new competitive conditions.

According to this, Sull argues that "Firestone's middle managers had no incentive to promote plant closures that jeopardized their jobs and communities. . . Instead of proposing plant closure, middle managers presented proposals for capacity additions and upgrades to improve their operations" (Sull, 1999).

FACTORS THAT AFFECT THE NATURE OF COMPETITORS' RESPONSE BEHAVIOR

The Nature of Competitors' Response Behavior

When competitors decide to respond, their response behavior can vary widely between two extremes, where imitation represents one end of the spectrum and differentiation represents the other. The more similar the competitors' technology and market strategy are to the pioneers', the more 'imitative' the competitors' responses. And the more dissimilar the competitors' technology and market strategy from the pioneers', the more 'differentiating' the competitors' responses.

As already introduced earlier in this chapter, the following factors affect the decision of each competitor:

(a) the pioneer's isolating barriers and licensing policy
(b) competitors' strengths and weaknesses in internal and external

complementary resources related to the old technology compared to those associated with the new technology

(c) the difference between the new and old technology in terms of the margins of development and new technology market opportunities.

When costs and risks of imitation are increased by these factors, competitors will decide to differentiate rather than imitate.

A Pioneer's Isolating Barriers and Licensing Policy

A pioneer's isolating barriers may increase both costs of imitation and costs of accessing the market related to the new technology. Vice versa, the licensing policy may decrease the costs of imitation and costs of accessing the new market.

The costs of imitation can increase with secrets, patenting, R&D investments, and learning or experience curves (Ghemawat and Spence, 1985). Important isolating barriers are managerial and organizational routines that the pioneer can develop because of the lead time it enjoys. When isolating barriers such as secrets, patents, R&D investments, and learning or experience curves are effective, competitors need more time and must invest more resources (financial, technological, legal, and so on) in imitating the knowledge related to the new technology.

Xerox's patenting policy allowed the firm to defend its first-mover advantages for a long time. To defend the knowledge on the basic Xerography process, Xerox patented a group of substitutive technologies, which defended the firm from the entry of new competitors (Bresnahan, 1985; Lieberman and Montgomery, 1988).

The pioneer's ability to gain advantages by pre-empting rivals in the acquisition of complementary resources or creating switching costs is a barrier that affects the competitors' costs in accessing the market related to the new technology (MacMillan, 1983). Pre-emption against rivals in accessing scarce assets (securing access to raw materials or components, dominating the supply chain, developing a dominant design, securing accelerated approval from national copyright agencies, expanding the scope of the product, proprietary processes, securing scarce and critical production skills, occupation of prime locations, and dominating distribution logistics) is a general mechanism that allows the pioneer to defend the advantage of being a first mover (MacMillan, 1988).

A useful pre-emption policy concerns complementary resources. Long relationships with specialized suppliers, expert researchers, important retailers, and so on increase the costs and time spent by competitors in order to seize advantages.

The switching costs are a second category of a pioneer's 'isolating barriers' in the new market. These costs arise from: (a) transaction costs or investments in adapting customer behavior to a pioneer's products; (b) learning a pioneer's product characteristics; and (c) a pioneer's loyalty programs. With switching costs, competitors must invest more resources and time in order to modify customer preferences. Pre-empting rivals in the acquisition of complementary resources or creating switching costs implies that the higher the costs of accessing the new technology and entering the related market, the lower the likelihood that competitors respond with speedy and a large number of imitations.

As MacMillan points out about IBM pre-empting policy, "IBM recognized a need for programming capabilities for its customers and preempted staunch support on the part of programmers and companies alike with its extensive programming schools" (MacMillan, 1983). IBM has a well-known pre-emptive policy that allowed the firm to dominate the mainframe computer industry for a long time.

Competitors' Strengths and Weaknesses in Internal and External Complementary Resources Related to the Old Technology Compared to those Associated with the New One

Competitors' strengths and weaknesses in internal complementary resources may be embodied in four dimensions: (1) employee knowledge and skills, (2) technical systems, (3) managerial systems, and (4) values and norms. External complementary resources lie in well-established and profitable relationships with specialized suppliers, expert researchers, important retailers, outstanding public and private research centers, expert customers, and other firms.

Usually, incumbents have resources related to the market of the old technology (Teece, 1986), while they do not possess the same amount and quality of knowledge on the new technology that the pioneer possesses. When a pioneer's isolating barriers are effective, competitors typically respond with differentiating initiatives (innovations in products and processes). Otherwise, if a pioneer's isolating barriers are ineffective, they are able to exploit complementary resources already accumulated to seize advantages of first movers in the market.

The story of EMI is meaningful in this sense. In the medical equipments industry, EMI failed in achieving sustainable advantages because Technicare Corporation, Pfizer Medical Systems, and General Electric were competitors with tremendous experience in the industry, high reputations among customers, a long history in the market, and strong financial resources. EMI lost in the marketplace because the firm was weaker in the technology infrastructure and marketing base compared to its competitors (Teece, 1986).

The Difference Between the New and Old Technology in Terms of Development Margins and Market Opportunities

Technological developments come from (a) new technological paradigms, (b) new technology improvements, and (c) technological standards. Each of these events reduces the risks and costs of entry in the new market.

In the personal computer industry, there were a lot of new entries after the IBM-Windows-Intel standard won the market battle against the Apple-Macintosh-Motorola standard. In the videogames market, every time the microelectronics manufacturers improved the velocity/capacity of chips, there were sequential attacks by new players (Atari, Nintendo, Sega, NEC, Sony, Microsoft).

While new technology developments decrease the risks and costs of imitation, the old technology margins of developments allow competitors to quickly respond to a pioneer's innovation with a differentiating behavior. This response is an opportunity that, in many circumstances, is undertaken by competitors.

Bower and Christensen discuss disk drive innovation, introduced new models of 5.25-inch drives at an accelerated rate and, in so doing, introduced an impressive array of sustaining technological improvements (Bower and Christensen, 1995). Even in the tire industry, US tire makers reacted to Michelin's innovation by improving the old technology. Instead of converting manufacturing to the radials, Firestone, Goodyear, Uniroyal, and BF Goodrich introduced belted bias tires that could be manufactured with minor modifications in existing production equipment (Sull, 1999).

Even if improvements of old technology allow competitors to respond to a pioneer's innovation quickly, the new technology overcomes the old technology performance in the long run, as the cases of personal computers and the disk drive discussed above show. Moreover, market opportunities related to the new technology decrease the costs and risks of accessing the new market or imitating the new technology (Utterback and Kim, 1986).

Market opportunities come from (a) a pioneer's investments, (b) evolution of customers' preferences, and (c) competitors' market redefinition. These elements affect the market growth, which reduces risks and costs of entry in new 'strategic windows' related to the innovation (Abell, 1978).

An example of market redefinition that allowed competitors to open a new window in the automatic teller machines industry (ATMs) is discussed by Abell:

Docutel supplied virtually all the ATM's in use up to late 1974. In early 1975, Docutel found itself losing market share to large computer companies such as Burroughs, Honeywell, and IBM as these manufacturers began to look at the banks' total EFTS (Electronic Funds Transfer System). They offered the bank a package of equipment representing a complete system of which the ATM was only one component. In essence their success may be attributed to the fact that they redefined the market in a way which increasingly appeared to disqualify Docutel as a potential supplier.

(Abell, 1978)

CONCLUSION

This chapter proposes a theoretical framework that provides a contribution to theory and practice by integrating two important research fields: first-mover advantages and interfirm rivalry.

The chapter contributes to the literature on first-mover advantages by fleshing out the dynamic process with which first-mover advantages are pursued, and contributes to the literature on interfirm rivalry by integrating the point of view of the firm that performs the action with those deciding to respond.

Issues for Future Research

Various theoretical and empirical contributions have already focused on relevant issues related to the competitive dynamics stimulated by a pioneer's innovation, but some fundamental explanations still lack theoretical and empirical contributions concerning the pioneer's and competitors' behavior.

For example, a relevant issue concerning the pioneer's behavior is related to this question: how does a pioneer's innovation affect industry attractiveness? In some cases, a pioneer's innovation affects, positively or negatively, industry attractiveness, and investigations on this issue could explain the conditions and factors affecting this process. Moreover, a related issue that needs more theoretical and empirical study concerns the pioneer's strategies before the competitors' respond. In many circumstances, this period represents an opportunity to create conditions helpful to maintain the early competitive advantage.

A different issue concerning the competitors' inertia is related to the following question: how can managerial filters be managed in order to avoid the delayed reaction of competitors? This issue opens further matters that can be investigated in the sphere of organizational behavior studies.

Finally, while there have been several research contributions concerning the responses of competitors (Cooper and Schendel, 1976; Robinson,

1988; Cooper and Smith, 1992; Bowman and Gatignon, 1995; Shankar, 1999), fewer studies have been focused on the pioneer's counter-moves. With the exception of analyses concerning pioneer marketing counter-moves to competitors' marketing reactions (Robinson and Gatignon, 1991; Shankar, 1997), few have investigated a pioneer's strategies in scenarios arising from competitors' imitative or differentiating responses.

Implications for Practice

3M, Sony and Cisco Systems are examples of firms that aggressively pursue first-mover advantages. These firms are able to manage the process of introducing new technologies in the market and challenge the incumbents. Other firms like IBM, Microsoft, Matsushita, and General Electric are examples of well-managed companies that are able to seize pioneers' competitive advantages.

What would explain the pioneer's advantages or incumbents' ability to respond? From the pioneer's point of view, the knowledge of factors affecting the competitive dynamics with incumbents increases managerial awareness of how the competitive advantage can be achieved and sustained. From the competitors' point of view, the knowledge of factors affecting the competitive dynamics with a pioneer increases managerial awareness of how first-mover advantages can be seized.

Managing the competition related to innovation is a complex matter, and involves making decisions on the timing of action, size of the market, and competitive posture. Moreover, after any action is taken, there are several factors that explain competitors' inertia and competitive dynamics. Finally, there are different strategies which are useful for pioneers to maintain the early market share and profits in the different scenarios that arise from the competitors' responses.

The framework proposed in this chapter considers some issues of the competitive dynamics stimulated by a pioneer's innovation. Several examples have shown how and when each issue of the framework affects a pioneer's or competitors' behaviors. The knowledge of the entire process initiated with the pioneer's technological innovation provides insight on how to manage the competition stimulated by technological innovation from the pioneer's or competitors' point of view.

REFERENCES

Abell, D.F. (1978), 'Strategic windows: the time to invest in a product or market is when a strategic window is open', *Journal of Marketing*, July.

Abell, D.F. (1980), *Defining the Business: The Starting Point of Strategic Planning*, Englewood Cliffs, N.J.: Prentice-Hall.

Ansoff, H.I. (1984), *Implanting Strategic Management*, Prentice-Hall.

Bain, J.S. (1956), *Barriers to New Competition*, Harvard University Press.

Baum, J.A.C. and H.J. Korn (1996), 'Competitive dynamics of interfirm rivalry', *Academy of Management Journal*, **39** (2).

Baum, J.A.C. and S.J. Mezias (1992), 'Localized competition and organizational failure in the Manhattan hotel industry, 1898–1900', *Administrative Science Quarterly*, **37** (4), 580–604.

Bettis, R.A. and D. Weeks (1987), 'Financial returns and strategic interaction: the case of instant photograph', *Strategic Management Journal*, **8**.

Bower, J.L. (1970), *Managing the Resource Allocation Process*, Boston, MA: Harvard Business School Press.

Bower, J.L. and C.M. Christensen (1995), 'Disruptive technologies: catching the wave', *Harvard Business Review*, January–February, 43–53.

Bresnahan, T.F. (1985), 'Post-entry competition in the plain paper copier market', *American Economic Review*, **75**, 15–19.

Brown, W.B. and N. Karagozoglu (1993), 'Leading the way to faster new product development', *Academy of Management Executive*, **7** (1).

Caves, R.E. and M.E. Porter (1977), 'From entry barriers to mobility barriers: conjectural decisions and contrived deterrence to new competition', *The Quarterly Journal of Economics*, **91** (2), 241–262.

Chen, M.-J., K.G. Smith and C.M. Grimm (1992), 'Action characteristics as predictors of competitive responses', *Management Science*, **38** (3).

Christensen, C.M. (1997), *The Innovator's Dilemma: When New Technologies Cause Great Firms to Fail*, Harvard Business Review Press.

Cooper, A.C. and D. Schendel (1976), 'Strategic responses to technological threats', *Business Horizons*, **19** (1).

Cooper, A.C. and C.G. Smith (1992), 'How established firms respond to threatening technologies', *Academy of Management Executive*, **6** (2).

Cusumano, M.A., Y. Mylonadis and R.S. Rosenbloom (1992), 'Strategic maneuvering and mass-market dynamics: the triumph of VHS over Beta', *Business History Review*, Spring.

D'Aveni, R. (1994), *Hypercompetition: Managing the Dynamics of Strategic Maneuvering*, New York: Free Press.

Day, G.S. (1986), *Analysis for Strategic Marketing Decisions*, St. Paul, MN: West Publishing.

Dixit, A. (1980), 'The role of investment in entry-deterrence', *The Economic Journal*, **90** (March).

Farrell, J. and G. Saloner (1985), 'Standardization, compatibility, and innovation', *Rand Journal of Economics*, **16**, 70–83.

Foster, R.N. (1986), *Innovation: The Attacker's Advantage*, New York: Summit Books.

Gatignon, H., E. Anderson and K. Helsen (1989), 'Competitive reaction to market entry: explaining interfirm differences', *Journal of Marketing Research*, **26** (February).

Ghemawat, P. (1984), 'Capacity expansion in the titanium dioxide industry', *Journal of Industrial Economics*, **33** (December).

Ghemawat, P. and A.M. Spence (1985), 'Learning curve spillovers and market performance', *Quarterly Journal of Economics*, **100**.

Gilbert, R.J. and D.M.G. Newbery (1982), 'Preemptive patenting and the persistence of monopoly', *American Economic Review*, **72** (June).

Glazer, A. (1985), 'The advantages of being first', *The American Economic Review*, **75** (3).

Golder, P.N. and G.J. Tellis (1993), 'Pioneer advantage: marketing logic or marketing legend?', *Journal of Marketing Research*, **30** (May).

Hamel, G. and C.K. Prahalad (1990), 'Strategic intent', *The McKinsey Quarterly*, Spring.

Harrigan, K.R. (1981), 'Barriers to entry and competitive strategies', *Strategic Management Journal*, **2** (4).

Harrigan, K.R. (1988), *Managing Maturing Businesses: Restructuring Declining Industries and Revitalizing Troubled Operations*, Lexington, MA: Lexington Books.
Haverman, H.A. (1993), 'Follow the leader: mimetic isomorphism and entry into new markets', *Administrative Science Quarterly*, **38** (4).
Helfat, C.E. (1997), 'Know-how and asset complementarity and dynamic capability accumulation: the case of R&D', *Strategic Management Journal*, **18** (5).
Judd, K.L. (1985), 'Credible spatial preemption', *Rand Journal of Economics*, **16**.
Karnany, A. and B. Wernerfelt (1985), 'Multiple-point competition', *Strategic Management Journal*, **6**, 87–96.
Kessler, E.H. and A.K. Chakrabarti (1996), 'Innovation speed: a conceptual model of context, antecedents and outcomes', *Academy of Management Review*, **21** (4).
Lambkin, M. (1988), 'Order of entry and performance in new markets', *Strategic Management Journal*, **9**.
Lieberman, M.B. and D.B. Montgomery (1988), 'First-mover advantages', *Strategic Management Journal*, **9**.
MacMillan, I.C. (1983), 'Preemptive strategies', *The Journal of Business Strategy*, **4** (2).
MacMillan, I.C. (1988), 'Controlling competitive dynamics by taking strategic initiative', *Academy of Management Executive*, **2** (2).
Nelson, R.R. and S.G. Winter (1982), *An Evolutionary Theory of Economic Change*, The Belknap Press of Harvard University Press.
Page, A. (1993), 'Assessing new product development practices and performance: establishing crucial norms', *Journal of Product Innovation Management*, **10**.
Parry, M.F. and F.M. Bass (1990), 'When to lead or follow? It depends', *Marketing Letters*, **1**.
Penrose, E.T. (1959), *The Theory of the Growth of the Firm*, New York: Wiley.
Peteraf, M.A. (1993), 'Intra-industry structure and response toward rivals', *Journal of Managerial and Decision Economics*, **14**, 519–528.
Porter, M.E. (1976), *Interbrand Choice: Strategic and Bilateral Market Power*, Cambridge, MA: Harvard University Press.
Porter, M.E. (1979), 'The structure within industries and companies' performance', *Review of Economics and Statistics*, **61**, 214–228.
Porter, M.E. (1980), *Competitive Strategy*, New York, N.Y.: Free Press.
Porter, M.E. (1985), *Competitive Advantage: Creating and Sustaining Superior Performance*, New York, N.Y.: Free Press.
Porter, M.E. (1985), 'Technology and competitive advantage', *Journal of Business Strategy*, **5**.
Reinganum, J.F. (1983), 'Uncertain innovation and the persistence of monopoly', *American Economic Review*, **73**.
Robinson, W.T. (1988a), 'Sources of market pioneer advantages: the case of industrial goods industries', *Journal of Marketing Research*, **25**.
Robinson, W.T. (1988b), 'Marketing mix reaction to entry', *Marketing Science*, **7**.
Robinson, W.T. and C. Fornell (1985), 'Sources of market pioneer advantage in consumer goods industries', *Journal of Marketing Research*, **25**.
Robinson, W.T., C. Fornell and M. Sullivan (1992), 'Are market pioneers intrinsically stronger than later entrants?', *Strategic Management Journal*, **13**.
Rumelt, R.P. (1987), 'Theory, strategy and entrepreneurship', in D.J. Teece (ed.), *Strategy & Organization for Industrial Innovation and Renewal*, Cambridge, MA: Ballinger.
Schelling, T.C. (1960), *The Strategy of Conflict*, Cambridge, MA: Harvard University Press.
Schmalensee, R. (1982), 'Product differentiation advantages of pioneering brands', *The American Economic Review*, **72** (3).
Schmalensee, R. (1983), 'Advertising and entry deterrence: an exploratory model', *The Journal of Political Economy*, **91** (4).
Schnaars, S.P. (1994), *Managing Imitation Strategies. How Later Entrants Seize Markets from Pioneers*, New York: The Free Press.
Schroeder, D.M. (1990), 'A dynamic perspective on the impact of process innovation upon competitive strategies', *Strategic Management Journal*, **11**.

Shankar, V. (1999), 'New product introduction and incumbent response strategies: their interrelationship and the role of multimarket contact', *Journal of Marketing Research*, **36**, 327–344.

Shapiro, C. (1989), 'The theory of business strategy', *RAND Journal of Economics*, **20** (1).

Smith, K.G., C.M. Grimm and M.J. Gannon (1992), *Dynamics of Competitive Strategy*, Newbury Park, CA: Sage.

Smith, K.G. and R.L. Wilson (1995), 'The predictive validity of the Karnani and Wernerfelt model of multi-point competition', *Strategic Management Journal*, **16**, 143–160.

Spence, M. (1981), 'The learning curve and competition', *Bell Journal of Economics*, **12**.

Sull, D.N. (1999), 'The dynamics of standing still: Firestone Tire & Rubber and the radial revolution', *Business History Review*, **73**.

Teece, D.J. (1980), 'Economics of scope and the scope of the enterprise', *Journal of Economic Behavior and Organization*, **1**.

Teece, D.J. (1982), 'Toward an economic theory of the multi-product firm', *Journal of Economic Behavior and Organization*, **3**.

Teece, D.J. (1987), 'Profiting from technological innovation: implications for integration, collaboration, licensing and public policy' in D.J. Teece (ed.), *Strategy & Organization for Industrial Innovation and Renewal*, Cambridge, MA: Ballinger.

Teece, D.J., G. Pisano and A. Shuen (1997), 'Dynamic capabilities and strategic management', *Strategic Management Journal*, **18** (7).

Urban, G.L., T. Carter, S. Gaskin and Z. Mucha (1986), 'Market share rewards to pioneering brands: an empirical analysis and strategic implications', *Management Science*, **32**.

Utterback, J.M. and L. Kim (1986), 'Invasion of a stable business by radical innovation', in P.R. Kleindorfer (ed.), *The Management of Productivity and Technology in Manufacturing*, Plenum Press.

Vesey, J.T. (1991), 'The new competitors: they think in terms of speed-to-market', *Academy of Management Executive*, **5** (2).

Zajac, E.J. and M.H. Bazerman (1991), 'Blind spots in industry and competitor analysis: implications of inter-firm (mis)perception to strategic decisions', *Academy of Management Review*, **16**.

PART 3

ADVANCED TOPICS IN COMPETITIVE STRATEGY RESEARCH

11 The evolving role of mergers and acquisitions in competitive strategy research

Olimpia Meglio and Arturo Capasso

INTRODUCTION

This chapter intends to investigate the role of strategic mergers and acquisitions (hereinafter M&As), traditionally viewed as a corporate strategy option, in sustaining competitive strategy, offering a description of the whole acquisition process and discussing the main and conflicting results produced by the abundant empirical research on this topic.

Mergers and acquisitions are nowadays frequent events in organizational lives. The two terms are normally used interchangeably in strategic management literature. Epstein (2004) claims that a distinction among mergers and acquisitions is necessary. Mergers of equals involve two entities of relatively equal stature coming together and taking the best of each company. An acquisition involves a much easier process of fitting one smaller company into the existing acquiring firm. This distinction, however, does not appear to be relevant when discussing the implications on the organizations involved, as both produce, at different pace and level, turmoil during the acquisition and integration problems once the deal is completed.

The established business literature considers M&As as a corporate strategy tool by which firms sustain and implement growth. Acquirers can gain immediate access to technologies, products, distribution channels, and desirable market positions. Acquisitions can bring into a company capabilities it finds hard to develop internally, and provide the opportunity to leverage the existing ones; under this regard, they help to gain or renew sustainable competitive advantages. This is consistent with the view of a firm as a set of capabilities embodied in an organizational framework. According to Haspeslagh and Jemison (1991) a clear understanding of which capabilities are central to a firm's competitive success makes it possible to understand how to renew such capabilities and develop a sound acquisitive strategy that creates value.

Despite the huge number of empirical researches yielded so far, the evaluation of M&As' performance for the acquiring firm is still an open issue.

237

Whatever the aggregate performance implication of acquisition activity, it is essential for strategic management scholars, as well as practitioners, to understand why some firms perform better than others in creating economic value from their acquisitions.

This chapter is structured as follows: first we present a brief literature review to account for recent advancement of theoretical and empirical studies about M&As and then we present an integrative framework to analyse the acquisition process and understand overall acquisition performance. Then a research agenda is provided.

THE EVOLUTION OF M&A LITERATURE: IS THERE A GAP TO FILL?

Mergers and acquisitions have been studied through several theoretical lenses, generating a vast amount of empirical studies and theoretical contributions that have produced a fragmented picture of this phenomenon (Capasso and Meglio, 2005). It has been analysed with different paradigms (although the functionalist one prevails), schools of thought, methods and units of analysis.

A recent meta-analysis of post-acquisition performance (King et al., 2004) indicates that, from a methodological standpoint, there is little overlap in the variables employed as predictors of acquisition performance. Moving from the previous meta-analysis on mergers and acquisitions (Datta et al., 1992), the authors argue that knowledge accumulation has been slower than expected, granted the amount of empirical research in this area, since new effects are sought over replication of known effects. Replicability plays a fundamental role in the research process, granting protection against uncertain assimilation of erroneous empirical results into the literature (Hubbard et al., 1998). As a consequence, no general theory on acquisitions has emerged yet (Bower, 2004; Javidan et al., 2004).

The multifaceted nature of acquisitive phenomena has encouraged the adoption of different perspectives (paradigms and theoretical lenses), research questions and methods. From a theoretical standpoint, this fragmentation has also prevented researchers from developing an integrative framework to analyse mergers and acquisitions except for the attempt of Larsson and Finkelstein (1999).

In this chapter, due to its aims and scope, we will provide only a selective literature review, accounting for recent advancements in M&A studies, focusing on strategic management and organizational behaviour literature. M&A research, however, has developed largely along these lines

Industrial organization

What are the effects of M&As on the economic system?
Extensive research about acquisition motives and performance

Financial economics

Do acquisitions create value for shareholders?
Surveys focused on acquiring's, target's shareholders or a combination of both

Strategic management

Variance approach: which factors either explain or predict acquisition performance?
Process approach: processual analysis applied to investigate M&As

Organizational behaviour

Analysis of organization- and individual- level effects:
Psychological reactions; resistance; cultural clash
Top management turnover, communication flow

Source: translated from Meglio (2004: 5).

Figure 11.1   Schools of thought in M&A studies

(Cartwright and Schoenberg, 2006), so, in some cases, it proves difficult to ascribe one contribution to a single school of thought.

The different schools of thought can be divided into two clusters (see Figure 11.1):

- economics-related: industrial organization (IO) and financial economics (FE);
- management-related: strategic management (SM) and organizational behaviour (OB).

IO and FE are mainly concerned with the effects of mergers and acquisitions: IO studies the impact of merger wave on the whole economic system (Scherer, 1980; Ravenscraft and Scherer, 1987 and 1989), while FE focuses on shareholders' value. Quantitative studies, generally employing an event study methodology, show that the target's shareholders earn abnormal returns, but no significant gain accrues to the acquirer's ones (Jarrell et al., 1988; Jensen and Ruback, 1983; Franks et al., 1991; Loderer and Martin, 1992; Agrawal et al., 1992; Mulherin and Boone, 2000). More recently, event studies report positive returns to acquirers, especially when the research setting is a particular industry or a geographic area, as reported in Kohers and Kohers's (2000, 2001) study on technology M&As; Goergen and Renneboog's (2003) on European transactions; Floreani and Rigamonti's (2001) on European insurance company mergers and Beitel et al.'s (2002) on European bank mergers.

Fragmentation strikingly emerges in the strategic management field, in which two different research approaches prevail (Tsoukas and Knudsen, 2002). The variance approach aims at uncovering variables explicative and predictive of the phenomenon investigated; M&A studies envisioned by this research approach typically test the relationship between a variable such as acquisition typology, resources redeployment, top management turnover, and integration capability and acquisition performance (Kusewitt, 1985; Chatterjee, 1986; Shelton, 1986; Seth, 1990a; Seth, 1990b; Bergh, 1997; Capron et al., 1998; Walsh, 1988; Haleblian and Finkelstein, 1999; Hayward, 2002; Singh and Zollo, 2004; Haleblian et al., 2006; Uhlenbruck et al., 2006), without providing conclusive results. Other studies, more descriptive in nature, highlight patterns of the most significant variables affecting mergers and acquisitions (Napier, 1989; Pablo, 1994).

More recently, we are witnessing an increasing interest in acquisitions as a substitute for R&D, brought about by the need to quickly build market positions due to shortening product life cycles (Bower, 2001). Academic literature about technology-driven acquisitions is still fragmented and in its infancy. We can account for studies based on large samples as well as case studies. Hitt et al. (1991, 1996) found that R&D investments decrease after the acquisition due to organization turmoil; Ahuja and Katila (2001) show that technology-driven acquisitions produce positive results, operationalized as number of new registered patents; Valentini (2005) focuses on financial performance to assess the success of technology-driven acquisitions, while Puranam et al. (2003, 2006) suggest that acquirers can resolve the coordination-autonomy dilemma by recognizing that innovation performance is dependent on the developmental stage of the acquired firm's innovation trajectories.

As for qualitative research, we can account for several studies. Ranft and Lord (2002) have developed an empirically grounded model of technology and capability transfer during acquisition implementation. Graebner and Eisenhardt (2004) offer the seller's perspective in the acquisition decision-making process, while Graebner (2004) provides a closer examination of the role of the acquired managers in creating value through acquisitions. Cassiman et al. (2005) show that technological and market relatedness between acquiring and target firms affects the organizational structure of R&D processes and the overall acquisition performance. Schweizer (2005) analyses the post-acquisition integration of biotechnology companies by pharmaceutical firms, arguing for a need to apply a hybrid integration approach with simultaneous short- and long-term actions.

The process approach is mainly interested in unravelling the mechanisms that yield a certain outcome. The seminal work of Jemison and Sitkin (1986) suggests that acquisitions can be referred to as processes; this implies that acquisition performance is affected by all the sub-processes which make up the whole M&A process. This approach has attracted many scholars to employ longitudinal case studies: Larsson (1990), Birkinshaw et al. (1997), Lohrum (1996) and Risberg (1999) engage in both retrospective and real-time reconstruction of two M&A events. Larsson (1990), Lorhum (1996) and Risberg's (1999) works are all based on a comparison of two cases; the analysis is conducted at multiple organizational levels of both acquiring and target firms. Empirical data allow an ex post reconstruction of acquisition processes. Birkinshaw et al.'s (1997) study shows how task and human integrations foster value creation. Yu et al. (2005) embarked upon an eight-year ethnographic study in a large healthcare system made up in a 1994 merger. The authors offer a description of different patterns observed during their bi-weekly meetings regarding how managers addressed the integration issues and defined the integration priorities. Finally, they identify vicious cycles of repeated conflicts in how organizational members made sense of integration issues. Kavanagh and Ashkanasy (2006) report a seven-year longitudinal study of mergers involving three large multi-site universities. Both qualitative and quantitative methods of analysis are used to examine the effects of leadership and change management on acceptance of cultural change by individuals. Findings indicate that in many cases the change is imposed on leaders themselves and it is often the pace of change that inhibits successful re-engineering of culture.

The organizational behaviour school is mainly concerned with both individual and organizational reactions to M&A, highlighting the possible negative chain reactions produced by an acquisition: merger syndrome, cultural clash and employee reactions (such as sabotage and absenteeism) are the prominent topics of this research stream (Marks and Mirvis, 1985; Nahavandi and Malekzadeh, 1988; Larsson et al., 2001). Other studies address the impact either of organizational culture (Chatterjee et al., 1992; Weber and Schweiger, 1992; Weber, 1996; Teerikangas and Very, 2006) or of national culture on acquisition performance (Olie, 1990; Very et al., 1993). Larsson and Lubatkin (2001) apply case survey analysis to a sample of 50 cross-border acquisitions to investigate the acculturation process. They found that acculturation benefits from social control mechanisms such as introduction programmes, training and cross-visits as well as similar socialization rituals. Participating in such activities allows employees to create a joint organizational culture, regardless of expectation of synergies, the relative organizational size and differences in nationalities and cultures.

Organizational scholars have recently challenged the monolithic vision of cultural fit, overcoming the notion of cultural clash, perceived as a sort of a theoretical 'deus ex machina' insufficient to explain the great variance in acquisition performances. Vaara et al. (2003) provide an alternative view to the dominant essentialist analysis of cultures and cultural differences, conceptualizing cultural identity-building as a metaphoric process. The research setting was a Finnish-Swedish merger. Data collected during a cultural seminar revealed specific cognitive, emotional and political aspects that probably would have remained hidden to more traditional research approaches. Moving from these attempts, Angwin and Vaara (2005) argue that culture has become a broad umbrella encompassing beliefs, norms, values, emotions, rules and routines without a clear specification. They suggest connectivity as a good metaphor that highlights the complexities of interconnected processes and synchronized activities in organizations and their contexts.

Riad (2005) argues that knowledge on organizational culture has acquired authority and constitutes a truth on mergers, a truth imbued with both enabling and constraining power effects. Drawing on ethnographic research into merger integration, these arguments are illustrated through two vignettes (surveillance and sanctuary) that represent the reproduction of, and resistance to, the truth effects of organizational cultures. Schweiger and Goulet (2005) carry out an exploratory study to systematically and empirically examine cultural learning interventions as they apply to the post-acquisition integration process. They argue that achieving an effective employee mindset toward acquisition may be less a process of choosing a culturally-compatible partner than it is an ability to manage cultural differences through cultural learning. The data collected during a longitudinal field experiment across three pairs of matched plants indicate that cultural distance can be overcome during the early stages of the integration process thanks to deep-level cultural learning intervention.

From this selective literature review it appears that much of the research on acquisitions addressed a variety of problems and dilemmas. However, researchers so far have failed to link these integration problems to the motives for acquisitions or to the types of resources being acquired. Instead, existing research tends to lump all types of acquisitions together and in so doing it tends toward overgeneralization and oversimplification. So it provides only a limited and insufficient understanding of this multidimensional phenomenon (Pablo and Javidan, 2004). The reality is that in any given acquisition, the combined firm will choose multiple levels and types of integration. As long as scholars limit themselves to categorizing integration approaches with single types or variables, the complex processes cannot be fully captured.

THE ACQUISITION PROCESS

Academics and practitioners often describe the acquisition process as a unifying process which is normally depicted as a sequence of discrete steps, as in Figure 11.2 (Graves, 1981; Marks, 1982; Buono and Bowditch, 1989; Haspeslagh and Jemison, 1991).

What seems and is generally depicted as a linear process is, however, complex and spiral: it is difficult to identify when each phase ends and the next starts. Moreover, phases do not neatly correspond with time: two events occurring at the same time can be referred to as different phases. This implies that different levels of merging firms and individuals can experience different phases at the same time (Risberg, 1999). Under this regard, the acquisition is not completed when the deal is signed.

In this chapter we apply a process approach to analysing mergers and acquisitions. This approach, rooted in Mintzberg and Water's (1985) image of strategy formation as a convergence of intended and emergent strategy, is mainly concerned with unravelling all the factors which explain how a strategy actually comes about. This approach takes further shape with acknowledging the importance of the context and the chronology of events.

Our framework, as depicted in Figure 11.3, suggests that acquisition performance is the outcome of all sub-processes in which can ideally be split the whole acquisition process, each of which is alone necessary, although not sufficient, to grant overall acquisition success. This does not mean that value creation is an additive process; it implies that many integration problems arise as a consequence of a poor analysis of acquisition candidates or a lack of due diligence. Moreover, it indicates that the pre-acquisition phase should be informed by integration processes risks, costs and implementation times. This framework also indicates the importance of triangulating different performance metrics, each reflecting different integration goals.

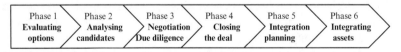

| Phase 1
**Evaluating
options** | Phase 2
**Analysing
candidates** | Phase 3
**Negotiation
Due diligence** | Phase 4
**Closing
the deal** | Phase 5
**Integration
planning** | Phase 6
**Integrating
assets** |

Figure 11.2   The acquisition process

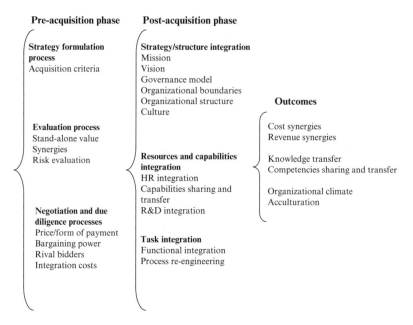

Source: Translation from Meglio (2004: 69).

Figure 11.3   Determinants of acquisition performance

For the sake of clarity, our analysis will go on examining each phase as a discrete step, highlighting possible trade-offs between different integration achievements.

The Pre-acquisition Phase

The process starts when the firm has to compare the various alternatives for growth (internal development, acquisition or an alliance) in terms of both opportunities and challenges. No alternative is in itself superior to any other; it depends on the resource endowment, time constraints and market conditions (Yip, 1982). In this perspective it is important to note that acquisitions are not a strategic choice but only a possible way to implement a growth strategy, provided that in so doing the economic value created is higher.

In the decision to carry out an acquisition, information plays a key role, as recognized in management literature. Information is increasingly seen as underlying many of the causes of M&As' poor record such as inadequate target screening, misjudgement of target value, overvaluation of synergies, ineffective negotiation, overpayment and hubris. Information

- **Which is the right acquisition candidate?**
- Resources and competencies complementarity
- Synergy exploitation
- Strategic/organizational/cultural fit
- Goals reached (which could not be attained by other options)
- Price

- **How to negotiate an effective agreement?**

- **Which is the integration model to implement?**

- **Which is the proper organizational model to adopt?**

- **What kind of 'human troubles' will the acquiring firm face?**

- **How to integrate functional areas?**

Figure 11.4   Acquisition criteria: an illustrative checklist

flows across the different actors involved, directly or indirectly, such as financial advisors or board interlocks, are also seen as crucial in the acquisition process.

Information economics (IE) contributes to our understanding of the role of information in the M&A process by outlining the role of adverse selection that arises from information asymmetries between sellers and acquirers (Akerlof, 1970). In parallel, strategic factor market (SFM) scholars have made great advances in understanding how an acquirer can obtain returns from its acquisitions relying on its informational advantage over rival bidders (Barney, 1991; Makadok and Barney, 2001). SFM outlines the role of the acquirer capability in scouting and evaluating the target's resources.

A timely piece of information can result in less competition for the target, while more private information available on targets is beneficial to the acquirer in assessing the value and eventually offering an appropriate price for the target. In this case the scouting skills of the acquiring firm's management assume a special importance.

If the acquisition looks like a sound strategy, a proper target has to be identified. A checklist with acquisition criteria can be a helpful tool to identify in advance the sources of value creation and destruction the acquisition will bring with it.

The tentative checklist provided above illustrates the main issues to address when selecting a partner, in the case of a 'deliberate' acquisitive strategy (Mintzberg and Waters, 1985). The selection of the right acquisition candidate is contingent on several factors such as strategic, organizational and cultural fit and synergy potential. Strategic fit is generally expressed in terms of different combination typologies (Lubatkin, 1983; Larsson, 1990; Salter and Weinhold, 1981; Haspeslagh and Jemison, 1991). Diversity in typologies arises from the combination of market and production relationships between merging companies; they represent desired benefits and integration needs after the deal is closed. Strategic fit, however, does not imply organizational fit, which focuses on the match between administrative and cultural practices and how personnel characteristics between merging firms may affect the ways they can be integrated (Jemison and Sitkin, 1986). Nahavandi and Malekzadeh (1986) classify acquisitions in terms of modes of acculturations. They take into account both acquiring and acquired firms' degree of multiculturalism, the acquisition typology and the perception of attractiveness of the acquirer by the acquired firm. Strategic, organizational and cultural fit alone do not guarantee value creation, which is strictly related to synergy exploitation.

Synergy is the additional value that is generated by combining acquiring and target firms that would not be available to these firms operating independently. The potential sources of synergy can be classified into two groups: operating and financial synergies. The former group affects the operations of the combined firms and includes economies of scale, increasing pricing power and higher growth potential. They generally result in higher expected cash flows. Financial synergies, on the other hand, are more focused and include tax benefits, diversification, a higher debt capacity and uses for excess cash. They result either in higher cash flows or lower discount rates. Synergies differ in terms of value creation likelihood and implementation costs: operating synergies are more difficult and costly to implement than financial ones. So a careful assessment of synergies can represent for the decision-makers an effective tool to negotiate a convenient deal, fixing an indication of the highest price for the deal.

Closing the Deal

Negotiating an agreement for an acquisition is usually a long and complicated task. Important terms include the price offered and the use of contractual devices to manage M&A risk.

The crucial aspect of the negotiation process is certainly the assessment of the offered price, especially when several potential buyers compete for the same target, as usually happens. In the short term, the offered price can play a key role in deciding who, among the potential buyers, will win the bid game, but in the long run it will heavily affect the value creation process and therefore acquisition success. If it is assumed that a deal will create economic value in absolute terms, it is straightforward that the price paid by the buyer to the seller determines their respective share of the value created, with the non-trivial time discrepancy that the seller gets its share immediately, whereas the buyer will have to put into practice the synergies only predicted in acquisition plans and embedded in the valuation of the target.

Competition for a certain target tends to eliminate all possible bidders' gains that are common to many potential buyers. According to Barney (1988), acquiring firms gain above normal returns from acquisitions only when private or uniquely valuable synergistic assets are involved. Privacy refers to information about the combination that is not available to potential outside bidders. Uniquely valuable synergy is created when no other combination of firms could produce the same value. If information is not private or if other equally synergistic combinations are possible in the market for corporate control, the target's price will be bid up to a point at which the value from potential synergy is absorbed by the acquisition price. Hitt et al. (1991) extend this line of reasoning, arguing that synergistic benefits from resource combinations are more likely to be private or uniquely valuable when based on complementarity rather than similarity in merging companies' assets.

Not only can the value created by synergies be different depending on the potential buyer but also transaction and integration costs might vary considerably as a result of cultural or organizational fitting. Furthermore, it should be considered that sometimes in valuing a target, a potential buyer has to take into account defensive implications. The assessment of the maximum price payable, in this hypothesis, considers the potential losses suffered by the buyer should the target company have been acquired by a competitor. This also explains why sometimes, after an initial tender offer for a company, other potential buyers are persuaded, or even compelled, to enter the bidding process.

Once the price is approximately set, the negotiation process should be extended to many other aspects, answering in advance those questions that might otherwise lead to uncertainty, inconsistent interpretations, disagreement, and, eventually, litigation. For this reason, due diligence normally supplements top management's strategic scrutiny. Due diligence is usually conducted during the period between the declaration of the initial intent to acquire and the closing of the transaction. Deal closure is contingent on a satisfactory due diligence report. This involves a detailed analysis of the condition of the target firm by representatives of the acquiring firm who verify financial records, analyse legal matters and investigate other potential problems. The information obtained during due diligence is generally not publicly available and hence should make possible a more careful assessment of the value the transaction might provide. Since the target has an incentive to make public any positive information, anything relevant uncovered during due diligence is usually unfavourable and should lower the value of the target for the acquirer. If a key goal of this phase is to discover and act on information that may lead to re-valuing the acquisition's feasibility and convenience, due diligence failures occur either when acquirers fail to discover new information that devalues the target firm or, having uncovered it, fail to react in an appropriate manner, i.e. by revising the price (Puranam et al., 2006).

Due diligence is not the only risk management tool to avoid valuation mistakes in M&A. Sometimes, in fact, the disagreement between the counterparts does not regard the past but the future performance of the acquired company. In this case, a possible solution relies on other M&A risk management tools like earnouts or collars. With the earnouts, the payment structure is typically contingent on future performance benchmarks. Earnouts are especially purposeful when the selling managers remain in charge; in this case earnouts and other contingent payment structures provide stronger performance incentives for selling managers as well as risk management devices for the buyer ones. Collars are generally used when acquisition payment is wholly or partially in acquiring company shares. If the buyer's share price falls or rises beyond predetermined triggers, collars grant either or both of the merging firms the right to renegotiate the deal. In this extreme case, a collar can be considered as an option to cancel a merger (Bruner, 2004).

The Post-acquisition Phase

After closing the deal, the acquirer must organize interactions and implement changes in processes and organizations that will allow synergies and forecasted cash flows to be realized. If any change is made or not made within the expected deadline for value creation, the acquisition can be, a posteriori, qualified as not worth the price paid. A fit does not automatically lead to beneficial acquisition outcomes. The paradoxical nature of synergy exploitation has been recently outlined by Shaver (2006), who starts his line of reasoning by considering the implication of interdependence brought about by post-merger integration. He distinguishes between two distinct effects: the contagion and the capacity effect. The former is intrinsically related to interdependence: this means that any change in competitive arena of one business is likely to have an impact across businesses. The latter is linked to resource slack reduction that decreases the chances that positive shocks in the business environment can be fully exploited because of capacity constraints. He challenges, although only theoretically, the conventional wisdom that a well-formulated and well-implemented acquisition strategy results in value creation. This paper is undoubtedly intriguing, but the lack of an empirical base makes us wonder, if not doubt, whether an acquisition necessarily reduces the resource slack due to the integration process. Resources, especially in horizontal mergers and acquisitions, are abundant and it is quite common that duplications need eliminating. Moreover, as for the contagion effect, managerial and knowledge transfer after an acquisition should help the new entity to react effectively to both positive and negative change in the competitive arena. In the absence of empirical data to support these propositions, we do think that integration can be key to the overall acquisition success.

The integration process refers to the process of asset rationalization, activity integration and employee acculturation that normally takes place after the deal has been signed. Haspeslagh and Jemison (1991: 106) define integration as an "interactive and gradual process in which individuals from two organizations learn to work together and cooperate in the transfer of strategic capabilities". Defining integration as interaction reflects the prominent role the human factor plays; this is consistent with Birkinshaw's (1999) distinction between task and human integration. Task integration refers to how the value-adding activities of the two companies are put together to generate synergies. It involves transferring capabilities from one company to the other, and sharing resources between the two. Quite often task integration also includes rationalization of activities, through downsizing and asset sales. Human integration refers to the process of generating satisfaction and, ultimately, shared identity among employees of the merged company. In the period immediately following the acquisition decision, the human integration process has to alleviate all the negative attitudes brought about by change and uncertainty. Afterwards, its objective switches toward the building of a unifying organizational culture.

The trade-off between economic and social aspects determines priority and time setting. The speed of integration has been found to significantly affect the integration's success (Homburg and Bucerius, 2006). If the integration team starts with rationalization (closing duplicate facilities, reducing overheads) it will make rapid progress on the cost side, but will face the prospect of an unenthusiastic and scared workforce. If the team starts with acculturation (building relationships between employees from the two firms, fostering a common culture) it will end up with happy employees but very few cost savings. And doing both at the same time may not be the answer indeed, because of the apparent hypocrisy of telling employees their involvement in the integration process is vital to the success of the enterprise, and in the next breath announcing that there will be a significant staff reduction. Many managers involved in acquisitions face this basic dilemma as task integration and human integration are often at cross-purposes. In the days following an acquisition announcement, for example, managers should meet one to one with every employee to allay understandable concerns. The demand for rapid action and cost control could, however, make such a move prohibitive. In contrast, closing one of the acquired firm's plants should help the task integration process, but will almost certainly hinder the human integration process, unless handled very carefully. Thus the ultimate goal of full task and human integration is clear, but the route chosen, and the trade-offs that route implies, are a source of continuous conflict for the individuals responsible for the integration process. This reinforces the importance of effectively balancing these opposing needs, according to the level of integration.

The choice of integration approach is one of the most critical in decision-making in an M&A context. Over- and under-integration can result in failure to create value or in value destruction. Integration approach recalls terms such as level of integration (Shrivastava, 1986; Pablo, 1994; Zollo and Singh, 2004), integration process modes (Haspeslagh and Jemison, 1991; Napier, 1989) and acculturation modes (Nahavandi and Malekzadeh, 1988). The integration typologies developed by Haspeslagh and Jemison have become very prominent among M&A scholars since they suggest four different integration modes based on two factors: strategic interdependence and organizational autonomy need. They reflect the acquiring firm's perspective, overlooking target firms' preferences. This perspective is taken into account by Nahavandi and Malekzadeh, who offer a more nuanced view of acculturation modes. These typologies, despite the undoubted merit of simplicity and parsimony, are not consistent with the ongoing nature of acquisition processes and do not exhaust their complexities. Given the multifaceted nature of mergers and acquisitions, acquiring companies need to apply a hybrid post-acquisition integration approach with simultaneous short- and long-term motives, orientations and segmentation at a different pace across different value chain components. Moreover, during the integration, action plans need to be adapted to new events or human reactions. Integration is a dynamic process of adjustment in a context of uncertainty and incomplete information. These interrelationships can be appreciated only by taking into account the actors involved at different organizational levels, and integration mechanisms put in use according to different purposes and different time frames, as depicted in Figure 11.5.

As for the actors in the integration process, we can identify three levels.

- Top management, responsible for defining the integration model, appointing the integration manager and approving his or her choices, such as the transition team leaders' appointments.

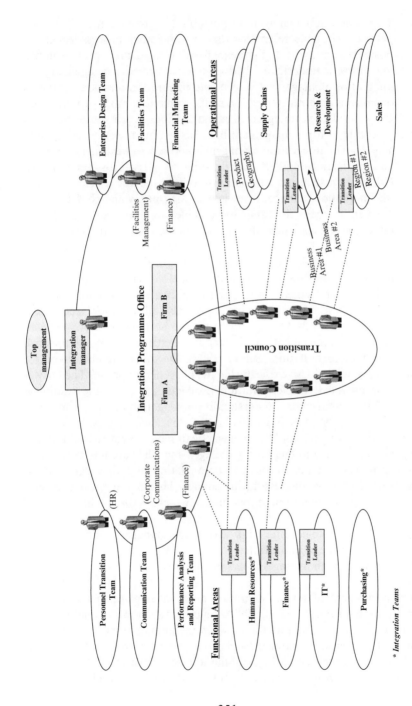

Figure 11.5   The integration programme structure

251

- The integration manager, responsible for running the integration process. The role resembles that of any other process-leadership position a company might create to drive any change-process implementation it undertakes. It does involve project management: the integration manager helps to create integration teams, consolidate operations and transfer critical skills from one company to the other. Yet, an effective integration manager does much more, not only reporting to top management but also helping to set the company's agenda. The integration manager should have an excellent decision-making instinct and distinctive skills to work cross-functionally. Critical is a strong trust relationship with the key executives, since the integration manager often acts as their proxy and confidant.
- Transition team leaders, responsible for undertaking specific integration tasks, under the integration manager's supervision.

The conventional view of the planned integration approach in M&A literature fits the traditional top-down models of change, according to which middle management limits itself to implement top management's plans. However, middle management may also play a more active role firstly because it needs to operationalise the strategic content (Meyer, 2006). Middle management can influence the strategic process upward, during strategy formulation (Schilit, 1987). Do middle managers play a destructive or a productive role during the post-merger phase? The answer cannot be univocal. Implementation problems are often the results of poor middle management understanding and commitment to strategy. However, recent studies have challenged this idea, suggesting a more nuanced view in which middle managers can have an active and influential role promoting and facilitating change, since they are uniquely suited to communicate change across the organization and they can address employees' emotional distress during change. This, of course, depends on middle managers' commitment to strategy, which, in turn, is linked to:

- how the strategic intent fits with what managers perceive as the interest of the organization
- how it fits with managers' personal interests.

The attainment of single integration goals takes place thanks to integration mechanisms (Larsson, 1990), which are the tools available to the acquirer to foster the interaction between the joining firms, the coordination of this interaction, and the collective, interpersonal and individual levels of the human side of the combination (see Table 11.1).

Communication is the vehicle to foster integration and change. Open

Table 11.1   Integration mechanisms

Integration mechanisms	Description	Purpose
Restructuring	Accumulation/stabilization of similar activities Combination/timing of flows of related activities	Asset rationalization
Formal planning	Formal pre-adjustment of activities to one another by specifying the actions in advance	Goal timing Ambiguity and uncertainty reduction
Management information system	Budget and reporting systems standardization	Improve communication process
Transition teams	They are made up of members from both organizations to leverage on the coordinative integration efforts	Flexible way of structuring the transmission of new information
Socialization	Improve the coordination of the firm interaction by creating a common orientation	Reduce employee resistance by enhancing acculturation
Mutual consideration	It is directed toward a more favourable employee interpretation	Reduce resistance by decreasing conflicts of interest
Human resource systems	Job design / reward systems / personnel policies / career planning	Reduce individual employee resistance

Source: Capasso et al. (2002: 534).

communication between the merging companies and within the acquired firm is a tool to minimize ambiguity following a deal. Mergers and acquisitions are often surrounded by uncertainty about the future. If nothing is communicated, employees seek their own answers and this can lead to rumours, which can increase anxiety instead of reducing it. Managers should communicate to all involved audiences – all relevant stakeholders – as soon as possible. Arguably, the goals and the content of the message, as well as the medium used, depend on the target audience as illustrated in the synopsis below.

Communication can be analysed from a process perspective too: this implies recognizing the need of different communication strategies for different acquisition phases (Sinetar, 1981). In the pre-merger phase a steady

Table 11.2   A communication plan

Target audience	Goals	Content	Medium
Top managers in both companies	Engage commitment	Merger goals Merger approach Golden parachutes plans	Cascade meetings Series of lunch meetings CEO confidential meetings
Transition leaders	Engage commitment Ensure understand their role	Merger goals Merger approach Individual team goals Team member selection criteria	Long meetings led by CEO
Employees	Ensure they know the basic merger goals Start constructive discussions	Merger goals Merger approach Future potential Personnel policies	Cascade meetings E-mails Face to face communications
Investors	Secure investors' support	Merger goals Merger approach Future potential	Press news Company reports Analysts' reports

communication that reassures employees is suitable, while during the transition one communication should direct them in the new organization. If used properly, Sinetar suggests that communication not only preserves morale but also prevents top management turnover.

ACQUISITION PERFORMANCE

Despite the great amount of theoretical and empirical studies, mergers and acquisitions are still shady to academics and practitioners. Two fundamental questions remain unresolved. How do we explain the great variance of acquisition performance? (In other words, why do some prominent acquirers, such as GE and Cisco, perform better than others?) And how do we measure acquisition performance?

Both these questions still wait for a conclusive answer. As for the first, some scholars (Haleblian and Filkenstein, 1999; Zollo and Singh, 2004; Capasso and Meglio, 2005; Haleblian et al., 2006) investigated if and under what conditions it is possible to learn to manage acquisitions, and how this affects acquisition performance. Academic studies are generally concerned with the learning processes of recurring events, which show a high degree of similarity. Yet acquisition processes are rare, heterogeneous and complex, with a high degree of causal ambiguity. According to the model proposed by Capasso and Meglio (2005), we can imagine a sort of continuum in which the learning investment increases as firms come to rely on articulation and codification rather than on the routinization process. An example is a brainstorming session organized to extract the lessons learned from managing an acquisition: it can be expensive in terms of both the direct cost (time devoted to this task) and the opportunity cost, measured as the sacrifice of time dedicated to active tasks. Our point of view is that firms undertake this investment only if they have been and will be frequent acquirers. Very recently, marketing scholars have proposed a different explanation to the great variance in acquisition performance, focusing their attention on the acquiring firm's profile. Sorescu et al. (2007) suggest that a firm-specific, market-driven variable – namely, product capital – affects acquisition performance and predicts which firms are better positioned to acquire in the first place.

The second question concerns the operationalization of acquisition performance construct. Basically, in M&A literature we found market- as well as accounting-based measures of value creation. The first, typically adopted in event study methodology, implies that the market knows the impact of acquisitions on the acquiring firm's value and reacts immediately after the announcement that the deal is signed. Our point of view is that this kind of measure is suitable when the primary goal of the acquisition is value capture, but it is ill-suited when the transaction is strategic and its effects will take years to unfold. In these circumstances it is difficult, if not impossible, to unravel confounding effects in long-term market returns.

As for accounting-based measures, we doubt that they can reflect entirely the dynamic of integration processes, in which many intangible factors are involved. They also suffer from the limits of backward looking measures.

Our point of view is that these metrics, when considered alone, are insufficient to depict such a complex and multifaceted phenomenon. In some cases, as in event studies, traditional metrics can offer a misleading measure of acquisition performance, granted the temporal gap between the conclusion of the deal and the end of integration processes.

Acquisition outcomes can be grasped only by multiple metrics which reflect each aspect of the acquisition process, according to the balanced scorecard philosophy (Gates and Very, 2003; Meglio, 2004). This sort of triangulation can serve to assess the overall acquisition performance as well as integration improvements during the post-acquisition phase, since each metric can be linked to a particular integration priority.

Table 11.3   Metrics of acquisition performance

Overall performance	Market returns
	Accounting-based measures: revenue, net income, operating income
Cost synergies	Economies of scale and scope
	Productivity increase
	Overhead reduction
	Headcount reduction
	Cost savings
Revenue synergies	Customer retention/new customer acquisition
	Turnover increase
	Customers' fidelity
	Customers' cross-selling
Organizational climate	Top management turnover
	Absenteeism rate
	Productivity rate
	Sabotage episodes
	Employees' satisfaction
Resources transfer/sharing/ exploitation	Knowledge transfer at R&D unit
	New products
	New patents
	Managerial skills and systems transfer

CONCLUSION

Mergers and acquisitions continue to be a highly popular strategic option for a firm's development. Paradoxically, acquisitions appear to provide at best a mixed performance for the stakeholders involved. As a consequence this topic is still intriguing for academics and practitioners. We contribute to the growth of this field of study by revolving our discussion around three issues that are key to understanding a multifaceted phenomenon such as the one at hand: namely the methods of inquiry, the performance construct and further research questions to address.

M&A as a key corporate strategy has attracted the interest and research attention of a broad range of management disciplines encompassing financial, strategic, behavioural, and cultural aspects of this inherently risky activity. As outlined previously, the huge bulk of theoretical and empirical contributions, most of which are based on cross-sectional data, has resulted in a fragmented literature, which varies along schools of thought, research questions addressed and methods employed. Despite the great interest in this topic, the existing research remains incomplete (King et al., 2004). As a matter of fact, extant research tends to lump all types of acquisitions together and, in doing so, it is prone to overgeneralization and oversimplification. Accordingly it provides only a limited and insufficient understanding of this multidimensional and dynamic phenomenon (Pablo and Javidan, 2004). As a consequence, we observe a compelling call for a greater recognition of processual and organizational dimensions of acquisitions, which could be best addressed by a longitudinal approach. Longitudinal research can help to better address the question of causality, produce a clearer understanding of processes, facilitate the development of dynamic models of change, and permit the identification of contextual constraints; therefore it will favour the design of effective M&A implementation plans. Unfortunately, qualitative and longitudinal studies of M&As are still uncommon. This is probably due to a cultural prejudice toward quantitative research and to the difficulties researchers face in negotiating and gaining access to merging companies for a long time.

As for the former aspect, we are currently witnessing a change in some of the top tier journals' editorial policies, such as *Academy of Management Journal, Strategic Management Journal, Organization Studies* and the *British Journal of Management*. From 2000 onwards we find prominent examples of longitudinal qualitative research on M&As, such as the works of Graebner (2004), Schweizer (2005), Yu et al. (2005) and Kavanagh and Ashkanasy (2006). We hope that this proclivity will be reinforced in the future.

As for the latter, the problem of gaining access, intrinsic to any research programme, is overemphasized when studying a change process. The increasing top management turnover during the integration process can make it necessary to renegotiate the access and eventually modify some details of the research project. These difficulties have probably prevented the development of programmatic longitudinal research apart from the extensive research activity developed by the M&A Consortium at the Strategic Management Research Center of Carlson School of Management, University of Minnesota. The works of Van de Ven and his colleagues on mergers and acquisitions in the healthcare sector constitute a prominent example of 'engaged scholarship' in which negotiating access is not only a way to get primary data but also a tool to improve research questions and raise new ones (Van de Ven, 2007). This should eventually help to build a bridge between academics and practitioners and develop rigorous and relevant research about M&As.

Another key aspect that deserves attention is the way acquisition performance is operationalized. Traditionally, empirical research has employed either accounting or market-based metrics to measure the overall acquisition performance. We contend that they both suffer from some shortcomings. As for the market-based methodology we doubt that financial markets are able to predict, a few days after the deal announcement, how effective and successful the acquirer will be at integrating the target company. And stretching the event window cannot be a proper answer indeed since it is almost impossible to detect confounding effects. As for the accounting-based metrics, they are typically backward looking and unable to account for intangible assets. Under this regard they provide only a weak picture of performance, especially when the acquisition is technology-driven. Triangulating performance metrics helps to reduce these limitations and offer a more complete picture of acquisition outcomes for each stakeholder involved and for different time frames.

Finally, there is a perspective completely overlooked in M&A studies: the role of prominent stakeholders like suppliers and customers and the effects of mergers and acquisitions on them. Mergers and acquisitions are not neutral for suppliers, especially in those industries where trustworthy relations with suppliers are a critical factor for success because important idiosyncratic investments are necessary in achieving an effective cooperation along the value chain. Similarly customers can be affected by M&A, especially when they involve mature industries and create dominant positions. In many cases, integration between merging companies involves the cannibalization of product lines and brings about accelerated product obsolescence, decreasing the product value for customers. This is an issue not only for Industrial Organization and Antitrust Law, but also for marketing researchers who could investigate the impact of mergers and acquisitions on customers who could suffer in many ways due to integration problems.

REFERENCES

Agrawal, A., J.F. Jaffe and G.N. Mandelker (1992), 'The post-merger performance of acquiring firms: a re-examination of an anomaly', *The Journal of Finance*, **47** (4), 1605–1621.
Ahuja, G. and R. Katila (2001), 'Technological acquisitions and the innovation performance of acquiring firms: a longitudinal study', *Strategic Management Journal*, **22**, 197–220.
Akerlof, G.A. (1970), 'The market for lemons: qualitative uncertainty and the market mechanism', *Quarterly Journal of Economics*, **84**, 488–500.
Angwin, D. and E. Vaara (2005), 'Introduction to the special issue. Connectivity in merging organizations: beyond traditional cultural perspectives', *Organization Studies*, **26** (10), 1445–1453.
Barney, J.B. (1988), 'Returns to bidding firms in mergers and acquisitions: reconsidering the relatedness hypothesis', *Strategic Management Journal*, **9**, 71–78.
Barney, J.B. (1991), 'Firm resources and sustained competitive advantage', *Journal of Management*, **17**, 99–120.
Bastien, D.T. (1987), 'Common patterns of behavior and communication in corporate mergers and acquisitions', *Human Resource Management*, **26** (1), 17–33.

Beitel, P., D. Schiereck and M. Wahrenburg (2002), 'Explaining the M&A – success in European bank mergers and acquisitions', working paper, University of Witten/Herdecke, Germany.

Bergh, D.D. (1997), 'Predicting divestiture of unrelated acquisitions: an integrative model of *ex ante* conditions', *Strategic Management Journal*, **18** (9), 715–731.

Birkinshaw, J. (1999), 'Acquiring intellect: managing the integration of knowledge intensive acquisitions', *Business Horizons*, May-June, 33–40.

Bower, J.L. (2001), 'Not all M&As are alike – and that matters', *Harvard Business Review*, March, 93–101.

Bower, J.L., 'When we study M&A, what are we learning?', in A.L. Pablo and M. Javidan (eds), *Mergers and Acquisitions: Creating Integrative Knowledge*, Oxford: Blackwell.

Bruner, R. (2002), 'Does M&A pay? A survey of evidence for the decision-maker', *Journal of Applied Finance*, **12**, 48–68.

Bruner, R. (2004), *Applied Mergers and Acquisitions*, New York: John Wiley & Sons.

Buono, A.F. and J.L. Bowditch (1989), *The Human Side of Mergers and Acquisitions*, San Francisco, CA: Jossey-Bass.

Calori, R., M. Lubatkin and P. Very (1994), 'Control mechanisms in cross-border acquisitions: an international comparison', *Organization Studies*, **15** (3), 361–370.

Cannella, A.A. and J.R. Hambrick (1993), 'Effects of executive departures on the performance of acquired firms', *Strategic Management Journal*, **14**, 137–152.

Capasso, A., E. Imperiale and O. Meglio (2002), 'Quality management in post-acquisition integration processes', *Proceedings of the 7th World Congress for Total Quality Management*, Verona, 320–335.

Capasso, A. and O. Meglio (2005), 'Knowledge transfer in mergers and acquisitions: how frequent acquirers learn to manage the integration process', in A. Capasso, G.B. Dagnino and A. Lanza (eds), *Strategic Capabilities and Knowledge Transfer Within and Between Organizations*, Cheltenham: Edward Elgar.

Capron, L., P. Dussage and W. Mitchell (1998), 'Resource redeployment following horizontal mergers and acquisitions in Europe and North America, 1988–1992', *Strategic Management Journal*, **19** (7), 631–663.

Cartwright, S. and C.L. Cooper (1993), 'The role of culture compatibility in successful organizational marriage', *Academy of Management Executive*, **7** (2), 57–70.

Cartwright, S. and R. Schoenberg (2006), 'Thirty years of mergers and acquisitions research: recent advances and future opportunities', *British Journal of Management*, **17**, S1–S5.

Cassiman, B., M.G. Colombo, P. Garrone and R. Veugelers (2005), 'The impact of M&A on the R&D process. An empirical analysis of the role of technological- and market-relatedness', *Research Policy*, **34**, 195–220.

Chatterjee, S. (1986), 'Types of synergy and economic value: the impact of acquisitions on merging and rival firms', *Strategic Management Journal*, **7**, 119–139.

Chatterjee, S., M. Lubatkin, D.M. Schweiger and Y. Weber (1992), 'Cultural differences and shareholder value in related mergers: linking equity and human capital', *Strategic Management Journal*, **13**, 319–344.

Chaudhuri, S. and B. Tabrizi (1999), 'Capturing the real value in high-tech acquisitions', *Harvard Business Review*, **5**, 15–21.

Datta, D.K. (1991), 'Organizational fit and acquisition performance: effects of post-acquisition integration', *Strategic Management Journal*, **12** (4), 281–297.

Datta, D.K. and J.H. Grant (1990), 'Relationships between type of acquisition, the autonomy given to the acquired firm, and acquisition success: an empirical analysis', *Journal of Management*, **16** (1), 29–44.

Epstein, M.J. (2004), 'The drivers of success in post-merger integration', *Organizational Dynamics*, **33** (2), 174–189.

Floreani, A. and S. Rigamonti (2001), 'Mergers and shareholders' wealth in the insurance industry', working paper, Universita Cattolica del S. Cuore.

Franks, J., R. Harris and S. Titman (1991), 'The post-merger share price performance of acquiring firms', *Journal of Financial Economics*, **29**, 81–96.

Gates, S. and P. Very (2003), 'Measuring performance during M&A integration', *Long Range Planning*, **36**, 167–185.

Goergen, M. and L. Renneboog (2003), 'Shareholder wealth effects of European domestic and cross-border takeover bids, finance working paper, European Corporate Governance Institute.

Graebner, M.E. (2004), 'Momentum and serendipity: how acquired leaders create value in the integration of technology firms', *Strategic Management Journal*, **25**, 751–777.

Graebner, M.E. and K.M. Eisenhardt (2004), 'The seller's side of the story: acquisition as courtship and governance syndicate in entrepreneurial firms', *Administrative Science Quarterly*, **49**, 366–403.

Habeck, M.M., F. Kroger and M.R. Tram (2000), *After the Merger*, London, UK: Financial Times, Prentice Hall.

Halebian, J. and S. Filkenstein (1999), 'The influence of organizational acquisition experience on acquisition performance: a behavioural perspective', *Administrative Science Quarterly*, **44**, 29–46.

Haleblian, J., J. Kim and N. Rajagopalan (2006), 'The influence of acquisition experience and performance on acquisition behavior: evidence from the US commercial banking industry', *Academy of Management Journal*, **49** (2), 357–370.

Hambrick, D.C. and A.A. Cannella (1993), 'Relative standing: a framework for understanding departures of acquired executives', *Academy of Management Journal*, **36** (4), 733–762.

Harrison, J.S., M.A. Hitt, R.E. Hoskisson and R.D. Ireland (2001), 'Resource complementarity in business combination: extending the logic to organizational alliances', *Journal of Management*, **27**, 679–690.

Haspeslagh, P.C. and D.B. Jemison (1991), *Managing Acquisitions*, New York: Free Press.

Hayward, M.L. (2002), 'When do firms learn from their acquisition experience? Evidence from 1990–1995', *Strategic Management Journal*, **23**, 21–39.

Hitt, M.A., R.E. Hoskisson, R.D. Ireland and J.S. Harrison (1991), 'Effects of acquisitions on R&D inputs and outputs', *Academy of Management Journal*, **34**, 693–706.

Hitt, M.A., R.E. Hoskisson, R. Johnson and D. Moesel (1996), 'The market for corporate control', *Academy of Management Journal*, **39**, 1084–1119.

Homburg, C. and M. Bucerius (2006), 'Is speed of integration really a success factor of mergers and acquisitions? An analysis of the role of internal and external relatedness', *Strategic Management Journal*, **27**, 347–367.

Hubbard, R., D.E. Vetter and E.L. Little (1998), 'Replication in strategic management: scientific testing for validity, generalizability and usefulness', *Strategic Management Journal*, **19**, 243–254.

Jarrell, G.A., J.A. Brickley and J.M. Netter (1988), 'The market for corporate control: the empirical evidence since 1980', *Journal of Economic Perspectives*, **2**, 49–68.

Javidan, M., A.L. Pablo, H. Singh, M. Hitt and D. Jemison (2004), 'Where we've been and where we're going', in A.L. Pablo and M. Javidan (eds), *Mergers and Acquisitions: Creating Integrative Knowledge*, Oxford: Blackwell.

Jemison, D.B. and S.B. Sitkin (1986), 'Corporate acquisitions: a process perspective', *Academy of Management Review*, **11**, 145–163.

Jensen, M.C. and R.S. Ruback (1983), 'The market for corporate control: the scientific evidence', *Journal of Financial Economics*, **11**, 5–50.

Kavanagh, M.H. and N.M. Ashkanasy (2006), 'The impact of leadership and change management strategy on organizational culture and individual acceptance of change during a merger', *British Journal of Management*, **17**, S81–S103.

King, D.R., D.R. Dalton, C.M. Daily and J. Covin (2004), 'Meta-analysis of post-acquisition performance: indications of unidentified moderators', *Strategic Management Journal*, **25**, 187–200.

Kohers, N. and T. Kohers (2000), 'The value creation potential of high-tech mergers', *Financial Analysts Journal*, **53** (3), 40–48.

Kohers, N. and T. Kohers (2001), 'Takeovers of technology firms: expectations vs. reality', *Financial Management*, Autumn, 35–54.

Krishnan, H.A., A. Miller and Judge (1997), 'Diversification and top management team complementarity: is performance improved by merging similar or dissimilar teams', *Strategic Management Journal*, **18** (5), 361–374.

Kusewitt, J.B. Jr (1985), 'An exploratory study of strategic acquisition factors relating to performance', *Strategic Management Journal*, **6**, 151–169.

Larsson, R. (1990), *Coordination of Action in M&A. Interpretive and System Approach Toward Synergy*, Lund Studies in Economics and Management 10, Lund University Press.

Larsson, R., M. Driver, M. Holmqvist and P. Sweet (2001), 'Career disintegration and reintegration in mergers and acquisitions: managing competence and motivational intangibles', *European Management Journal*, **19** (6), 609–618.

Larsson, R. and S. Filkenstein (1999), 'Integrating strategic, organizational, and human resource perspectives on merger and acquisitions: a case survey of synergies realization', *Organization Science*, **10** (1), 1–26.

Larsson, R. and M. Lubatkin (2001), 'Achieving acculturation in mergers and acquisitions: an international case survey', *Human Relations*, **54** (12), 1573–1607.

Loderer, C. and K. Martin (1992), 'Post-acquisition performance of acquiring firms', *Financial Management*, Autumn, 69–79.

Lohrum, C. (1996), 'Post-acquisition integration: towards an understanding of employee reactions', doctoral dissertation. Research Reports 65, Swedish School of Economics and Business Administration, Helsinki, Finland.

Lubatkin, M.H. (1983), 'Mergers and the performance of the acquiring firm', *Academy of Management Review*, **8**, 218–225.

Makadok, R. and J.B. Barney (2001), 'Strategic factor market intelligence: an application of information economics to strategy formulation and competitor intelligence', *Management Science*, **47** (12), 1621–1638.

Marks, M.L. (1982), 'Merging human resources: a review of current research', *Mergers & Acquisitions*, **17**, 38–44.

Marks, M.L. and P. Mirvis (1985), 'Merger syndrome: stress and uncertainty', *Mergers & Acquisitions*, Summer, 50–55.

Meglio, O. (2004), *Il Processo di Integrazione Post-acquisizione. Profilo Teorico ed Esperienze Aziendali*. [The post-acquisition integration process. Theories and experiences], Padova: CEDAM.

Meyer, C.B. (2006), 'Destructive dynamics of middle management intervention in post-merger processes', *Journal of Applied Behavioral Science*, **42** (4), 397–419.

Mintzberg, H. and J.A. Waters (1985), 'Of strategies, deliberate and emergent', *Strategic Management Journal*, **6** (3), 170–184.

Mirvis, P. and M.L. Marks (1986), 'Merger syndrome: management by crisis (part 2)', *Mergers & Acquisitions*, **20** (3), 70–76.

Moeller, S., F. Schlingemann and R. Stulz (2003), 'Do shareholders of acquiring firms gain from acquisitions?', working paper, Ohio State University.

Mulherin, J.H. and A.L. Boone (2000), 'Comparing acquisitions and divestitures', *Journal of Corporate Finance*, **6** (6), 117–139.

Nahavandi, A. and A.R. Malekzadeh (1988), 'Acculturation in mergers and acquisitions', *Academy of Management Review*, **13** (1), 79–90.

Napier, N.K. (1989), 'Mergers and acquisitions, human resources issues and outcomes: a review and a suggested typology', *Journal of Management Studies*, **26** (3), 271–289.

Olie, R. (1990), 'Culture and integration problems in international mergers and acquisitions', *European Management Journal*, **8** (2), 219–235.

Pablo, A.L. (1994), 'Determinants of acquisition integration level: a decision-making perspective', *Academy of Management Journal*, **37** (4), 803–836.

Pablo, A.L. and M. Javidan (eds) (2004), *Mergers and Acquisitions: Creating Integrative Knowledge*, Oxford: Blackwell.

Puranam, P., B.C. Powell and H. Singh (2006), 'Due diligence failure as a signal detection problem', *Strategic Organization*, **4** (4), 319–348.

Puranam, P., H. Singh and M. Zollo (2003), 'A bird in the hand or two in the bush? Integration trade offs in technology-grafting acquisitions', *European Management Journal*, **21** (2), 179–184.

Puranam, P., H. Singh and M. Zollo (2006), 'Organizing for innovation: managing the coordination-autonomy dilemma in technology acquisitions', *Academy of Management Journal*, **49** (2), 263–280.

Ranft, A.L. and M.D. Lord (2002), 'Acquiring new technologies and capabilities: a grounded model of acquisition implementation', *Organization Science*, **13**, 420–442.

Ravenscraft, D. and F.M. Scherer (1987), *Mergers, Sell-offs, & Economic Efficiency*, Washington, D.C.: the Brookings Institute.

Ravenscraft, D. and F.M. Scherer (1989), 'The profitability of mergers', *International Journal of Industrial Organization*, **7**, 101–116.

Riad, S. (2005), 'The power of organizational culture as a discursive formation in merger integration', *Organization Studies*, **26** (10), 1529–1554.

Risberg, A. (1999), *Ambiguities Thereafter – An Interpretive Approach to Acquisitions*, Lund Studies in Economics and Management 46, Lund University Press.

Roll, R. (1986), 'The hubris hypothesis of corporate takeovers', *Journal of Business*, **59**, 197–216.

Sales, A.L. and P.H. Mirvis (1985), 'When cultures collide: issues in acquisition', in J.R. Kimberly and R.E. Quinn (eds), *New Futures: The Challenge of Managing Corporation Transitions*, Homewood, IL: Dow Jones Irwin.

Salter, M.S. and W.A. Weinhold (1981), 'Choosing compatible acquisitions', *Harvard Business Review*, Jan-Feb, 117–127.

Saxton, T. and M. Dollinger (2004), 'Target reputation and appropriability: picking and deploying resources in acquisitions', *Journal of Management*, **30** (1), 123–147.

Scherer, F.M. (1980), *Industrial Market Structure and Economic Performance*, Chicago: Rand McNally.

Schilit, W.K. (1987), 'An examination of the influence of middle-level managers in formulating and implementing strategic decisions', *Journal of Management Studies*, **24**, 271–293.

Schweiger, D.M. and A.S. De Nisi (1991), 'Communication with employees following a merger: a longitudinal field experiment', *Academy of Management Journal*, **34** (1), 110–135.

Schweiger, D.M. and P.K. Goulet (2005), 'Facilitating acquisition integration through deep-level cultural learning interventions: a longitudinal field experiment', *Organization Studies*, **26** (10), 1477–1499.

Schweiger, D.M. and Y. Weber (1989), 'Strategies for managing human resources during mergers and acquisitions: an empirical investigation', *Human Resource Planning*, **12** (2), 69–86.

Schweizer, L. (2005), 'Organizational integration of acquired biotechnology companies in pharmaceutical companies: the need for a hybrid approach', *Academy of Management Journal*, **48** (6), 1051–1074.

Seth, A. (1990a), 'Value creation in acquisitions: a reexamination of performance issues', *Strategic Management Journal*, **11**, 99–115.

Seth, A. (1990b), 'Source of value creation in acquisitions: an empirical investigation', *Strategic Management Journal*, **11**, 431–446.

Shaver, M.J. (2006), 'A paradox of synergy: contagion and capacity effects in mergers and acquisitions', *Academy of Management Journal*, **31** (4), 962–976.

Shelton, L.M. (1988), 'Strategic business fit and corporate acquisitions: empirical evidence', *Strategic Management Journal*, **9** (3), 279–287.

Shrivastava, P. (1986), 'Post-merger integration', *Journal of Business Strategy*, **7** (1), 65–76.

Sorescu, A.B., R.K. Chandy and J.C. Prabhu (2007), 'Why some acquisitions do better than others: product capital as a driver of long term stock returns', *Journal of Marketing Research*, **1** (44), 57–72.

Teerikangas, S. and P. Very (2006), 'The culture-performance relationship in M&A: from yes/no to how', *British Journal of Management*, **17**, S31–S48.

Tsoukas, H. and C. Knudsen (2002), 'The conduct of strategy research', in A. Pettigrew, H. Thomas and R. Whittington (eds), *Handbook of Strategy and Management*, London: Sage.

Uhlenbruck, K., M.A. Hitt and M. Semadeni (2006), 'Market value effects of acquisitions involving internet firms: a resource-based analysis', *Strategic Management Journal*, **27**, 899–913.

Vaara, E. (2001), 'Role-bound actors in corporate combinations: a sociopolitical perspective on post-merger change processes', *Scandinavian Journal of Management*, **17**, 481–509.

Vaara, E., J. Tienari and R. Santti (2003), 'The international match: metaphors as vehicles of social identity-building in cross-border mergers', *Human Relations*, **56** (4), 419–451.

Valentini, G. (2005), 'Mergers & acquisitions and technological performance', *Academy of Management Best Paper Proceedings.*

Van de Ven, A.H. (1992), 'Suggestions for studying strategy process: a research note', *Strategic Management Journal*, **13**, 169–188.

Van de Ven, A.H. (2007), *Engaged Scholarship: Creating Knowledge for Theory and Practice*, New York: Oxford University Press.

Very, P., R. Calori and M. Lubatkin (1993), 'An investigation of national and organizational culture influences in recent European mergers', *Advances in Strategic Management*, **9**, 323–346.

Very, P., M. Lubatkin, J. Calori and J. Veiga (1997), 'Relative standing and the performance of recently acquired European firms', *Strategic Management Journal*, **18** (8), 593–614.

Walsh, J.P. (1988), 'Top management turnover following acquisitions', *Strategic Management Journal*, **9** (2), 173–183.

Weber, Y. (1996), 'Corporate cultural fit and performance in mergers and acquisitions', *Human Relations*, **49** (9), 1181–1202.

Weber, Y. and D.M. Schweiger (1992), 'Top management culture conflict in mergers and acquisitions', *The International Journal of Conflict Management*, **3** (4), 285–301.

Yip, G.S. (1982), 'Diversification entry: internal development versus acquisition', *Strategic Management Journal*, **3** (4), 331–345.

Zollo, M. and Singh (2004), 'Deliberate learning in corporate acquisitions: post-acquisition strategies and integration capability in US bank mergers', *Strategic Management Journal*, **25**, 1233–1256.

Zollo, M. and S.J. Winter (2002), 'Deliberate learning and the evolution of dynamic capabilities', *Organization Science*, **13**, 339–351.

12 Strategic implications of alliance formation and dynamics: a comprehensive review[1]

Africa Ariño and Esteban García-Canal

INTRODUCTION

Until the early 1980s, very little attention was paid to analyzing the strategic alliances (SAs) and cooperative agreements between firms. Nevertheless, from that moment onwards, there was an increasing interest in SAs and the number of papers on that topic has grown exponentially. The main reason for this growth was the importance that SAs began to gain, as the number of agreements of all kinds became larger, even in circumstances where they had not occurred up to that point, as in the case of SAs created by large corporations in order to develop new technologies or to coordinate their international strategies. Due precisely to the growth in this stream of research, this seems to be an appropriate moment to review this literature in order to synthesize the main advances in our knowledge of SAs. Thus, this chapter is organized around the main lines of the field including research on the logic of alliance formation, their governance form, and dynamic and performance issues.

THE LOGIC OF ALLIANCE FORMATION

Why do companies engage in SAs? There are many ways to approach this question. We will focus on SAs as a mechanism to deal with uncertainty, and as a vehicle to access requisite resources. In so doing, we will review some extant theoretical perspectives on SA formation including real options theory, transaction cost economics, the resource-based perspective, the learning-race view, the knowledge-access perspective, and the relational view.

Two types of uncertainty surround any transaction: environmental uncertainty, and behavioral uncertainty. The first one refers to uncertainty about future states of nature. It results from exogenous sources that rest outside an organization's control and are hard to anticipate (e.g. Krishnan et al., 2006), and it resolves with the passage of time (Santoro and McGill,

2005). Under conditions of high environmental uncertainty, real options theory helps explain the formation of SAs as a way to maintain flexibility while opening options for the future. This view of SAs was first advanced by Kogut (1991), and was followed by a number of studies (e.g. Chi and McGuire, 1996; Santoro and McGill, 2005). Kogut (1991) conceived joint ventures (JVs) as a real option to expand in the face of future market and technological developments. A JV grants a company the option of future expansion and growth if the environmental uncertainty resolves favorably, while limiting the downside risk associated with investing in a volatile environment. Instances of high environmental uncertainty include (1) a firm's expansion to new geographical markets, and (2) the technological progress to which certain industries are subject. First, and beyond a company's own lack of familiarity with new markets, entering certain countries entails a high uncertainty due to the volatility of economic conditions that results in an uncertain demand, to exchange rate fluctuations, and to political risk. Second, technological uncertainty results in alternative potential technological trajectories. A company may ensure its entry into any of these trajectories by means of a network of SAs, while limiting the investment committed to any one of them.

The second type of uncertainty – behavioral uncertainty – refers to the difficulty in anticipating and understanding a party's actions (e.g. Krishnan et al., 2006). It is endogenous to the transacting parties, and is reduced by their actions (Santoro and McGill, 2005). Behavioral uncertainty is at the heart of transaction cost economics, which conceives it as present in transactions involving a high degree of asset specificity, assuming uncertainty and bounded rationality (Williamson, 1985). The optimal governance choice is that which minimizes the sum of production and transaction costs. Hennart (1988) was among the first to apply the transaction cost logic to explain SA formation – or more specifically, JV formation. Behavioral uncertainty drives the choice of governance form, while exogenous uncertainty is viewed as aggravating other conditions, especially asset specificity (Cuypers and Martin, 2006). Specific assets have economic rents associated with them. When two parties engage in a transaction, a situation of bilateral monopoly is created. The party contributing the specific assets runs the risk of expropriation of those rents if the other party behaves opportunistically. JVs are the optimal form under conditions of intermediate product market inefficiencies, when the intermediate products being transacted are firm-specific and have the characteristics of public goods (Hennart, 1988). In JVs, alignment of incentives is achieved by mutual hostage positions.

The transaction cost explanation of SA formation has been criticized for focusing on efficiency seeking instead of value creation (Zajac and

Olsen, 1993). From a resource-based perspective, SAs are seen to create value through the novel combination of resources contributed by the partners. Das and Teng (2000) outline the literature that draws from this perspective. Valuable resources are characterized by their scarcity and relevance in the product market; the competitive advantage they convey will be sustainable to the extent that they are durable and difficult to transfer and to imitate. By definition, this type of resource is difficult to find in the market, and costly for a firm to develop both in terms of time and economic resources. Under these conditions, SAs become a suitable mechanism for firms to access requisite resources.

Knowledge-based resources lend themselves to being shared in the context of an SA. From a resource-based view, they have the characteristics of valuable resources just described. From a transaction cost perspective, they tend to be firm-specific, and have the characteristics of public goods – necessary conditions for an SA to be formed. A discussion that has emerged in the literature relates to whether firms should internalize these resources or whether it is enough for companies to access them. The learning-race perspective conceives SAs as transitory vehicles for organizational learning. This view was first proposed by Hamel (1991), and followed by Khanna et al. (1998). From this perspective, partners to an SA engage in a learning race. The partner outcompeting the other in either acquiring the counterpart's knowledge or appropriating the joint learning developed within the SA wins the race. As that partner has internalized the requisite resources, the SA has no longer a raison d'etre for the winning partner. Some authors (e.g. Hennart et al., 1999) have questioned the presumption that most SAs are of the learning-race type. Others (e.g. Baden-Fuller and Grant, 2004) espouse the view that the advantage of SAs over both hierarchies and markets resides precisely in that they are a vehicle for accessing knowledge rather than acquiring it, as SAs may combine the benefits of knowledge specialization and those of flexible integration. At the end of the day, underlying is an efficiency argument for a particular case.

Others see the relationship that develops through an SA as a resource in and of itself. This stream constitutes the so-called relational *view*. The relationship has the characteristics of an asset "whose effective exploitation in the pursuit of value requires the incurrence of expenditures specifically dedicated toward developing and advancing the relationship" (Madhok and Tallman, 1998: 331). Such an asset has the potential to generate new value creation opportunities to the extent to which partners "combine, exchange, or invest in idiosyncratic assets, knowledge, and resources/capabilities, and/or they employ effective governance mechanisms" (Dyer and Singh, 1998: 662). The relationship creates an interaction platform that allows partners to generate and transfer knowledge and information, thus augmenting their innovativeness and flexibility (Lorenzoni and Lipparini, 1999).

ALLIANCE STRUCTURAL CHOICES

Research on alliance structural choices has been dominated by studies on the choice of governance form (e.g. Hennart, 1988; Pisano, 1989; Gulati, 1995; García-Canal, 1996; Oxley, 1999). The key research question underlying these studies is under what conditions an equity-based JV is preferable to a purely contractual SA. The choice of one or another will determine the institutional context – in this case, a hybrid one in between markets and hierarchies – within which a transaction will take place (Williamson, 1985). However, whether an SA takes the form of a JV or of a purely contractual SA, contracts will be designed that will specify the terms of exchange, and the allocation of risks and gains (James, 2000). Despite their importance to SA structuring, only recently have SA contracts received attention from researchers (e.g. Lerner and Merges, 1998; Ariño and Reuer, 2006a). In this section we will review extant researches related to both the choice of governance form, and to SA contracts – see Ariño and Reuer (2006b) for a collection of state of the art research on alliance governance and contracts. The main contributions in these two branches of this research line are analyzed in the following subsections.

The Choice of a Governance Form

As we just mentioned, the choice of a governance form is one of the most frequently analyzed research problems in the SA field. In particular, the literature has revolved around the conditions that determine the choice between the creation of a JV and the use of a purely contractual agreement to organize the SA activities. The question has been considered from a number of theoretical perspectives, including transaction cost economics, social network theory, and the organizational design approach. Transaction cost economics (Williamson, 1985) has been the main theoretical framework used in this literature. The pioneering works (Hennart, 1988; Pisano, 1989), starting from the classic distinction between markets and hierarchies, assimilate JVs to hierarchies, and attribute to JVs similar properties to those identified in hierarchies in the study of vertical integration. Social network theory (Burt, 1982; Granovetter, 1985) appears as an alternative to analyze governance choice in the context of the network of relationships companies are embedded in (e.g. Gulati, 1995). Finally, the principles of the organizational design approach (Thomson, 1967) permeate another group of studies that emphasizes the usefulness of JVs in solving the coordination problems derived from task uncertainty and interdependence (Casciaro, 2003; Gulati and Singh, 1998).

The empirical evidence is far from conclusive regarding the factors that determine the governance choice. Still, there seems to be convergence around a number of conditions. For instance, the choice of a JV seems to be preferable relative to a purely contractual SA if the SA involves several functional areas, products, technologies, or partners (Colombo, 2003; Croisier, 1998; García-Canal, 1996; Oxley, 1999; Oxley and Sampson, 2004; Pisano, 1989). These results may be expected from a transaction cost perspective, as well as from an organizational design one, as under those conditions coordination and/or motivation problems tend to increase.

Interestingly, although similar coordination problems also arise when the collaboration covers several countries, the different studies have not obtained conclusive results for this factor (Croisier, 1998; García-Canal, 1996). Moreover, results related to certain partner characteristics are also inconclusive. For instance, the empirical evidence is mixed regarding the influence of factors such as whether the partners are previous competitors (Colombo, 2003; Oxley and Sampson, 2004), collaborators (Colombo, 2003; García-Canal, 1996; Gulati, 1995; Gulati and Singh, 1998; Oxley and Sampson, 2004), or have the same nationality (Gulati, 1995; Oxley and Sampson, 2004). Results relating to the existence of previous cooperative relationships among the partners deserve special attention. According to social network theory, such relationships would imply a lower probability of creating JVs relative to the creation of a purely contractual SA. However, only the works of Gulati (1995) and Gulati and Singh (1998) offer evidence supporting the argument.

The different empirical studies have not tested the exact same hypothesis. However, common to all of them is their approach to JVs as an organizational option to solve a latent conflict in any collaboration: the allocation of coordination and control rights and distribution of cooperation rents. Given that all partners are directly involved in the performance of the activities, none of them will have the full capacity to direct them or will be the only residual claimant. This generates a latent conflict for the control of the activities and the distribution of the profits earned.

If the SA adopts the form of a JV, an administrative hierarchy will be established to ensure control rights to supervise and manage the use of the pooled resources. In addition, the ownership structure of the JV establishes a criterion for distributing SA rents. Setting up this hierarchy, however, has two drawbacks. On the one hand, there are some start-up and operating costs pertaining to the new company – which must be assumed by the partners – and that sometimes exceed the coordination and control benefits stemming from the formation of the JV (Reuer and Ariño, 2002). On the other hand, the joint ownership of the venture implies that all partners hold a stake in the residual value of the cooperative project without specifying *ex ante* performance requirements (Kogut, 1988). Relying exclusively on contractual agreements requires that partners negotiate control rights and rent distribution criteria at the time of signing the contract, specifying all possible compensations in the relationship, and anticipating solutions for the potential contingencies that could arise. Otherwise, they may be exposed to re-negotiations and subsequent conflicts.

For this reason, a JV will be a more attractive option for partners in complex SAs: those in which it is difficult to specify *ex ante* behavioral and performance requirements. In the remaining cases, relying exclusively on contractual agreements will constitute the best option, because partners can define control rights and rent distribution criteria by means of contracts, and besides, the two disadvantages derived from the establishment of the administrative hierarchy we have just mentioned are avoided.

The institutional environment also plays a critical role in the effectiveness of contractual agreements (Henisz and Williamson, 1999). In fact, recent contributions in the field of the Economics of Intellectual Property Rights (e.g. Lerner and Merges, 1998) highlight the critical role played by intellectual property rights in assuring the effectiveness of contractual agreements. In fact, empirical research shows that JVs are more frequently used in countries in which the effectiveness of the intellectual property rights system is negligible (Oxley, 1999; Hagedoorn et al., 2005).

The Literature on SA Contracts

Another branch of the literature on the governance of SAs has analyzed the clauses and specific content of the contracts that regulate SAs (for a broader review of alliance contractual design, see Ariño and Reuer, 2006a). SA contracts may serve two important purposes. First, they provide an opportunity to define partner expectations and to help them plan their activities. Second, in the case of SA break-up, they may provide guidance to the courts on what the partners' intentions were. Typical contract terms include the parties' roles and responsibilities, the allocation of decision and control rights, contingency planning, how the parties will communicate, and how they will resolve disputes (Argyres and Mayer, 2007).

Early studies of SA contracts treated them as a variable that helped explain certain SA attributes or outcomes. For instance, Parkhe (1993) treats contractual safeguards as an *ex post* attempt to deter opportunism, and finds that contractual safeguards are positively linked to the perception of opportunistic behavior, and negatively to the payoff from unilateral cooperation and the shadow of the future. Deeds and Hill (1998) provide a similar treatment; however, their results show a non-significant relationship between the use of contractual safeguards and perceived opportunism. Reuer and Ariño (2002) find that SAs with more extensive contractual safeguards *ex ante* are less likely to experience contractual re-negotiations throughout their life than those with less complex contracts.

More recently, attention has turned to examine contract characteristics per se. Poppo and Zenger (2002) claim the need to develop precise measures of contractual clauses. Subsequently, a few studies have examined the multidimensionality of alliance contracts. Luo (2005) identifies three such dimensions: term specificity, contingency adaptability, and contractual obligatoriness. Reuer and Ariño (2007) distinguish two such dimensions which they call enforcement and coordination provisions. Hagedoorn and Hesen (2007) review a reduced number of SA contracts including two of equity JVs, two of non-equity partnerships, and two license contracts. They compare such contracts in terms of the following provisions: adaptation clauses, damage measures, warranties, dispute settlement mechanisms, property rights, and revision clauses. They suggest that equity JVs and non-equity partnerships follow a relational contracting perspective, while licenses are more attuned to classical contracting.

The role of formal contracts in connection to relational governance has also received increasing attention. On the one hand, some argue that the two are substitutes. The initial seed for this view may be traced back to the work of Macaulay (1963) who argues that an excessive reliance on formal governance may banish relational norms. Gulati (1995) claims that relational norms can substitute for hierarchical contracts in many instances. On the other hand, others argue that formal contracts and relational governance are complementary. For instance, Poppo and Zenger (2002) find support for the complementarity between contractual complexity and relational governance. Luo (2002: 917) concludes that "[w]ithout contracts, cooperation will lack an institutional framework to proceed. Without cooperation, contracts cannot encourage long-term evolutions of IJVs." Carson et al. (2006) argue that formal and relational contracts are not simply substitutes; rather, each is favored under certain environmental contingencies. One of the ways in which the two may be complementary is through the contracting process. According to Mayer and Argyres (2004: 407), "the contracting process promotes expectations of cooperation and generates commitment to the relationship." Carson et al. (2006) also emphasize the importance of the contracting process for coordination purposes. We turn now to review the literature related to SA processes.

ALLIANCE PROCESS DYNAMICS

"The interplay between structure and process is the defining feature of any fundamental transformation in interorganizational relationships" (Zajac and Olsen, 1993: 144). After a long period during which most of the research efforts related to the decision of whether to form an SA, and of which type, a series of studies subsequent to that by Zajac and Olsen (1993) have built a body of research around processes at work at different SA stages. Three distinct stages can be identified, whatever names they take (Salk, 2005): formation, execution, and change or discontinuation. Throughout these stages, processes of sense-making, mutual understanding, and commitment take place (Ring and Van de Ven, 1994).

Formation processes are the least explored. One critical reason for this is the difficulty researchers have in accessing requisite data. Formation processes include internal sense-making regarding the adequacy of forming an SA, assessment of potential partners, active sense-making about the joint activities, and efforts to build relational quality that will feed the operational stage (Ring, 2000). Doz et al. (2000) investigate formation processes in R&D consortia, and find two different formation pathways which they label emergent and engineered.

Most of the SA process research focuses on the execution stage. Doz (1996) explores how learning processes mediate between initial conditions and SA outcomes. Building on Ring and Van de Ven (1994) and Doz (1996), Ariño and de la Torre (1998) propose an evolutionary model of interfirm collaboration that helps explain the genesis of relational quality, as well as SA dissolution. Kumar and Nti (1998) examine outcome and process discrepancies that may emerge as the partners interact, and argue that discrepancies drive alliance evolution. This stream of literature focuses on inter-partner dynamics, and is in close connection to the relational view of SAs.

Regarding change or discontinuation, Yan and Zeng (1999) denounce a lack of attention to these processes, with research that is static in character, and focused on the outcome. They claim the need of a process-based approach that portrays the causes and dynamic development of instability. Inkpen and Beamish (1997) explain instability in terms of shifts in partner bargaining power associated with learning that eliminates a partner's dependence on the other one. Das and Teng (2000) explain SA instabilities in terms of the tensions generated by three pairs of forces: cooperation vs competition, rigidity vs flexibility, and short-term vs long-term orientation. We turn next to review the literature considering SA change or discontinuation as an outcome, as well as the literature on SA performance.

Alliance Instability and Performance

The high instability and discontinuation of SAs have sprung a large number of studies about the factors that motivate their success or failure, or at least their instability and evolution. However, the studies that follow this research line have come across an important methodological problem, namely finding an objective, reliable and valid criterion to measure SA performance. Thus, before discussing the determinants of SA instability and performance, we offer a brief review of the performance measures used (more comprehensive reviews may be found in Geringer and Hebert, 1991, and Ariño, 2003).

On the Measurement of Alliance Performance

A large segment of the empirical research on SA performance has focused on JVs, since it is easier to obtain information about this type of SA than about purely contractual ones. Still, it is not easy to find an objective indicator of JV performance. JV dissolution and/or certain changes in the property structure were taken as such indicators (e.g. Blodgett, 1992; Park and Russo, 1996), although they have been criticized by some. With regard to JV termination, it has been said that JVs are inherently unstable (Gomes Casseres, 1987): they are created because the partners need to combine their resources, and their termination may just indicate that they are not necessary any more – perhaps because the partners have acquired those resources through organizational learning. Because of this, JV termination or property change cannot be interpreted as a failure; at least not for all of the partners. On the other hand, the use of changes in the property structure as a performance indicator presents the additional problem of being influenced by other factors, such as the partners' different bargaining power and the relative importance of their contributions (Geringer and Hebert, 1991).

In any event, it is hard to find any objective measure of SA performance void of disadvantages. This is the case when measuring the stock market reaction to SA formation announcements (e.g. Koh and Venkatraman, 1991), which is an *ex ante* measure of performance that can be used only when the partners are public companies. Due to these shortcomings of objective measures, subjective measures of performance, normally based on partners' perception of alliance outcomes, have been increasingly used. Next we summarize the main findings of three main groups of studies: (1) studies on so-called objective measures of SA performance, such as instability and duration; (2) studies on the stock market reaction to alliance formation; and (3) studies relying on *ex post* assessments of SA organizational effectiveness.

Studies Based on Objective *Ex Post* Measures of SA Performance

Studies on objective measures of SA performance may be grouped around two stages: a first stage associated with the analysis of JV instability, and a second in which JV duration becomes the focus of research questions. Initial research focused its attention on JV instability, although this instability was imprecisely defined. Some studies focused on changes in the JV ownership structure (e.g. Blodgett, 1992; Hennart et al., 1998). Other studies focused on termination either due to sale to a third party or to dissolution (e.g. Gomes-Casseres, 1987; Kogut, 1988), whereas still others simply studied terminations resulting from dissolution (Reynolds, 1984; Kogut, 1989). In many cases, analysis of instability was carried out employing descriptive techniques – mainly frequencies and contingency tables – estimating instability or mortality ratios of between 29 and 55 percent. In these studies, greater instability was observed in JVs with size differences among the partners (Kogut, 1988), and in those created in developing countries (Beamish, 1988). The relationship between instability and the ownership structure of the JV was also examined, although contradictory results were obtained. Whereas some (e.g. Kogut, 1988) found greater stability in JVs with a dominant partner, others (e.g. Blodgett, 1992) detected greater stability in those with an equitable ownership structure. The stability of JVs was also compared with that of wholly owned subsidiaries, with the former showing greater instability than the latter (Gomes-Casseres, 1987).

The weakness in the theoretical connection between instability and performance of the agreement has subsequently been highlighted (for a review, see Yan and Zeng, 1999). On the one hand, the dissolution of a JV may be associated with partners having fulfilled their proposed goals, making cooperation no longer necessary. This does not necessarily imply failure, at least not for all of the partners (Gomes-Casseres, 1987). In addition, the JV may be valid under certain conditions, although if these conditions change cooperation may no longer make sense. Even in these cases, the creation of a JV might have been a good decision, having helped protect the firms from uncertainty as suggested by the real options approach (Kogut, 1991). On the other hand, survival of a JV could be a consequence of success or just due to commitment escalation even if performing poorly (Inkpen and Ross, 2001).

In a second stage, studies of objective measures of SA performance turned their attention to SA duration, which became a research issue in its own right. At the same time, researchers began to use more sophisticated statistical techniques, such as econometric duration models. Since the mid 1990s, empirical studies have mainly focused on analyzing the influence that certain factors have on JV duration (e.g. Kogut, 1989; Blodgett, 1992; Park and Russo, 1996; Hennart et al., 1998; Hennart and Zeng, 2002). Among the factors that have been studied, we find: cultural distance, experience (either in the host country or in the management of JVs or SAs in general), number of partners, competition among these, distribution of equity, previous SAs between the partners, or size. However, empirical evidence is non-conclusive for most of these factors (see Valdés and García-Canal 2006 for a review).

Studies on the Stock Market Reaction to Alliance Formation

A second group of studies on SA dynamics and performance analyze the stock market reaction to SA formation, taking this as an *ex ante* measure of SA performance. At the first stage, exploratory studies pursued the measurement of the abnormal returns from SA formation as the main research question (e.g. McConnell and Nantel, 1985). These studies found low or insignificant returns on alliance formation, as did subsequent studies on this topic.

At a second stage, studies of value creation carried out in the 1990s tried to identify not only the abnormal returns from SA formation, but also the factors that may lead to the creation or destruction of value in an SA. Although it is not easy to identify neatly defined trends from these results, the market seems to react more positively to those attributes that increase potential synergies from the SA, even if these increase exposure to opportunistic behavior and SA complexity. This is the case of technological activities (e.g. Das et al., 1998; Merchant and Schendel, 2000), direct competition (Koh and Venkatraman, 1991), or partners' intangible assets (Chen et al., 2000). Although the evidence for some of these attributes is mixed – for a more detailed review see Vidal and García-Canal (2003) – there are more results in favor of than in opposition to the synergy argument. In contrast, the market does not seem to react negatively to the presence of factors that increase the complexity of the SA like cultural distance, despite the fact that SAs have high coordination costs (Kim and Park, 2002; Merchant and Schendel, 2000).

Studies Based on *Ex Post* Assessments of SA Organizational Effectiveness

Finally, a third group of studies analyzes SA dynamics and performance relying on *ex post* assessments of SA organizational effectiveness.
Studies dealing with this issue have contributed to the development of
the relational view, a theoretical approach to which we referred earlier
in this chapter. These studies, based on primary data, had the advantage
of exploiting more detailed data than the previous ones, usually based
on secondary data. Parkhe's (1993) work shows how SA performance is
a complex issue dependent on partners' cooperative behavior, which is
based on both previous interactions between partners and expectations
regarding future benefits. One of the main factors analyzed within this
research line as determinants of the performance of SAs is the number
of partners (see Beamish and Kachra, 2003 for a review). An interesting finding of this research line is that the critical factors leading to SA
effectiveness are different in dyadic and multi-party SAs. García-Canal et
al. (2003) found that trust and relational embeddedness between partners
significantly influence the effectiveness of dyadic JVs, while monitoring
mechanisms are pivotal in the case of multi-party JVs.

CONCLUSIONS

In the past few years there has been a growing interest in the study of SAs by
different fields of management and economics. Thus, SAs have gone from
being a marginal topic of study to a subject of special attention. Although
research has been motivated by the importance that SAs have achieved as
a corporate practice, the development of new theoretical approaches has
contributed in a remarkable way to studying them in depth.

In this chapter we have studied four research lines that analyze different
aspects of this topic. For each one of them, the main theoretical approach
was identified and the main contributions were systematized and integrated. Each line has contributed to enlarge our knowledge of SAs and
interorganizational relations.

Further advancement of our knowledge of SAs may be pursued along
a number of avenues. Here, we suggest two of them. One area we deem
critical is the interaction between SA structural features and management
processes. While each of these aspects has received research attention,
most of the studies have looked at them separately, as our review shows.
Some authors maintain that structure is the key driver of SA performance
(e.g. Hennart and Zeng, 2005), and dismiss the significance of the influence that processes may have. Others complain about a generalized lack of

understanding of the methods required to understand processes (e.g. Salk, 2005). We are witnessing how the two streams of research slowly begin to cross paths. As a sample indicator, the 2007 Academy of Management meetings included a symposium organized by Fabrice Lumineau and Joanne Oxley in which the papers presented had a common focus on the influence of agreement structures on post-formation processes in interfirm relationships. Further opportunities include research on contracting as a process, the outcome of which goes beyond a legal document to encompass a psychological contract which results from sense making processes. Others (e.g. Contractor, 2005) have proposed related lines of inquiry such as how contractual provisions influence partner behavior, or how negotiation processes influence structures.

A second avenue for further research relates to SAs as a key mechanism to compete in ecosystems. As industries converge it becomes virtually impossible for any single company to possess in-house all of the requisite capabilities needed to succeed in these new competitive arenas. Thus, more and more companies will have to turn to SAs as building bricks of open business models. What is novel to these networks of SAs is the mutual interdependencies they create which go beyond those created by the underlying dyadic relationships. We know little about how to manage these complex networks of SAs. Although the formation of these alliance networks has been analyzed previously (see for instance Nohria and García-Pont, 1991), the role that these networks can play in firms' competitive strategies has not been fully studied. In addition, these alliance networks constitute a real challenge for the studies dealing with alliance performance, as new performance measures that take into account not only the interdependencies that may exist between all of the alliances created by a single firm but also the whole implications of alliances for a firm's competitiveness need to be developed.

NOTE

1. Financial support provided by the Spanish Ministry of Education and Science (Projects ECO-2011-23220 and complementary action ECO-2011-13361-E, and ECO-2010-18718) is gratefully acknowledged.

REFERENCES

Argyres, N.S. and Mayer, K.J. (2007), 'Contract design capability as a firm capability: an integration of learning and transaction cost perspectives', *Academy of Management Review*, **32**, 1060–1077.

Ariño, A. (2003), 'Measures of strategic alliance performance: an analysis of construct validity', *Journal of International Business Studies*, **34** (1), 66–79.
Ariño, A. and J. de la Torre (1998), 'Learning from failure: towards an evolutionary model of collaborative ventures', *Organization Science*, **9**, 306–325.
Ariño, A. and J.J. Reuer (2006a), 'Alliance contractual design' in O. Shenkar and J.J. Reuer (eds), *Handbook of Strategic Alliances*, London: Sage.
Ariño, A. and J.J. Reuer (eds) (2006b), *Strategic Alliances: Governance and Contracts*, New York: Palgrave Macmillan.
Baden-Fuller, C. and R.M. Grant (2004), 'A knowledge accessing theory of strategic alliances', *Journal of Management Studies*, **41** (1), 61–84.
Beamish, P.W. (1988), *Multinational Joint Ventures in Developing Countries*, London, UK: Routledge.
Beamish, P.W. and A. Kachra (2003), 'Number of partners and JV performance', *Journal of World Business*, **39** (2), 107–120.
Blodgett, L.L. (1992), 'Factors in the instability of international joint ventures: an event history analysis', *Strategic Management Journal*, **13**, 475–481.
Burt, R.S. (ed.) (1982), *Toward a Structural Theory of Action*, New York, USA: Academic Press.
Carson, S.J., A. Madhok and T. Wu (2006), 'Uncertainty, opportunism, and governance: the effects of volatility and ambiguity on formal and relational contracting', *Academy of Management Journal*, **49**, 1058–1077.
Casciaro, T. (2003), 'Determinants of governance structure in alliances: the role of strategic, task, and partner uncertainties', *Industrial and Corporate Change*, **12**, 1223–1251.
Chen, S., W. Kim, C. Lee and G. Yeo (2000), 'Investment opportunities, free cash flow and market reaction to international joint ventures', *Journal of Banking and Finance*, **24**, 1747–1765.
Chi, T. and D.J. McGuire (1996), 'Collaborative ventures and value of learning: integrating the transaction cost and strategic option perspectives on the choice of market entry modes', *Journal of International Business Studies*, **27** (2), 285–307.
Colombo, M.G. (2003), 'Alliance form: a test of the contractual and competence perspectives', *Strategic Management Journal*, **24**, 1209–1229.
Contractor, F.J. (2005), 'Alliance structure and process: will the two research streams ever meet in alliance research?', *European Management Review*, **2** (2), 123–129.
Croisier, B. (1998), 'The governance of external research: empirical test of some transaction-cost related factors', *R&D Management*, **28**, 289–298.
Cuypers, I.R.P. and X. Martin (2006), 'Strategic alliance governance: an extended real options perspective', in A. Ariño and J.J. Reuer (eds), *Strategic Alliances: Governance and Contracts*, New York: Palgrave-Macmillan.
Das, S., P. Sen and S. Sengupta (1998), 'Impact of strategic alliances on firm valuation', *Academy of Management Journal*, **41**, 27–41.
Das, T.K. and T. Bing-Sheng (2000), 'Instabilities of strategic alliances: an internal tensions perspective', *Organization Science*, **11**, 77–101.
Deeds, D.L. and C.W.L. Hill (1998), 'An examination of opportunistic action within research alliances: evidence from the biotechnology industry', *Journal of Business Venturing*, **14**, 141–163.
Doz, Y.L. (1996), 'The evolution of cooperation in strategic alliances: initial conditions or learning processes?', *Strategic Management Journal*, **17** (supl.), 55–83.
Doz, Y.L., P.M. Olk and P.S. Ring (2000), 'Formation processes of R&D consortia: which path to take? Where does it lead?', *Strategic Management Journal*, Special Issue, **3**, 239–266.
Dyer, J.H. and H. Singh (1998), 'The relational view: cooperative strategy and sources of interorganizational competitive advantage', *Academy of Management Review*, **23**, 660–679.
García-Canal, E. (1996), 'Contractual form in domestic and international strategic alliances', *Organization Studies*, **17**, 773–794.

García-Canal, E., A. Valdés-Llaneza and A. Ariño (2003), 'Effectiveness of dyadic and multi-party joint ventures', *Organization Studies*, **24** (5), 743–770.
Gomes-Casseres, B. (1987), 'Joint venture instability: is it a problem?', *Columbia Journal of World Business*, **22**, 97–144.
Granovetter, M. (1985), 'Economic action and social structure: the problem of embedded-ness', *American Journal of Sociology*, **91**, 481–510.
Gulati, R. (1995), 'Does familiarity breed trust? The implications of repeated ties for contractual choice in alliances', *Academy of Management Journal*, **38**, 85–112.
Gulati, R. and H. Singh (1998), 'The architecture of cooperation: managing coordination costs and appropriation concerns in strategic alliances', *Administrative Science Quarterly*, **12**, 781–814.
Hagedoorn, J., D. Cloodt and H. van Kranenburg (2005), 'Intellectual property rights and the governance of international R&D partnerships', *Journal of International Business Studies*, **36**, 175–186.
Hagedoorn, J. and G. Hesen (2007), 'Contract law and the governance of inter-firm technology partnerships – an analysis of different modes of partnering and their contractual implications', *Journal of Management Studies*, **44** (3), 342–366.
Hamel, G. (1991), 'Competition for competence and interpartner learning within international strategic alliances', *Strategic Management Journal*, **12**, 83–103.
Henisz, W.J. and O.E. Williamson (1999), 'Comparative economic organization within and between countries', *Business and Politics*, **1**, 261–276.
Hennart, J.F., D.J. Kim and M. Zeng (1998), 'The impact of joint venture status on the longevity of Japanese stakes in US manufacturing affiliates', *Organization Science*, **9** (3), 382–395.
Hennart, J.F., T. Roehl and D.S. Zietlow (1999), '"Trojan horse" or "workhorse"? The evolution of US–Japanese joint ventures in the United States', *Strategic Management Journal*, **20**, 15–29.
Hennart, J.F. and M. Zeng (2002), 'Cross-cultural differences and joint venture longevity', *Journal of International Business Studies*, **33** (4), 699–716.
Hennart, J.F. and M. Zeng (2005), 'Structural determinants of joint venture performance', *European Management Review*, **2** (2), 105–115.
Inkpen, A.C. and P.W. Beamish (1997), 'Knowledge, bargaining power, and the instability of international joint ventures', *Academy of Management Review*, **22** (1), 177–202.
Inkpen, A.C. and J. Ross (2001), 'Why do some strategic alliances persist beyond their useful life?', *California Management Review*, **44** (1), 132–148.
James, H.S. Jr (2000), 'Separating contract from governance', *Managerial and Decision Economics*, **21**, 47–61.
Khanna, T., R. Gulati and N. Nohria (1998), 'The dynamics of learning alliances: competition, cooperation, and relative scope', *Strategic Management Journal*, **19**, 193–210.
Kim, K. and J. Park (2002), 'The determinants of value creation for partner firms in the global alliance context', *Management International Review*, **42** (4), 361–384.
Kogut, B. (1988), 'Joint ventures: theoretical and empirical perspectives', *Strategic Management Journal*, **9**, 319–332.
Kogut, B. (1989), 'The stability of joint ventures: reciprocity and competitive rivalry', *Journal of Industrial Economics*, **38** (12), 183–198.
Kogut, B. (1991), 'Joint ventures and the option to expand and acquire', *Management Science*, **37** (1), 19–33.
Koh, J. and N. Venkatraman (1991), 'Joint venture formations and stock market reactions: an assessment in the information technology sector', *Academy of Management Journal*, **34**, 869–892.
Krishnan, R., X. Martin and N.G. Noorderhaven (2006), 'When does trust matter to alliance performance?', *Academy of Management Journal*, **49** (5), 894–917.
Kumar, R. and K.O. Nti (1998), 'Differential learning and interaction in alliance dynamics: a process and outcome discrepancy model', *Organization Science*, **9** (3), 356–367.
Lerner, J. and R.P. Merges (1998), 'The control of technology alliances: an empirical analysis of the biotechnology industry', *Journal of Industrial Economics*, **46**, 125–156.

Lorenzoni, G. and A. Lipparini (1999), 'The leveraging of interfirm relationships as a distinctive capability: a longitudinal study', *Strategic Management Journal*, **20**, 317–338.

Luo, Y. (2002), 'Contract, cooperation, and performance in international joint ventures', *Strategic Management Journal*, **23**, 903–919.

Luo, Y. (2005), 'How important are shared perceptions of procedural justice in cooperative alliances?', *Academy of Management Journal*, **48** (4), 695–709.

Macaulay, S. (1963), 'Non-contractual relations in business', *American Sociological Review*, **28**, 55–70.

Madhok, A. and S.B. Tallman (1998), 'Resources, transactions and rents: managing value through interfirm collaborative relationships', *Organization Science*, **9**, 326–339.

Mayer, K.J. and N.S. Argyres (2004), 'Learning to contract: evidence from the personal computer industry', *Organization Science*, **15**, 394–410.

McConnell, J. and J. Nantel (1985), 'Common stock returns and corporate combinations: the case of joint ventures', *Journal of Finance*, **14**, 519–536.

Merchant, H. and D. Schendel (2000), 'How do international joint ventures create shareholder value?', *Strategic Management Journal*, **21**, 723–737.

Nohria, N. and C. García-Pont (1991), 'Global strategic linkages and industry structure', *Strategic Management Journal*, **12**, 105–124.

Oxley, J.E. (1999), 'Institutional environment and the mechanisms of governance: the impact of intellectual property protection on the structure of inter-firm alliances', *Journal of Economic Behaviour & Organization*, **38**, 283–309.

Oxley, J.E. and R.C. Sampson (2004), 'The scope and governance of international R&D alliances', *Strategic Management Journal*, **25**, 723–749.

Park, S.H. and M.V. Russo (1996), 'When competition eclipses cooperation: an event history analysis of joint venture failure', *Management Science*, **42**, 875–890.

Parkhe, A. (1993), 'Strategic alliance structuring: a game theoretic and transaction cost examination of interfirm cooperation', *Academy of Management Journal*, **36** (4), 794–829.

Pisano, G.P. (1989), 'Using equity participation to support exchange: evidence from the biotechnology industry', *Journal of Law Economics and Organization*, **35**, 109–126.

Poppo, L. and T. Zenger (2002), 'Do formal contracts and relational governance function as substitutes or complements?', *Strategic Management Journal*, **23**, 707–725.

Reuer, J. and A. Ariño (2002), 'Contractual renegotiations in strategic alliances', *Journal of Management*, **28**, 47–68.

Reuer, J. and A. Ariño (2007), 'Strategic alliance contracts: dimensions and determinants of contractual complexity', *Strategic Management Journal*, **28** (3), 313–330.

Reynolds, J.I. (1984), 'The pinched shoe effect of international joint ventures', *Columbia Journal of World Business*, **19** (2), 23–29.

Ring, P.S. (2000), 'The three T's of alliance creation: task, team and time', *European Management Journal*, **18**, 152–163.

Ring, P.S. and A. Van de Ven (1994), 'Developmental processes of cooperative interorganizational relationships', *Academy of Management Review*, **19**, 90–118.

Salk, J.E. (2005), 'Often called but rarely chosen: alliance research that directly studies process', *European Management Review*, **2** (2), 117–122.

Santoro, M.D. and J.P. McGill (2005), 'The effect of uncertainty and asset co-specialization on government in biotechnology alliance', *Strategic Management Journal*, **26** (13), 1261–1269.

Thompson, J.D. (ed.) (1967), *Organizations in Action*, New York, US: McGraw-Hill.

Valdés, A. and E. García-Canal (2006), 'Direct competition, number of partners and longevity of stakes in joint ventures', *Management International Review*, **46** (3), 307–326.

Vidal, M. and E. García-Canal (2003), 'Transaction costs and value creation in global alliances: a relational approach', *Management Research*, **1** (1), 45–60.

Williamson, O.E. (ed.) (1985), *The Economic Institutions of Capitalism: Firms, Markets, Relational Contracting*, New York, US: Free Press.

Yan, A. and M. Zeng (1999), 'International joint venture instability: a critique of previous

research, a reconceptualization and directions for future research', *Journal of International Business Studies*, **30** (2), 397–414.
Zajac, E.J. and C.P. Olsen (1993), 'From transaction cost to transactional value analysis: implications for the study of interorganizational strategies', *Journal of Management Studies*, **30**, 131–147.

13 Innovation and technology management in competitive strategy research
Bruno Cassiman and Maria Chiara Di Guardo

INTRODUCTION

How to achieve competitive advantage is the fundamental question of strategic management and the key to a successful entrepreneurship. The issue has been studied extensively but still provides a challenging topic for both scholars and managers. In times when technology constantly generates new business opportunities and markets rapidly reach new horizons, firms scramble to follow the pace, searching the most fruitful strategic moves to gain advantage over their competitors.

Unfortunately, when facing the impressive rise in competition over recent decades (D'Aveni, 1994), as well as an increased pace of technological change (Iansiti, 1995), the traditional sources of competitive advantage (Brown and Eisenhardt, 1995) seem to no longer provide long-term security and firms are turning to innovation as a new lever to drive their growth and preserve their market share. As Brown and Eisenhardt (1995: 344) point out, "[innovation] is among the essential processes for success, survival and renewal of organizations, particularly for firms in either fast-paced or competitive markets". Nowadays there seems almost a general consensus on how innovation may positively affect firm performance (Porter and Stern, 2001). Too often, however, it is presented as the panacea for all ills while new findings are clearly showing that investing in R&D and innovation by itself cannot suffice to reach success. Particularly illuminating is a recent study by Booz, Allen and Hamilton, on the 1000 publicly held companies from around the world with the highest budgets for research and development (Global Innovation 1000), which found that there seems to be no relationship between R&D spending on the one hand, and the primary measures of economic or corporate success, such as growth, enterprise profitability, and shareholder return on the other (Jaruzelski et al., 2005). While at first sight these findings seem shocking, firms are slowly realizing that successful innovation – implementation and commercialization of new ideas – and R&D are not equivalent.

The key to a successful innovation must in fact be sought in the development and integration of new knowledge in the innovation process and the access to such resources. While in the past, established firms typically relied on internally developed technological and innovative capabilities (Mowery et al., 1998; Nelson, 1990), recently, resorting to external sources of knowledge and innovation has become increasingly relevant (Porter and Stern, 2001) in the strategic actions of many firms. Thus, the innovation process is increasingly involving partners from outside a firm's boundaries, including research organizations, business partners, customers, rivals, academics, and firms in unrelated industries (Odagiri, 2003; Chesbrough, 2003; Linder et al., 2003). Recent work provides evidence on how opening the firm's boundaries may be used to extend the innovation capacity of the firm (e.g. Rigby and Zook, 2002; Chesbrough, 2003) and suggests that a viable innovation strategy incorporates the need for external vs internal technology development and suggests when to alternate between these two knowledge-sourcing modes. Not surprisingly, even the largest and most technologically self-sufficient organizations make no exception and acquire knowledge from beyond their boundaries.

Although prior studies (e.g. Nagarajan and Mitchell, 1998; Beneito, 2003; Pisano, 1990; Veugelers and Cassiman, 1999) have attempted to understand the factors that influence the way in which firms select their innovation activities – deciding between in-house R&D, cooperation, R&D contracting and licensing etc. – the topic of how to actually organize the innovation strategy, i.e. the combination of these different activities and their performance effect, is still very much debated.

In order to analyze the relationship between innovation strategy and competitive advantage we focus on those conditions that make an 'open innovation' strategy viable. We argue that strategy scholars and managers should draw more on the innovation management literature for a deeper insight into innovation strategies that are successful under these new circumstances. In particular, exploring the typical dimensions highlighted in the innovation management literature of technological change, timing and different units of analysis (industry, firm and set of firms affected by technological change), we develop insights for a firm's innovation strategy when a more open innovation strategy might lead to a sustainable competitive advantage.

We first introduce our perspective on open innovation, focusing primarily on the motives and modes that push organizations to adopt this innovation model. We then provide an overview of the importance of open innovation strategy, classifying the different studies according to the level of the variables considered that affect the innovation strategy: environment and industry, firm characteristics, and technology characteristics. We next indicate the potential problems associated with open innovation and unfold the links between open innovation and firm performance while introducing a model to identify the factors that can help in designing the most suitable innovation strategy. Finally, we propose new avenues for research to advance the study of open innovation from a strategic organization perspective.

SOURCING EXTERNAL KNOWLEDGE: MOTIVES AND MODES

Faced with ever-shortening product life cycles, accelerated technology change, increased competition, shifting demographics and deregulation, businesses are finding their markets in turmoil. Many large companies with excellent performance records are feeling pressure on their financial returns and worry about their products and services sinking virtually to 'commodity' status. Under such conditions of rapid change, it should come as no surprise that innovation and technologies are receiving substantial attention.

Within this context, possible explanations for the increasing importance of the external sourcing of technology can be found both on the supply and the demand side. The former is driven, among other things, by an increase in scientific knowledge in almost all major disciplines, creating new sources of innovation, available for tapping by interested parties, often in seemingly unrelated fields (Chatterji, 1996). As a result, markets for technologies are emerging and developing in several high tech industries (Arora et al., 2001). In this chapter, however, we will concentrate on the demand side of this evolution. Higher competition and a growing pressure on costs, coupled with the necessity of being responsive to local and global markets, requires a faster development cycle (Iansiti, 1995), an increasing complexity and multidisciplinarity of resources and the search for risk-sharing technological policies (Veugelers and Cassiman, 1999). In addition, firms need a wide range of approaches to maximize the returns to internal innovations – which cannot always be internally commercialized – including selling technology on the external market or even giving away technology to stimulate demand for other products (West and Gallagher, 2006). Finally, for many companies the recourse to external technologies is linked to the need for maintaining or improving product margins and to the belief that utilizing more technology from outside the firm is critical for profitable growth (Chesbrough and Crowther, 2006).

Different modes through which firms may source external knowledge for use in their innovation process may be adopted. Besides internal development, which creates the needed absorptive capacity, firms may undertake cooperative agreements, or they may make use of the market. In the latter case, firms may either buy a specific set of knowledge or technology (R&D contracting and licensing), or they may buy out entire firms. Each strategy enables the firm to gain access to specific benefits. For instance, firms will forge linkages to gain access to those capabilities that they perceive will lead to an improved competitive position and a greater chance of mitigating competitive uncertainty (Nohria and Garcia-Pont, 1991). In addition, failure in the market for knowledge causes firms to buy and sell entire businesses rather than exchange discrete resources (Capron et al., 1998).

MULTI-LEVEL DRIVERS OF AN OPEN INNOVATION STRATEGY

Various perspectives and key variables have been used to gain insight into innovation behavior. In particular, we can classify the different studies according to the level of the variables considered that affect the innovation strategy: environment and industry, firm characteristics, and technology characteristics.

The first group of studies focuses on industry characteristics with respect to the surrounding environment. Pisano (1990) and Beneito (2003) argue that the in-house organization of R&D activities is more likely the more competitive is the environment firms evolve in. In parallel Bayona et al. (2001) and Miotti and Sachwald (2003), among others, provide evidence that firms belonging to sectors with a higher technological intensity have a greater propensity to establish external knowledge-sourcing strategies. Sakakibara (2001) also points out that firms in R&D-intensive industries conduct cooperative R&D projects in order to enter new R&D-intensive industries. Deeper in detail, Nagarajan and Mitchell (1998) indicate industry 'technological regime' as the main driving factor, and then argue that equity alliances are used in regimes encompassing technological change; internal R&D dominates when technological change is incremental; and non-equity alliances are prevalent during periods of complementary technological change (radical changes that have a greater effect on the firm's complementary activities than on its core resources or capabilities). Powell et al. (1996) show that in regimes of rapid technological development, research breakthroughs are so broadly distributed that no single firm has all the internal capabilities and knowledge needed for success. In such an environment, the locus of innovation is found in a network of inter-organizational relationships. Innovation behavior is influenced by the positions held by organizations in a broader, market-related context. For instance, Stuart (1998) argues that firms in technologically 'crowded' positions and with high prestige form technological alliances at a higher rate.

A second group of studies considers firms' characteristics as the principal variables for determining the R&D strategy. Among these, firms' age is a relevant predictor: young firms are in fact likely to be most affected by key external relationships (Eisenhardt and Schoonhoven, 1996), mainly because they are resource constrained (McDougall et al., 1994), and because they strongly depend upon knowledge to survive and grow (Autio et al., 2000). Pisano (1990), however, found that bio-tech companies with more R&D experience rely more on internal sourcing. This result is explained by the author in a behavioral-theory-of-the-firm framework where bounded rationality prevents firms from making the necessary adjustments and they continue to behave according to routines developed in the past (Bromiley, 2005). Finally, past choices and sourcing history are thought to increase organizational inertia and thus are likely to guide future decisions along the historical paths (Steensma and Fairbank, 1999).

The possible role of size, although highly correlated with firm age, is more controversial. Large firms are expected to have a higher 'absorptive capacity' (Cohen and Levinthal, 1990), but are also endowed with the necessary technical and financial resources to carry out their own R&D realizing scale advantages in R&D in-house. This dilemma is not unanimously resolved in empirical studies: whereas the work conducted by Robertson and Gatignon (1998), inter alia, does not support this correlation, Hagedoorn and Schankeraad (1994) and Colombo and Garrone (1998) find a positive relationship between firms' size and cooperation in R&D (see also Arora and Gambardella, 1990; Gambardella, 1992; Cockburn and Henderson, 1998). In line with the latter work, Almeida et al. (2003) find that larger firms are more likely to build on external knowledge, and West and Gallagher (2006) highlighted that large IT firms with a broad scope of products became involved in open innovation strategy because they could not ignore any significant source of external innovation available to rivals. At the same time their analysis of smaller firms did not provide any particular insight due to the absence of clear regularities in the data. On the contrary, Rothwell and Dodgson (1991) focus their work on the specific problems facing small and medium-sized firms when establishing external linkages. The authors show how in-house technical skills – complementary between in-house and external know-how accumulation, and appropriate technology strategies in guiding the accumulation process – are related to the external sourcing activities of the firm.

A third and final group of studies concentrates on technology characteristics. Schilling and Steensma (2002) suggest that technology's uniqueness, commercial uncertainty, and imitability should favor internal solutions while Delmas (1999) adds that tacit, complex, and strategic technologies are more likely developed through alliances rather than acquired through contracts. Cassiman et al. (2009) show that the form of governance employed in managing R&D projects depends on the projects' knowledge attributes, and that, while in order to develop new knowledge different external partners may be more productive, the recourse to external sourcing is less frequent when building strategic knowledge.

A technology characteristic that has received considerable attention and relates to the issue of appropriation is the likelihood of spillovers. Some researchers (De Bondt, 1997; D'Aspremont and Jacquemin, 1988; Shapiro and Willig, 1990) argue that on the one hand, a lower expected level of appropriability may lead to a lower effort in R&D and to a general tendency to internalize the process, while on the other hand, spillovers may augment the benefit of cooperation. Others suggest that often what might appear as involuntary spillovers are actually well-regulated knowledge flows across firms which can be managed deliberately (Cassiman and Veugelers, 2002; Breschi and Lissoni, 2001). Pisano (1990) finds that small-numbers bargaining problems and appropriability issues influence dramatically the pharmaceutical companies in their decisions regarding procurement of biotech R&D. By the same token, but referring to the information technology industry, Ulset (1996) reaches similar conclusions and maintains that the benefits of R&D outsourcing in terms of quicker access to more advanced technology can seldom be achieved without additional (transaction) costs. Nonetheless, such costs can either be managed or avoided by strengthening administrative control rights or switching to vertical integration.

OPEN INNOVATION AND INNOVATION PERFORMANCE

Although literature has paid some attention to the factors that influence the adoption of different innovation activities, relatively little empirical work has addressed the performance implications[1] of these decisions since the seminal work of T. Allen (Argote et al., 2003; Keller, 1994; Peterson, 1993). Arguments emphasizing the benefits of acquiring external R&D competences assume that many critical capabilities reside outside the boundaries of the firm and that appropriation problems are minimal. In these settings, performance is directly tied to the ability to identify, isolate, and solve a specific set of independent technical problems. In contrast, arguments extolling the benefits of internal development assume that the most valuable capabilities reside within the firm and that appropriation problems are significant. In such case, the principal advantage of internal organization derives from the ability to provide enhanced information transfer and coordination across activities within the production system, therefore implying that performance is principally driven by second- and higher-order interactions among a set of value-chain activities (De la Mothe and Link, 2002).

The concept of absorptive capacity enriches the picture, suggesting that internal and external technology do not affect firms' performance independently, and that firms' ability to profit from external know-how is largely a function of the firms' level of prior related knowledge (Cohen and Levinthal, 1990; Kamien and Zang, 2000; Zahra and George, 2002). The existence of external knowledge provides no benefits per se to the firm if the firm cannot identify the relevant knowledge and incorporate it into its innovation activities (West and Gallagher, 2006). In addition, a higher internal technological capacity is often coupled with a better protection of developed knowledge through secrecy, complexity, or lead time, and with a superior ability to appropriate the returns of innovation (Cassiman and Veugelers, 2006). Therefore, the higher the level of internal R&D, the higher the potential return from external activities. The reverse relationship – that is, the effect of the level of external activities on the return of in-house R&D – also finds support. More convincingly, Veugelers (1997) finds that cooperation in R&D has no significant effect on own R&D unless firms have their own R&D infrastructure, in which case cooperation stimulates internal R&D expenditures. These results support the idea that absorptive capacity is necessary to be able to capitalize on the complementarities between internal and external know-how. In this line, the literature highlights that, for example, the not-invented-here syndrome (Harrigan, 1985), a severe barrier to innovation, can also be mitigated if external partners are involved early in the process (Katz and Allen, 1982). Nevertheless, a clear causality is hard to distinguish.

Some studies do explore directly the effect of a specific innovation activity on technological performance. Hitt et al. (1991, 1996) and Valentini (2005) analyze the effect of M&A on patenting output. Valentini (2005) finds that the success of the innovation process depends on the chances to create and capture value from innovations. Following Teece (1986) he finds that complementary resources between targets and acquirers may provide unique synergies for value creation and value capture. Technological resources allow the creation of more value through innovations, while complementary assets allow more value to be captured from innovations, fostering firms' incentives in the innovation process. Moreover, firms that decide to acquire external knowledge without investing in internal capabilities (that is, to acquire external resources in substitution of internal development) are in a worse position to create potential synergies: internal and external innovation activities are thus complementary. Stuart (2000) assesses the effect of technological alliances on innovation productivity, showing that well-endowed firms like those that possess a large stock of technological resources can produce the best ex-post results for their associates.

Recent studies also provide mounting evidence about the potential for combining internal and external sourcing modes as complementary innovation activities (Arora and Gambardella, 1990; Granstrand et al., 1992; Veugelers and Cassiman, 1999), and the return from external activities is higher when these activities are coupled with internal R&D (Cassiman and Veugelers, 2006). Arora and Gambardella (1990) provide evidence that in the biotech industry the different possible strategies to acquire external linkages in R&D (agreements with other firms, research agreement with universities, investments in the capital stock of new firms, and acquisition of small firms) are complementary, and that each strategy enables the firm to gain access to a specific set of tangible and/or intangible resources. Analyzing a sample of Belgian firms, Cassiman and Veugelers (2006) find that, not only are internal and external activities correlated, but also that those firms that combine internal and external activities outperform those firms that do not integrate different activities in their innovation management process. Also Cassiman and Veugelers (2006) find that complementarity matters more for firms that find scientific information more important for the innovation process (they find that the nature of complementarity depends on important contextual variables such as the importance of scientific information for the innovation process).

While there is strong evidence favoring complementarity between innovation activities, the exact mechanism when a more open innovation strategy dominates a more selective single R&D sourcing strategy is still debated. R&D outsourcing stresses the advantage of tapping existing and often more specialized knowledge if available. This leads to time gains and lower innovation costs to the extent that economies of scale in R&D can be more efficiently exploited. However technology outsourcing may create considerable transaction costs: ex ante in terms of search and negotiation costs and ex post in executing and enforcing the contract. Next to asset specificity, the typical uncertain and complex nature of R&D projects exacerbates these problems. Hence, R&D contracting is more likely to occur for generic, non-firm specific R&D that allows for specialization advantages, such as routine research tasks like materials testing, and process innovation rather than product innovations (Mowery and Rosenberg, 1989). Cohen and Klepper (1996) however argue that the returns to process R&D are less saleable in disembodied form, given a less effective patent protection. In addition, when the appropriation regime is tight, as it is in the pharmaceutical industry, and when assets complementary to the technology are in competitive supply, the small-numbers bargaining hazards are minimized and external technology sourcing is more probable (Teece, 1986; Pisano, 1990).

The value created by an open innovation strategy is contingent upon the situation and it differs across performance dimensions. Actually, it may even appear that crossing organizational boundaries has a negative impact on performance. M&A may in fact decrease the importance, the generality, and the originality of the inventions produced (Valentini, 2005). However, shifting the boundaries of R&D can bring about important efficiency gains in the production of knowledge by providing access to complementary knowledge, assets and capabilities. And it is particularly so when technology grafting is coupled with internal R&D activities.

To analyze these seemingly contradicting observations, the next section highlights the need to consider some new factors that can explain the role of innovation and technology management in competitive strategy research.

WHAT FACTORS CAN HELP IN DESIGNING THE MOST SUITABLE INNOVATION STRATEGY?

The apparently contradicting results highlighted in the previous literature review – some of which indicate that opening the boundaries of innovation has a positive impact on performance and others that hint at just the opposite – call for a deeper analysis of the factors and contingencies that can explain how firms should organize their R&D activities and what factors can help firms to design the most suitable innovation strategy.

To do so, this chapter proposes an element of novelty with respect to prior literature. It characterizes the outcome of the innovation process as essentially dependent on a set of fundamental dimensions drawing directly from the analysis of the technological change literature. In fact, complementing the strategy literature which is broadly concerned about how to build a competitive advantage, the technology literature informs on how technological change is achieved or survived and provides a different perspective to help understand the issue. An analysis of the main contributions suggests that three fundamental dimensions have to be taken into account when dealing with this phenomenon: a) type of technological change, b) timing and dynamics, and c) unit of analysis.

The first dimension relates to the type of technological change. For instance, the change could be embodied into radical innovations (e.g. Romanelli and Tushman, 1994; Anderson and Tushman, 1990) or could encompass a broader concept of innovation that includes incremental or modular innovation (e.g. Henderson and Clark, 1990; Christensen, 1997). The second dimension conveys the relevance of a temporal component. Prior studies have focused either on the innovation-generating moment (e.g. Romanelli and Tushman, 1994) or on the diffusion phase and its consequences (e.g. Afuah and Bahram, 1995; Tripsas and Gavetti, 2000). Finally, the various studies on innovation adopt different units of analysis. These include: individual firms (e.g. Abernathy and Clark, 1985), the industry at large (e.g. Dosi, 1982), and the set of firms affected by the change (e.g. Afuah and Bahram, 1995). Each unit of analysis provides a different emphasis and suggests different directions for developing the innovation strategy of the firm. The analysis of each of the above dimensions in a common framework not only is useful in categorizing prior literature, but also provides helpful insights into the factors that may influence the way in which firms organize their innovation strategy.

Technological Change

Prior studies have zeroed in either on the radical innovation / technological change generating phase or on the diffusion phase and its consequences. It is important to tease out these two phases because they differ in terms of the mechanism leading to competitive advantage and innovation strategy. When technological ferment begins, prior knowledge and competencies may no longer be valuable in the new competitive system that is gradually taking shape (Christensen et al., 1998). Much of the literature depicts incumbents going into decline, while new entrants exploit the new technology and rise to market dominance (Hill and Rothaermel, 2003).

If radical technological innovation is successful in the marketplace, it frequently constitutes a discontinuity that dramatically alters the established demand and supply conditions. Radical innovations do not have an established market that gives them a clear target, and there are numerous technological uncertainties (Tushman and Romanelli, 1985). Established firms frequently do not have the culture, structures and attitudes to succeed in creating new markets: pioneers are usually new firms (Rosenbloom and Christensen, 1998; Sull et al., 1997). Over the years, the reasons why companies may fail to create new markets or technologies or why they fail to adapt to them have been thoroughly analyzed. Reasons include a different value system, an obsolete mental model, inertia or prior commitments (e.g. Henderson, 1993; Tripsas and Gavetti, 2000; Christensen and Bower, 1996). The focus for this chapter, however, is on whether firms can have better chances to succeed in these conditions by opening the innovation boundaries. Indeed, radical technological change may render internal resources obsolete (Tushman and Anderson, 1986), and push for external sourcing to access complementary technological resources. Robertson and Gatignon (1998) do argue that alliances will be preferred over internal development when technological uncertainty increases. Nevertheless, internal development is favored over alliances as asset specificity and measurement problems increase, indicating that opening the innovation process to external knowledge and resources might not work unconditionally in these circumstances.

Timing and Dynamics

Secondly, the entry timing dimension is fundamental in clarifying whether firms have better chances of success if they open the innovation boundaries. Pioneers should understand when a new technological market can be created analyzing established firms' strategies and consumers' preferences and their match. Established firms, on the contrary, should time their entry to coincide with the growth of the mass market (Markides and Geroski, 2003). What can make established firms successful is taking an early market out of the hands of the pioneers and scaling it up into a mass market. The widely held belief that pioneers enjoy first mover advantages is not always correct. In both cases, for pioneers and established firms, opening the innovation activities is crucial to their success.

Pioneers do not have the resources to create mass markets, while established firms typically do not have the resources to create a new niche, as argued above. Only through a careful strategic analysis of entry timing can firms beat their competitors. Once the market is set up, relative stability is created (Anderson and Tushman, 1990) and existing resources become fundamental. To compete for resources, the firm must own specific valuable assets in short supply. However, this is not a sufficient condition. Sustained competitive advantage requires that the condition of heterogeneity be preserved (Peteraf, 1993). In the case of technology then, the appropriability of its value in the face of spillovers, leakage and imitation is of paramount importance. Appropriability is the property of knowledge and of the environment in which one operates, that allows an invention to be protected against imitation (Dosi, 1988). Once an innovation enters the public domain it may well become visible and accessible to the world. As a consequence, the benefits of its value could spill over to other organizations. However, to invest in technological resources, firms must be able to appropriate the returns sufficiently to make the investment worthwhile (Levin et al., 1987). Without appropriability, valuable technological resources cannot secure a competitive advantage. At the same time, appropriability fosters investments in resources.

Timing considerations highlight how two different challenges are at stake. On one hand, firms can exploit technological change to build a competitive advantage. But on the other, firms should also be able to defend (or even build) competitive advantage in the face of (exogenous) technological change. The exploration and the exploitation of the technological trajectories have a direct effect on the open innovation strategy (Chesbrough and Crowther, 2006). Open innovation allows firms to explore new technological trajectories but might hurt their exploitation potential if unable to appropriate the returns of this exploration. While pioneering firms should focus on their appropriation potential within their innovation strategy, incumbent firms should probably be more open to external knowledge and resources to reinforce their exploration potential.

Unit of Analysis

The occurrence of 'battles for dominance' between two or more rival technologies leads us to a third dimension shedding light on the innovation strategy of firms, i.e. the different units of analysis: individual firms, the industry at large, and the set of firms affected by the change. To date most of the effort in this area has been focused on identifying the different factors that affect the final outcome of a technology battle: technological superiority, firm resources, institutions' role, etc. (Suarez and Utterback, 1995; Schilling, 1998; Shapiro and Varian, 1999; Scott, 1994; Scherer, 1992). Contrarily, insufficient insight has been provided as to how these factors put forward different directions for the innovation strategy. For example, in several high-tech markets the value of the product (or service) increases with the number of adopters. This change in value is called a network effect (Katz and Shapiro, 1985). For instance, the willingness of a consumer to pay for an operating system (say, Windows) increases with the number of consumers who adopt the same operating system. An increasing number of markets are taking on the characteristics of networks, and this should make executives reconsider the way they bring innovations to market (Chakravorti, 2004). Think of the battle for the internet browsers: Netscape entered first and had valuable resources. Nonetheless, Microsoft won the battle with Explorer. Not only are markets increasingly becoming networked, but 'old' networked industries are characterized by a renewed competition with new entrants and new standards (i.e. Linux vs Microsoft).

In such networked markets, opening the boundaries becomes even more important than in traditional industries. As the interconnections between players increase, the payoffs on each player's choices depend more and more on the others' decisions. Firms involved in open-source software, for example, often make investments that will be shared with real and potential rivals. West and Gallagher (2006) identify four strategies firms employ – pooled R&D/product development, spinouts, selling complements and attracting donated complements – to address the challenges of an open innovation strategy.

Understanding the competitive environment and the industry in which firms are immersed (industry change vs firm-level changes) as well as that of potential competitors with substitutes or of complementors may also provide useful information. The technology literature suggests that cooperation is a more convenient innovation strategy in some sectors than in others (e.g. Gans et al., 2002), and that global industries favor open innovation models because they achieve economies of scale more swiftly than in the traditional closed model and promote more powerful standards and dominant designs (Anderson and Tushman, 1990; Gassmann, 2006). Nevertheless, we believe there remains an interesting potential for tying back industry-level analyses and effects to implicit innovation strategy recommendations. Shapiro and Varian (1999) have probably illustrated this most prominently for the case of information industries.

CONCLUSION AND AVENUES FOR FUTURE RESEARCH

A systematic review of the literature on the shifting boundaries of innovation should contribute to and provide insights for future work to at least three streams of research: the strategy literature, the knowledge management literature, and the theory of the firm literature.

Ultimately, the strategy field seeks to explain why some companies outperform others and how they build a sustainable competitive advantage. A fundamental question this chapter answers is: how does innovation strategy contribute to competitive advantage? As expected, there is no unconditional lesson. Managers should appreciate the different dimensions of technological performance, assess their needs along these dimensions, and choose their innovation strategy accordingly. As we know, business strategy is about trade-offs. Innovation strategy makes no exception and implies some trade-offs as well, mainly summarized by the old dilemma between short- and long-term. A careful balance between openness and internal development is therefore necessary to meet the demand of today's and tomorrow's technological success. Moreover, although there is some evidence at the firm level supporting the positive relationship between the combination of innovation activities and performance, the factors that explain these phenomena at a more micro level are still not clear. Many important (and interesting) questions remain: What drives the complementarity between innovation activities (i.e. which mechanisms are responsible for these efficiencies created through the integration and combination of different innovation activities)? And at which organizational level are innovation activities complementary (i.e. at which level are the effects of integration and combination of different activities important)?

This chapter also contributes to the knowledge management literature. Knowledge has been shown to be an important contingent variable influencing organizational design in different technological settings (Birkinshaw et al., 2002; Zander and Kogut, 1995). R&D generates new knowledge and helps to assimilate existing knowledge (Cohen and Levinthal, 1990). And firms' innovation strategy depends on the characteristics of the productive knowledge on which they are based and the means that are effective in protecting knowledge assets (Winter, 1997). But while the fact that innovation and knowledge are intrinsically linked is widely recognized, less is known about how knowledge could or should influence the organization of the innovation process. There is still little evidence on the effects of the use of external knowledge on performance (Argote et al., 2003). In particular, recent studies cast some doubt on the effectiveness of sourcing external knowledge. Menon and Pfeffer (2003), for instance, argue that external knowledge is often overvalued. Internal knowledge is more readily available and therefore subject to greater scrutiny – in this way, its flaws are more easily discovered – while external knowledge is scarcer and thus appears more valuable and unique. Furthermore, knowledge transfer still seems to be much easier inside an organization than between organizations (Song et al., 2003). The issue of the effect of external knowledge on performance should therefore be better scrutinized, as this chapter highlights unresolved puzzles involving the relationship between knowledge sourcing and innovative performance.

Finally, the chapter also offers insight for future research on the theory of the firm. In the past, the literature has primarily used transaction cost economics (Williamson, 1975 and 1985) as the dominant framework for explaining the organizational form of the innovation process. However, other contributions underline that this framework cannot render a full account of a tremendously complex phenomenon like organizational boundaries (e.g. Holmstrom and Roberts, 1998; Madhok, 2002). Transaction cost economics fails to highlight that firms differ in their resources, and that it takes time for organizations to create and enhance capabilities through experience, learning, and investments. As Coase (1988, 1990) himself has highlighted, it is also necessary to consider that firms have different production costs for different activities, and that these are largely determined by the other activities that the firms have undertaken. Organizational boundaries are thus responsive to more than hold-up problems (Holmstrom and Roberts, 1998; Conner and Prahalad, 1996). In environments where know-how is the key asset, building specific assets, rather than protecting them, may be the main issue. This bodes well for future research exploring value creation mechanisms in conjunction with value appropriation, rather than the strong focus on value appropriation up to now in this literature.

NOTE

1. There is still little agreement about what 'innovation performance' means. The range of indicators adopted in the literature varies widely: financial performance, market shares, new products introduced into the market, patents, GDP growth, and so on. In addition, the time lag between innovative efforts and performance is often so large, and so industry specific, that it remains just very hard to produce reliable estimates.

REFERENCES

Abernathy, W.J. and K.B. Clark (1985), 'Innovation: mapping the winds of creative destruction', *Research Policy*, **14**, 3–22.
Afuah, A. and N. Bahram (1995), 'The hypercube of innovation', *Research Policy*, **24**.
Almeida, P., G. Dokko and L. Rosenkopf (2003), 'Startup size and the mechanisms of external learning: increasing opportunity and decreasing ability?', *Research Policy*, **32** (2), 301–315.
Anderson, P. and M.L. Tushman (1990), 'Technological discontinuities and dominant designs: a cyclical model of technological change', *Administrative Science Quarterly*, **35** (4), 604–634.
Argote, L., B. McEvily and R. Reagans (2003), 'Managing knowledge in organizations: an integrative framework and review of emerging themes', *Management Science*, **49**, 571–582.
Arora, A. and A. Gambardella (1990), 'Complementarity and external linkages: the strategies of the large firms in biotechnology', *Journal of Industrial Economics*, **38**, 361–379.
Arora, A., A. Fosfuri and A. Gambardella (2001), 'Markets for technology and their implications for corporate strategy', *Industrial and Corporate Change*, **10**, 419–451.
Autio, E., H.J. Sapienza and J. Almeida (2000), 'Effects of age at entry, knowledge intensity and imitability on international growth', *Academy of Management Journal*, **43**, 909–924.
Bayona, C., T. Garcia-Marco and E. Huerta (2001), 'Firms' motivations for cooperative R&D: an empirical analysis of Spanish firms', *Research Policy*, **30**, 1289–1307.
Beneito, P. (2003), 'Choosing among alternative technological strategies: an empirical analysis of formal sources of innovation', *Research Policy*, **32**, 693–713.
Birkinshaw, J., R. Nobel and J. Ridderstrale (2002), 'Knowledge as a contingency variable: do the characteristics of knowledge predict organization structure?', *Organization Science*, **13**, 274–289.
Breschi, S. and F. Dissoni (2001), 'Knowledge spillovers and local innovation systems: a critical survey', *Industrial and Corporate Change*, **10** (4), 975.
Brown, S. and K. Eisenhardt (1995), 'Product development: past research, present findings, future directions', *The Academy of Management Review*, **20** (2), 343–378.

Capron, L., P. Dussauge and W. Mitchell (1998), 'Resource redeployment following horizontal mergers and acquisitions in Europe and the United States, 1988–1992', *Strategic Management Journal*, **19**, 631–661.

Cassiman, B. and R. Veugelers (2002), 'R&D cooperation and spillovers: some empirical evidence from Belgium', *American Economic Review*, **92** (4), 1169–1185.

Cassiman, B. and R. Veugelers (2006), 'In search of complementarity in the innovation strategy: internal R&D and external knowledge acquisition', *Management Science*, **52** (1), 68–82.

Cassiman, B., M.C. Di Guardo and G. Valentini (2009), 'Organizing R&D projects to profit from innovation insights from co-opetition', *Long Range Planning*, **42** (2), 216–230.

Chakravorti, B. (2004), 'The new rules for bringing innovations to market', *Harvard Business Review*, **82**, 58–67.

Chatterji, D. (1996), 'Accessing external sources of technology', *Research and Technology Management*, 48–56.

Chesbrough, H. (2003), *Open Innovation*, Boston, MA: Harvard Business School Press.

Chesbrough, H. (2006), *Open Business Models: How to Thrive in the New Innovation Landscape*, Boston, MA: Harvard Business School Press.

Chesbrough, H.W. and A.K. Crowther (2006), 'Beyond high tech: early adopters of open innovation in other industries', *R&D Management*, **36** (3), 229–236.

Chesbrough, H., W. Vanhaverbeke and J. West (eds) (2006), *Open Innovation: Researching a New Paradigm*, Oxford: Oxford University Press.

Christensen, C.M. (1997), *The Innovator's Dilemma When New Technologies Cause Great Firms to Fail*, Boston, MA: Harvard Business School Press.

Christensen, C.M. and J.L. Bower (1996), 'Customer power, strategic investment, and the failure of leading firms', *Strategic Management Journal*, **17** (3), 197–229.

Christensen, C.M., F.F. Suárez and J.M. Utterback (1998), 'Strategies for survival in fast-changing industries', MIT ICRMOT working paper WP#152–96.

Coase, R. (1988), 'The nature of the firm: influence', *Journal of Law, Economics, and Organization*, **4**, 33–48.

Coase, R. (1990), 'Accounting and the theory of the firm', *Journal of Accounting and Economics*, **12**, 3–13.

Cockburn, I. and R. Henderson (1998), 'Absorptive capacity, coauthoring behavior, and the organization of research in drug discovery', *Journal of Industrial Economics*, **46**, 157–182.

Cohen, W.M. and S. Klepper (1996), 'Firm size and the nature of innovation within industries: the case of process and product R&D', *The Review of Economics and Statistics*, **78**, (2), 232–244.

Cohen, W.M. and D.A. Levinthal (1990), 'Absorptive capacity: a new perspective on learning and innovation', *Administrative Science Quarterly*, **35** (1), 128–152.

Colombo, M. and P. Garrone (1998), 'A simultaneous equations model of technological agreements and infra-mural R&D', in M. Colombo (ed.), *The Changing Boundaries of the Firm*, London: Routledge, pp. 140–157.

Conner, K.R. and C.K. Prahalad (1996), 'A resource based theory of the firm: knowledge versus opportunism', *Organization Science*, **7**, 477–501.

D'Aspremont, C. and A. Jacquemin (1988), 'Cooperative and noncooperative R&D in duopoly with spillovers', *American Economic Review*, **78**, 1133–1137.

D'Aveni, R.A. (1994), *HyperCompetition. Managing the Dynamics of Strategic Manoeuvring*, New York: The Free Press.

De Bondt, R. (1997), 'Spillovers and innovative activities', *International Journal of Industrial Organization*, **15** (1), 1–28.

De la Mothe, J. and A.N. Link (eds) (2002), *Networks, Alliances, and Partnerships in the Innovation Process*, Boston, MA: Kluwer Academic.

Delmas, M.A. (1999), 'Exposing strategic assets to create new competencies: the case of technological acquisition in the waste management industry in Europe and North America', *Industrial and Corporate Change*, **8**, 635–652.

Dosi, G. (1982), 'Technological paradigms and technological trajectories', *Research Policy*, **11**, 147–162.

Dosi, G. (1988), 'Sources, procedures, and microeconomic effects of innovation', *Journal of Economic Literature*, **26**, 1120–1171.

Eisenhardt, K.M. and C. Schoonhoven (1996), 'Resource-based view of strategic alliance formation: strategic and social effects in entrepreneurial firms', *Organization Science*, **7**, 136–150.

Gambardella, A. (2002), 'Successes and failures in the markets for technology', *Oxford Review of Economic Policy*, **18** (1), 52.

Gassmann, O. (2006), 'Opening up the innovation process: towards an agenda', *R&D Management*, **36** (3), 223–238.

Granstrand, O., E. Bohlin, C. Oskarsson and N. Sjoberg (1992), 'External technology acquisition in large multi-technology corporations', *R&D Management*, **22**, 111–133.

Hagedoorn, J. and J. Schakenraad (1994), 'The effect of strategic technology alliances on company performance', *Strategic Management Journal*, **15**, 291–309.

Harrigan, K. (1985), 'An application of clustering for strategic group analysis', *Strategic Management Journal*, **6** (1), 55–74.

Henderson, R. (1993), 'Underinvestment and incompetence as responses to radical innovation: evidence from the photolithographic alignment equipment industry', *RAND Journal of Economics*, **24** (2), 248–270.

Henderson, R. and K.B. Clark (1990), 'Architectural innovation: the reconfiguration of existing product capabilities and the failure of established firms', *Administrative Science Quarterly*, **35**, 9–30.

Hitt, M., R. Hoskisson, R. Ireland and J. Harrison (1991), 'Effects of acquisitions on R&D inputs and outputs', *Academy of Management Journal*, **34**, 693–706.

Hitt, M., R. Hoskisson, R. Johnson and D. Moesel (1996), 'The market for corporate control and firm innovation', *Academy of Management Journal*, **39**, 1084–1119.

Holmstrom, B. and J. Roberts (1998), 'The boundaries of the firm revisited', *Journal of Economic Perspectives*, **12**, 73–94.

Iansiti, M. (1995), 'Shooting the rapids: managing product development in turbulent environments', *California Management Review*, **38** (1), 37–58.

Jaruzelski, B., K. Dehoff and R. Bordia (2005), *The Booz Allen Hamilton Global Innovation 1.000: Money isn't Everything*. Strategy + business 41.

Kamien, M.I. and I. Zang (2000), 'Meet me halfway: research joint ventures and absorptive capacity', *International Journal of Industrial Organization*, **18** (7), 995.

Katz, M.L. and C. Shapiro (1985), 'Network externalities, competition, and compatibility', *American Economic Review*, **75** (3), 424–440.

Katz, R. and T.J. Allen (1982), 'Investigating the Not Invented Here (NIH) syndrome: a look at the performance, tenure, and communication patterns of 50 R&D project groups', *R&D Management*, **12** (1), 7–20.

Keller, R. (1994), 'Technology-information processing fit and the performance of R&D project groups: a test of contingency theory', *Academy of Management Journal*, **37**, 167–179.

Levin, R., A. Klevorick, R. Nelson and R. Winter (1987), 'Appropriating the returns from industrial research and development', *Brookings Papers on Economic Activity*, Special Issue.

Linder, J.C., S. Jarvenpaa and T.H. Davenport (2003), 'Toward an innovation sourcing strategy', *MIT Sloan Management Review*.

Madhok, A., (2002), 'Reassessing the fundamentals and beyond: Ronald Coase, the transaction cost and resource-based theories of the firm and the institutional structure of production', *Strategic Management Journal*, **23**, 535–550.

Markides, C. and P. Geroski (2003), 'Teaching elephants how to dance and other silly ideas', *Business Strategy Review*, **14** (3), 49–53.

McDougall, P.P., S. Shane and B.M. Oviatt (1994), 'Explaining the formation of international new ventures: the limits of theories from international business research', *Journal of Business Venturing*, **9**, 469–487.

Menon, T. and J. Pfeffer (2003), 'Valuing internal versus external knowledge', *Management Science*, **49**, 497–513.

Miotti, L. and F. Sachwald (2003), 'Cooperative R&D: why and with whom? An integrated framework of analysis', *Research Policy*, forthcoming.

Mowery, D.C. and N. Rosenberg (1989), 'New developments in US technology policy: implications for competitiveness and international trade policy', *California Management Review*, **32** (1), 107–125.

Mowery, D.C., J.E. Oxley and B.S. Silverman (1998), 'Technological overlap and interfirm cooperation: implications for the resource-based view of the firm', *Research Policy*, **27** (5), 507–523.

Nagarajan, A. and W. Mitchell (1998), 'Evolutionary diffusion: internal and external methods used to acquire encompassing, complementary and incremental technological changes in the lithotripsy industry', *Strategic Management Journal*, **19**, 1063–1077.

Nelson, R. (1990), 'US technological leadership: where did it come from and where did it go?', *Research Policy*, **19**, 193–214.

Nohria, N. and C. Garcia-Pont (1991), 'Global strategic linkages and industry structure', *Strategic Management Journal*, **12**, 105–24.

Odagiri, H. (2003), 'Transaction costs and capabilities as determinants of the R&D boundaries of the firm: a case study of the ten largest pharmaceutical firms in Japan', *Managerial and Decision Economics*, **24** (2,3), 187.

Peteraf, M. (1993), 'The cornerstones of competitive advantage: a resource-based view', *Strategic Management Journal*, **14** (3), 179–191.

Peterson, J. (1993), 'Assessing the performance of European collaborative R&D policy: the case of Eureka', *Research Policy*, **22**, 243–264.

Pisano, G. (1990), 'The R&D boundaries of the firm: an empirical analysis', *Administrative Science Quarterly*, **35**, 153–176.

Porter, M.E. and S. Stern (2001), 'Innovation: location matters', *Sloan Management Review*, **42** (4), 28–43.

Powell, W.W., K.W. Koput and L. Smith-Doerr (1996), 'Interorganizational collaboration and the locus of innovation: networks of learning in biotechnology', *Administrative Science Quarterly*, **41**, 116–145.

Rigby, D. and C. Zook (2002), 'Open-market innovation', *Harvard Business Review*, October, 80–89.

Robertson, T.S. and H. Gatignon (1998), 'Technology development mode: a transaction cost conceptualization', *Strategic Management Journal*, **19**, 515–531.

Romanelli, E. and M. Tushman (1994), 'Organizational transformation as punctuated equilibrium: an empirical test', *Academy of Management Journal*, **37** (5).

Rothwell, R. and M. Dodgson (1991), 'External linkages and innovation in small and medium-sized enterprises', *R&D Management*, **21** (2) 125–138.

Sakakibara, M. (2001), 'Cooperative research and development: who participates and in which industries do projects take place?', *Research Policy*, **30**, 993–1018.

Schilling, M. and H.K. Steensma (2002), 'Disentangling the theories of firm boundaries: a path model and empirical test', *Organization Science*, **13**, 387–401.

Shapiro, C. and H.R. Varian (1999), *Information Rules: A Strategic Guide to the Network Economy*, Boston, MA: Harvard Business School Press.

Shapiro, C. and R. Willig (1990), 'On the antitrust treatment of production joint ventures', *The Journal of Economic Perspectives*, **4** (3), 113–131.

Song, J., P. Almeida and G. Wu (2003), 'Learning-by-hiring: when is mobility more likely to facilitate interfirm knowledge transfer?', *Management Science*, **49**, 351–365.

Steensma, H.K. and J.F. Fairbank (1999), 'Internalizing external technology: a model of governance mode choice and an empirical assessment', *Journal of High Technology Management Research*, **10** (1), 1–35.

Stuart, T.E. (1998), 'Network positions and propensities to collaborate: an investigation of strategic alliance formation in a high-technology industry', *Administrative Science Quarterly*, **43**, 668–698.

Stuart, T.E. (2000), 'Interorganizational alliances and the performance of firms: a study of growth and innovation rates in a high-technology industry', *Strategic Management Journal*, **21**, 791–811.

Sull, D.N., R.S. Tedlow and R.S. Rosenbloom (1997), 'Managerial commitment and technological change in the US tire industry', *Industrial and Corporate Change*, **6**, 461–501.

Teece, D. (1986), 'Profiting from technological innovation: implications for integration, collaboration, licensing and public policy', *Research Policy*, **15** (6).

Tripsas, M. and G. Gavetti (2000), 'Capabilities, cognition, and inertia: evidence from digital imaging', *Strategic Management Journal*, **21** (10/11).

Tushman, M.L. and P. Anderson (1986), 'Technological discontinuities and organizational environments', *Administrative Science Quarterly*, **31**, 431–465.

Ulset, S. (1996), 'R&D outsourcing and contractual governance: an empirical study of commercial R&D projects', *Journal of Economic Behavior and Organization*, **30**, 63–82.

Valentini, G. (2005), 'Mergers & acquisitions and technological performance', *Academy of Management Conference Best Papers Proceedings*.

Veugelers, R. (1997), 'Internal R&D expenditures and external technology sourcing', *Research Policy*, **26** (3), 303–326.

Veugelers, R. and B. Cassiman (1999), 'Make and buy in innovation strategies: evidence from Belgian manufacturing firms', *Research Policy*, **28**, 63–80.

West, J. and S. Gallagher (2006), 'Challenges of open innovation: the paradox of firm investment in open-source software', *R&D Management*, **36** (3), 319–331.

Williamson, O.E. (1975), *Markets and Hierarchies: Analysis and Antitrust Implications*, New York: The Free Press.

Williamson, O.E. (1985), *Economic Institutions of Capitalism*, New York: The Free Press.

Winter, S. (1997), 'Knowledge and competence as strategic assets', in D.J. Teece (ed.), *The Competitive Challenge*, Cambridge, MA: Ballinger, pp. 159–184.

Zahra, S.A. and G. George (2002), 'Absorptive capacity: a review, reconceptualisation, and extension', *Academy of Management Review*, **27** (2), 185–203.

Zander, U. and B. Kogut (1995), 'Knowledge and the speed of the transfer and imitation of organizational capabilities: an empirical test', *Organization Science*, **6**, 76–92.

14 Corporate governance issues in competitive strategy research
Igor Filatotchev

INTRODUCTION

The last decade has witnessed an explosion in both policy and research devoted to corporate governance. The main objective of this chapter is to review various literatures looking at the interdependencies of corporate governance and the firm's competitive strategy with a particular focus on the governance roles of boards and large shareholders. It also discusses contingencies and complementarities related to the practices of corporate governance in terms of their effects on business strategy and its organizational outcomes.

From a theoretical point of view, most of the empirical literature on corporate governance has been rooted in agency theory, and is concerned with linking different aspects of corporate governance with firm performance. Three fundamental behavioural assumptions about agents and principals underlie agency theory: both agents and principals are assumed to be (a) rational and (b) self-interested, whereas the agent is assumed to be (c) more risk-averse than the principal (Jensen and Meckling, 1976). It is therefore argued that, in situations in which there is a conflict of interest between the agents and principals, the former are likely to select self-serving actions at the expense of the latter's welfare (Fama, 1980; Fama and Jensen, 1983). This stream of research identifies situations in which shareholders' and managers' goals are likely to diverge, and examines mechanisms that can mitigate managers' self-serving behaviour (Shleifer and Vishny, 1997). The assumption here is that, by managing the principal-agency problem between shareholders and managers, firms will operate more efficiently and perform better. To constrain managerial opportunism, shareholders may use a diverse range of corporate governance mechanisms, including monitoring by boards of directors and mutual monitoring by managers (Fama and Jensen, 1983) as well as monitoring by large outside shareholders (Demsetz and Lehn, 1985). In addition, internal governance mechanisms may include various equity-based managerial incentives that align the interests of agents and principals (Jensen and Murphy, 1990). Finally, external factors, such as the threat of takeover (Shleifer and Vishny, 1997), product competition (Jensen, 1993), and managerial labour markets (Fama, 1980) may constrain managerial opportunism. Rediker and Seth (1995) suggest that combinations (or bundles) of internal and external governance mechanisms may reduce principal-agent costs and align the interests of principals and agents.

Although economics and the corporate finance perspective have traditionally dominated corporate governance research, strategic management is rapidly catching up and makes further important advances in terms of linking governance with business strategy. It increasingly recognizes corporate governance as an important organizational factor affecting the firm's performance and long-term survival. Some recent papers have begun to combine the resource-based and agency perspectives, to explain entrepreneurial behaviour (Zhara and Filatotchev, 2005), strategic choice and organizational structure and network dynamics (Filatotchev and Toms, 2003). From a resource-based perspective, governance choices may affect the creation of economic rents by providing access to valuable, rare, costly to imitate, and non-substitutable resources as well as mediating their appropriation. From an agency perspective, managers may appropriate a disproportionate share of such rents. Greater shareholder value may be realized where compensation structures reflect firm-specific managerial risk (Castanias and Helfat, 2001) or where there are design differences between boards able to recruit skilled directors who can generate economic rents and boards focused only on minimizing agency conflicts, for example through appointment of outsiders (Barney et al., 2001). Zahra and Filatotchev (2004) argue that corporate governance systems and organizational learning are interdependent, and in some cases may substitute or complement each other. A knowledge-based analysis of governance recognizes the importance of strategic context and the relevance of different types of knowledge at different stages of the firm's life cycle.

These arguments suggest that the firm's competitive dynamics and corporate governance changes are inter-linked, and the firm's life cycle may go hand in hand with dramatic shifts in its governance system. The valuable resource base accessible by the firm, where extensive, consists of organization-specific idiosyncratic resources, including 'tacit' knowledge (Castanias and Helfat, 1991; Barney, 1997). Such resources might include specialized production facilities, trade secrets and engineering experience (Teece et al., 1997) and human capital assets (Teece, 1980). Internal knowledge, where valuable, has the characteristic of being difficult to imitate, reflecting the heterogeneous nature of assets advocated in the resource-based theory of the firm. Alternatively, where the resource base is narrower, resources come from outside the organization, and possess external economy of scale characteristics. Such external pools of knowledge usually have a public good element, such as local concentrations of experience and skilled labour. These definitions subsume the wealth creation roles of corporate governance within a resource and knowledge-based view of the firm. To complement this view, the agency framework deals with the accountability aspect and refers to the wealth protection dimension of the governance function, contrasting situations with limited transparency, where principal-agent-based monitoring mechanisms are inchoate or ineffective with high transparency and accountability where these are more developed and effective.

Within this diverse literature, which is focused on the wealth creation and wealth protection function of corporate governance practices, the governance roles of corporate boards and major shareholders have received particular attention. These two important aspects of corporate governance are discussed in the following sections.

THE BOARD OF DIRECTORS

Corporate governance research that examines the impact of board characteristics and composition on critical decisions has predominantly adopted an agency theory rationale. Board monitoring has been centrally important in corporate governance research, with boards of directors described as "the apex of the internal control system" (Jensen, 1993: 862). Boards represent an organization's owners and are responsible for ensuring that the organization is managed effectively. Thus, the board is responsible for adopting control mechanisms to ensure that management's behaviour and actions are consistent with the interests of the owners. Important control mechanisms are the selection, evaluation and if necessary removal of a poorly performing CEO and top management, the determination of managerial incentives and the monitoring and assessment of organizational performance (Mizruchi, 1983; Zahra and Pearce, 1989). The main driver of these control mechanisms is the board's obligation to ensure that management operates in the interests of the company's shareholders – an obligation that is met by scrutiny, evaluation, and the regulation of top management's actions by the board (Hillman and Dalziel, 2003).

Management research has suggested that boards can extend their involvement beyond monitoring and controlling top management to the provision of ongoing advice and counsel to executive directors on strategic issues (Johnson et al., 1996; Westphal, 1999; Zahra and Pearce, 1989). Advice and counsel from non-executive directors can broaden the range of strategic options considered by management and help management to identify new strategic opportunities (Judge and Zeithaml, 1992; Pfeffer and Salancik, 1978). Strategy researchers indicate that a board of directors may also play an important role in establishing relationships between the organization and its external environment. Resource-dependence theory proposes that organizations are dependent upon resources in the environment for their survival and views directors as instruments, which organizations can use to deal with external dependencies (Dalton et al., 1999; Hillman and Dalziel, 2003; Pfeffer and Salancik, 1978). Directors, in this view, help to secure valuable information and resources and provide access to key constituents (Hillman et al., 2000). Again, these roles of boards regarding service, strategy and resources should lead to an improvement in the firm's competitiveness and performance. Moreover, despite the focus on shareholder interests and the board, outside of the USA or UK, it should be noted that board composition often involves a wider spectrum of stakeholders and, more specifically, includes employee representatives in Scandinavian countries, Germany, Austria, and the Netherlands (Jackson, 2005). Here, board behaviour may substantially depart from the agency theory perspective to consider the governance of a wider range of managerial objectives.

The strategic management research on the governance roles of the board has focused on three main themes: the effects of board composition and structural parameters on business strategy; relationships between board characteristics, such as diversity, external ties, etc. and the firm's competitiveness and performance; and links between board processes and organizational outcomes.

Board Composition and Strategic Decisions

A decision-centred perspective on the governance roles of corporate boards suggests that, rather than examining a board's monitoring effectiveness by using the firm's financial performance as a proxy, a more accurate evaluation can be gained by examining discrete decisions that involve a potential conflict of interest between management and shareholders (Deutsch, 2005; Mallette and Fowler, 1992; Sundaramurthy, 1996). Such decisions will be referred to as 'critical decisions'. The rationale behind this line of inquiry is that, whereas board monitoring has a direct effect on firms' critical decisions, it has only an indirect effect on firm performance. Moreover, a company's financial performance is influenced by a multitude of endogenous and exogenous factors beyond the composition of its board (Kosnik, 1987).

Prior strategy research has indicated that independent directors are involved in strategic change, restructuring, and corporate entrepreneurship (Pearce and Zahra, 1992; Hoskisson et al., 2002; Tihanyi et al., 2003).

Gibbs (1993), in a study of strategic restructuring in large USA firms, provides evidence that board independence is positively associated with re-focusing strategies and an increase in financial leverage that reduces the firm's free cash flow. Goodstain and Boeker (1991), in their study of 327 hospitals in the USA, provide evidence that independent boards are positively associated with strategic restructuring measured in terms of changes in the breadth of products and services an organization offers.

However, more recent studies suggest that board structure may have a selective effect on different types of strategies. For example, a number of studies associate board independence with diversification and M&A strategies (Baysinger et al., 1991; Beekun et al., 1998; Hill and Snell, 1988; Hoskisson et al., 1994; Judge and Zeithaml, 1992; Pearce and Zahra, 1992; Sanders and Carpenter, 1998; Hoskisson et al., 2002; Tihanyi et al., 2003; Zajac and Westphal, 1996). Studies of R&D expenditure suggest that innovation intensity, on the other hand, is positively associated with insider-dominated boards (Baysinger et al., 1991). Baysinger and Hoskisson (1990) suggest that the superiority and quality of inside directors' information combined with their specific risk preferences may explain these differential effects of board structure on various types of business strategies.

Both financial economists and strategy researchers investigate the effects of board independence on the adoption of the anti-takeover defences. Takeover defences are adopted to deter hostile takeovers. Indeed, Pound (1987) found that takeover defences decrease the likelihood of takeover attempts by 26 per cent. Whereas CEOs favour takeover defences because they protect their positions and provide greater freedom from the disciplining influence of the market for corporate control, it has been argued that takeover defences have negative effects on shareholders' wealth (Mallette and Fowler, 1992). For example, research indicates that poison pills, a common takeover defence, have a significant negative effect on a firm's stock price. Furthermore, stock prices typically decline following court decisions that validate poison pills and rise after court decisions that invalidate them. This negative wealth effect may stem from the fact that firms that adopt a poison pill are less likely to be targets of acquisition. Shivdasani (1993) suggests that board independence affects takeover probabilities by influencing both the quality of the company's management and the process of takeover. However, other empirical studies by Buchholtz and Ribbens (1994) and Mallette and Fowler (1992) provide ambiguous results.

A central task of effectively functioning boards is the removal of poorly performing executives. Boards with greater structural independence may be more able to remove ineffective executives prior to a crisis reaching the point of corporate bankruptcy. This action may prove critical in reversing a financial decline, since deficiencies within the top management team may be related to firm failure. A substantial number of studies are focused on board structure effects on the probability of the CEO turnover (Alexander et al., 1993; Fizel and Louie, 1990; Mangel and Singh, 1993; Sanders and Carpenter, 1998; Weisbach, 1988; Young et al., 2000). In his meta-analysis of board independence effects on strategic decisions, Deutsch (2005) uses 16 different studies to support the assumption that more independent boards are associated with a higher probability of CEO turnover. Another stream of research links board structure with executive compensation. Although it is often argued that a high level of total compensation enables firms to attract and retain high-quality CEOs, the elevated levels of remuneration awarded to CEOs of publicly traded corporations is often criticized (Deutsch, 2005), suggesting that some firms systematically overpay their executives and that these firms could have secured the service of the same CEO at substantially lower costs to shareholders. Because CEOs prefer the highest compensation level possible, vigilant board monitoring is expected to result in lower levels of CEO compensation. A number of authors analyse the effects of board independence on the level of CEO compensation (Conyon and Peck, 1998; Fizel and Louie, 1990; Mangel and Singh, 1993; Sanders and Carpenter, 1998). However, no systematic relationship was found between the two variables.

Board Characteristics, Business Strategy and Performance

Although agency theorists emphasize the core board's function as a monitoring and control mechanism, there is growing recognition in management research and an upper echelon perspective (e.g. Carpenter and Westphal, 2001; Daily and Dalton, 1992; Geletkanycz and Hambrick, 1997) that board directors also constitute a critical organizational resource. Rooted in behavioural and socio-economic research, stewardship theory holds a less self-centred view of managerial behaviour than does agency theory. The stewardship framework suggests that, whereas managers are expected to adopt self-serving behaviour as a response to highly threatening situations, they tend to serve the good of the organization in situations where only relatively minor conflicts of interest exist (Anderson and Reeb, 2002; Davis et al., 1997; Deutsch, 2005). Acting as stewards, executive directors may collaborate with independent board members who provide industry-specific expertise and objective advice, and act as advocates for corporate health and viability.

More recent resource-dependence, behavioural and socio-cognitive views on corporate boards have extended agency research by suggesting that pro-active behaviour by non-executive directors depends not only on the extent of board independence, but also on the strategic perspective and base of experience they bring to the organization (Carpenter, 2002; Carpenter and Westphal, 2001; Carpenter et al., 2003; Westphal and Zajac, 1995; Westphal, 1999; Golden and Zajac, 2001). The resource-dependency view emphasizes that, in addition to control functions, the board may also play service and strategic roles in the decision-making process (Pfeffer, 1972; Pfeffer and Salancik, 1978; Provan, 1980), especially at those points in the life cycle of the firm that involve strategic transition (McNulty and Pettigrew, 1999). Pye (2001) suggests that in order to 'add value' to the board, non-executive directors are expected to bring a background of executive experience of running other firms. Previous studies identify four types of resources that are provided by boards: (1) advice and counsel; (2) legitimacy; (3) channels for communicating information between the firm and external organizations, and (4) assistance in obtaining resources or commitments from important stakeholders outside the firm (Hillman et al., 2000; Lynall et al., 2003).

Therefore, according to socio-cognitive and resource perspectives, outside board members' experience may not only improve their monitoring efficiency, but also substitute for a relative lack of executives' business experience or contacts (Carpenter et al., 2003; Shivdasani and Yemack, 1999). Within this research, structural board characteristics are not as important as factors associated with the board's human and social capital, such as board size, demography characteristics and business links outside the focal firm (Carpenter and Westphal, 2001). These characteristics underpin the service, strategy and resource roles of boards and should lead to an improvement in the firm's competitiveness and performance.

Resource-dependence theory has been the primary foundation for the perspective that larger boards will be associated with higher levels of firm performance (Dalton et al., 1999; Pfeffer, 1972; Pfeffer and Salancik, 1978; Provan, 1980). In this view, board size may be a measure of an organization's ability to form environmental links to secure critical resources. From the monitoring perspective, a number of authors suggest that larger boards are not as susceptible to managerial domination as their smaller counterparts (Zahra and Pearce, 1989). Daily et al. (2002) and Daily and Dalton (1992 and 1994) find positive effect of board size on financial performance in large samples of firms in the USA. Golden and Zajac (2001) find a non-linear (inverted U-shape) relationship between board size and strategic change. Using 27 board size-related studies in their meta-analysis, Dalton et al. (1999) found a significant positive effect of board size on performance. However, agency researchers are more sceptical about the effects of board size on the monitoring capacity of independent directors

(Jensen, 1993). When boards become too big, agency problems (such as director free-riding) increase within the board, and it becomes more symbolic and less part of the management process (Hermalin and Weisbach, 2003). Yermack (1996) reports that there is a significant negative relationship between board size and Tobin's Q. Judge and Zeithaml (1992) report that large boards are less likely to be involved in strategic decision, a finding also supported by Goodstain and Boeker (1991). Therefore, the organizational outcome of board size remains an empirical issue.

Research on the service, expertise and counsel roles of the board emphasizes that directors may provide a quality of support and advice to the CEO otherwise unavailable from other corporate staff (Dalton et al., 1998 and 1999; Hillman and Dalziel, 2003; Lorsh and MacIver, 1989; Zahra and Pearce, 1989). The effectiveness of these support and service roles of the board, in turn, depends on the board's cumulative human capital that is often linked to various board demography characteristics, such as tenure, professional diversity, and so on. Boards that are composed of lawyers, financial representatives, top management of other firms, public affairs specialists and so on, may be more effective in terms of bringing important expertise, experience and skills to facilitate advice and counsel. This research emphasizes that board structural characteristics (e.g. the proportion of independent directors, separate CEO and chairperson) are less relevant compared to the quality of the board's cumulative human capital. A number of studies argue that board diversity in terms of directors' professional experiences should lead to more efficient service, expertise and counsel roles of the board and, as a result, to better performance (Carpenter, 2002; Baysinger and Hoskisson, 1990; Wagner et al., 1998; Westphal, 1999).

Another stream of research links the board's human capital with a number of 'demographic' factors, such as directors' age and tenure, although empirical evidence linking these factors with performance outcomes is rather limited. Pfeffer (1983) and Finkelstein and Hambrick (1996) argue that greater tenure of board members is associated with greater rigidity, increased commitment to established practices and procedures, and increased insulation towards new ideas. However, Hambrick and Mason (1984) and Hambrick and D'Aveni (1992) suggest that longer tenure provides directors with much more comprehensive access to a richer stock of remembered information, relative to what a novice can access. Golden and Zajac (2001), in their study of strategic change in USA hospitals, find a curvilinear relationship between the average tenure and strategic restructuring: as average board member tenure increases, its effect on strategic change is positive for boards with lower levels of tenure, and negative for boards with higher levels of tenure. Similarly, these authors present evidence of non-linear effect of directors' age on strategic change: as the average age of board members increases, its effect on strategic change is positive for younger boards, and negative for older boards. Generally, existing research considers board diversity and limits on board members' tenure and age as 'good' corporate governance drivers.

A board's social/relational capital is another important factor essential for the provision of resources, advice and counsel. This factor is usually associated with external directorships and other extra-organizational ties held by the firm's directors. First, resource-based research provides evidence that board interlocks are associated with effective capital acquisition (Filatotchev and Toms, 2003; Mizruchi, 1996). Second, building cognitive capacity by importing knowledge from the outside becomes vital for the long-term survival of the firm (Carpenter, 2002). This import may be facilitated by appointing non-executive directors who have served on the boards of other, well-established firms, or who have important professional and social links that may be used strategically by the firm. The links that non-executive directors have with the firm's environment can be used to obtain important information and strategic expertise (Golden and Zajac, 2001; Pettigrew, 1992). Carpenter and Westphal (2001) and Westphal (1999) find that boards consisting of directors with ties to strategically related organizations were able to provide better advice and counsel, which is positively related to firm performance. Third, board social capital has been linked to the provision of firm legitimacy and reputation. Social network theory emphasizes the importance of network formation in terms of reputation, trust and mutual inter-dependence (Geletkanycz and Hambrick, 1997; Lynall et al., 2003). Therefore, having directors with extensive extra-organizational ties may be an important factor associated with the resource and service roles of boards.

Some authors, however, are cautious with regard to the possible governance implications of board interlocks. A 'class hegemony' perspective suggests that, by inviting their friends from other companies to sit on the focal firm's board, executives re-enforce their power within the organization (Pettigrew and McNulty, 1995; Useem, 1993). Hermalin and Weisbach (2003), for example, provide evidence that CEO pay at a given company increases when the given company's board contains directors who are CEOs of firms on whose boards the CEO of the given company sits. In this context, previous research emphasizes the importance of both the intensity of non-executive directors' external ties (for example, an average number of board 'interlocks' held by a non-executive director) and their diversity, such as directors' membership in social and political elites, professional services organizations, etc., in addition to their board interlocks (Carpenter, 2002; Daily et al., 1999; Filatotchev and Bishop,

2002; Pettigrew, 1992; Zahra and Pearce, 1989). Certo (2003) and Certo et al. (2001) find that firms with prestigious and diverse boards experience better performance at their initial public offering (IPO). Filatotchev and Bishop (2002) draw similar conclusions in their study of IPOs in the UK. Higgins and Gulati (1999) suggest that board interlocks are particularly important for young, entrepreneurial firms that are in search of resources and legitimacy.

Although there seems to be general agreement in the governance literature that boards deal with strategic issues, the extent of the board's involvement in strategic decision-making is disputed. Lorsch and McIver (1989) argued that the board's primary role is in advising and evaluating strategy, rather than in initiating strategy. Demb and Neubauer's (1992) research on boards of directors from a number of European countries found that setting strategic direction was considered an important role of the board. However, overall they found a wide variety of views on how boards should be involved in strategy. At one end of the spectrum, the board was perceived as rather passive and uninvolved while at the other end the board was regarded as initiating, decisive and fully responsible for strategic decision-making.

A growing number of papers move away from research on the organizational outcomes of board structure and demographic characteristics to greater focus on board processes and functions. This research aims to shed light on a number of relatively under-researched issues that Pettigrew (1992: 176) raised in his study on managerial elites, such as: why do boards look the way they do? How do particular constellations of human resource assets on the board occur and build up? How does executives' power affect the control relationships between team members and the board? These questions extend discussion beyond the relatively narrow boundaries of agency theory. Indeed, a growing number of studies suggest that the agency framework should be used in conjunction with complementary theories (Daily et al., 2003; Pettigrew, 1992), including behavioural (e.g. Hambrick and Mason, 1984; Sanders and Carpenter, 2003) and socio-cognitive research (Carpenter et al., 2003; Carpenter, 2002) in examining governance-related issues.

THE GOVERNANCE ROLES OF BLOCKHOLDERS AND SHAREHOLDER ACTIVISM

There is a growing body of research in the economics and management literature that links the pattern and amount of stock ownership with managerial behaviour and, eventually, corporate performance (see Dalton et al., 2003, and Short, 1994, for a comprehensive survey). The concentration of ownership may be an effective approach to controlling the agency problems caused by the separation of risk-bearing and decision functions in firms (Demsetz, 1983; Tihaniy et al., 2003). However, because most of the previous research in the corporate governance area is focused on corporations with diffused ownership within the framework of the conventional USA/UK model of corporate control, little is known about the behaviour of joint stock firms with concentrated ownership (Holderness and Sheehan, 1988). In terms of issues related to the ownership structure and identities of the major groups of shareholders, previous research has recognized several possible governance roles for large-block shareholders, some of which are likely to be value-enhancing while others are likely to have negative effects (see Shleifer and Vishny, 1997, for an extensive discussion).

Strategic management provides another important stream of research that links ownership patterns with the firm's strategic decisions. For example, using structural equation modelling, Hoskisson et al. (1994) show that large-block shareholders help mitigate against poor strategy, such as diversification, to evolve into poor performance, therefore decreasing the magnitude of restructuring. Hill and Snell (1988) find that ownership concentration is positively correlated with R&D expenditures, specialization and relatedness in a sample of 94 firms in research-intensive industries. According to Black (1992), institutional investors have demonstrated a decided propensity to restrain managerial appetite for value-destroying mergers and acquisitions.

Some researchers have indicated, however, that concentrated shareholding may create a trade-off between incentives and entrenchment (La Porta et al., 2000a; Short, 1994). For example, using a variety of linear regressions, Morck et al. (1988) suggest that there is an incentive effect of managerial ownership on performance (measured in terms of Tobin's Q) in the 0 to 5 per cent ownership range, negative relation in the 5 to 25 per cent range, and a further positive relation beyond 25 per cent. Building on this theoretical framework, the empirical study by McConnell and Servaes (1990) finds a significant curvilinear relation between Tobin's Q and the share of common stock owned by the managers. In addition, there is evidence that concentrated non-managerial ownership can also harm market valuation (Roe, 1990).

In particular, lack of diversification and limited liquidity mean that large shareholders are affected adversely by the company's idiosyncratic risk (Maug, 1998). To compensate for this risk they may use an opportunity to collude with managers or shift wealth from minority shareholders to themselves. For example, Pound (1988) argues that large institutional investors and unaffiliated blockholders are likely to side with management (the strategic-alignment hypothesis). Likewise, blockholders may be influenced by other existing business relationships with management (the conflict-of-interest hypothesis). Building on this research, some authors point out that ownership concentration per se may negatively affect the value of the firm when majority shareholders have a possibility to abuse their position of dominant control at the expense of minority shareholders (Bebchuk, 1994; Stiglitz, 1985). As a result, at some level of ownership concentration the distinction between insiders and outsiders becomes blurred, and blockholders, no matter what their identity is, may have strong incentives to build coalitions with managers and divert resources in ways that make them better off at the expense of other shareholders. La Porta et al. (2000) suggest that in this environment firms with concentrated owners would face difficulty raising equity finance, since minority investors fear expropriation by managers and concentrated owners, and, as a result, profitable new ventures will be forsaken.

A number of empirical studies failed to confirm positive links between ownership concentration and performance. For example, Demsetz and Len (1985) find no association between ownership concentration and accounting profit rate in their sample of 511 large USA firms. Using a large sample of Forbes 800 firms and controlling for the endogenous nature of large-block shareholding, Agrawal and Knoeber (1996) do not find any significant effects of ownership concentration and a variety of performance measurements. Bethel and Liebeskind (1993) examine strategic restructuring in a panel of a large USA firm and suggest that institutional investors did not serve to discipline managers. They also provide evidence that concentrated shareholders normally support managers in their quest for growth. In addition, Dalton et al. (2003) applied meta-analytical procedures to 229 studies related to equity holdings and firm financial performance. Their tests do not provide support for the hypothesized relationship between share ownership by large blockholders and a number of performance proxies that include Tobin's Q, returns on assets, equity, sales, investment, etc. The authors conclude that, "the results of our meta-analyses do not support agency's theory proposed relationship between ownership and firm performance" (p. 23).

A number of more recent studies tried to find explanations for this inconsistency in theoretical predictions and empirical evidence with regard to the governance roles of concentrated owners. Jensen (1993) has questioned the promise of shareholder activism in general, and institutional investor activism in particular. Their increasing reliance on indexing investment strategies suggests that they believe that, on average, their portfolio of firms will yield returns comparable to those for the market as a whole, regardless of the governance structure of their portfolio firms. Black (1992) documents an increasing importance of exit strategies for the fund managers as opposed to shareholder activism. Daily et al. (2003) also suggest that shareholder activism can be much more costly than pure reliance on indexing strategies. Some authors challenge the very foundations of the 'blockholders–firm performance' hypothesis. More specifically, previous research treats ownership concentration as exogenous and does not address the issue of what affects ownership concentration for a given firm. A number of authors have suggested that firm characteristics such as size, investment needs, industry, location and so on, may determine its ownership structure (Demsetz and Lehn, 1985). In other words, a firm's ownership structure is an equilibrium response to its operating characteristics and competitive environment (Short, 1994), and the direction of causality between ownership concentration and firm characteristics is not entirely resolved by papers using cross-sectional variations in ownership.

Despite these empirical and theoretical arguments against shareholder activism hypotheses, a growing number of studies point out that the answer may be in the types of blockholders and what they actually do in terms of governing the firms in which they invest. Most research on the performance effects of large-block share ownership has not differentiated among types of investors. Only recently have studies acknowledged that the identity of such owners has important organizational implications because different owners may have different objectives and decision-making horizons (Hoskisson et al., 2002; Tihanyi et al., 2003). For example, banks and investment trusts may behave differently in terms of their strategic preferences (see Chang, 2003; and McConnell and Servaes, 1990, for a discussion).

Some authors (e.g. Brickley et al., 1988; David et al., 1998) differentiate between 'pressure-resistant', 'pressure-sensitive' and 'pressure-indeterminate' institutional investors. Pressure-resistant institutions, such as public pension funds, mutual funds, foundations and endowments, are unlikely to have strong business links with their investors, and they may have stronger influence on strategy choices and their performance outcomes (Dalton et al., 2003; Hoskisson et al., 2002). Johnson and Greening (1999) also indicate that a pension and investment fund manager's objective is a high relative performance of their portfolio firms because of their own reward system. They are the most likely among institutional investors to monitor organizational decision makers and to be labelled 'activist institutional investors' (Brickley et al., 1988). On the other hand, pressure-sensitive investors such as insurance companies and banks are likely to have business relationships with the firms in which they invest (Kroszner and Strahan, 2001). Because they often have an obligation to support the management's agenda, their governance role tends to be more passive compared to activist investors (Tihanyi et al., 2003). Corporate pension funds typify the pressure indeterminate institutional investor category. Relationships between the funds and the firms in which they invest may exist, and they are unlikely to actively challenge firm decision makers (Dalton et al., 2003).

Daily et al. (2003) and other authors suggest that only pressure-resistant investors behave in line with the assumptions of agency arguments related to the governance roles of blockholders. Hoskisson et al. (2002), for example, provide empirical evidence which suggests that managers of public pension funds prefer internal innovation and investment in R&D, whereas professional investment funds' managers prefer external innovations such as M&A. Wahal (1996) finds that pension funds moved away from takeover-related proxy proposals in the late 1980s and toward governance-related proxy proposals in the 1990s, suggesting that their managers are interested in active voice and less interested in short-term arbitrage. Research by Woidtke (2002) supports this view. Tihaniy et al. (2003) provide evidence of long-term strategic orientation of pension funds compared to other institutional investors.

Another stream of research in economics and finance suggests that private equity firms and venture capitalists may have a particularly strong impact on the process of corporate governance development because of their early involvement in the strategic development of the portfolio firm. They also gain a detailed knowledge and substantial decision-making rights in firms that they finance (Lerner, 1995). In particular, private equity firms impose contractual restraints on managerial discretion, including the use of staged investment, an enforceable nexus of security covenants, and the option to replace the entrepreneur as manager unless key investment objectives are met (see Megginson and Weiss, 1991, for a discussion). Since these special rights end at the time of an exit, when the need for oversight is particularly great, outside investors may compensate for a relative loss of control by strengthening other governance mechanisms, such as increasing the IPO firm's board independence (Black and Gilson, 1998). In addition, they often influence the distribution of the firm's shares in the process of IPO (Brav and Gompers, 1997). Therefore, private equity firms represent an ultimate version of pressure-resistant investors, although in the UK their investments are mainly confined to entrepreneurial ventures, buy-outs and public-to-private transactions.

A number of studies identify individual or group blockholders as another important type of pressure-resistant investors. These investors hold 5 per cent or more of a given firm's equity. Demsetz (1983) suggests that the substantial wealth they have at risk implies that benefits of monitoring will outweigh associated costs. Therefore, they have a stronger incentive than even activist institutional investors to engage in control activities (Dalton et al., 2003). Pound (1992) suggests that blockholders demonstrate their ability to effect changes in the composition of boards and corporate constitutions. Bethel and Liebeskind (1993) provide empirical evidence that blockholders' equity was associated with pro-active restructuring strategies in their panel of 388 Fortune 500 firms. Their evidence is consistent with the argument that large blockholders play a critical role in monitoring and redirecting corporate strategy.

Family owners represent an important subset of individual and group blockholders. A number of researchers express concerns about the problems associated with family control, and the increased likelihood of the abuse of managerial power. Research from North America in particular (e.g. Morck et al., 1988; Smith and Amoako-Adu, 1999) provides evidence of the negative effect of a controlling family on corporate performance. In addition, strategy research identifies family firms to be altruistic in the relationship between parents and their children (Schulze et al., 2003), which may have an impact on the effective succession process when the founder retires. Moreover, family interest may dominate the interest of non-family shareholders, since the concentration of personal and family wealth in owner-managed firms normally creates a preference for income and for wealth preservation over other dimensions of firm performance such as maximization of dividend payments to outside shareholders (Carney and Gedajlovic, 2003). Finally, family control tends to shield a firm from the disciplinary pressure of the market for corporate control since concentrated share ownership reduces the probability of a hostile take-over (Gomez-Mejia et al., 2003).

However, whether families or professional managers run companies better for society in general is still open to debate. During the current prolonged recession, corporate scandals and the collapse of stock markets have resulted in a return to the kind of values prevalent in family-owned companies. Family businesses that survived their own internal succession dramas have tended to take a longer-term view rather than live and die by stock market evaluation of their performance. Because of the extension of altruism from the family system to the firm, owners in the current generation have the tendency and obligation to reserve wealth for the next generation. As a result, family firms often possess longer horizons compared to non-family firms. Family firms, therefore, represent a special class of large shareholders that may have a unique incentive structure, a strong voice in the firm, and powerful motivation of managers. Anderson et al. (2003) suggest that these characteristics can alleviate agency conflicts between the firms' debt and equity claimants and reduce the agency costs of debt.

In addition, strategy analysis of corporate governance (Filatotchev and Bishop, 2002) view family control as less of a problem as it is a potential provider of more useful resources and enhancement of firm value. Furthermore, through family networks, uncertainties and complexity are reduced because information is shared and circulated among the participants in the network, resulting in better monitoring of activities both within and between firms. Some more recent empirical studies provide evidence that controlling family ownership is associated with better performance (Chang, 2003; Joh, 2003; Carney and Gedajlovic, 2002).

Finally, some recent studies emphasize that firms may have multiple large shareholders. Some researchers suggest that it may be optimal to have more than one large owner in terms of the effectiveness of corporate governance. When control is dissipated among several large investors, a decision to behave opportunistically requires the consent of a coalition of investors, and this coalition might hold enough cash flow rights to choose to limit expropriation of the remaining shareholders and pay the profits as efficient dividends (La Porta et al., 2000b). In this particular case, a relatively low entrenchment effect associated with small shareholdings of the coalition's members may be dominated by the Jensen-Meckling incentives generated by the combined coalition's share ownership. For example, Bennedsen and Wolfenzon (2000) suggest a theoretical model explaining an alignment effect of a coalition of large shareholders, that is a positive relation between the cash flow stake of the controlling coalition and total firm value.

CORPORATE GOVERNANCE AND BUSINESS STRATEGY: CONTINGENCIES AND COMPLEMENTARITIES

A number of authors suggest that the effects of corporate governance factors, such as board structure and characteristics, on business strategy and performance may be contingent on various organizational factors such as the firm's size, age, industry, growth/decline phase, etc. In particular, the scale and diversity of large firms may cloud any relationship between board composition and performance. However, in smaller, entrepreneurial firms, boards could more easily meet their resource, counselling and control roles. Boards of smaller, less complex firms would enjoy more discretion with fewer vested interests within the firm (Dalton et al., 1998). Consistent with this perspective, recent meta-analysis has found that the relationship between board size and firm performance is stronger for smaller, as compared to larger, firms (Dalton et al., 1999). Daily and

Dalton (1992) provide evidence of a positive relationship between both the number and proportion of independent directors and price-earnings ratio in a sample of small firms. IPO research in the USA and UK (Certo, 2003; Certo et al., 2001; Filatotchev and Bishop, 2002) discovers that newly listed companies with more diverse and independent boards have better performance.

Some researchers emphasize that board governance may be particularly important in the environment of organizational decline or bankruptcy (Daily and Dalton, 1994; Filatotchev and Toms, 2003; Hambrick and D'Aveni, 1992). In their study of UK textile companies in the environment of industrial decline, Filatotchev and Toms (2003) show that the 'survivors' had relatively larger boards and significantly larger board diversity measured in terms of outside directorships held by individual directors compared to the 'early exits'. These authors argue that board 'interlocks' helped companies to restructure and survive. Daily and Dalton (1994) and Dalton et al. (1999) suggest that board size may play an important role in crisis situations since, from a resource-dependency view, larger boards may provide more diverse networking links to resource providers. Gilson (1990) and Hermalin and Weisbach (2003) find that following a bankruptcy or private restructuring, debtholders take an active role in the firm's governance, including appointing a number of directors.

Finally, an emerging research on the life cycle of corporate governance (Filatotchev and Wright, 2005; Lynall et al., 2003) suggests the notion of a number of firm life cycle stages where different forms of corporate governance may be required. Corporate governance may thus need to be viewed as a dynamic system that may change as firms evolve over these stages. The firm's evolution is accompanied by changes in ownership structure, board composition, the degree of founder involvement, and so on. The balance of the accountability and enterprise roles of the various governance elements may change over this life cycle through establishment, growth, maturity and decline. For example, the knowledge contribution of boards may be more important in growing entrepreneurial firms than in firms facing more mature markets. However, the monitoring roles of the board may be particularly important at maturity stage. Therefore, there may be a number of optimal board configurations, depending on a particular stage of the firm's life cycle.

In the vast majority of governance-related papers a particular aspect of corporate control, such as board structure or composition, is related to performance measurements. Some authors have recognized that governance mechanisms operate interdependently, with the overall effectiveness depending on a simultaneous operation of several mechanisms in limiting managerial opportunism (Rediker and Seth, 1995; Walsh and Seward,

1990). Since alternative control mechanisms exist, greater use of one mechanism need not be positively related to firm performance. Where one specific mechanism is used less, others may be used more, resulting in equally good performance (Agrawal and Knoweber, 1996). Different governance mechanisms can replace or complement each other (Dalton et al., 2003; Hoskisson et al., 2002), and the cost-benefit trade-offs among a variety of governance mechanisms would determine their use.

A limited number of papers explore these substitution and complementarity effects empirically. Deutsch (2005) finds complementarity between board composition and executive pay. Rediker and Seth (1995) in their study of 81 bank holdings in the USA find a substitution effect between governance effects of independent boards and large-block investors. These studies suggest that a combination (or bundles) of governance mechanisms may reduce principal-agent costs and align interests of principals and agents. Just as with the contingencies literature discussed above, governance practices here are not seen as universally applicable. Rather than isolated 'best practices', corporate governance practices become effective only in particular combinations. Complementarities concern such interactions between practices, and how these interdependencies align governance to potentially diverse organizational environments. Although the effectiveness of corporate governance practices depends on a 'fit' with or adaptation to different contingencies and costs, complementarities suggest a further mutual enhancement such that the joint presence of two or more practices increases their effectiveness within the boundaries of particular costs and contingencies.

DISCUSSION AND FUTURE RESEARCH

The various theoretical perspectives reviewed in this chapter generally share one common element: their authors have highlighted the importance of contextual factors in corporate governance research that is based on different organizational environments. An important implication of their arguments is that these should not be treated, in methodological or theoretical terms, simply as control variables in understanding otherwise universal relationships. Rather, they suggest that theoretical and empirical research should progress to a more context-dependent understanding of corporate governance and that this, in turn, will prove very useful for practitioners and policy makers interested in applying corporate governance to particular situations. In this regard, recent methodological advances in studying configurations through set-theoretic methods represent a very fruitful avenue for further research. A potentially more contentious argument is that understanding effectiveness or performance requires greater sensitivity to how corporate governance affects different aspects of performance in different contexts. For example, whereas return on equity may be relevant for the corporate governance of mature firms, younger entrepreneurial firms' performance may be better measured by innovation. Likewise, the existence of diverse stakeholder relationships implies that corporate governance should be associated with different distributive outcomes.

Grounding corporate governance in organizational theory has important implications for the future study of strategic effects of governance as well as its organizational outcomes, such as performance. First, this grounded framework can be applied to the study of governance processes in diverse forms of organization, such as entrepreneurial firms or multinational firms, which have been overlooked in the corporate governance literature. It also allows us to compare similarities and differences of corporate governance within and across industries, as well as in broader sets of national institutions and regulation. Second, strategic management research suggests that the resource- and knowledge-based perspectives and their interaction with institutional theory constitute a useful extension to a field previously dominated by agency theory. These studies go some way towards addressing this need for an organizational approach to corporate governance, but there is still much to be explored. Theory as well as empirical research should progress to a more context-dependent understanding of corporate governance and this, in turn, will prove very useful for practitioners and policy makers interested in applying corporate governance in particular situations. In theoretical terms, more attention must be paid to the diversity of empirical results and these differences must be more explicitly built into theoretical models.

In empirical terms, recent methodological advances may help operationalize and test more complex and context-depending theories in ways that are hard to apply in large-scale sample-base research, which often relies on very broad proxies for context factors. Understanding effectiveness requires greater sensitivity to how corporate governance affects different aspects of effectiveness for different stakeholders and in different contexts. For example, whereas return on equity may be relevant for the corporate governance of mature firms, younger entrepreneurial firms' performance may be better measured by innovation and growth. A balance between different functions of governance may also change when the firm evolves from its entrepreneurial stage through an IPO to growth and maturity stages. Likewise, corporate governance is likely to be associated with different distributive outcomes among corporate stakeholders, which reflects how risks and rewards to their relative resource contributions are governed.

CONCLUSION

Traditional corporate governance research, especially within the agency theory, was often criticized for its lack of systematic attention to contextual factors grounded in diverse organizational environments. While the open-systems approach to understanding organizations and their environments has been a staple of organization theory, similar lines of inquiry remain surprisingly underdeveloped within the corporate governance literature. In this chapter, we have reviewed various literatures looking at environmental interdependencies of corporate governance and the firm's competitive strategy in terms of contingencies and complementarities related to the two well-known practices of corporate governance. In order to take systematic account of these factors in future empirical studies, studies of corporate governance must explore the patterned variation of corporate governance practices, their combinations, and their effectiveness in terms of alignment of organizations with a more contextualized view of organizational environments.

REFERENCES

Admati, A., P. Pfleiderer and J. Zechner (1994), 'Large shareholder activism, risk sharing, and financial market equilibrium', *Journal of Political Economy*, 102, 1097–1130.
Agrawal, A. and C. Knoeber (1996), 'Firm performance and mechanisms to control agency problems between managers and shareholders', *Journal of Financial and Quantitative Analysis*, 31, 377–395.
Alchian, A.A. and H. Demsetz (1972), 'Production, information costs, and economic organization', *American Economic Review*, 62, 777–795.
Alexander, J.A., M.L. Fennell and M.T. Halpern (1993), 'Leadership instability in hospitals: the influence of board-CEO relations and organizational growth and decline', *Administrative Science Quarterly*, 38, 74–99.
Anderson, R., S. Mansi and D. Reeb (2003), 'Founding family ownership and the agency costs of debt', *Journal of Financial Economics*, 68, 263–285.
Baysinger, B.D and R.E. Hoskisson (1990), 'The composition of boards of directors and strategic control: effects on corporate strategy', *Academy of Management Review*, 15, 72–87.
Baysinger, B.D., D.R. Kosnik and T.A. Turk (1991), 'Effects of board and ownership structure on corporate R&D strategy', *Academy of Management Journal*, 34, 205–214.
Bazerman, M. and F. Schoorman (1983), 'A limited rationality model of interlocking directorates', *Academy of Management Review*, 8, 206–217.
Bebchuk, L. (1994), 'Efficient and inefficient sales of corporate control', *Quarterly Journal of Economics*, 109, 957–994.
Beekun, R.I., Y. Stedham and G.J. Young (1998), 'Board characteristics, managerial controls and corporate strategy: a study of US hospitals', *Journal of Management*, 24, 3–19.
Bennedsen, M. and D. Wolfenzon (2000), 'The balance of power in closely held corporations', *Journal of Financial Economics*, 58, 113–139.
Bethel, J.E. and J. Liebeskind (1993), 'The effects of ownership structure on corporate restructuring', *Strategic Management Journal*, 14, 15–31.

Black, B.S. (1992), 'Agents watching agents: the promise of institutional investor voice. UCLA', *Law Review*, **39**, 811–839.

Black, B.S. and R.J. Gilson (1998), 'Venture capital and the structure of capital markets: banks versus stock markets', *Journal of Financial Economics*, **47**, 243–277.

Brav, A. and P.A. Gompers (1997), 'Myth or reality? The long-run underperformance of initial public offerings: evidence from venture and nonventure capital-backed companies', *Journal of Finance*, **52**, 1791–1821.

Brickley, J., R. Lease and C. Smith (1988), 'Ownership structure and voting on anti takeover amendments', *Journal of Financial Economics*, **20**, 267–291.

Buchholtz, A.K. and B.A. Ribbens (1994), 'Role of chief executive officers in takeover resistance: effects of CEO incentives and individual characteristics', *Academy of Management Journal*, **37**, 554–579.

Carney, M. and E. Gedajlovic (2002), 'The coupling of ownership and control and the allocation of financial resources: evidence from Hong Kong', *Journal of Management Studies*, **39** (1), 123–146.

Carpenter, M.A. (2002), 'The implications of strategy and social context for the relationship between top management team heterogeneity and firm performance', *Strategic Management Journal*, **23**, 275–284.

Carpenter, M.A. and J.D. Westphal (2001), 'The strategic context of external network ties: examining the impact of director appointments on board involvement in strategic decision-making', *Academy of Management Journal*, **44**, 639–660.

Carpenter, M.A., T.G. Pollock and M.M. Leary (2003), 'Testing a model of reasoned risk-taking: governance, the experience of principals and agents, and global strategy in high-technology IPO firms', *Strategic Management Journal*, **24**, 803–820.

Certo, T.S. (2003), 'Influencing initial public offering investors with presige: signaling with board structures', *Academy of Management Review*, **28** (3), 432–446.

Certo, T.S., C.M. Daily and D.R. Dalton (2001), 'Wealth and the effects of founder management among IPO-stage new ventures', *Strategic Management Journal*, **22**, 641–658.

Chaganti, R., S. Mahajan and S. Sharma (1985), 'Corporate board size, composition and corporate failures in retailing industry', *Journal of Management*, **22**, 400–417.

Chang, S. (2003), 'Ownership structure, expropriation, and performance of group-affiliated companies in Korea', *Academy of Management Journal*, **46**, 238–254.

Chrisman, J.J. and J. Leslie (1989), 'Strategic, administrative, and operative problems: the impact of outsiders on small firm performance', *Entrepreneurship Theory and Practice*, **4** (2), 37–51.

Cochran, P.L., R.A. Wood and T.B. Jones (1985), 'The composition of boards of directors and the incidence of golden parachutes', *Academy of Management Journal*, **28**, 664–671.

Conyon, M.J. and S.I. Peck (1998), 'Board control, remuneration committees, and top management compensation', *Academy of Management Journal*, **41**, 146–157.

Daily, C.M. and D.R. Dalton (1992), 'The relationship between governance structure and corporate performance in entrepreneurial firms', *Journal of Business Venturing*, **7** (5), 375–386.

Daily, C.M. and D.R. Dalton (1994), 'Bankruptcy and corporate governance: the impact of board composition and structure', *Academy of Management Journal*, **37**, 1603–1617.

Daily, C.M., D.R. Dalton and A.A. Canella (2003), 'Corporate governance: decades of dialog and data', *Academy of Management Review*, **28** (3), 371–398.

Daily, C., D. Dalton and N. Rajagopalan (2003), 'Governance through ownership: centuries of practice, decades of research', *Academy of Management Journal*, **46**, 151–158.

Daily, C.M., J.L. Johnson and D.R. Dalton (1999), 'On the measurements of board composition: poor consistency and a serious mismatch of theory and operationalization', *Decision Sciences*, **30**, 83–106.

Daily, C.M., P. McDougall, J.G. Covin and D.R. Dalton (2002), 'Governance and strategic leadership in entrepreneurial firms', *Journal of Management*, **28** (3), 387–412.

Dalton, D., C. Daily, S. Certo and R. Roengpitya (2003), 'Meta-analysis of financial performance and equity: fusion or confusion?', *Academy of Management Journal*, **46**, 13–26.

Dalton, D.R., C.M. Daily, A.E. Ellstrand and J.L. Johnson (1998), 'Meta-analytic review of board composition, leadership structure, and financial performance', *Strategic Management Journal*, **19**, 269–290.

Dalton, D.R., C.M. Daily, J.L. Johnson and A.E. Ellstrand (1999), 'Number of directors and financial performance: a meta-analysis', *Academy of Management Journal*, **42**, 674–686.

David, P., R. Kochhar and E. Levitas (1998), 'The effects of institutional investors on level and mix of CEO compensation', *Academy of Management Journal*, **41**, 200–208.

Davis, J.H., F.D. Schoorman and L. Donaldson (1997), 'Towards a stewardship theory of management', *Academy of Management Review*, **22**, 20–47.

Demb, A. and F.F. Neubauer (eds) (1992), *The Corporate Board. Confronting the Paradoxes*, New York: Oxford University Press.

Demsetz, H. (1983), 'The structure of ownership and the theory of the firm', *Journal of Law and Economics*, **26**, 375–390.

Demsetz, H. and K. Lehn (1985), 'The structure of corporate ownership: causes and consequences', *Journal of Political Economy*, **93**, 1155–1177.

Fama, E.F. (1980), 'Agency problems and the theory of the firm', *Journal of Political Economy*, **88**, 288–307.

Fama, E.F. and M.C. Jensen (1983), 'Separation of ownership and control', *Journal of Law and Economics*, **26**, 301–325.

Filatotchev, I. and K. Bishop (2002), 'Board composition, share ownership and "underpricing" of UK IPO firms', *Strategic Management Journal*, **23**, 941–955.

Filatotchev, I. and S. Toms (2003), 'Corporate governance, strategy and survival in a declining industry: a study of UK cotton textile companies', *Journal of Management Studies*, **40** (4), 895–920.

Filatotchev, I. and M. Wright (eds) (2005), *Corporate Governance Life-cycle*, Cheltenham: Edward Elgar.

Finkelstein, S. and D.C. Hambrick (eds) (1996), *Strategic Leaderships: Top Executives and their Organizations*, Minneapolis: West Educational Publishing.

Fizel, J.L. and K.K.T. Louie (1990), 'CEO retention, firm performance, and corporate governance', *Managerial and Decision Economics*, **11**, 167–176.

Gibbs, P.A. (1993), 'Determinants of corporate restructuring: the relative importance of corporate governance, takeover threat, and free cash flow', *Strategic Management Journal*, **14**, 51–68.

Gilson, S.C. (1990), 'Bankruptcy, boards, banks and blockholders', *Journal of Financial Economics*, **27**, 355–387.

Golden, B.R. and E.J. Zajac (2001), 'When will boards influence strategy? Inclination × power = strategic change', *Strategic Management Journal*, **22**, 1087–1111.

Gomes-Mejia, L., M. Larraza-Kintana and M. Makri (2003), 'The determinants of executive compensation in family-controlled public corporations', *Academy of Management Journal*, **46**, 226–237.

Goodstain, J. and W. Boeker (1991), 'Turbulence at the top: a new perspective on governance structure changes and strategic change', *Academy of Management Journal*, **34**, 306–330.

Hambrick, D.C. and R.A. D'Aveni (1992), 'Top team deterioration as part of the downward spiral of large corporate bankruptcies', *Management Science*, **38**, 1445–1466.

Hambrick, D.C. and P. Mason (1984), 'Upper echelons: the organization as a reflection of its top managers', *Academy of Management Review*, **9**, 193–206.

Hermalin, B.E. and M.S. Weisbach (2003), 'Boards of directors as an endogenously determined institution: a survey of the economics literature', *Economic Policy Review*, **9**, 7–26.

Higgins, M.C. and R. Gulati (1999), 'Getting off to a start: the effects of upper echelon affiliations on prestige of investment bank and IPO success', working paper, Harvard Business School.

Hill, C.W.L. and S.A. Snell (1988), 'External control, corporate strategy, and firm performance in research-intensive industries', *Strategic Management Journal*, **9**, 577–590.

Hillman, A.J. and T. Dalziel (2003), 'Boards of directors and firm performance: integrating agency and resource dependence perspectives', *Academy of Management Review*, **28** (3), 383–396.

Hillman, A.J., A.A. Cannella Jr. and R.L. Paetzold (2000), 'The resource dependence role of corporate directors: strategic adaptation of board composition in response to environmental change', *Journal of Management Studies*, **37**, 235–255.

Holderness, C.G. and D.P. Sheehan (1988), 'The role of majority shareholders in publicly held corporations', *Journal of Financial Economics*, **20**, 317–346.

Hoskisson, R.E., R.A. Johnson and D.D. Moesel (1994), 'Corporate divestiture intensity in restructuring firms: effects of governance, strategy and performance', *Academy of Management Journal*, **37**, 1207–1251.

Hoskisson, R.E., M.A. Hitt, R.A. Johnson and W. Grossman (2002), 'Conflicting voices: the effects of institutional ownership heterogeneity and internal governance on corporate innovation strategies', *Academy of Management Journal*, **45**, 697–716.

Jensen, M.C. (1993), 'The modern industrial revolution, exit, and the failure of internal control systems', *Journal of Finance*, **48**, 831–880.

Jensen, M.C. and W. Meckling (1976), 'Theory of the firm: managerial behavior, agency costs, and ownership structure', *Journal of Financial Economics*, **3**, 305–360.

Johnson, J.L., C.M. Daily and A.E. Ellstrand (1996), 'Board of directors: a review and research agenda', *Journal of Management*, **22**, 409–438.

Johnson, R. and D. Greening (1999), 'The effects of corporate governance and institutional ownership types on corporate social responsibility', *Academy of Management Journal*, **42** (5), 564–576.

Judge, W.Q. Jr. and C.P. Zeithaml (1992), 'Institutional and strategic choice perspectives on board involvement in the strategic decision process', *Academy of Management Journal*, **35**, 766–794.

Kosnik, D.R. (1987), 'Greenmail: a study in board performance in corporate governance', *Administrative Science Quarterly*, **32**, 163–185.

Lerner, J. (1995), 'Venture capitalists and the oversight of private firms', *Journal of Finance*, **50**, 301–318.

Lorsch, J.W. and E. MacIver (eds) (1989), *Pawns or Potentates. The Reality of America's Corporate Boards*, Boston, MA: Harvard Business School.

Lynall, M.D., B.R. Goden and A.J. Hillman (2003), 'Board composition from adolescence to maturity: a multitheoretic view', *Academy of Management Review*, **28** (3), 416–431.

Mallette, P. and K.L. Fowler (1992), 'Effects of board composition and stock ownership on the adoption of poison pills', *Academy of Management Journal*, **35**, 1010–1035.

Mangel, R. and H. Singh (1993), 'Ownership structure, board relationship and CEO compensation in large US corporations', *Accounting and Business Research*, **23**, 339–350.

Maug, E. (1998), 'Large shareholders as monitors: is there a trade-off between liquidity and control?', *Journal of Finance*, **53**, 65–92.

McConnell, J.J. and H. Servaes (1990), 'Additional evidence on equity ownership and corporate value', *Journal of Financial Economics*, **27**, 595–612.

McNulty, T. and A. Pettigrew (1999), 'Strategists on the board', *Organization Studies*, **20**, 47–74.

Megginson, W.L. and K.A. Keiss (1991), 'Venture capitalist certification in initial public offerings', *Journal of Finance*, **46**, 879–903.

Mizruchi, M. (1983), 'Who controls whom? An examination of the relationship between management and boards of directors in large American corporations', *Academy of Management Review*, **8**, 426–435.

Mizruchi, M. (1996), 'What do interlocks do? An analysis, critique, and assessment of research on interlocking directorates', *Annual Review of Sociology*, **22**, 271–298.

Morck, R., A. Shleifer and R. Vishny (1988), 'Management ownership and market valuation: an empirical analysis', *Journal of Financial Economics*, **20**, 293–316.

Pearce, J.A. and S.A. Zahra (1991), 'The relative power of CEOs and boards of directors: associations with corporate performance', *Strategic Management Journal*, **12**, 135–153.

Pettigrew, A.M. (1992), 'On studying managerial elites', *Strategic Management Journal*, **13**, 163–182.

Pettigrew, A. and T. McNulty (1995), 'Power and influence in and around the boardroom', *Human Relations*, **48**, 845–873.

Pfeffer, J. (1972), 'Size and composition of corporate boards of directors: the organization and its environment', *Administrative Science Quarterly*, 17, 218–222.

Pfeffer, J. and G. Salancik (eds) (1978), *The External Control of Organizations: A Resource Dependence Perspective*, New York: Harper & Row.

Pound, J. (1988), 'Proxy contests and the efficiency of shareholder oversight', *Journal of Financial Economics*, 20, 237–265.

Provan, K. (1980), 'Board power and organizational efficiency among human service agencies', *Academy of Management Journal*, 23, 221–236.

Pye, A. (2001), 'A study in studying corporate boards over time: looking backwards to move forwards', *British Journal of Management*, 12, 33–45.

Rediker, K.J. and A. Seth (1995), 'Boards of directors and substitution effects of alternative governance mechanisms', *Strategic Management Journal*, 16, 85–99.

Roe, M.J. (1990), 'Political and legal restraints on ownership and control of public companies', *Journal of Financial Economics*, 27, 7–42.

Sanders, G.W. and M.A. Carpenter (2003), 'Strategic satisficing? A behavioral–agency theory perspective on stock repurchase program announcements', *Academy of Management Journal*, 46, 160–178.

Schulze, W., M. Lubatkin and R. Dino (2003), 'Exploring the agency consequences of ownership dispersion among the directors of private family firms', *Academy of Management Journal*, 46, 217–229.

Shivdasani, A. (1993), 'Board composition, ownership structure, and hostile takeovers', *Journal of Accounting and Economics*, 16, 167–198.

Shivdasani, A. and D. Yermack (1999), 'CEO involvement in the selection of new board members: an empirical analysis', *Journal of Finance*, 54, 1829–1853.

Shleifer, A. and R. Vishny (1997), 'A survey of corporate governance', *Journal of Finance*, 52, 737–783.

Short, H. (1994), 'Ownership, control, financial structure and the performance of firms', *Journal of Economic Surveys*, 8, 203–249.

Stiglitz, J.E. (1985), 'Credit markets and the control of capital', *Journal of Money, Credit and Banking*, 17, 133–152.

Sundaramurthy, C. (1996), 'Corporate governance within the context of antitakeover provisions', *Strategic Management Journal*, 17, 377–394.

Tihanyi, L., R. Johnson, R. Hoskisson and M. Hitt (2003), 'Institutional ownership differences and international diversification: the effects of boards of directors and technological opportunity', *Academy of Management Journal*, 46, 195–211.

Useem, M. (ed.) (1993), *Executive Defence, Shareholder Power and Corporate Reorganization*, Cambridge, MA: Harvard University Press.

Wagner, J.A., J.L. Stimpert and E.I. Fubara (1998), 'Board composition and organizational performance: two studies of insider/outsider effects', *Journal of Management Studies*, 35, 655–677.

Wahal, S. (1996), 'Pension fund activism and firm performance', *Journal of Financial and Quantitative Analysis*, 31, 1–23.

Walsh, J.P. and J.K. Seward (1990), 'On the efficiency of internal and external corporate control mechanisms', *Academy of Management Review*, 15, 421–458.

Weisbach, M.S. (1988), 'Outside directors and CEO turnover', *Journal of Financial Economics*, 20, 431–460.

Westphal, J.D. (1999), 'Collaboration in the boardroom: behavioral and performance consequences of CEO-board social ties', *Academy of Management Journal*, 42, 7–24.

Westphal, J.D. and E.J. Zajac (1995), 'Who shall govern? CEO/board power, demographic similarity, and new director selection', *Administrative Science Quarterly*, 40, 60–83.

Woidtke, T. (2002), 'Agents watching agents? Evidence from pension fund ownership and firm value', *Journal of Financial Economics*, 63, 99–131.

Yermack, D. (1996), 'Higher market valuation of companies with a smaller board of directors', *Journal of Financial Economics*, 40, 185–211.

Young, G.J., Y. Stedham and R.I. Beekun (2000), 'Boards of directors and the adoption of a CEO performance evaluation process: agency and institutional theory perspectives', *Journal of Management Studies*, **37**, 277–295.

Zahra, S.A. and I. Filatotchev (2004), 'Governance of the entrepreneurial threshold firm: a knowledge-based perspective', *Journal of Management Studies*, **41** (5), 883–895.

Zahra, S.A. and J.A. Pearce (1989), 'Boards of directors and corporate financial perform- ance: a review and integrative model', *Journal of Management*, **15**, 291–334.

Zajac, E.J. and J.D. Westphal (1996), 'Director reputation, CEO-board power, and the dynamics of board interlocks', *Administrative Science Quarterly*, **41**, 507–529.

15 Entrepreneurial issues in competitive strategy research
Mario Sorrentino

LINKING ENTREPRENEURSHIP AND WEALTH CREATION: THE STRATEGIC ENTREPRENEURSHIP CONCEPT

One of the greatest challenges that firms have to face is that of producing wealth in the current highly uncertain, rapidly changing environment. The objective of this chapter is to analyse how being entrepreneurial can lead firms to establish competitive advantage and create wealth in the current competitive environment. This objective implies not only investigating what being entrepreneurial means, but also focussing on how entrepreneurial strategies pursued by firms can lead to competitive advantage able to produce wealth in uncertain and rapidly changing markets.

In high uncertainty the probability distribution of events that are important for the firm's decision-making process is not only unknown but unknowable (Buchanan and Vanberg, 1991), mainly due to a lack of information about cause and effect relationships (Hoskisson and Busenitz, 2002). By contrast, the rapidity of change means sudden modifications in key variables for interfirm competition and discontinuities in phenomena that affect their behaviour. In competitive contexts dominated by uncertainty and rapid change the duration of product life-cycles is reduced, as are firms' response times to environmental pressures. In terms of competitive dynamics, uncertainty, rapid change and speed in decision-making generate conditions of hypercompetition (D'Aveni, 1994) whose main effect on organizational performance is to make competitive advantages temporary, advantages that in more stable environmental conditions would be sustainable in time. In general, in such environmental conditions it is increasingly difficult for firms to produce wealth.

At the same time, however, uncertainty and rapid change also offer firms opportunities from which they can gain new competitive advantages. Indeed, although an uncertain environment threatens the sources of competitive advantage, the environment itself requires that firms compete continuously in the market of opportunities offered precisely by uncertainty and change. Managing to capture such opportunities underpins the capacity of firms to search for competitive advantage which, though destined to be swiftly eroded, allows them to attain a better performance than that of rival firms. McGrath and MacMillan (2000) argue that firms that manage to focus on and capture the benefits of uncertainty and rapid change show an entrepreneurial mindset – that is, a way of thinking about managing firms that systematically searches for attempts to exploit high-potential opportunities that originate from uncertain environments.[1]

Being entrepreneurial therefore means that firms have both organizational and cognitive abilities that allow them to recognize high-potential opportunities that rivals have not observed from uncertain and fragmented environmental conditions (Alvarez and Barney, 2002) and choose between different specific ways to exploit such opportunities. In this vein, following Shane and Venkataraman's definition (2000), the subject matter of entrepreneurship can be identified as having to do with the discovery and exploitation of opportunities and the modes of action used to exploit such opportunities. These modes entail not only the creation of new independent ventures but also the development of new entrepreneurial units within established firms – namely, internal corporate ventures.[2]

Thus, entrepreneurship entails the study of how new enterprises, whether new independent start-ups or internal ventures, discover and exploit opportunities that rivals have not discovered or have underexploited. In order to maximize wealth creation, these new enterprises competing in the market for opportunities need to continuously establish competitive advantage. Thus, if the study of entrepreneurship is to be linked with wealth creation issues (Hitt et al., 2002), we must focus on the ways in which the discovery and exploitation of opportunities can lead to establishing even temporary competitive advantage. Given that the search for competitive advantage is one of the main issues in strategic management studies, one can recognize the existence of a strategic side of entrepreneurship. Ultimately, the concept of strategic entrepreneurship (Hitt et al., 2001 and 2002) deals not only with opportunity discovery and exploitation – that is, entrepreneurial actions – but also with strategic actions through which new ventures (both independent start-ups and internal ventures) develop competitive advantage able to produce wealth in dynamic and rapidly changing markets. Hitt et al. (2001: 481) view strategic entrepreneurship as "the integration of entrepreneurial (i.e. opportunity-seeking actions) and strategic (i.e. advantage-seeking actions) perspectives to design and implement entrepreneurial strategies that create wealth". While entrepreneurial actions focus on the entrepreneurial abilities that account for the discovery of the opportunity and creation of the new enterprise, strategic actions focus on actions that will help firms to compete against rivals in the future.

Focussing on the link between entrepreneurial actions and strategic actions, the strategic entrepreneurship approach provides interesting insights to explore both new independent ventures and internal corporate ventures. In particular, what appears critical is to create a link between the creation of new enterprises and their performance, intended as the ability to establish competitive advantage and generate enhanced wealth. The next section analyses this link, focussing on the interface between entrepreneurial abilities and the strategic theory of competitive advantage. Drawing on this link, subsequent sections investigate how both new independent ventures and internal corporate ventures can be effectively implemented to create new enterprises that generate economic value and wealth.

ENTREPRENEURIAL CAPABILITIES AS DYNAMIC CAPABILITIES

Recent developments in strategic management studies have led to a rethinking of the explanation of competitive advantage supplied by the resource-based view according to which persistent performance differences among firms are a function of the idiosyncratic and specific resources owned or controlled by the firm in its product market strategy (Wernerfelt, 1984; Barney, 1986 and 1991; Mahoney and Pandian, 1992; Peteraf, 1993; Amit and Schoemaker, 1993). According to the resource-based theory, firms' sustainable competitive advantage originates from leveraging on and using resources and assets that are rare, valuable, imperfectly imitable, and non-transferable, and performance differences are a consequence of the ability of firms to exchange heterogeneous resources in highly imperfect markets. In this view, competitive advantages are a function of the resource positions held by firms and take the form of economic rents that can be sustained for a long time. However, recent developments have led to the argument that, rather than the static ownership of specific resources, performance differentials among firms are related to the capacity to continually adapt and renew resources and skills in response to sudden environmental changes. In hypercompetition contexts, what seems to most affect firms' competitive advantage is their ability to integrate and reconfigure internal and external know-how so as to rapidly address changing environments (Teece et al., 1997). The dynamic capabilities approach (Teece and Pisano, 1994; Teece et al., 1997; Kogut and Zander, 1992) underlines the fact that firms need to reconfigure their own asset structure and perform continuous changes – it is this capacity to generate new combinations of resources and skills which generates competitive advantage. Competitive dynamics chiefly occur in the form of innovative competition in which, rather than economic rent, it is possible to earn Schumpeterian rent. Such rents do not last long and continually have to be fuelled by firms with new combinations of resources and skills, given that environmental change means their original resources can no longer sustain their competitive advantage. What generates differential positions between firms is not the exploitation of a stock of owned or controlled resources but rather the firm's ability to use and reconfigure such resources in time, thereby generating new capabilities. Valuable assets thus depend on the actual development and deployment of firm resources, and understanding how firms re-direct and renew their resources and skills so as to respond to a rapidly changing environment lies at the base of competitive advantage. Under this rationale, it becomes crucial to focus on managerial and organizational processes and on learning dynamics that allow continual renewal and adaptation to changes in the environment. In fact, both organizational processes and learning dynamics may embody capabilities by which resources and skills are continuously integrated to compete in the market of opportunities created by change and uncertainty.

The dynamic capabilities approach provides interesting insights to create a link between the creation of new enterprises (entrepreneurial actions) and their performance intended as the ability to achieve competitive advantage and wealth creation (strategic actions). Understanding how entrepreneurial actions can be linked to competitive advantage can be easier if one considers entrepreneurial abilities as dynamic capabilities with which firms compete in rapidly changing environments. Indeed, entrepreneurship understood as the ability to exploit opportunities by means of appropriate action would seem to account for competitive advantage in highly dynamic environments in which Schumpeterian-type competition prevails. In such environments, the capability of integrating resources and skills with stimuli from the external environment chiefly depends on the firm's ability to discover and exploit opportunities – that is, on entrepreneurial capabilities. It is worth noting that such capabilities, which are the focus of the following sections, derive from the possibility of acting upon the firm's basic capabilities, recombining them creatively so as to capture opportunities offered by change and uncertainty. Therefore, entrepreneurial capabilities can be configured as dynamic metacapabilities – that is, higher-level idiosyncratic capabilities of integrating different lower-level capabilities (Dagnino, 2005) which provide the firm with the possibility to create value in uncertain environments. This possibility is linked to the fact that entrepreneurial action behind the creation of a new enterprise (whether new independent ventures or internal ventures) is characterized by substantial causal ambiguity which makes it difficult, if not impossible, to understand the links between actions and results. Causal ambiguity of entrepreneurial processes and actions (Alvarez and Busenitz, 2001) is fuelled by non-transferable tacit knowledge, social complexity and specificity factors (Reed and DeFilippi, 1990). These factors make it difficult for rival firms to imitate and allow continuous development of isolation mechanisms which, albeit temporary, generate wealth over time for the firm.

Entrepreneurial abilities can thus be considered dynamic capabilities with which firms compete and generate wealth in rapidly changing and uncertain markets. These abilities are needed to facilitate the discovery and recognition of new opportunities and exploitation of these opportunities with the creation of a new enterprise – the latter being either a new independent venture or a new entrepreneurial venture within an established firm.

Importantly, both the discovery of opportunities and the process of combining resources for the new enterprise reveal many differences a____ d-ing to whether the way opportunities are exploited entails the creation of a new independent firm or an internal corporate venture. In particular, three main differences can at least be highlighted. First, in independent start-ups the discovery and recognition of opportunities not observed by others chiefly reflect the dynamic interaction of the individual and the opportunity (Sarason et al., 2006), while in internal ventures the ability to discover and recognize opportunities is chiefly an organizational resource of the established firm. In fact to be able to continually explore new strategic opportunities, established firms have to overcome organizational rigidities which tend to make them concentrate on accumulated resources and ongoing activities, thereby generating organizational inertia, lack of experimentation and general resistance to innovation (Ireland et al., 2003). Second, in new independent firms the process of combining resources to launch the new venture almost always occurs in conditions of resource scarcity while this does not hold for large firms that promote internal ventures. Indeed, for these firms there are fewer resource constraints for launching initiatives, and it is thus easier to produce differential value for the market and acquire positions of competitive advantage. Third, internal ventures often have low degrees of flexibility since they are promoted within a pre-existing organizational structure, while this does not apply to independent start-ups which are very flexible and entrepreneurial. Therefore, analysis of entrepreneurial capabilities and their link with wealth creation necessarily differs, depending on whether one considers new independent firms or new entrepreneurial units within established firms. In this vein, the next section focuses on new independent ventures, while the fourth section analyses internal ventures. Nevertheless, though it is necessary to keep the treatment of new ventures and internal ventures distinct, in both cases the aim is to focus on the entrepreneurial capabilities that appear to integrate the need to be entrepreneurial with the need to establish competitive advantage and generate enhanced wealth in dynamic environments. In other words, in both settings the aim is to explore how entrepreneurial strategies can be effectively implemented to create new enterprises that generate economic value and wealth.

EXPLORING ENTREPRENEURIAL CAPABILITIES IN NEW VENTURES

New venture firms are typically considered the nexus of entrepreneurial actions. The emergence of a new venture is a direct consequence of the discovery and exploitation of an entrepreneurial opportunity. The ability to recognize entrepreneurial opportunities is often linked to the entrepreneurial alertness of individual entrepreneurs (Kirzner, 1997) – the superior ability to identify when new products or services become feasible and valuable to the market. In this context, individual creativity and imagination play a decisive role. Previous studies have cast light on the nature of entrepreneurial opportunities (Shane and Venkataraman, 2000; Sarasvathy and Venkataraman, 2001), on both the individual and environmental factors that explain the birth of a new enterprise (Cooper, 1995) and on the possibility of considering the start-up of a new venture as a process (Bhave, 1994). Nevertheless, despite extensive investigations, what still needs to be clarified is the ability of new ventures to achieve competitive advantage and actually generate wealth – the issue of new venture post-entry performance. In terms of the strategic entrepreneurship perspective, this issue directly concerns the strategic side of new ventures as it focusses on the advantage-seeking actions that these ventures find it difficult to implement. While often good at identifying opportunities, new independent ventures need to develop advantage-seeking behaviour to successfully exploit identified opportunities (Matricano, 2010).

A reasonable way to investigate how new venture firms can generate enhanced wealth is to focus on entrepreneurial capabilities that seem to better adapt to and capture benefits from the environmental conditions in which the creation of the new independent firm takes place. To effect this focus we need first of all to dwell on the nature of the new venture start-up process. This process – of acquiring resources to exploit the entrepreneurial opportunity through the new venture – can be considered as an investment decision. Two main conditions characterize this investment decision.

First, this decision is dominated by uncertainty as relevant information for the creation of the new venture is very often unknown (Knight, 1921). This is what happens when entrepreneurs are unable to assess key issues of the new venture such as the technical feasibility or market appeal of the venture. In this case, key uncertainties relate to the organization's capabilities, for example ability to manufacture or sell the product. Under this 'internal' uncertainty, realizing the investment – that is, acquiring resources – is the only way to assess the key issues for the development of the new venture and reduce uncertainty associated with subsequent investments (Dixit and Pindyck, 1994; McGrath, 1997a).

Second, the investment decision aimed at acquiring resources for the new venture is irreversible. The financial resources available to independent neo-entrepreneurs are almost always scarce and the opportunity cost of investment decision is high. Consequently, progressively acquired resources are a constraint for the new venture since additional resources with which to make possible substitutive investments are non-existent or scarce. Hence, as far as possible, the initial investment should represent a lower proportion of resources than what is believed to be available for start-up, and bigger investments may be postponed until critical external uncertainties are resolved (Dixit and Pindyck, 1994).

Thus high uncertainty and irreversible investment decisions characterize the emergence of new independent ventures. The uncertainty and irreversibility of the start-up investment essentially have two implications. First, the state of internal uncertainty which affects new ventures may be reduced only by making the investment; secondly, the irreversibility of investments may be tackled by ensuring that initial investment accounts for a small share of available resources. In this setting, real options logic (Trigeorgis, 1993; Bowman and Hurry, 1993) proves to be an investing behaviour that generates enhanced wealth for new ventures. Like investing in a financial option, real options logic entails making small investments that give you the right to make a decision later (McGrath and MacMillan, 2000). The investment rationale based on real options is represented by a metaphor – the option chain (Bowman and Hurry, 1993) – which lends itself to being effectively used for new ventures (McGrath, 1996 and 1997a). According to this metaphor the firm, depending on its own resources and capabilities, identifies and recognizes certain investment opportunities, defined as 'shadow options'. Faced with a shadow option, the entrepreneur can make a small exploratory investment by which the business idea is tested. This experimental investment should be such as to make more information available on the feasibility of the venture without being so high as to bind the entrepreneur irreversibly. Thus the entrepreneur manages to create a growth option with scarce resources, given that the small initial investment gives the possibility (without obligation) of capturing later development opportunities which, through the investment undertaken, are better assessed. If the information that is generated subsequent to the experimental investment reduces uncertainty, the entrepreneur invests more, having drawn on the information emerging from the test. The option created with the small starting investment is thus exercised by large-scale investing in the venture on the basis of information and the learning processes obtained with this small investment. However, if the information is unsatisfactory or does not allow the feasibility of the venture to be assessed more reliably, the larger investment is not made. Thus, real options logic helps entrepreneurs to effectively deal with the uncertainties associated with the exploitation of the entrepreneurial opportunities and the irreversible nature of resource acquisition for new ventures.

In order to be captured, the benefits of real options logic require selected capabilities by entrepreneurs. A first capability arising from the real options rationale is the need to maximize learning. Only if the entrepreneur maximizes learning from information available from experimental investment can the firm be more confident in its allocation decision for further investments. Even if relevant, information that is available from the small initial investment is very likely still uncertain. Thus, in order to maximize learning, the entrepreneur may benefit from using heuristics to piece together scant ambiguous information. In fact, being based on simplifying strategies that individuals use to make strategic decisions when less complete or uncertain information is available (Alvarez and Busenitz, 2001), heuristics enable entrepreneurs to make sense of uncertain and complex situations building from limited and less accurate information (Baron, 1998). Research on entrepreneurial cognition has shown that the use of heuristics in decision-making is virtually the only way for entrepreneurs to progress (Busenitz and Barney, 1997), and often leads to new insights and unexpected decisions. Thus, higher-level learning for entrepreneurs is inevitably linked with the use of heuristics in decision-making (Alvarez and Busenitz, 2001). Both the ability to maximize learning and the use of heuristics are entrepreneurial capabilities that allow the new venture to actually capture the benefits of real options logic. Having argued that this logic proves to be a new venture investing strategy that generates wealth in uncertain business environments, the ability to maximize learning and use of a heuristic-based decision style can both be considered as dynamic capabilities as they appear to be critical for the new ventures to compete and generate wealth.

A second ability that seems to be critical for real options logic is entrepreneurial networking. The role of networks in the entrepreneurial process has been considered of paramount importance since the very first studies in entrepreneurship (Birley, 1985; Aldrich et al., 1987; Dubini and Aldrich, 1991). However, the link between the ability to establish relationships with external entities and the real options logic in the context of new ventures has been less investigated. The system of social relations with external entities and individuals to which the entrepreneurial group has access (Starr and MacMillan, 1990; Antoncic and Hoang, 2003) and with which it interacts to promote the interests of the organization is of crucial importance to obtain as much information as possible from the exploratory investment. This investment must be made in strict contact with external interlocutors considered important for the growth of the new venture. Take the case in which the exploratory investment concerns the development of a prototype of an innovative, highly complex product in which there are serious uncertainties as to its technical feasibility and its commercial attractiveness. In these circumstances, the possibility of creating a prototype able to supply interesting information depends on the capacity to involve potential customers and/or professional experts. Interaction with the former will provide information on product marketability, besides possible input on improving the product itself; in some cases, the help received could also be partial or total financing of the costs of developing the prototype. By contrast, involvement of qualified experts may reduce the margins of uncertainty concerning the technical specifications which the product should have.

Should the making of the exploratory investment manage to attenuate several factors of uncertainty, the results obtained must in turn be shared with outsiders so as to generate further information with which the uncertainty can be further reduced and subsequent investments can be appraised more reliably. In the above case, joint development of the prototype with experts or some key potential customers could ascertain the technical feasibility of the product and signal good commercial potential. The value of these results increases if they are disclosed to potential investors, for whom availability of a prototype which has already received positive technical and market feedback constitutes an interesting element for assessing the venture, probably much more important than a detailed business plan. In the same vein, the ability to attract outside finance into the business will be greater when the costs of producing the prototype have been covered by potential product purchasers who believed in the entrepreneurial idea to the point of investing their own capital to test it; or when, though not having financed the costs of developing the prototype, future customers have advanced the value of one or more orders to the new venture in its start-up. In more general terms, it is through the social network that neo-entrepreneurs are able to obtain information from the exploratory investment with which to decide on a sounder basis whether to continue the investment. A strong propensity to interact with external entities increases the option value created with the exploratory investment since, other things being equal, a more forceful use of social relationships produces more information and allows the subsequent investment to be made in conditions of less uncertainty. Thus, recourse to networking allows the strategic benefits of applying real options logic to be captured by new ventures. Consequently, the ability to maximize social networking may be viewed as a dynamic capability of new ventures.[3]

Third, applying real options logic to new venture investment also calls for the use of an 'asset parsimony' approach. In general terms, this approach is based on minimizing investment in fixed and liquid assets per unit of output. Thus, assets are minimized in relation to a firm's output (Hambrick and MacMillan, 1984). This objective is achieved by splitting the investment into many small incremental investments, postponing those that are greater and preferring the acquisition of assets that generate variable (as with leasing) rather than fixed costs. The investment is made by acquiring at the lowest possible cost only those assets which are strictly necessary to produce the desired output – larger-scale investments are made when permitted by the financial flows from the investment (Hambrick and MacMillan, 1984; MacMillan, 1986). Since the rationale of real options logic is to make a small exploratory investment which is far lower than the resource endowment envisaged to achieve *in toto* the start-up investment, to make this investment asset parsimony logic is necessary. Thus, the entrepreneur's ability to use an asset parsimony approach appears to be a critical capability of the new venture.[4]

Table 15.1 summarizes the relevant conditions that characterize the emergence of new independent firms and the selected entrepreneurial capabilities that can lead to generating wealth in the creation of these firms.

Table 15.1   Critical entrepreneurial capabilities in new independent firms

Relevant conditions that characterize the emergence of new independent ventures	Selected entrepreneurial capabilities that generate wealth
• High internal uncertainty • High external uncertainty • Irreversible investment decisions	• Use of real options logics • Maximize learning • Use of heuristics • Maximize social networking • Asset parsimony

EXPLORING ENTREPRENEURIAL AND ORGANIZATIONAL CAPABILITIES IN INTERNAL CORPORATE VENTURES

The Difficulties in Promoting Internal Corporate Ventures

Internal corporate venturing occurs when employees with a business idea are systematically encouraged to pursue and then commercially exploit that idea within the corporate structure (Miles and Covin, 2002). The basic idea of internal venturing is to create within the established organization the new venture creation's context in which employees who propose a business idea act and behave as internal entrepreneurs. This means that the firm has to give a substantial degree of autonomy and responsibility to these employees (Block and MacMillan, 1983). In this section, the focus is on internal ventures – that is, on new entrepreneurial ventures that originated within the organization and were funded and developed utilizing the firm's internal resources. External forms of corporate venturing in which the firm acquires or takes an equity position in an external venture (Miles and Covin, 2002) or cooperative forms of venturing (e.g. alliances, joint ventures) (Hoskisson and Busenitz, 2002) are not considered. Indeed, these forms of venturing do not entail the creation of a new enterprise. Since it has been argued that entrepreneurship entails the discovery of opportunities and the exploitation of such opportunities through the development of a new enterprise, external and cooperative venturing do not fit with the subject matter of entrepreneurship.

In the first section of this chapter it was argued that internal venturing is the entrepreneurial strategy with which existing firms show an entrepreneurial mindset – that is, the entrepreneurial strategy with which firms systematically search for and attempt to exploit high-potential opportunities that originate from uncertain and dynamic environments (McGrath and MacMillan, 2000). Firms that commit substantial resources to internal venturing identify and discover business opportunities by leveraging on business ideas proposed by self-selected employees who are in a good position to detect opportunities (Stevenson and Jarillo, 1990) and wish to act as internal entrepreneurs. Through the launch and hopefully the commercial development of a portfolio of internal ventures firms exploit such opportunities with a view to establishing competitive advantage and generating wealth at the corporate level. Thus, internal venturing fits the concept of strategic entrepreneurship as it deals with discovery of the opportunity and creation of the new venture (entrepreneurial actions) as well as the search for competitive advantage and wealth creation (strategic actions).

Besides being a valuable entrepreneurial strategy for firms – especially large ones – competing for opportunities deriving from highly uncertain and dynamic markets, there are several motives that induce firms to promote internal venturing. These include pursuing growth aspirations (Burgelman, 1983; Miles and Covin, 2002), promoting innovation (Miles and Covin, 2002), favouring desirable cultural change and organizational climate as well as developing human resources within the organization. From a strategic perspective, internal venturing is a powerful route for developing the organization's knowledge and capabilities (Burgelman, 1983; McGrath et al., 1994; McGrath, 1997b and 1999). The development of a portfolio of highly innovative ventures, more or less related to the firm's ongoing business (Burgelman, 1983), positively influences the development of new organizational knowledge and capabilities. Internal ventures provide a continuous opportunity to extend the firm's knowledge base and generate new knowledge leveraging on the corporation's own entrepreneurial potential. Often tacit, this knowledge represents much of what the firm knows about the competition in its industry, technological evolution and the assessment of entrepreneurial opportunities arising from a rapidly changing environment. Thus, internal venturing enhances the firm's ability to continuously renew and reconfigure internal and external capabilities in order to compete in uncertain business environments. In other words, internal venturing can be considered a dynamic capability (Teece et al., 1997) for firms which aim to create wealth.

However, increasing numbers of established firms are experiencing disappointment in their efforts to promote internal venturing and are turning to external forms of venturing (Miles and Covin, 2002). The significant difficulties encountered by firms in internal venturing started as early as the late 1970s, in which many of the corporate venturing programmes launched during the 1960s and early 1970s by about 25 per cent of Fortune 500 firms were abandoned. Subsequent years showed further cycles of corporate venturing (Burgelman and Valinkangas, 2005) in which the renewed interest of firms was then followed by abandonment and closure (Chesbrough, 2000).

Difficulties and critical dimensions of internal venturing are various in nature. A more acknowledged critical issue is financial returns. As for new independent ventures, the likelihood of internal venture failure is high – this means that the returns from such investments are highly uncertain (Block and MacMillan, 1993). Moreover, internal ventures typically do not exhibit positive returns until years seven or eight (Biggadike, 1979). Other major difficulties that existing firms meet in their efforts to launch internal ventures include core rigidities that contribute to organizational inertia, and high resource commitments.

The inability to deal with these critical dimensions prevents the firm benefiting from the strategic implications of internal venturing. In other words, internal venturing capability inadequacies do not allow venturing to actually become a dynamic capability of established firms which aim to behave entrepreneurially and create competitive advantage in uncertain environments. To really affect a firm's wealth creation, this form of venturing requires selected capabilities. The next section focusses on these capabilities.

Implementing Internal Venturing

The first major difficulty that firms encounter in promoting internal venturing is to implement a large number of innovative ideas and projects with which to seek to identify and capture opportunities from the external environment. Stimulating innovative projects on the part of one's employees clashes with the tendency of organizations to accumulate and exploit existing resources and capabilities and rule out exploring new opportunities which entail the acquisition of new resources and capabilities. Core capabilities on which the firm tends to focus may change into core rigidities (Leonard-Barton, 1992) which generate resistance to innovation, thereby underlying organizational inertia which impedes the promotion and development of a large number of highly experimental internal ventures. Stimulating innovative projects and overcoming resistance to change and innovation are often linked to the firm's capacity to substantially change the characteristics of the organizational context (Kuratko et al., 1990; Birkinshaw, 1996). In particular, firms able to stimulate widespread entrepreneurial behaviour have changed their organizational context, introducing managerial practices with high organizational impact from which there clearly emerges the level of commitment of the firm's top management towards the proposing of ideas and the search for opportunities. Such practices include the possibility for employees to allocate part of their time to developing ideas and personal projects, the management's willingness to assess the ideas emerging, complete tolerance shown towards mistakes and failure, acceptance of non-orthodox employee behaviour – in the sense of a lack of respect for organizational procedures – if aiming to test an innovative idea, adoption of innovative behaviour on the part of top management, and the possibility of encouraging and developing internal ventures even if unrelated to their core activities which may be abandoned retroactively if held to be non-strategic (Brazeal, 1993; Burgelman, 1983; Rind, 1981; Miles and Covin, 2002). The need thus emerges for a disciplined approach to systematically identify opportunities that may be entered in an opportunity register – an inventory of potentially attractive new business opportunities which provides the firm with a rich set of potential innovative projects to choose from (McGrath and MacMillan, 2000). In general, all these managerial practices require selected capabilities by top management and generate high costs for the firm. To ensure the widespread emergence of innovative ideas and projects that can be converted into internal ventures, considerable commitment is required of the firm's top management both in terms of personal involvement and willingness to invest high organizational resources.

It is precisely the need to invest large quantities of resources which represents a second major barrier for firms seeking to promote internal venturing effectively. Besides the organizational resources required to create a favourable context for putting forward ideas, financial resources need to be available to withstand the sunk costs linked to the high failure rates of internal ventures. Even if each failed or interrupted internal venture means, taken individually, a negligible loss of resources, systematic promotion of a portfolio of internal ventures requires the firm's willingness to incur considerable sunk costs. Hence it is particularly important for firms to minimize the waste of financial resources without, however, neglecting the possibility of exploring all the ideas and business opportunities that seem promising. In these circumstances, two selected abilities stand out. First, firms greatly benefit from using real options logic in managing the portfolio of internal initiatives (McGrath and MacMillan, 2000). As Ireland et al. (2003: 969) state, "Successful use of an option approach minimizes the waste of resources while increasing the likelihood that the firm concentrates on its most valuable entrepreneurial opportunities". Secondly, in the presence of a multitude of internal ventures the firm's ability to rapidly disinvest when needed becomes extremely critical. Indeed, allowing widespread project pains, caused by delays in disinvestment decisions, may generate sunk costs that cannot be borne by the firm.[5]

A third critical issue of internal venturing is that of disappointing financial returns, which can induce firms to forgo engaging in internal ventures. As stated above, low financial returns are mainly due to the high likelihood of internal venture failure. The returns from such investments are often highly uncertain and have multi-year payback periods. However, in terms of the strategic entrepreneurship perspective, the real nature of internal venture investments is such that quick financial returns cannot be a reasonable driver for engaging in internal venturing. Indeed, returns from internal venturing investments need to be better assessed in terms of new knowledge generated by the ventures (McGrath et al., 1992). If quick financial returns is the chief motivation for venturing, then external forms of corporate venturing are more suitable than internal venturing (Miles and Covin, 2002). What appears to be critical in promoting internal venturing is the ability of the firm to acquire, assimilate and exploit new knowledge generated by the portfolio of internal ventures in order to gain insights into emerging opportunities (Burgelman and Valinkangas, 2005) and create innovation and value. Obviously, the lower the level of relatedness between the internal ventures and the firm (Sorrentino and Williams, 1995; Thornhill and Amit, 2000), the more the new knowledge will be perceived as external knowledge and the more learning the firm must undertake to internalize this knowledge. This means that returns from internal venturing (the ability to create value from knowledge generated by ventures) are a function of the firm's ability to absorb and internalize this external knowledge. Absorptive capacity is an organization's ability to recognize, assimilate and exploit external knowledge for commercial use (Cohen and Levinthal, 1990). This capacity has been defined as "a set of organizational routines and processes by which firms acquire, assimilate, transform, and exploit knowledge to produce a dynamic organizational capability" (Zahra and George, 2002: 186). Thus, being conceptualized as a dynamic capability, the firm's absorptive capacity is of paramount importance for firms promoting internal ventures as it mediates the relationship between the firm's efforts to engage in internal venturing and its ability to capture benefits from internal venturing for strategic purposes. Firms that continuously engage in internal venturing and that have better absorptive capacities than their competitors exploit opportunities by absorbing and transforming knowledge so that it can be competitively exploited. Being stimulated by internal ventures, the learning that these firms must undertake to internalize and exploit external knowledge may be termed 'learning by venturing'.[6]

Table 15.2 summarizes the difficulties that characterize the promotion of internal corporate ventures and the selected capabilities that can lead

Table 15.2   Critical entrepreneurial and organizational capabilities in internal venturing

Difficulties that characterize the promotion of internal ventures	Selected entrepreneurial and organizational capabilities that overcome difficulties and generate wealth
• Core rigidities and resistance to innovation • High resource commitments and high sunk costs • Disappointing and highly uncertain financial returns	• Ability to change organizational context • Top management commitment • Use of real options logic • Ability to promptly terminate ventures • Absorptive capacity

to generating wealth in the development of these ventures. Given that in internal venturing new enterprises take place within an established organization, these capabilities refer not only to entrepreneurial but also to organizational abilities.

CONCLUSIONS

The uncertain and turbulent competitive environment requires firms to act entrepreneurially. For individuals or firms, being entrepreneurial means grasping business opportunities arising from uncertainty and change which are not exploited by others, and exploiting such opportunities by developing new entrepreneurial enterprises. Such new enterprises may involve both new independent firms and internal ventures promoted by established firms.

In adopting a strategic perspective, this chapter has argued that the link between entrepreneurship and competitive advantage means focussing on entrepreneurial and organizational capabilities that appear to allow new independent firms and internal ventures to create wealth in uncertain environments. This chapter has proposed identification of such capabilities. In new ventures, discovery of opportunities is mainly identified with the entrepreneur's individual capabilities. The process of combining resources which characterizes the start-up of a new venture very often occurs in a condition of resource scarcity. In highly uncertain environments, resource scarcity and the consequent irreversibility of choices made by the entrepreneur suggest investment behaviour based on real options logic. However, to produce value, this makes it necessary to activate entrepreneurial capabilities to leverage on social networking, use heuristics and adopt asset parsimony logic in acquiring resources. In internal venturing promoted by established firms, the capacity to effectively discover opportunities requires both organizational and entrepreneurial abilities. Core rigidities, organizational inertia and resistance to change make the discovery and subsequent exploitation of business opportunities difficult. Given the high incidence of internal venture failure, internal venturing also generates high sunk costs and modest financial returns. Empirical evidence shows that firms that have overcome such difficulties have developed organizational and entrepreneurial capabilities on several fronts. The ability to stimulate the continual search for opportunities requires an active, deliberate role on the part of top management and appropriate investments to change the organizational context. By contrast, effective management of an internal venture portfolio appears related to the firm's ability to minimize the waste of resources without forgoing all the business opportunities that seem more promising. In turn, this capability is related to the use, once again, of real options logic and the firm's ability to swiftly interrupt less worthwhile ventures, overcoming resistance to disinvestment.

Identification of the critical capabilities contributes to our understanding of how firms that wish to act entrepreneurially can establish and sustain competitive advantage and create wealth. For new independent entrepreneurs and for corporate executives who wish to effectively manage their firm's venturing activity, the development of the entrepreneurial and organizational capabilities herein described should lead them to gain a competitive advantage through the successful discovery and exploitation of opportunities.

Given the importance of its implications, the analysis presented herein requires research to better understand the relationships posed. In particular, future research might focus on further clarifying the conditions under which some of the entrepreneurial and organizational capabilities that have been highlighted may be revealed to be more relevant than others in leading to competitive advantage. For new independent ventures, additional promising research objectives include the understanding of how the relevance of selected entrepreneurial abilities may vary according to various contextual factors like the new firm's entry size, the type of industry, the degree of environmental munificence, and the entrepreneur's background and motivation. In the same vein, future research on internal venturing might be targeted to investigate the relationship between the critical capabilities herein described for promoting internal ventures and factors like the firm's strategy at the corporate level, the growth prospects of the core business and the amount of uncommitted financial resources. Hopefully this work will encourage research to address such issues and others concerning the link between entrepreneurship and competitive strategy.

NOTES

1. Given that in these environments there is no pre-existing universe of possibilities to explore, firms create such a universe, often unintentionally and leveraging on human imagination, transforming contingent and individual aspirations into possible specific goals and opportunities – what is called the process of effectuation (Sarasvathy and Venkataraman, 2001).
2. Another way of exploiting opportunities is to sell them to existing firms (markets). However, as it is not based on direct exploitation of the opportunity, this mode does not imply the development of a new enterprise. Given that there seems to be growing consensus among influential scholars that entrepreneurship research should focus on new enterprises and their role in furthering economic progress, the sale of opportunities should not be considered entrepreneurship.

3. Importantly, social relationships promoted by new ventures with external entities are highly idiosyncratic. The ties created depend on the entrepreneurs and their ability to contact a certain network of external interlocutors which is not accessible to other possible neo-entrepreneurs with the same entrepreneurial idea. Relations activated with the exploratory investment thus increase the causal ambiguity of the new venture. By preventing imitation on the part of other firms, causal ambiguity favours the search for competitive advantage.

4. A decisive role in applying parsimony logic is played once again by the entrepreneur's networking capability. Indeed, it is through the system of embedded relations that one seeks to reduce the cost of the resources required to make the exploratory investment. Recourse to the social capital of the neo-entrepreneur and the adoption of resource cooptation strategies (Starr and MacMillan, 1990) allow enough low-cost resources and assets (know-how, unused equipment, financial capital, etc.) to be obtained to launch the venture experimentally. In some cases, involving external interlocutors means that the entrepreneur can make the experimental investment by chiefly using the resources of others (MacMillan, 1986).

5. The decision to interrupt internal ventures is far from easy since it encounters resistance and barriers both from the internal entrepreneurs and from top management. As regards the former, high project expectations and the desire to avoid failure lead them to oppose the decision to terminate the project. As for top management, resistance to disinvestment is chiefly connected to the need to avoid admitting errors made in assessing internal ventures.

6. It is worth noting that, if the returns from internal venturing are to be assessed in terms of knowledge generated by ventures, then firms may benefit from failed ventures in the same way they benefit from successful initiatives. The experience of venture failure often generates valuable new tacit knowledge, and the potential for firms to learn from this knowledge is high (McGrath, 1997b). Thus, firms may benefit from conducting post-mortem learning activities with the team in place aimed at both spreading valuable new knowledge in the rest of the firm and deploying failed internal entrepreneurs on the discovery and exploitation of new opportunities (Chesbrough, 2000).

REFERENCES

Aldrich, H., B. Rosen and W. Woodward (1987), 'The impact of social networks on business foundings and profits', in N. Churchill, J. Hornaday, O.J. Krasner and K. Vesper (eds), *Frontiers of Entrepreneurship Research*, Wellesley, MA: Babson College, pp. 154–168.

Alvarez, S. and L.W. Busenitz (2001), 'The entrepreneurship of resource-based theory', *Journal of Management*, **27** (6), 755–775.

Alvarez, S.A. and J.B. Barney (2002), 'Resource-based theory and the entrepreneurial firm', in M.A. Hitt, R.D. Ireland, S.M. Camp and D.L. Sexton (eds), *Strategic Entrepreneurship: Creating a New Mindset*, Oxford: Blackwell Publishers, pp. 89–105.

Amit, R. and P.J.H. Schoemaker (1993), 'Strategic assets and organizational rents', *Strategic Management Journal*, **14** (1), 33–46.

Antoncic, B. and H. Hoang (2003), 'Network-based research in entrepreneurship. A critical review', *Journal of Business Venturing*, **18** (2), 165–187.

Barney, J.B. (1986), 'Strategic factor markets: expectations, luck and business strategy', *Management Science*, **32** (10), 1231–1241.

Barney, J.B. (1991), 'Firm resources and sustained competitive advantage', *Journal of Management*, **17** (1), 99–120.

Baron, R. (1998), 'Cognitive mechanisms in entrepreneurship: why and when entrepreneurs think differently than other people', *Journal of Business Venturing*, **13** (4), 275–294.

Bhave, M.P. (1994), 'A process model of entrepreneurial venture creation', *Journal of Business Venturing*, **9** (3), 223–242.

Biggadike, R. (1979), 'The risky business of diversification', *Harvard Business Review*, **57** (3), 103–111.
Birkinshaw, J. (1996), 'Model of corporate entrepreneurship and organization context development', working paper, The Institute of International Business, Stockholm School of Economics.
Birley, S. (1985), 'The role of networks in the entrepreneurial process', *Journal of Business Venturing*, **1** (1), 107–116.
Block, Z. and I.C. MacMillan (eds) (1993), *Corporate Venturing: Creating New Business within the Firm*, Cambridge, MA: Harvard Business School Press.
Bowman, E.H. and D. Hurry (1993), 'Strategy through the option lens: an integrated view of resource investments and the incremental-choice process', *Academy of Management Review*, **18** (4), 760–782.
Brazeal, D.V. (1993), 'Organizing for internally developed corporate ventures', *Journal of Business Venturing*, **8** (1), 75–90.
Buchanan, J.M. and V.J. Vanberg (1991), 'The market as a creative process', *Economics and Philosophy*, **7**, 167–186.
Burgelman, R.A. (1983), 'A process model of internal corporate venturing in the diversified major firm', *Administrative Science Quarterly*, **28** (2), 223–244.
Burgelman, R.A. and L. Valikangas (2005), 'Managing internal corporate venturing cycles', *MIT Sloan Management Review*, **46** (4), 26–34.
Busenitz, L. and J. Barney (1997), 'Differences between entrepreneurs and managers in large organizations: biases and heuristics in strategic decision-making', *Journal of Business Venturing*, **12** (1), 9–30.
Chesbrough, H. (2000), 'Designing corporate ventures in the shadow of private venture capital', *California Management Review*, **42** (3), 31–49.
Cohen, W.M. and D.A. Levinthal (1990), 'Absorptive capacity: a new perspective on learning and innovation', *Administrative Science Quarterly*, **35** (1), 128–152.
Cooper, A.C. (1995), 'Challenges in predicting new firm performance', in I. Bull, H. Thomas and G. Willard (eds), *Entrepreneurship. Perspective on Theory Building*, Oxford: Pergamon Elsevier, pp. 109–124.
Dagnino, G.B. (2005), 'Coupling combinative and relational capabilities in interorganizational best practice transfer: an evolutionary perspective', in A. Capasso, G.B. Dagnino and A. Lanza (eds), *Strategic Capabilities and Knowledge Transfer between Organizations: New Perspectives from Acquisitions, Networks, Learning and Evolution*, Cheltenham, UK: Edward Elgar.
D'Aveni, R.A. (ed.) (1994), *Hypercompetition. Managing the Dynamics of Strategic Maneuvering*, New York: The Free Press.
Dixit, A. and R. Pindyck (eds) (1994), *Investment under Uncertainty*, Princeton, NJ: Princeton University Press.
Dubini, P. and H. Aldrich (1991), 'Personal and extended networks are central to the entrepreneurial process', *Journal of Business Venturing*, **6** (5), 305–312.
Hambrick, D.C. and I.C. MacMillan (1984), 'Asset parsimony. Managing assets to manage profits', *Sloan Management Review*, **25** (2), 67–74.
Hitt, M.A., R.D. Ireland, S.M. Camp and D.L. Sexton (2001), 'Strategic entrepreneurship: entrepreneurial strategies for wealth creation', *Strategic Management Journal*, **22**, 479–491.
Hitt, M.A., R.D. Ireland, S.M. Camp and D.L. Sexton (2002), 'Strategic entrepreneurship: integrating entrepreneurial and strategic management perspectives', in M.A. Hitt, R.D. Ireland, S.M. Camp and D.L. Sexton (eds), *Strategic Entrepreneurship: Creating a New Mindset*, Oxford: Blackwell Publishers, pp. 89–105.
Hoskisson, R.E. and L.W. Busenitz (2002), 'Market uncertainty and learning distance in corporate entrepreneurship entry mode choice', in M.A. Hitt, R.D. Ireland, S.M. Camp and D.L. Sexton (eds), *Strategic Entrepreneurship: Creating a New Mindset*, Oxford, UK: Blackwell Publishers, pp. 151–172.
Ireland, R.D., M.A. Hitt and D.G. Sirmon (2003), 'A model of strategic entrepreneurship: the construct and its dimensions', *Journal of Management*, **29** (6), 963–989.

344 *Handbook of research on competitive strategy*

Kirzner, I. (1997), 'Entrepreneurial discovery and the competitive market process: an Austrian approach', *Journal of Economic Literature*, **35** (1), 60–85.

Knight, F.H. (ed.) (1921), *Risk, Uncertainty and Profits*, Chicago: University of Chicago Press.

Kogut, B. and U. Zander (1992), 'Knowledge of the firm, combinative capabilities, and the replication of technology', *Organization Science*, **3** (3), 383–397.

Kuratko, D.F., R.V. Montagno and J.S. Hornsby (1990), 'Developing an intrapreneurial assessment instrument for an effective entrepreneurial environment', *Strategic Management Journal*, **11**, 49–58.

Leonard-Barton, D. (1992), 'Core capabilities and core rigidities: a paradox in managing new product development', *Strategic Management Journal*, **13**, 111–125.

MacMillan, I.C. (1986), 'To really know about entrepreneurship let's study habitual entrepreneurs', *Journal of Business Venturing*, **1** (3), 241–243.

Mahoney, J.T. and J.R. Pandian (1992), 'The resource based view within the conversation of strategic management', *Strategic Management Journal*, **13**, 363–380.

Matricano, D. (2010), 'Achieving and sustaining new knowledge development in high-expectation start-ups', *Industry and Higher Education*, **24** (1), 47–53.

McGrath, R.G. (1996), 'Option and the entrepreneur: toward a strategic theory of entrepreneurial wealth creation', *Academy of Management Proceedings*, Academy of Management.

McGrath, R.G. (1997a), 'A real options logic for initiating technology positioning investments', *Academy of Management Review*, **22** (4), 974–996.

McGrath, R.G. (1997b), 'Advantage from adversity: learning from disappointments in internal corporate ventures', *Journal of Business Venturing*, **10** (2), 121–142.

McGrath, R.G. (1999), 'Falling forward: real options reasoning and entrepreneurial failure', *Academy of Management Review*, **24** (1), 13–30.

McGrath, R.G. and I.C. MacMillan (eds) (2000), *The Entrepreneurial Mindset*, Boston: Harvard Business School Press.

McGrath, R.G., S. Venkataraman and I.C. MacMillan (1992), 'Measuring outcomes of corporate venturing: an alternative perspective', working paper, Snider Entrepreneurial Center, University of Pennsylvania.

McGrath, R.G., S. Venkataraman and I.C. MacMillan (1994), 'The advantage chain: antecedents to rents from internal corporate ventures', *Journal of Business Venturing*, **9** (5), 351–369.

Miles, M.P. and J.G. Covin (2002), 'Exploring the practice of corporate venturing: some common forms and their organizational implications', *Entrepreneurship Theory and Practice*, **26** (3), 21–40.

Peteraf, M.A. (1993), 'The cornerstones of competitive advantage: a resource-based view', *Strategic Management Journal*, **14** (3), 179–191.

Reed, R. and R.J. DeFillippi (1990), 'Causal ambiguity, barriers to imitation, and sustainable competitive advantage', *Academy of Management Review*, **15** (1), 88–102.

Rind, K.W. (1981), 'The role of venture capital in corporate development', *Strategic Management Journal*, **2** (2), 169–180.

Sarason, Y., T. Dean and J.F. Dillard (2006), 'Entrepreneurship as the nexus of individual and opportunity: a structuration view', *Journal of Business Venturing*, **21** (3), 286–305.

Sarasvathy, S.D. and S. Venkataraman (2001), 'Strategy and entrepreneurship: outline of an untold story', in M.A. Hitt, E. Freeman and J.S. Harrison (eds), *Handbook of Strategic Management*, Oxford: Blackwell.

Shane, S. and S. Venkataraman (2000), 'The promise of entrepreneurship as a field of research', *Academy of Management Review*, **25** (1), 217–226.

Sorrentino, M. and M.L. Williams (1995), 'Relatedness and corporate venturing: does it really matter?', *Journal of Business Venturing*, **10** (1), 50–73.

Starr, J.A. and I.C. MacMillan (1990), 'Resource cooptation via social contracting: resource acquisition strategies for new ventures', *Strategic Management Journal*, **11**, 79–92.

Stevenson, H. and J. Jarillo (1990), 'A paradigm of entrepreneurship: entrepreneurial management', *Strategic Management Journal*, **11**, 17–27.

Teece, D.J. and G. Pisano (1994), 'The dynamic capabilities of the firm: an introduction', *Industrial Corporate Change*, **3** (3), 537–556.
Teece, D.J., G. Pisano and A. Shuen (1997), 'Dynamic capabilities and strategic management', *Strategic Management Journal*, **18** (7), 509–533.
Thornhill, S. and R. Amit (2000), 'A dynamic perspective of internal fit in corporate venturing', *Journal of Business Venturing*, **16** (1), 25–50.
Trigeorgis, L. (1993), 'The nature of option interactions and the valuation of investments with multiple real options', *Journal of Financial and Quantitative Analysis*, **28** (1), 1–20.
Wernerfelt, B. (1984), 'A resource-based view of the firm', *Strategic Management Journal*, **5** (2), 171–180.
Zahra, S.A. and G. George (2002), 'Absorptive capacity: a review, reconceptualization, and extension', *Academy of Management Review*, **27** (2), 185–203.

16 Family business and competitive strategy research[1]

Giorgia M. D'Allura and Alessandro Minichilli

INTRODUCTION

The global competitive game requires firms to explicitly develop or implicitly adopt and pursue competitive strategies. Such strategies rely on core competencies, resources, and other capabilities held by the firm in order to effectively compete in the global markets and to achieve the firm's ultimate goals. Similarly to other firms, family firms need to identify and organize resources in order to build their competitive advantage. Family firms may differ from non-family as the controlling family is likely to have an influence over the strategic management process.[2] This influence is the consequence of the converging interests, priorities, values and strategic vision of the family unit into the business. According to family business scholars, differences between family and non-family firms are likely to exist with respect to the set of goals, the way the process is realized, and the actors involved in the process. In addition, the family unit is believed to influence every step of the process (Harris et al., 1994). The influence the family unit exerts on the strategic decision process has often been underestimated in past research and only few studies adopted a comparative approach to explore differences in strategies and policies of family vis-à-vis non-family firms. Despite the lack of comparative studies, the family business literature provides a careful consideration and description of strategic choices in family firms.

Scholars in the field have observed that family firms are rich in intangible resources, which have the potential to generate distinctive resources over their non-family rivals (Habbershon et al., 2003). This approach is based on a resource-based view of the firm[3] and relies on the concept of 'familiness' (Habberson and Williams, 1999). The familiness of a firm has been portrayed as the systemic influence generated by the interaction of three sub-systems: the family unit, the business entity, and the individual family members (Habbershon et al., 2003). This interaction has the potential to generate an idiosyncratic pool of resources and capabilities. In a resource-based frame, the identification of family firm-specific pools of resources and capabilities "is a useful model for thinking about how systemic family influence creates the potential for advantage and corresponding performance outcomes" (Habbershon et al., 2003: 458). The concept of 'familiness' emphasizes the family unit as one of the most relevant variables in the study of family business.[4]

In addition, in our chapter we are interested in better understanding how family firms' unique bundles of resources are translated into competitive advantage, and to what extent they lead to effective and competitive strategic choices. Since the family firm reflects both the aspirations and capabilities of its family members, we believe that strategic decisions result from interactions within the family unit as a social group (Chrisman et al., 2003). In this direction, our chapter explores the characteristics of the family unit which lead to competitive strategic choices. To this end, we will discuss the relevance of the family unit as a decision maker in the family-owned firm decision process. Our argument is that 'familiness' creates an advantage if family units are able to pursue a 'distinctive familiness' that holds the potential for providing firms with a competitive advantage (Habbershon et al., 2003). In our view, three core variables define the potential to generate 'distinctive familiness' over non-family firms. They are the level of commitment the family unit has to the business, the need of distinctiveness it pursues, and the long term vision it has. The use of a series of anecdotal case studies supports and reinforces our arguments. Moreover, it shows how family firms have a preference towards differentiation strategies as a result of the family unit involvement in the business.

The remainder of the chapter is structured as follows. The second section presents a literature review on family business and competitive strategy research helpful to understand the state of the art in the family business competitive strategy research. The third section illustrates the characteristics of the family unit in its role of decision maker to analyze the decision-making process within the family firm. In the fourth section, we present various anecdotal case studies to support our arguments. In the fifth and final section, we portray some concluding remarks and marshal a few directions for future family business competitive strategy research.

THE COMPETITIVE STRATEGY OF FAMILY BUSINESS: BACKGROUND LITERATURE

Family business scholars rely on consolidated frameworks such as those of Porter (1980)[5] and of Miles, Snow and colleagues (1978) aimed at exploring the role of competitive strategies in family firms. The contributions relying on Porter's framework to analyze the competitive choices of family firms consistently argued for a family firm's orientation towards differentiation strategies emphasizing quality over low cost or diversification strategies

(Moores and Mula, 1998; Ward, 1997). As a general tenet, family firms are believed to focus on what has been defined as 'high quality strategy' (Upton et al., 2001). A number of studies have emphasized the importance of the family name on the product or service delivered to markets as an indicator of quality. Hence, most controlling families consider themselves to be innovative in the market, and they often describe their business strategy as 'first to market' or 'early followers' (Teal et al., 2003). Conversely, other scholars explored the competitive choices of the family firm through the strategic orientation framework (Miles et al., 1978). This framework characterizes four possible stereotypes of firms, labeled as 'prospectors', 'analyzers', 'defenders' and 'reactors'.[6] In this respect, a number of studies in family business research classified family firms as 'defenders'. This framework has also been widely used for comparative studies between family and non-family firms. Daily and Dollinger (1992), for instance, found a high representation of family firms among the 'defenders', while professionally managed firms were often classified among the 'reactors'. Gudmundson et al. (1999), then, found no significant differences between family and non-family firms on strategic orientation. Rather, they found the customer groups to be a driver for strategic orientation, and showed how family firms focusing on business customers had a significantly higher tendency towards a 'prospector' orientation. McCann et al. (2001), then, analyzed the strategic orientation among family firms through self-assessment techniques. They asked family firms' managers to rank 16 priorities in terms of their importance to business goals, and reported that the majority of the family firms characterized themselves as adopting a 'prospector' or 'defender' strategy.

More recently, management scholars examined the family firms' competitive advantage drawing up the resource-based lenses. Among them, Sirmon and Hitt (2003) highlighted the existence of five resources and attributes of family firms, and concluded that these attributes were the unique characteristics that provided family firms with potential advantages over non-family firms.[7]

The previous arguments show how family business scholars consistently tried to support the existence of a difference between family and non-family firms with respect to their competitive advantage and strategic choices. Nonetheless, they failed to identify any significant difference in the strategic decision process of family vis-à-vis non-family firms. Our argument is that family units have a potential to generate 'distinctive familiness' as long as they have the ability to bring their values, goals, needs and visions in the strategic decision-making process. Based on this assumption, we focus on the family unit as the decision-making body, in order to understand the determinants of competitive advantage and strategic choices. Since we rely on the idea that family firms' uniqueness arises from the integration of the family unit in the business life (Habbershon and Williams, 1999), the next paragraph will discuss which family unit characteristics have the potential to determine competitive advantage and to influence the competitive strategic choices, and how. Consistent with our arguments above, level of commitment, need of distinctiveness and long-term vision are core variables to define the family unit potential to determine 'distinctive familiness' and advantage-based rents.

THE FAMILY UNIT AS THE DECISION-MAKER IN THE FAMILY BUSINESS

The resource-based view of the firm argues that variations in firms' performance relate more to firms' unique resources and capabilities than to structural characteristics of the industries they are part of. According to this, firms acquire different resources and develop unique capabilities to survive, compete and succeed.[8] Therefore, firms competing within the same industry have different bundles of resources and develop distinctive characteristics. Following these assumptions, we have observed that the relationship between the family and the business has been studied as a potential source of advantage or disadvantage with respect to other firms with different ownership structures. Along this line, the owner family is generally the decision-making unit in the family firm (Habbershon et al., 2003), and its decision-making process relies on values and norms that strictly relate to the family viewed as a social system. In order to appreciate this influence in the strategic competitive choices, it is helpful to identify the values and norms of the family system that influence its strategic decision making and the firm potential to build a 'distinctive familiness'.

Scholars in the family business field have observed that the family unit conceived as a social system emphasizes the importance of satisfying different sets of needs. Among those needs, the family unit wishes primarily to instill both the current and prospective personal welfare and allow a reasonable economic wealth to all its members.[9] When a family unit is involved in a business, it is important to understand which of the social family needs have an influence on the business-related choices, and to what extent. The 'overlapping circles model' has been the standard theoretical model to describe the intersection among the family unit, the business entity and its management.[10] According to this model, several risks may arise when the family unit pursues the supremacy of its own needs over the business needs. For instance, parental relationships inside family firms create opportunities for entrepreneurs, founders and family CEOs to entitle family members with benefits that they would not have received in non-family firms.[11] Under these circumstances, the firm's growth and competitiveness run the risk to be compromised, and conflicts inside the family unit are likely to arise, especially with respect to legacy-related issues.

Such a negative view of the family involvement in the strategic decision process has been criticized in other studies emphasizing the positive effects family units have over the business entity. Family culture and family values such as the sense of belonging, the wish to create wealth for the family, the employees and all the other relevant stakeholders, and the wish to be socially recognized entrepreneurs are among the competitive resources of the so-called 'family entrepreneurship'. The positive view of family unit involvement in the business emphasizes the intention to keep the business in the family, the building of a strong corporate culture and reputation, and the long-term time horizon (Hoopes and Miller, 2006; Miller and Le Breton-Miller, 2006). All the previous elements portray the family unit as a decision-making body in which family culture and values represent the roots of competitive advantage. Following this line, we identified three variables as proxies of family culture and values, and of the firm's 'familiness'. They are:

1) the level of commitment;
2) the need for distinctiveness;
3) the long-term vision.

We believe that these three variables represent sources of competitive advantage because of their influence in the strategic decision-making process. Moreover, they have the potential to define the bundle of family firms' distinctive resources and capabilities, and thus to define the competitive advantage potential of the 'distinctive familiness'.

The Level of Commitment

Commitment to the business is one of the main variables driving the decision making in the family businesses. Family relationships enhance loyalty and increase trust (LaChapelle and Barnes, 1998). Family firms are believed to have greater commitments to their missions as a consequence of heritage of their founders' beliefs (Schein, 1983). Consistently, family members are more than employees because they are owners and they have strong connections to each other and to the business.

In this chapter, we define family commitment as the extent to which family members identify themselves in the family business as compared to other professional or personal factors (D'Allura, 2004). We observe that kinship among family members strengthens the need of individuals to work with the family business because they cannot afford to leave (continuance commitment). They strongly identify with the firm they own, and consequently develop affective emotions towards the firm itself (affective commitment). Finally, the relationship among family members develops a sense of connection for each individual to work in the family business because of pressures from other family members (normative commitment).

Under these circumstances, family business researchers observed that family firms have maintained a long tradition of providing quality and value to the consumer as a consequence of a sense of commitment to the family business and its success (Ward and Aronoff, 1991).

The Need for Distinctiveness

Another element affecting family decision process is the family need for distinctiveness. The need for distinctiveness is the family owners' need to distinguish themselves in their arena both at the business and at the social level, especially in local communities. Being an entrepreneur in a local community requires investments in reputation[12] and consequently, family firms are often very generous in their neighboring.[13]

The need of distinctiveness goes beyond the need entrepreneurs have to distinguish in local communities, and relates also to the family identity. Families find that such activities reinforce relationships, build family pride, and even provide an element of pure enjoyment. Family members are 'often primarily motivated by their sense of belonging in a group that possesses the uniquely meaningful opportunity to sustain and extend a legacy of values' (Aronoff, 2004: 57). Family business inward orientation also defines the need for distinctiveness. For instance, the choice to use the family name as the company brand relates to the need for distinctiveness and affects the identity of family members. Being associated with defective or inferior products becomes a reflection of themselves.[14] Founders and owners having their names on buildings makes them more conscious of their standing in the community and more jealous of their reputation. Thus, the family will find it unattractive to pursue only short-term financial gains if doing so might tarnish the firm's standing. The family need for distinctiveness makes the family business interest to the quality of their products and services much higher.

The Long-Term Vision

A third important characteristic of family firms is the long-term vision the family unit has in the strategic decisions regarding growth targets, investment projects and other strategic choices. That is why family-owned firms are often said to have longer-term visions than non-family ones (Hoopes and Miller, 2006). The arguments supporting the previous statement are reported as follows. First, family firms benefit from the overlap with the family unit. Despite the potential increase in agency costs due to 'altruistic transfers' (Schulze et al., 2003), such overlap should ensure alignment of interests between the family unit and the business entity. Second, family firms are relatively free from the constraints of shortsighted managers obsessed by quarterly financial performance targets. In this respect, family firms may be less reactive to economic financial and market instability, since they pursue long-term value-creating objectives (Ward, 1997).[15] Third, the stability of the family leadership limits the managerial turnover[16] and fosters relationships with core customers and markets in the long term[17] as well as a consistent family leadership. Fourth, family firms have a higher attitude to invest in long-term opportunities (Dreux, 1990). Family firms have so-called 'patient capital' (de Visscher et al., 1995), that is the willingness to wait longer than most other investors for a return on the employed capital. A testimony of the long-term vision of family firms is the evidence that they survive very long (Hoopes and Miller, 2006).

The basic argument of this chapter is that the family's competitive strategy decision-making process is shaped by the level of commitment, the need for distinctiveness and the long-term vision the family brings into the business. Along this line, the source of the competitive advantage heavily relies on the way the family units emphasize the three elements we have introduced. The level of commitment relates to the family unit embeddedness within the firm. Family members are emotionally involved in the firm, and often have a 'filial love' for the firm they own. As a consequence, the level of commitment is supposed to strengthen the efforts and the performance of family members, and enhance their commitment to the firm's success and long-term value creation.

Most of the previous elements also define the kind of strategic orientation family firms have as a result of the family unit involvement in the business. Our argument is that, in those firms, the choice of the competitive strategy is related to the characteristics of the family units we identified above. Specifically, a high level of commitment emphasizes the need for distinctiveness and the long-term vision as relevant predictors of differentiation strategic choices. Conversely, low commitment to the firm reduces the emphasis on the need for distinctiveness and the long-term vision. Under these circumstances, family members do not feel the need to continue the family tradition and to bond ties with their customers, and rather prefer short-term profits and private benefits. Thus, we argue that the three variables we identified positively relate to the tendency family firms have to differentiate. In the next section, we will introduce some anecdotal evidence that supports these arguments.

THE TENDENCY OF FAMILY FIRMS TO DIFFERENTIATE: ANECDOTAL EVIDENCE

In this section we present some anecdotal case studies about family businesses. To appreciate the level of commitment over time, we have selected family firms that have been in operation for at least three generations. In fact, we believe that the need for distinctiveness and the long-term vision are related more to the first generation than to the next. Thus, the presence of various generations explains a higher level of commitment to the business that can foster our prediction about the differentiation strategy. To develop unique capabilities a family business needs time; thus, 'familiness' needs more appreciation in the oldest family companies.

Let us consider the case of ultra-centenary firms, like for instance Barone Ricasoli, which has produced wines since 1141 and is currently owned and managed by a member of the founding family, Francesco Ricasoli (who is the 32nd Baron in the line of the family dynasty). They clearly show over past centuries considerably high continuance and affective commitment towards their business, along with long-term vision on the evolution of the business itself. Other family examples support this argument. The Antinori family, for instance, has been in the wine business since Giovanni di Piero Antinori joined the Florentine Guild of Vintners more than 600 years ago. Similarly, Fortunato Amarelli created 'Amarelli' with his son in Rossano in 1731, harvesting liquorice to sweeten his land. In these cases, the remarkable commitment and the long-term vision to the business have secured the family tradition to survive over many centuries. The level of commitment also relates to the need for distinctiveness and the long-term vision.

Founders often have a high need for distinctiveness, which is usually transferred to the family and, consequently, to the firm. The use of the family name and the association of the family unit with the products and/ or services offered, drives family units to place prominent emphasis on quality and innovation. The founder and the family members feel the need to deliver quality to the customers, with the purpose to build trust among the core customers and to enhance the family's reputation in the marketplace. The search for quality directly implies the search for differentiation, since the family firm's purpose is to create value for its customers through products and/or services with distinctive features with respect to its competitors.

Let us consider the Hallmark example. When Joyce Hall created his famous greetings cards, his purpose was to communicate intimate sentiments to customers. Despite the presence of other funny or colored greeting cards in the market, he was the first to express emotions related to special occasions in people's lives. The quality of his greeting cards was far superior to competitors', in terms of quality of materials, printout, and especially the message they wanted to communicate. Joyce Hall and his staff have since devoted extreme care to every detail, and his family members continue today with this tradition as a family value. Similar to Joyce Hall, several families who have their names on their products and services devote particular care to the quality of those products and services in the need to distinguish from other 'anonymous' competitors. The Ferragamo clothes distribution chain is one of those examples.

The long-term vision of family firms leads to continuous improvements in products and/or services. In a family firm, the family unit is hardly motivated by pure short-term financial profits, and is willing to invest over time to create a brand and a product that customers consider a synonym of quality, which represents a tradition in the markets the firm operates in. For these features, family entrepreneurs have often been defined as 'patient' entrepreneurs, since they are more willing to wait than others in periods of crisis or financial distress. The long-term vision enhances the attention to quality, to create solid ties with the core customers and to keep these ties stable even in times of crisis.

Commitment, need for distinctiveness and long-term vision also enable family firms to create emotional ties with their customers. Estée Lauder, for instance, emphasizes familiar relationships with its customers through the use of beauty consultants, who help clients to choose the beauty products that best fit their needs. In other cases, relationships with customers are strengthened through explicit mentions of the family ownership. Overall, the need for distinctiveness and the long-term vision are closely related to a differentiation strategy.

CONCLUSION AND FURTHER RESEARCH

This chapter has proposed possible variables to distinguish the competitive strategic choices of family firms as compared to firms with different ownership structures. Specifically, we have focused on the characteristics that drive the decision-making process in family firms, and thus define both the potential for competitive advantage and the way family firms select their competitive strategy. Family firms are characterized by the presence of the family unit in the ownership structure and, often, also in the management. As a consequence, the family unit drags its values, norms, traditions and managerial styles into the business.

Past literature on family firms has long tried to understand whether the presence of a controlling family brings advantages or disadvantages to the firm. With respect to this, a major stream of research has often indicated the need to limit as much as possible the interference of the family in the day-to-day managerial choices of the firm. Recently, resource-based arguments have emphasized the positive sides of 'familiness' and its potential to explain the advantages that firms take from their controlling families in terms of unique or distinctive resources and capabilities that lead the firm itself to advantage-based rents (Habbershon et al., 2003). Specifically, we argued how most of the family firms' values, norms and traditions have a potential to determine a 'distinctive familiness'. To this purpose, we identified three core variables defining the family unit behavior: level of commitment, need for distinctiveness and long-term vision. The level of commitment relates to the emotional ties the family has to the firm it owns, and is strengthened by the will of family members to take part in the entrepreneurial project of the family unit. The need for distinctiveness relies on the need to successfully position in the marketplace and to gain a social recognition. The choice to use the family name highlights the will to build a long-lasting self-fulfilling tradition and to perpetuate this tradition of distinctiveness over time.

Finally, the long-term vision characterizes family ownership in its will to secure rents and occupation for future generations. Overall, these elements represent a source of competitive advantage for the family firm, and are likely to determine a firm's strategic orientation towards differentiation strategies in the case of high-level family commitment. The thorough review of earlier studies and anecdotal evidence we presented in this chapter give preliminary support to our arguments.

NOTES

1. This chapter is the result of a theoretical effort of both authors. However, Giorgia Maria D'Allura wrote sections 3, 4 and 5; while Alessandro Minichilli wrote sections 1 and 2.
2. The strategic management process consists of three basic steps. The first step deals with the selection of the strategic goals the firm wants to pursue; the second refers to the formulation of strategies to follow the strategic goals of the firm; the third consists in the implementation phase of the competitive strategies selected in the second step. For each of the previous steps several alternatives are provided, and thus selection and evaluation of alternatives are essential to have a consistent control over the process, to make adjustments where required, and to keep the process effective (Andrews, 1971).

3.   The resource-based view of the firm has emerged as a major paradigm in the strategic management field in the 1990s (Barney, 1991; Wernerfelt, 1984). This view asserts that firms differ according to their resource endowments and that this resource heterogeneity give rise to differential performance (Barney, 1986; Rumelt, 1987). Thus, from the resource-based model, each organization is a collection of unique resources and capabilities that provides the basis for its strategy and that is the primary source of its returns.

4.   The systemic approach we argue for challenges the traditional dualistic view of the family firm which considers the contextual existence of the family unit and the business, but hardly assumes the lack of boundaries among those entities (Lansberg, 1983). The comprehensive view of family units and business entities shows how the behavior of any part of the system will influence and be influenced by all the other parts of the system. As a consequence, the family unit will influence and be influenced by the business and vice versa.

5.   Porter (1980) notably suggested four possible business-level strategies. He argued that a firm could carry out either the cost leadership or the differentiation strategy. He then distinguished between cost leadership and differentiation in the broad market from narrower cost leadership or differentiation strategies targeted to a particular segment of the market. He also referred to the targeting of a narrow market segment as a focus strategy.

6.   Miles et al. classify companies into four strategic types: 1. Defender: it is a mature company in a mature industry that tries to protect its market position through efficient production, strong control mechanisms, continuity, and reliability. 2. Prospector: it is the company that seeks to exploit new opportunities, to develop new products and/or services, and to create new markets. 3. Analyzer: it is a company that avoids excessive risks but excels in the delivery of new products and/or services. 4. Reactor: the companies having little control over their external environment, lacking the ability to adapt to external competition and lacking in effective internal control mechanisms.

7.   They are: a) human capital, b) social capital, c) patient capital, d) survivability capital, and e) the governance structure.

8.   More specifically, the resource-based view suggests that a competitive advantage often results from the ambiguity that arises from a firm's technical complexity and/or its social complexity (Colbert, 2004). In applying the resource-based view to the study of family firms, we consider the family system's characteristics as variables that influence the decision making.

9.   The ways to achieve those general purposes vary across different family units, according to their will to focus exclusively on primary needs or to aim at the satisfaction of high-level needs. High-level needs require the family to commit on wealth creation in order to sustain family members in their wish to achieve high education, status, and social recognition (Kepner, 1983).

10. According to this model, family firms differ from each other on the extent to which the family is willing to separate the social sphere of the family unit from the business sphere of the firm. It means basically recognizing the business as a separate entity, with different sets of stakeholders' expectations from the family unit. The managerial professionalism, the motivation to include other shareholders than family members in the ownership structure, or the will to list in a stock market to sustain the firm's growth are among the decisions showing the commitment the family firm has to keep the family unit, the business entity and its management separate from each other (Gersick et al., 1997).

11. Among these benefits, common altruistic transfers include: i) safe employment, even without passing through regular selection procedures; ii) access to high-level positions, even without the required knowledge and skills; iii) pecuniary benefits, perks and other misappropriations; iv) unethical or harmful behaviors like shirking or, the opposite, empire-building with the funding (and at the risk) of the family firm (e.g. Davis, 1983; Lansberg, 1983).

12. This may be due to the fact that they often supply local markets, in which their presence should be highly visible. Lyman (2001) observed that family firms' sense of responsibility towards the community is positively related to family members' participation in community-based groups.
13. For instance, they give endowments and donations to scholarships for the children of employees as a sign of appreciation for those who have made the firms' success possible (Ward and Aronoff, 1993).
14. Lyman (1991) found significant differentiation among family and non-family firms in terms of customer care arising from the sensitivity that the quality of customer service echoed on the owner.
15. The benefits related to the possibility to have a long-term vision are also likely to depend upon the number of non-family managers involved in the business. Despite the benefits of more professional management, non-family managers often suffer internal competition from family members, and strongly believe that they will be excluded from the upper managerial positions (Chua et al., 2003). Therefore, they might be tempted to outperform competitors, at least in the short run, in order to enhance their reputation and to be more attractive in the managerial job market.
16. The relationship between owners and managers in family firms is different in nature from non-family public companies (Poza et al., 1997). Hence, the trust relationship with the entrepreneur and other family representatives lowers the likelihood of replacements caused by failures in meeting short-term performance targets (Vilaseca, 2002).
17. Lyman (2001) suggests that the family participation in the local community (see sections about the level of commitment and the need of distinctiveness) sustains the family business's reputation as a superior supplier and high-quality service to their community members.

REFERENCES

Andrews, K.R. (ed.) (1971), *The Concept of Corporate Strategy*, Homewood: Irwin.
Aronoff, C. (2004), 'Self-perpetuation family organization built on values: necessary condition for long-term family business survival', *Family Business Review*, **17** (1), 55–59.
Barney, J. (1986), 'Strategic factor markets: expectations, luck, and business strategy', *Management Science*, **32** (10), 1231–1241.
Barney, J. (1991), 'Firm resources and sustained competitive advantage', *Journal of Management*, **17** (1), 99–120.
Chua, J.H., J.J. Chrisman and P. Sharma (2003), 'Succession and nonsuccession concerns of family firms and agency relationship with nonfamily managers', *Family Business Review*, **16** (2), 89–107.
Colbert, B.A. (2004), 'The complex resource-based view: implications for theory and practice in strategic human resource management', *Academy of Management Review*, **29**, 341–358.
D'Allura, G.M. (ed.) (2004), 'Ownership configurations in family firms: the role of the evolution dynamics of the family', unpublished PhD dissertation, University of Catania.
Daily, C.M. and M.J. Dollinger (1992), 'An empirical examination of ownership structure in family and personally managed firms', *Family Business Review*, **5** (2), 375–386.
Davis, P. (1983), 'Realizing the potential of the family business', *Organizational Dynamics*, **12** (1), 47–56.
De Visscher, F.M., C.F. Aronoff and J.L. Ward (1995), 'Financing transitions: managing capital and liquidity in the family business', *Family Business Leadership Series*, Marietta, GA: Business Owner Resources.
Gersick, K.E., J. Davis, M.M. Hampton and I. Lansberg (eds) (1997), *Generation to Generation: Life Cycles of the Family Business*, Boston: Harvard Business School Press.
Habberson, T. and M.L. Williams (1999), 'A resource-based framework for assessing the strategic advantages of family firms', *Family Business Review*, **12** (1), 1–22.

Habberson, T.G., M. Williams and I.C. MacMillan (2003), 'A unified systems perspective of family firm performance', *Journal of Business Venturing*, **18** (4), 451–465.

Harris, D., J.L. Martinez and J.L. Ward (1994), 'Is strategy different for the family owned businesses?', *Family Business Review*, **7** (2), 159–176.

Hoopes, D.G. and D. Miller (2006), 'Ownership preferences, competitive heterogeneity, and family-controlled business', *Family Business Review*, **19** (2), 89–101.

Kepner, E. (1983), 'The family and the firm: a co-evolutionary perspective', *Organizational Dynamics*, **12** (1), 57–70.

LaChapelle, K. and L.B. Barnes (1998), 'The trust catalyst in family-owned business', *Family Business Review*, **11** (1), 1–17.

Lansberg, I. (1983), 'Managing human resources in family firms: the problem of institutional overlap', *Organizational Dynamics*, **12** (1), 39–46.

Lyman, A.F. (1991), 'Customer service: does family ownership make a difference?', *Family Business Review*, **4** (3), 303–324.

Miles, R.E., C.C. Snow, A.D. Meyer and H.J. Coleman Jr. (1978), 'Organizational strategy, structure, and process', *Academy of Management Review*, **3** (3), 546–562.

Miller, D. and I. Le Breton-Miller (2006), 'Family governance and firm performance: agency, stewardship, and capabilities', *Family Business Review*, **19** (1), 73–87.

Moores, K. and J. Mula (1998), 'Strategy diversity in Australian family owned businesses: impact of environmental induced constraints', *Bond Management Review*, **5** (2), 25–33.

Porter, M.E. (ed.) (1980), *Competitive Strategy*, New York: The Free Press.

Schein, E.H. (1983), 'The role of the founder in creating organization culture', *Organizational Dynamics*, **5** (1), 13–28.

Schulze, W.S., M.H. Lubatkin and R.N. Dino (2003), 'Toward a theory of agency and altruism in family firms', *Journal of Business Venturing*, **18** (4), 473–490.

Sirmon, D.J. and M.A. Hitt (2003), 'Managing resources: linking unique resources, management, and wealth creation in family firms', *Entrepreneurship Theory and Practice*, **27** (4), 339–358.

Tagiuri, R. and J.A. Davis (1992), 'On the goals of successful family companies', *Family Business Review*, **5** (1), 43–62.

Teal, E.J., N. Upton and S.L. Seaman (2003), 'A comparative analysis of strategic marketing practices of high-growth US family and non-family firms', *Journal of Developmental Entrepreneurship*, **8** (2), 177–195.

Upton, N., E.J. Teal and J.T. Felan (2001), 'Strategic and business planning practices of fast growth family firms', *Journal of Small Business Management*, **39** (1), 60–72.

Vilaseca, A. (2002), 'The shareholder role in the family business: conflict of interest and objectives between nonemployed shareholders and top management team', *Family Business Review*, **15** (4), 299–320.

Ward, J.L. (1997), 'Growing the family business: special challenges and best practices', *Family Business Review*, **10** (4), 323–337.

Ward, J.L. and C.E. Aronoff (eds) (1991), *Family Business Succession: The Final Test of Greatness (Business Owners Resources)*, XXX.

Ward, J.L. and C.E. Aronoff (1993), 'Philanthropy with purpose – charitable contributions by family businesses', *Nation's Business*, **81** (6), 60.

Wernerfelt, B. (1984), 'A resource-based view of the firm', *Strategic Management Journal*, **5**, 272–280.

17 Multinational firms and competitive strategy research
Grazia D. Santangelo

INTRODUCTION

Strategy-making in multinational enterprises (MNEs) involves adopting a specific set of goals (such as internationalization, responsiveness and global integration) in order to build up and maintain a sustainable competitive advantage. Given the distinctive feature of the MNE (i.e. multi-country operations carried out through a network of multiple units), the achievement of these goals as well as of many others which may arise in the management of MNEs' activities strongly depends on the MNE's internal and external organizational strategy. The former concerns the structure and design of the organization as well as the strategic role that subsidiaries come to play within the MNE's internal network. Both these aspects change as the internationalization of the firm evolves. Research on corporate organization has, indeed, documented major changes in the structure of the corporation and the role of its wholly owned subsidiaries over the past few decades. As far as external organizational strategy is concerned, for multinational (like for domestic) firms, strategic goals have been increasingly achieved by linking up to other actors, as reflected by the expanding resort to external network arrangements (Dyer and Singh, 1998). Such networks may be differently defined according to the relational (either business or social) and governance (alliances, industry network, clusters, etc.) boundaries adopted. Among those external organizational strategies, strategic alliances involving MNEs have witnessed a boom in the last decades.

This chapter surveys MNEs' competitive strategy research. The discussion is split into three main sections. The first section illustrates the international strategic goals imposing strategic choices to the MNEs. Section two deals with corporate internal organizational strategy by focusing on the changing organization of the MNE internal structure and the role of its wholly owned subsidiaries. The third section is devoted to international strategic alliances as an external organizational strategy of the MNE. As far as this final topic is concerned, if some overlaps inevitably rise between this chapter and the one from Africa Ariño and Esteban García-Canal the distinctive feature of our discussion lies in our focus on cross-border alliances. The final section also discusses the issue of MNEs in clusters.

INTERNATIONAL STRATEGY ISSUES

The 1970s theoretical development in International Business (IB) hardly evoked the concept of strategy at all. In those days, strategy was hardly defined and the term was either interchangeably used with the expression 'chosen course of action' or, if used on its own, indicated the crucial importance of a given decision (Buckley and Casson, 2001). Since the 1980s such a concept has, instead, increasingly come to play a central role in the research field on MNEs, as witnessed by the flourishing of a sizeable number of studies explicitly addressing MNE strategy (e.g. Kobrin, 1994; Buckley and Ghauri, 2004; Ricart et al., 2004).

The recognition of a multinational strategy calls for the application of a strategy analysis framework to the decision MNEs confront. Therefore, as for domestic firms, for each set of goals MNEs' strategy analysis goes through four phases: identification and use of resources and capabilities, analysis of industries and competition, elaboration of strategic options, and strategic choice-making. However, although relying on the application of classic strategic analysis, research on international strategy is distinct from research on domestic strategy. The distinct feature of international (as opposed to domestic) strategy lies in the kind of goals MNEs set and the institutional environment where they operate (Tallman and Yip, 2001; Santangelo and Meyer, 2011). More specifically, once a firm decides to go international, its goals are sequentially related to the geographical dispersion of its activities (i.e. in which country to locate its operation), the responsiveness to the host markets (i.e. to what extent to adapt its operations to local market specificities) and the integration of its activities across borders (i.e. how to coordinate its intrafirm network of activities across countries). In what follows, classic strategic analysis is applied in order to evaluate the strategic choices faced in the accomplishment of these goals.

Driven either by the desire to access larger markets, or particularly valuable tangible and/or intangible resources, firms decide to geographically disperse their activities (i.e. to become internationalized) to increase and sustain their competitive advantage. In achieving this goal, the MNE needs to define and exploit unique resources and capabilities which it either owns or has access to (Prahalad and Hamel, 1990; Teece et al., 1997). Successful internationalization calls indeed for the identification of a firm-specific advantage relative to each potential host location and for an industry analysis in order to learn about the opportunities for extra profits (Porter, 1986; Yip, 1992). To this end, MNEs need to collect information in order to make strategic decisions about two strategic options: the choice of the location to enter and the choice of entry mode. As far as the former is concerned, when choosing the location to enter MNEs need to consider the strategic importance of this location in terms of market, resources, assets and efficiency. However, nowadays choosing a location hardly implies the sacrifice of another. The pervasiveness of information and communications technology (ICT) together with current trade liberalization allows MNEs to set up simultaneously in more than one country (rather than proceed sequentially), thus simultaneously exploiting the different advantages rising from different entries. The choice of entry modes is about the selection of more or less committing forms of market penetration running from export entry modes (e.g. distributors, subsidiaries) through contractual entry modes (e.g. licensing, franchising) to investment entry modes (greenfields, mergers and acquisitions, and joint ventures) (see Root, 1987 and 1994 for a review). The choice of one type over the other may have an impact on the success of the internationalization strategy. The adoption of specific entry mode may be also driven by the nationality of the MNE (Makino and Neupert, 2000) as well as by local market features such as common language, close culture and geographical proximity (Kogut and Singht, 1988; Gatignon and Anderson, 1998).

The responsiveness goal is about the ability of the firm to adapt to differentiated market demands since, as it goes internationally, the firm faces consumers' heterogeneity across locations. The risk of a complete adaptation is encompassed in the reduction of the MNE to atomistic business units enjoying little synergies between them and facing high costs due to the loss of economies of integration (Barba Navaretti and Venables, 2004). In this sense, the integration-responsiveness tension (Prahalad and Doz, 1987) within the MNE needs to be closely watched and permanently balanced. Following strategy analysis methodology, in order to achieve the responsiveness goal, resources and capabilities enabling the MNE to adapt successfully to the host needs and desires should be leveraged. In this perspective, the MNE has to decide to what extent to subsidize the activities of its subsidiaries and how much to delegate to its subsidiaries' managers. Similarly, analysis of the industry and competitors should be carried out beyond the local market where adaptation is sought, by also considering the global industry where powerful competition may arise. In this context, the strategic option is about the degree of adaptation to reveal locally, as analysed by the country of origin effect literature (Johansson, 1989). Thus, MNEs may want to claim a full adaptation to the local market or to emphasize their country of origin. The former may be, for instance, the case of MNEs operating in locations showing specific comparative advantages in the industry in question by comparison with the country of origin (e.g. MNEs from developing countries operating in developed economies). The latter may occur when MNEs show specific comparative advantages in the country of origin by comparison with the host location (e.g. MNEs from developed countries investing in less developed economies).

The global integration goal is complementary to the local adaptation one, in that it is about the integration of MNEs' activities across borders. The main motivations underpinning this issue draw on efficiency considerations (i.e. economies of scale through large operation across countries) (Bartlett and Ghoshal, 1989) as well as differentiation strategies (i.e. cost benefits and access to new capabilities rising from the combinations of skills and resources from many locations) (Kogut, 1985). Whatever the motivation, the solution of the global integration issue requires resources and capabilities that need to be freed by the current management of corporate activities or directly allocated to a globally integrated management depending on whether the MNE runs its activities along a multilocal value chain or has just started its operations. Similarly, resources and capabilities can be developed by accessing location-bound advantages and then transferred throughout the MNE's network. The strategic goal of global integration also calls for an analysis of the industry of operation of the MNE and related competitors, since different industries show different degrees of globalization across countries.[1] The options the MNE confronts concern the choice of globalizing production (along a global value chain) and standardizing products (Kogut, 1985; Barlett and Goshal, 1989), globalizing marketing activities (following a standardized approach across different national markets (Jain, 1989; Yip, 1999)), and globally coordinating competitive moves (Hamel and Prahalad, 1985) and market participation (Porter, 1980).

CORPORATE ORGANIZATIONAL STRATEGY: THE INTERNAL NETWORK

The literature on the MNE's organization has developed around an evolutionary perspective, in that it understands the multinational as an organization that changes over time under differently specified selection mechanisms, which make firms in the same trajectory share common organization patterns (Westnery and Zaheer, 2001). The major difference within this stream of literature concerns the nature of the selection mechanisms, portrayed as internal by the early studies of the 1960s and 1970s, and as external by the work developed in the 1980s. A more complex picture was, instead, drawn in the 1990s as a result of the difficulty to treat empirically the MNE as a comprehensive unit of analysis due to the corporate evolution occurring at the same time.

The common element of the early approaches to MNE organization lies in the unilinear character of the organizational evolution. Drawing on Chandler's *Strategy and Structure* (1962) and further elaborated by Fouraker and Stopford (1968) and Stopford and Wells (1972), a first stream of research focused on the formal structure of organization, which evolved from the individual enterprise to a more sophisticated global matrix characterized by high product diversification and great internationalization of production activities. The internal mechanism allowing this evolution from one stage to another was identified by this model in the management stresses due to diversification. Although sharing the unilateral evolutionary pattern, the Swedish school (Johanson and Vahlne, 1977) focused on the evolution of value-adding activities increasingly dispersed in progressively less similar locations through operations requiring greater involvement of corporate ownership. In this case, the internal driver was the enrichment of managerial capabilities and knowledge, and the development of organizational routines favouring internationalization. A further line of research proposed by Perlmutter (1969) shifted the focus to managerial culture, distinguishing different attitudes of corporate executives shaping (and, thus, embodied in) different organizational models. All three approaches were further developed in later years, as witnessed by the work of Egelhoff (1982), Kogut (1983) and Hedlund (1986).

In the 1980s a gradual shift was observed in the source of the selection mechanism promoting the changing of the MNE's organization, although the unilinear character of the evolutionary process was maintained. The first studies flourishing in this period (Prahalad, 1976; Prahalad and Doz, 1987 and Doz et al., 1981) shared the view that MNEs' organization changes as a result of the conflict between external environmental forces, namely the political imperative rising from the request of adjustment of host governments and the economic imperative dictated by the market. On the grounds of these two external forces, later named responsiveness and integration respectively, strategic guidelines were proposed to different industries according to the prevalence of one over the other force, as well as to firms within industries once accounting for managers' 'administrative heritage' (Barlett, 1983). The integration-responsiveness framework developed by Bartlett and Ghoshal (1989) also identified four organizational models of the MNE, mirroring different strategies: the multinational whose strategy was based on responsiveness to local market, the international whose strategy was based on home country leadership, the global whose strategy was based on scale economies, and the transnational whose strategy was based on balancing responsiveness, scale and learning.

The establishment of the MNE as a large internationalized firm shifted the focus of analysis away from the internationalizing enterprises toward the strategic competitive advantage of the international firm (Kogut, 1985; Hedlund, 1986; Kogut and Zander, 1993). Thus, a first stream of research, starting from the 1980s transnational model, addressed the managerial challenges of the international firm by looking, for instance, at the internationalization of R&D (e.g. Cantwell, 1989) and at the connection between the transnational model and the organization of R&D activity (Nonaka, 1990; Granstrand et al., 1990). The strategic role of organization was also explored in these years by institutional theorists (e.g. DiMaggio and Powell, 1983) who have argued that economic environmental pressures on organizational evolution had been over-emphasized at the expense of the pressures coming from similar organizations (i.e. other MNEs, the headquarters and/or other MNEs' units) to adapt to them (Rosenzweig and Singh, 1991). The 1990s also witnessed a growing interest in knowledge generation and transfer within the MNE in the strategy field (Teece et al., 1997). This stream of research looks at the MNE as an integrated network of R&D and production (Cantwell, 1989; Teece, 1996; Patel and Pavitt, 1991), where knowledge creation activities are locally specialized and internationally dispersed across major national and sub-national centers. Accordingly, these authors contend that the international network of MNE subsidiaries replaced the system of miniature replica, thus strategically changing the subsidiary role.

The Strategic Role of the MNE Subsidiary

Little space was devoted to the MNE subsidiary, at least until the early 1980s. Before then, the subsidiary came into the story as far as the MNE-subsidiary relationships (e.g. Hedlund, 1986; Gates and Egelhoff, 1986; Prahalad and Doz, 1981) were concerned. Nonetheless, the early studies adopting the MNE subsidiary as a unit of analysis recognized that subsidiaries can play different roles (Poynter and Rugman, 1983). Moving from this position, a large empirical literature investigating the role taken by subsidiaries within the MNE has flourished starting from the 1990s. Such a stream of research aimed at identifying centers of excellence distinguishing specific subsidiaries (e.g. Holm and Pedersen, 1999), different roles of R&D units (Nobel and Birkinshaw, 1998; Kuemmerle, 1999), and the emergence of regional and divisional headquarters in subsidiaries (e.g. Schutte, 1998; Forsgren et al., 1995). Linked to pre-1980s research on the MNE's organization, another line of empirical research has looked at the headquarters–subsidiary relationship (e.g. Kim and Mauborgne, 1991; Gupta and Govindarajan, 1999). Aspects related to the evolution of the subsidiary's role over time (Birkinshaw and Hood, 1997; Peters, 1999; Cantwell and Mudambi, 2005) and the flows of information between the subsidiary and its network have also been addressed (Gupta and Govindarajan, 1991; Szulanski, 1996). However, this vast empirical literature lacked solid theoretical foundations due to the difficulty of applying firm-level theories to the subsidiary unit as in the case of internationalization theory (Buckley and Casson, 1976) and the resource-based view of the firm (Teece et al., 1997). Similarly, theoretical approaches that avoided treating the subsidiary as a subordinate unit (such as the network perspective (Ghoshal and Barlett, 1990)) show, nonetheless, some drawbacks due to the descriptive methodological approach adopted.

Despite of the lack of theoretical underpinning, the empirical evidence on research on MNE subsidiaries discussed above points out that subsidiaries may enjoy different degrees of freedom. The greater their freedom, the more capable the subsidiary is to determine its own strategy within the constraints fixed by the headquarters and the market. Subsidiary strategy is about choosing a market position relative to its customers and competitors on the grounds of the available and foreseen resources and capabilities (Porter, 1990). However, as Birkinshaw (2001) points out, nowadays, on the one hand, MNE subsidiaries are less free to set their market strategies, which are more and more centrally managed; on the other, their resources and capabilities are embedded in the local context and their development and enhancement are completely controlled by subsidiary managers which, unlike headquarters managers, fully understand them. By creating a mismatch between subsidiaries' market position and resources and capabilities, this situation has been solved by increasingly involving subsidiary managers in market decisions in order to avoid duplications of product lines and by integrating R&D and business units in order to facilitate knowledge development and transfer within the MNE's internal network.

CORPORATE ORGANIZATIONAL STRATEGY: THE EXTERNAL NETWORK

Strategic alliances have been recognized as a main feature of the new phases of the capitalist system where competitiveness is increasingly pursued through cooperation (Dunning, 1995 and 1997). The distinctive features of MNEs' (as opposed to domestic firms') strategic alliances lies in their cross-border nature. Cross-border alliances may be, for instance, a better strategy than foreign direct investment if the location advantage cannot be completely captured by the foreign investor because it is specific to domestic firms (Dunning, 1993). Strategic alliances are collaborative agreements aiming at value creation in order to improve partners' positioning relative to their rivals (Kogut, 1988). This definition implies that, subsequent to the alliance formation, the partners remain distinct entities (unlike, for example, in the case of mergers and acquisitions where one of the two disappears) although they are tied to each other by mutual interdependence. This last aspect plays a major role in terms of management control, the organizational process through which each party attempts to influence the other in order to achieve its objectives and satisfactory performance (Yan and Gray, 1994) by means of formal (involving explicitly information transfer) and informal (usually organizationally embedded) mechanisms (Makhija and Ganesh, 1997).[2] The extent to which partner firms draw on these mechanisms greatly depends on the degree of mutual trust, which, requiring familiarity and mutual understanding, is highly time- and context-specific (Nootemboom et al., 1997). Therefore, if mutual trust has been recognized as an essential ingredient of successful partnering (Buckley and Casson, 1988; Inkpen and Beamish, 1997; Madhok, 1995), in cross-border strategic alliance its role is amplified. Socio-cultural proximity, which is likely to imply organizational fit, is supposed to increase the compatibility between international partners (e.g. Barkema and Vermeulen, 1997; Lane and Beamish, 1990) and thus mutual trust. Conversely, socio-cultural differences are likely to increase partners' compatibility problems and mistrust between them, leading to alliance instability and termination. However, it has been pointed out that consistent empirical evidence does not cover these aspects, most likely as a result of measurement difficulties (Osborn and Hagendoorn, 1997).

The strategic objectives of alliances have been identified as: the reduction of risk since each partner is not bearing the full cost of the project which, conversely, is shared between them; gaining scale economies by joining partners' activities; and building up a reputation by partnering with established firms in a specific sector or with local firms in a potential new market. However, drawing on the resource-based view (Penrose, 1959; Prahalad and Hamel, 1990) and dynamic capability theory (Teece et al., 1997) a growing stream of literature has recognized alliances' strategic objective in the access to partners' knowledge with the ultimate aim of maximizing value creation in the long run. In this perspective, firm learning yielding to long-term competitive gains has been acknowledged as a strategic rationale for alliance formation by an extensive body of theoretical research (Kogut, 1988; Inkpen, 2000; Parkhe, 1991; Mody, 1993) and empirical studies (Dodgson, 1993; Hamel, 1991; Mowery et al., 1996; Simonin, 1999; Santangelo, 2000; Narula and Santangelo, 2009). This literature argues that alliances can create powerful learning opportunities (Dyer and Singh, 1998; Inkpen, 1998) by enabling firms to adopt and develop their own internal capabilities. In support of this view, it has been noted that the new wave of strategic alliances between MNEs has been far more oriented towards joint technological development and interfirm cooperation in learning, and has been relatively less motivated by the joint exercise of market power, by comparison with the international cartels of the interwar years (Hagedoorn and Schakenraad, 1990; Cantwell and Barrera, 1998). Accordingly, the growth in the number of technology-based interfirm alliances has mainly been recorded in science-based fields such as ICT (Hagedoorn and Schakenraad, 1992; Hagedoorn, 1993; Duysters and Hagedoorn, 1995). As a result of the greater role of basic science in technology, firms need to have some mastery of a wider range of disciplines. Therefore, the new role of technological systems together with the rise in technological internationalization and greater costs of R&D budgets marked a new avenue in technological development, which goes beyond the boundaries of a particular firm. As highlighted by Porter and Fuller (1986), the rate of technological change is a main determinant of the growth of strategic alliances in the sense that corporate competitive advantage is mainly related to the rate of increase in knowledge rather than to the absolute increment of the stock of knowledge.

Whatever the nature of the strategic rationale, governance structure may be differently specified to achieve the same objective (Buckley and Casson, 1996; Hennart, 1998). On the one hand, to achieve a given goal multinational firms may choose to partner in one occasion and to draw on wholly owned subsidiaries or market-based contracts in others. On the other, when choosing to partner the organizational arrangements may vary from one setting to another. Technology partnering in high-tech sectors, for instance, is highly characterized by contractual agreements by comparison with medium- and low-tech sectors where the adoption of joint ventures is rather large (Harrigan, 1988; Hagedoorn and Narula, 1996). Transaction cost theory has explained differences in structural choices on the grounds of Williamson's (1975 and 1981) argument of the minimization of the sum of production and transaction costs. As far as the choice between alliances and other organizational structures is concerned, alliances can be a favorite option when aiming at a rapid establishment of competitive advantage (Contractor, 1990; Madhok, 1997) as in industries where rapid structural changes are taking place. Similarly, alliances may be a more efficient alternative when the final goal goes beyond firm-specific assets and also involves other businesses (Chi, 1994; Hennart, 1988). Empirical evidence on the adoption of different alliance structures concludes that more equity governance modes are preferred when substantial relational-specific investments are involved, while firms seem to opt for more bilateral contractual forms of cooperation under uncertain conditions in order to preserve flexibility and ease of adjustment (Cantwell and Colombo, 2000; Colombo, 2003). However, it has been argued that explaining structural change merely on the grounds of microeconomic process neglects historical and behavioral aspects which may bear significant insights for the understanding of the cases at hand (Inkpen, 2001). Therefore, far from being concurrent, strategic and structural explanations are nowadays seen as complementary.

MNEs in Clusters

John Dunning's eclectic paradigm (1977) makes a strong point on the different location advantages each firm may enjoy. By providing a comprehensive framework of MNEs' activities, the eclectic paradigm moves away from the predictive theories of MNEs and identifies the determinants of international production in ownership, location and internalization (OLI) advantages. Due to the drastic technological, economic and political changes of the past two decades as well as the theoretical attempts (new trade theory, economic geography, and international political economy) to further analyze and integrate this aspect into mainstream research, L advantages have gained increasing relevance in academic investigation (Narula and Santangelo, 2012). Among the changes that have geared the rethinking of L advantages, the emergence of knowledge as a crucial asset and the technological revolution starting in the late 1960s have doubtless played a major role. These two aspects have, indeed, generated concurrent centripetal and centrifugal forces in the sense that, if technological advantage has eased the transfer of knowledge across and within borders, the production of knowledge is still locally embedded. Nonetheless, spatial aspects have not, as yet, become a mainstream preoccupation of IB theory, where geography is defined simply in terms of home versus foreign country and the sub-national unit of analysis has been traditionally neglected.

The growing interest in local industrial agglomeration in IB literature has been mainly inspired by Michael Porter's (1990 and 1998) cluster theory, which has dominated much of the recent literature on this subject by providing a way to address the L advantage of the OLI paradigm at the sub-national level. A central claim of Porter's theory is that a competitive region (that is, a region bearing potential to enhance the competitive advantage (Porter, 1985) of the firm (Porter, 1990, 1998a and b)) is characterized by the presence of an industrial cluster which provides the individual firm with valuable local resources, inputs, infrastructure and opportunities for learning from other local firms and institutions. Such learning mechanisms mainly function through intentional and unintentional knowledge inflows and may lead to virtuous cycles, continuously feeding advantages to investing in particular areas over other alternative locations. This implies that cluster formation and development have a strong element of irreversibility and firms have over time an increasing advantage in locating in such clusters (Santangelo, 2002). However, research carried out so far on the geography of MNEs has questioned Porter's theory (Alcacer and Chung, 2007; Baum and Haveman, 1997; Shaver and Flyer, 2000; Chung, 2001) in that the involvement of MNEs in clusters is very sensitive to the nature of the industry structure in which the firm operates (Cantwell and Kosmopoulou, 2002) as a result of potential loss due to knowledge spillovers to corporate competitors. Therefore, major differences in MNEs' location behavior have been recorded between intra- and inter-industry geographical agglomerations (Cantwell and Kosmopolou, 2002; Cantwell and Santangelo, 2002; Cantwell and Iammarino, 2003), pointing out that in oligopolistic industries firms do not colocate their value-added activities with those of their competitive rivals (Narula and Santangelo, 2009; Cantwell and Santangelo, 2000; Simmie, 1998).

Although the sub-national unit of analysis has been adopted only recently in the IB field, a growing number of studies focusing on the role of MNEs in emerging clusters has flourished (Arora et al., 2000; Athreye, 2001; Bresnahan et al., 2001; Santangelo, 2004, 2009, 2011; Tallman et al., 2004, 2009, 2011; Arora and Gambardella, 2005). Within this line of research greater attention has been paid to the creation of local linkages, traditionally recognized as crucial to local economic development for the sake of localized spillovers (Blomström and Kokko, 1998; UNCTAD, 2001). Empirical and analytical studies have shown that the presence of foreign-owned multinationals may lead to productivity or efficiency benefits in the local firms of the host economy as a result of forward or backward linkages with multinationals' affiliates (Rodriguez-Clare, 1996; Markusen and Venables, 1999; Alfaro and Rodriguez-Clare, 2004). In these cases, local firms are forced to use existing technologies and resources more efficiently or to search for more efficient technologies as a result of more severe competition in the host market. Similarly, research has shown that the creation of local linkages by foreign MNEs may promote imitation, reverse engineering and involuntary diffusion of information on advanced technologies and managerial techniques (Mansfield and Romeo, 1980; Jenkins, 1990; Dunning, 1993). A more recent stream of literature (e.g. Feldman, 1993; Anselin et al., 1997) has also explored a further type of potential benefits linkages creation between foreign-owned multinationals and local actors. Such benefit arising from science-technology spillovers (Jaffe et al., 1993) tends to rise in locations where there is a university presence or other sources of publicly funded R&D are strong (Anselin et al., 1997; Santangelo, 2004).

CONCLUSIONS AND FUTURE RESEARCH

This chapter has surveyed the literature on MNEs' competitive strategy research, which applies the classical strategy analysis framework to the MNE's decision-making process aiming at the achievement of strategic goals. While this methodology is common to any firm (domestic or multinational), the distinctive feature of the multinational's choice problem lies in its choice of goals and the environment where it operates. The chapter has also covered the literature on MNEs' internal organization since the structure and design of corporate organization affect the accomplishment of corporate strategic goals. On the grounds of the evolution of the MNE's organizational structure and design, attention has been paid to the changing role of the wholly owned subsidiary within the internal multinational network. Finally, the chapter has dealt with the issue of international strategic alliances as a form of external organization strategy as well as of MNEs in clusters.

If those are the 'hot' themes developed by MNE competitive strategy research in the last decades, new avenues of research have also started to emerge as a result of technological, political and economic changes in the international arena. In today's knowledge-intensive economy, MNEs' success is challenged by new players, such as startups or divisions of existing corporations, which can also achieve global stature by tapping pockets of technology and market intelligence scattered around the world (Doz et al., 2001). Therefore, the competitive strategy to be followed seems the metanational one, aiming at connecting and leveraging dispersed pockets of untapped knowledge around the world, rather than the former multinational strategy grounded on the dispersion of headquarters or subsidiary knowledge across the world.

Within this perspective, one avenue of future research which has already emerged and started to grow can be identified in the stream of studies on re-location and de-localization of low-and high-value activities (Contractor et al., 2010). This calls for a thorough analysis of the new onshoring and offshoring strategies of multinationals currently re-designed with the ultimate aim of tapping into knowledge niches dispersed around the world. However, if this phenomenon directly involves the MNE, it also impacts on its home country corporate network by both enriching it due to reverse technology transfer and threatening it due to a possible hollowing out (D'Agostino et al., 2010; D'Agostino and Santangelo, 2012).

The meta-national nature of MNEs' strategy imposes a restructuring of the multinational's internal and external network, and, consequentially, of the related strategies. On the one hand, the rationalization of the IT, human resource management, service retailing, accounting, finance, sales and after-sales services divisions has changed the role of multinational subsidiaries which nowadays are mainly involved in developing operations which can uniquely arise and maintain the long-term advantage of the multinational by differentiating themselves from their foreign suppliers. On the other hand, such rationalization has implied an amplification of the multinational external network, which may eventually transform the MNE in a virtual entity acting as a 'hub' of a dense external network, through which sourcing activities complementary to its core competencies are sourced.

The increasing involvement of MNEs in emerging economies has also invigorated the debate on corporate social responsibility, whose outcome can easily affect corporate strategy. A greater sensitivity to corporate social responsibility issues bears major implications for multinationals strategy in countries such as India and China, which are key locations in today's economy.

NOTES

1. It should be also mentioned that some scholars (e.g. Rugman, 2000) strongly oppose the global industry nature, arguing in favor of the regionalization of industries.
2. For a comprehensive review on research on control and coordination mechanisms in multinationals see Martinez and Jarillo (1989).

REFERENCES

Alcacer, J. and W. Chung (2007), 'Location strategies and knowledge spillovers', *Management Science*, **53** (5), 760–776.
Alfaro, L. and A. Rodríguez-Clare (2004), 'Multinationals and linkages: an empirical investigation', *Economia*, **4** (2), 157–163.
Anselin, L., A. Varga and Z. Acs (1997), 'Entrepreneurship, geographic spillovers and university research: a spatial econometric analysis', ESRC Centre for Business Research, University of Cambridge Working Papers, 59.
Arora, A. and A. Gambardella (eds) (2005), *From Underdog to Tigers: The Rise and Growth of the Software Industry in Some Emerging Economies*, Oxford, UK: Oxford University Press.
Arora, A., A. Gambardella and S. Torrisi (2000), 'In the footsteps of Silicon Valley? Indian and Irish software in the international division of labour', SIEPR Discussion Paper No. 00–41.
Athrey, S. (2000), 'Agglomeration and growth: a study of the Cambridge high-tech cluster', SIEPR Discussion Paper No. 00–042.
Barba Navaretti, G. and A. Venables (eds) (2004), *Multinational Firms in the World Economy*, Princeton: Princeton University Press.
Barkema, H.G. and F. Vermeulen (1997), 'What differences in the cultural backgrounds of partners are detrimental for international joint venture?', *Journal of International Business Studies*, **28**, 845–864.
Bartlett, C.A. (1983), 'MNCs: get off the reorganization merry-go-round', *Harvard Business Review*, **61** (2), 138–146.
Bartlett, C.A. and S. Ghoshal (eds) (1989), *Managing Across Borders; The Transnational Solution*, Boston, MA: Harvard Business Press.

Baum, J. and H. Haveman (1997), 'Love thy neighbor? Differentiation and agglomeration in the Manhattan hotel industry, 1898–1990', *Administrative Science Quarterly*, **42**, 304–338.

Birkinshaw, J.M. (2001), 'Strategy and management of subsidiaries', in A.M. Rugman and T.L. Brewer (eds), *Oxford Handbook of International Business*, Oxford, UK: Oxford University Press.

Birkinshaw, J.M. and N. Hood (1997), 'An empirical study of development processes in foreign owned subsidiaries in Canada and Scotland', *Management International Review*, **37** (4), 339–364.

Blomström, M. and A. Kokko (1998), 'Multinational corporations and spillovers', *Journal of Economic Surveys*, **2** (2), 1–31.

Bresnahan, T., A. Gambardella and A. Saxenian (2001), 'Old economy inputs for new economy outputs: cluster formation in the new Silicon Valleys', *Industrial and Corporate Change*, **10** (4), 835–860.

Buckley, P.J. and M.C. Casson (eds) (1976), *The Future of Multinational Enterprise*, London: Macmillan.

Buckley, P.J. and M.C. Casson (1988), 'A theory of cooperation in international business', in F. Contractor and P. Lorange (eds), *Cooperative Strategies in International Business*, Lexington, Mass: Lexington Books, pp. 31–54.

Buckley, P.J. and M.C. Casson (1996), 'An economic model of international joint venture strategy', *Journal of International Business Studies*, **27**, 849–876.

Buckley, P.J. and M.C. Casson (2001), 'Strategic complexity in international business', in A.M. Rugman and T.L. Brewer (eds), *Oxford Handbook of International Business*, Oxford, UK: Oxford University Press, pp. 88–126.

Buckley, P.J. and P.N. Ghauri (2004), 'Globalisation, economic geography and the strategy of multinational enterprises', *Journal of International Business Studies*, **35**, 81–98.

Cantwell, J.A. (ed.) (1989), *Technological Innovation and Multinational Corporation*, Oxford: Basil Blackwell.

Cantwell, J.A. and M.P. Barrera (1998), 'The localisation of corporate technological trajectories in the interwar cartels; co-operative learning versus an exchange of knowledge', *Economics of Innovation and New Technology*, **6** (2), 257–290.

Cantwell, J.A. and M.G. Colombo (1998), 'Technological and output complementarities, and inter-firm co-operation in information technology ventures', *Journal of Management and Governance*, **4**, 117–147.

Cantwell, J.A. and S. Iammarino (eds) (2003), *Multinational Corporations and European Regional System of Innovation*, London, UK: Routledge.

Cantwell, J.A. and E. Kosmopoulou (2002), 'What determines the internationalization of corporate technology?', in M. Forsgren, H. Håkanson and V. Havila (eds), *Critical Perspectives on Internationalisation*, London: Pergamon.

Cantwell, J.A. and R. Mudambi (2005), 'MNE competence-creating subsidiary mandates', *Strategic Management Journal*, **26**, 1109–1128.

Chandler, A.D. (ed.) (1962), *Strategy and Structure*, Cambridge, MA: MIT Press.

Chi, T. (1994), 'Trading in strategic resources: necessary conditions, transaction cost problems, and choice of exchange structure', *Strategic Management Journal*, **15**, 217–290.

Chung, W. (2001), 'Mode, size and location of foreign direct investments and industry markups', *Journal of Economic Behaviour and Organization*, **45** (2), 185–211.

Colombo, M.G. (2003), 'Alliance form: a test of the contractual and competence perspective', *Strategic Management Journal*, **24**, 1209–1229.

Contractor, F.J. (1990), 'Contractual and cooperative forms of international business: toward a unified theory of modal choice', *Management International Review*, **30** (1), 31–54.

DiMaggio, P. and W.W. Powell (1983), 'The iron cage revisited: institutional isomorphism and collective rationality in organizational fields', *American Sociological Review*, **48** (2), 147–160.

Dodgson, M. (1993), 'Learning, trust and technological collaboration', *Human Relations*, **46**, 77–95.

Doz, Y., C. Bartlett and C.K. Prahalad (1981), 'Global competitive pressure vs. host country demands: managing tensions in multinational corporations', *California Management Review*, **23** (3), 63–74.

Doz, Y., J. Sanots and P.J. Williamson (eds) (2001), *From Global to Metanational: How Companies Win in the Knowledge Economy*, Boston, MA: Harvard Business Press.

Dunning, J.H. (ed.) (1993), *Multinational Enterprises and the Global Economy*, Wokingham: Addison-Wesley Publishers Ltd.

Dunning, J.H. (1995), 'Reappraising the eclectic paradigm in an age of alliance capitalism', *Journal of International Business Studies*, **26** (3), 461–491.

Dunning, J.H. (ed.) (1997), *Alliance Capitalism and Global Business*, London: Routledge.

Duysters, G. and J. Hagedoorn (1995), 'Strategic groups and inter-firm networks in international high-tech industries', *Journal of Management Studies*, **32** (3), 359–381.

Dyer, J.H. and H. Singh (1998), 'The relational view: co-operative strategy and source of inter-organizational competitive advantage', *Academy of Management Review*, **23** (4), 660–679.

Egelhoff, W.G. (1982), 'Strategy and structure in multinational corporation: a revision of the Stopford and Wells model', *Administrative Science Quarterly*, **27** (3), 435–458.

Feldman, M. (1993), 'An examination of the geography of innovation', *Industrial and Corporate Change*, **2**, 451–470.

Forsgren, M., U. Holm and J. Johanson (1992), 'Division headquarters go abroad: a step in the internationalisation of the multinational corporation', *Journal of Management Studies*, **32** (4), 475–491.

Fouraker, L.E. and J.M. Stopford (1968), 'Organizational structure and the multinational strategy', *Administrative Science Quarterly*, **13** (1), 47–64.

Gates, S. and W.G. Egelhoff (1986), 'Centralisation in headquarter-subsidiary relationships', *Journal of International Business Studies*, **17** (2), 71–92.

Gatignon, H. and E. Anderson (1988), 'The multinational corporation's degree of control over foreign subsidiaries: an empirical test of a transaction cost explanation', *Journal of Law, Economics, and Organization*, **4**, 305–336.

Ghoshal, S. and C.A. Bartlett (1990), 'Multinational corporation as an international network', *Academy of Management Review*, **15** (4), 603–625.

Granstrand, O., P. Patel and K.L.R. Pavitt (1997), 'Multi-technology corporation: why they have "distributed" rather than "distinctive core" competencies', *California Management Review*, **39**, 8–25.

Gupta, A.K. and V. Govidarajan (1991), 'Knowledge flows and the structure of control within multinational corporations', *Academy of Management Review*, **16** (4), 443–457.

Gupta, A.K. and V. Govidarajan (1999), 'Feedback-seeking behaviour within multinational corporations', *Strategic Management Journal*, **20** (3), 205–225.

Hagedoorn, J. (1993), 'Strategic technology alliances and modes of co-operation in high-technology industries', in G. Grabher (ed.), *The Embedded Firm*, London: Routledge.

Hagedoorn, J. and R. Narula (1996), 'Choosing organizational modes of strategic technology partnering: international and sectoral differences', *Journal of International Business Studies*, **27** (2), 264–284.

Hagedoorn, J. and J. Schakenraad (1990), 'Inter-firm partnerships and co-operative strategies in core technologies', in C. Freeman and L.L.G. Soete (eds), *New Explorations in the Economics of Technical Change*, London: Frances Pinter.

Hagedoorn, J. and J. Schakenraad (1992), 'Leading companies and networks of strategic alliances in information technologies', *Research Policy*, **21**, 163–190.

Hamel, G. (1991), 'Competition for competence and inter-partner learning within international strategic alliances', *Strategic Management Journal*, **12**, 83–104.

Hamel, G. and C.K. Prahalad (1985), 'Do you really have a global strategy?', *Harvard Business Review*, July–August, 139–148.

Harrigan, K.R. (1988), 'Strategic alliances and partner asymmetries', in F.J. Contractor and P. Lorange (eds), *Cooperative Strategies in International Business*, Boston, MA: Lexington Books.

Hedlund, G. (1986), 'The hypermodern MNC: a heterarchy?', *Human Resource Management*, **25**, 9–25.

Hennart, J.F. (1988), 'A transaction cost theory of equity JVs', *Strategic Management Journal*, **9**, 361–374.

Holm, U. and T. Pedersen (eds) (1999), *The Emergence and Impact of Centres of Excellence*, London: Macmillan.

Inkpen, A.C. (1998), 'Learning and knowledge acquisition through international strategic alliances', *Academy of Management Executive*, **12** (4), 69–80.

Inkpen, A.C. (2000), 'Learning through joint ventures: a framework of knowledge acquisition', *Journal of Management Studies*, **37**, 1019–1043.

Inkpen, A.C. (2001), 'Strategic alliances', in A.M. Rugman and T.L. Brewer (eds), *Oxford Handbook of International Business*, Oxford, UK: Oxford University Press.

Inkpen, A.C. and P.W. Beamish (1997), 'Knowledge bargaining power and international joint ventures stability', *Academy of Management Review*, **22**, 177–202.

Jaffe, A.B., M. Trajtenberg and R. Henderson (1993), 'Geographical localisation of knowledge spillovers, as evidenced by patent citations', *Quarterly Journal of Economics*, **58** (3), 577–598.

Jain, S.C. (1989), 'Standardisation of international marketing strategy: some research hypotheses', *Journal of Marketing*, **53**, 70–79.

Jarillo, J.C. and J.I. Martinez (1989), 'Different role for subsidiaries: the case of multinational corporation', *Strategic Management Journal*, **11**, 501–512.

Jenkins, R. (1990), 'Comparing foreign subsidiaries and local firms in LDCs: theoretical issues and empirical evidence', *Journal of Development Studies*, **26**, 205–228.

Johansson, J.K. (1989), 'Determinants and effects of 'made' in label', *International Marketing Review*, **6** (1), 47–58.

Johansson, J.K. and J.E. Vahlne (1977), 'The international process of the firm: a model of knowledge development and increasing foreign market commitments', *Journal of International Business Studies*, **8** (1), 23–32.

Kim, C. and R. Mauborgne (1991), 'Implementing global strategies: the role of procedural justice', *Strategic Management Journal*, **12**, 125–144.

Kobrin, S.J. (1994), 'Is there a relationship between a geocentric mind-set and multinational strategy?', *Journal of International Business Studies*, **25**, 493–511.

Kogut, B. (1983), 'Foreign direct investment as a sequential process', in C. Kindleberger and D. Audretsch (eds), *The Multinational Corporation in the 1980s*, Cambridge, MA: Cambridge University Press.

Kogut, B. (1985), 'Design global strategies: comparative and competitive value added chains', *Sloan Management Review*, Summer, 27–38.

Kogut, B. (1988), 'Joint ventures: theoretical and empirical perspectives', *Strategic Management Journal*, **9**, 319–322.

Kogut, B. and H. Singh (1988), 'The effect of national culture on the choice of entry mode', *Journal of International Business Studies*, **19** (3), 411–432.

Kogut, B. and U. Zander (1993), 'Knowledge of the firm and the evolutionary theory of the multinational corporation', *Journal of International Business Studies*, **24** (4), 625–645.

Kuemmerle, W. (1999), 'The drivers of foreign direct investment into research and development: an empirical investigation', *Journal of International Business Studies*, **30** (1), 1–24.

Lane, H.V. and P.W. Beamish (1990), 'Cross-cultural cooperative behaviour in joint ventures in LDCs', *Management International Review*, **30**, 87–102.

Madhok, A. (1995), 'Revisiting multinational firms' tolerance for joint ventures: a trust-based approach', *Journal of International Business Studies*, **6**, 117–138.

Madhok, A. (1997), 'Cost, value and foreign market entry mode: the transaction and the firm', *Strategic Management Journal*, **18**, 39–61.

Makhija, M.V. and U. Ganesh (1997), 'The relationship between control and partner learning in learning-elated joint ventures', *Organizational Science*, **5**, 508–520.

Makino, S. and K.E. Neupert (2000), 'National culture, transaction costs, and the choice between joint venture and wholly owned subsidiary', *Journal of International Business Studies*, **31** (4), 705–713.

Mansfield, E. and A. Romeo (1980), 'Technology transfer to overseas subsidiaries by US based firms', *Quarterly Journal of Economics*, **95** (4), 737–750.

Markusen, J. and A.J. Venables (1999), 'Foreign direct investment as a catalyst for industrial development', *European Economic Review*, **43**, 335–356.

Mody, A. (1993), 'Learning through alliance', *Journal of Economic Behaviour and Organization*, **20**, 151–170.

Mowery, D.C., J.E. Oxley and B.S. Silverman (1998), 'Technological overlapping and inter-firm co-operation: implications for resource-based view of the firm', *Research Policy*, **27** (6), 507–523.

Narula, R. and G.D. Santangelo (2009), 'Location, collocation and R&D alliances in the European ICT industry', *Research Policy*, **38** (2), 393–403.

Narula, R. and G.D. Santangelo (2012), 'Location and collocation advantages in international innovation', *Multinational Business Review*, **20** (1), 6–25.

Nobel, R. and J. Birkinshaw (1998), 'Patterns of control and communication in international research and development units', *Strategic Management Journal*, **19** (5), 479–498.

Nonaka, I. (1990), 'Managing globalization as a self-renewing process: the experience of Japanese MNCs', in C. Barlett, Y. Doz, and G. Hedlund (eds), *Managing the Global Firm*, London: Routledge.

Nootemboom, B., H. Berger and N.G. Noorderhaven (1997), 'Effects of trust and govern-ance on relational risk', *Academy of Management Journal*, **40**, 308–338.

Osborn, R. and J. Hagendoorn (1997), 'The institutionalization and evolutionary dynam-ics of interorganizational alliances and network', *Academy of Management Journal*, **40**, 261–278.

Parkhe, A. (1991), 'Interfirm diversity, organizational learning, and longevity in global stra-tegic alliances', *Journal of International Business Studies*, **22**, 579–602.

Patel, P. and K.L.R. Pavitt (1991), 'Large firms in the production of the world's technology: an important case of non-globalisation', *Journal of International Business Studies*, **22**, 1–21.

Penrose, E. (ed.) (1959), *The Theory of the Growth of the Firm*, Oxford: Basil Blackwell.

Permultter, H. (1969), 'The tortuous evolution of the multinational corporation', *Columbia Journal of World Business*, **5** (1), 9–18.

Peters, E. (1999), 'Plant subsidiary upgrading: some evidence from the electronic industry', in N. Hood and S. Young (eds), *The Globalization of Multinational Enterprise Activity and Economic Development*, London: Macmillan.

Porter, M.E. (ed.) (1980), *Competitive Strategies: Techniques for Analysing Industries and Competitors*, New York: The Free Press.

Porter, M.E. (ed.) (1985), *Competitive Advantage,* New York: The Free Press.

Porter, M.E. (1986), 'Changing patterns of international competition', *California Management Review*, **28** (2), 9–40.

Porter, M.E. (1990), *The Competitive Advantage of Nations*, New York: The Free Press.

Porter, M.E. (1998a), 'Clusters and the new economics of competition', *Harvard Business Review*, **76** (6), 77–90.

Porter, M.E. (1998b), 'Competing across locations', in M.E. Porter, *On Competition*, Cambridge, MA: Harvard Business School Press, pp. 309–348.

Porter, M.E. and M.B. Fuller (1986), 'Coalitions and global strategy', in M.E. Porter (ed.), *Competition in Global Industries*, Boston, MA: Harvard Business School Press.

Poyntner, T.A. and A.M. Rugman (1982), 'World product mandates: how will multination-als respond?', *Business Quarterly*, Autumn, 54–61.

Prahalad, C.K. (1976), 'Strategic choices in diversified MNCs', *Harvard Business Review*, **54** (4), 67–78.

Prahalad, C.K. and Y. Doz (1981), 'An approach to strategic control in MNCs', *Sloan Management Review*, Summer, 5–13.

Prahalad, C.K. and Y. Doz (eds) (1987), *The Multinational Mission: Balancing Local Demands and Global Vision*, New York: The Free Press.

Prahalad, C.K. and G. Hamel (1990), 'The core competence of the corporation', *Harvard Business Review*, **68** (3), 76–91.

Rodriguez-Clare, A. (1996), 'Multinationals, linkages and economic development', *American Economic Review*, **86** (4), 852–873.

Rosenzweig, P. and J. Singh (1991), 'Organizational environments and the multinational enterprise', *Academy of Management Review*, **16** (2), 340–361.

Ricart, J.E., M.J. Enright, P. Ghemawat, S.L. Hart and T. Khanna (2004), 'New frontiers in international strategy', *Journal of International Business Studies*, **35**, 175–200.

Root, F. (ed.) (1987), *Entry Strategy for International Markets*, Lexington, MA: Jossey-Bass.

Rugman, A.M. (ed.) (2000), *The End of Globalisation*, London: Random House Business Books.

Santangelo, G.D. (2000), 'Corporate strategic technological partnerships in the European information and communications technology industry', *Research Policy*, **29** (9), 1015–1031.

Santangelo, G.D. (2002), 'The regional geography of corporate patenting in information and communications technology (ICT): domestic and foreign dimension', *Regional Studies*, **36** (5), 495–514.

Santangelo, G.D. (2004), 'FDI and local capabilities in peripheral regions – the Etna Valley case', *Transnational Corporations*, **13** (1), 73–106.

Santangelo, G.D. (2009), 'MNCs and linkages creation: evidence from a peripheral area', *Journal of World Business*, **44** (2), 192–205.

Santangelo, G.D. (2011), 'The tension of information sharing: effects on subsidiary embeddedness', *International Business Review*, **21** (2), 180–195.

Santangelo, G.D. and K. Meyer (2011), 'Extending the internationalization process model: increases and decreases of MNE commitment in emerging economies', *Journal of International Business Studies*, **42** (7), 894–909.

Schutte, H. (1998), 'Between headquarters and subsidiaries: the RHQ solution', in J.M. Birkinshaw and N. Hood (eds), *Multinational Corporate Evolution and Subsidiary Development*, London: Macmillan, pp. 102–137.

Shaver, J.M. and F. Flyer (2000), 'Agglomeration economies, firm heterogeneity and foreign direct investment in the United States', *Strategic Management Journal*, **21** (12), 1175–1193.

Simmie, J. (1998), 'Reasons for the development of "islands of innovation": evidence from Hertfordshire', *Urban Studies*, **35** (8), 1261–1289.

Simonin, B.L. (1999), 'Ambiguity and the process of knowledge transfer in strategic alliances', *Strategic Management Journal*, **20** (7), 595–623.

Stopford, J.M. and L.T. Wells (eds) (1972), *Managing the Multinational Enterprise: Organization of the Firm and Ownership of the Subsidiaries*, New York: Basic Books.

Szulanski, G. (1996), 'Exploring internal stickiness: impediments to the transfer of best practices within the firm', *Strategic Management Journal*, **17**, 27–44.

Tallman, S.B. and G.S. Yip (2001), 'Strategy and multinational enterprises', in A.M. Rugman and T.L. Brewer (eds), *Oxford Handbook of International Business*, Oxford, UK: Oxford University Press.

Tallman, S., M. Jenkins, N. Henry and S. Pinch (2004), 'Knowledge, clusters and competitive advantage', *Academy of Management Review*, **29** (2), 258–271.

Teece, D.J. (1996), 'Firm organization, industrial structure and technological innovation', *Journal of Economic Behavior and Organization*, **31** (2), 193–224.

Teece, D.J., G. Pisano and A. Shuen (1997), 'Firm capabilities, resources, and the concept of strategy', *Strategic Management Review*, **18** (7), 509–533.

Westerney, D.E. and S. Zaheer (2001), 'The multinational enterprise as an organization', in A.M. Rugman and T.L. Brewer (eds), *Oxford Handbook of International Business,* Oxford, UK: Oxford University Press, pp. 349–379.

Williamson, O.E. (ed.) (1975), *Markets and Hierarchies: Analysis and Antitrust Implications*, New York: The Free Press.

Williamson, O.E. (1981), 'The economics of organization: the transaction cost approach', *American Journal of Sociology*, **87** (3), 548–577.

Yan, A. and B. Gray (1994), 'Bargaining power, management control, and performance in the United States–China joint ventures: a comparative case study', *Academy of Management Journal*, **37**, 1478–1517.

Yip, G.S. (ed.) (1992), *Total Global Strategy: Managing for Worldwide Competitive Advantage*, Englewood Cliffs, New Jersey: Prentice Hall.

PART 4

METHODOLOGICAL ISSUES IN COMPETITIVE STRATEGY RESEARCH

18 The use of quantitative methodologies in competitive strategy research
Roberto Ragozzino, Asda Chintakananda and Jeffrey J. Reuer

INTRODUCTION

During the past two decades, there has been growing interest in the field of strategy, and scholars in the area have brought forth significant advancements on both the theoretical and the empirical sides of research. With respect to the latter, the improved availability of archival data has also opened the door to new questions that could not be effectively addressed previously. As a result of this evolution, empirical work in strategy research has advanced dramatically and has transformed from being conducted predominantly through case studies during the 1960s and 1970s, to large-scale studies using cutting-edge quantitative methods (Hitt et al., 1998).

The objective of this chapter is to provide insights on the methodological development of quantitative methodologies in strategy research over the last 16 years (1990–2005). Understanding how the field has evolved not only allows us to take stock of the progress made by research to date, but it can also offer important prescriptive guidance to researchers committed to advancing our knowledge in the future. In the subsequent sections, we will discuss the various types of quantitative methodologies employed in strategy research between 1990 and 2005, and we will highlight several noteworthy trends that have emerged over this time period.

Aside from surveying some of the developments in the field, we will also draw a comparison to the work of Scandura and Williams (2000), who conducted a similar study for the area of management broadly defined. Our objectives are to (1) compare and contrast management and strategy from a historical perspective, and (2) offer insights as to how these differences may unfold in the future. This supplemental analysis will also be made in relation to the discussion on the state-of-the-art strategy research by Hitt et al. (1998), in order to determine whether the methodological advances undertaken in our field have been consistent with the guidance offered by these authors.

METHODS

In order to arrive at a systematic classification of the various quantitative methodologies used in strategy research, we began by conducting a content analysis of every article published in the *Strategic Management Journal* (SMJ) for the period of 1990–2005. As we will discuss in the results section of this chapter, for purposes of comparability and consistency with prior work, we further broke down the 16-year time period into four separate time intervals (1990–1993, 1994–1997, 1998–2001, and 2002–2005). The advantage of narrowing our survey to SMJ is that, unlike other premier management journals such as the *Academy of Management Journal* (AMJ), *Administrative Science Quarterly* (ASQ), *Organization Science* (OS), and *Management Science* (MS), SMJ specializes in strategy research and this focus helps us to avoid the pitfalls of having to determine which articles published in the other management journals should or not be counted as applicable for our study. Our usage of SMJ is also consistent with a prior investigation by Wiersema and Bowen (1997), who studied empirical strategy research by reviewing SMJ articles from 1993 to 1995.

There are at least two other interesting implications associated with our focusing on SMJ and strategy research: first, this approach allows us to relate our results to an earlier discussion on future trends in strategy research offered by Hitt et al. (1998). Second, as a result of our relatively narrow focus we are able to compare our findings to the broader set of research methods used in general management studies, which Scandura and Williams (2000) previously investigated. Their study included other areas of management such as organizational theory, organizational behavior, and human resource management; their survey also covered a broader set of journals (i.e., *Academy of Management Journal, Administrative Science Quarterly, Organization Science*, and *Management Science*).

Our initial sample consisted of a total of 1004 articles published in SMJ between 1990 and 2005. Each article was classified into one of four broad categories: formal theory/literature review, issue introductions and editorial commentaries, qualitative research, and quantitative research. Given our interest in the latter, we excluded articles belonging to any of the first three categories, and this step left us with a final sample of 709 research papers that employed quantitative methodologies.

The procedure employed for the subsequent analyses is consistent with prior work in the area and involves the following steps: First, we reviewed all of the 709 quantitative research studies and classified each based on the method employed. We relied upon a classification scheme developed by McGrath (1981) and subsequently adopted and modified by Scandura and Williams (2000). Second, we complemented this taxonomy with the research methods classifications proposed by Hitt et al. (1998). The following section of the chapter and Figures 18.1 and 18.2 provide a detailed description of the specific variables we constructed, as well as a description of the way in which we categorized the various statistical techniques used in the articles we surveyed. As a check, upon completing the steps described above, we conducted an electronic search for each of the categorized methods within the SMJ archive, in order to capture any errors or omissions that might have occurred. Finally, we summed up entries in the individual categories to obtain a count of the times each method was used in the articles employing quantitative methodologies.

Coding

We collected seven variables for all of the 1004 articles that were published in SMJ between 1990 and 2005. First, we coded each article according to its overall purpose and separated research notes from full-length research articles. We also categorized papers depending upon whether they were conceptual, experimental, or empirical articles, and then, for this last category, we further broke down the articles that were purely quantitative versus qualitative in nature, or studies that used a combination of both quantitative and qualitative research techniques. We relied on this coding in order to narrow the 1004 articles to 709 research articles that employed quantitative methods. Then, we examined all quantitative research articles in detail and divided them according to the data collection strategy employed: sample surveys, secondary archival data, primary data, judgment tasks, and/or experiments and simulations. The steps we just illustrated are consistent with prior work by McGrath (1981) as well as Scandura and Williams (2000). Next, we noted whether the sample used in each article was cross-sectional and/or longitudinal in nature.

The last two variables detail the analytical procedures used by researchers to test their hypotheses, as described in the research methodology section of each article. We made an effort to ensure that the constructed variables reflect the descriptions of the procedures used in the testing of the hypothesized relationships rather than merely procedures used in the validation of the sample or used for other purposes not related to the actual testing of hypotheses. As an illustration, analytical procedures were coded as 'ANOVA' if the research article used an ANOVA procedure to test the theorized relationship between two variables. However, if an ANOVA procedure was used as part of the descriptive statistics or for other purposes besides hypothesis testing, then ANOVA was not coded.

Article format	Type of research	Type of empirical research	Research strategy employed	Time frame of study	Type of research methods employed	Categorizations of research methods employed
Research note	Conceptual	Quantitative	Sample survey	Cross-sectional	- see figure 18.2 -	
Research article	Experimental	Qualitative	Primary data	Longitudinal/panel		
	Empirical	Both	Secondary data			
			Experiments and simulations			

Figure 18.1 Framework for content analysis

In the case of multiple analytical procedures being used to test hypotheses, we recorded all of the procedures used. For example, if both ANOVA procedures and hierarchical linear modeling were used to test hypothesized relationships, then analytical procedures were coded as 'ANOVA' and 'hierarchical linear modeling'.

As a next step, we grouped our categorized analytical procedures into a broader taxonomy, following Scandura and Williams (2000) and Hitt, Gimeno and Hoskisson (1998). Under this taxonomy, procedures such as *t*-tests, ANOVA, and MANOVA were categorized into one group labeled 'analysis of variance'. Simple, multiple, hierarchical, moderated and mediated regressions were categorized as 'linear regression techniques'. Other categorizations were as follows: the 'non-parametric techniques and interpretive analysis' group included procedures such as descriptive statistics, content analysis, validity tests, and casual mapping. The 'linear techniques for categorical dependent variables' group included logistic regressions and probit analysis. The 'factor analytic and clustering technique' group included confirmatory factor analysis and discriminate analysis. 'Multiple levels of analysis' included hierarchical linear modeling and within and between analysis. 'Structural equation modeling and path analytic procedures' are combined into one group, as are 'time series and event analysis procedures'. The above examples are illustrative in nature. Moreover, other analytical techniques (e.g. meta-analysis, simulations, policy capturing, co-integration analysis, and variance decomposition) were not grouped into any broader categories. Other techniques that were either seldom used (e.g. Iterative Kolmogorov-Smirnov (IKS) analysis, stochastic frontier estimation, and the Del Method) or that did not fall into any of the above categories were classified as 'others'. Figure 18.2 provides a detailed description of each of these categories.

RESULTS

Trends in Strategic Management Research

In this section, we analyze the trends of strategy research based on our content analysis of articles appearing in the four-year intervals of 1990–1993, 1994–1997, 1998–2001, and 2002–2005. In general, the usage of quantitative methods has been predominant in strategy research and the usage of such methods has increased since the early 1990s (Table 18.1). For instance, in the early 1990s, quantitative methodologies accounted for 81 percent of all research and this proportion rose to 93 percent in the last period considered. In contrast, the use of qualitative research declined

Analysis of variances	Regressions	Techniques for categorical dependent variables	Meta-analysis	Non-parametric techniques & interpretive analysis	Factor analysis and clustering techniques
ANOVA	Simple/ multiple	Logistic regression	Meta-analysis	Comparison of means	Exploratory/ Confirmatory
MANOVA	Hierarchical	Binary logit		MTMM	Discriminant analysis
MANCOVA	Moderated/ Mediated	Binary probit		Analysis of maps	Clustering
T-test	2SLS	Multinomial logit		Cross-tab regression	
F-test	3SLS	Multinomial probit		Validity test	
	Partial least squares	Ordered logit		Co-plot Methods	
	Maximum likelihood estimation	Binomial logistic regression		Chow test	
	Seemingly Unrelated Regression Estimator	Negative binomial regression		Pooled distance matrix	
	Generalized Least Squares	Tobit model		Casual mapping	
	Least Absolute Deviation	Ordered probit		Descriptive Statistics	
		Poisson		Content analysis	
				Cross-tabulation	
				Smallest space analysis	
				Data envelopment analysis	

Figure 18.2   Framework for analytical techniques

Structural equation modeling / path analysis	Time series / event analysis	Multiple level of analysis	Simul-ation	Conjoint analysis/ policy capturing	Variance composi-tion	Others
SEM	Survival analysis	Hierarchical linear modeling	Computer simulation	Conjoint analysis	Variance decom-position	IKS
	Event history analysis	Within and between analysis	Monte Carlo	Policy capturing		UCINETIV
	MLR event time regression	Within group analysis				Stochastic Frontier Estimation
		Simul-taneous equation estimation				The Del Method
		Bayesian hierarchical model				

Table 18.1   Trend of empirical approaches

Empirical approach[1][2]	1990–1993	1994–1997	1998–2001	2002–2005	Total
Quantitative only	81%	85%	88%	93%	87%
Qualitative only	17%	13%	12%	7%	12%
Both	1.8%	2.1%	0.5%	0.4%	1.1%

Notes:
1   Aggregate information includes empirical analysis only
2   n=175 (1990–1993), 196 (1994–1997), 209 (1998–2001), and 233 (2002–2005)

Table 18.2   Trend of data collection

Research strategy[1][2]	1990–1993	1994–1997	1998–2001	2002–2005	Total
Sample survey	24.5%	25.3%	37.2%	26.7%	28.6%
Field study					
Primary (i.e. interviews)	3.5%	5.4%	5.5%	6.5%	5.4%
Secondary (i.e. archival)	72.7%	78.3%	67.2%	77.9%	74.2%
Experiments and simulations	7.0%	2.4%	0.5%	1.8%	2.7%

Notes:
1   Aggregate information includes empirical analysis only
2   n=143 (1990–1993), 166 (1994–1997), 183 (1998–2001), 217 (2002–2005)

Table 18.3   Trend of research time frames

Time frame[1][2]	1990–1993	1994–1997	1998–2001	2002–2005	Total
Longitudinal	35.7%	36.7%	43.2%	41.9%	39.8%
Cross-sectional	62.9%	62.7%	56.3%	56.7%	59.2%

Notes:
1   Aggregate information includes empirical analysis only
2   n=143 (1990–1993), 166 (1994–1997), 183 (1998–2001), 217 (2002–2005)

from 17 percent in the early 1990s to only 7 percent in the period of 2002–2005. Interestingly, the usage of both quantitative/qualitative methods in individual articles also declined from 1.8 percent in the early 1990s to only 0.4 percent in the final period considered.

Strategy research has relied mostly on secondary data: When we consider the entire 16-year time frame, archival sources made up approximately 75 percent of the total, and this figure did not vary significantly

Table 18.4   Trend of multiple/single analytical techniques

	1990–1993	1994–1997	1998–2001	2002–2005	Total
Single methods	84.6%	80.1%	79.8%	76.5%	79.8%
Multiple methods	15.4%	19.9%	20.2%	23.5%	20.2%

across the four time intervals. In contrast, sample surveys remained the next most used source of data, averaging 29 percent of the total and peaking at 37 percent in the period 1998–2001. Other less recurring sources of data were field studies and interviews (5 percent of total), as well as experiments and simulations (3 percent of total). Finally, the proportion of research that employed longitudinal datasets has increased since the early 1990s, going from roughly 36 percent to 42 percent in the period 2002–2005.

Analytical Approaches

Turning our attention to the statistical techniques adopted by strategy researchers, our findings indicate that linear regression techniques have been the dominant approach in strategy work. In fact, their use has increased from 34 percent in the early 1990s to 46 percent in the period 2002–2005. In comparison, the use of other methods such as analysis of variance, non-parametric and interpretive analysis, and factor analytic and clustering techniques has steadily declined over time, going from 20 percent to 14 percent, from 16 percent to 6 percent, and from 14 percent to 4 percent, respectively in the same time window. Similarly, the use of simple correlation coefficient analyses as a direct hypothesis-testing technique has declined from 8 percent during the early 1990s to zero in more recent times. The use of methods that account for imperfect measurement of strategic constructs (i.e. EFA, CFA) and specialized designs (analysis of maps, smallest space analysis) has decreased from 19 percent to 3 percent in the latest time period.

Our analysis continues with the incidence of regression analyses characterized by a discrete dependent variable, such as logit and probit models, Poisson regressions, and negative binomial regressions. The findings show a strong increase in these techniques from a mere 6 percent during the early 1990s to about 28 percent during the period of 2002–2005. Furthermore, advanced techniques that measure choices or changes over time such as event history analysis doubled from 7 percent in the early 1990s to 14 percent in the latest period. Lastly, other complex econometric methods, aimed at uncovering casual relationships such as simultaneous equations

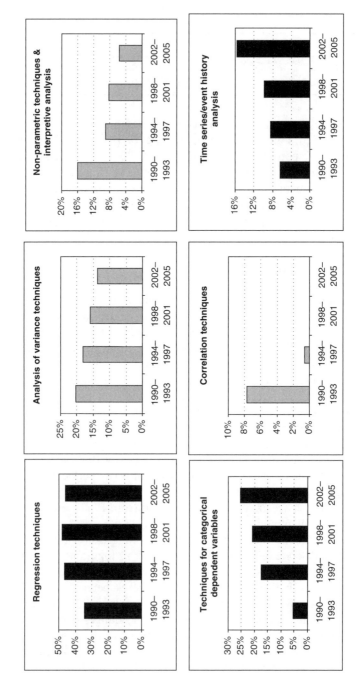

Non-parametric techniques & interpretive analysis

Time series/event history analysis

Analysis of variance techniques

Correlation techniques

Regression techniques

Techniques for categorical dependent variables

388

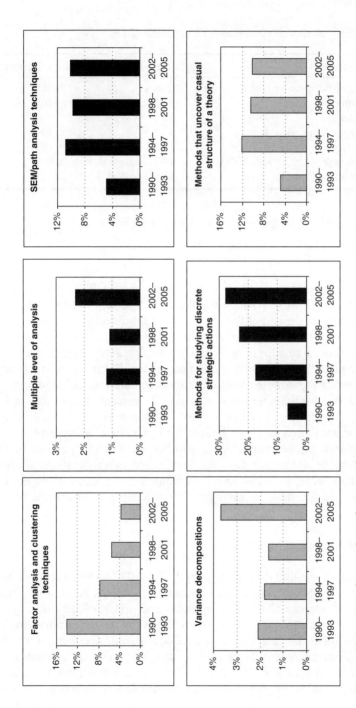

Figure 18.3   Trend in analytical approaches

Table 18.5   Research strategies for the period of 1995–1997

Research strategy[1]	Strategy[2]	General management[3]
Formal theory/literature review	20.69%	18.70%
Sample survey	18.23%	3.60%
Field study		
Primary (i.e. interviews)	5.91%	40.90%
Secondary (i.e. archival)	51.72%	26.60%
Judgment task	1.97%	20.00%
Experiments and simulations	1.48%	10.00%

Notes:
1   Aggregate information includes all conceptual and empirical analysis
2   n=203
3   Source: Scandura & Williams (2000), n=411

models, seemingly unrelated regression estimation (SURE), and structural equation modeling (SEM) have doubled from 5 percent to 10 percent from the beginning to the end of the 16 years we considered.

Aside from the changes in the use of analytical techniques that we outlined above, the adoption of multiple analytical techniques in a single research project has also become commonplace. For instance, while only 15 percent of the sample employed multiple analytical techniques in the early 1990s, this number rises to about 24 percent during the period 2002–2005. Additional analysis reveals that in most cases, studies that rely on more than a single technique for hypothesis testing tend to pair linear regression techniques with another method (63 percent of the total). Among all the pairings with linear regression techniques, analysis of variance techniques and linear techniques for categorical dependent variables are the most recurring, at 39 percent and 26 percent of the total.

Strategy vs. General Management Research

Table 18.6 shows that during the period 1995–1997, strategy research had a higher reliance on archival data and sample surveys, and less emphasis on experiments, simulations, judgments, and primary field studies than general management research. Around half of the strategy studies employ archival data as the data source, compared with only one fourth for those of general management studies, while sample surveys are the next most widely used method (i.e. 18 percent). This last figure is quite large compared to general management research, as sample surveys account for only

Table 18.6   Time frame of studies for the period of 1995–1997

Time frame[1]	Strategy[2]	General management[3]
Cross-sectional	58.14%	85.60%
Longitudinal	41.86%	14.40%

Notes:
1   Aggregate information includes empirical analysis only
2   n=129
3   Source: Scandura & Williams (2000), n=334

Table 18.7   Data analytical approaches for the period of 1995–1997

Analytical procedure[1]	Strategy[2]	General management[3]
Analysis of variance techniques	17.05%	13.80%
Regression techniques	48.06%	42.40%
Correlation techniques	0.78%	1.80%
Meta-analysis	0%	0.60%
Techniques for categorical dependent variables	17.05%	6.90%
Non-parametric/interpretive techniques	8.53%	11.10%
Factor analysis/clustering techniques	6.98%	5.10%
Structural equation/path analysis techniques	11.63%	8.70%
Time series/event history techniques	9.30%	7.50%
Multiple level of analysis	0.78%	1.80%
Computer simulation techniques	0.78%	0.30%
Variance composition	2.33%	0%

Notes:
1   Aggregate information includes empirical analysis only
2   n=129
3   Source: Scandura & Williams (2000), n=334

around 4 percent of research studies during this time period, as reported by Scandura and Williams (2000). Additionally, although over one fourth of general management research relies on experiments, simulations, and judgment tasks, less than 5 percent of strategy research uses these data-gathering approaches. When comparing our findings with Scandura and Williams' in the corresponding time frame, it is interesting to note that 42 percent of the strategy research employs a longitudinal sample, compared to just 14 percent of general management research (see Table 18.7).

Table 18.8   Data analytical approaches for the period of 1995–1997

Analytical procedure[1]	Strategy[2]	General management[3]
Analysis of variance techniques	17.05%	13.80%
Linear regression techniques	48.06%	42.40%
Correlation techniques	0.78%	1.80%
Meta-analysis	0%	0.60%
Linear techniques for categorical dependent variables	17.05%	6.90%
Non-parametric/interpretive techniques	8.53%	11.10%
Factor analytic/clustering techniques	6.98%	5.10%
Structural equation/path analytic techniques	11.63%	8.70%
Time series/event history techniques	9.30%	7.50%
Multiple level of analysis	0.78%	1.80%
Computer simulation techniques	0.78%	0.30%
Variance composition	2.33%	0%

Notes:
1   Aggregate information includes empirical analysis only
2   n=129
3   Source: Scandura & Williams (2000), n=334

Analytical Approaches

Turning our attention to the several methodologies employed by strategy research vis-à-vis general management work, the results show that the strategy studies have a greater adoption rate of linear regression techniques and structural equation/path analytical techniques, whereas general management studies use non-parametric and interpretive analysis to a greater extent (see Table 18.8). However, there do not appear to be significant differences in usage of linear regression techniques (i.e. 48 percent for strategy and 42 percent for general management), although linear techniques for categorical dependent variables are more widely used in strategy research than in general management research (17 versus 7 percent respectively).

Time series and event studies, which rely on time-dependent estimation, are more widely used in strategy research (12 percent) than in general management research (8 percent), and variance decomposition techniques, while not frequently used in strategy work (i.e., 2.3 percent) are not at all present in general management research.

DISCUSSION

The results of our survey highlight the key developments experienced by quantitative strategy research over time, as well as offering interesting differences between this area of research and the broader management field. First, we show that secondary archival data have been the predominant source of data throughout the 16-year window we cover. In contrast, research in general management has tended to rely on primary data (e.g. interviews), experiments, and simulations to a much greater extent. Snow and Thomas (1994) predicted that the use of mixed data sources, such as field research methods, archival data, interviews, and sample surveys/ questionnaires will continue to be used heavily in developing and testing new strategy theories. It has also been suggested that the internet will enhance researchers' ability to conduct experiments and sample surveys through virtual exercises and web-based surveys (Scandura and Williams, 2000). Although we do not directly test the veracity of these predictions, our results show that the effects of the internet have not resulted in a higher incidence of experimentation and sample surveys in strategy research. This finding might be explained in part based on the inherent challenges of capturing firm-level constructs by way of field experiments and surveys (Hitt et al., 1998).

Although it was predicted that the combined usage of qualitative/ quantitative data approaches would increase over time (Hitt et al., 1998), as the richness of qualitative data has the potential to complement other sources of data (e.g. Lee, 1999), our results run counter to these predictions. We suspect that this finding can be explained by the abundance of readily available archival data that can be applied to quantitative methods. In contrast, qualitative data is often time-consuming to gather (Miles, 1979), it lacks standard protocols and its interpretation tends to be subject to uncertainty (Barr, 2004; Miles, 1979). It is also possible that authors use combined data collection approaches in their research yet choose to present findings in separate articles focused on either quantitative or qualitative data.

Turning to longitudinal data, the findings demonstrate that strategy research has utilized longitudinal datasets more frequently than has general management research. We suspect that this difference is the result of the greater need for strategy work to capture spurious and environmental effects that can affect firms' choices and outcomes (Carmer and Fahey, 1995; Rumelt and Wensley, 1981). This sort of unobserved heterogeneity can be difficult to account for using cross-sectional data (Hitt et al., 1998), and might at least partially explain our result.

Since the adoption of longitudinal data, research in strategy has also increasingly utilized a number of more dynamic and more sophisticated analytical methods in general over the past two decades. While prior work had argued that strategy work had placed excessive emphasis on cross-sectional data and simple regression techniques (Hill and Hansen, 1992; Lubatkin and Chatterjee, 1991; Camerer and Fahey, 1985), the field has clearly made a turn in recent years: we report a marked increase in the use of time series econometrics, discrete choice models, methods that uncover the casual structure of relationships, and methods that account for imperfect measurement of constructs. This trend is consistent with the guidance put forth by Hitt et al. (1998), and it has begun to address Bergh's (1995) criticism that strategy research does not sufficiently capture temporal dimensions that are inherent in longitudinal relationships.

We also report an increase in the use of nonlinear models aimed at the study of firms' discrete choices, such as logistic regression, multinomial logit models, and Poisson or negative binomial regressions. These approaches have become more commonplace thanks in part to the greater availability of fine-grained data on strategic actions (Hitt et al., 1998). Moreover, our results point to a higher usage of methods that uncover the casual structure of the relationships between variables, which include path analysis techniques, structural equation modeling, and seemingly unrelated regression estimation (SURE). The trend in the usage of these methods, especially structural equation modeling, has slightly increased since the early 1990s. However, there has been a negligible change in the adoption of these methods in the latter part of our sample, and this might be explained by some of the complexity inherent in these methods (Shook et al., 2004). However, as researchers become more adept at using these approaches, we expect that this trend will increase, as these methods have the potential to provide better theoretical understanding of newer relationships between firms' discrete choices, underlying factors, and outcomes (Hitt et al., 1998).

While this study provides a comprehensive survey of the quantitative methodologies adopted by strategy research during 1990–2005, there are some limitations that are important to note. First, as with any research that requires coding and judgment, there exists the potential for errors in the process of categorizing the research, particularly since a single coder was used for this chapter. As noted previously, we have sought to be consistent with prior work and as objective as possible in our approach. Furthermore, the narrow scope of our survey vis-à-vis previous similar studies reduces the potential for errors in classifying each research article we examined. However, despite our efforts, we recognize that some subjective judgment had to be made through the process, and these steps might increase the possibility of errors. Second, it is important to consider that the shifts in methodological practices we report may be driven by factors other than developments in the literature per se (doctoral education, tenure requirements, and so on). However, as a first analysis of recent trends in strategy research, our work highlights the important advances that empirical research in strategy has witnessed. In the future, as scholars draw from better data sources and continue to adopt increasingly more sophisticated methodological techniques, we expect that more light will be shed on firms' strategies and their competitive advantages.

CONCLUSION

This chapter discusses the developments in the usage of quantitative methodologies in competitive strategy research published in the *Strategic Management Journal* over the past 16 years. In essence, our analysis reveals that while linear regression has been the dominant approach in competitive strategy research, there has been an increasing use of more novel and advanced techniques, such as survival analysis, structural equation modeling, and binomial regressions. We have also found that research papers tend to draw more from multiple analytical techniques than they used to in the earlier period we investigate. On the contrary, more descriptive statistical tools such as correlation coefficient analyses, analysis of variance, and non-parametric and interpretive analysis have been on the decline. Finally, our data and results suggest that strategy research has continued to draw from archival data at an increasing pace over the time period we consider, which has in turn facilitated studies conducted on a larger scale and with greater statistical power. We attribute this trend both to the enhanced availability and reliability of such data, as well as to the tradeoffs that using qualitative data sources present for academics in our area of research.

Although the primary purpose of our work is to present the facts of how strategy research has evolved over time, and not draw causal inferences or judgments, we consider most of the findings we report to be positive for the field. Many of the tools that have been introduced to strategy research have helped scholars to ask a broader set of questions and explore them empirically with much greater depth and precision. We expect strategy research to continue to build upon its knowledge base in a similar fashion in the future.

REFERENCES

Barr, P. (2004), 'Current and potential importance of qualitative methods in strategy research', in D.J. Ketchen and D.D. Bergh (eds), *Research Methodology in Strategy and Management*, Oxford, UK: Elsevier.

Bergh, D.D. (1995), 'Problems with repeated measures analysis: demonstration with a study of the diversification and performance relationship', *Academy of Management Journal*, **38**, 1692–1708.

Camerer, C. and L. Fahey (1985), 'The regression paradigm: a critical appraisal and suggested directions', in J. Grant (ed.), *Significant Developments in Business Policy Research*, Greenwich, CT: JAI Press.

Gulati, R., P.R. Lawrence and P. Puranam (2005), 'Adaptation in vertical relationships: beyond incentive conflict', *Strategic Management Journal*, **26** (5), 415–440.

Hill, C.W.L. and G.S. Hansen (1991), 'A longitudinal study of cause and consequences of changes in diversification in the US pharmaceutical industry 1977–1986', *Strategic Management Journal*, **12**, 187–199.

Hitt, M.A., J. Gimeno and R.E. Hoskisson (1998), 'Current and future research methods in strategic management', *Organizational Research Methods*, **1** (1), 6–44.

Lee, T. (ed.) (1999), *Using Qualitative Methods in Organizational Research*, Thousand Oaks, CA: Sage.

Lubatkin, M.H. and S. Chatterjee (1991), 'The strategy–shareholder value relationship: testing temporal stability across market cycles', *Strategic Management Journal*, **12**, 251–270.

McGrath, E.J. (1981), 'The study of research choices and dilemmas', *American Behavioral Scientist*, **25** (2), 179–210.

Miles, M.B. (1979), 'Qualitative data as an attractive nuisance: the problem of analysis', *Administrative Science Quarterly*, **24** (4), 590–601.

Rumelt, R.P. and R. Wensley (1981), 'In search of the market share effect', *Academy of Management Proceedings*, 2–6.

Scandura, T.A. and E.A. Williams (2000), 'Research methodology in management: current practices, trends, and implications for future research', *Academy of Management Journal*, **43** (6), 1248–1264.

Shook, C.L., D.J. Ketchen, T.M. Hult and K.M. Kacmar (2004), 'An assessment of the use of structural equation modeling in strategic management research', *Strategic Management Journal*, **25** (4), 397–401.

Snow, C.C. and J.B. Thomas (1994), 'Field research methods in strategic management: contributions to theory building and testing', *Journal of Management Studies*, **31** (4), 457–480.

Wiersema, M.F. and H.P. Bowen (1997), 'Empirical methods in strategy research: regression analysis and the use of cross-section versus pooled time-series, cross-section data', in M. Ghertman, J. Obadia and J.L. Arregle (eds), *Statistical Models for Strategic Management*, Dordrecht, Netherlands: Kluwer Academic Publishers, pp. 201–220.

Williams, L.J., M.B. Gavin and N.S. Hartman (2004), 'Structural equation modeling methods in strategy research: applications and issues', in D.J. Ketchen and D.D. Bergh (eds), *Research Methodology in Strategy and Management*, Oxford, UK: Elsevier.

19 Semiotic methods and the meaning of strategy in firm annual reports

Maria Cristina Cinici and Roger L. M. Dunbar

This chapter explores the reasons why the research methods inspired by semiotics, i.e. the study of the principles of signification (Saussure, 1916), can be conceived as useful tools in the field of competitive strategy.[1] It specifically concerns written strategy, although we are aware that semiotics is interested in every kind of text (both oral and written) and applies "in any system of signs, whatever their substance and limits; images, gestures, musical sounds, objects, and the complex associations of all of these, which form the content of ritual, convention or public entertainment. These constitute, if not *languages*, at least systems of signification" (Barthes, 1967: 9).

This research analyses written competitive strategy as it is described in firms' annual reports to shareholders.

Annual reports provide updates on firm activities and results over a specific time period and deliver information about what a firm has achieved, what it is trying to achieve, and how it is going about achieving it. They do so by presenting a letter by the chairperson explaining the firm's behavior, financial reports, discussions and analyses of these reports, and general information about the firm's facilities and activities.

An annual report is intended to help shareholders figure out firm strategy as well as monitor and assess the agency relationship that they have with the firm's board of directors and top management (Jensen and Meckling, 1976). Top management prepares an annual report to satisfy a legal requirement and to persuade shareholders that, as agents, the board of directors and the firm's managers have pursued a firm strategy that served shareholder interests as well as possible. The legal requirement and the agency relationship both affect the strategy information included in annual reports. Beyond these influences, however, there are also many opportunities for top managers to decide what strategy information they want to present in annual reports and how they present it.

By approving the firm's annual report, shareholders affirm the strategy taken by their agents, the firm's board of directors and top management, and implicitly endorse their future plans for the firm. In fact, until shareholders approve the firm's annual report, they have not reconfirmed the agency relationship. Aware of this, a firm's board of directors and top managers usually prepare annual reports carefully and then depict the approval process as something that everyone should take for granted. Yet, should shareholders automatically accept the annual report and so confirm the competitive strategy taken by the firm's board and top management? How confident should one be that the annual report will include the strategy information needed to understand the condition of the firm? To the extent matters are controversial, are annual reports likely to explain the whole firm strategy, or are they likely to skim over some issues and frame them in ways intended to gain shareholder endorsement? To the extent that firm annual reports omit information or include misleading information, a semiotic analysis examining strategy signification processes is expected to be able to identify where, why and how this is likely to occur.

We shall use both generative (Barthes, 1964; Greimas, 1966) and interpretive semiotics (Peirce, 1931; Eco, 1976) to explain strategy communication and explore the annual report content and presentation choices and consider the implications. The structural frameworks developed by Greimas (1966, 1970) help uncover the underlying forces and the associated oppositions that influence the content of annual report messages. The frameworks developed by Saussure (1916) help explain how various narrative structures make situations more understandable. The frameworks developed by Barthes (1964, 1966) show how word use and framing make narratives more convincing, while the semiotics of Peirce (1931) and Eco (1976, 1984b) help to explain how people interpret the strategy information presented to them. In this chapter, we discuss how these theoretical ideas influence annual report content and firm strategy presentation and propose issues open for future research.

COMMUNICATING FIRM STRATEGY THROUGH LANGUAGE AND NARRATIVE

Firm annual reports contain a mission statement and a strategic vision (Fisher, 1984) and explain and justify the competitive strategy the firm is pursuing (D'Aveni and MacMillan, 1990; Salancik and Meindl, 1984). Appearing at regular and predetermined intervals and describing firm behavior and performance over a specific time period for shareholders, investors, and others (Bettman and Weitz, 1983), annual reports constitute an institutionalized source of information about firm strategy.

Somewhere in the annual report, managers usually describe firm strategy by constructing a narrative to portray what firms have done and achieved over the past year (Czarniawska, 1997; Mazza, 1999; Segars and

Kohut, 2001). A narrative includes a sequenced set of events (Pentland, 1999) built around an underlying plot that has sufficient continuity to ensure that the significance of each event is clear. The narrative explains, for example, what the firm was trying to do at the beginning of the year, how situations then developed, and what the situation was at the end of the year. The narrative construction is around a plot that depicts the interplay over time of two sets of entities, i.e., the firm's actions (its strategy) and environmental events (the actions of competitors, the effects of government policies, technological developments, and so forth). These entities mutually affect each other over time and the narrative presents top management's views concerning how this process occurred, and what the consequences are.

Discussions in annual reports provide top managers with an opportunity to formally address the issues they believe are or should be of interest to shareholders and so they are not simply ceremonial. The firm strategy presented in an annual report is a constructed account that identifies what management believes are significant events and issues and how they are linked by causes and ends (Barthes, 1953). The account will explain how the firm has taken various initiatives and has dealt with various struggles between counteracting forces. It often culminates in a summary of how things stand at the end of the particular year (Greimas, 1970). The particular plot line clarifies the top management's perspective on the struggle and generates expectations for shareholders in terms of ongoing developments and likely conclusions. By being built around a plot, a narrative is easier for shareholders to comprehend (Bremond, 1966).

In presenting firm strategy as a constructed narrative in an annual report, management chooses between two forms: the personal and the apersonal (Barthes, 1966). If annual reports adopt the apersonal form, the narrative is presented in the third person, e.g., "The firm achieved...," and the firm's strategy will be constructed as if it was something objective even though it is still management's account and interpretation (Barthes, 1953). A choice of the apersonal form may be important, however, because it implies an agency relationship not only between shareholders and top management, but also directly between top managers and the firm and, implicitly, these two agency relationships oppose one another. That is, while shareholders supposedly oversee top managers, they are also dependent on the account that top managers prepare in order to understand the firm. By choosing the apersonal form, top managers communicate that they not only have an agency relationship with the firm but also that shareholders depend upon their superior knowledge to manage their agency relationship (Salancik and Meindl, 1984). Through using the apersonal form, then, top managers implicitly raise questions about whether there is any supervising power available to shareholders in their legal agency relationship with top managers. In other words, is the principal a principal, and the agent an agent?[2]

If top management adopts the personal presentation form, in contrast, they directly confirm their agency relationship with shareholders (Pentland, 1999). Accounts can then report not only on how top management has directed the firm to act, explore and achieve on behalf of shareholders, but also top managers can personalize their account mentioning thoughts, reactions and interpretations they have had in response to unfolding events while fulfilling their agency responsibilities (Chase, 2005). They may report, for example, how they were disappointed in particular outcomes and they may mention the motivations that led to particular strategy decisions (Propp, 1958). By including top managers' reactions to events and their motivations for the future, texts not only confirm the agency relationship but also present a more personal, vivid and motivated account of what occurred than is possible using the apersonal form.

Having chosen a plot and a presentational form, managers then use annual reports to achieve the following (Barthes, 1967).

1. To fix shareholder perceptions of firm strategy. If shareholders could observe firm behavior, they would choose which actions and/or decisions they would look at (Barthes, 1964). But because shareholders can neither see the strategy a firm pursues nor know what is important, they rely on top management to tell them. Annual reports oblige by encouraging shareholders to focus upon the actions and decisions top management considers important, e.g. the report might focus on the implications for the firm of entering foreign markets or participating in a new joint venture. The intent in an annual report is to focus and fix shareholder attention on the events that top management thinks are important.
2. To broadly inform shareholders about strategic decisions and actions that may be taken that will affect or change the firm. This is because the mark of a good agent is not to surprise their principal – the shareholders. Hence, top management discusses in broad terms the strategic decisions and changes that are under consideration so that shareholders do not feel surprised if and when such actions are taken (Hambrick and Finkelstein, 1987).
3. To explain why things are going to develop in specific ways, thereby establishing management's strategic understanding and ability to exercise control in the minds of shareholders. This situation occurs when management predicts how specific firm actions will cause certain events (Weiner, 1979). Annual reports can explain, for example, how and why (a) a locus of causality is internal or external to a firm, (b)

whether this cause is stable over time, and (c) whether and how firm management can control this causal factor. Such pieces of information keep shareholders informed of the issues top management is dealing with and of the control levers that it has access to.

4. To explain the wider environment to shareholders and the implications of this for what the firm can and must do. As there is a gap between shareholder expectations and actual firm behavior, top management must justify and explain current competitive strategies that have not led to desired results (Staw et al., 1983) and this usually brings up consideration of developments in the broader environment along with their implications. Managers construct explanations using labels, for example, to identify and classify events as problems, threats or opportunities, and to characterize the firm as having specific strengths that enable logical responses to these events. Such accounts provide content and language to talk about the firm's situation (D'Aveni and MacMillan, 1990).

5. To explain transformational organizational changes and, in particular, decisions to change or abandon institutionalized and taken-for-granted structures, e.g. why it makes sense to relocate a head office to a new city, for example (Palmer et al., 2004). Such accounts will usually emphasize the particular firm needs that the transformational change will deal with and how this action is in the shareholders' best interests. It will most likely explain matters in terms of being steps that further shareholders' interests irrespective of what may be happening in the external environment, further attempting to confirm appropriate agency behavior.

6. To highlight specific actions that top management believes are particularly valuable at the present time for current strategic decision-making, e.g. an important acquisition, the reduction of firm debt. By stressing how specific steps have immediate current impact, reports imply top management is aware of and dealing with current concerns. If a firm launches new products, for example, then if top managers provide no further explanation, shareholders may think that product launches are routine events. But if top management highlights why a particular product family introduction is strategically significant, by implication, additional new product introductions may also have strategic significance to shareholders.

7. To confirm, in the minds of shareholders, a sense for top management's expertise, competence and effectiveness (Pfeffer, 1981). This is most often done by signaling institutional status. Members of top management may mention positions that imply, for example, that they are highly capable and widely respected. Annual reports may also

touch upon issues like corporate governance, fiduciary responsibilities, and the regulations the firm must comply with in terms of accounting and financial controls, again to emphasize top management's knowledge and concern for shareholder interests (Salancik and Meindl, 1984). Another way top managers confirm positive expectations about their competence is by taking credit for positive events while eschewing blame for negative events. Top managers also stay very realistic and do not make reckless promises or do other things that would raise unrealistic expectations. While annual reports can imply many things, they do not usually directly lie (Bettman and Weitz, 1983).

As concerns structuralist semiotics, therefore, the intent of the annual report is not only to inform shareholders about firm strategy and what has happened to the firm, but also to avoid leaving strategy and past courses of action open to additional shareholder interpretation. Rather, the report endeavors to direct shareholders' attention to particular strategic actions and decisions that top management believes are important. The choice of a particular plot and presentational format establishes top management's perspective and its view of the relationship with shareholders. Through the annual report, the aim is to persuade shareholders to adopt and endorse top management's understanding of the firm's strategy.

SIGNIFYING FIRM STRATEGY IN THE SEMIOTIC SQUARE

While a variety of ideas and perspectives are presented in annual reports depicting firm strategy, the reporting task itself takes place in a specific institutional context, i.e. shareholders have an agency relationship with the firm's top management and board of directors. As a consequence, while a variety of views may be presented in the annual report, the strategy presentation itself is constrained by the opposing forces that underlie and structure the agency relationship and the associated reporting task.[3] A structural analysis aims to reveal how given the agency relationship and reporting task, all strategy presentations will spring from a common grammar: "the content of the actions changes all the time, the actors vary, but the enunciation-spectacle remains always the same, for its permanence is guaranteed by the fixed distribution of the roles" (Greimas, 1966: 175).

This common and unchanging grammar – the deep structure underlying the annual report – is depicted by Figure 19.1, a semiotic square, which identifies the counteracting forces that underlie and guide reports

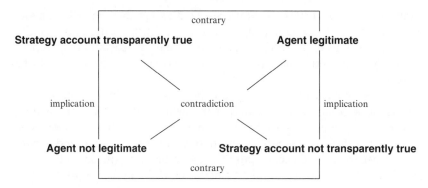

Figure 19.1   Semiotic square: the countervailing forces underlying firm annual report content

prepared in the context of the agency relationship between top management and shareholders (Greimas, 1966). In this depiction, the sender and reader of the report are excluded (Greimas, 1970). Two assumptions then underlie the construction of this semiotic square for identifying and assessing the content and strategy presentation of annual reports:

1. as the firm's annual report is generated by top management in their role as agents of shareholders, the aim of the report is to persuade the principals, i.e. the firm's shareholders, to accept the strategy of top management and so reconfirm top management and the board of directors as shareholder agents;
2. to support reconfirmation, top management claims that the strategy account in the annual report is transparent and true and, as agents for shareholders, they have behaved appropriately and legitimately. These 'oppositions' – an emphasis on a transparent and true account and agent legitimacy and appropriateness – are assumed to be the driving forces underlying the strategy content included in the firm's annual report.

The dominant positive value is a strategy account that is transparent and true, presenting all of the relevant facts concerning the firm. This value pole is located at the upper left corner of the square. Top management also seeks to communicate to shareholders that as agents, top managers have consistently acted appropriately and legitimately to further shareholder interests. This 'contrary' value that top management also seeks to communicate occupies the upper right corner of the square.[4] As well as the two contraries at the top of the semiotic square, the lower sections include contradictions of these two contraries, i.e. the 'agents are not legitimate' and the 'strategy account is not transparently true'. These possibilities occupy positions in the square that are diagonal to the values they oppose and they imply additional possibilities concerning how strategy might be perceived.

One can unpack the semantic content possibilities by moving around the semiotic square and considering the fields of difference, opposition, and implication established by the opposing force structures. Each side of the semiotic square identifies alternative values for annual report truth and transparency and agent legitimacy and reliability, and so each defines an alternative scenario that might emerge, embedding the report. Starting from the top and the upper left pole, for example, the semiotic square maps four plausible scenarios for annual report content.

(a) At the top of the square, an annual report presents an account that explains firm strategy and the results it has achieved, and it depicts top managers as legitimate agents. As the firm's strategy makes sense and top managers have affirmed their commitments in support of shareholder interests, this should ensure shareholders' acceptance of the firm's annual report (Feldman and March, 1981). It is the 'expected and normal' situation that, ideally, can be taken for granted.

(b) On the left hand side of the square, while annual reports present a transparent strategic account, there may be doubts about the claim of agent legitimacy. Perhaps top managers are paid very high salaries and have other perks that go way beyond what most people enjoy. Even if the annual report account is true and transparent, by giving themselves outrageous rewards and benefits managers may at least appear to have behaved disrespectfully of shareholder interests. This may lead to questions about whether firm executives as agents support shareholder interests.

(c) At the bottom of the square, the annual report account is not considered true and transparent and top managers are not considered to have behaved appropriately and legitimately. In the 2008 sub-prime mortgage crisis, for example, top bank managers reported billions of dollars in write-offs, and then later wrote off still more billions even as many continued to be richly rewarded based on their compensation agreements. The semiotic square outlines the structure of this situation where shareholders are likely to expect resignations and firings, e.g. during the sub-prime crisis, many prominent banking CEOs either resigned or were forced to resign.

(d) On the right hand side of the square, top managers are perceived to have behaved appropriately and consistently, but the strategy account is not perceived to be true and transparent, i.e. for some reason it lacks credibility. Perhaps disclosures are missing, or perhaps the firm strategy explanations seem inconsistent with assessments in the media made by analysts or commentators and available to shareholders. These are grounds for questioning the annual report and its message.

(e)   The diagonal lines in Figure 19.1 represent direct contradictions in the values underlying the annual report message. Fiol (1989: 284) argued, however, that any meaning emerging from contradictions is necessarily unstable. One cannot conceive of how a 'transparent and true account' and a 'not transparent and true account,' for example, could meaningfully co-exist for very long. Rather, the contradiction will be resolved so that the report is considered to be either transparent and true, or not transparent and not true and so these contradictions do not generate meaningful scenarios.

This specific semiotic square is a structure of immanence rather than manifestation, i.e. its terms – its value poles – are established prior to when the firm strategy is communicated rather than becoming perceptible based on an analysis of the words actually used in the annual report. The immanence structure reflects the agency relationship of top management and the board of directors with shareholders. The structure then defines the values influencing the communication content and presentation that takes place between top management and shareholders. Any communication that is a manifestation of the underlying agency relationship, e.g. an annual report, will reflect the same opposing value poles (Greimas, 1966).

To understand strategy as it is described in annual reports, then, is not merely to follow the content of the communicated accounts. It is also to recognize that in constructing such accounts, there is an implicit vertical axis, the relation between agent and principal that necessarily mediates everything reported. One moves from the surface level, i.e. the level of the narrative reporting developments in the firm over the year, to the deep level, i.e. the level of strategy signification, where the opposing forces center around top management's fundamental task of gaining and retaining shareholder belief and trust (Greimas, 1966). Seen from this perspective, the annual report to shareholders is necessarily a mediated and not an objective account. The strategy report is constructed at óne level to tell shareholders what has happened but due to the agency relationship, the content at another level is managed so as to be pleasing to shareholders, to generate their trust and gain their approval, in order to secure reconfirmation of the agency relationship.

READING AND INTERPRETING COMPETITIVE STRATEGY

While the semiotic square outlines various potential scenarios that may be generated by communications, the readers of the annual report – the shareholders – determine the strategy communication that is actually accomplished. While top management attempts to influence and satisfy shareholder expectations in the way that they construct the strategy presentation, shareholders as readers then make up their minds about the communication.

In reading annual reports, shareholders assess the verisimilitude of the strategic narrative (Bruner, 1986). Specifically, does the story ring true in terms of what the firm has done in the past, in terms of what this management team has promised, and in terms of what has been reported about the firm and its strategy in the media? In terms of agent legitimacy and appropriateness, shareholders consider the institutional legitimacy of the symbols of social rank that are held by members of the board of directors and by top management. Most shareholders accord legitimacy to the top managers and directors whose background and experience include degrees from good universities, who have affiliations with institutionally accepted and powerful organizations, who have achieved exceptionally in a particular field, and who present themselves as free of any association with scandal.

Annual reports signal the truth and legitimacy of firm strategy in various ways. For example, they are announced in advance and then issued as promised on particular days by firm headquarters. Shareholders expect to see an annual report signed by the firm's chairman or CEO – the person who has primary responsibility for firm strategy. In practice, however, while a chairman or CEO may sometimes take up a pen and write the letter to shareholders, this is unusual. Even though the signature of the firm chairperson or CEO is there, the annual report is most often a product jointly developed by members of the top management team with the assistance of firm public relations experts. This is because an annual report constitutes an institutional rather than an individual communication (Bettman and Weitz, 1983; Staw et al., 1983). The question is whether readers of the annual report – shareholders, analysts and investors – will read and interpret firm strategy as it was intended to be understood. As they are aware not only of the content of the annual report but also of the implications of the underlying forces guiding top management's communication efforts, they will be aware of the mediation affecting the communication and hence how this necessarily has the potential to alter and distort messages contained in the annual report.

One of the main functions of the annual report is to describe and justify the firm's competitive strategy to shareholders and to explain the results actually achieved (Barry and Elmes, 1997; Brannen, 2004). Readers will have their own expectations about what the annual report should contain, however, so although the firm's strategic situation may be complex and may have developed on many dimensions, top management cannot include all of these details in an annual report. This is because what top management provides and what shareholders want to receive is a translation of the complex experiences that occurred for the firm over the past year into a predictably ordered, simplified, rational explanation so that what occurred can be easily understood. Managers as agents have to make the unfamiliar familiar by structuring the narrative contained in annual reports to make the firm strategy understandable, legitimate and familiar (Salancik and Leblebici, 1988).

Annual reports construct an image in readers' minds of a rational firm in a rational world that in fact includes agents and objects (spatial dimension) that change in ways that cannot be fully predicted due to unfolding events (temporal dimension). Consistently and unless otherwise explained, however, responses to these unfolding events are rational and in this sense subject to managerial control. Most often, then, the report uses narrative discourses to represent, explain and justify actions taken that imply appropriate managerial control. The narratives are usually temporally structured accounts – with a beginning, middle, and an end – complete with a sequence of events, central characters, organizational context, and a plot with crisis and resolutions (Czarniawska, 1997). They are structured accordingly around (a) the narrative subject, namely the firm strategy and what it seeks to do; (b) the ultimate object or goal of the narrative, such as profitability, growth, new business success and so on; always taking account of the targets of the annual reports, i.e. the shareholders.

Such a 'closed' annual report is an assemblage of familiar strategy meanings that shareholders expect to passively decipher and responsively accept as conventional practice. The closed report aims at eliciting 'obedient cooperation' from shareholders (Eco, 1984b), by imposing limits on what they can think about and furnishing readers with a report that reduces freedom to interpret (Barthes, 1966).

A closed report offers a limited range of strategy meaning leaving much unsaid, as shareholders are presented with and are then forced to accept a particular text. It can be conceived as a 'readerly' text in that the strategy and the explanation seem reasonable enough so shareholders as dependent consumers accept the account (Barthes, 1964). The report may offer a representation of the firm's image and identity (Dutton and Dukerich, 1991; Gioia and Thomas, 1996) emphasizing, for instance, the integrity of management, the community spirit management fosters, and so forth. It may also emphasize the role top management plays in making firm success possible, and it may explain the wider role that a firm plays in particular social contexts (Barley, 1983).

Generally, a closed report uses institutionalized symbols and artifacts to construct and signal the legitimacy of the firm as it is run by top management (Daft, 1983; Zott and Huy, 2007). For example, as new managers are appointed, an inauguration ceremony may highlight the importance of the event and reconfirm top management's legitimacy. A closed report also frames situations and the actions taken so as to imply that shareholder interests are consistent with broader social values. In discussing potentially controversial events such as CEO succession and other managerial changes, business divestments, plant closures and acquisitions (Smircich and Stubbart, 1985), the firm's priorities emphasizing increased shareholder value will be emphasized no matter what costs such actions may entail. Within a context emphasizing shareholder interests, such mediated communication facilitates targeted understanding and view acceptance. Readers soon recognize the framing that the annual report emphasizes and often, rightly, take it for granted their top management will always emphasize shareholder interests when explaining what they have done and as a result, as other perspectives are missing, the story provided is necessarily incomplete (Aldrich and Fiol, 1994).

Top management has wide latitude in determining an annual report's content and it is also their chance to explain the firm strategy in ways that convince shareholders of their views. For instance, top management might narrate the divestment of some firm activity as an attempt to focus only on businesses with high returns. Alternatively, the same divestment could be presented as an example of a policy to divest activities not related to the firm's core business. Just about any rationalization that uses institutionalized expressions like 'divestment', 'growth', 'concentration,' or 'core business' along with institutionalized arguments that relate them to shareholder interests will sound familiar and seem sensible to many shareholders, thus achieving verisimilitude. In contrast, anything not framed in a logical, rational manner using institutionalized expressions and logics is likely to sound unfamiliar and generate questions. One cannot report too much detail and too much about local conditions for this moves the annual report to the unfamiliar and this generates questions.

Annual reports can fail to convince and so leave shareholders feeling that based on the content, they must produce strategy meanings for themselves (Barthes, 1964). Various codes, the different circumstances that occasion the delivery of annual reports, and the initiatives displayed by readers in making presuppositions and abductions, all influence attributions of meaning (Eco, 1984b). As shareholders have doubts about the annual report, they use the information in it to confirm their doubts, so they are able to reinterpret and elaborate firm strategy on what has been presented. They can also reinterpret firm strategy by translating reported firm events and developing new understandings based on alternative values and emphases, different logics and assessment criteria (Eco, 1984b). Also as they read annual reports, readers can draw on their own experience to continually shift focus – and hence change the organizing principle around which they understand the firm. Such an interpretation process might generate merely a state of indeterminacy based on different meanings that contrast with the perspective on the firm presented by managers.

While readers cannot change the content of annual reports, they can raise questions about what annual reports encourage them to think (Eco, 1976). Shareholder interpretations of firm strategy can even contradict management's interpretations, as proposed in an annual report. Such challenges will probably also raise questions about the practical legitimacy of the top managers, themselves, and their commitment to shareholder interests, at least as shareholders understand these interests. As shareholders see management's activities as generating unfavorable outcomes and no compensating benefits, they will eventually consider firm strategy as undesirable, improper, and inappropriate and so top management tries to use communication to avoid such a state of affairs.

Shareholders expect that, in most annual reports, managers will make the firm's image explicit, and will stress or amplify a set of firm strategy directions that in fact they already know and expect. If expected directions or firm actions conceived as crucial are not in fact mentioned or discussed, or if events expected to occur do not in fact take place, an account lacks verisimilitude. Shareholders then create a strategy image of the firm for themselves. Sometimes the reports' narratives can even contradict the received image of the firm thereby producing in shareholders a compensatory firm strategy's connotation that is the result of a compromise.

While open and closed strategy reports represent two types of narrative structures, in reality the practice of generating and interpreting firm strategy represents a graded continuum of possible interaction between the maximal freedom and the most repressive conformity requests (Eco, 1984b).

FUTURE RESEARCH USING SEMIOTIC FRAMEWORKS

Writing and analyzing annual reports is a bit like writing and analyzing a theatrical play; there are two different schools of thought. On the one side, there is Aristotelian theatre, which obscures its own constructive rules and tends to present itself as a self-contained, objective set of sequenced events. On the other side, there is the Brechtian theatre, which reveals the efforts required to produce the scene uncovering the contrary forces, even lies, on which for centuries the Aristotelian theatre has been based but were hidden from view.

Firm strategy as it is reported in firm annual reports is comparable to Aristotelian theatre. A semiotic analysis of firm strategy leads, in contrast, to a more Brechtian analysis, a reconstruction of the semiotic character of the forces underlying firm strategy and a discovery of how these processes are constantly operating and play a continual role in transforming the way strategy is presented as factual evidence. In fact, even though the analysis focuses on sentences and utterances, the subject unfolds at two levels – one level is about the language, what is said and what it means, but the other level is about the agency relationships and obligations that underlie the processes of strategy communication and signification. The main result is that words accounting for firm strategy in annual reports are not just related to strategy. They also report actions to a specific and powerful audience in a formalized way. Accordingly, the research object is not simply to focus on the terminology used, but also on the code used and in particular, the firm strategy that it eventually signifies.

Actually, a scholar that semiotically scrutinizes firm strategy has to tackle both theoretical and practical hitches. The former is strictly related to the breadth of a semiotic enquiry. If semiotics wishes to find a place in the field of competitive strategy research complementing long-established research methods, it should be compatible with any other explorations of strategy signification. The latter reside in the potential receivers of semiotic research. The need for formalization and the stress on the uniqueness of the texts' concepts will appear as extremely qualitative to scholars who usually adopt traditional methods.

Nevertheless, as an objective and thorough method, semiotics has significant potential for future research on competitive strategy. First, it can broaden the perspectives currently pursued in the strategy field by complementing, methodologically speaking, popular quantitative methods and longitudinal field studies. The scholar who carries out a semiotic analysis of strategy does not consider measures that indicate strategic success from a shareholder's point of view. They will, of course, be there. From an epistemological point of view, his attention is focused on the presentation of firm strategy, which is affected by the agency relationship context. He or she defines the elements of the semiotic square as the basis of strategic discourses, analyzes their interrelations and emphasizes their consistencies so as to achieve both the formulation of an empirical method and the comprehension of the data. A semiotic analysis clarifies the strategic context and the competitive strategy choices that a firm wants readers of its reports to believe it is making.

In this respect, how the firm and the CEO present themselves in the annual report signals how the relationship between managers and share-holders is conceptualized and impacts strategy communication (Barthes, 1964; Eco, 1976). The agency relationship implies that top managers cannot manage unless shareholders express confidence in them as agents by accepting their strategy accounts. Depending on the language used, the annual report may suggest different types of relationship and may disclose more or less strategy information. For example, sometimes the letter is framed as a personal communication (a letter to shareholders might say I or we, for example, and it could address the sharehold-ers as 'you') or alternatively, it could use the third person to construct the whole of the strategic narrative ("the firm started the year. . . ."). Such framings highlight on the one hand, how managers exercise influ-ence over strategic decisions and have reactions to them and, on the other, they depict strategy as something that is objective and factual, as something that occurs and is monitored, rather than as something that is subject to direct managerial influence. That is, the framings reflect different ontological assumptions about how the nature of strategy is conceived (Fiol, 1989).

Second, semiotics provides insights concerning how annual reports should look, given they are mediated by an agency relationship. Semiotics offers the conceptual and practical tools to highlight the linguistic struc-tures upon which firm strategy communications are based and these are always mediated rather than objective (Eco, 1976). Semiotics is also crucial in discovering further mechanisms through which underlying structures may be concealed or transformed in obvious rules or in shared principles applied in particular situations. It helps to look at firm strategy not only as a way of investigating the surrounding world, but also as a discourse regarding the surrounding world, and like any discourses, as a corpus of concepts susceptible to analysis and deconstruction. Semiotics moves researchers' attention from conscious linguistic phenomena to the infrastructures that unconsciously managers apply to their discourses. A research on competitive strategy inspired by semiotics focuses on the specific way managers communicate and give sense to firm strategy. As a result, a semiotic research is always specific to the context in which the phenomenon occurs. The meanings managers attach to the words of letters to shareholders, though idiosyncratic, are then analyzed within an analytical framework, the semiotic square, which systematically supports further reflections and generalizations (Fiol, 1991).

Third, semiotics might help us to consider how readers eventually interpret the communicated strategy. Eco (1978 and 1984) reflected on the role that the structuralist perspective assigns to readers such as shareholders in interpreting texts. Our arguments have stressed that, as far as possible, management tries to control the meaning that shareholders attribute to strategy through annual reports. The deep structure shows how the context requires the text to converge on particular meanings. Nevertheless, each shareholder can interpret the annual report themselves as no text can be interpreted according to the utopia of a definite, original, and final authorized meaning (Eco, 1984b). According to this perspective, firm reports appear truly complex in that the results they deliver are ambiguous and, although the subject matter is technical, the readership is broad. The narrative conclusion can be neither deduced nor predicted (Ricoeur, 1981). The annual report's conclusion must be acceptable to shareholders. Given the many forces impinging on communications between top managers and shareholders, the understandings of a firm's experience that shareholders gain are probably at best plausible possibilities (Peirce, 1931).

NOTES

1. Semiotics was founded by Ferdinand de Saussure (1916), who conceived it as the mother of linguistics, and by Charles Sanders Peirce (1931), who saw semiotics as a philosophical field related to logic. The result has been alternative and complementary perspectives: structural semiotics (Barthes, 1964) extended to generative semiotics as proposed by Algirdas Greimas (1966 and 1983), and interpretive semiotics developed by Umberto Eco (1976). The two perspectives share an interest in signs and signification. They differ in that generative semiotics focuses on the structures underlying communication, while interpretive semiotics focuses on how people ascertain meaning by examining gaps between messages received and messages sent.
2. As regards the use of the third person in the narrative, Barthes (1953: 40) argued: "The reader will perhaps recall a novel of Agatha Christie in which all the invention consisted in concealing the murderer beneath the use of the first person of the narrative. The reader looked for him behind every 'he' in the plot while the murderer was all the time hidden under 'I'. Agatha Christie knew well that in a novel, we expect the 'I' to play the role of spectator and we expect the 'he' to act, i.e., potentially, be the murderer".
3. Structures can be observed in arrangements of entities which embody the following fundamental ideas: (a) the idea of wholeness, the sense of internal coherence; (b) the idea of transformation, because new material is constantly processed by and through structures; (c) the idea of self-regulation, in the sense that structure makes no appeal beyond itself in order to validate its transformational procedure (Hawkes, 1977).
4. Greimas (1966: 19) wrote: "We perceive differences and thanks to that perception, the world takes shape in front of us, and for our purposes."

REFERENCES

Aldrich, H.E. and C.M. Fiol (1994), 'Fools rush in? The institutional context of industry creation', *Academy of Management Review*, **19** (4), 645–670.
Barley, S. (1983), 'Semiotics and the study of occupational and organizational cultures', *Administrative Science Quarterly*, **28** (3), 393–413.
Barry, D. and M. Elmes (1997), 'Strategy retold: toward a narrative view of strategy discourse', *Academy of Management Review*, **22** (2), 429–452.
Barthes, R. (1953), *Le Degré Zéro de L'écriture*, Paris: Editions du Seuil.
Barthes, R. (1964), *Eléments de Sémiologie*, Paris: Editions du Seuil.
Barthes, R. (1966), Introduction à l'analyse structurale des récits, *Communications* 8.
Barthes, R. (1967), *Système de la Mode*, Paris: Editions du Seuil.
Bettman, J.R. and B.A. Weitz (1983), 'Attributions in the board room: causal reasoning in corporate annual reports', *Administrative Science Quarterly*, **28** (2), 165–183.
Brannen, M.Y. (2004), 'When Mickey loses face: recontextualization, semantic fit, and the semiotics of foreignness', *Academy of Management Review*, **29** (4), 593–616.
Bruner, J.S. (1986), *Actual Minds, Possible Worlds*, Cambridge, MA: Harvard University Press.
Bruner, J.S. (1990), *Acts of Meaning*, Cambridge, MA: Harvard University Press.
Chase, S.E. (2005), 'Narrative inquiry: multiple lenses, approaches, voices', in N.K. Denzin and Y.S. Lincoln (eds), *Qualitative Research*, third edition, London, UK: Sage Publications.
Czarniawska, B. (1997), *Narrating the Organization: Dramas of Institutional Identity*, Chicago, US: University of Chicago Press.
Czarniawska, B. (1998), *A Narrative Approach to Organization Studies*, London, UK: Sage Publications.
D'Aveni, R.A. and I.C. MacMillan (1990), 'Crisis and the content of managerial communications: a study of the focus of attention of top managers in surviving and failing firms', *Administrative Science Quarterly*, **35** (4), 634–657.
Daft, R. (1983), 'Symbols in organizations: a dual-content framework of analysis', in L. Pondy, P. Frost, G. Morgan and T. Dandridge (eds), *Organizational Symbolism*, Greenwich, CT, US: JAI Press.
Dutton, J.E. and J.M. Dukerich (1991), 'Keeping an eye on the mirror: image and identity in organizational adaptation', *Academy of Management Journal*, **34** (3), 517–554.
Eco, U. (1976), *A Theory of Semiotics*, Bloomington: Indiana University Press.
Eco, U. (1984), *Semiotics and the Philosophy of the Language*, London, UK: Benjamins Publishing.
Eco, U. (1984b), *The Role of the Reader: Explorations in the Semiotics of Texts*, Bloomington: Indiana University Press.
Feldman, M.S. and J.G. March (1981), 'Information as signal and symbol', *Administrative Science Quarterly*, **26** (2), 171–186.
Fiol, C.M. (1989), 'A semiotic analysis of corporate language: organizational boundaries and joint venturing', *Administrative Science Quarterly*, **34**, 277–303.
Fiol, C.M. (1991), 'Seeing the empty spaces: towards a more complex understanding of the meaning of power in organizations', *Organization Studies*, **12** (4), 547–566.
Fisher, W. (1984), *Human Communication as Narration: Toward a Philosophy of Reason, Value and Action*, Columbia, SC: University of South Carolina Press.
Freeman, R.E. (1984), *Strategic Management: A Stakeholder Approach*, Boston, MA: Pitman.
Gioia, D.A. and J.B. Thomas (1996), 'Identity, image, and issue interpretation: sensemaking during strategic change in Academia', *Administrative Science Quarterly*, **41** (3), 370–403.
Greimas, A.J. (1966), *Sémantique Structurale*, Paris: Larousse.
Greimas, A.J. (1970), *Du Sens: Essais Sémiotiques*, Paris: Editions du Seuil.
Hambrick, D. and S. Finkelstein (1987), 'Managerial discretion: a bridge between polar views of organizational outcomes', *Research in Organizational Behavior*, **9**, 369–406.

Jensen, M.C. and W. Meckling (1976), 'Theory of the firm: managerial behavior, agency costs, and capital structure', *Journal of Financial Economics*.
Martens, M.L., J.E. Jennings and P.D. Jennings (2007), 'Do the stories they tell get them the money they need? The role of entrepreneurial narratives in resource acquisition', *Academy of Management Journal*, **50** (5), 1107–1132.
Mazza, C. (1999), *Claim, Intent, and Persuasion*, Norwell, MA: Kluwer Academic Publishers.
Palmer, I., A.W. King and D. Kelleher (2004), 'Listening to Jack: GE's change conversations', *Journal of Organizational Change Management*, **17** (6), 593–614.
Peirce, C.S. (1931), *Collected Writings*, Cambridge, MA: Harvard University Press.
Pentland, B.T. (1999), 'Building process theory: from description to explanation', *Academy of Management Review*, **24** (4), 711–724.
Pfeffer, J. (1981), 'Management as symbolic action: the creation and maintenance of organizational paradigms', in B.M. Staw and L.L. Cummings (eds), *Research in Organizational Behavior*, vol. 3, 1–52, Greenwich, CT: JAI Press.
Propp, V. (1958), *Morphology of the Folktale*, Austin, TX: University of Texas Press.
Salancik, G.R. and J.R. Meindl (1984), 'Corporate attributions as strategic illusion of management control', *Administrative Science Quarterly*, **29** (2), 238–254.
Saussure, F. (de) (1916), *Course de linguistique générale*, Paris: Gallimard.
Segars, A.H. and G.F. Kohut (2001), 'Strategic communication through the world wide web: an empirical model of effectiveness in the CEO's letter to shareholders', *Journal of Management Studies*, **38** (4), 535–556.
Smircich, L. and C. Stubbart (1985), 'Strategic management in an enacted world', *Academy of Management Review*, **10** (4), 724–736.
Staw, B.M., P.I. McKechnie and S.M. Puffer (1983), 'The justification of organizational performance', *Administrative Science Quarterly*, **28** (4), 582–600.
Zott, C. and Q.N. Huy (2007), 'How entrepreneurs use symbolic management to acquire resources', *Administrative Science Quarterly*, **52** (1), 70–105.

20 The role and impact of computer simulation modeling in competitive strategy research
J. Richard Harrison and Gordon Walker

For decades, business and military leaders have utilized computer simulations to understand and anticipate strategic dynamics in the process of formulating and evaluating competitive strategy (Reibstein and Chussil, 1999). Academic researchers also have a history of using simulation methodology to study competitive strategy. They develop formal models of organizational processes, including strategic behavior, and use simulations to explore the competitive implications of the models. The first effort of this nature was by Cyert and March (1963), who developed a simulation model of price and output. In their model, pricing strategy is influenced by the price behavior of competitors. Another prominent example of the early application of computer simulation to competitive strategy is Nelson and Winter (1982), who developed models of Schumpeterian competition and used simulations to examine the implications for technological innovation and industry concentration.

In spite of these early contributions, however, a relatively small proportion of research in competitive strategy is based on computer simulations. We believe that this methodology has the potential to contribute more to the understanding of competitive strategy. In this chapter, we will describe computer simulations, discuss some of the recent applications of simulations to competitive strategy, and consider how we think computer simulations could help to advance agendas in several current areas of strategic theory and research.

COMPUTER SIMULATIONS

Theories of competitive strategy frequently describe organizational outcomes such as performance as the result of the interactions of multiple interdependent processes operating simultaneously. Even when the individual processes can be well specified, their interaction typically produces nonlinear system behavior with feedback. Such systems are usually analytically intractable, but their behavior can be assessed using numerical methods – specifically, through the use of computer simulation or computational modeling (Axelrod, 1997). This approach has been used in physics since the development of the digital computer in the late 1940s, and has become an accepted and widely used method for scientific work in the natural sciences (Harrison et al., 2007).

The application of simulation methodology to competitive strategy requires the specification of a formal dynamic model: a precise formulation of the processes through which the values of variables change over time, based on theoretical reasoning. The formal model may specify mathematical relationships, such as equations, or sets of explicit computational rules, such as 'when X occurs, then do Y,' or a combination of the two. The model is then translated into computer code and the resulting program is run on the computer for multiple time periods to produce the outcomes of interest.[1]

DEFINITION

Formally, we define a computer simulation as a computational model of system behavior coupled with an experimental design.[2] The computational model consists of the relevant system components (variables) and the specification of the processes for changes in the variables. The equations or rules for these processes specify how the values of variables at time $t + 1$ are determined, given the state of the system at time t. In stochastic models, these functions may depend partly on chance; the equation for the change in a variable's value may include a disturbance term to represent the effects of uncertainty or noise, or a discrete process such as the failure of a firm may be modeled by an equation that gives the probability or rate of mortality. The model's functions typically require the investigator to set some parameters (coefficients) so that computations can be carried out.

The experimental design consists of five elements: initial conditions, time structure, outcome determination, iterations and variations. The computational model specifies how the system changes from time t to time $t + 1$, but not the state of the system at time 0, so initial conditions must be specified.

The time structure sets the length of each simulation time period and the number of time periods in the simulation run. The length of the time period links the simulation to observation; for example, it may be desirable for mortality rates in a simulation to correspond with the realistic mortality rates for a firm. Once the time period is determined, the number of time periods to be simulated can be set to obtain the desired total duration of the simulation run, or a rule may be established to stop the run once certain conditions (e.g. system equilibrium) are met.

The outcomes of interest are often some function of the behavior of the system, and need to be calculated from system variables. Outcomes may be calculated for each time period or only at the end of the run, depending on the simulation's purpose.

Simulation models may be either stochastic or deterministic. Stochastic models contain probabilistic components, so that the behavior of a model in any particular instance depends to some extent on chance. Stochastic simulations typically use Monte Carlo methods, relying on the idea that the probabilistic components have distributions that can be sampled to obtain input values for these components in a model using random number generators. The simulation outcomes will vary somewhat from run to run depending on the random numbers generated, so the results of one run may not be representative of the average system behavior. To assess average system behavior as well as variations in behavior, multiple iterations are necessary; that is, the simulation run must be repeated many times (using different random number streams) to determine the pattern of outcomes. Deterministic models have no probabilistic elements and produce the same outputs each time, so they need to be run only once for a given model.

Finally, the entire simulation process described above may be repeated with different variations. For two reasons, both the parameter values and the initial conditions can be varied. First, the behavior of the system under different conditions may be of interest; the examination of such differences is often a primary reason for conducting simulation experiments. The second reason for introducing variations involves examining how sensitive the behavior of the system is to the choices of parameter settings and initial conditions; this type of variation is called sensitivity analysis.

After the simulation runs are completed, the results may be subjected to further analysis. Graphical analysis is a common method for analyzing simulation data. Since interactive systems typically produce nonlinear behavior, estimation using the general linear model may not be appropriate except for comparing the model findings with empirical work using linear models.

TYPES OF SIMULATION MODELS

While a number of typologies of simulation models have been proposed (see Burton, 2003; Cohen and Cyert, 1965; Macy and Willer, 2002; Davis et al., 2007), we will discuss three commonly used types: (1) agent-based models; (2) systems dynamics models; and (3) cellular automata models.

1. *Agent-based models*. Agent-based models focus on modeling the behaviors of adaptive actors (agents) who make up a social system and who influence one another through their interactions (Macy and Willer, 2002). One example is firms competing in an industry. The behavior of the system is not modeled directly, but is an emergent property of the interaction of the agents. The outcomes of interest may be the consequences of the interactions for the actors, or the consequences for the social system as a whole.
2. *Systems dynamics models*. These focus on modeling the behavior of the system as a whole, rather than modeling the behaviors of actors within the system (see Forrester, 1961). They simulate the processes that lead to changes in the system over time. Systems dynamics models are typically presented in diagrams of variables connected with arrows – including feedback loops – that show the directions of influence of variables on one another, and then each influence component is formalized.
3. *Cellular automata models*. Cellular automata models are based on a grid, with each square in the grid representing a cell. The model specifies how each cell changes from being occupied by an actor, or not, in each time period as a function of the characteristics of neighboring cells. In other words, influence is limited to localized interactions. These localized interactions, however, can influence the evolution of the system over time.

SIMULATION STUDIES IN COMPETITIVE STRATEGY

Simulation is a useful methodology for developing competitive theory and for exploring the implications of models of competitive behavior. Competition is inherently a complex phenomenon, and simulations are uniquely suited to the analysis of complex interactive systems. A simulation model can specify a variety of influences and processes involved in competitive behavior, such as pairwise interactions between the multiplicity of individual competitors in an industry, and can determine the consequences of these interactions for both the competitors and for the industry as a whole using computational methods.

Using simulation methods, researchers can study theories of competitive strategy in ways that are difficult or perhaps impossible with empirical methods. For example, the behaviors of competitive processes over extended time frames can be examined. The effectiveness of strategies under different sets of conditions – such as different levels of uncertainty, different organizational or industry structures, or different patterns of industry entry and exit – can be analyzed. The performance implications of major changes, such as diversification or technological change, can be assessed. Undertaking any of these efforts, of course, requires the specification of a formal simulation model.

Simulation can also be used to explore a subtler issue. Any stochastic behavior, including competition, can lead to a distribution of outcomes. In the real world, when we observe the state or evolution of an industry, we are observing only a single realization from the distribution of possible outcomes. Analyzing what we observe may result in inaccurate inferences about the nature of the processes which caused the outcome. Factors such as path dependence or random chance can produce an industry trajectory that may not be typical of the underlying processes that shape an industry's evolution. By running many iterations of a stochastic model to derive the distribution of possible outcomes, a simulation can help us to understand the range of variation implicit in the processes we postulate.

Prevalence of Simulation Approaches in Strategy

As we have mentioned, a relatively small proportion of research in competitive strategy is based on computer simulation methods. Figure 20.1 shows the proportion of simulation studies appearing in the *Strategic Management Journal* in the past ten years. The proportion is highest in 2003, with nearly 4 percent (three of 79 articles) using simulation methods. For five of the ten years examined, no simulation articles were published. Of course, simulation-based strategic research also appears in other journals; we simply chose SMJ, as the leading strategy journal, to illustrate this point.

CONTRIBUTIONS OF SIMULATION RESEARCH

Despite the small proportion of simulation studies relative to other types of studies, there are actually a substantial number of simulation analyses, and they have made important contributions to the strategy literature. In addition to the work by Cyert and March (1963) and Nelson and Winter (1982) discussed earlier, more recent work has contributed in several areas. Table 20.1 summarizes some more recent simulation studies relevant to competitive strategy. Many of these studies use complex simulation

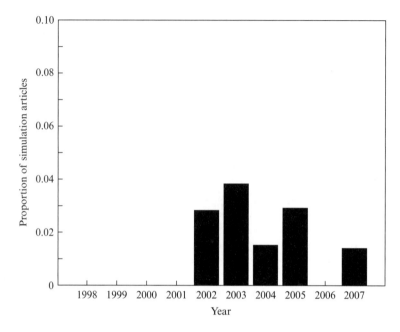

Figure 20.1   Simulation-based articles in Strategic Management Journal *by year*

models and address several related issues. Accordingly, the summaries are simplifications rather than full descriptions, and reflect our judgments of the key features of interest. No attempt has been made to summarize the findings of the studies, which are often contingent on variations in parameter settings and initial conditions in complex ways. The table is intended to provide an overview of the topics of these studies and to serve as a guide for those interested in additional information.

We should also note that it was necessary to establish some boundaries in determining what types of studies to include in the table, since many simulations have been conducted in areas with implications for competitive strategy. Here, we attempted to select studies with the most direct relevance to competitive strategy.

Of particular interest in Table 20.1 is the strategy topic to which a simulation study pertained. The category scheme of strategy topics comes from the chapters in Walker (2008). The most relevant were: *strategic positioning*, which entails providing value to a customer at a specific cost and whose goal is competitive advantage; *industry analysis*, which means the forces in an industry – e.g. Porter's five forces – that influence the firm's market position or viability; *competing over time*, which indicates

Table 20.1 Simulation-based strategy studies

Author(s)	Actor modeled	Modeling context	Key variable(s)	Outcome(s)	Model type	Strategy topic
Burton and Obel (1980)	Firm	Technology decomposability	Structure	Profits	Agent-based	Execution
Lant and Mezias (1990)	Firm	Discontinuous change	Adaptation, imitation	Performance	Agent-based	Competing over time (search)
March (1991)	Individual, organization	Exploration and exploitation	Learning rate	Knowledge, organizational performance	Agent-based	Competing over time (search)
Merten (1991)	Firm	Multipoint competition	Portfolio structure	Revenue	Systems dynamics	Diversification
Mezias and Glynn (1993)	Business unit	Search domain	Innovation routines	Performance	Agent-based	Competing over time (search)
Levy (1994)	Supply chain	Chaos theory	Inventory level	Stability	Systems dynamics	Execution
Carroll and Harrison (1994)	Organization	Competition between populations	Population density	Population dominance	Agent-based	Competing over time (industry evolution)
McCloughan (1995)	Firm	Entry, exit and growth	Growth	Size distributions, industry concentration	Agent-based	Competing over time (industry evolution)
Lomi & Larsen (1996)	Organization	Entry, exit, proximity	Population density	Degree of population density	Cellular automata	Competing over time (industry evolution)

Table 20.1 (continued)

Author(s)	Actor modeled	Modeling context	Key variable(s)	Outcome(s)	Model type	Strategy topic
Lomi & Larsen (1997)	Decision maker	Prisoner's dilemma	Strategic change	Propagation of organizational strategy	Cellular automata	Competing over time (industry evolution)
Carley & Lin (1997)	Decision maker	Decision context, information accuracy	Decision	Decision accuracy	Agent-based	Execution
Levinthal (1997)	Firm	NK landscape	Organizational design	Selection based on fitness	Agent-based	Competing over time (search)
Sastry (1997)	Organization	State variables	Punctuated organizational change	Performance	Systems dynamics	Execution
Brush & Bromiley (1997)	Variance components	Predicting business performance	Corporate parent variance component	Component distance from zero	Simple equation	Diversification
Lomi, Larsen & Ginsberg (1997)	Decision maker	Decision context	Adaptation	Decision effectiveness	Systems dynamics	Execution
Malerba, Nelson, Orsenigo & Winter (1999)	Firm	Competition, customer segmentation	Budget allocation decisions in R&D, marketing	Profits	Agent-based	Competing over time (industry evolution)
Rivkin (2000)	Firm	NK landscape	Complexity	Strategy design imitation	Agent-based	Competing over time (search)

Rivkin (2001)	Firm	NK landscape with varying complexity	Complexity	Replication Imitation	Agent-based	Competing over time (search)
Adner & Levinthal (2001)	Firm	Segmented consumer market	Product functionality and price, product and process innovation investment mix	Price-cost margin	Agent-based	Strategic positioning
Strang & Macy (2001)	Firm	Heterogeneity in firm competence and innovation effectiveness	Firm performance	Performance level	Agent-based	Competing over time (industry evolution)
Lee & Harrison (2001)	Firm	Fitness landscape, entry and exit	R&D investment in innovation and imitation	Strategic group formation, firm growth	Agent-based	Competing over time (industry evolution)
Malerba & Orsenigo (2002)	Firm	Competing firms	Budget allocation decisions in R&D, marketing	Profits	Agent-based	Competing over time (industry evolution)
Adner (2002)	Firm	Competition, customer segmentation	Product and process investment	Profits	Agent-based	Competing over time (search)
Repenning (2002)	Firm	Innovation implementation	Commitment to innovation	Results	Systems dynamics	Execution

Table 20.1 (continued)

Author(s)	Actor modeled	Modeling context	Key variable(s)	Outcome(s)	Model type	Strategy topic
Lee, Lee & Rho (2002)	Firm	Double peaked industry landscape	Strategic choice	Emergence of strategic groups	Agent-based	Competing over time (industry evolution)
Zott (2003)	Firm	N-firm competitive landscape	Dynamic capability	Fitness	Agent-based	Competing over time (search)
Dosi, Levinthal, & Marengo (2003)	Decision maker	NK landscape	Task decomposition	Organizational fitness	Agent-based	Competing over time (search)
Knott (2003)	Firm	N-firm competitive landscape	Knowledge stocks	Knowledge growth, industry heterogeneity	Agent-based	Competing over time (industry evolution)
Johnson & Hoopes (2003)	Firm	Hotelling model of consumer taste	Managerial cognition	Strategic similarity in industry	Agent-based	Competing over time (industry evolution)
Lee, Lee & Lee (2003)	Firm	Network externalities	Investment in technology	Sales	Agent-based	Strategic positioning
Rivkin & Siggelkow (2003)	Firm structure	NK landscape	Interdependence in organizational design elements	Firm stability vs. search efforts	Agent-based	Execution
Seshadi & Shapira (2003)	Manager	Alternative hierarchies	Organization design	Idea combination in organizations	Agent-based	Execution

Study	Unit	Context	Variable	Outcome	Method	Theme
Siggelkow & Levinthal (2003)	Firm structure	NK landscape	Centralized, decentralized, and reintegrated designs	Search performance of firm	Agent-based	Execution
Lin & Carley (2003)	Decision maker	Decision context	Organization design	Organizational performance	Agent-based	Execution
Denrell (2004)	Firm	Resource accumulation	Resource stock	Interfirm heterogeneity, profitability	Agent-based	Competing over time (industry evolution)
Ethiraj & Levinthal (2004)	Organizational structure	NK landscape	Design modularity	Organizational fitness, performance	Agent-based	Execution
Miller & Arikan (2004)	Firm	Stochastic technology space	Technology search options	Performance	Systems dynamics	Competing over time (search)
Harrison (2004)	Firm	Industry evolution	Growth	Size distributions, industry concentration	Agent-based	Competing over time (industry evolution)
Gary (2005)	Firm	Implementing related diversification	Diversification	Performance	Systems dynamics	Diversification
Gavetti, Levinthal & Rivkin (2005)	Firm	NK landscape	Policy decisions	Performance	Agent-based	Competing over time (search)
Siggelkow & Rivkin (2005)	Firm	NK landscape, environmental turbulence and complexity	Organization design	Speed vs. breadth of search	Agent-based	Execution

how a firm makes investments over time to improve its market position, and often in the context of the stages of industry evolution; *strategy execution*, whose elements determine the capabilities and resources that produce the firm's market position; and *diversification*, which, along with the associated topic of multibusiness firms, applies directly to the problems of growth through the addition and management of new businesses. This categorization scheme covers a broad swath of the strategy field and is useful for showing how simulation research pertains to it. Several simulation studies spanned more than one topic; in such cases, our sense of the study's most important contribution guided the topic classification.

Table 20.1 shows that by far the most frequently studied topic is competing over time. Twenty-four of the 41 simulation studies listed involve either adaptive firm level search for improved policies (11 articles) or the evolution of industry structure (13 articles). Why are these topics so prevalent in the simulation literature? The obvious answer is that simulation methodologies involving repeated trials can easily model how a system changes over time. They are therefore highly amenable to both problems of search over a landscape of potential solutions, connoting change over time, and problems of temporal stochastic variation in industry characteristics.

In general, the literature on search focuses on firm policy or technology choice from a range of alternatives structured in ways that reflect theoretical issues. The studies take one of three basic approaches. The first focuses on the modality of search or innovation (March, 1991; Mezias and Glynn, 1993; Zott, 2003; Miller and Arikan, 2004; Gavetti et al., 2005). In this case, how a firm innovates or adapts, for example through exploration or exploitation (March, 1991) or through analogy or incrementally (Gavetti et al., 2005), influences its success rate. Second, studies examine whether a strategy's characteristics, particularly complexity, influence its probability of success (Levinthal, 1997; Dosi et al., 2003), its ability to self-replicate (Rivkin, 2001), and its ability to be imitated (Rivkin, 2000 and 2001). Last, several articles have focused on innovation in the context of changing market conditions. Lant and Mezias (1990) examine how firms adapt to discontinuous market change, while Adner (2002) shows that customer segmentation based on technological preferences can lead to different paths of innovation among competing firms, with particular relevance to the emergence of disruptive technologies.

The evolution of industry structure has also been a recurrent theme in simulation-based research. While these studies emphasize competing over time, they are also a form of industry analysis because they address the forces that shape industry structure. Five interesting approaches are evident. First, from different perspectives, several studies have examined the persistence of heterogeneous firms. Both Knott (2003) and Strang and Macy (2001) show that heterogeneity can emerge and persist due to repeated, path dependent innovation, although these studies differ in the benefit from the investments made. As a counterpoint, Denrell's (2004) results indicate that enduring heterogeneity can emerge by following a random walk. The second theme concerns the emergence of strategic groups. Lee et al. (2002) model the development of groups as determined by dynamic capabilities, while Lee and Harrison (2001) show that groups can persist through path dependent investments. The third theme is 'history-friendly' modeling, which entails creating formal models of competition in an industry (pharmaceuticals, computers) and using these models to simulate observed industry evolution (Malerba et al., 1999; Malerba and Orsenigo, 2002). In another approach emphasizing history, Carroll and Harrison (1994) explore how path dependence can lead to the dominance of competitively inferior populations. The fourth theme examines the implications of Gibrat's law of firm growth and its variants; McCloughan (1995) and Harrison (2004) study the implications of alternative firm growth processes for size distributions and industry concentration over time. The final theme is localized competition, modeling how localized interaction influences industry structure (Lomi and Larsen, 1996) and the diffusion of competitive strategy (Lomi and Larsen, 1997; Johnson and Hoopes, 2003).

Given the extensiveness of simulation research on topics related to competing over time, how much more can be fruitfully done? The answer is: a great deal, primarily because of the inherent flexibility of simulation as a method. However, an important question inherent in these studies concerns whether the number of trials necessary for convergence reflects the number of decisions a real organization would make. One can always argue that each trial represents a draw from an underlying distribution; however, because time is the explicit dimension in the simulations, interpretability of the results requires that a single agent make decisions repeatedly. If the decisions do not involve large investments, this assumption might be plausible; but if major inputs are necessary, it seems unlikely that a manager or firm could make as many decisions as the designs of some studies require. Nonetheless, the benefit of simulation remains: it can create scenarios that are theoretically important but unlikely to be observed in reality. For this reason, the results for intertemporal competition remain compelling.

The second most prevalent topic found in the simulation literature is strategy execution (12 articles). By far the dominant theme regarding execution is organization design, and the question most often posed regarding design, not surprisingly, is its relationship to search. The key elements of design in many studies are the modularity and complementarity of its components. Siggelkow and Levinthal (2003) examine how well firms with different organizational structures (centralized, decentralized, partially centralized) perform in exploring an environment that has changed radically. Rivkin and Siggelkow (2003) explore how various configurations of design elements trade off extensive search and organizational stability. In turn, Ethiraj and Levinthal (2004) show how degrees of design modularity influence innovation and performance, and Siggelkow and Rivkin (2005) explore the performance of organization designs in more or less turbulent environments. These studies all use agent-based modeling in an NK landscape as an analytical approach. Focusing only within the organization, Burton and Obel (1980) test Williamson's M-form hypothesis for different levels of decomposability of technology, and Seshadri and Shapira (2003) explore the implications of different hierarchical structures on the flow of project proposals in an organization. Finally, Carley and Lin (1997) show how organization design can affect the accuracy of individual judgments, and Lin and Carley (2003) examine how organization design affects performance for organizations under stress.

The four remaining simulation studies of strategy execution have disparate topics. Sastry (1997) examines the management of strategic reorientation, Lomi et al. (1997) address learning dynamics, Repenning (2002) studies the implementation of innovations, and Levy (1994) analyzes the trend in inventory levels in a firm's supply chain. The first three of these use systems dynamics tools, while the last is guided by chaos theory.

Strategy execution implies that the firm has, either implicitly or explicitly, targeted the market position it wants to achieve and is building or reinvesting in the capabilities required to get there. Organization design is central to this effort. Although simulations of design have attempted to map its critical aspects – vertical hierarchy, modularity, interdependency – it is not always clear why an organization might choose one or another of these in order to build the capabilities necessary for achieving a particular market position. From a strategic perspective, organization design has an economic rationale, and such a motivation is missing from these studies.

Further, it is curious that simulation studies do not contain other aspects of execution, such as incentives (see Rivkin and Siggelkow, 2003, for an exception[3]). Strategy execution involves an array of parameters, including resources such as fixed technology assets, for guiding the behavior of organizational members towards a specific goal. To understand better how these elements work in concert, it would be useful to broaden the specifications of simulation models so that the interplay between, say, incentives, interdependencies among activities and technological inputs can be explored.

The two remaining strategy topics that have attracted simulation researchers – strategic positioning and diversification – have stimulated only a modicum of interest. In contrast to general models of competition over time, strategic positioning entails specifying a particular structure of customer preferences that guides firm investment decisions. Adner and Levinthal (2001) examine how firms change their product's price and technology in response to customer segmentation on the basis of sensitivity to improvements in functionality. Similarly, Lee et al. (2003) explore how firm investments in alternative technologies are related to tradeoffs by customers between technology performance and the benefits of network externalities. In both these studies, alternative customer choices are important for firm investments, following a demand-based approach to explaining investment decisions.

As for diversification, three studies have looked at a disparate set of topics. Merten (1991) examines how the business portfolios of two competitors change over time; Brush and Bromiley (1997) show that corporate effects on the variation in business performance are often underestimated in variance components models; and Gary (2005) analyzes the implications of interbusiness relatedness for corporate performance. Given the extensive empirical research on diversification, it is striking how little attention it has attracted in the simulation literature.

GAPS IN THE SIMULATION LITERATURE

Even though simulations have covered a wide swath of strategy topics, there are many others that have simply not been addressed. Most of those studied are central to the traditional strategy literature, but much might be gained from analyzing more nascent strategy themes from a simulation perspective. We suggest a number of these below.

One strategy topic that has received no attention in the simulation literature is interfirm contracting and, more generally, issues regarding the boundaries of the firm. Williamson's (1975 and 1985) transaction cost theory of vertical integration has been the dominant approach to analyzing organizational boundaries. In Williamson's work, this theory has lacked a regular functional form, and therefore has been less amenable to simulation than two other theories that have emerged in economics: Grossman and Hart's (1986) property rights theory and Holmstrom and Milgrom's (1994) theory of incentives. However, recently, Whinston's (2003) formalization and elaboration of the transaction cost framework has made it clearer analytically. His match of transaction cost and property rights models to data from empirical studies raises as many questions about how these theories apply to various vertical integration decisions as it provides answers. Moreover, Makadok and Coff's (2007) expansion of Holmstrom and Milgrom's (1994) theory has shown how it might intersect with ideas based on both property rights and on transaction costs. This recent progress in formalizing these theories, and the difficulty of finding data to test them, suggests that there are substantial opportunities for simulation research on this topic.

A second and related area of research pertains to strategic alliances. Although the alliance literature has in general eschewed formal models (but see Lin et al., 2007, for an initial effort to model alliance networks), the burgeoning literature on incomplete contracting (see Hart, 1995) has not. As an intermediate governance form, alliances almost by definition involve the kind of relationship-specific investments that incomplete contracting models assume. Moreover, recent research by Argyres et al. (2007) shows that contracting terms can change in an interpretable way over time. How the path of these changes, in the context of various forms of investment, affects the performance of the relationship raises a range of possible simulation topics.

Finally, a topic of strategy research that could be explored through simulation involves the costs and benefits of geographical location. The basic cluster benefits of specialized supply, labor pooling and technology spillovers are dependent on a range of conditions whose relative importance remains speculative. Simulations of various models built from the existing conceptual literature would be illuminating. Moreover, competition among clusters for the siting of promising technologies, firms, or activities – a topic with broad practical appeal – would be a natural extension of simulation research on the implications of geography for strategy.

CONCLUSION

In this chapter, we have described the methodology of computer simulation modeling and have discussed its applications to research in competitive strategy. Its major advantages for strategy research are that it explicitly incorporates the complex and dynamic nature of strategy and it frees the researcher from analytical tractability and empirical constraints through its use of computational methods, opening up a range of new research possibilities.

While simulation has been relatively underutilized as a tool for studying strategy, it has nevertheless made important contributions to understanding strategic behavior, particularly competition over time and the execution of strategy. For these topics and others we have identified in this chapter, simulation methodology has the potential to yield further insight.

Simulation analysis, like other research methodologies, has its limitations. These include problems with model specification, empirical grounding and verification due to observation and measurement issues, and interpretation of complex models and findings. Still, we believe that simulation offers a promising and largely unexplored avenue for furthering the research agenda in strategy.

NOTES

1. We restrict our attention to discrete-time simulations, the prevalent approach, which use predetermined time intervals (e.g., a simulation day, month, or year) and update the state of the system each time interval as the simulation clock advances during the computer run.
2. This definition and its explanation are based on Harrison et al. (2007).
3. Dosi et al. (2003) also consider incentives in search performance.

REFERENCES

Adner, R. (2002), 'When are technologies disruptive? A demand-based view of the emergence of competition', *Strategic Management Journal*, **23**, 667–688.
Adner, R. and D.A. Levinthal (2001), 'Demand heterogeneity and technology evolution: implications for product and process innovation', *Management Science*, **47**, 611–628.
Argyres, N.S., J. Bercowitz and K.J. Mayer (2007), 'Complementarity and evolution of contractual provisions: an empirical study of IT services contracts', *Organization Science*, **18**, 3–19.
Axelrod, R. (1997), *The Complexity of Cooperation: Agent-based Models of Competition and Collaboration*, Princeton, US: Princeton University Press.
Brush, T.H. and P. Bromiley (1997), 'What does a small corporate effect mean? A variance components simulation of corporate and business effects', *Strategic Management Journal*, **10**, 825–835.
Burton, R.M. (2003), 'Computational laboratories for organization science: questions, validity and docking', *Computational and Mathematical Organization Theory*, **9**, 91–108.
Burton, R.M. and B. Obel (1980), 'A computer simulation test of the M-form hypothesis', *Administrative Science Quarterly*, **25**, 457–466.
Carley, K.M. and Z. Lin (1997), 'A theoretical study of organizational performance under information distortion', *Management Science*, **43**, 976–997.
Carroll, G.R. and J.R. Harrison (1994), 'On the historical efficiency of competition between organizational populations', *American Journal of Sociology*, **100**, 720–749.
Cohen, K.J. and R.M. Cyert (1965), 'Simulation of organizational behavior', in J.G. March (ed.), *Handbook of Organizations*, Chicago, US: Rand McNally, pp. 305–334.
Cyert, R.M. and J.G. March (1963), *A Behavioral Theory of the Firm*, Englewood Cliffs, US: Prentice Hall.
Davis, J.P., K.M. Eisenhardt and C.B. Bingham (2007), 'Developing theory through simulation methods', *Academy of Management Review*, **32**, 480–499.

Denrell, J. (2004), 'Random walks and sustained competitive advantage', *Management Science*, **50**, 922–934.

Dosi, G., D.A. Levinthal and L. Marengo (2003), 'Bridging contested terrain: linking incentive-based and learning perspectives on organizational evolution', *Industrial and Corporate Change*, **12**, 413–436.

Ethiraj, S.K. and D. Levinthal (2004), 'Bounded rationality and the search for organizational architecture: an evolutionary perspective on the design of organizations and their evolvability', *Administrative Science Quarterly*, **49**, 404–437.

Forrester, J.W. (1961), *Industrial Dynamics*, Cambridge, US: MIT Press.

Gary, M.S. (2005), 'Implementation strategy and performance outcomes in related diversification', *Strategic Management Journal*, **26**, 643–664.

Gavetti, G., D.A. Levinthal and J.W. Rivkin (2005), 'Strategy making in novel and complex worlds: the power of analogy', *Strategic Management Journal*, **26**, 691–712.

Grossman, S. and O. Hart (1986), 'The costs and benefits of ownership: a theory of vertical and lateral integration', *Journal of Political Economy*, **94**, 691–719.

Harrison, J.R. (2004), 'Models of growth in organizational ecology: a simulation assessment', *Industrial and Corporate Change*, **13**, 243–261.

Harrison, J.R., Z. Lin, G.R. Carroll and K.M. Carley (2007), 'Simulation modeling in organizational and management research', *Academy of Management Review*, **32**, 1229–1245.

Hart, O. (1995), *Firms, Contracts and Financial Structure*, Oxford, UK: Oxford University Press.

Holmstrom, B. and P. Milgrom (1997), 'Multi-task principal-agent analyses: incentive contracts, asset ownership and job design', *Journal of Law, Economics and Organization*, **7**, 24–52.

Johnson, D.R. and D.G. Hoopes (2003), 'Managerial cognition, sunk costs, and the evolution of industry structure', *Strategic Management Journal*, **24**, 1057–1068.

Knott, A.M. (2003), 'Persistence heterogeneity and sustainable innovation', *Strategic Management Journal*, **24**, 687–705.

Lant, T.K. and S.J. Mezias (1990), 'Managing discontinuous change: a simulation study of organizational learning and entrepreneurship', *Strategic Management Journal*, **11**, 147–179.

Lee, J. and J.R. Harrison (2001), 'Innovation and industry bifurcation: the evolution of R&D strategy', *Industrial and Corporate Change*, **10**, 115–149.

Lee, J., J. Lee and H. Lee (2003), 'Exploration and exploitation in the presence of network externalities', *Management Science*, **49**, 553–570.

Lee, J., K. Lee and S. Rho (2002), 'An evolutionary perspective on strategic group emergence', *Strategic Management Journal*, **23**, 727–746.

Levinthal, D.A. (1997), 'Adaptation on rugged landscapes', *Management Science*, **43**, 934–950.

Levy, D. (1994), 'Chaos theory and strategy: theory, application, and managerial implications', *Strategic Management Journal*, **15**, 167–178.

Lin, Z. and K.M. Carley (2003), *Designing Stress Resistant Organizations*, Boston, US, Dordrecht, The Netherlands, and London, UK: Kluwer.

Lin, Z., H. Yang and I. Demirkan (2007), 'The performance consequences of ambidexterity in strategic alliance formations: empirical investigation and computational theorizing', *Management Science*, **53**, 1645–1658.

Lomi, A. and E.R. Larsen (1996), 'Interacting locally and evolving globally: a computational approach to the dynamics of organizational populations', *Academy of Management Journal*, **39**, 1287–1321.

Lomi, A. and E.R. Larsen (1997), 'A computational approach to the evolution of competitive strategy', *Journal of Mathematical Sociology*, **22**, 151–176.

Lomi, A., E.R. Larsen and A. Ginsberg (1997), 'Adaptive learning in organizations: a system dynamics-based exploration', *Journal of Management*, **23**, 561–582.

Macy, M.W. and R. Willer (2002), 'From factors to actors: computational sociology and agent-based modeling', *Annual Review of Sociology*, **28**, 143–166.

Makadok, R. and R. Coff (2007), 'Both market and hierarchy: a formal theory of hybrid governance forms', working paper, Emory University.

Malerba, F., R. Nelson, L. Orsenigo and S. Winter (1999), '"History-friendly"models of industry evolution: the computer industry', *Industrial and Corporate Change*, **8**, 3–40.

Malerba, F. and L. Orsenigo (2002), 'Innovation and market structure in the dynamics of the pharmaceutical industry and biotechnology: towards a history-friendly model', *Industrial and Corporate Change*, **11**, 667–703.

March, J.G. (1991), 'Exploration and exploitation in organizational learning', *Organization Science*, **2**, 71–87.

McCloughan, P. (1995), 'Simulation of concentration development from modified Gibrat growth-entry-exit processes', *Journal of Industrial Economics*, **43**, 405–433.

Merten, P.P. (1991), 'Loop-based stragegic decision support systems', *Strategic Management Journal*, **12**, 371–386.

Mezias, S.J. and M.A. Glynn (1993), 'The three faces of corporate renewal: institution, revolution, and evolution', *Strategic Management Journal*, **14**, 77–101.

Miller, K.D. and A.T. Arikan (2004), 'Technology search investments: evolutionary, option reasoning, and option pricing approaches', *Strategic Management Journal*, **25**, 473–485.

Nelson, R.R. and S.G. Winter (1982), *An Evolutionary Theory of Economic Change*, Cambridge, US: Belknap Press of Harvard University Press.

Reibstein, D.J. and M.J. Chussil (1999), 'Putting the lesson before the test: using simulation to analyze and develop competitive strategies', *Competitive Intelligence Review*, **10**, 34–48.

Repenning, N.P. (2002), 'A simulation-based approach to understanding the dynamics of innovation implementation', *Organization Science*, **13**, 107–127.

Rivkin, J.W. (2000), 'Imitation of complex strategies', *Management Science*, **46**, 824–844.

Rivkin, J.W. (2001), 'Reproducing knowledge: replication without imitation at moderate complexity', *Organization Science*, **12**, 274–293.

Rivkin, J.W. and N. Siggelkow (2003), 'Balancing search and stability: interdependencies among elements of organizational design', *Management Science*, **49**, 290–311.

Sastry, M.A. (1997), 'Problems and paradoxes in a model of punctuated organizational change', *Administrative Science Quarterly*, **42**, 237–275.

Seshadri, S. and Z. Shapira (2003), 'The flow of ideas and timing of evaluation as determinants of knowledge creation', *Industrial and Corporate Change*, **12**, 1099–1124.

Siggelkow, N. and D.A. Levinthal (2003), 'Temporarily divide to conquer: centralized, decentralized, and reintegrated organizational approaches to exploration and adaptation', *Organization Science*, **14**, 650–669.

Siggelkow, N. and J.W. Rivkin (2005), 'Speed and search: designing organizations for turbulence and complexity', *Organization Science*, **16**, 101–122.

Strang, D. and M.W. Macy (2001), 'In search of excellence: fads, success stories, and adaptive emulation', *American Journal of Sociology*, **107**, 147–182.

Walker, Gordon (2008), *Modern Competitive Strategy* (3rd edition), New York: McGraw-Hill.

Whinston, M. (2003), 'On the transaction costs of vertical integration', *Journal of Law, Economics and Organization*, **19**, 1–23.

Williamson, O.E. (1975), *Markets and Hierarchies: Analysis and Antitrust Implications*, New York, US: Free Press.

Williamson, O.E. (1985), *The Economic Institutions of Capitalism*, New York: Free Press.

Zott, C. (2003), 'Dynamic capabilities and the emergence of intraindustry differential firm performance: insights from a simulation study', *Strategic Management Journal*, **24**, 97–125.

PART 5

COMPETITIVE STRATEGY AT THE INTERSECTION BETWEEN RESEARCH AND PRACTICE: A LOOK INTO THE FUTURE

21 The management of trust in competitive strategy research: why it is important and what is new
Sandro Castaldo and Katia Premazzi

INTRODUCTION

This chapter discusses how trust, intended as a fundamental resource, plays an important role in both gaining and sustaining a firm's competitive advantage in the current networking economy.

One of the phenomena that best characterizes markets today is the exponential development of their complexity level, which directly affects the behavior of economic subjects. The most prominent implication is that the network of relationships in which a firm is nested, together with its networking inclination and ability, is crucial for achieving a competitive advantage (Dyer and Singh, 1998; Morgan and Hunt, 1999). Such a relational network constitutes a sort of 'mine' to be exploited in order to engender the resources that feed sustainable competitive advantages in current complex markets. These cognitive resources are generally knowledge- and trust-based.

Firms that realize the importance of such networks will take steps to actively engage in and create networks with other firms or subjects who are characterized by complementary cognitive resources (Arora and Gambardella, 1994).

Two main factors drive this trend:

- Knowledge-based factors engendering a 'science-pushed' networking trend;
- Customer-based factors favoring a 'demand-pulled' networking trend.

As firms are incapable of autonomously managing the increasing level of environmental complexity, they therefore require specialization in the production of knowledge. Hence their need to liaise in networks and integrate complementary competencies and expertise in order to set up the resources required to face tougher competitive contexts. This need represents a knowledge-based (or science-pushed) vector that drives the constitution of networks of subjects with complementary cognitive resources.

The needs of the customers rise in complexity, too. Demand needs appear with increased frequency in bunches. This creates a customer-based (or demand-driven) vector, which contributes to the tendency towards networking. This tendency not only expands the relational bandwidth that connects a set of firms seeking to satisfy a common cluster of needs, it also reduces the cognitive distance between the firm and its customers.

In order to meet the complexity of needs expressed by customer demand, the firm-market relationship must undergo radical change. Unilateral and instantaneous relations will have to become long-term bilateral relations with customers actively interacting with a network of firms, thus contributing to their knowledge endowment. By reducing the cognitive distance, firms and customers become the co-producers of the reticular knowledge base. Evidence drawn from the virtual economy clearly indicates the development of such a trend, which induces firms, customer communities, and individual customers to liaise and cooperate in the generation of innovation (Lacobucci, 1998; Achrol and Kottler, 1999; Sawhney and Prandelli, 2000). This seems specifically true of the lead users (von Hippel, 1988): particularly advanced end users directly committed to the development process of product innovation.

The capability to connect with the final market, and for all economic subjects to contribute to the basic resources required for the efficient functioning of value-creation processes are essential to a firm's survival and growth. Trust plays a fundamental role in such a scenario. In the new 'network economy', the environmental and scientific complexity undergoes a transformation that is driven by the specialization process: this translates into a relational network complexity. Trust is crucial for such articulated bonds to make the entire system work effectively and efficiently. Thus, the growing level of environmental uncertainty increases the relevance of trust as a relational asset. Trust becomes a key intangible resource for the network itself and for all the involved subjects. It is the one factor capable of prescribing and governing the growing relational complexity in the competitive arena.

First, we have to understand what trust is. The first section of this chapter provides a definition of trust, and the second proposes a typology based on its nature. In the third section, we discuss why trust is considered one of the basic resources that a firm must develop. In other words, we summarize the main positive consequences of trust in a competitive or market context. The final section of the chapter illustrates strategies and practices that a firm can follow to engender trust, thus feeding its resource endowment.

WHAT IS TRUST? TRUST AS A COMPLEXITY AND UNCERTAINTY ABSORBER

In this section, we take into account the most common definitions of trust, and discover that trust may absorb complexity and uncertainty, which enables networks to be activated and function.

Analyzing the various definitions of trust proposed in the management literature, trust emerges as a certainty to foresee future trustees' behaviors. Thus, trust affects the reliability of a subject's promises, or the guarantee that she or he will behave with respect for her or his obligations. Indeed, scholars who have adopted the rational choice model have defined trust as a particular level of subjective probabilities, assigned by an agent (the trustor) to a given outcome of an action performed by one or more different agents (the trustee), both before (or independently of) observing that action and in a context in which the specific action affects the action of the first agent (Gambetta, 1988). Therefore, trust represents that threshold of the subjective probability distribution of someone else's actions that, once crossed, supports an expectation for cooperation that in turn induces us to cooperate (Galeotti, 1990). Trust is therefore essential to achieve cooperation within a network.

In order to establish the theoretical relevance of the trust concept, the expectations for the actions of party B (trustee), that influence party A (trustor) while achieving her or his goals, cannot be verified before A's decision has been made (Williams, 1989). In fact, the impossibility of controlling someone else's actions is critical to the definition of trust: if I can control what others will do before I choose what to do, trust loses its power (Dasgupta, 1989: 66). The fundamental prerequisite of trust is thus equated to the existence of an uncertainty situation, in other words, facing a risky circumstance in which the possible damage could be greater than the hoped for advantages (Deutsch, 1958 and 1962; Golembiewski and McConkie, 1975; Luhmann, 1989; Andaleeb, 1992).

Most definitions of trust proposed in the management literature require the presence of external risk as a prerequisite of trust. In fact, uncertainty is fundamental to the effective value of trust within a subject's decision process. If someone were omniscient, her or his selection among alternative behaviors would be performed in a situation of perfect certainty, and trust would not be required (Lewis and Weigert, 1985). However, trust plays a very useful role every time a situation is uncertain and risky. It reduces the inner complexity of interaction systems, helping the interested parties to establish specific expectations for their mutual future behavior. Hence, trust acts as a complexity absorber: it reduces the level of interactional uncertainty (Luhmann, 1979 and 1991; Mishra, 1996).

In view of the centrality of risk as a gauge of the utility and relevance of trust, some authors conceptualize trust in terms of expectation certainty about the trustee's future actions. As the fundamental trigger activating trust, the presence of risk is bound to have an attenuating function, which generates an element of certainty with regard to the counterpart's future responses. Thus, until further information can be acquired, trust is used to reduce the risk level caused by the uncertainty associated with a situation that would either induce the parties to remain inactive or, ultimately, delay a decision until a more certain future.

Thus, trust is a prerequisite for decisions and actions (e.g. sharing information) to be taken within networks. However, after a decision to trust has been made, a new kind of risk emerges. Relational, or internal, risk is revealed as the trustor accepts a situation of vulnerability in relation to the counterpart. Vulnerability occurs when, as a result of the trustee's opportunistic behavior, the trustor risks suffering greater damages than the advantages derived by choosing to trust. Thus risk, in situations that require a high level of trust, is generally associated with the trustor's vulnerability or with the uncertainty regarding an achieved outcome (Doney et al., 1998).

More precisely, the logical nexus that links risk to trust is conceptualized as follows: while external risks foster the opportunity to trust, giving to the latter concept some practical relevance, the existence of trust makes risk taking decisions and behaviors both possible and cognitively acceptable (Rosseau et al., 1998: 395). There is therefore a circular relationship between risk and trust. Risk determines the need for trust, which in turn negatively affects the perceived risk level, establishing the prerequisites needed by the actors to develop behaviors that imply individual vulnerability (and thus the existence of external risk) in cognitive situations of apparent certainty.[1]

The activation of a trust-based behavior is therefore only possible in both the presence of a potential risk (as perceived by a subject) and the presence of trust. Moreover, trust implies a partial substitution of an unmanageable external risk with a relational risk, which is more cognitively manageable, as it is correlated to the situation of vulnerability felt by the trustor. Without trust, the latter would face an external risk.

To sum up, in the current market scenario, firms perceive a high level of external risks that appear tough to manage. Trust may represent a way to cope with such external risks, by transforming them into more manageable, relational risks. It remains to be explained what the bases, or the drivers, of trust and trusting behaviors are, especially within network relationships.

In the following section, we will show that there are different bases of trust that may evolve with the development of relationships, thus engendering different types of trust.

TRUST TYPOLOGIES

Trust is not a static construct: it is dynamic. The trust determining a certain relationship between subjects usually changes over time (longitudinal perspective) and across situations. For example, trust tends to evolve as long as the relationship history continues, as it cultivates interactive experience. Consequently, it is possible to find different meanings associated with the word trust, as these variations reflect its nature.

A common distinction found in literature differentiates between trust's contents or, more precisely, the nature of trust's cognitive antecedents. This has revealed three types of trust: calculus-based trust (rational or deterrence-based), knowledge-based trust (cognitive trust), and identification-based trust (sometimes referred to as normative trust and goodwill trust) (Lewicki and Bunker, 1996; Shapiro et al., 1992; Sheppard and Tuchinsky, 1996; Lane, 1998; Child, 1998; Sako, 1991 and 1998; Sako and Helper, 1998).[2]

The first typology refers to trust that is exclusively based on economic evaluations and rational calculations. In some cases, the trustor may find it convenient to trust another party (even when she or he can only count on limited knowledge), because the potential losses induced by trusting are lower than the potential advantages of behavior based on trusting. In sum, the trustor is coerced into trusting the counterpart because this decision can generate future returns that are far greater than the possible damages.

An alternative approach links trust less to one's own personal convenience and more to the counterpart's perceived convenience. In this variation, which is closer to the definition of deterrence-based trust, a person trusts another mainly because the trustee's potential losses, in case of unreliable behavior (e.g. a reputation loss as a consequence of dissatisfactory events), are equal to or greater than the trustee's advantages gained by exploiting the trustor's vulnerability.

Calculus-based trust is typical of initial relationships: convenience calculus mitigates the lack of information and direct knowledge of the other party. In reality, this situation could be defined as non-trust, because it is exclusively based on economic convenience and is the product of a rational decision (Williamson, 1993). Alternatively, it could be defined as proto-trust, due to its activation in the absence of personal experience: it occurs during the first stage of a relationship.

The second typology, knowledge-based trust or cognitive trust, is evident when the interactive experience of the parties allows them to develop specific knowledge of the counterpart's characteristics, behaviors and, more importantly, competencies and skills. Above all, to trust means to recognize that the trustee has the needed knowledge to execute the activities required by the trustor completely and satisfactorily. Therefore, the awareness of the other party's competency, as required by the task at hand, facilitates a decision to trust that is not exclusively based on economic and rational processes, but grounded in more solid conceptual elements: the knowledge of the other party's competency profile.

This task-specific type of trust is usually placed in those who are believed competent in a given field: in order to safeguard a positive outcome, a trustor will delegate the execution of activities appropriate to the trustee's competencies. For example, this trust typology is implicitly considered in the context of brand extension policies, which require a perceptual fit between the brand and the extension target category. In particular, this fit mostly concerns a verifiable compatibility between the competencies associated with the firm in its original field of endeavor and those that are considered fundamental for the presentation of an offer qualitatively whole and evenly capable of satisfying customers in a new business arena.[3]

The last typology of trust is more abstract and thus more easily transferable. As this trust is less burdened by task and performance specificity, it is based on identification and personal values. This value-based trust is normally acquired during the most advanced stages of a relationship, when the parties involved have built a consistent level of interdependence. This level is reached when a single subject not only has knowledge of a trustee's competencies, but also a trustee's values and cultural orientations. This type of trust, therefore, does not involve specific activities or relational contexts; rather, it widens the relationship potential bandwidth and extension opportunities of the parties involved. While knowledge-based trust induces a perception of the trustee as reliable with regard to specific activities associated with his or her recognized competency set, trust based on identification and personal values makes recognition of the counterpart's reliability more abstractly categorized, that is to say, without reference to a specific performance. Consequently, the activity and performance spectrum conveyed by this type of relationship is much wider, thus increasing the relationship value and potential.[4]

Similarly, Huemer's (1998 and 2000) proposed distinction between predictive trust (Sitkin and Roth, 1993) and the explorative trust may be partly traced to the previous distinction. The former corresponds to calculative and knowledge-based trust, and is based on certainty about the expectations raised by a subject. Thus, predictive trust stabilizes relationships, promotes exchanges, and reduces the transactional costs. Nevertheless, when only the predictive dimension of trust is considered, we cannot appreciate trust's true potential in terms of innovative activities and ambiguous relational contexts. Actually, the circumstances in which predictive trust is considered *by itself* are uncertain and in constant change. This is in contrast with the tendency to stabilization and inertia associated with trust's predictive functions. In fact, to explore the boundaries beyond a firm's current knowledge and known options, a type of trust that is not anchored in prior knowledge is required. Huemer (2000) suggests the introduction of explorative trust. Although explorative trust is somewhat similar to the more abstract type of trust (the value-based typology), it is much more flexible than its predictive counterpart as it is free from the concept of risk. If the only trust developed is exclusively predictive – therefore based on the capacity to duplicate activities undertaken in the past in order to reduce the exchange of embedded risks – the inevitable result is a tendency to stabilize and reproduce the relationship, even when this is not functional to the management of uncertainties, such as those typically generated by innovation processes (Castaldo and Verona, 2001). Uncertainty can be managed by activating trust's explorative dimension (March, 1991). Only then is it possible to follow unknown development paths, attract new relationships, and fully value complexity and change within the new scenarios of the connection economy (Vicari, 2001). In turn, explorative mechanisms open up new opportunities to follow radically new learning vectors, eschewing simple incremental solutions based on prior knowledge development paths.

In the new economic scenario, trust becomes a firm's basic resource as it enables the competitive advantage that has been defined as relationship-based (Hunt and Morgan, 1995; Morgan and Hunt, 1999; Dyer and Singh, 1998). In order to understand why this occurs, it is necessary to look at the possible consequences of accrued trust on organizational processes and value generation.

TRUST VALUE

The effects of accrued trust can be analyzed within the firm and referred to the management of external relations (with other firms and with the customers). The available literature distinguishes the major advantages of trust development for a certain firm with respect to its different domains: a) intra-organizational relationships, b) inter-organizational relationships, and c) relationships developed with the firm's customers.

With regard to intra-organizational relations (a), it has been widely proven (Das and Teng, 1998; Doney et al., 1998; Maverson et al., 1996; McAllister, 1995; Perrone and Chiacchierini, 1999) that trust may:

– facilitate management coordination among different organizational units;
– improve the organizational climate by reducing the level of inter-functional conflicts;
– enable more effective and efficient inter-function teamwork;
– contribute to an effective implementation of strategies that support the plan implementation phase;
– determine organizational citizenship and extra role behaviors;
– reduce control-based monitoring and defensive behaviors.

These effects make the organized activities more effective and improve efficiency as, in a climate based on trust relations, control costs decrease and conflict solutions are arrived at quicker.

With regard to inter-organizational relations (b), the development of trust contributes to:

– limiting transaction costs, especially in organizational situations when there is a high level of uncertainty;
– facilitating long-term relationships, thus reducing conflicts that are non-functional to the partnership goals;
– stimulating collaboration among firms, significantly contributing to the success of strategic alliances;
– simplifying knowledge transfer and joint learning.

(Anderson and Narus, 1990; Doney et al., 1998; Dore, 1983; Ganesan, 1994; Gulati, 1995; Jap, 1999 and 2001; Moorman et al., 1992 and 1993; Morgan and Hunt, 1994; Ring and Van de Ven, 1992).

This makes the relational activity both more effective and less expensive, and has positive implications in terms of opportunities for economic value generation and cost reduction in the case of inter-organizational collaboration initiatives.

In relation to demand (c), trust generates important consequences for the firm by enhancing customers' loyalty (Anderson and Sullivan, 1993; Johnson et al., 1995; Srivastava et al., 1998):

– an increased differentiation, extension and relationship-associated learning potential, thus obtaining a premium price;
– a more reduced price sensitivity;
– a higher propensity to consumption;

- a favorable reputation, spreading positive information on the firm, partially replacing marketing investments;
- a reduction of sales and assistance costs;
- a trading-up propensity, i.e. purchasing higher quality goods within the same product line;
- a cross-buying propensity, i.e. purchasing other goods or services offered by the same firm;
- a knowledge-sharing propensity, i.e. activating co-evolutionary processes between demand and supply, based on knowledge exchange and integration.

Such effects may enhance the value generated by the firm, either by increasing efficiency (for example, by reducing customer management costs and replacing other communication investments due to a positive reputation), or by increasing revenue sources (due to other cross-buying opportunities and lower price sensitivity).

Finally, it can be useful to examine the effects of trust and loyalty on the customer equity value, the value generated by a single customer (or even a specific segment of the demand), calculated according to the net cash flows she or he can guarantee throughout the lifetime of her or his relationship with the firm.

Such value is determined by the difference between the margins generated by a single customer and the activation, development and maintenance costs that a customer determines (Wayland and Cole, 1997: 101):

$$CE = \sum_{t=1}^{n} P_t(Q_t M_t) d^t - \sum_{t=1}^{n} (S_t + F_t) d^t - A_t$$

where:

P = probability of purchase by the customer in the ith period;
Q = expected purchasing volume throughout the relationship cycle;
M = unit margins after taxes;
t = period (year) of the relationship;
n = total number of the relationship's periods;
S = customer development cost;
F = customer retention cost;
A = customer activation cost (connection phase);
d = discount rate $[1/(1+k)]$.

An increase in trust can positively affect every element of the above-mentioned value.

Upon increasing the trust level of its customer base, a firm enjoys an increase in:

- the likelihood of purchases by its customers (P);
- the expected quantity of purchases over the whole relationship (Q), for example due to the cross-buying phenomena;
- unit margins (M), for example, due to reduced price sensitivity;
- the overall relationship duration (n).

At the same time, customer development costs (S) are bound to decrease: a customer can be easily induced to broaden both the scope of the relationship and the range of products and services purchased by the single supplier. It also costs less to activate customers (A) and gain their loyalty (F), by taking advantage of positive word of mouth and the new customers' greater positive disposition induced by the firm's market reputation. Finally, the discount rate (represented by $d = 1/(1+k)$) drops as well.[5]

Thus, it is clear that trust actually translates into an economic value for a firm.

Given the positive consequences of trust on a firm's internal and external relationships, it can be useful to identify some strategies and practices that a firm can follow in order to engender this valuable intangible asset. In the following section, we will contrast the two most common approaches, and exemplify how they can be implemented in practice by means of different tactics.

TRUST BUILDING

Before focusing on the identification of strategies, it is advisable to discuss the actual possibility, and consequent opportunity, for a firm to perform deliberate actions of trust development. Some scholars believe that this is not an adequate strategy, because as soon as one deliberately chooses behaviors of this type, the resulting trust is both artificial and bound to the (egotistical) goals of the trustees and is therefore fully alien to the pure concept of trust. Conversely, we believe that trust management is not only feasible, but it also represents a functional orientation of economic system development. This term refers to the development of 'true' trust, not a trust façade, which hides opportunistic behaviors (Hardy et al., 1998). A trust façade is not true trust, because the trustee risks a quick termination of the relationship with the trustors that she or he has duped, as soon as they identify his or her true intentions (as this is inevitable due to the vigilant trust that characterizes the initial developmental stages of a relationship).

Based on the antecedents of trust (transparency, honesty, competencies, personal values, lack of opportunism, fairness, integrity, and mutual satisfaction), trust development conversely allows for the establishment of long-term relationships. This very demanding goal has positive implications for economic systems, organizations, and individuals alike. Indeed, it is difficult to find a good reason why a firm should not adopt such trust strategies and policies, and enjoy their positive effects at the ambience level – diffusing a trust climate favorable to exchanges and characterized by greater transparency – and for the parties involved in the relationship (as seen earlier, true trust benefits both trustee and trustor).

Having established the importance and opportunity of trust building as an element that helps to organize the growing complexity of individual choices and reduce their uncertainty, it is important to review the modalities of its effective realization. Those who are interested in trust management agree on the critical role played, at the individual level, by the development of trust expectations toward the counterpart. To this effect, it is possible to isolate two basic approaches, which should not be considered alternative or exclusive:

1)   those based on antecedent activation;
2)   those that identify growth strategies integrating those that are driver-based.

Activating the Antecedents or Drivers of Trust

Trust – defined as certainty of the behavior of others – is mainly conditioned by the following aspects:

−   past experiences with the counterpart (length of the relationship) and relative level of satisfaction regarded as a behavioral antecedent;
−   the trustee's perceived capabilities and competencies, which allow him or her to express behaviors in line with expectations;
−   the counterpart's motivations to pursue joint goals without opportunistic behaviors (an aspect often defined as goodwill);
−   the trustee's perceived integrity and values.

According to the literature, these seem to be the fundamental antecedents of trust.

In situations characterized by a high content of interpersonal contacts, these determinants are heavily influenced by the behaviors and personal characteristics of the subjects involved in the relationship (for example, honesty and sympathy).

There are also some determinants that, in reality, are generating circular relations with trust. This seems to be specifically true with regard to the counterpart's perceived fairness and justice; communication transparency and intensity; past satisfaction level (this element is the most direct link with the behavioral-type determinants); and cooperative initiatives. These variables, undoubtedly representing some of the antecedents of trust, cannot be considered as determinants alone. Rather, these variables both determine the level of trust and are conditioned by it, thus dynamically generating circular causality relationships. Therefore, trust is a stock variable of the relationship that, if there were a system to detect and account for intangible resources, would be included with a firm's patrimonial assets. In such a metaphor, the experiences of satisfaction, perceived fairness, cooperative initiatives, and communication represent quantity flows, or dynamic capabilities (Teece et al., 1997); alternatively, the processes that enrich the patrimony of trust linked to the relationship (customers' trust), may in turn generate more consistent flows of fairness, satisfaction, cooperation, and communication. Such greater flows further enhance the trust level, thus triggering a recursive process that self-generates the resources linked to the relationship along an auto-poietic path of development (Vicari, 1991: 75). Therefore, in a dynamic perspective, the variables linked by a circular causal relationship to trust represent the antecedents of trust at time t_0, at the beginning of the relationship. In a more advanced stage, they can become the consequences of trust, once the relation between the parties has been better consolidated. It is trust itself (by now consolidated) that warrants the counterpart's perceived fairness, communication quality, and the partner's satisfaction and cooperative propensity.

This highlights the critical role of longitudinal analysis, because, by distinguishing the different evolutionary stages of the relationship, it is possible to better understand the causality linking its constructs.

The first approach to trust building requires the identification of the most central drivers or antecedents: those that have the most consistent perceptive leverage within the semantic network that defines the concept of trust. Consequently, firms need to take appropriate actions, with a clear understanding of their role as hygienic factor or as a motivator, in order to stimulate such drivers. Motivators are essential elements in the development of trust, while hygienics are factors that prevent distrust (Sirdeshmukh et al., 2002).

In this regard, it seems useful to mention the process by which new trust relationships are forged with unknown subjects, whom an actor initially contacts in a virtual environment (McKnight et al., 1998; Tan and Santosa, 2001). In this case, the level of uncertainty is considerable and, consequently, the need for trust is quite high. Consequently, the parties must find the operational modalities that work best to activate the appropriate trust drivers. Naturally, the partner's newness presents an inevitable gap in reference to both past experiences and satisfaction: two of the fundamental elements needed to build a trust relationship. To bridge this gap, alternative mechanisms must be found, producing the trusting climate needed to establish online relationships and enacting the connection potential offered by virtual environments. Some of these actions may involve either the use of rating modalities and participant pre-selection to mitigate the problematic lack of previous contacts with the counterpart, or the organization of a forum in which to exchange information and generate that level of mutual knowledge that is vital to building a collaborative climate. The following represent further modalities of positive impact on trust antecedents: signaling the competitors' offers, strictly selecting the participants of marketplace and virtual communities, advising postponement of the purchase of the firm's products, and revealing the risks of performing a given transaction (Reichheld and Schefter, 2000; Urban et al., 2000; Prandelli and Verona, 2001; Tan and Santosa, 2001). These forms of behavior establish the prerequisites of a recursive trust production process, bound to territorially defined markets, which allows the creation of wider, trust-based virtual markets.

Trust Growth Strategies

The second approach includes several strategies of trust enhancement, which extend beyond the simple activation of trust drivers, that all exploit a peculiarity of trust. Trust is a moral resource that is not consumed with use; it is enhanced through use (Dasgupta, 1989; Gambetta, 1989; Nooteboom et al., 1997). Trust can be increased through auto-poietic processes. Therefore, continuous use of trust, starting with a trust presupposition, and trusting can be regarded as strategies that develop trust. The following examples will illustrate how this occurs.

Successive confirmations of trust in someone strengthens the trust in this subject and increases the multiplicity of positive experiences. Consequently, trust is fed by the continuous creation of new expectations regarding the counterpart (making new promises), and the adoption of behaviors capable of continuously satisfying the expectations thus created. This is an example of what we mean by continuously using trust.

In addition, trust depends on the expectations that an actor formulates a priori.[6] If a firm is regarded as scarcely reliable, it is likely that this hypothesis will be confirmed, whether or not it is objectively tested. In fact, it is most likely that organizations or individuals will share experiences with subjects whom they trust. Subsequent positive experiences will deepen that initial trust.[7] Firms that are not trusted, and therefore with which no experience has occurred, have no chance to modify such initial negative perceptions (whether these are motivated or not); these negative perceptions are strengthened.[8] This is an example of a trust-presupposition.

In a similar way, distrust is characterized by a self-realizing property that generates a congruent reality (Gambetta, 1989: 305). An initial belief, as hypothesized by an individual or firm, affects trust growth paths.[9] In fact, as long as the relationship evolves positively, as long as a party does not betray the other's trust, each partner is induced to continue interacting with the counterpart, whose behavior is easily predicted, being constantly aligned with his or her promises. If counterparts lack the same learning level, relationships with other subjects will be avoided. This also explains the difficulties encountered in entering a market or expanding the market share in industries characterized by strongly consolidated trust relationships, because these relations make it difficult to bridge the gap between a firm's partners and those who would like to be its new counterparts. In these contexts, trust plays a decisive role in attenuating competitive interdependencies. This function is particularly significant when the relationship concerns especially complex tasks, which demand a consistent learning effort from the involved actors. In these cases, it is far more economical to continue trusting those who were trusted in the past as a cognitive shortcut than to start new relationships that would require significant effort in terms of learning and building what we defined as knowledge-based trust.

Finally, the trusting strategy may be explained as: placing trust in ourselves or in the counterpart as a way to increase trust itself. The amount of trust bestowed upon a firm by others depends on the trust that the relevant firm has in itself and, in particular, in its capability to perform tasks of interest to external subjects (Lehrer, 1997). As previously mentioned, capabilities and knowledge are major components of trust: if the trustee does not trust his or her own capabilities, it seems likely that external actors will sense an ability gap, thus opening the way to distrust or, at best, hopeful trust as defined by Andaleeb (1992).

Furthermore, trust is a reciprocity-based resource: the enhancement of trust in a party facilitates trust bestowing in the opposite direction (Gambetta, 1989). Consequently, in order to increase the trust in an actor, the latter needs to trust the trustor (although this step alone is not sufficient to achieve that goal).[10] Triggering this virtuous cycle is crucial for trust relationship consolidation, and its translation in collaborative behaviors. In situations in which an actor shows preset distrust toward the counterpart, the process of mutual trust building might be stillborn.[11]

To sum up, a firm may follow one or both of the two main approaches: acting on the determinants (drivers or antecedents) of trust, especially the most pivotal ones, or exploiting the autopoietic properties of trust by choosing among diverse alternatives (continuously using trust, starting with a trust-presupposition, or trusting oneself and the counterpart).

Considering the importance of trust in the current market environment as a source of competitive advantage, the following section aims to sum up some managerial implications by suggesting guidelines for the policies of trust management.

CONCLUSION: TOWARD THE STRATEGIC MANAGEMENT OF TRUST

The policies of trust management may be structured in two fundamental phases:

a) an analytical phase, aimed at measuring trust and the connections with its related variables;
b) a definition phase of trust development strategies.

a) A trust measurement and detection system needs to be developed first of all. To this end, it is required to detect the construct consistence and quality (typologies). It is crucial to clarify the concept meaning and its analytical dimensions in a way that defines the object to be measured, and develop solid detection systems. Subsequently, from a managerial perspective, it is appropriate to verify the logical link connecting the construct and its consequences, in terms of both functional implications and economic value. To this effect, firms need to be aware of the economic impact of trust, as well as its benefits, both cognitive (uncertainty reduction, conflict control, and commitment enhancement) and behavioral (collaboration, partnership activation, and loyalty). In fact, only a full understanding of trust, or real, benefits makes it possible to reach that fundamental level of commitment that is needed to implement effective development strategies, and to make the single operational units involved in the innovative process of trust production accountable and to control them. Finally, firms need to quantify both the relation between the construct and its cognitive and behavioral antecedents, and the impact of the moderating and amplifying variables (Baron and Kenny, 1986). To sum up, it is appropriate to reconstruct the antecedents (semantic network structure) underlying the trust concept, as well as detect their relative leverage.

b) In dealing with trust development policies, it is, for simplicity's sake, useful to distinguish between the relationship's internal elements and external factors.

As previously mentioned, policies promoting internal factors can be focused on the activation of drivers and the transversal strategies (continuous use of trust, starting from a trust presupposition, and trusting oneself and the counterpart).

Particular relevance should be attributed to managing the various relational interfaces and the trust mimicry. For example, a manufacturer of consumer goods, marketed through self-service distribution formats, relates to customers via the support of the product itself and through ad campaigns or other forms of communication (including direct communication). In contrast, a retailer interacts with customers through: assortment (single brands, even private labels), stores (space, layout, equipments, etc.), salespeople (adding an interpersonal dimension to the relational interface), and various in-store and out-of-store means of communication. Ultimately, the relational interface available to the retailer is generally much richer and more varied than that of a brand. The retailer can count on personal, firm, product trust and so on, elements that increase his or her trust mimicry tools. Nevertheless, in view of the possible poor integration of messages signaled by the various interfacing elements and salespeople's equally possible opportunistic exploitation of the personal trust that they have developed with the customers, this potential is also more complex to manage. These remarks highlight the radical change in relational interfaces caused in e-commerce, which, despite virtual reproductions, still lacks instances of physical contact (product-support, point of sale, sales personnel, etc.). It seems relatively simple to foresee the changes thus introduced in trust production mechanisms.

Naturally, trust development processes and strategies should be designed by paying explicit attention to the relationship's life cycle and the different constructs associated with its phases (trust based on calculus, knowledge, and values). These designs should gradually increase the abstraction of trust contents.

These processes underlie the policies of trust extension, which is focused on widening the relationship scope. An interesting example of trust abstraction policy is offered by Migros, the largest retail group in Switzerland. Since its founding, Migros has sought to build a typology of trust characterized by a high level of abstraction. Migros has always been a synonym of a socially responsible (ethically and environmentally) and consumerist firm that promotes and defends the interests of its consumers (this is similar to the French retailer, Leclerc). For example, in several product divisions, Migros has developed strict codes of conduct to which its suppliers must subscribe and adhere. In order to fulfill these goals, the firm usually collaborates with institution-partners (mostly non-profit), that act as guarantors, vouching for the credibility of the firm's commitment to the public. In addition, Migros has deliberately decided not to market products that may be considered harmful to its customers' health, such as cigarettes and hard liquor. The strong trust connection that customers feel toward the firm allows Migros to satisfy wide and highly structured clusters of customer needs. It suffices to say that, in addition to distributing only privately labeled products (some well-known industrial brands are present due to co-branding), Migros offers its customers financial services, insurance coverage, and tour packages, as well as training and educational services for the youth, and baby caring facilities.

Within the domain of trust development policies, special consideration should be reserved for the multi-layered nature of relationships and the interdependencies that can be established between those levels. For example, when a customer trustor faces an unknown salesperson, his or her trust in the organization brand naturally prevails, producing a trust transfer from the inter-organizational to the inter-personal level (and vice versa in a particular situation). Obviously, even in this case, perceptive weight and leverage should be considered. In fact, there are mutual interdependences between the antecedents, which refer to the individuals and relate to the organization. These interdependences determine a more structured and complex multi-layered semantic network that, when the relation is characterized by a significant personal presence, needs to be very carefully managed. To avoid such problems, some retailers have recently proposed counter-trend sale solutions.

While these solutions seem to be less effective in terms of mere customer satisfaction, they tend to minimize the contact with the customer (for example, in the fresh grocery category). Thus, these firms attempt to avoid becoming the hostages of salespeople, who are capable of managing the relationship with the customer with respect to the sale of products, at a personal level, as such a relationship requires significant amounts of trust. By reducing the salesperson's presence in the management of customer relations, the trust guarantor role is largely transferred to the retailer brand. Conversely, an evolutionary trend of opposite valence seems to characterize the world of manufactured brands. Many firms are increasingly trying to personalize the relationship with their customers, associating their brands with that of personal profiles considered reliable (testimonials sometimes fully identify with the entrepreneur). In this way, a firm attempts to virtually spread the relational interface width and enhance its trust mimicry tools, as well as to personify its image profile, thus drawing from trust determinants normally associated with personal value and characteristics.

Finally, with regard to external policies of trust production, it is essential for a firm to join or even create networks capable of obtaining an external image of reliability, on which its trust profile can depend. At the same time, it is worth monitoring the level of institutional trust by properly activating the most favorable environments of trust.

From our perspective, a topic that seems to be particularly relevant is the possibility for a single firm to exhibit behaviors that foster a compensatory type of trust or induce the creation of a favorable climate within a more limited environmental network in the presence of a significant level of institutional distrust (systemic trust). This will insulate the firm from phenomena that seriously undermine greater institutional trust. This possibility presents difficulties directly correlated to the magnitude of institutional instability and requires long-term interventions to create more cohesive relational environments characterized by a trust value profile. The extended time span of this intervention need not depend on an instability-causing event, but requires anticipatory actions in the context of a deliberate strategy for the continuous production of a trust environment that is both favorable and redundant.

As these brief remarks demonstrate, although trust management is very complex to analyze, it represents an exciting vector of deeper knowledge about trust and provides the fundamental input needed to implement truly trust-based behaviors and firm policies. Therefore, this work opens new pathways for further research on stimulating construct of trust.

NOTES

1. Some scholars have pointed out that the circular relationship between risk and trust is the basis for a paradox that underlies the very concept of trust. While trust reduces the level of risk, *ex post* it loses its utility, because it has neutralized the fundamental reason behind the need to trust, that is: risk itself. This consideration does not seem to have any conceptual value as, first of all, these two aspects (trust and risk) represent facets of the same phenomenon. The possible conclusion of a trust relationship, and the subsequent lack of trust it implies, would inevitably lead to a re-emersion of an external risk and to the interruption of individual behaviors due to the high level of uncertainty that would develop.
2. This classification further elaborates on the distinction between reliability-based and value-based trust, originally proposed by Sitkin and Roth (1993). Calculative trust and knowledge-based trust further distinguish the first type (based on predictability), even though they are quite different. In fact, the former is exclusively based on economic calculation, while the latter is based on perceptions of the other party's competence. Contrarily, value-based trust coincides with trust based on identification and personal

values. The tripartition now introduced is easily referenced to a distinction between calculative trust and relational trust proposed by Rousseau et al. (1998), where the second typology includes both knowledge-based and value-based trust.

3. Actually, a correct perception of the trustee's competence profile requires a certain level of trust, also regarding one's skill in recognizing someone else's capabilities (a type of self-confidence about one's capacity to signal decoding), as much as the other party's signaling of transparency or assumed lack of willful distortion of the latter's competencies, thus acting as a clean player.

4. Kramer et al. (1996: 373) further classify this last level of trust and, more generically, identity-based trust into four subcategories (reciprocity-based trust, elicitative trust, compensatory trust, noncontingent or moralistic trust).

5. The evaluation of the nexus between trust growth and the variation of customer equity's single components could be an interesting subject for empirical analysis. A revamping of the above-mentioned formula has been recently suggested by Costabile (2001: 154). This author underlines the appropriateness of differentiating between the current customer equity, calculated according to the already described modalities, and the potential customer equity. The latter also includes the options of broadening the relationship scope derived from the development of trust (and trust abstraction policies).

6. Einhorn and Hogarth (1978) offered an empirical confirmation of this statement.

7. In this regard, Berger and Luckmann's (1967) considerations of image are particularly interesting and can be easily extended to the concept of trust. Essentially trust presents many analogies to image, due to its synthetic nature and regardless of its reference to a cognitive scheme. Image is characterized by its tendency to further strengthen and, once consolidated, to self-realization. Indeed, it generates a finalized behavior that, if successful, tends first to justify and then to strengthen itself. Images that generate strong, visible, and successful actions have a prophetic allure: they self-realize. See Berger and Luckmann (1967, quoted by Normann, 1984: 129).

8. Einhorn's example (1982: 282) about a waiter working in a crowded restaurant helps to clarify this matter. Not having the time to offer good service to all his customers, the waiter tries to foresee (prophesize) which ones are more likely to leave a good tip. He reserves his best service for them to the detriment of the rest. If the tip amount depends on the rendered service quality, the customers' behavior cannot but confirm the waiter's initial assessment.

9. On the subject's capability to self-determine events, see also Watzlawick (1981), Luhmann (1989), Gambetta (1989), and Einhorn and Hogarth (1978).

10. In a series of experiments on interpersonal relationships, based on the prisoner's dilemma, Boyle and Bonacich (1970) have verified that cooperative behavior is always characterized by mutuality.

11. Interesting empirical research by Kelley and Stahelski (1970) has demonstrated that competitive individuals most often assume that the counterpart's behavior is hostile. This assumption leads these individuals to be distrustful, making it impossible to have a relationship based on cooperation. In contrast, more cooperative personalities regard others in a more balanced light, distinguishing cooperative from competitive people. This attitude greatly facilitates the triggering of a trust relationship based on cooperative behavior.

REFERENCES

Achrol, R.S. and P. Kotler (1999), 'Marketing in the network economy', *Journal of Marketing*, **63**, 146–163.

Andaleeb, S.S. (1992), 'The trust concept: research issues for channel of distribution', in J.N. Sheth (ed.), *Research in Marketing*, vol. 11, Greenwich, CT: Jai Press Inc., pp. 1–34.

Anderson, E.W. and M.W. Sullivan (1993), 'The antecedents and consequences of customer satisfaction for firms', *Marketing Science*, Spring, 125–143.

Anderson, J.C. and J.A. Narus (1990), 'A model of distributor firm and manufacturer firm working partnerships', *Journal of Marketing*, **54**, 42–58.

Arora, A. and A. Gambardella (1994), 'The changing technology of technological change: general and abstract knowledge and the division of innovative labour', *Research Policy*, **23** (5), 523–532.

Bacharach, M. and D. Gambetta (2001), 'Trust as type detection', in C. Castelfranchi and Y.H. Tan (eds), *Trust and Deception in Virtual Societies*, Dordrecht: Kluwer Academic Publisher, pp. 1–26.

Barney, J.B. and M.H. Hansen (1994), 'Trustworthiness as a source of competitive advantage', *Strategic Management Journal*, **15**, 175–190.

Baron, R.M. and D.A. Kenny (1986), 'The moderator-mediator variable distinction in social psychological research: conceptual, strategic, and statistical consideration', *Journal of Personality and Social Psychology*, **51** (6), 1173–1182.

Boyle, R. and P. Bonacich (1970), 'The development of trust and mistrust in mixed-motive games', *Sociometry*, **33** (6), 123–139.

Castaldo, S. and G. Verona (2001), 'L'innovazione nell'economia della virtualità', in S. Vicari (ed.), *Economia Della Virtualità*, Milan: EGEA, pp. 89–125.

Child, J. (1998), 'Trust and international strategic alliances: the case of Sino-foreign joint ventures', in C. Lane and R. Bachmann (eds), *Trust Within and Between Organizations. Conceptual Issues and Empirical Applications*, Oxford: Oxford University Press, pp. 241–272.

Costabile, M. (ed.) (2001), *Il Capitale Relazionale*, Milan: McGraw Hill.

Das, T.K. and B.S. Teng (1998), 'Between trust and control: developing confidence in partner cooperation in alliances', *Academy of Management Review*, **23** (3), 491–512.

Das, T.K. and B.S. Teng (2001), 'Trust, control and risk in strategic alliances: an integrated framework,' *Organization Studies*, **22** (2), 251–283.

Dasgupta, P. (1989), 'La fiducia come bene economico', in D. Gambetta (ed.), *Trust. Making and Breaking Cooperative Relations*, Oxford: Blackwell, pp. 63–94.

Deutsch, M. (1958), 'Trust and suspicion', *The Journal of Conflict Resolution*, **2**, 265–279.

Deutsch, M. (1962), 'Cooperation and trust: some theoretical notes', in J.R. Marshall (ed.), *Nebraska Symposium on Motivation*, Lincoln: University of Nebraska Press.

Doney, P.M. and J.P. Cannon (1997), 'An examination of the nature of trust in buyer-seller relationships', *Journal of Marketing*, **61**, 35–51.

Doney, P.M., J.H. Cannon and M.R. Mullen (1998), 'Understanding the influence of national culture on the development of trust', *Academy of Management Review*, **23** (3), 601–620.

Dore, R. (1983), 'Goodwill and the spirit of market capitalism', *The British Journal of Sociology*, **34** (4), 459–482.

Dyer, J.H. and H. Singh (1998), 'The relational view: cooperative strategy and sources of interorganizational competitive advantage', *Academy of Management Review*, **4**, 660–679.

Einhorn, H.J. (1982), 'Learning from experience and suboptimal rules in decision making', in D. Kahnerman, P. Slovic and A. Tversky (eds), *Judgement Under Uncertainty: Heuristics and Biases*, Cambridge, Illinois: Cambridge University Press, pp. 268–283.

Einhorn, H.J. and R.M. Hogart (1978), 'Confidence in judgment: persistence of the illusion of validity', *Psychological Review*, **85** (5), 395–416.

Galeotti, A.E. (1990), 'Fidarsi è bene', *Stato e Mercato*, **28** (4), 117–126.

Gambetta, D. (1989), 'Possiamo fidarci della fiducia?', in D. Gambetta (ed.), *Trust. Making and Breaking Cooperative Relations*, Oxford: Basil Blackwell Ltd (Italian translation: *Le strategie della fiducia. Indagini sulla razionalità della cooperazione*, Torino: Einaudi, pp. 275–309, Italian edition).

Ganesan, S. (1994), 'Determinants of long-term orientation in buyer-seller relationships', *Journal of Marketing*, **58** (4), 1–19.

Golembiewski, R.T. and M.M. McConkie (1975), 'The centrality of interpersonal trust in group processes', in C.L. Cooper (ed.), *Theories of Group Processes*, New York: John Wiley & Sons, pp. 131–186.

Gulati, R. (1995), 'Does familiarity breed trust? The implications of repeated ties for contractual choice in alliances', *Academy of Management Journal*, **38** (1), 85–112.

Hardy, C., N. Phillips and T. Lawrence (1998), 'Distinguishing trust and power in interorganizational relations: forms and façades of trust', in C. Lane and R. Bachmann (eds), *Trust Within and Between Organizations. Conceptual Issues and Empirical Analysis*, Oxford: Oxford University Press, pp. 64–87.

Huemer, L. (ed.) (1998), *Trust in Business Relations. Economic Logic or Social Interaction?*, Umeå: Boréa Bokförlag.

Huemer, L. (2000), 'Beyond predictability: employing trust in business relationships', working paper, Norwegian School of Management, Sandvika.

Hunt, S.D. and R.M. Morgan (1997), 'Resource-advantage theory: a snake swallowing its tails or a general theory of competition?', *Journal of Marketing*, **61**, 74–82.

Iacobucci, D. (1998), 'Interactive marketing and the meganet: networks of networks', *Journal of Interactive Marketing*, **12** (1), 5–16.

Jap, S.D. (1999), 'Pie-expansion efforts: collaboration processes in buyer-supplier relationships', *Journal of Marketing Research*, **36** (11), 461–475.

Jap, S.D. (2001), '"Pie sharing" in complex collaboration contexts', *Journal of Marketing Research*, **38** (2), 86–99.

Johnson, M.D., E.W. Anderson and C. Fornell (1995), 'Rationale and adaptive performance expectations in a customer satisfaction framework', *Journal of Consumer Research*, March, 695–707.

Kelley, H.H. and A.J. Stahelski (1970), 'Social interaction basis of cooperators' and competitors' beliefs about others', *Journal of Personal and Social Psychology*, **16** (1), 66–91.

Kramer, R.M., M.B. Brewer and B.A. Hanna (1996), 'Collective trust and collective action: the decision to trust as a social decision', in R.M. Kramer and T.R. Tyler (eds), *Trust in Organizations: Frontiers of Theory and Research*, California: Sage Publications, pp. 357–389.

Lane, C. (1998), 'Introduction: theories and issues in the study of trust', in C. Lane and R. Bachmann (eds), *Trust Within and Between Organizations. Conceptual Issues and Empirical Analysis*, Oxford: Oxford University Press, pp. 1–30.

Lehrer, K. (ed.) (1997), *Self Trust. A Study of Reason, Knowledge, and Autonomy*, Oxford: Clarendon Press.

Lewicki, R.J. and B.B. Bunker (1996), 'Developing and maintaining trust in work relationships', in R.M. Kramer and T.R. Tyler (eds), *Trust in Organizations: Frontiers of Theory and Research*, California: Sage Publications, pp. 114–139.

Lewis, J.D. and A. Weigert (1985), 'Trust as a social reality', *Social Forces*, **63** (4), 967–985.

Luhmann, N. (ed.) (1980), *Trust and Power*, New York: Wiley.

Luhmann, N. (1989), 'Familiarital, confidare e fiducia: problemi e alternative', in D. Gambetta (ed.), *Trust. Making and Breaking Cooperative Relations*, pp. 123–140.

Luhmann, N. (ed.) (1991), *Risk: A Sociological Theory*, Berlin: Walter de Gruyter.

March, J.G. (1991), 'Exploration and exploitation in organizational learning', *Organization Science*, **2** (1), 71–87.

McAllister, D.J. (1995), 'Affect- and cognition-based trust as foundations for interpersonal cooperation in organizations', *Academy of Management Journal*, **38** (1), 24–59.

McKnight, D.H., L.L. Cummings and N.L. Chervany (1998), 'Initial trust formation in new organizational relationship', *Academy of Management Review*, **23** (3), 473–490.

Meyerson, D.K., E. Weick and R.M. Kramer (1996), 'Swift trust and temporary groups', in R.M. Kramer and T.R. Tyler (eds), *Trust in Organizations: Frontiers of Theory and Research*, California: Sage Publications, pp. 166–195.

Mishra, A.K. (1996), 'Organizational responses to crisis: the centrality of trust', in R.M. Kramer and T.R. Tyler (eds), *Trust in Organizations: Frontiers of Theory and Research*, California: Sage Publications, pp. 261–287.

Moorman, C., R. Deshpandè and G. Zaltman (1993), 'Factors affecting trust in market research relationships', *Journal of Marketing*, **57** (1), 81–101.

Moorman, C., G. Zaltman and R. Deshpandè (1992), 'Relationship between providers and users of market research: the dynamics of trust within and between organizations', *Journal of Marketing Research*, **29** (8), 314–329.

Morgan, R.M. and S.D. Hunt (1999), 'Relationship-based competitive advantage: the role of relationship marketing in marketing strategy', *Journal of Business Research*, **46**, 281–290.

Nooteboom, B., H. Berger and N.G. Noorderhaven (1997), 'Effects of trust and governance on relational risk', *Academy of Management Journal*, **40** (2), 308–338.

Normann, R. (ed.) (1984), *Service Management. Strategy and Leadership in Service Businesses*, New York: John Wiley & Sons.

Perrone, V. and C. Chiacchierini (1999), 'Fiducia e comportamenti di cittadinanza organizzativa. Un'indagine empirica nella prospettiva della rete degli scambi sociali', *Economia & Management*, **4**, 87–100.

Reichheld, F. and P. Schefter (2000), 'E-loyalty. Your secret weapon on the web', *Harvard Business Review*, **7–8**, 105–113.

Ring, P.S. and A.H. Van de Ven (1992), 'Structuring cooperative relationships between organizations', *Strategic Management Journal*, **13**, 483–498.

Rousseau, D.M., S.B. Sitkin, R.S. Burt and C. Camerer (1998), 'Not so different after all: a cross-discipline view of trust', *Academy of Management Review*, **23** (3), 393–404.

Sako, M. (1991), 'The role of "trust" in Japanese buyer-supplier relationships', *Ricerche Economiche*, **45** (2–3), 449–474.

Sako, M. (1998), 'Does trust improve business performance?', in C. Lane and R. Bachmann (eds), *Trust Within and Between Organizations. Conceptual Issues and Empirical Analysis*, Oxford: Oxford University Press, pp. 88–117.

Sako, M. and S. Helper (1998), 'Determinants of trust in supplier relations: evidence from the automotive industry in Japan and the United States', *Journal of Economic Behavior & Organization*, **34**, 387–417.

Sawhney, M. and E. Prandelli (2000), 'Beyond customer knowledge management: customer as knowledge co-creators', in Y. Malhotra (ed.), *Knowledge Management and Virtual Organizations*, Hershey, PA: Idea Group Publishing, pp. 258–281.

Shapiro, D., B.H. Sheppard and L. Cheraskin (1992), 'Business on a handshake', *Negotiation Journal*, **8** (4), 365–377.

Sheppard, B.H. and M. Tuchinsky (1996), 'Micro-OB and the network organization', in R.M. Kramer and T.R. Tyler (eds), *Trust in Organizations: Frontiers of Theory and Research*, California: Sage Publications, pp. 140–165.

Sirdeshmukh, D., J. Singh and B. Sabol (2002), 'Consumer trust, value, and loyalty in relational exchange', *Journal of Marketing*, **66** (1), 15–37.

Sitkin, S.B. and N.L. Roth (1993), 'Explaining the limited effectiveness of legalistic "remedies" for trust/distrust', *Organizational Science*, **4**, 367–392.

Srivastava, R.K., T.A. Shervani and L. Fahey (1998), 'Market-based assets and shareholder value: a framework for analysis', *Journal of Marketing*, **1**, 2–18.

Tan, Y.H. and S. Santosa (2001), 'A trust model for first trade transactions in electronic commerce', workshop on trust within and between organisations, Vrije Universiteit Amsterdam, The Netherlands, 29–30 November.

Teece, D.J., G. Pisano and A. Shuen (1997), 'Dynamic capabilities and strategic management', *Strategic Management Journal*, **18**, 509–533.

Troilo, G. (ed.) (2001), *Marketing Knowledge Management*, Milan: Etas.

Urban, G.L., F. Sultan and W.J. Qualls (2000), 'Placing trust at the center of your internet strategy', *Sloan Management Review*, Fall, 39–48.

Vicari, S. (ed.) (1991), *L'impresa Vivente. Itinerario di una Diversa Concezione*, Milano: Etas.

Vicari, S. (ed.) (2001), *Economia della Virtualità*, Milan: Egea.

Von Hippel, E. (ed.) (1988), *The Sources of Innovation*, Oxford: Oxford University Press.

Watzlawick, P. (1981), 'Le profezie che si autodeterminano', in P. Watzlawick (ed.), *Die Erfundene Wirklichkeit*, Munich: Piper.

Williams, B. (1989), 'Strutture formali e realtà sociale', in D. Gambetta (ed.), *Trust. Making and Breaking Cooperative Relations*, pp. 5–18.

Williamson, O.E. (1993), 'Calculativeness, trust, and economic organization', *Journal of Law and Economics*, **36**, 453–486.

22 Competing through business models[1]
Ramon Casadesus-Masanell and Joan E. Ricart

Business model innovation is becoming one of the main forces driving strategic renewal efforts of businesses around the world. IBM's 2006 *Global CEO Study*, for example, shows that top management in a broad range of industries is actively seeking guidance on how to innovate in their business models to improve their ability to both create and capture value.

While the expression 'business model' has been part of the business jargon for a long time, there is no widely accepted definition of what it means. Its origins can be traced back to the writings of Peter Drucker (1954), but the notion has gained prominence amongst both academics and practitioners only in the last decade. This is not to say that organizations did not have or use business models prior to this recent wave of interest, but business models of industry players were for the most part similar and, as such, the notion was not the focus of attention.

Advances in information and communication technologies have driven the recent interest in business model design and business model innovation. Many of the so-called 'e-businesses' constitute new business models (Evans and Wurster, 1997; Varian and Shapiro, 1999). Shafer et al. (2005) present 12 recent definitions of business model and find that eight are related to e-business. Of course not all business model innovations are IT-driven; other forces such as globalization and deregulation have also resulted in new business models and fed the interest in this area.

New strategies for the bottom of the pyramid in emerging markets (Ricart et al., 2004) have also steered researchers and practitioners towards the systematic study of business models. Most academics working in this area agree that for firms to be effective in such 'different' environments companies need to develop novel business models (Prahalad and Hart, 2002; London and Hart, 2003). In fact, socially motivated enterprises that aim to reach the bottom of the pyramid constitute an important source of business model innovations (Hart and Christensen, 2002; Prahalad, 2005).

Although it is uncontroversial that for organizations to thrive, managers must have a good understanding of how business models work, the academic community has offered little insight on this issue so far. In truth little is understood about what constitutes a superior business model, not even about what a business model really is. This chapter attempts to remedy this state of affairs.

WHAT IS A BUSINESS MODEL?

Although there is no generally accepted definition of business model, practitioners and academics often talk loosely of a business model as 'the way the firm operates.' While we share this view, we must provide a more concrete definition to make progress. Towards this end, we review existing work and base our definition on earlier notions.

Magretta (2002) defines business models as "stories that explain how enterprises work." This author goes back to Peter Drucker and defines a good business model as one that provides answers to the following questions: Who is the customer and what does the costumer value? What is the underlying economic logic that explains how we can deliver value to customers at an appropriate cost? Magretta's implicit idea is that business model refers to the logic by which the organization earns money. While not formal, Magretta's approach highlights two fundamental questions any business model should answer: one related to the value provided to the client and the other to the organization's ability to capture value in the process of serving customers.

While Magretta's definition is broad and imprecise, Amit and Zott's (2001) is narrow (as it focuses on e-businesses) but precise. These authors review the contributions of several theories including virtual markets, Schumpeterian innovation, value chain analysis, the resource-based view of the firm, dynamic capabilities, transaction cost economics, and strategic networks. As they point out, every theory contributes elements to the notion but none, by itself, explains completely the nature of business models. Amit and Zott analyze a sample of USA and European e-business models to highlight the drivers of value creation and present the following integrative definition: "A business model depicts the content, structure, and governance of transactions designed so as to create value through the exploitation of business opportunities" (2001:511). Transaction content refers to the goods or information being exchanged, as well as to the resources and capabilities required. Transaction structure refers to the parties that participate, their links, and the way they choose to operate. Finally, transaction governance refers to the way flows of information, resources, and goods are controlled by the relevant parties, the legal form of organization, and the incentives to the participants.

As mentioned above, Shafer et al. (2005) uncovered 12 definitions published from 1998 to 2002, and they developed an affinity diagram to identify four major categories common to all or most definitions: strategic choices, creating value, capturing value, and the value network. Therefore, consistent with the intuitive view of the concept, a business model is defined by strategic choices, sometimes made by a network of organizations, that explain value creation and value capture. From this we conclude that one important component of business models is the concrete choices made by management on how the organization must operate. For example, choices regarding compensation practices, procurement contracts, location of facilities, assets employed, extent of vertical integration, or sales and marketing initiatives are, for the most part, choices made by management that define the way the firm operates.

Choices, however, are not the sole constituent of business models. As all authors highlight, choices must be connected to value creation and value capture, or to alternative goals the firm may want to pursue. And just as causes have effects in the physical world, management choices have consequences. For example, the provision of high-powered incentives (a choice) has implications regarding the willingness to exert effort or to cooperate with coworkers (consequences). Likewise, pricing policies (choices) have obvious implications regarding sales volume which, in turn, affects the economies of scale and bargaining power enjoyed by the firm (two consequences). Because consequences (such as low cost or a culture of frugality) are usually employed to describe the way the firm operates, we include them in our definition of a business model.

In sum, a business model consists of: (1) a set of choices and (2) the set of consequences derived from those choices.

For the purposes of illustration, and somewhat loosely, think of a company as a machine.[2] Of course, real organizations are different from machines in many important respects but, as will become clear, the comparison is useful. In this analogy, a business model refers to how the machine is assembled (choices regarding how the machine is put together) and how the different elements work together (consequences of the choices). There are a zillion different ways a machine can be constructed, with different levels of redundancy, specific mechanisms, quality of components and so on. Different machine configurations have different direct consequences and this affects the overall level of efficiency (speed, input efficiency, noise, quality of output. . .).

It is useful to distinguish different types of choices and consequences. There are three types of choices: policies, assets, and governance of assets and policies. Consequences, on the other hand, are classified into flexible and rigid.

Policies refers to courses of action adopted by the firm regarding all aspects of its operation. Examples of policies include: opposing the

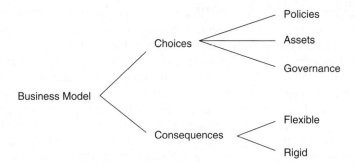

Figure 22.1   Elements of a business model

emergence unions, locating plants in rural areas, encouraging employees to fly tourist class, providing high-powered monetary incentives, or flying to secondary airports. Assets (physical) refers to tangible resources such as manufacturing facilities or a satellite system for communicating between offices.[3] By governance of assets and policies we mean the structure of contractual arrangements that confer decision rights regarding policies or assets. For example, a given business model may contain as a choice the use of certain assets such as a fleet of trucks. The fleet can be owned by the firm or leased from a third party. As the literature on transaction cost economics demonstrates (see for example Williamson, 1980), seemingly innocuous differences in governance of assets and policies may have a dramatic effect on the effectiveness of a given business model.

A consequence is flexible if it is sensitive to the choices that generate it. For example, large volume is a consequence of a policy of low prices. If the policy changes to high prices, volume is likely to fall rapidly. In contrast, a rigid consequence is one that does not change rapidly with the choices that generate it. For example, a culture of frugality is a consequence that changes only slowly with the choices that generate it. Perhaps a more tangible example is an installed base of PCs, which is (partly) a consequence of prices set by Intel and Microsoft for the microprocessor and the operating system, respectively. As prices change, the installed base changes slowly: it is a rigid consequence. Clearly, no consequence is purely flexible or purely rigid. All consequences are somewhere in between, it is a matter of degree.

BUSINESS MODEL REPRESENTATIONS

A useful way to represent business models is by means of a causal loop diagram (Baum and Singh, 1994): choices and consequences linked by arrows representing causality. However, except possibly for the simplest organizations, such a representation rapidly becomes highly complex and often intractable. In principle, one could make the effort of listing every choice made by management (although this would take a very long time). More difficult, perhaps, is to list the set of all consequences of those choices and to spell out exactly how choices (and different combinations of choices) deliver those consequences and how exactly consequences (and different combinations of consequences) enable choices. In most businesses there are large numbers of choices and consequences. An analysis and evaluation of an organization's business model that takes into consideration every choice and every consequence is just impractical: nothing meaningful can be concluded by considering choices and consequences in full richness of detail.

To overcome this issue, we work with representations of business models (or models of business models). A business model representation consists of (i) choices (generally a subset of all choices), (ii) consequences (generally a subset of all consequences), and (iii) theories.

Notice the third element: theories. Theories are suppositions on how choices and consequences are related. For example, a theory may be that as R&D expenditures increase, products with innovative features are brought to market. In the causal loop diagram, we would have an arrow from 'high R&D expenditures' to 'innovative products.' In many cases theories are commonly accepted relationships open to little discussion.[4] Other times, however, they are controversial. In the 1960s, Sam Walton believed that large volumes of merchandise would be bought in rural areas if discount stores were located there. At the time, most people did not share this view. (See Bradley et al., 1994.)

Notice also that theories do not appear in the definition of a business model. A business model is made up of choices and consequences, but these are the actual choices and actual consequences as they are truly related. Business model refers to the real relationships. A business model representation, on the other hand, refers to a model of the business model. A business model representation integrates theories of causality that are believed to be true by the business model designer or analyst. If later they fail to hold up, there will be a break in the logic and business model failure (partial or complete).

As mentioned above, we do not include every choice and consequence in the business model representation. There are two main ways to move from the full, true detail of a business model to a simplified, tractable representation: aggregation and decomposability. In most instances, business model representations make simultaneous use of both approaches.

Aggregation

Aggregation works by bunching together detailed choices and consequences into larger constructs. For example, specific incentive contracts (which may be unique to every individual in the organization) may be bunched together into a choice called 'high-powered incentives.' This captures the idea that on average contracts impose high-powered incentives onto the workforce. In the business model representation, instead of detailing every contract offered to every individual, we simply write one choice: high-powered incentives. This allows a simplified representation that enhances our understanding of the organization.

One can think of aggregation as 'zooming out' and looking at the (real) business model from a distance. As the analyst zooms out, details blur and larger objects (aggregations of details) become clear. If one keeps one's nose close to every choice and consequence, it is impossible to see the larger picture and understand how the business model works. On the other hand, if one looks at the business model from very far away, all interesting details are lost. It is more an art than a science to find the right distance from which to assess a given business model. How much to zoom out generally depends on the question the analyst is trying to address.

In what follows we use the expression 'level of aggregation' to refer to the extent to which we zoom out from the full business model. A high level of aggregation refers to looking at the business model from a large distance. A low level of aggregation refers to being close to the details. As we point out below, high levels of aggregation are needed when analyzing interaction between business models of different players (or competition through business models).

Decomposability

Sometimes business models are decomposable in the sense that different groups of choices and consequences do not interact with one another and thus can be analyzed in isolation. In this case, depending on the question to be addressed, representing just a few parts of an organization's business model may be appropriate. Clearly, this simplifies the analyst's task considerably. For example, in the case of Ryanair developed below, there are few interactions between Ryanair's choices on related businesses such as car rentals or accommodation or ancillary business by others and Ryanair's operative choices related directly to the management of the airline. Given this, one can understand the working of Ryanair's model without the need to be absolutely comprehensive.

Decomposability also allows the study of individual business units in multi-business organizations. For example, below we represent Microsoft's business model for operating systems and productivity applications for the PC (at a high level of aggregation). Microsoft is in many other businesses such as videogame systems or operating systems for personal digital assistants. Although there are interactions between all of these businesses, these may not be central to the particular question being addressed by the analyst and may be ignored.

In what follows, we will abuse language and refer to business model representations as, simply, business models. In doing this, we are assuming that the representation does a good job of portraying the organization's true business model.

An example: Ryanair

To illustrate our notion of a business model, consider Ryanair in 1999 as described in Rivkin's (2000) classic. Important choices in Ryanair's business model include: low fares, flying to secondary airports, all passengers treated equally, nothing is free, no meals, short haul flights, standardized fleet of Boeing 737s, low commissions to travel agencies, non-unionized, high-powered incentives, and spartan headquarters. Consequences of those choices include: low variable and fixed cost, reputation for reasonable fares, combative management team and large volume. Considering what we know about the industry, we develop theories on how choices and consequences are related. For example, an arrow from low fares (choice) to high volume (consequence) reflects the theory that the demand function for flights is downward sloping. We employ a causal loop diagram to represent Ryanair's business model (see Figure 22.2).

Choices are in bold and underlined, rigid consequences are in boxes, and flexible consequences are plain text. Notice that the representation does not include every choice made by Ryanair, nor every consequence. We have made use of aggregation and decomposability.

In sum, the causal loop diagram represents theories linking choices and consequences that allow us to conjecture that Ryanair is able to offer service at a very low cost without lowering too much willingness to pay by customers in the target segment.

We should point out that the absence of arrows also implicitly defines theories. For example, Ryanair's choices of standardized fleet and the use of secondary airports are unrelated, even if they may reinforce one another by leading to low maintenance cost and rapid turnovers. However, the assumption is that these choices are independent. For simplicity, in the diagram, we do not spell out these 'absent arrow' theories.

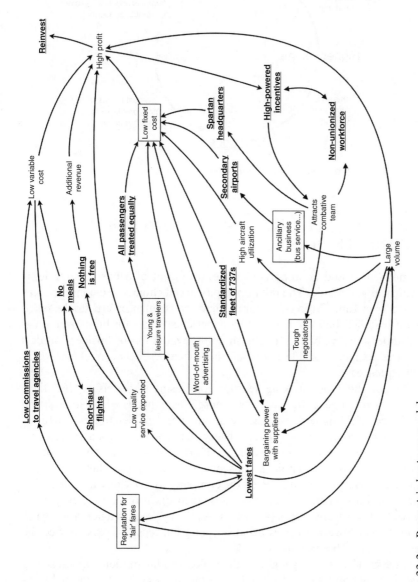

Figure 22.2   Ryanair's business model

467

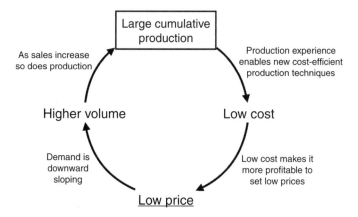

Figure 22.3   Example of a virtuous cycle

VIRTUOUS CYCLES – THE DYNAMICS OF BUSINESS MODELS

By now, it should be apparent that our concept of a business model is intrinsically dynamic. The relationship between choices and consequences occurs over time. Moreover, some 'rigid' consequences are stocks (such as an installed base or cumulative experience) that are built over time. An understanding of the functioning and evaluation of business models requires explicit consideration of the dynamics between choices and consequences.

One of the most striking features of business models is that their dynamics often generate feedback loops. This happens when, in addition to choices yielding consequences, consequences enable choices. Virtuous cycles are feedback loops that in every iteration strengthen some components of the model. For example, Honda historically set low prices for its motorcycles (a choice), consequences were high volume and high cumulative output which allowed the company to move down the learning curve, and low cost. Low cost (a consequence), in turn, enabled Honda to profitably set low prices (a choice). As the cycle spun again and again, Honda kept lowering prices because (marginal) cost decreased.[5] See the representation diagram in Figure 22.3.

Once virtuous cycles get going, they take on a life of their own. Just as a fast-moving body is hard to stop because it possesses kinetic energy,[6] well-functioning virtuous cycles cannot easily be brought to a halt.

Virtuous cycles are especially desirable when they affect the growth of consequences related to goals that the firm seeks to accomplish. For example, Figure 22.2 demonstrates that Ryanair's business model possesses many important virtuous cycles that lead to low cost. The following are examples of virtuous cycles in Figure 22.2 that 'pass through' low cost, one cornerstone of Ryanair's model:

- Cycle 1: ***low fares*** → high volume → bargaining power with suppliers → low fixed cost → ***low fares*** → . . .
- Cycle 2: ***low fares*** → high volume → high aircraft utilization → low fixed cost → ***low fares*** → . . .
- Cycle 3: ***low fares*** → large volume → ancillary businesses develop → ***fly to secondary airports*** → low fixed cost → ***low fares*** → . . .
- Cycle 4: ***low fares*** → attracts young and pleasure travelers → ***all passengers treated equally*** → low fixed cost → ***low fares*** → . . .
- Cycle 5: ***low fares*** → low quality service expected → ***no meals*** → low variable cost → ***low fares*** → . . .

As we discuss below, a desirable feature of business models is the generation of virtuous cycles that move the organization towards fulfilling its goals, whatever those may be.

BUSINESS MODEL EVALUATION

We have defined a business model as a set of choices and the consequences associated with those choices. Clearly, because every organization makes choices and these choices have consequences, every organization has some business model. The question is then: what constitutes a good business model? How can we tell a good from a bad business model?

We begin by considering business models ignoring how they may be affected by those of other players. In other words, we consider an organization's business model in an interaction vacuum and discuss four related desirable features: alignment to goal, reinforcement, virtuousness, and robustness. We later move to include other players and provide a framework to evaluate business models in interaction. While considering business models in isolation is artificial, the analysis of business model interaction adds enough complexity to justify the approach.

BUSINESS MODEL EVALUATION – ANALYSIS IN ISOLATION

Alignment to Goal

Alignment to goal refers to business model choices delivering consequences that move the organization towards achieving its objectives. An organization may possess a terrific business model that works very smoothly. However, if the organization's goal is different from what the business model delivers, then alignment to goal fails and the business model is just not appropriate.

Possible goals include, but are not limited to, profit maximization, a better environment, and a pleasant place to work. The community of Linux developers (an organization that competes against Microsoft's Windows), for example, is more concerned about adding useful new features to the operating system, its robustness, minimization of bugs, and maximization of available complements rather than cost minimization or profit maximization.

Organizations often have multiple goals. The balance between different goals may itself be a goal. Notice the trivial fact that, in most cases, goals are consequences, not choices: a firm that tries to maximize profit, for instance, is not choosing profit directly; profits arise endogenously as a function of choices made by the firm. In many cases, alignment to goal is obvious. Ryanair's goal of high growth and profitability in the airline industry requires low costs. Everything in Ryanair's business model is geared towards delivering low cost.

Of course there are organizations that develop business models that fail to satisfy alignment to goal. Xerox Corporation, for example, set up Xerox Labs in the 1970s as instruments for innovation with the objective of developing new, profitable businesses. While Xerox did come up with many breakthrough innovations, it was unable to generate new businesses and capture value from those.

Reinforcement

Reinforcement refers to choices complementing each other well. Reinforcement is closely related to the well-known idea in strategy of internal consistency (Porter, 1985 and 1996). It is worth defining clearly what we mean by two choices complementing one another. Let A and B be two choices. Let C be all other choices made by the firm. Finally, let o(A, B, C) be a measure or score of how close the organization's goal is satisfied when choices are A, B and C. A larger score means better performance.

Obviously, o(.) is a consequence. We say that B complements A if o(A, B, C) – o(0, B, C) > o(A, 0, C) – o(0, 0, C) where 0 stands for the absence of the choice.[7] Our notion of complementarity is local in the sense that it depends on the set C: A and B may be complementary given C = C_1, but not complementary when C = C_2. For example, suppose A is low price and B is heavy advertising. Let o(A, B, C) be market share. A and B are complementary in the sense that the effect of a low price on market share is likely to be larger when there is heavy advertising. Likewise, the effect of heavy advertising on share is stronger when prices are low. In business model representations we sometimes write A ↔ B to denote complementarity. We do this to economize writing. A more elaborate diagram would have the entire chain from every choice to every consequence.

An obvious example of lack of reinforcement would occur if Ryanair decided to provide a level of comfort comparable to that of full-fare carriers such as British Airways. Increasing the level of comfort would require reducing the number of seats in planes, offering food, coffee, baggage transfer, and, perhaps, flying to primary airports. These choices would undermine the low-cost structure. As a consequence, Ryanair would not be able to maintain its low fares; volume would fall, affecting incentives, economies of scale, and reputation.

As a second example, consider high-powered incentives, a choice that results in large effort exertion. A side effect of high-powered incentives is that it often results in less willingness to cooperate and help each other. In organizations with business models that do not rely on cooperation, high-powered incentives will generally be appropriate (at least for a portion of the workforce). Absence of reinforcement implies the presence of opportunities to improve the business model by discontinuing some choices and adding new ones. Business models develop through time. Early identification of tensions due to inconsistencies is fundamental to manage their development.

Virtuousness

Virtuousness refers to the presence of virtuous cycles (positive feedback loops) that help a business model gain strength over time. In the case of Microsoft, for example, there are two complementary virtuous cycles: the first is related to operating systems and the second to productivity applications. Virtuousness is a dynamic version of reinforcement.

Business models endowed with virtuous cycles that lead to better fulfillment of objectives often imply growth. Growth takes place as rigid consequences directly related to goals become stronger. Examples include positive feedback loops that generate bargaining power (with, say, suppliers) or network effects such as in the case of online auction sites such as eBay. We have already pointed out many of Ryanair's virtuous cycles above. Interestingly, many of the cycles run through low cost and low fares. As a consequence as the cycles spin, Ryanair finds it easier to reach its goal of low cost and high profitability.

Porter cautions managers about the 'growth trap,' the idea that a fixation for growth without consideration of how it furthers the development of competitive advantage may lead to deterioration of that very advantage (Porter, 1996). While growth, per se, may be a poor goal to pursue, an implication of virtuous business models is growth. In a sense, growth and virtuousness are indissoluble. The ultimate goal should never be growth but the pursuit of a strategy that generates virtuous cycles that help the organization create and capture increased value over time.

Robustness

Robustness refers to the ability of the business model to sustain its effectiveness over time. Ghemawat (1999) has identified four generic threats to sustainability: imitation, holdup, slack, and substitution. To check for robustness we ask: how well does the business model fend off each threat?[8]

Imitation is the drive of competitors to replicate a firm's successful business model. However damaging imitation may potentially be, there are reasons why business models might be hard to copy. The presence of rigid consequences is the first such reason. Rigid consequences such as experience, reputation, culture, or privileged relationships do not change rapidly with the choices that generate them. They take a long time to build. Experience, for instance, requires the accumulation of output, which is time-consuming. Therefore, it may be hard for the imitator to reconfigure its choices and build rigid consequences similar to those of the focal firm rapidly enough so as to become a viable competitor.

In the case of Ryanair one can easily see that many of its rigid consequences are difficult to replicate. Reputation for reasonable fares takes time to develop; an installed base of young pleasure travelers is not easy to build when it must be stolen from such an aggressive incumbent; low cost deriving from airport selection and the fleet or key negotiations with some suppliers are all but easy to develop. Clearly, rigid consequences act as important deterrents to imitation in this case. This barrier to imitation is even stronger when rigid consequences are part of virtuous cycles that spin fast.

A second barrier to imitation is reinforcement. A business model with many elements that are highly complementary to each other is generally hard to imitate. A competitor who intends to replicate the model must copy many choices simultaneously for them to have an effect comparable to what is observed in the focal firm. The reason is that complementarity between A and B depends on C (the other choices made by the organization). Thus, to get the benefit of A and B together, C must also be in place. The third barrier is the mere complexity of the business model. A business model with many interacting elements may be hard to understand and replicate. Causal ambiguity may lead imitators to wrong choices and deficient imitation. Walmart's business model has many important rigid consequences such as a frugal culture, a reputation for everyday low prices or large bargaining power with suppliers. Furthermore, it has many complementary virtuous cycles that reinforce one another. In addition, the model is complex. These features make Walmart's model difficult to imitate.

The second threat to sustainability is holdup. Holdup refers to customers, suppliers, complementors, or other industry participants capturing value created by the focal firm through the exercise of bargaining power. Holdup is especially threatening when the firm has invested in relationship-specific assets, which make it hard to walk away or find alternative trading partners.

Protection against holdup can be developed through choices related to the governance of assets and activities. Vertical integration and/or contracting with multiple parties (both business model choices) can help avoid dependence that leads to holdup. We should point out, however, that commitments are often important components of strategy. Thus it may be impossible for a firm to have a business model with no specific investments or vulnerability to holdup.

A third generic threat to robustness is slack, or organizational complacency. Protection against slack arises from the right mix of incentives and monitoring (business model choices). As mentioned above, low-powered incentives may also protect from slack if a culture of hard work (which is a rigid consequence) has been developed through other choices. The case of Irizar (see the Appendix) illustrates this point very clearly.

The last generic threat identified by Ghemawat is substitution. Substitution refers to decreased value perceived by customers because of the presence of other products. For example, air travel is a substitute for railway travel. The shuttle service between Boston and New York reduces willingness to pay and demand for Amtrak services between these two cities. As technologies, customer needs, or regulatory barriers evolve, unforeseeable substitutes emerge. Substitutes are often hard to identify.

To deal well with substitution threats, successful business models often have 'competitive sensors' that alert their presence. Microsoft is perhaps the clearest example of an organization that is especially good at detecting (and responding) to substitution threats. When a substitute emerges that is superior, it may be necessary to implement changes in the focal firm's business model to deal with it. Business model plasticity is thus desirable. Plasticity requires the absence of rigid consequences which, as we discussed above, are desirable to deal with the imitation threat. Barriers to imitation may become important impediments to effectively respond to substitution, and vice versa.

Walmart is an interesting case of fighting substitution, a fundamental threat in retailing as different formats (specialty stores, department stores, discount stores) appear to have dominated the industry at different times. Walmart has sensed new ideas well, copied them fast, and perfected them. Walmart adopted the warehouse club format in the early 1980s with Sam's Clubs, a concept created by Sol Price a few years earlier with Price Club. Sam Walton moved later to super-centers, a concept invented in Europe. In the meantime Walmart tested several alternative formats that eventually discontinued (Bradley and Ghemawat, 1994).

Zara provides an interesting counter-example to the idea that the presence of rigid consequences implies that a business model is ill-suited to respond to the substitution threat.[9] One important rigid consequence in Zara's business model is the organization's ability to learn customers' preferences and respond to them in real time by coming up with new designs that are manufactured immediately. This rigid consequence allows Zara to sense and respond and thus deal with substitute products better than traditional clothing chains such as The Gap or Benetton. Notice that this consequence helps Zara respond to product substitution threats, but not necessarily to business model substitution.

Business Model Effectiveness

The *effectiveness* of a business model is measured by the extent to which it satisfies the four evaluation criteria outlined above: alignment to goal, reinforcement, virtuousness, and robustness. To end the section on analysis in isolation, we discuss some features of Ryanair's business model that deliver effectiveness. First, reinforcement and virtuousness are satisfied as there are many virtuous cycles and no vicious cycles. Because there are redundant virtuous cycles, if any one cycle is threatened by competitors' actions, there are many other cycles that ensure that profitability is protected. Second, many of the virtuous cycles pass through low fares, large volume, and low cost, three elements directly related to profitability, which is Ryanair's main goal.

Third, there are many rigid consequences making imitation difficult. A virtuous cycle made up of flexible consequences can more easily be disrupted than one with rigidities. The use of secondary airports, for example, promotes the development of ancillary services such as transportation to the city (for example, since Ryanair's arrival to Girona – a city some 100 kms away from Barcelona – a bus service from BCN city center to the airport that coordinates with Ryanair's departures and arrivals priced at just €11 has developed). A simple lowering of competitors' fares does not make these ancillary services disappear. The word of mouth advertising that takes place because of the ridiculously low fares that Ryanair has does not vanish immediately if competitors also lower their prices.

A significant holdup problem may arise in airlines if pilots get together to request higher pay. Ryanair's choices, such as avoiding unions or having high-powered incentives and consequences such as the culture of high productivity that it has developed, make holdup and slack less likely to happen to Ryanair than to traditional flag-carriers, adding to robustness. Finally, while substitution is possible by, for example, high speed trains connecting cities served by Ryanair, the fact that its fares are extremely low together with having few delays (a consequence of choices such as flying to secondary airports and having a standardized fleet of 737s) make substitution less harmful than to full-fare airlines serving similar routes.

BUSINESS MODEL EVALUATION – ANALYSIS IN INTERACTION

After having discussed the evaluation of business models in isolation, we now move to the study of business models in interaction. The effectiveness of a business model depends to a large extent on the design of the business models of other players with which it interacts. Business models do not operate in a vacuum. For example, the success of Linux is not only dependent on the organization of open source software development and distribution but also on how Linux's business model interacts with that of Microsoft. Microsoft's business model makes possible some actions that affect the ability of Linux to grow to exploit network effects.

Notice first that business model interaction can potentially be very complex. To the intricacy of business models in isolation (with their multiple choices and consequences) there is the added complexity of how choices affect consequences of other players and how choices of other players affect the focal organization's consequences. As we discussed above, business models considered in isolation are almost always so complex that we have to make use of aggregation and decomposition in our representations so that we have tractable objects to work with. The analysis of business model interaction is much more involved because, in addition to the full richness of business models, there is the full richness of interactions.

Strategy, Tactics, and Business Model

We adopt the notion of strategy introduced by Porter (1996:68): "strategy is the creation of a unique and valuable position, involving a different set of activities." Thus, a firm's strategy results in a particular set of choices which, together with their consequences, constitutes a business model. In other words, a strategy is a (contingent) plan of action, one where the elements of choice are policies, assets, and governance structures. The firm's business model is a reflection of its strategy (Casadesus-Masanell and Ricart, 2010; Casadesus-Masanell and Zhu, 2010). For example, when the Ryan brothers were at the brink of bankruptcy in the early 1990s, their strategy was to transform their company from a standard full-service airline struggling to just be better (lower cost and better service) than existing competitors to one radically different by adopting the Southwest's no-frills model. In the mid 1990s, after the transformation, Ryanair had a new business model.

Similar to strategy, tactics are also courses of action. The difference is that the action sets available for tactics are constrained by the business model in place. That is, tactics are courses of action that take place within the bounds drawn by the firm's business model. Consider, for example, Le Cirque du Soleil. Le Cirque may have a goal to reach the $2 billion revenue mark. If the plan of action to reach this goal is simply continuing business as usual (carefully selecting a number of cities where shows will be performed), we call such a plan tactics. The plan is tactical and not strategic because it does not require changes in the organization's business model, which is the object of strategy. In the short and medium terms, the organization's business model places constraints on what the firm can do. The remaining scope for action is what we refer to as tactics.

To clarify the distinction between strategy, business model, and tactics, let's bring back the analogy between business models and machines introduced earlier. Specifically, think of an automobile as a business model. The way the automobile is built places constraints on what the driver can do, it determines the action set for tactics. For example, a large, powerful SUV makes it hard for a driver to maneuver on the narrow streets of Barcelona's Gothic Quarter. A small, less powerful compact car would make this task far less cumbersome. As a matter of fact, there are tactics possible with the compact car (such as driving through a really narrow street) that are impossible (not in the action set) with the large SUV. The shape of the automobile (an element of how the machine is built – its business model) places hard constraints to what the driver can do. At the same time, the powerful SUV allows the driver to enjoy the Pyrenees more fully than the small, compact car. Imagine now that prior to operating the automobile, the driver could modify the features of the car: shape, power, consumption, noise. . . Such modifications would constitute strategies. In summary: the design and building of the car is strategy; the car itself is the business model; and driving the car is tactics.

Just as Porter (1996) points out, strategy requires strong leadership as it often calls for substantial tradeoffs. In addition, it is usually hard to foresee all the effects that strategies have on tactics. Moreover, strategies often entail commitments that are hard to reverse. Tactics, on the other hand, are generally less consequential, easier to implement, and easier to understand. They fall many times under the responsibility of middle management. In fact, a large portion of the literature on the economics of industrial organization and game theory is devoted to the study of tactics.[10]

Both strategy and tactics have deliberate and emergent elements. Consider, for example, the competition between Toyota and General Motors in the 1970s and 1980s. At the beginning, both organizations were competing with similar business models, but slowly Toyota began developing a different set of choices until reaching the so-called lean manufacturing model. Part of Toyota's strategy was emergent and part was the result of deliberate design.

Interaction

Intuitively, two organizations interact when performance depends on the presence of the other. Put more simply: two organizations interact when they affect one another. Interaction can be with competitors, suppliers, complementors, or distributors (to mention just a few possibilities). Moreover, interaction may entail competition or cooperation and both may be for value capture or for value creation.

Following our distinction between business model, strategy and tactics, we present two different but related concepts of interaction. Tactical interaction refers to organizations affecting each other by acting within the bounds set by their business models. In most cases, tactical interaction concerns the use of variables such as price, advertising, or R&D intensity. The choice of these variables is constrained by the business models of the affected organizations. Strategic interaction, on the other hand, refers to organizations affecting each other by modifying their business models. Therefore, strategic interaction concerns the use of policies, assets, and governance structures to compete or cooperate.

Before discussing interaction, however, we need to present the notion of business model interdependence.

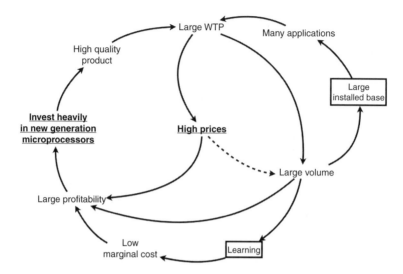

Figure 22.4   High-level representation of Intel's business model

Business Model Interdependence

Business models of two firms are interdependent when some consequences are common to both firms' models. In other words, the business models of two firms are interdependent when they 'touch' each other. For a concrete example, consider Microsoft and Intel's client PC businesses in the mid 1990s. Figure 22.4 captures the essence of the dynamics of Intel's business model (at a high level of aggregation). The representation stresses two choices: heavy investment in new generation microprocessors and relatively high microprocessor prices.

Microsoft's business model is fundamentally different to Intel's because, in addition to deriving revenue and profit from sales of PCs (every new PC sold has a Microsoft operating system), Microsoft also derives profit from selling applications and upgrades to the installed base of PCs. Figure 22.5 is a high-level representation of Microsoft's business model. Choices are underlined.

In this stylized representation we have included three main choices: investment in new generation operating systems, relatively low operating system prices, and relatively high application software prices. Notice that there are several virtuous cycles. As the installed base grows, it is increasingly difficult for competitors to catch up with Microsoft. Over time, Microsoft becomes stronger.

The diagram reveals that Microsoft has an incentive to set low prices

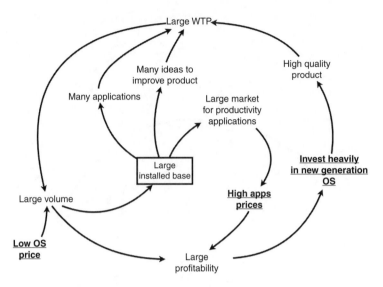

Figure 22.5   High-level representation of Microsoft's business model

for operating systems to grow the installed base. Microsoft then sets high prices for the applications (mainly productivity applications) and makes money from the large installed base of PCs.

Figure 22.6 shows that Intel and Microsoft's business models are linked together. The diagram is strictly a combination of both companies' business model representations shown above. The linkages are: willingness to pay for the PC and volume of PCs sold. The figure makes clear that the ability of Intel's (Microsoft's) business model to generate profit depends not only on the design and implementation of Intel's model (Microsoft's) but also on how it interacts with Microsoft's (Intel's) model. In other words, Intel and Microsoft's business models are interdependent: Microsoft's choices (i.e. OS pricing and investment in and timing of release of new operating systems) affect the working of Intel's business model and vice versa.[11]

Specifically, the volume of PCs sold at any given time period depends on the prices set by Intel and Microsoft for the microprocessor and operating system, respectively. Given a willingness to pay for a PC, the more Intel charges for the microprocessor, the less value is left for Microsoft to capture through OS prices (and vice versa). This implies that there is potential conflict between Intel and Microsoft regarding pricing. Likewise, willingness to pay for a PC is highly dependent on how well Intel and Microsoft's microprocessor and operating system work together. This depends on how well Intel and Microsoft coordinate the release of new generation processors and operating systems.

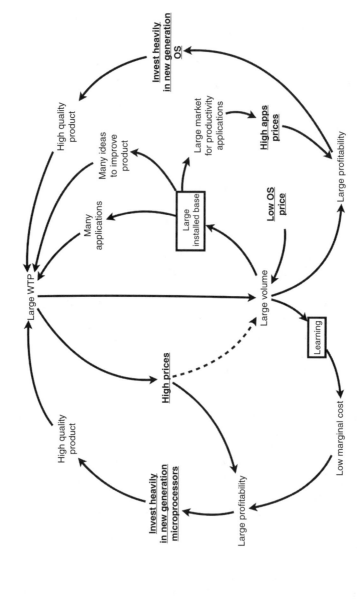

Figure 22.6   Links between Intel and Microsoft's business models

In the late 1990s and beginning of the 2000s, Microsoft reduced business model interdependence with that of Intel by helping a third player, AMD, thrive. In this new context (Intel, Microsoft, and AMD), interdependence between Microsoft and Intel became much lower compared to when AMD was a marginal player. On the other hand, Intel's (and AMD's) interdependence with Microsoft's business model remained large: taking Microsoft out of the picture renders Intel and AMD's microprocessors valueless. Intel's recent support of Linux (through Intel Capital, for example) and Apple's move to Intel architecture chips should reduce the degree of interdependence between its business model and that of Microsoft.[12]

Another example of business model interdependence is that of bricks and mortar book distributors such as Barnes & Noble (B&N) and internet distributors such as Amazon. The nature of interdependence is quite asymmetric. Amazon's business model attracts some segments of clients away from Barnes & Noble, but it also serves other markets. So we have intermediate negative interdependence of Amazon over Barnes & Noble. However, interdependence of Barnes & Noble over Amazon, while still negative, is close to 0. If Barnes & Noble disappeared the effect on Amazon would be small.

We end this section with a summary of the main ideas. First, there is a wide array of players with which a focal firm's business model may be interdependent (competitors, substitutes, complementors, customers and suppliers). Two business models are interdependent if they are connected. Traditional analyses tend to focus on interdependences between competitors and, to a lesser extent, between buyers and sellers. Less attention has been given to complements (such as Intel and Microsoft) or substitutes. Second, the intensity of interdependence is endogenous as it depends on how players have decided to configure their business models. (We study this issue below when we discuss strategic interaction.) Third, interdependencies may be positive or negative. Two business models may reinforce each other (cooperation) and help one another to 'work better' or they may detract from each other (competition).

Tactical Interaction

Tactical interaction refers to organizations affecting each other by acting within the bounds set by their business models. If the business models of the firms under consideration are not interdependent, then there cannot be tactical interaction. The links between business models allow tactics of one firm to affect the working of the other firm's model. When contact points are absent, tactics have no effect on each other. Of course, even in the absence of interdependence, there is a direct effect of tactics on the organization employing them.

Aggressiveness refers to the capacity of a firm to affect the working of other players' business models by use of tactics. Conversely, defensiveness refers to how well a firm can fend off or take advantage of the 'moves' of players with which it interacts given its business model. Aggressiveness and defensiveness are generally not symmetric. When the business models of firms interacting are distinct, it is most likely that aggressiveness and defensiveness will be asymmetric. Furthermore, aggressiveness and defensiveness depend on the specific players under consideration. A's business model may result in substantial aggressiveness and defensiveness when in interaction with player B, but not when interacting with C.

Aggressiveness and defensiveness depend on the business models of the firms under consideration. There are two reasons for this. First, the breadth of tactical actions available depends on the business model. Second, the configuration of the firms' models determines the intensity of business model interdependence; and, as we pointed out above, the presence of interdependence is a necessary condition for tactical interaction.

The business model of firm A is said to be consistent for a given interaction with B, if it displays an appropriate balance between aggressiveness and defensiveness. Firm A's business model is consistent (overall) if it is consistent for all relevant interactions it may face. Consistency captures the capacity of the business model to continue being effective taking into account the possible strategic interactions that may potentially take place.

Strategic Interaction

As mentioned above, 'strategy' refers to the process of crafting an organization's business model. Thus, a strategy is a plan of action where the elements of choice are policies, assets, and governance structures. Correspondingly, *strategic interaction* refers to how changes in a firm's business model affect the working of another firm's business model.

IESE Business School may consider increasing the salary levels of assistant professors by, say, 20 percent (as part of a new policy that alters its current business model). If this wage increase affects the working of LBS's business model, we say that there is strategic interaction between IESE and LBS (concerning IESE's wages for assistant professors).

Strategic interaction is concerned with the choice of policies, assets, and governance structures. And while organizations do not affect each other directly through changes in their business models, there is an indirect effect through the resulting business models as new intensity levels of interdependence and tactical interaction ensue.

Thus, as it concerns competitive (and cooperative) interaction, there are two ways in which strategies affect outcomes. First, strategies affect the degree of business model interdependence present between any two players. In other words, business model interdependence is endogenous.[13] Second, strategies determine the extent to which business models exhibit (tactical) aggressiveness and defensiveness. It is important to notice that the intensity of interdependence, aggressiveness, and defensiveness between players A and B is not chosen by A alone or B alone, but depends (simultaneously) on the strategies followed by both A and B; that is, their strategic interactions.

The following are a few of the many ways in which firms may act to reduce business model interdependence.

- Modifying their own business model so that the organization moves to spaces where there are fewer points of contact between business models. For instance, Cirque du Soleil's business model does not interact much with that of traditional circuses. The search for these spaces with few negative interactions is the key insight of *Blue Ocean Strategy* (Kim and Mauborgne, 2005).

- Adding elements in your business model that help other players thrive so that no one player has a large effect on the score of the focal firm. Consider once again the relationship between Intel and Microsoft and think of the role played by AMD. The more AMD is a close substitute for Intel, the lower the interaction between Microsoft and Intel. In the extreme case where Intel and AMD are perfect substitutes, if Intel vanished, Microsoft's score would not be affected. In general, a firm decreases its interdependence with a complementor when substitute complementors appear. Similarly, a firm decreases its dependence of a key supplier when substitute suppliers appear.

Other standard ways to reduce interdependence are: keeping capacity low in commodity industries, growing the market or increasing horizontal and vertical product differentiation.

Of course, the points above can be reversed and act as ways to increase interdependence. Increased business model interdependence is desirable when the interactions are positive (complementary). Intel Capital, for example, is the flipside of *Blue Ocean Strategy* in the sense that Intel is populating the 'ocean' in a way that there are as many players with which it interacts as possible. The interactions in this case are complementary and therefore help all players in that ecosystem thrive.

Strategic interaction, as we have defined it, corresponds to the intuitive notion of competition through business models: modifying my own business model to affect your choices while at the same time reacting to changes in your business model.

Competition through business models is difficult to deal with. While the concept of best response is easy to define for tactics (as the action sets and payoffs are relatively easy to determine), best response functions for strategies are often very hard to figure out. The reason is that, in the case of strategies, the action spaces are huge and the interactions between different choices complex. As a consequence, it is practically impossible to come up with one's own (let alone other players') payoff functions. The implication is that strategy search is only vaguely related to classic optimization or game theory. Contrary to the case of tactics, finding appropriate strategies is much more of a creative process than one of calculation. Together with leadership, inspiration and imagination are the main features that strategists must possess.

The proliferation of managerial books on strategy innovation is related to the difficulty in deriving best responses. Much of the recent managerial literature on innovation is concerned with altering business models (even as it often refers to business models superficially). Yip (2004) claims that strategy practice can gain light by understanding business models. Recent authors such as McGrath and McMillan (2005) and Govindojaran and Trimble (2005) develop techniques to help companies come up with such strategies. Even authors from operations management such as Lee (2004) point out that radical changes in some parts of a firm's business model can have tremendous performance implications. At some level, this managerial literature is all about proposing avenues to make operational the future of competition as described by Prahalad and Ramaswamy (2004).

CONCLUSIONS

The reasons for the renewed interest in business models are clear: on the one hand, the competitive environment is becoming increasingly complex, giving rise to hyper-competition (Thomas and d'Aveni, 2004), which is characterized by difficulties in sustaining competitive advantage as new business models substitute for established ways to compete. In addition, the recent ICT revolution opens broad opportunities to configure choices in radically different ways (Malone, 2004). Enablers of new business models are becoming readily accessible in an environment where business model innovations are increasingly important for survival.

Firms experiment and learn to change and transform their business models to adapt to the needs of complex new competitive environments

(Rindova and Kotha, 2001). Firms are increasingly looking at the periphery for innovative ideas (Foster and Kaplan, 2001). In this co-evolution of firms, competitors, complementors, and environment (Lewin and Volberdra, 1999), it is necessary to emphasize exploration over exploitation (March, 1991). As firms are forced to explore more they must become more entrepreneurial. The essence of entrepreneurship is the design of effective business models.

Entrepreneurship is all about discovering (and exploiting) existing opportunities and/or creating such opportunities. For example, Ryanair wanted to exploit the opportunities opened by air traffic deregulation in Europe, but discovered the hard way (as it was close to bankruptcy in 1991) the need to use an unconventional business model. Alternatively, some entrepreneurs create an opportunity by inventing new business models. This is the case of Irizar's Koldo Saratxaga as described in the appendix. Pressed to recover Irizar from bankruptcy and, at the same time, keep high-value jobs in the Basque Country, Koldo invented a radically new business model.

To sum up, firms face a tough environment where innovation and entrepreneurship are fundamental. Our concept of business model is a tool for managers to deal with these complexities. We have developed a notion of business model and introduced a method for representation. We have also introduced criteria to evaluate their effectiveness in isolation. Finally, we have presented an approach to study the complex interactions between business models of different players. In summary, we have developed a set of tools to understand the process of business model innovation, competition, and cooperation. We hope that the ideas in this chapter will help managers to better face this difficult but fundamental task.

NOTES

1. We thank Giambattista Dagnino, Pankaj Ghemawat, Costas Markides, Jan Rivkin, and seminar participants at IESE's Brown Bag Seminar series and the 2007 Meetings of the Academy of Management (Philadelphia). Casadesus-Masanell is grateful to the HBS Division of Research. This chapter presents a summary of research by the authors on business models and competitive interaction. See Casadesus-Masanell and Ricart (2008a, 2008b, and 2008c) and Casadesus-Masanell and Ricart (2010).
2. For-profit organizations are often referred to as money-making machines.
3. Notice that intangible assets such as experience, brand equity, or even the value of patents are consequences (generally rigid), not choices.
4. Notice that disciplines such as economics, sociology, or psychology are, for the most part, devoted to generating theories. For example, there is a large body of economic literature devoted to understanding how incentives affect performance. These theories are distilled in our business model representation by use of a simple arrow (or a few arrows) connecting choices and consequences. Disciplines look at the arrows with great

care but have little concern about how arrows interact with one another and contribute to making the whole of a business model.
5. See Christiansen and Pascale (1983).
6. Kinetic energy is the energy that a body possesses by virtue of its movement.
7. Notice the assumption that objectives are quantifiable. Sometimes objectives are easily quantifiable (at least conceptually) such as value creation or value capture (profit maximization). Quantification is less direct in other cases. For example, one main goal of Greenpeace may be a better environment and this may be hard to measure objectively.
8. Even if competition and the context where the business model evolves are relevant to address the question of sustainability, for expositional clarity we discuss robustness here by considering the business model of the focal firm in isolation from those of other players with which it interacts.
9. For a detailed description of Zara's business model, see Ghemawat and Nueno (2003).
10. In industrial organization and game theory, however, strategy is a contingent plan of action, regardless of whether this plan is strategic (from a Porterian point of view) or tactical (as defined above).
11. This analysis is based on Casadesus-Masanell and Yoffie (2007). For more details on this example, see Casadesus-Masanell et al., "Wintel (A), (B), (C), (D), (E), and (F) (TN)." Harvard Business School Teaching Note 706–495.
12. For details on competitive interaction between Microsoft, Intel, and AMD see Casadesus-Masanell et al. (2007).
13. Note that most of the literature on industrial organization assumes exogenous interdependence.

REFERENCES

Amit, R. and C. Zott (2001), 'Value creation in e-business,' *Strategic Management Journal*, **22**, 493–520.
Andrews, K. (ed.) (1971), *The Concept of Corporate Strategy*, Irwin: Dow-Jones.
Baum, J.A.C. and J.V. Singh (1994), 'Organization-environment coevolution,' in J.A.C. Baum and J.V. Singh (eds), *Evolutionary Dynamics of Organizations*, New York: Oxford University Press.
Bower, J. (1972), 'Crown Cork & Seal and the metal container industry,' *Harvard Business School* case 373–077.
Bradley, S., P. Ghemawat and S. Foley (1994), 'Wal-Mart Stores, Inc,' *Harvard Business School* case 794–024.
Brandenburger, A. and B. Nalebuff (1996), 'Value-based business strategy,' *Journal of Economics & Management Strategy*, **5**, 5–24.
Casadesus-Masanell, R. and P. Ghemawat (2006), 'Dynamic mixed duopoly: a model motivated by Linux vs. Windows,' *Management Science*, **52** (7), 1072–1084.
Casadesus-Masanell, R., B. Nalebuff and D.B. Yoffie (2010), 'Competing complements,' Harvard Business School Working paper, No. 09–009, July 2008 (revised March 2010).
Casadesus-Masanell, R. and J. Mitchell (2006), 'Irizar in 2005,' *Harvard Business School* case pp. 706–424 and teaching note 706–446.
Casadesus-Masanell, R. and J.E. Ricart (2008a), 'Competing through business models (A),' *Harvard Business School* note 708–452.
Casadesus-Masanell, R. and J.E. Ricart (2008b), 'Competing through business models (B),' *Harvard Business School* note 708–475.
Casadesus-Masanell, R. and J.E. Ricart (2008c), 'Competing through business models (C),' *Harvard Business School* note 708–476.
Casadesus-Masanell, R. and J.E. Ricart (2010), 'From strategy to business models and onto tactics,' Special Issue on Business Models, *Long Range Planning*, **43** (2), 195–215.

Casadesus-Masanell, R. and D.B. Yoffie (2007), 'Wintel: cooperation and conflict,' *Management Science*, **53** (4), 584–598.

Casadesus-Masanell, R. and F. Zhu (2010), 'Strategies to fight ad-sponsored rivals,' *Management Science*, **56** (9), 1484–1499.

Caves, R.E. (1984), 'Economic analysis and the quest for competitive advantage,' *American Economic Review*, **13**, 127–132.

Christiansen, E.T. and R.T. Pascale (1983), 'Honda (A),' *Harvard Business School* case 384–049.

Drucker, P. (ed.) (1954), *The Practice of Management*, New York: Harper and Row Publishers.

Evans, P.B. and T.S. Wurster (1997), 'Strategy and the new economics of information,' *Harvard Business Review*, Sept.–Oct., 71–82.

Foster, R. and S. Kaplan (2001), *Creative Destruction from Built-to-Last to Built to Perform*, London: Financial Times Prentice Hall, Random House, Aug.

Ghemawat, P. (1991), *Commitment: The Dynamic of Strategy*, New York: The Free Press.

Ghemawat, P. (1999), *Strategy and the Business Landscape*, New York: Prentice Hall.

Ghemawat, P. and J.L. Nueno (2003), 'ZARA. Fast fashion,' *Harvard Business School* case 703–497.

Govindajaran, V. and C. Trimble (2004), 'Strategic innovation and the science of learning,' *MIT Sloan Management Review*, Winter, 19–80.

Guth, W.D. (1964), 'Crown Cork & Seal Company (A),' *Harvard Business School* case 310–013.

Hart, S. and C. Christensen (2002), 'The great leap: driving innovation from the base of the pyramid,' *MIT Sloan Management Review*, **44** (1), 51–56.

IBM Global Business Services, *Expanding the Innovation Horizon: The Global CEO Study 2006*, New York: IBM Corporation, 2006.

Kim, W.C. and R. Mauborgne (eds) (2005), *Blue Ocean Strategy: How to Create Uncontested Market Space and Make Competition Irrelevant*, Boston, MA: Harvard Business School Press.

Kim, W.C., R. Mauborgne and B.M. Bensau (2002), 'Even a clown can do it,' INSEAD case 302–057–8.

Lee, H.L. (2004), 'The triple-A supply chain,' *Harvard Business Review*, October, 1–12.

Lewin, A.Y. and H.W. Volberda (1999), 'Prolegomena and coevolution: a framework for research on strategy and new organizational forms,' *Organization Science*, **10** (5), 519–534.

London, T. and S. Hart (2003), 'Reinventing strategies for emerging markets: beyond the transnational model,' *Journal of International Business Studies*, September, 350–370.

Magretta, J. (2002), 'Why business models matter,' *Harvard Business Review*, May, 86–92.

Malone, T.W. (ed.) (2004), *The Future of Work*, Boston, MA: Harvard Business School Press.

March, J.G. (1991), 'Exploration and exploitation in organizational learning,' *Organization Science*, **2** (1), 71–87.

McGrath, R.G. and C. Macmillan (eds) (2005), *MarketBusters: 40 Strategic Moves That Drive Exceptional Business Growth*, Boston, MA: Harvard Business School Press.

Porter, M.E. (ed.) (1985), *Competitive Advantage*, New York: The Free Press.

Porter, M.E. (1996), 'What is strategy?' *Harvard Business Review* pp. 61–78.

Prahalad, C.K. and S. Hart (2002), 'The fortune at the bottom of the pyramid,' *Strategy & Business*, **26**, 2–14.

Prahalad, C.K. (ed.) (2005), *The Fortune at the Bottom of the Pyramid: Eradicating Poverty through Profits*, Philadelphia: Wharton School Publishing.

Prahalad, C.K. and V. Ramaswamy (eds) (2004), *The Future of Competition: Co-Creating Unique Value with Customers*, Boston, MA: Harvard Business School Press.

Ricart, J.E., M. Enright, P. Ghemawat, S. Hart and T. Khanna (2004), 'New frontiers in international strategy,' *Journal of International Business Studies*, **35** (3), 175–200.

Rindova, V.P. and S. Kotha (2001), 'Continuous "morphing": competing through dynamic capabilities, form, and function,' *Academy of Management Journal*, **44** (6), 1263–1280.

Rivkin, J.W. (2000), 'Dogfight over Europe: Ryanair (C),' *Harvard Business School* case 700–117.
Shafer, S.M., H.J. Smith and J.C. Linder (2005), 'The power of business models,' *Blue Horizons*, **48**, 199–207.
Thomas, L.G. and R. D'Aveni (2004), 'The rise of hypercompetition from 1950 to 2002: evidence of increasing structural destabilization and temporary competitive advantage,' Tuck School of Business working paper, Dartmouth College, Hanover, NH, October.
Varian, H.R. and C. Shapiro (eds) (1999), *Information Rules: A Strategic Guide to the Network Economy*, Boston, MA: Harvard Business Press.
Williamson, O.E. (ed.) (1985), *The Economic Institutions of Capitalism*, New York: The Free Press.
Yip, G.S. (2004), 'Using strategy to change your business model,' *Business Strategy Review*, **15** (2), Summer, 17–24.
Zott, C. and R. Amit (2007), 'Business model design and the performance of entrepreneurial firms,' *Organization Science*, **18** (2), 181–199.
Zott, C. and R. Amit (2008), 'The fit between product market strategy and business model: implications for firm performance,' *Strategic Management Journal*, **29** (1), 1–26.

APPENDIX

An Example: Irizar

Irizar is a highly successful manufacturer of bodies for luxury motor coaches. Under the leadership of Mr. Koldo Saratxaga, Irizar emerged from near bankruptcy in 1991 to become "probably now the most efficient coachbuilder in the world," according to *The Economist Intelligence Unit* (2000: 172). Irizar has received several recognitions such as the overall winner of the European Quality Award in 2000 (granted by the European Foundation for Quality Management, EFQM). The company also clinched the title as the best European coach of the year in 2004.

When Saratxaga joined Irizar in 1991, the company was on the verge of bankruptcy. In the late 1980s, after a series of ill-conceived strategic moves, the company posted a series of large losses. Several of Irizar's executives defected to set up a new company which quickly won over some of Irizar's key customers. When Irizar's leadership changed twice in 1990, morale hit an all-time low, and the organization's members seriously doubted its future. Even though the company was a cooperative, the organizational structure emulated that of a traditional limited liability corporation with a functional hierarchy, top-down decision-making processes, and limited worker involvement in decision making. At the time, Irizar was producing 226 coaches per year to five distinct markets with an employee base of 286 people.

Within the first four weeks of arriving at Irizar, Saratxaga decided that major changes were needed to save the organization. Installing a system focused on customer loyalty, strict quality adherence, and an empowered workforce, Irizar enjoyed spectacular revenue growth, with a 23.9 percent compound annual growth rate over 14 years (Saratxaga's tenure), growing to 310 million Euros by 2004. Producing 1600 coaches in 2005, Irizar considered itself to be 'a business project based on people.'

Irizar's new business model under Saratxaga was characterized by the following set of choices (for details, see Casadesus-Masanell and Mitchell, 2006):

1. *Self-managed teams*. All work is done by teams that set their own goals, decide how to organize, choose the team leader.
2. *No clocking-in and clocking-out*. Teams decide when to begin work and when to end. There is an understanding that on average individuals should work eight hours per day.
3. *No hierarchy, no bosses*. Flat organizational structure. Three levels only. No bosses, just coordinators.
4. *Open floor plant*. Organization of physical space resembles organization. No walls. All in one level only. No assigned parking spaces.
5. *No paid overtime*. Teams often work overtime, but receive no additional pay.
6. *Decentralized decision making*. Most members allowed to make important decisions on Irizar's behalf.
7. *Obsession about communication*. All information available to members. Lots of meetings to inform and discuss business performance. Internal magazine. General assemblies.
8. *Workers' cooperative*. Workers own the assets and make financial contribution to join.
9. *Low-powered (extrinsic) incentives*. Pay scale is 1:3, amazingly flat.
10. *No firing*. After tenure is granted (three years' probation) nobody is ever fired.
11. *One product for all markets*. One coach model to serve all markets.
12. *A Constitution ('Strategic Thoughts')*. Document entitled 'Strategic Thoughts' is a short Constitution detailing what Irizar is all about.
13. *No evaluations*. Nobody is evaluated after tenure.
14. *Heavy use of outsourcing*. Most repetitive tasks are outsourced.
15. *Located in small town*. Ormaiztegi. Small/isolated plant in Spain's Basque Country.
16. *High prices*. Relatively high prices.
17. *Profit sharing*. Some level of profit (and losses) sharing to complement wage.

The *choices* listed above indicate how the Irizar machine was set up. To understand what the machine does, however, we need to look at the

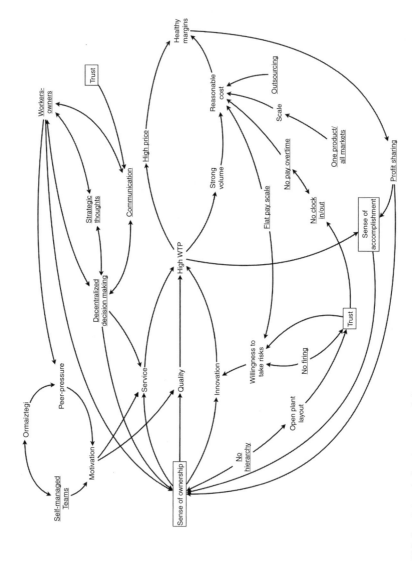

Figure A22.1   Irizar's business model representation

consequences of these choices. The *representation* in Figure A22.1 shows how choices and consequences are related and, thus, how the machine works.

Notice that the main virtuous cycle in the above representation (in bold) passes through (a) willingness to pay, (b) cost, and (c) price. Thus value creation and value capture grow as the cycle spins. Supporting the main cycle there is a large set of *complementary choices* (such as the firm's location in a small town, self-managed teams, no firing, no clocking-in or clocking-out. . .) *that with their consequences help that cycle spin faster and more robustly*.

By redesigning how Irizar worked, Saratxaga effectively created a new *business model*. When faced with the dilemma of how to save Irizar from bankruptcy, Saratxaga could have set up a very different business model from the one that he put in place (perhaps one with a functional organizational form, high-powered incentives, vertical decision making, vertically integrated, that built basic coaches for the Spanish market). Therefore, the redesign exercise that transformed Irizar from the 'machine' that Saratxaga found when he joined in 1991 to the operation that was in place in 2005 was *strategy*.

Strategy is often defined as a contingent *plan of action* designed to achieve a particular goal. As Caves (1984) and Ghemawat (1991) point out, an essential element of strategy is the set of *committed choices* made by management. Similarly, Porter (1996: 68) states: "strategy is the creation of a unique and valuable position, *involving a different set of activities*" (emphasis added). Saratxaga made a number of important *choices* that committed the whole organization to a course of action and that positioned the firm uniquely in the industry. These choices (which we have listed above) explain the underlying logic of value creation and value capture at Irizar. They define Irizar's scope (one high-quality product addressed to customers in all geographies who look for luxury, long-range coaches) and the key ways to serve this segment by creating an offering based on service, quality and innovation. As we add granularity to the description of Irizar's business model (by, essentially, considering additional choices) we obtain a better understanding of the resources and capabilities that the firm developed over time, how those supported the value activities, and how the value activities ended up delivering a product with high willingness to pay. The committed *choices* have direct *consequences* and those consequences eventually enable choices. Therefore, the strategy is reflected in the business model that allows the organization to reach its goals. Thus, *a firm's business model is a reflection of its strategy*.

23 Coopetition: nature, challenges, and implications for firms' strategic behavior and managerial mindset
Giovanni Battista Dagnino,
Maria Chiara Di Guardo and Giovanna Padula

INTRODUCTION

Dating back to Brandenburger and Nalebuff (1996)'s seminal work, management scholars have started recognizing that interfirm interdependences across multiple industries are characterized by strictly intertwined features of competition and cooperation. Coopetition is the way these interfirm interdependences have been labeled (e.g. in Brandenburger and Nalebuff, 1996). While the 'flavor' of coopetition has been to some extent present in the elaboration of thought since the work of Adam Smith (see our comments below on Smith's 1759 *Theory of Moral Sentiments*), the recent and steady increase in the attitude of firms to cooperate has made this phenomenon increasingly visible and has started sparking considerable interest in coopetition as a stream of research on its own.

We claim that understanding interfirm interdependences as a coopetitive game provides new challenges in the strategic behavior of the firms and call for the need to develop a novel managerial mindset and a coopetitive strategy (Dagnino, 2007). Whereas various authors (Brandenburger and Nalebuff, 1996; Lado et al., 1997; Bengtsson and Kock, 1999; Gnyawali and Madhavan, 2001) have emphasized the growing importance of coopetition for today's interfirm dynamics, scientific investigation on the issue of coopetition is at the beginning of its lifecycle (Walley, 2007; Tidstrom, 2008). Accordingly coopetition is a theme that tends to attract increasing attention from both strategy research (Baglieri et al., 2008) and practice (Dagnino and Rocco, 2009).

This chapter contributes to the debate on coopetition by providing an analytical understanding of the nature of coopetition and claiming for the need to recognize its challenging implications for strategy. By suggesting that coopetition is a matter of "incomplete interest (and goal) congruence" shaping firms' interdependence (Padula and Dagnino, 2007), we point out that coopetition does not simply emerge from coupling competition and cooperation issues, but it rather implies that cooperation and competition merge together to form a new kind of strategic interdependence between firms, giving rise to a coopetitive system of value creation (Dagnino, 2009). This argument recognizes the emergence of a *new managerial mindset* to steer interfirm dynamics.

Incidentally, it is interesting to recall that, as early as the nineteenth century, two founding fathers and early presidents of the USA, John Adams and Thomas Jefferson, were meaningfully termed as 'rival friends'. Actually, they had initially been good friends and then fierce political opponents in different periods of their long lifetimes. Notwithstanding that, at the sunset of their lives they started and maintained an intense correspondence, wherein each of them, while accepting to openly and serenely confront with the other's opinion, retained his appraisal on a variety of subject matters.

The remainder of this chapter is organized as follows. The second section provides analytical content to the concept of coopetition viewed as the synthesis between two opposite, ideal perspectives: competition and cooperation. In doing so, it elucidates the limitations of the two perspectives and moves to show analytically how these restrictions are overcome and accommodated within the new understanding of firm dynamics provided by coopetition. The third section extracts some basic properties that idiosyncratically shape the structure of coopetition, while the fourth section illustrates the challenges to firms given by coopetition. In this section, we assert the need to develop a novel managerial mindset that may guide the new coopetitive strategic behavior. Concluding remarks on the future paths of the issue of coopetition are supplied in the last section.

INTERFIRM COOPETITION DYNAMICS UNVEILED

We suggest that coopetition is a synthesis between two contradictory perspectives that have shaped strategic thinking in the last few decades: the competitive perspective and the cooperative perspective. In this vein, coopetition results from overcoming the limitations outspreading from such extreme understandings of interfirm dynamics provided by the competitive and cooperative perspectives and show the advantage to depict a more realistic comprehension of the interdependences across firms as they manifest in the actual world.

Competitive Perspective: Nature and Limitations

Business success in strategic management has been traditionally thought of as the result of competitive interdependences characterized by the following features: 1) win-lose game business; i.e., the success of a firm comes out at the expenses of other firms; 2) negative interdependences; i.e., the competitive behavior of the other categories of actors that populate the competitive environment of a firm and generate negative effects on the profits of that firm; 3) game of business that is about value distribution; i.e., competitive interdependences are driven by strategic maneuvers exclusively bound to capture value. Briefly, these three features provide an image of competition as a zero-sum game structure characterized by a completely divergent interest structure. Yet, the observation of a variety of different business experiences demonstrates that the interdependences across rival firms hardly show a strict zero-sum game structure, and firms may engage in strategic actions for the achievement of mutual benefits on the basis of common interests.

Some of these actions are not driven by the explicit intent to cooperate and pursue a common interest, but they show an emergent effect of providing mutual benefits within a wider community of industry competitors. An example in this direction is provided by the repositioning campaign of an orange juice from a juice for breakfast to a fresh beverage suitable for a larger variety of uses. This repositioning strategy enacted by an industry competitor enabled an increase in the overall sales volumes of the orange juice that was (at least potentially) beneficial for all the main producers of orange juice. This campaign represents a competitive action that generated value at the beverage industry level, qualifying positive interdependences across the main industry players in a win-win game structure. Then, each industry player set specific maneuvers bound to attract the customers' preferences and determine their market shares, affecting the actual distribution of the value generated by that campaign among the main orange juice producers. These maneuvers characterized negative interdependences across the industry players in a win-lose game structure.

Other manifestations of strategic behavior that generates positive interdependences across rivals in a win-win game structure are supplied by strategic alliances and other forms of partnerships whereby competitors develop cooperative relationships explicitly bound to pursue common benefits. For example, in the information and communication technology (ICT) industry, the main mobile wireless telephones manufacturers in the world, Nokia, Ericsson, and Motorola, made a joint-venture, called Symbian, with Psion, the leading company in mobile digital computing. Its vision statement is "to set the standard for mobile wireless operating systems and to enable a mass market for Wireless Information Devices." The Symbian joint-venture was born to compete with the standard for mobile wireless operating systems based on Windows (Ancarani and Shankar, 2003) and its collaboration primary motive is to put together resources to enhance its partners' capability to clash Microsoft's technology development strength.

The three mobile phone operators in the French market – Orange, SFR and Bouygues Telecom – initiated a cooperation project, motivated to enhance the telecommunications services offered to their clients and thus increase their profits in the saturated French market. These rival firms decided to cooperate in such a way as to offer the best homogenous public wi-fi service covering the whole country. Cooperation between these rival operators unifies the complementary innovative techniques and the different experiences that each member has in different processes (De Ngo and Okura, 2008). In November 2006, the three mobile operators (Bouygues Telecom, Orange and SFR), in collaboration with two banking networks (BNP Paribas and Crédit Mutuel-CIC), launched an initiative for testing a common solution for contactless payment by mobile phone.

In the smart card industry, actors cooperate to design, implement, and deploy smart card applications, while simultaneously competing to capture the largest share of the value created by these applications (M'Chirgui, 2004). Similarly, life insurance firms may divulge their private information to their rivals in order to reduce the incidence of insurance fraud, whilst competing vigorously over insurance premiums and quality (De Ngo and Okura, 2008). Cooperation across competitors is also apparent in the global airlines industry where airlines basically cooperate inside three major competing alliance constellations: OneWorld, Skyteam and StarAlliance (Lazzarini, 2007).

While cooperating, the partnering firms actually pursue a common interest and define a context of positive interdependences within a win-win game structure. Of course, while cooperating on some businesses, they remain strict competitors with opposite interests on other businesses. Even more, their status of competitors requires them to manage carefully their cooperative relationships – by controlling the flows of knowledge across their firm boundaries for instance (Hamel, 1991) – to avoid that cooperating on some businesses may be detrimental to the other businesses. In fact, as firms cooperate with rival firms, they may actually end up realizing that they have contributed to strengthen their competitors (Dowling et al., 1996; *Economist*, 1999). Hence, cooperation across rivals defines a context of strictly intertwined positive and negative interfirm interdependences with both common and private benefits pursued simultaneously.

Cooperative Perspective: Nature and Limitations

The harshly competitive understanding of firm interdependence as a zero-sum game structure was first challenged by an opposite perspective juxtaposing the role of cooperation to achieve a business success (e.g. Contractor and Lorange, 1988; Hakansson and Snehota, 1995; Doz and Hamel, 1998). Yet, while providing the advantage of shedding light on the limitations of a strict competitive perspective, this alternative line of reasoning shows theoretically the opposite limitation of emphasizing the mutual advantages of firms cooperating for a common interest while neglecting the negative, competitive issue that actually arises within a cooperative game structure (Padula and Dagnino, 2009).

In fact, business success within this perspective is thought of as the result of interfirm interactions characterized as follows: 1) a purely win-win game of business; i.e. success of a firm adds to the value of other firms; 2) positive interdependences; i.e. cooperative behavior across firms generates positive effects on the profits of those firms; 3) game of business that is about value creation; i.e. cooperative interdependences are driven by strategic maneuvers exclusively bound to generate joint value. In a few words, in a strict cooperative perspective firms interact within a positive-sum game structure characterized by a completely convergent interest structure.

Yet, a close look at cooperation actually reveals that the interdependences across cooperating firms are far from showing the ideal, positive features implicitly assumed by a strict cooperative perspective. Ample empirical evidences show that, while cooperating, firms also face serious challenges that actually move their game structure away from the ideal positive interdependences and fully convergent interests assumed by a harsh cooperative perspective. The examples and discussions provided to illustrate the limitations of a strict competitive perspective already have shed some light on the limitations of the cooperative perspective. In fact, we have argued that, while cooperating, rival firms maintain negative interdependences on several aspects of their business.

We supply additional evidences and discussions on the limitations of a strict cooperative perspective by examining the nature of interdependences across two additional categories of industry players: those with whom a firm may have vertical cooperation linkages (cooperation with its customers and suppliers) and those with whom a firm may have horizontal cooperation relationships (cooperation with other firms from beyond the industry).

The intrusion of competitive issues within vertical cooperative relationships
Several contexts may reveal the existence of win-win interdependences between a firm and its customers: interactions whereby a firm helps its customers improve their quality products, production efficiency, supply

management efficiency, etc. Searches for positive interdependences in the supplier-customer relationships have tremendously increased in the past decade (e.g. Capon, 2001), thereby leading to an increasingly diffused shift in marketing management logic from simple adaptation to customer needs to anticipation of customer needs in the attempt to assist customers to achieve their business objectives (Cova et al., 2002). In this customer management reasoning, supplier-customer interdependences are embedded in a long-run partnership requiring the two firms to share (or even jointly develop) future strategies, technology and resources. This circumstance implies that each firm is involved early in the other firm's product development cycle and that significant amounts of both routine and sensitive information flow between the two organizations.

Several cases employing this rationale of serving customers are easy to cite. Armstrong World Industries operates a management development program aimed at improving the skills of its key customers' mid-level and senior managers. To the extent that management skill is improved, the customers benefiting from this program perform better and Armstrong's business prospects are therefore enhanced. Alcatel developed the 'All-in-One Service' providing the telecom operators with an extensive set of services assisting them to reduce time-to-market, cut cost, achieve optimum quality of service and efficient customer care. By doing so, Alcatel's customers are posited in a better position to face the increasing competition in the telecom markets and the greater pressures from the telecom operators' increasingly demanding customer side, and to get increased revenues. At the same time, by broadening its rationale to assist its customers from simply selling products to helping them achieve their objectives, Alcatel increases its business opportunities with its current customers and is in a better position to attract new prospects.

In each of these examples, the supplier firm was able to deepen its relationships with its customers. As this logic adds value to the customers, price and other manifestations of competitive pressures on the supplier firm's business are mitigated and negative interdependences across the two business players weakened. Yet, this win-win logic of business is also associated with negative interdependences that exert pressures on the part of the supplier firm. One of the more important sources of the pressures at hand is provided by the supplier firms' limitations of business opportunities with other customers. In fact, this extreme win-win logic of assisting a customer is characterized by high degree of interaction and information exchange between the supplier firm and the customer firm. The downside of such close relationships is that the customer may require the supplier firm not to enter business relationships with its competitors. Conversely, other potential customers may not accept such close relationships between a potential supplier and one of their competitors. In either case, such business logic, while on the one side strengthening the positive interdependences within a supplier-customer relationship, on the other side raises negative pressures with respect to the supplier firm's overall business practices as it places limitations on the supplier firm's potential market opportunities.

A firm's interdependences with its suppliers are the mirror image of the interdependences it has with its customers that we examined earlier. Indeed, while in the previous case the firm took the role of supplier in the supplier-customer relationship, in this case we analyze its customer role within the same relationship. Firms may develop cooperative relationships with their suppliers that may trigger product quality enhancement, production efficiency, and other business improvements that help them achieve their objectives. At the same time, by enabling other firms to make business, suppliers strengthen their business opportunities with these firms. Northern Italy's long-standing clusters of manufacturing businesses across a wide variety of industries, with their close relationships with Italian machine-tool manufacturers, are a fruitful context to observe these kinds of relationships. The importance of exchanging information and cooperation with the machine suppliers is paramount across many downward industries, from clothes to glasses, from jewellery to food and pharmaceuticals to give a few examples. Yet, whereas this information exchange enables the suppliers to serve better their customer base and mitigate prices and other competitive pressures within the supplier-customer dyad, it also adds other sources of competitive pressures as it strengthens the suppliers' ability to serve better their customer firms' competitors.

In their efforts to keep up with the demands of the more sophisticated Italian goldsmiths, suppliers such as IECO and Sisma have been able to dominate their business, providing about 80 percent of the total world market of equipment for gold jewelry making. At the same time, while obtaining higher quality offers, jewel manufacturers have helped their customers to serve better their competitors worldwide. Hence, the examples above clearly show the intrusion of negative, competitive interdependences within a context of cooperative customer-supplier relationships.

The intrusion of competitive issues within horizontal cooperative relationships

While the cooperative perspective has found intense application in the realm of buyer-seller relationships, it has sparked even greater interest within the context of horizontal relationships. An interesting case in this latest vein is provided by the emergence and development of the PC industry, and the interdependences across IBM – one of the leading firms in the industry – and its two conventional main partners: Intel (which provided the microprocessor) and Microsoft (which provided the operating system).

IBM decided to enter the microcomputer market in 1981, when three other competitors – Apple, Commodore and Radio Shack – had already been four years on the market and were starting prospering. Differently from its main competitors, IBM entered the market with a strategy that put forth an open architecture and reliance on outside providers for all components. As regards the core components of the computer system, the microprocessor and the operating system, IBM relied respectively on Intel's 8-bit chip and Microsoft's MS-DOS. Though IBM had already developed the semiconductors and software competence for its mainframe and minicomputer markets, its choice to rely on external source, instead of adapting its internal competence for the PC market, was explained by the interest of speeding up the product to the mass consumer market and to benefit from the recently created external economies. Not only did those relationships allow IBM to reduce its investment and the time to market of its product, but they helped it to establish the dominant archi-tecture of the entire microcomputer industry. By 1984, three years after the introduction of the PC, IBM had in fact succeeded in replacing Apple as the leader of microcomputers, with a 26 percent market share of the entire PC business. One year after, IBM's market share had achieved 41 percent. On the other hand, Intel's and Microsoft's starting growth laid in their relationships with IBM and their agreement with the latter to use their products as the core component solution of the IBM architecture. Unmistakably, a win-win game structure with positive interdependences between IBM and its main partners arose in the beginning of the industry development and enabled to set IBM architecture as the dominant design of the whole PC industry.

With the IBM standard widespread in the industry, a new competitive landscape emerged that opened the room to huge negative interdepend-ences between IBM and its main partners (Intel and Microsoft). First, the PC industry started entering a fierce price competition. Besides this, as compatibility had been reached, PC manufacturers could purchase the same microprocessors from Intel and the same operating system from Microsoft. Put in other terms, as IBM battled to reveal the supremacy of IBM architecture, the value distribution of the industry was increasingly benefiting its partners, Intel and Microsoft. To manage its profit squeeze, IBM decided then to advance its PC architecture, but both Intel and Microsoft, which helped establish the original architecture, this time did not follow IBM's lead. An increasing divergence in the interest structure of the industry players arose and the interdependences between IBM and its two major partners turned to be mainly negative.

In 1991, IBM allied with Motorola and Apple to develop an alternative, more powerful, microprocessor that would strike at Intel's supremacy. By the rules of agreement, IBM was to design the processor – termed Power PC – to meet the needs of Apple's PC, while Motorola was to become the second manufacturing source of chips for IBM, Apple and the open market. For this purpose, IBM would have deployed the competences developed for the design and the production of the processor which had been developed for the workstation market. With this alliance, IBM reshaped its decade-old relationship with Intel. Intel quickly responded to that challenge in 1993 by releasing a new, far more powerful (though also more expensive) microprocessor, the Pentium. Pentium was designed to be compatible with all major operating systems including both those developed by Microsoft and Unix, which was intended to spread among the new workstation market. By means of this initiative, in 1994 Intel was capable to hold 74 percent of the world wide microprocessor market.

The development of IBM-Microsoft interdependence shows a larger degree of ambiguity vis-à-vis IBM-Intel interdependence, though both share the fact that they ultimately turned to perform from positively to negatively. The first evidence of negative pressures can be traced in the mid-1980s when IBM and Microsoft signed a joint development agreement for the development of OS/2, the new operating system for the IBM next computer generation. In the meantime Microsoft was developing a graphical user interface project, called Windows, which Bill Gates had offered to IBM but IBM had declined. The new OS/2 operating system was designed for an older chip generation, 8-bit 286.

Why did Microsoft agree to write OS/2 in a 286 assembler program, if it had developed a new operating system, Windows 386, for the newer chip generation, Intel's 16-bit 386? First, for many observers this development was a crucial learning experience essential to Microsoft for properly developing the proprietary Windows system. Second, to others it was a strategic move by Microsoft, which was in fact interested to ensure the failure of OS/2 in order to crack their IBM-related business. Subsequently, Bill Gates was incensed when, in the spring of 1988, IBM joined with DEC, Apple and Hewlett-Packard in the so-called Open Software Foundation. The association was targeted to give birth to a single Unix standard that would challenge DOS, OS/2 and, ultimately, Windows.

In the summer of 1990, Gates was again at IBM's headquarters outlining his plans to challenge, with IBM's support, Novell, a start-up that had quickly become the dominant firm in the new networking software technology and was leading the way in developing operating systems for client-server systems. Again he was rebuffed. Later in 1990, Gates broke openly with IBM, about six months after Microsoft introduced Windows 3.0. IBM's OS/2 had appeared in late 1987 and, by 1990, it had only about 1 percent of the installed base of operating systems. Windows 3.0 became instead an instant success and emerged as the standard personal computer operating system worldwide. In the early 1990s, Microsoft was using its learned internal capabilities not only to develop next generation operating systems, such as Windows 95 for PCs, but also to commercialize operating systems for workstations (Windows NT) and a wide variety of third-party software applications. At the same time, Gates was using Microsoft's learned internal capabilities to intensify his moves into closely related software applications markets.

By this systematic and methodical description of the emergence and development of a strategic partnership between two relevant firms pooling together complementary resources from distinct although convergent industries, we observe that cooperation strategies are far from qualifying a positive interdependence within a completely convergent interest structure. Alternatively, serious negative, competitive issues arise from within a cooperative context, and a mix of intertwined positive and negative interdependences arise and shape a partially convergent interest structure.

Overcoming the Limitations of the Competitive and Cooperative Perspectives: The Nature of Coopetition

The discussion above on the limitations of the two opposite perspectives and on the complexity of the hybrid structure supplemented by positive and negative interdependences provides a clearer image of actual interfirm interdependence. Actually it presents the characteristics that follow:

1. a mix of win-lose and win-win business games, so interfirm dynamics have the potential of adding value to and detracting value from the other firms;
2. interfirm interdependences may have positive and negative outcomes; strategic firm behavior generates both positive and negative effects on the profits of other firms;
3. interfirm interdependences generate strictly intertwined dynamics of value generation and value distribution: firms' strategic actions are a matter of creating value by 'enlarging the pie of business' and capturing the value by trying to appropriate the bigger slice of it.

The features reported heretofore depict the essence of a coopetitive perspective of interfirm interdependences. The perspective suggests that firms operate within a context of a partially convergent interest structure, whereby the opportunities for pursuing mutual benefits are often coupled together with tight trade-offs across opposite, divergent requirements.

While a few authors pioneered the efforts in this direction (Hamel et al., 1989), Brandenburger and Nalebuff (1996) were the ones who actually introduced the term coopetition in managerial discourse. They inaugurated the notion of coopetition essentially in order to elucidate the strategic interplay among 'coopetitors'. According to Afuah (2000), the word coopetitors is used in the place of the phrase 'suppliers, customers and complementors' (the manufacturers of goods which are complementary to the goods produced by the firm at hand). Brandenburger and Nalebuff used the term coopetitors to embrace – in addition to suppliers, customers and complementors – a fourth pivotal group of strategic players: the firm's coopetitors. They suggested that strategy analysis needs to take into account five different kinds of players: the firm, its customers, its competitors, its suppliers and its complementors. Distancing from a simple replication of the widely recognized idea of stakeholders, they modeled a structure of multiple relationships in which the firm is embedded.

In defining coopetition, we call attention to the analysis of interest and goal structures of the actors involved in the coopetitive game structure. Whereas both competitive and cooperative perspectives focus on entirely diverging or entirely converging interest structures respectively, we argue that coopetition represents an *integrative theoretical bridge* which stretches to join the two countervailing perspectives mentioned[1] since it acknowledges that firm interdependence arises from a partially congruent interest structure (Padula and Dagnino, 2007; Dagnino, 2009).

Coopetition is viewed as a much-needed attempt to rebalance the collaborative bias affecting the cooperation perspective as well as to rebalance the antagonistic bias affecting the competitive perspective. Regarding the former bias, the cooperative perspective has actually focused its attention on the joint value creation benefits of cooperating, whereas it has largely overlooked to derive analytically how the value jointly created by the partner firms is translated into actual benefits at the individual firm level (Tsai, 2002). The coopetitive perspective stresses that the supreme interests of a partner are not necessarily aligned with the supreme interest of the other partner(s). This partial or incomplete interest congruence requires explicitly taking into consideration distribution of value across the partnering firms and the related *fairness problem* arising from sharing the jointly developed value within the cooperative game structure (Grandori and Neri, 1999). In other words, the coopetitive perspective pays attention to the positive-but-variable game structure. This structural variability enlightens the presence of uncertainty due to the competitive pressures of firms' interdependence, provided that it is not known ex ante

Table 23.1   A comparative analysis of competition, cooperation and coopetition

	Perspectives		
	Competition	Cooperation	Coopetition
Structure of interdependence	win-lose	win-win	win-win/win-lose
Nature of interdependence	fully negative	fully positive	positive/negative
Function	value distribution	value generation	value generation/ value distribution
Structure of interests	fully divergent	fully convergent	partially convergent
Overall game structure	zero-sum	positive	positive-but-variable

to what extent each partner would benefit from cooperation compared to the other(s).

Regarding the latter bias, emphasis has always been placed on competitive behavior aimed at achieving above-normal profits, either by developing a better fit with the industry structure (Porter, 1980) or by building hard-to-copy competencies (Wernerfelt, 1984; Barney, 1991; Peteraf, 1993), and has instead neglected the positive side of competitive maneuvering, whereby common benefits across the rival firms may be actually obtained either intentionally or non-intentionally.

THE STRUCTURE OF COOPETITION AND THE SMITHIAN ARGUMENT

We believe that firms' interdependence as arising from a coopetitive game defined by a partially congruent interest structure is not a new phenomenon. In fact, the sudden emergence and steady growth of strategic alliances and other forms of cooperative agreements in the last couple of decades have not created this phenomenon; instead they have just contributed, substantially, to make the coopetitive nature of firms' interdependences much more visible. Our assumption that the coopetitive game structure is an old, long-standing phenomenon is revealed by the understanding of the nature of competition in the Smithian perspective. Indeed, as Sen (1984: 93) has pointed out:

> When we carry out an exchange, we do achieve what we set out to achieve, and in the process we have helped each other. In more complex cases too – with

many agents and with production in addition to trade – the market works on the basis of *congruence of interests* of different participants. That is the essence of the Smithian perspective: different people have common interest in exchange and the market gives them the opportunity to pursue their *common interest* – with success *not* failure. Of course they also have conflicting interests in many other matters, but the market is not concerned in resolving these conflicts. (emphasis added)

The above quote reports an important part of the message of Smith's (1759) *Theory of Moral Sentiments* as it allows to bypass the problem of altruism. Even if any single firm has no direct concern for the welfare of others, it has an interest in their success because of the opportunity of exchange and growth that may result from having the market system work efficiently. For the same reason, firms have an interest in the success, not only of firms with complementary capabilities, but also of their rivals (Loasby, 2004: 14).

The Smithian argument is congruent with our image of coopetition as a game structure defined by a partial congruence of interests. Based on this image, coopetition appears to be far more complex than the two baseline components of competition and cooperation, as it defines a game structure wherein opportunity for pursuing mutual benefits is often coupled together with tight trade-offs across opposite, divergent requirements. On the ground of these features, a coopetitive game structure seems to be characterized by three basic properties (Castaldo and Dagnino, 2009):

1. inner complexity;
2. relative instability;
3. requisite contextuality.

First, since it is the upshot of two seemingly contradictory behaviors, the structure of coopetition exhibits a degree of inner complexity which goes far beyond the complexity usually shown by each of its two components (competition and cooperation). As Herbert Simon (1996) has pointed out, any adaptive entity contains an adaptive inner environment. Complex systems are nested hierarchies that contain other complex systems: the subsystems are therefore subject in turn to evolutionary pressures. Coopetition is a complex system of interacting, co-adapting firms in which the coopeting firms are complex subsystems embedded in coopetitive context. Additionally, the theory of complex systems allows us to define the coopetitive arenas as self-designing and self-organizing entities: dynamic spaces that continuously shape and reshape themselves and their dynamics in connection with the other (coopetitive and non-coopetitive) spaces. Coopeting firms coevolve with one another because the changes in the behaviors of firms transform the individual interest functions and such a shift alters other firm behaviors (Anderson, 1999: 223). As a consequence, a coopetitive context evolves over time through the entry, exit and transformation of firms. Accordingly, coopetitive contexts are systems performing emergent properties.

The second coopetition property is its relative instability. In fact for the reasons above, coopetitive contexts may also be highly erratic and unstable evolving from competition to cooperation and vice versa (Das and Teng, 2000). In their attempt to explore the drivers underlying the emergence of competitive issues within a cooperative game structure, Padula and Dagnino (2007) develop a theory that emphasizes the relative instability of a competitive game structure and provide a rationale of this instability. More generally, coopetition is by no means a long-standing and relatively stable condition where firms may live in a peaceful unremitting and semiautomatic routine: it is more a temporary unstable condition that – if graphically symbolized in an imaginary continuous line – virtually evolves from any of the extremes (a strict competition or a strict cooperation), mixes the two, and comes back to one of the extremes again. Under coopetition, both structures, the competitive one and the cooperative one, are always considered emergent structures; they may come to the surface even unexpectedly, and then hide back and disappear as they have come to light, bringing nonetheless relevant behavioral consequences. For their distinctive structural traits in which novelty and diversity may emerge from firm interactions, as a matter of course coopeting firms' transformation, innovation and change cannot be fully planned ex ante or entirely governed by managerial intervention. Coopetition usually requires flexible adjustments and the foresight-driven ability to master emergent unanticipated behaviors and unintended consequences, which may occur as results of human action but not of human design (Hayek, 1945). Managers facing a coopetitive context need to know that they have to fine tune and adapt as they are not able to steer completely the unpredictable development of coopetitive processes.

Finally the third coopetition property is requisite contextuality. The evolution of the structure of coopetition is tightly coupled with the specific circumstances of time and place (or the context) in which it occurs. This is nothing but the initial definition of the property that we indicate as requisite contextuality of coopetitive contexts. This means that the context of coopetition is not one that may be labeled as entirely history-free: it is instead profoundly embedded in definite historical contexts. Each coopetitive context is in fact rich of local circumstances of space and time. Each coopetitive set of actions is epitomized by shared contexts and experience fields which craft the glue of coopetitive contexts. By accepting firms interacting in specific contexts that are simultaneously competitive and cooperative, coopetition drives out firm coevolution and coevolutionary processes. By promoting the balance of cooperation and competition among firms, coopetition offsets the firms' dynamic development over time. By enhancing knowledge flows and exchanges among firms, coopetition helps generate new and local solutions to old and new problems (new products/processes/routines).

The three fundamental properties of a coopetitive game structure heretofore reported contribute to characterize in depth the structure of coopetition as they make clear some essential features which lie at the basis of the evolution of coopeting firms. In particular, since they typify a state of affairs in which strategic interaction and dynamic intersections, situational indeterminism and shared ecosystems are concurrently present, coopetition complexity and instability are of central importance if observed in the light of partial interests or goal alignment. Similarly, as regards the property of contextuality, making use of a strategic behavior that is consistent with the requirements of coopetitive interfirm dynamics, we may feel more soundly positioned to understand how the contextualization of coopetitive contexts becomes of paramount importance whenever, by considering definite conditions of space and time, we are able to achieve better recognition of specific evolutionary business relationships at both the firm and the personal levels.

CHALLENGES RAISED BY COOPETITON AND THE QUEST FOR A NOVEL MANAGERIAL MINDSET

In a strict competitive perspective, there is no room for a cooperative intent as success is thought of as accruing to the better performing firms at the expense of the less performing ones. Conversely, cooperation defines itself as excluding a priori competition. The cooperation plea is to share efforts and resources in order to achieve a mutual objective shared between parties. Gain repartition in cooperation does not consider having a winner and a loser to the advantage of the winner, but a reciprocal relational intent ascribed to the advantage of all the partners.

Since the concepts of competition and cooperation are, by definition, fundamentally different and at odds, their integration in a single unifying concept leads necessarily to convey a paradoxical and complex approach, or what the renowned Florentine humanist Nicola Cusano incidentally termed *coincidentia oppositorum*: the coincidence of the opposites. This implies fundamental change in the cognitive maps of actors in order for them to accommodate coopetitive behavior; and radical change in the standard managerial *doxa* dominated by the time-honored Aristotelian strictly dichotomist conception (competition vs. cooperation, theory vs. practice and so on).

Mixing simultaneously competition and cooperation (and acting concurrently in a competitive and cooperative way) is something that implies some kind of *cognitive revolution*. In fact, it is cognitively much easier to simplify the relations among competitors by defining them as 'enemies', according to a military metaphor that rules out cooperation, or as 'colleagues' or 'partners', according to a communitarian metaphor that excludes competition. Developing research on coopetition leads necessarily to a re-examination and a novel definition of the rules of interaction among firms that require novel managerial mindset for the simultaneous development of competitive and cooperative behaviors. This new representation of the relations among competing firms lays down managerial problems at both the individual level and at the collective level. At the individual level, it could be arduous for a firm's employees to subsume and embrace the new complexity vis-à-vis a more trivial representation that simply considers the competitors as rivals to fight and defeat. At the collective level, we are required to conceive new ready-to-use management tools that allow grasping coopetitive dynamic interaction and developing simultaneously competitive and cooperative behaviors.

This kind of cognitive revolution contains a condition of *cognitive dissonance*; in other words we recognize that it comes out when we are in the presence of high-complexity and paradoxical behavior (Chen, 2008). Coopetition stresses the need to overcome the "oversimplified framework that lies at the base of the conventional approaches (competition and cooperation) and proposes a description of more complex market structures where cooperation and competition merge together to form an entirely new perspective" (Dagnino, 2007: 4). Hence, in a coopetitive game structure, firms (and their managers and entrepreneurs) are encouraged to develop a novel managerial mindset which can enable them to actually operate within a context of partially convergent interest structure, while opportunities for pursuing mutual benefits are often coupled together with tight tradeoffs across opposite, divergent requirements. The example of EADS (the company that holds the major stake in Airbus Industries) shows how Germany and France have been able to manage simultaneously cooperation and competition at governmental level by means of a dual governance system. The simultaneity of cooperation and competition is equally at the center of the development of 'competitive areas and regions' within the European Union and across the Atlantic among the US and the EU.

CONCLUSION

In this chapter, we have provided analytical content to the concept of coopetition and emphasized the challenges that coopetition raises for the renewal of the managerial mindset and firm behavior in a way that fits with the opposite requirements of dealing simultaneously with the tensions of competitive and cooperative issues. We have also claimed that rethinking the business context in terms of coopetition and renewing managerial orientation accordingly is not simply a way to defend themselves from threatening changes in the business context features, but a grand managerial and entrepreneurial opportunity that is virtually capable to increase considerably firms' ability to consistently improve the strategic understanding of today's hypercompetitive economic and technological ecosystems and to successfully operate within them (D'Aveni et al., 2010; Adner and Kapoor, 2010).

Coopetition has recently sparked a great deal of interest across management scholars and practitioners and driven the development of a field of research specifically focused on the appreciation of the coopetitive nature of interfirm interdependences and business contexts (see for example the special issues of *International Studies of Management and Organization* 2007, and *Management Research* 2008, respectively).

Although interesting advances have been obtained in this field of studies, we acknowledge that research on coopetition is still in its infancy and that there is a number of factors that have hitherto prevented a more fluid assimilation of the notion of coopetition in strategic management investigation and practice. First, ideological barriers. Strategic thinking has been in fact traditionally based on the deterministic and dichotomy-rooted mainstream economics, which is arduous to overcome. Second, psychological barriers. As we know, the long-lived black-and-white conception of the world rules out contradictory and paradoxical behavior and thwarts the acceptance of the word coopetition and of coopetition strategy. Third and finally, organizational and structural barriers. Firms' purposeful strategic design stems from the previous dominant logics that permeate the way businesses are actually structured and organized within the firms' boundaries.

In this respect, Yami et al. (2008) stressed that a full-size challenge for research on coopetition is to develop a scientific cross-theory and interdisciplinary conceptual basis. Broadening the theoretical basis of research on coopetition and deepening the implications of coopetitive strategic behavior for both scholars, executives, entrepreneurs and policy makers is a promising and fruitful line of inquiry for future research in the coopetition parole.

NOTE

1. We acknowledge that a couple of slightly different approaches on coopetition have been proposed in the last decade. For a review of these perspectives, see Dagnino et al. (2007).

REFERENCES

Adner, R. and R. Kapoor (2010), 'Value creation in innovation ecosystems: how the structure of technological interdependence affects firm performance in new technology generation', *Strategic Management Journal*, **31**, 306–333.

Afuah, A. (2000), 'How much do your co-opetitors' capabilities matter in the face of technological change?', *Strategic Management Journal*, **21** (3), 397–404.

Ancarani, F. and V. Shankar (2003), 'Symbian: customer interaction through collaboration and competition in a convergent industry', *Journal of Interactive Marketing*, **17** (17), 56–76.

Anderson, P. (1999), 'Complexity theory and organization science', *Organization Science*, **10** (3), 216–232.

Baglieri, D., G.B. Dagnino, M. Giarratana and I. Gutierrez (2008), 'Guest editors' introduction on coopetition strategy. Stretching the boundaries of coopetition', *Management Research*, **7** (3), 157–163.

Barney, J.B. (1991), 'Firm resources and sustained competitive advantage', *Journal of Management*, **17**, 99–120.

Bengtsson, M. and S. Kock (1999), 'Cooperation and competition in relationships between competitors in business networks', *Journal of Business and Industrial Marketing*, **14** (3), 178–190.

Brandenburger, A.M. and B.J. Nalebuff (1996), *Co-opetition*, New York: Doubleday.

Brandenburger, A.M. and S. Stuart (1996), 'Value-based business strategy', *Journal of Economics & Management Strategy*, **5** (1), 5–14.

Capon, N. (2001), *Key Account Management and Planning: The Comprehensive Handbook for Managing Your Company's Most Important Strategic Asset*, New York: The Free Press.

Castaldo, S. and G.B. Dagnino (2009), 'Trust and coopetition: the strategic role of trust in interfirm coopetitive dynamics', in G.B. Dagnino and E. Rocco (eds), *Coopetition Strategy: Theory Experiments and Cases*, London: Routledge, pp. 74–100.

Chen, M.J. (2008), 'Reconceptualizing the competition–cooperation relationship: a transparadox perspective', *Journal of Management Inquiry*, **17** (4), 288–304.

Cova, B., P. Ghauri and R. Salle (2002), *Project Marketing: Beyond Competitive Bidding*, Chichester: John Wiley and Sons.

Dagnino, G.B. (2007), 'Preface. Coopetition strategy: toward a new kind of interfirm dynamics?', *International Studies of Management and Organization*, **37** (2), 3–10.

Dagnino, G.B. (2009), 'Coopetition strategy: a new kind of interfirm dynamics for value creation', in G.B. Dagnino and E. Rocco (eds), *Coopetition Strategy: Theory Experiments and Cases*, London: Routledge, pp. 25–43.

Dagnino, G.B., M.C. Di Guardo and M. Galvagno (2008), 'Coopetition capabilities in action: the cases of Wintel and Mactel', paper presented at the Third EIASM International Workshop 'Coopetition strategy: stretching the boundaries of coopetition', Carlos III University, Madrid, February 7–8.

Dagnino, G.B., F. Le Roy and S. Yami (2007), 'La dynamique des stratégies de coopétition', *Revue Française de Gestion*, **33** (176), 87–98.

Dagnino, G.B. and E. Rocco (2009), 'Introduction: coopetition strategy in theory and in practice', in G.B. Dagnino and E. Rocco (eds), *Coopetition Strategy: Theory Experiments and Cases*, London: Routledge.

Das, T.-K. and B. Teng (2000), 'Instabilities of strategic alliances: an internal tensions perspective', *Organization Science*, **11** (1), 77–101.

D'Aveni, R.A., G.B.Dagnino and Ken G. Smith (2010), 'The age of temporary advantage', *Strategic Management Journal*, Special issue, **31**, 1371–1385.

Dowling, M.J., W.D. Roering, B.A. Carlin and J. Wisnieski (1996), 'Multifaceted relationships under coopetition. Description and theory', *Journal of Management Inquiry*, **5**, 155–167.

Doz, Y.L. (1996), 'The evolution of cooperation in strategic alliances: initial conditions or learning processes?', *Strategic Management Journal*, **17**, 55–83.

Doz, Y.L. and G. Hamel (1998), *Alliance Advantage: The Art of Creating Value Through Form and Action*, Boston: Harvard Business School Press.

Economist (1999), 'The complication of clustering', January 2–8, 57–58.

Gnyawali, D.R. and R. Madhavan (2001), 'Cooperative networks and competitive dynamics: a structural embeddedness perspective', *Academy of Management Review*, **26** (3), 431–445.

Grandori, A. and M. Neri (1999), 'The fairness properties of interfirm networks', in A. Grandori (ed.), *Inter-firm Networks*, London: Routledge.

Gulati, R., N. Nohria and A. Zaheer (2000), 'Strategic networks', *Strategic Management Journal*, **21**, 203–215.

Håkansson, H. (1993), 'Network as a mechanism to develop resources', in P. Beije, J. Groenewegen and O. Nuys (eds), *Networking in Dutch Industries*, Leven-Apeldorn: Garant, pp. 207–223.

Hamel, G. (1991), 'Competition for competence and inter-partner learning within international strategic alliances', *Strategic Management Journal*, **12**, 83–104.

Hamel, G., Y. Doz and C.K. Prahalad (1989), 'Collaborate with your competitors and win', *Harvard Business Review*, **67** (1), 133–139.

Hayek, F.A. (1945), 'The use of knowledge in society', *American Economic Review*, **35** (4), 519–530.

Jorde, T. and D.J. Teece (1989), 'Competition and cooperation: striking the right balance', *California Management Review*, **31** (3), 25–38.

Khanna, T. (1998), 'The scope of alliance', *Organization Science*, **9**, 340–355.

Khanna, T., R. Gulatiand and N. Nohria (1998), 'The dynamics of learning alliances: competition, cooperation and relative scope', *Strategic Management Journal*, **19**, 193–210.

Koza, M.P. and A.Y. Lewin (1998), 'The co-evolution of strategic alliances', *Organization Science*, **9**, 255–264.

Lado, A.A., N. Boyd and S.C. Hanlon (1997), 'Competition, cooperation, and the search for economic rents: a syncretic model', *Academy of Management Review*, **22** (1), 110–141.

Lazzarini, S.G. (2007), 'The impact of membership in competing alliance constellations: evidence on the operational performance of global airlines', *Strategic Management Journal*, **28** (4), 345–368.

Loasby, B.J. (2004), 'Entrepreneurship, evolution and the human mind', paper presented at the International Schumpeter Society, Bocconi University Milan, June 9–12.

Luo, Y. (2004), 'A coopetition perspective of MNC-host government relations', *Journal of International Management*, **10** (4), 431–451.

M'Chirgui, Z. (2004), 'The economics of smart card industry: towards coopetitive strategies', Universités d'Aix-Marseille II and III, working paper n.5.

Ngo, D.D. and M. Okura (2008), 'Coopetition in a mixed oligopoly market', paper presented at the Third EIASM International Workshop 'Coopetition strategy: stretching the boundaries of coopetition', Carlos III University, Madrid, February 7–8.

Padula, G. and G. Dagnino (2007), 'Untangling the rise of coopetition. The intrusion of competition in a coopetitive game structure', *International Studies of Management and Organization*, **37** (2), 32–52.

Penrose, E.T. (1959), *The Theory of the Growth of the Firm*, Oxford: Basil Blackwell.

Peteraf, M. (1993), 'The cornerstones of competitive advantage: a resource-based view', *Strategic Management Journal*, **14** (3), 179–191.

Porter, M.E. (1980), *Competitive Strategy. Techniques for Analyzing Industries and Competitors*, New York: Free Press.
Sen, A. (1984), *Resources, Values and Development*, Cambridge, MA: Harvard University Press.
Simon, H.A. (1996), *The Sciences of the Artificial*, Cambridge, MA: MIT Press.
Smith, A. (1776/1937), *The Theory of Moral Sentiments*, Edinburgh and London.
Tidstrom, A. (2008), 'Perspectives on coopetition on an actor and operational level', *Management Research*, **6** (3), 205–215.
Tsai, W. (2002), 'Social structure of coopetition within a multiunit organization: coordination, competition, and intraorganizational knowledge sharing', *Organization Science*, **13** (2), 179–190.
Walley, K. (2007), 'Coopetition: an introduction to the subject and an agenda for research', *International Studies of Management and Organization*, **37** (2), 11–31.
Wernerfelt, B. (1984), 'A resource based view of the firm', *Strategic Management Journal*, **5**, 171–180.
Yami, S., L. Lehmann-Ortegaand and G. Naro (2008), 'Coopetitive dynamic capabilities: the MSI case in the mechanical industry', paper presented at the Third EIASM International Workshop 'Coopetition strategy: stretching the boundaries of coopetition', Carlos III University, Madrid, February 7–8.

24 Crossing boundaries between contemporary research in strategy and finance: connecting the firm's financial structure and competitive strategy
Maurizio La Rocca and Elvira Tiziana La Rocca

INTRODUCTION

This chapter responds to the general call for integration between finance and strategy by examining how financial decisions are related to corporate strategy (Kochhar and Hitt, 1998).[1] With relatively few exceptions, strategic management and finance appear to be in schizophrenic tension, if not in direct opposition (Ward and Grundy, 1996). Bettis (1983) argued that modern financial theory and strategic management are based on very different paradigms, resulting in opposing conclusions. The conflicting state of these two knowledge systems might not matter if managers were able to make the linkages between strategy and finance with ease in practice (Grundy, 1992). But the few (empirical) studies available suggest that general managers do not find these linkages at all easy to make.

The polarity between finance and strategy, two areas of research that have been traditionally studied in a separate fashion, is just apparent. Conversely, these two research and teaching areas present manifold connections, and it is relevant to understand the way in which these areas function individually and interrelate.

In particular, the link between financial decisions and strategy is largely unexplored. An extremely relevant topic, notoriously controversial, to the academic and business communities relates to capital structure decisions and their effects on firms' creation of value. A firm's capital structure refers, generally, to the mix of its financial liabilities. In analysing capital structure we focused on the type of funds, debt or equity, used in the firm for financing. Debt and equity are the two major classes of liabilities, with debtholders and shareholders representing the two types of investors in the firm. Each of these is associated with different levels of risk, benefits, and control. While debtholders exert lower control, they earn a fixed rate of return and are protected by contractual obligations with respect to their investment. Shareholders are the residual claimants, bearing most of the risk, and, correspondingly, have greater control over decisions.

Heretofore, financial theorists suggested that, in perfect and efficient markets, financing decisions may be irrelevant for firms' strategy (Modigliani and Miller, 1958); however, in the real business world such choices may differentially affect firm value, explicitly because there are several imperfections (Myers and Majluf, 1984). Several strategy scholars have argued that financial decisions have strategic importance (Barton and Gordon, 1987; Bromiley, 1990; Kochhar, 1996), especially in affecting corporate governance (Jensen, 1986). Oviatt (1984) suggested that a theoretical integration between the two disciplines is indeed possible, and that according to the way managers, firms' financial stakeholders and firms' non-financial stakeholders interrelate, transaction cost economics and agency theory provide possible avenues. Barton and Gordon (1987) pointed out that corporate strategies complement traditional finance paradigms and enrich the understanding of a firm's capital structure decisions. In addition to tax reasons, the value of a firm can be affected by financing decisions in the moment that information asymmetries between the firm's management and its stakeholders are noted, or when 'real' decisions differ from financing decisions, because of agency problems, for example, or whether costs of financial distress are generated due to debt. Therefore, it is important to better understand the potential interrelation between capital structure and corporate strategy.

In general, the literature on finance and strategy analyses how the strategic actions of key players (managers, shareholders, debtholders, competitors, workers, suppliers, etc) affect firm value and the allocation of value between claimholders.[2] It is possible to provide a different role to these corporate players according to how close they are to the core of the corporation; if they are the corporation's owners, as shareholders and debtholders, or if they are at the boundary of the core, as suppliers, competitors, customers, etc. Specifically, capital structure decisions can concern value creation process (1) influencing efficient investments decisions according to the existence of conflict of interest between managers and financial stakeholders (shareholders and debtholders) and (2) affecting the relationship with non-financial stakeholders, as suppliers, competitors, customers, etc.

From one side, this chapter describes the factors affecting agency problems with the financial stakeholders, explaining how debt can cause shareholders (managers) to take on projects that are too risky and to pass up profitable investments, but also identifying various situations in which debtholders and shareholders may disagree on the decision to liquidate the firm. The interactions between managers, shareholders and bondholders can influence the process of identifying, selecting and choosing investment projects and, as a result, the processes of value creation.[3] The presence of these conflicts, together with information asymmetries and incomplete contracting, can give rise to suboptimal investment strategies that do not maximize the firm's value but rather benefit only a specific category of subjects.

On the other side, debt policy can affect the non-financial stakeholders' behaviour and the competitiveness in the product market, directly influencing the firm's competitive strategy and, as a consequence, the processes of value creation. A new line of research has analysed the possible connections between capital structure, stakeholder theory, market structure, and a firm's strategic behaviour. First of all, capital structure affects the behaviour of non-financial stakeholders, as claimants to the firm's cash flows in addition to shareholders and bondholders. Second, debt level affects market structure and thus leads to either higher or lower industry concentration levels. In addition, capital structure can serve as a way to commit to a certain product-market strategy. According to the underlying assumptions of this notion, leverage will cause firms to behave more or less aggressively, which makes competition tougher or softer. The interaction between how a corporation is financed and how it is viewed by its non-financial stakeholders suggests that capital structure decisions must be incorporated into the overall corporate strategy of the firm. Therefore, the chapter describes how the firm's financial situation is likely to affect its sales, its ability to attract employees and suppliers, the competitors' behaviour in the market, and, in general, the ability of a firm to operate its business profitably.

In all the cases it is important to realize, and be aware of, the role of capital structure in mitigating corporate governance problems and leveraging the firm's competitive advantage.

This chapter intends to discuss these interactions and the consequences on the value processes. The rest of the chapter is organized as follows: the second section highlights how the interaction between managers, shareholders and debtholders affects capital structure and investment decisions, creating the so-called problems of underinvestment and overinvestment. The third section focuses on the interaction between how a corporation is financed and how it is viewed by its non-financial stakeholders, suggesting that capital structure decisions must be incorporated into the overall corporate strategy of the firms. The final section discusses the main conclusions, providing directions for future research.

FINANCIAL POLICY AND INVESTMENT: THE EFFECT OF THE RELATION AMONG MANAGERS, SHAREHOLDERS AND DEBTHOLDERS

The interactions among managers, shareholders and debtholders, and the related conflicts of interests, influence capital structure, corporate governance activities and strategy plans, which, in turn, could give rise to inefficient managerial decisions and suboptimal investments that generally fall under the categories of problems of underinvestment and overinvestment.

Especially in regards to capital structure planning, the conflicting relationship between managers, shareholders and debtholders could bring managers to act: 1) in their own interests, by choosing suboptimal projects that do not provide an adequate yield level but that are low risk, thus ignoring shareholder preference for riskier projects;[4] 2) in the interest of shareholders, by making investment decisions that maximize equity value and not firm value and, when operating in inefficient markets, could cause them to make suboptimal choices that damage debtholders.[5] In this latter case, value is destroyed because of the different objective functions of shareholders and debtholders. It is the contrasting goals to be achieved that cause distortions in the corporate strategy formulation. The incentive to maximize equity value is not necessarily coherent with the incentive to maximize firm value. As is well known, firm assets value can be broken down into equity value and debt value; thus, strategies that reduce debt value and leave firm value as it was, increase equity value by transferring wealth from the debtholders to the shareholders.

Overinvestment Problems

Problems in overinvestment have to do with the possibility that management can abuse its decision-making power by adopting unprofitable investments (managerial overinvestment), that could damage the interests of the shareholders, or overly risky projects (risk shifting or asset substitution) in favour of the shareholders but against the interests of the debtholders (Jensen and Meckling, 1976; Galai and Masulis, 1976; Jensen, 1986; Stultz, 1990).

Managerial overinvestment
When considering the hypothesis where ownership and control are separated, the problem of managerial overinvestment consists of a conflict of interest that primarily influences the relationship between the managers, who have control over the firm, and the shareholders, who are the owners of the firm (Jensen, 1986). Instead, in a context where property and control

substantially coincide (owner-managed firms), the conflict of interest has to do with the relationship between internal shareholders, the group in control or managers and entrepreneurs, and external shareholders who do not participate in firm management (Jensen and Meckling, 1976). The problem of managerial overinvestment is based on the hypothesis that managers emphasize the importance of their role, different from that of the shareholders, which gives rise to a conflict of interest *in nuce* that will produce opportunistic behaviour that can lead to a decrease in the firm's total value when the chance arises (Jensen and Meckling, 1976).[6] Overinvestment problems can take various forms. Jensen (1986) connects overinvestment to how managers use the financial resources that the firm produces. When profitable investment projects and growth opportunities are lacking, managers prefer to use the free cashflow (available cashflow that is in excess of the resources that are necessary to handle the firm's investments at a positive net present value) for opportunistic purposes, instead of giving it back to the shareholders through dividends.[7] As Jensen (1986) and Stulz (1990) point out, firm expansion beyond what may be considered an optimal level and the increase of resources directly under managerial control would create higher salaries and would offer greater power and prestige to those who run the firm (the empire-building phenomenon). The propensity towards empire building tends to stimulate managers to invest all available resources (the free cashflow) in projects that increase the firm's size but not its value. Essentially, managers tend to invest even in negative present value projects so long as they can increase the firm's size and thus their own private benefits (Degryse and De Jong, 2001). Managerial overinvestment can also take on other forms. For example, Shleifer and Vishny (1989) assert that managers prefer investing in projects that are even of negative net present value but that increase their own human capital, making firm activity inseparable from their personal skills (entrenchment). These authors define managerial entrenchment as a set of self-defence mechanisms that management creates by deciding on firm development strategies so as to emphasize their own competencies and skills, rather than choosing strategies that are in the firm's interest.[8] In this way a dependent type of relationship is created, which attributes importance to the managers' skills independently of whether or not they are capable of maintaining the firm's competitive advantage.

In these types of situations debt, as pointed out by Jensen (1986), can help reduce overinvestment problems by limiting managerial discretion in using agency resources. In fact, making recourse to debt represents an indirect means of control and discipline of managerial behaviour by limiting their tendency to use free cashflow inefficiently, since it must first of all be used for interest and loan capital reimbursement.[9]

Overinvestment in risky projects: incentives for risk shifting

Overinvestment in risky projects (called also *risk shifting* or *asset substitution*) produces a conflict of interest between shareholders and debtholders and increases the possibility that managers, after having contracted a debt and while acting in ownership interest, transfer the value from debtholders to shareholders through another rise in leverage, thus increasing the risk of distress and bankruptcy, or undertake new investment projects that are riskier than the firm's average ones (Jensen and Meckling, 1976). Therefore, when firms are indebted, an *ex post* (with respect to debt contracting) risk increase can, *ceteris paribus*, transfer earnings from debtholders to shareholders (Galai and Masulis, 1976). In fact, different levels of risk connected to investment decisions made by managers influence the conflict of interest between debtholders and shareholders, since riskier investment and financing policies that increase share value and decrease debt value transfer wealth from debtholders to shareholders.

Jensen and Meckling (1976) show how, due to equity's limited liability, shareholders (and the managers that act in their interests) are encouraged to approve projects that are riskier than the ones initially proposed before the debt was underwritten.

This mechanism is based on the fundamental difference between equity and debt, that can be found in the different type of sensitivity they show with respect to the firm's level of risk; in fact, while equity value grows when there is higher risk, debt value decreases when the volatility of the firm's activities increases (Jostarndt, 2002).

Shareholders increase their wealth by increasing the volatility of the firm's activities, that then means they approve projects that are too risky and thus end up distorting investment policy. Therefore, shareholders of indebted firms can obtain most of the benefits inherent in a risky project when it is successful, and can avoid totally bearing the costs of unsuccessful projects, transferring them to debtholders thanks to their limited liability (Jensen and Meckling, 1976).

Underinvestment Problems

Underinvestment problems have to do with the agency relationship between shareholders and debtholders, following the hypothesis that managers act in shareholder interest (underinvestment à la Myers, also called debt overhang), or else between new and old shareholders, when managers act in the interests of the old ones (underinvestment in risky projects or risk avoidance).

Underinvestment à la Myers or debt overhang

Myers, in his 1977 study, was the first to point out the possibility that high debt relationships can stimulate managers to reject positive net present value projects, which ends up decreasing firm value. The presence of 'risky' debt,[10] that shows a lower market value than the nominal one, has a particularly negative influence on firms' investment choices.

Myers' (1977) analysis is based on the concept that firm value is made up of assets in place and growth opportunities (based on the future ability to make profitable investments). Growth opportunities are compared to options, whose present value is a result of not only the expected cash flow, but also the probability that the firm actually takes advantage of them. In other words, the value of growth opportunities depends on investments made at the manager's (decision maker's) discretion, who has the power to exercise these options.[11] The way that the assets in place are financed, and thus the way the firm's capital is structured, influences the ability to create and take advantage of growth opportunities, since in this manner pressure is put on the quality of the firm's decision making.

Myers (1977) shows that, when there is risky debt, managers who act in shareholder interest tend to follow a biased decision-making process, which leads them to reject profitable investments that could offer positive net worth to the firm's value. In other words, shareholders of firms who have risky debt are not willing to finance projects, thus taking on the cost, that would exclusively or mostly benefit the firm's debtholders; in these cases, the net present value of the project, while positive, would allow the debt's market value to rise up to the corresponding nominal value, without producing other benefits for the shareholders. In fact, risky debt would act as a sort of 'tax' on the profits derived from the new investments, since most of the value created would only serve to allow debtholders to recover their loan (Stein, 2001).

In such a situation the investment would be made only when the net present value is positive and higher than the debt's nominal value (Myers, 1977; Bekovitch and Kim, 1990). In fact managers, as a general rule, would tend to choose investments whose net present value offers a residual payoff to shareholders, while it is also positive and thus can cover the debt value.

The presence of risky debt creates, *ex post*, potential situations where management can serve shareholders' interests only by making suboptimal decisions for all the stakeholders (Myers, 1977). Therefore, firms that are indebted would not be able to finance positive net present value investment projects, thus losing growth opportunities and, in the long run, value.

Underinvestment in risky projects: incentives for risk avoidance

Brito and John (2002) show how the presence of risky debt does not always create risk shifting, but that in some contexts it can generate situations of risk avoidance (underinvestment in risky projects) that are opposite to the former.

Incentives for risk shifting traditionally have been analysed (Jensen and Meckling, 1976) with theoretical models based on finite periods (periods 0 and 1), without considering the firm as an entity in continuous evolution and thus not taking into account the presence of growth opportunities that can come up in the future, which are a fundamental component of the firm's value.

On the basis of these considerations Brito and John (2002) re-examine incentives for risk shifting in a model where during the final period the firm still shows growth opportunities that have not yet been realized, and show how these have a very strong impact on agency costs determined by risky debt. In fact, these growth opportunities can eliminate the underinvestment problem described by Myers (1977) and reduce the problem of risk shifting, by sometimes converting it into opposite situations of risk avoidance.[12]

Although risk-shifting problems seem to be particularly relevant, it can be observed in economic reality that often these types of indebted firms adopt a conservative and prudent investment policy, where they try to focus on the core business by selling extra assets and reducing, instead of increasing, the firm's risk (Brito and John, 2002).

While incentives for risk shifting are generated by the shareholders' awareness that they are in any case protected by the principle of limited liability (put options on firm activity), risk avoidance attitudes are produced by the fear that growth opportunities may be lost if the firm were to be put up for sale.

The impact of risky debt on firm decision making depends on whether or not there are future opportunities for investment of value; excessively risky investment policies could damage the firm's possibility to survive at least up until the time when such growth opportunities can be taken advantage of. Entrepreneurs can obviously take advantage of such growth opportunities only if they manage to keep control of the firm, i.e. keep it from going bankrupt; in fact, financial distress and eventual bankruptcy could lead to liquidation and debtholders could become the owners of the firms. The entrepreneurs' commitment is thus towards saving the firm's future ability to obtain those financial resources necessary to be able to take advantage of growth opportunities.

The main conclusion reached by Brito and John (2002) is that the presence of growth opportunities that have not yet been taken advantage of has a notable impact on agency costs of risky debt: firms with low growth prospects that operate in mature sectors and with high leverage are stimulated to overinvest in risky projects (risk shifting), whereas to the contrary, firms with good economic prospects are stimulated to underinvest and to avoid overly risky investments (risk avoidance).

Incentives for risk avoidance, which are generally the result of information asymmetries, allow us to understand why firms with high levels of risky debt and growth opportunities not yet taken advantage of adopt quite conservative investment policies.

Overinvestment and Underinvestment: Determining Factors and Consequences

From one side, when a firm has risky debt and scarce growth opportunities, managers, acting in shareholder interests, could reject positive net present value investment projects (underinvestment à la Myers), because the value created would be advantageous only for the firm's debtholders and would not avoid distress. They could also decide to promote high-risk investment policies (risk shifting) that take away value from debtholders and maximize equity value. However, if growth opportunities are high, managers can end up choosing conservative investment policies so as to avoid risking losing their control over the firm (risk avoidance). Thus, the main source of these types of distortions lies in the presence of risky debt, i.e. in high levels of debt whose market value is lower than the nominal one and therefore difficult for the firm to handle (crisis situations or financial distress).

On the other side, where firms with low debt levels, high liquidity but low prospects for growth opportunities are concerned, and especially in the case of mature firms, managers could undertake negative net present value investment projects for purely opportunistic reasons (empire building). The origins of managerial overinvestment can be found in the type of decision-making power that management has, that allows it to engage in investments for its own benefit. In this case, as noted by Jensen (1986) and Stulz (1990), an increase in leverage disciplines management's behaviour; in fact, the presence of debt obliges managers to always be able to pay interest rates and meet deadlines and thus increases their commitment towards more efficient company management. Table 24.1 synthesizes and confronts the main characteristics of such problems.

The benefits of debt can be found in how they allow problems of managerial overinvestment to be foreseen and prevented when there is a lack of future growth opportunities, while its costs lie in the risk of not being able to undertake positive net present value investment projects because of debt overhang problems or in incentives to make other types of inefficient investment decisions (risk shifting). The existence of a trade-off between the costs and benefits of debt thus becomes evident (Stultz, 1990). The

Table 24.1 Problems of under- and overinvestment: characteristics, determining factors and consequences

	Overinvestment		Underinvestment	
	Empire building or managerial overinvestment (Jensen, 1986; Stulz, 1990)	Risk shifting or overinvestment in risky projects (Jensen and Meckling, 1976)	Underinvestment à la Myers or debt overhang	Risk avoidance or underinvestment in risky projects (Brito and John, 2002)
Subjects in agency relations	Managers against shareholders (and debtholders)	Managers with shareholders against debtholders	Managers with shareholders against debtholders; present shareholders against new shareholders	Managers against shareholders (and debtholders)
Determining factors	Leverage: low / Growth opportunities: low / Cashflow availability: high	Leverage: high / Growth opportunities: low (high risk but unprofitable growth opportunities) / Cashflow availability: low	Leverage: high / Growth opportunities: low / Cashflow availability: low	Leverage: high / Growth opportunities: high / Cashflow availability: low
Type of firm	Firms that rarely make recourse to debt and that operate in sectors that have scarce growth prospects	Firms that make quite a bit of recourse to debt, especially when in financial difficulty, and that operate in high risk sectors	Firms that make quite a bit of recourse to debt, especially when in financial difficulty, and that operate in sectors with good economic potential	Both young firms with high growth potential (high tech) and mature ones (resulting from LBO)
Influence on value	Choice of projects with negative net present value	Choice of high risk projects, with low probabilities of being successful or even with negative net present value	Refusal towards positive net present value investment projects	Refusal towards risky investment projects but with positive net present value
Role of debt	Reduces such problems due to its ability to discipline management	Exascerbates such problems	Exascerbates such problems	Exascerbates the problem

Source: our elaboration.

Table 24.2   *Classification of deviant investment behaviours on the basis of investment stock and risk*

Deviations from optimal levels in firm investment policy regarding:		
the firm's level of investments undertaken	⟹ Managerial *overinvestment* (Jensen, 1986; Stulz, 1990)	*Underinvestment* (Myers, 1977)
the firm's risk profile	⟹ *Risk shifting* (Jensen and Meckling, 1976)	*Risk avoidance* (Brito and John, 2002)

Source: Brito and John (2002).

benefits of debt would become obvious in how management efficiently exercises its control over firm activity. On the other hand, high debt could increase the risk that positive net present value investment projects are rejected or that excessively risky projects are accepted.

Therefore, problems of incomplete contracts, information asymmetries and conflicts of interest between managers, shareholders and debtholders can give rise to inefficient investment choices both when there is a high and a low level of debt.

As observed by Brito and John (2002), deviations from optimal investment policies, whether or not their determining factors are different, can be classified under two dimensions (Table 24.2): on the basis of the quantity of the resources invested in firm activity and according to the level of risk that the various investment choices can produce.

The first dimension takes into consideration the type of influence the conflict of interest between managers, shareholders and debtholders has on the level of the investments made by the firm, or rather on the tendency to engage in investment projects that are of different economic sizes, thus countering managerial underinvestment (Myers, 1977) problems with overinvestment ones (Jensen, 1986). In Myers' model, the sum total of resources destined to new investments is inferior to what would be desirable and thus negatively influences the firm's ability to take advantage of growth opportunities. In this case, a lower number of projects are undertaken with respect to an 'optimal' investment level, which blocks positive processes of creation of economic value. To the contrary, managerial overinvestment always is connected to the firm's investment level, but in this case managers' preference for empire building may bring them to invest more resources than would be considered optimal, and to engage even in negative net present value projects if they increase the firm's size and allow the managers to enjoy more private benefits.

The second dimension has to do with the risk profile of financed projects rather than influencing the amount of resources that will be used for investments, which mostly causes problems of risk shifting (Jensen and Meckling, 1976). In this case the risk/return profile will be the one that will change, by stimulating investment projects that show a risk level that is different from the firm's average one and that is, above all, different from the one that was *ex ante* appreciated by the firm's investors. In fact, risk-shifting problems have to do precisely with the transference of value from debtholders to shareholders through an added increase in leverage that increases the risk of distress and bankruptcy, or through the acceptance of new investment projects that are riskier than the firm's average ones. To the contrary, Brito and John (2002) show that situations of risk avoidance are more common where managers tend to engage in secure investments or in ones that are less risky than the firm's average ones, so as to protect their control over the company and avoid that others can eventually benefit from future growth opportunities.

It is interesting to observe how each deviation from the optimal investment level has a different motivation. For example, in underinvestment problems the shareholders and managers underinvest, since most of the benefits would go to the debtholders, and thus prefer to issue dividends before they lose all control of the firm. Where the risk avoidance problem is involved, the shareholders and managers avoid risky projects for the opposite reason: they don't want to lose control of the firm.

Table 24.3 shows the contexts in which inefficient investment choices are made. In firms that are having financial problems (close to bankruptcy) but that still have high growth opportunities, incentives for risk avoidance are the main determining factor behind suboptimal investment choices; to the contrary, in firms with low economic prospects incentives for managerial overinvestment, risk shifting and underinvestment become dominant,

Table 24.3   Relationship between growth prospects, financial condition and investment choices

Impact of growth opportunities and financial distress on firm investment policy		Growth opportunities	
		High	Low
Financial conditions	Positive	Optimal investment policy	Managerial overinvestment
	Negative	Risk avoidance	Risk shifting and underinvestment (Myers)

Source: Brito and John (2002).

depending on whether the firm is in optimal financial shape (with lots of available cash) or is, rather, in financial difficulty (close to bankruptcy).

Therefore, firms' reactions to situations of financial distress strongly depend on economic prospects. In a situation of risky debt where there are few possibilities for growth, incentives for risk shifting and underinvestment become paramount, since the firm could end up not being able to take over the value created by the investments (in that they would benefit only the debtholders). Otherwise it would engage in investments with high yield prospects but that at the same time are much more volatile than the average risk level of the firm's activities. If growth opportunities are good, management will prefer to protect their control over the firm and avoid that others can take advantage of the future benefits of growth opportunities. If financial conditions are positive – i.e. if the firm has a good cash-flow that can be used freely once the debt has been covered – the absence of valuable investment prospects could stimulate management to waste cash in organizational inefficiencies instead of returning it to the shareholders, or use it for investments that do not recover the cost of the capital.

FINANCIAL POLICY AND CORPORATE STRATEGY: THE EFFECT OF THE RELATION AMONG MANAGERS AND NON-FINANCIAL STAKEHOLDERS

Beside the role of financial stakeholders (shareholders and debtholders) in influencing capital structure decisions and a firm's value, financial policy is also affected by non-financial stakeholders.[13] These have no direct monetary stake in the firm and no direct influence on the firm's financial policy (no decision or voting power). However, a firm's capital structure can affect non-financial stakeholders directly, for instance by affecting the probability of default on their explicit and implicit claims on the firm, as well as indirectly, for instance by influencing the firm's production and pricing decisions. Non-financial stakeholders, as a result, are interested in the firm's financing choices because they can be hurt by a firm's financial difficulties. Consequently, firms may be forced (implicitly) to take the interests of their non-financial stakeholders into account in formulating financial policy.

Figure 24.1 provides a broad overview of the relations between the firm, its non-financial stakeholders and its financial stakeholders.

As highlighted by the prestigious and still relevant survey of Harris and Raviv (1991) on capital structure determinants, one of the distinctive categories of determinants that deserve more attention is related to products

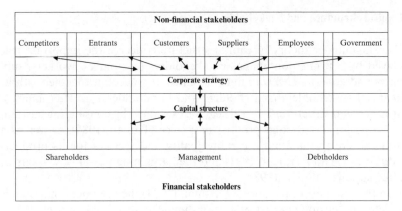

Source: modified from Franck and Huyghebaert (2004).

Figure 24.1 *Overview of the relation between capital structure, financial stakeholders and non-financial stakeholders*

and product-market characteristics. In their conclusion, the two authors refer to the role of these characteristics as the most promising for future research on capital structure:

> In our view, models which relate capital structure to products and inputs are the most promising. This area is still in its infancy and is short on implications relating capital structure to industrial organization variables such as demand and cost parameters, strategic variables, etc.

This observation seems still valid and in vogue (Istaitieh and Rodriguez-Fernandez, 2006).

The interrelationship between the financial and real decisions of firms comes from the role of financial instruments in conveying information (on a firm's profitability) to investors as well as to product-market rivals, consumers, and suppliers (Istaitieh and Rodriguez-Fernandez, 2006). Indeed, firms can use their financial policy towards product-market participants (customers, suppliers, employees, competitors) to solve asymmetric information and agency problems. In addition, capital structure can serve as a signalling device to these non-financial stakeholders, and thereby affect their behaviour.

The literature that links capital structure and product-market factors relates some elements of modern financial theory to stakeholder theory, industrial organization, and the strategic management of firms. Particularly interesting are the studies on how the design of capital structure is affected by non-financial stakeholders as well as competitive dynamics in the product market.

Capital Structure and Stakeholder Theory

The stakeholder theory of capital structure concerns the important role played by a firm's non-financial stakeholders (customers, workers, suppliers and government) who must be taken into account together with its financial stakeholders (shareholders and bondholders) in determining a firm's capital structure. This role can be explained by considering customers' need for a particular product or service (Titman, 1984), as well as a firm's desire to maintain a certain quality and services for its products (Maksimovic and Titman, 1991) and the bargaining power of workers or other suppliers (Sarig, 1998).

In the seminal contribution of Titman (1984) the argument that debt is affected by customers and other non-financial stakeholders is explained as follows. For firms that market durable or unique goods, a firm's liquidation, as a consequence of a financial crisis, may impose costs on its customers, who may not be able to obtain the product, parts, and/or related services, but also on its suppliers, who may have to stop doing business with the firm, and finally on its employees, if the firm offers them fewer opportunities for advancement. The idea is that a firm's liquidation decision may impose costs on other stakeholders, especially the customers, workers or suppliers who make firm-specific investments. These costs might be transferred to shareholders by customers, demanding lower prices for the firm's product, by suppliers, who may be reluctant or who may even stop doing business with the firm, or by potential employees who avoid seeking jobs in these firms. In particular, customers, who can predict firms' behaviour from their knowledge of their financial status, may be reluctant to do business with firms that are threatened with bankruptcy or in financial difficulties and would pay less for the firms' products in the market (Maksimovic and Titman, 1991). Therefore, firms may deliberately use financial instruments to convey information to customers as well as the marketing agents and distributors about their quality, and thus the firm might have an interest in maintaining a low debt level to keep far away the probability of distress.

The stakeholders' views are particularly important for firms whose products need future servicing like automobiles and computers, or whose product quality is important but difficult to observe like prescription drugs. Financial distress, as a consequence of a high leverage, will also be costly for firms that require their employees and suppliers to invest in product-specific training and physical capital, specialized to the firms' needs. This idea suggests why some firms choose not to borrow when banks are willing to provide debt financing at attractive terms or when tax shields are relevant. On the other hand, financial distress should be less costly for firms that produce non-durable goods like agricultural products, or services that are not particularly specialized like hotel rooms, or whose quality can easily be assessed. These firms should have relatively more debt in their capital structure.

In terms of bargaining power with the employees, it is generally assumed that financial distress can benefit some firms by improving their bargaining positions with their stakeholders. By increasing leverage, the firm can reduce its employees' demands by exploiting their fear that a wage increase will push the firm towards bankruptcy (Dasgupta and Sengupta, 1993). Without attractive alternative sources of employment, unionized employees gain less from achieving higher wages if this result substantially increases the probability that the firms will become bankrupt. For the same reasons, government can be pushed to provide subsidies, such as loan guarantees, to a number of distressed firms to keep them far from failing.

To the contrary, some studies in this area (Sarig, 1998) argue that skilled employees of highly leveraged firms can negotiate better contract terms than can employees of identical, but less leveraged, firms. This is because highly leveraged firms are more susceptible to employees' threats to seek alternative employment than are less leveraged firms. As a result, highly leveraged firms, whose employees are presumably more specialized, use relatively little debt in their capital structure.

Capital Structure and Corporate Strategy

The link between corporate strategy and capital structure was developed mainly in the 1980s, while the main contributions start in the 1990s. Generally, little attention was paid to the role of corporate strategy on financial choices. In particular, studies on the interaction between diversification and capital structure became of interest due to their associated strategic implications regarding corporate governance. Indeed, starting with the study of Jensen and Meckling (1976), financial choices have been evaluated because of the close interaction between capital structure and management choices. In the 1980s, other researchers, motivated by the connection between investment and financial choices, highlighted the link between capital structure and diversification (Oviatt, 1984; Titman, 1984; Jensen, 1986; Barton and Gordon, 1987; Williamson, 1988; Titman and Wessels, 1988; Gertner et al., 1988).

The effect of diversification on capital structure choices has been explained mostly through the coinsurance effect (Lewellen, 1971; Bromiley, 1990), the transaction cost theory (Williamson, 1988; Balakrishnan and Fox, 1993), and by applying the agency cost theory (Jensen, 1986; Kochhar, 1996). The coinsurance effect deals with the reduction of operating risk due to the imperfect correlation between the different cashflows of a firm running diverse businesses (Lewellen, 1971; Kim and McConnell, 1977). It is more relevant for firms that develop unrelated diversification strategies because the lack of correlation between businesses is greater: these firms should be able to assume more debt (Kim and McConnell, 1977; Bergh, 1997).[14] The transaction cost approach deals with the governance of contractual relations in transactions between two parties (Williamson, 1988). In particular, by matching corporate finance theory and strategy theory, this approach examines a firm's financial decisions in terms of its specific assets, considering debt and equity as alternative governance structures (Markides and Williamson, 1996). Firms diversify their activities in response to the presence of an excess of unutilized assets, and the kind of diversification strategy depends on the characteristics of these resources (Chatterjee and Wernerfelt, 1991).[15] Therefore, the transaction cost approach, considering debt as a rule-based governance structure and equity as a discretionary governance device, supports the use of debt to finance non-specific assets and the use of equity to finance specific ones (Williamson, 1988).[16] As a consequence, in the presence of highly specific assets (mainly associated to related-diversified firms), that keep a limited liquidation value in case of default, equity is the preferred financial instrument because such assets cannot be easily re-employed. In contrast, in the presence of general purpose assets (mainly associated to unrelated-diversified firms), more valuable as collateral and able to retain their value in the event of liquidation or default, debt is the preferred financing tool (relationship with debtholders, based on the availability of non specific assets, are cheaper).[17] Agency cost theory, rooted in the existence of conflicts of interest between shareholders and managers (Jensen and Meckling, 1976),[18] provides a further theoretical scheme that supports the influence of diversification strategy on capital structure (Kochhar, 1996; Kochhar and Hitt, 1998). Jensen (1986) pointed out the disciplining role of debt on managerial behaviour, in that it reduces managerial discretion regarding free cashflow. Thus, the Jensen perspective supports the positive role of debt in reducing the ability of a manager to realize detrimental diversification strategies, especially unrelated ones. As a consequence, the result of diversification on the debt/equity choice can be interpreted according to the monitoring effect. Stakeholders, and in particular shareholders, are assumed to have the capability to affect the strategic decisions of managers, in a way to avoid that a diversification strategy, especially unrelated, is realized for opportunistic behaviours. Consequently, shareholders will promote the use of debt as a device to discipline managerial behaviour, limiting diversification decisions (especially unrelated).[19]

Capital Structure and Competitive Strategy

An important player affecting corporate financing decisions are the firm's competitors. If investment decisions, incentive to take on a risky project, and liquidation choice are influenced by a firm's leverage, and thus influence the action of its competitors, then leverage choice may be a strategic tool that grants a competitive advantage. Firms may affect both market structure and the competitiveness of an industry by strategically changing their financial behaviour, depending on their own capital structure and that of their rivals. A firm's financial structure influences production and pricing decisions as well as a firm's pre-commitment to a certain strategic output or price level; it also affects entry and exit decisions through incumbent predatory behaviour.

The relationship between market structure and capital structure can be explained by taking into consideration how, during an industry recession, more highly leveraged firms tend to experience lower operating profits and lose more market share than their more conservatively financed competitors – an effect that is exacerbated by product differentiation and industry concentration (Opler and Titman, 1994). Unleveraged rivals can try to take advantage of the situation by using aggressive behaviour to weaken the financial position of a competing firm. As a result, financially strong (unleveraged) firms, in an effort to drive out (highly leveraged) competitors vulnerable to financial distress (in particular those firms with specialized products), may take advantage of distress periods to aggressively advertise or price their products.[20] In a highly competitive environment, low-leveraged firms may engage in predatory practices in order to exhaust financially highly leveraged firms and drive them out of the market. The predatory policy of conservatively financed firms is especially effective in industries in which customers and other stakeholders are concerned about the long-term viability of the firms with which they do business. Telser (1966), implicitly assuming capital market imperfections, argued that, as a rule, a firm entering the market has a more vulnerable financial structure than does an incumbent.[21] Therefore, an incumbent with deep pockets can engage in predatory practices, such as a price war or increasing its output, to exhaust the entrant financially and drive it out of the market, at least temporarily (Poitevin, 1989).[22] Foresighted firms use low debt levels as a strategic instrument to signal their solvency and toughness to the market, thus deterring any predatory action and risk of aggressive behaviour by rivals.

Leverage affects the competitive dynamics of an industry in a non-trivial way: in some situations it forces firms to become more aggressive competitors, in others less aggressive. In an industry in which the aggregate demand for a product is extremely uncertain, greater output generally increases risk because it leads to higher profits when product demand turns out to be strong, but lower profits when demand turns out to be weak. Hence, since higher leverage increases a firm's appetite for risk (see risk-shifting problems in the previous paragraph), the greater a firm's leverage, the greater its incentive to produce at a high level of output. Competitors, observing a firm's high leverage ratio, will realize that the firm is going to boost production. Not wishing to drive the price down to the point where no firm profits, the competitors may accommodate the firm's high output by producing at a lower level.

Furthermore, competition and debt can be considered as a trade-off (Nickell, 1996). According to the incentive theory and the agency model, a high level of competition in the product market can replace leverage as a disciplinary mechanism for managers à la Jensen (1986), thereby inducing more efficient behaviour.

CONCLUSIONS

Strategy and finance are growing closer but rarely together. The time has come when it has become necessary to match strategy and investment plans with financing requirements, complementing external sources of finance to strategies for corporate development. A good integration between strategy and finance dimensions can be tantamount to turning out to be a competitive weapon.

The interaction between financing and real decisions creates a situation in which high or low debt can compromise a firm's ability to take advantage of strategic options. The need to study in greater depth the interaction between real decisions and financing, with respect to interactions with financial and non-financial stakeholders, is a topic of interest to academics and to the business community.

The common theme here is that a firm's financial policy and its ability to support the value creation process are affected by its relationship with (1) financial stakeholders, referring to shareholders and debtholders, and (2) non-financial stakeholders, such as customers, workers, and suppliers.

Debt leverage generates, along with tax benefits, a series of responsibilities and incentives in business management activities that can affect the relationship between managers and stakeholders and, as a consequence, the process of value creation.

The first part of this chapter has focused on the cost and thus the investment distortions that arise because of the conflicts of interest between management, shareholders, and debtholders. To the extent that lenders anticipate how debt distorts investment incentives, shareholders will bear

the costs of the investment distortions caused by their firm's capital structure. A firm with an incentive to make investment decisions that reduce the
value of its debt will be subject to higher borrowing costs and may at times be
unable to obtain debt financing. As a consequence, firms have an incentive
to design their capital structures such as to minimize these investment distortions. This is a well-known topic in management and finance, and in this
chapter it is discussed with reference to the main literature. We have pointed
out the causes, determining factors, and effects that ensue in response to
problems arising from the interaction between financial stakeholders.

A high-leveraged firm can engage actions that are harmful to its shareholders or debtholders but also to its non-financial stakeholders such as
customers, employees, and suppliers. Indeed, the conflicts arising between
managers, shareholders and debtholders do not appear to be the major
source of trouble with debt financing for many firms. A high-leveraged
firm can find it difficult to get more external finance and may find it more
costly to efficiently carry out its day-to-day business.

The second part of the chapter has analysed the role of non-financial
stakeholders in influencing capital structure decisions. The types of products a firm sells, the nature and degree of output-market competition,
uncertainty in the product market, and other aspects of the firm's overall
strategy have a relevant influence on capital structure, along with taxes,
information asymmetries, and agency costs. At the same time, theoretical
work has shown an alternative, opposing relationship. Thus, depending on
the underlying assumptions, corporate debt can increase or decrease firm
aggressiveness. Furthermore, capital structure influences the probability
of predation and market exit.

The chapter examines the situations in which firms should limit their
desire to use debt financing, and in contrast, explains why many firms
choose to maintain a low debt ratio even when lenders are willing to
provide debt capital at attractive terms. To summarize, the potential
interaction between managers, financial stakeholders, and non-financial
stakeholders influences capital structure, corporate governance activities,
and value creation processes. These in turn may give rise to inefficient
managerial decisions or they may shape the industry's competitive dynamics to achieve a competitive advantage.

In our view, this chapter is an overture to further and more detailed
empirical study, able to explore how strategy and finance can be welded
more closely together. Research in this boundary area has been heretofore
largely theoretical, but the subject deserves further empirical examination.
A robust research design and data set may offer interesting approaches
to understanding how product-market behaviour affects capital structure. Future research could simultaneously and empirically study a

two-directional effect, considering endogeneity problems, in which debt level affects and is affected by non-financial stakeholders or, in general, by the firm's strategic behaviour in the product market. Additionally, most of the reports in the literature have so far examined how the debt-equity mix drives these decisions, but other aspects of the financing mix may also play a role. Further studies evaluating the role of capital structure on product-market behaviour may benefit from taking into account debt mix, debt maturity structure, debt seniority structure, covenants, and so on.

One final consideration should be of interest: decision making regarding capital structure is not simply a matter of deterministic, prescriptive principles, due to the complex number of forces that influence firm relations and managerial activity. It is, rather, an art that, despite all the innovations in financial engineering and changes in the competitive context, are part of today's financial world and cannot be separated from the intellectual skill of good financial managers.

NOTES

1. Finance allows organizations to quantitatively understand firms' strategic initiative impact on corporate value.
2. Financial policy decisions of firms are the product of deliberate choices in a strategic environment that features numerous other actors, each armed with their own disparate agenda.
3. When a firm is defined as a 'nexus of contracts' (Jensen and Meckling, 1976) all those who have an interest in the firm's activities are part of the whole of explicit and implicit contracts that a firm is made up of. In this sense, managers are different from all the other stakeholders, since they hold a central position of coordination and execution of all the firm's contracts. Managers have direct control over business activity (even though the shareholders, or suppliers of risk capital, have indirect control); thus it is their specific task to make strategic decisions regarding firm development and to plan resource allocation. This does not always happen, due to the fact that often opportunistic interests bring them to use firm resources inappropriately, by allocating them poorly and by making suboptimal investment decisions that diminish firm value.
4. As is well known, managers are economic subjects that are more averse to risk than shareholders, in that it is impossible for them to diversify company risk through investment differentiation. In this case, when having to choose between two projects they will tend to prefer low-risk investments that are most likely to be successful, due to the fact that most of the managers' personal earnings depend on the firm's fate.
5. In particular, managers could choose not to support safe projects with positive present net value if that would mean causing an increase in debt value with respect to an insignificant (in terms of absolute value) increase in equity value. In other cases, managers, by acting in the interests of shareholders, could accept risky projects with negative net present value that could significantly damage debt value and transfer earnings from the debtholders to the shareholders.
6. Beyond their goal of maximizing stock value, managers consider the firm a source of economic profit, of self-esteem and, more generally, as a means to increase their own human capital (Jostarndt, 2002). For this reason, managers sometimes end up making inefficient decisions whose only objective lies in increasing their own private profits, with no regard for the eventual consequences that can damage the shareholders.

7. For example, the resources mentioned could be used to make the main offices more elegant, buy expensive automobiles, increase the number of employees that will be under their direct control, use company jets for private purposes, etc.

8. For example, managers that have a high number of shares can defend themselves from or completely avoid any sort of hostile takeover by maintaining their job even when they are operating inefficiently; the fact they can avoid this mechanism makes room for opportunistic behaviour.

9. A high level of recourse to debt capital, while assuring a fixed recurring outflow of financial resources that are thus no longer available to managers, stimulates management's commitment to avoid situations of economic distress and bankruptcy, means that company management is more exposed to capital market evaluations (Jensen, 1986) and represents a positive sign for the capital market, which results in share appreciation (Ross, 1977).

10. As Myers points out (1977), there are no underinvestment problems if the debt's market value corresponds to its nominal value, i.e. in the presence of a safe debt. Eventual transfers of wealth from debtholders to shareholders could come about only when there is risky debt, for example when the yield value is at 90 with respect to a market value of 50; in these cases, managers could adopt inefficient investment strategies that favour shareholders.

11. Therefore Myers asserts that firm value depends on activities that can be considered call options (growth opportunities), in the sense that their value is at least partially derived from the firm's investment decisions.

12. The concept of risk avoidance, recently brought to light thanks to the contributions of Brito and John (2002), represents an interesting topic for future research, in that it needs more in-depth study on both a theoretical and an empirical level.

13. Two comprehensive surveys of theoretical and empirical works on this topic are the one of Istaitieh and Rodriguez-Fernandez (2006), and Franck and Huyghebaert (2004).

14. Consistent with this argument, several studies (Kim and McConnell, 1977; Bergh, 1997 and Alonso, 2003) have found that the coinsurance effect is one of the most important value-increasing sources associated with unrelated diversification. Firms that follow unrelated diversification can issue more debt and benefit from the fiscal advantages related to debt financing (Bergh, 1997). The tax liability of the diversified firm may be less than the cumulated tax liabilities of the different (single) business units.

15. An excess of highly specific assets is more likely to lead to related diversification because these assets can only be transferred across similar businesses. Conversely, an unrelated diversification strategy should be based on the presence of an excess of non-specific assets.

16. Debt financing requires a firm to make interest and principal payments according to a schedule stipulated in the contract; in the event of default, debtholders may exercise their pre-emptive claims against the firm's assets (Shleifer and Vishny, 1989). At the same time, the shareholders bear a residual-claimant status with regard to earnings and to assets liquidation; their relations with the firms last for the lifetime of the business.

17. For instance, in the case of financial distress, a firm that operates in three sectors – grocery, mechanical and pharmaceutical – and that has basically general purpose assets, has the opportunity to liquidate the assets easily and quickly (as it is useable in many activities and industry sectors). As a consequence, the higher capacity to meet the scheduled debt payment, thanks to general purpose asset liquidity, provides security for the loan provided, reducing the cost of capital and increasing the debt capacity.

18. Managers, acting as agents, may make non-profitable investments, which are inconsistent with the objective of value creation for shareholders (the principal); while shareholders are strictly interested in the maximization of shareholder value, managers consider the firm as an instrument to increase their wage, self-esteem, private benefits, and, generally, their human capital value. In paying attention to all these benefits, of which just one is based on shareholder value, managers may exhibit opportunistic behaviours.

19. A diversified firm, especially if organized in unrelated business segments, will increase the use of debt, under the influence of the stakeholders, to constrain potential

opportunistic behaviours of the management, by the increased amount of interest payment at the due deadline (Jensen, 1986). Therefore, debt prevents managers from using diversification to destroy value (for private benefit).
20. The incentives of rivals are greater in concentrated markets, because there are greater gains to be made from such a strategy.
21. With perfect financial markets this strategy cannot succeed, because the entrant can always secure financing as long as its entry is profitable.
22. Once again, when an incumbent firm observes the entrant's leveraged financial structure, it increases its output, thus lowering the latter's cashflow and making its default more likely. Therefore, predatory incentives are an increasing function of the entrant's debt level.

REFERENCES

Balakrishnan, S. and I. Fox (1993), 'Asset specificity, firm heterogeneity and capital structure', *Strategic Management Journal*, **14**, 3–16.
Barton, S. and P. Gordon (1987), 'Corporate strategy: useful perspective for the study of capital structure?', *Academy of Management Review*, **12**, 67–75.
Bergh, D. (1997), 'Predicting divestiture of unrelated acquisitions: an integrative model of ex-ante conditions', *Strategic Management Journal*, **18**, 715–731.
Berkovitch, E. and E.H. Kim (1990), 'Financial contracting and leverage induced over and under investment incentives', *Journal of Finance*, **45** (3), 1145–1186.
Bettis, R. (1983), 'Modern financial theory, corporate strategy and public policy: three conundrums', *Academy of Management Review*, **8**, 406–415.
Brito, J.A. and K. John (2002), 'Leverage and growth opportunities: risk avoidance induced by risky debt', working paper, University of New York, Salomon Centre, Stern School of Business.
Bromiley, P. (1990), 'On the use of financial theory in strategic management', in P. Shrivastava and R. Lamb (eds), *Advances in Strategic Management*, **6**, 71–98.
Chatterjee, S. and B. Wernerfelt (1991), 'The link between resources and type of diversification: theory and evidence', *Strategic Management Journal*, **12**, 33–48.
Dasgupta, S. and K. Sengupta (1993), 'Sunk investment, bargaining and choice of capital structure', *International Economic Review*, **34**, 203–220.
Degryse, H. and A. De Jong (2001), 'Investment spending in the Netherlands: asymmetric information or managerial discretion?', working paper, Erasmus University, Rotterdam.
Franck, T. and N. Huyghebaert (2004), 'On the interactions between capital structure and product markets: a survey of the literature', *Tijdschrift voor Economie en Management*, **49** (4), 727–787.
Galai, D. and R. Masulis (1976), 'The option pricing model and the risk factor of common stock', *Journal of Financial Economics*, **3** (3), 545–580.
Gertner, R., R. Gibbons and D. Scharfstein (1988), 'Simultaneous signalling to the capital and products markets', *RAND Journal of Economics*, **19**, 173–190.
Grinblatt, M. and S. Titman (eds) (2001), *Financial Markets and Corporate Strategy*, Boston: McGraw-Hill.
Grundy, A. (eds) (1996), *Corporate Strategy and Financial Decisions*, London: Kogan Page.
Harris, M. and A. Raviv (1991), 'Capital structure and the informational role of debt', *Journal of Finance*, **45**, 321–349.
Istaitieh, A. and J. Rodriguez-Fernandez (2006), 'Factor-product markets and firms' capital structure: a literature review', *Review of Financial Economics*, **15**, 49–75.
Jensen, M. (1986), 'Agency costs of free cash flow, corporate finance, and take-overs', *American Economic Review*, **76**, 323–329.

Jensen, M. and W. Meckling (1976), 'Theory of the firm: managerial behaviour, agency costs and ownership structure', *Journal of Financial Economics*, **3**, 305–360.

Jostarndt, P. (2002), 'Financing growth in innovative industries: agency conflicts and the role of hybrid securities – empirical evidence from Nasdaq convertible debt offerings', working paper, Fisher Center for the Strategic Use of Information Techology, Haas School of Business.

Kim, E. and J. McConnell (1977), 'Corporate mergers and the coinsurance of corporate debt', *Journal of Finance*, **32**, 349–365.

Kochhar, R. (1996), 'Explaining firm capital structure: the role of agency theory vs transaction cost economics', *Strategic Management Journal*, **17**, 713–728.

Kochhar, R. and M. Hitt (1998), 'Linking corporate strategy to capital structure: diversification strategy, type and source of financing', *Strategic Management Journal*, **19**, 601–610.

Lewellen, W. (1971), 'A pure financial rationale for the conglomerate merger', *Journal of Finance*, **26**, 521–537.

Maksimovic, V. and S. Titman (1991), 'Financial policy and reputation for product quality', *Review of Financial Studies*, **4**, 175–200.

Markides, C. and P. Williamson (1996), 'Corporate diversification and organizational structure: a resource-based view', *Academy of Management Journal*, **39**, 340–367.

Modigliani, F. and M. Miller (1958), 'The cost of capital, corporation finance and the theory of finance', *American Economic Review*, **48** (3), 291–297.

Myers, S. (1977), 'Determinants of corporate borrowing', *Journal of Financial Economics*, **5**, 146–175.

Myers, S. and Majluf (1984), 'Corporate financing and investment decision when firms have information that investors do not have', *Journal of Financial Economics*, **13** (2), 187–221.

Nickell, S. (1996), 'Competition and corporate finance', *Journal of Political Economy*, **104**, 724–746.

Opler, T. and S. Titman (1994), 'Financial distress and corporate performance', *Journal of Finance*, **49**, 1015–1040.

Oviatt, B. (1984), 'On the integration of financial management and strategic management', *Academy of Management Best Paper Proceedings*, 27–31.

Poitevin, M. (1989), 'Financal signalling and the "deep pocket" argument', *RAND Journal of Economics*, **20** (1), 26–40.

Ross, S. (1977), 'The determination of financial structure: the incentive signaling approach', *Bell Journal of Economics*, **8**, 1–32.

Sarig, O. (1998), 'The effect of leverage on bargaining with a corporation', *Financial Review*, **33**, 1–16.

Shleifer, A. and S. Vishny (1989), 'Management entrenchment: the case of manager-specific investments', *Financial Economics*, **25**, 123–147.

Stulz, R. (1990), 'Managerial discretion and optimal financing policies', *Journal of Financial Economics*, **26**, 3–27.

Telser, L. (1966), 'Cutthroat competition and the long purse', *Journal of Law and Economics*, **9**, 259–277.

Titman, S. (1984), 'The effect of capital structure on a firm's liquidation decision', *Journal of Financial Economics*, **13** (1), 137–151.

Titman, S. and R. Wessels (1988), 'The determinants of capital structure', *Journal of Finance*, **43**, 1–19.

Ward, K. and A. Grundy (1996), 'The strategic management of corporate value', *European Management Journal*, **14** (3), 321–330.

Williamson, O.E. (1988), 'Corporate finance and corporate governance', *Journal of Finance*, **43** (3), 567–591.

25 Does firm ownership matter? Investors, corporate governance and strategic competitiveness in privately-held firms
Rosario Faraci and Wei Shen

INTRODUCTION

Modern capitalism relies primarily, but not exclusively, on various models of investor-owned firms (Hansmann, 1996) ranging from privately-held to public corporations. However, the spectrum of ownership forms is even broader since it includes also employee-owned, producer-owned, consumer-owned, government-owned and a various set of non-profit organizations. Nevertheless similar in their organizational structure, investor- and non-investor-owned firms are different in terms of rights exerted over the company and of using the relative power to protect these rights.

For instance, publicly-held corporations and large cooperatives may be similar because they both deal with a dispersed ownership that delegates professional management to direct the firm, but they are significantly different from each other. Publicly-held firms are an example of investor-owned companies where owners have the right to claim for residual earnings, while cooperatives are consumer-, producer- or employee-owned organizations where owners do not have the same right, because the distribution of profits is not allowed by law. In addition, cooperatives are a powerful example of workplace democracy that is becoming common in countries that have experienced the fall of communist regimes.

According to these premises, the governance boundaries of the firm, or the scope of the governance functions, the use of internal and additional governance mechanisms and the nature of the governance ties, are affected and they, in turn, influence the firm's competitiveness. Competitiveness is a multifaceted construct that affects organizational, strategic, financial, and economic aspects of the firm. When looking at the entire competitive process, ownership is an important governance variable that influences the whole process.

This chapter deals primarily with the most common forms of investor-owned firms, known around the world as privately-held corporations. Most firms are in fact privately-held, including some of the world's largest companies, like Microsoft, BMW, VW, and FIAT (La Porta et al., 1999), especially in Europe (Thomsen and Pedersen, 2000; Faccio and Lang, 2002) and Asia (Claessens et al., 2000). Privately-held firms do not constitute a homogenous group, because they range from entrepreneurial start-ups to large, established, family-owned firms to companies recently making a transition from one type of private ownership to another (Uhlaner et al., 2007). Control in these firms can be exerted through different means – shares, multiple classes of shares, pyramidal structures, holdings through multiple control chains, and cross-holdings. Even most public corporations have a private investor as their ultimate owner. For instance, a study by Faccio and Lang (2002) of 5232 publicly-traded corporations showed that Western European firms (in 13 countries) are family controlled in 44.29 percent of the observations. Similar results have been found in a study by Claessens et al. (2000) of 2980 listed firms in nine Asian countries.

Surprisingly, privately-held firms received less attention in strategy research, getting only a greater interest in entrepreneurship studies, because private ownership is the source of financing for small and medium-sized enterprises. Unlike publicly-held companies, those privately-held have a more concentrated and long-lasting ownership structure. However, ownership concentration is not the unique feature of the privately-held firms, because even public companies may overcome the problem of distribution of stock ownership through a large block-holder (usually a family or an institutional investor). A fast-growing literature, mostly in the finance area, has examined the claim that publicly-owned firms with a large family block-holder may perform better (Anderson and Reeb, 2003; Miller et al., 2007; Thomsen and Pedersen, 2000). Similar results have been observed when the large-block shareholder is an institutional investor. Even with a concentrated ownership structure, public corporations are different from privately-held firms because they tend to deal with a transient ownership (Porter, 1992) and the ownership concentration is only a governance mode that allows owners to maximize their wealth through higher returns on their investment.

In contrast, privately-held companies rely more on a stable and long-lasting ownership structure and composition that allow the owners to be more powerful and to exert a strong commitment to the firm. In addition, most privately-held firms are not incorporated and, even if incorporated, ownership stakes are not easily tradable. Furthermore, a controlling shareholder is given control rights in excess of their cashflow rights.

This chapter aims to analyze, from a conceptual perspective, whether corporate ownership matters for the competitiveness of privately-held companies. The study transcends the simple relationship between corporate ownership and firm performance, which is the common approach taken by studies in the finance realm. Instead, our analysis is closer to previous studies that investigated how the ownership structure affects the efficiency and the strategic development of a firm (Hill and Snell, 1989). Our intention is to access the ownership 'black box' and to explore how corporate ownership of privately-held firms influences their governance boundaries that, in turn, affect their competitiveness. In order to do that, we look at different owners' behaviors and attitudes. The specific research focus allows us to understand that, even if they have the same rights, owners tend to behave differently. Such heterogeneity in owner behavior is important to understand how the governance boundaries of the firms, the scope of the governance functions, the use of internal and other governance mechanisms and the nature of the governance ties, are shaped and influenced by the proprietors.

Our interest for such a topic comes from various streams of research which find their origins in corporate governance studies. First, most privately-held firms around the world are family businesses and there is substantial evidence that family-owned and controlled firms tend to behave (and to perform) differently than non-family companies (Miller et al., 2007). Second, since publicly-held companies are no longer managed in the best interests of their owners, therefore the congruency of interests between top executives and shareholders has been challenged throughout the years (Jensen, 1989). Third, we believe that the rise of so-called 'institutional capitalism' in privately-held firms deserves more consideration, because numerous private equity and venture capitalist firms have invested (and are continuing to invest) their cash in privately-held companies, while their general partners, i.e. institutional investors, are becoming the most powerful stockholders of many public corporations (Useem, 1996). Fourth, we observe that several firms are in transition, not only in emerging economies, where by definition corporate ownership is fluctuant due to institutional changes, but also in well-established and developed countries, where most privately-held firms experience sequence of changes in share ownership.[1]

Such evolving patterns of ownership have a significant impact on the monitoring, control and financing of the firms. Last but not least, many changes occurred at the level of corporate governance systems (i.e. the ease of property rights transfers, some fiscal advantages associated with the succession, new codes of conduct for firms, and so on) that make firms more transparent and accountable to investors. It means that almost all the categories of investors may access privately-held firms more easily and, on the other side, the traditional owners of these firms are less reluctant to change the ownership composition because additional financial resources can come not only from the debt but also from the outside equity.

The remainder of this chapter is organized as follows. In the second section, we define the conceptual perimeter of corporate ownership, intended as a governance structure, as we focus primarily on the heterogeneous attitudes and behaviors of the various corporate owners and investors. This implicitly means that, beyond the traditional agency theory perspective, we consider as relevant a broad spectrum of other economic and behavioral theories of the firm. Particularly, we are interested in the owners' commitment to the firm. The third section reviews the most known theories dealing with privately-held firms that treat corporate ownership as an independent variable in research design. Such theories largely fall into two categories: those deriving from economic analyses; and others spreading out instead from the behavioral sciences. The fourth section examines how corporate ownership works with other conventional and, as well, non-conventional governance devices in order to influence the main governance functions of a firm: i.e., the monitoring and control exerted by owners and other investors.

We assume that how corporate governance matters for a firm's strategic competitiveness is better understood when a firm is considered as a nexus of investments that varies over time along a succession of evolving patterns of monitoring, control and financing. The fifth section deals with the relationship between corporate ownership and firm competitiveness. We acknowledge that such a relationship is more complex than has been thought in most studies, where the variance in firm performance was explored in terms of various types of ownership structure. Conversely, our effort goes beyond such simple association as it investigates a broader concept of firm competitiveness, including the results, processes, and potential dimensions. The final section draws a few conclusions and points out some of the limitations of our approach to firm ownership.

THE CONCEPTUAL PERIMETER OF CORPORATE OWNERSHIP AS GOVERNANCE STRUCTURE

Corporate ownership is a contextual variable as well as a governance variable. As we have mentioned earlier, corporate ownership can assume different forms, depending on whether firms are investor-owned (e.g. public corporations and privately-held firms) or non-investor-owned (e.g. producer-, consumer-, or employee-owned firms as well as a broad range of cooperatives, governmental and non-governmental organizations). Owners have primarily two formal rights: to control the firm and to appropriate the firm's profits or residual earnings (Hansmann, 1996).

As a contextual variable, corporate ownership is the result of the institutional settings at a country level. Accordingly, in a given country some ownership issues, such as the dominance of a specific business ownership form over others, the level of ownership concentration, the protection of minority shareholders and the easiness of property rights transfers among different investors, are mainly the result of how corporate governance works at the institutional level. For instance, La Porta et al. (1999) noted that similar geographical clusters by legal determinants tend to apply the same features of corporate ownership at the country level. Depending on different legal systems, corporate ownership may be the exclusive means of owners in exerting control over the company, the mode of wielding commitment to the firm or, more simply, a way of monitoring how a financial investment is doing.

As a governance variable, corporate ownership can be seen alternatively as an instrument for shareholders (Keasey and Wright, 1993) or other external stakeholders (Freeman and Reed, 1983), or as a mechanism to support what is the best for the firm per se (Pfeffer and Salancik, 1978). The first definition relies on the idea that the firm is an instrument of external actors; therefore corporate ownership defines the relationships among different corporate stakeholders and determines their relative power balance (Kroll et al., 1997). The second definition considers the firm as an independent entity; corporate ownership is accordingly a source of power that can be used to support or oppose management. Salancik and Pfeffer noted that "ownership represents a source of power used either to support or oppose management, depending on how it is concentrated and used. In general, the more concentrated the ownership is the more potent potential support or opposition" (Salancik and Pfeffer, 1980: 655). According to the second definition, corporate ownership affects the firm's governance boundaries which in turn influence the firm's competitiveness.

More broadly, when looking at corporate ownership as a governance variable, we realize that owners do matter, particularly in investor-owned firms that are privately-held. Formal rights – to control the firm and to appropriate the firm's profits – interfere with claims of other firms' stakeholders and primarily of the employees and the management. Various categories of investors may share the same privileges and it could be a source of conflicts among them. When the management of the company is delegated to professionals, further conflicts may arise between managers and proprietors.

The existing body of studies mainly focuses its attention on large publicly-held companies because, since the seminal work of Berle and Means (1932), they have been considered the most reliable examples of modern corporations. In conventional theory of the firm, it is presumed that organizations are managed in the best interests of their owners

(Marris, 1964). In those firms, corporate ownership is dispersed among a myriad of shareholders. Consequently, many authors argued that the distribution of stock ownership has important implications in firms' efficiency and strategic development (Galbraith, 1967; Pfeffer and Salancik, 1978; Williamson, 1964), while others have argued that the distribution of ownership is irrelevant (Demsetz, 1983; Demsetz and Lehn, 1985; Fama, 1983; Jensen and Meckling, 1976). Due to the fact that shareholders have minimal or no control over the company, conflicts arise between the owners (the principal) and the managers (the agent). In order to mitigate or reduce such conflicts the principal incurs agency costs to enhance monitoring and to exert some control over the company. Thus, both external and internal corporate governance devices largely fall into these agency costs: the board of directors, executive compensation, the market for corporate control and other mechanisms that generally increase the firm's accountability.

Nonetheless, the majority of existing firms in all countries are not listed in the stock market. Most firms are privately-held and the ultimate owner is an individual, a family, or a team of individuals and families. In some cases, there is even a discrepancy between the firms' ownership and control, and the ultimate owner exerts control exceeding the level of the possessed stake. In these firms, agency conflicts arising from diverging rights into the company are minimal, because the management of the firm is strictly controlled by the ultimate owners or coincides with them. In these firms, who are the owners matters more than in publicly-held corporations. Different owners have different behaviors and attitudes and the difference can be the origin of conflicts. For instance, when the ultimate owner of a company is an individual (the entrepreneur or the founder), he or she may be interested in the firm's survival, even if the firm's financial, economic and operating performance is lower than expected. The family as ultimate owner of a firm tends to create an overlap between the interests of the firm and those of the family members. In addition, when the attitudes and behaviors of the different family members are divergent, some agency conflicts arise even in these privately-held firms. Different behaviors and attitudes arise when the ultimate owner is a financial company. A bank, a private equity firm, or a venture capitalist may exert only the monitoring or head the control depending on how their financial interests fit the firm's goals.

The taxonomy of corporate ownership within privately-held firms is not exhaustive. For instance, firms may be dependent on a parent company, or they can be affiliated with a business group and both these configurations can be private. Accordingly, the magnitude of agency conflict can increase. Many firms may experience evolving patterns of monitoring, control and financing since they rely on a succession of changes in the ownership of shares. An entrepreneurial firm can be started by a lone founder or a founding team (for instance in the case of academic start-ups or biotech firms), then participated in by another individual investor (perhaps a business angel or another entrepreneur), further venture-backed, and finally it may go public or be sold to another company (Mayer, 2005).

A family firm is born as a company started by a lone founder, then it becomes a family business when other family members operate the company. It may experience both the transfer of the shares' ownership among the family members and the internal succession from the founder to the heir apparent (Lansberg, 1999). Depending on the business lifecycle (Mueller, 1972) and on the profitability of the company, a family business can be targeted by a private equity or venture capital firm, then it may go public, being sold to other companies or perpetuate the family involvement over the business.

When it is seen as a governance variable, corporate ownership matters since it influences the governance boundaries of the entire firm. As will be examined in the next section, the firm's ownership structure and composition influence the use of other governance devices, the latitude of the governance functions, and the nature of the governance ties among the different investors. In other words, particularly in the world of privately-held firms, corporate ownership is very pervasive. If the firm is possessed by a sole individual, the behavior and the attitude of the owner shape completely the firm's strategy, organization and competitiveness. If the firm includes different investors in addition to the ultimate owners, the firm's governance boundaries are influenced by the diversity of shareholders. Some investors may be interested only in monitoring the firms as they are more sensitive to contractual arrangements that protect their investments. Other investors may be interested in sharing with the owners a portion of the firm's control, so that they may be more responsive to relational arrangements that assure a more direct control over the company. These issues are of extreme importance when a privately-held firm is targeted by outside investors, as in the case of private equity or venture capital firms.

ECONOMIC AND BEHAVIORAL THEORIES OF PRIVATELY-HELD OWNERSHIP

This section reviews the existing literature on corporate ownership along two important areas of research: economic and behavioral theories. The economic theories emphasize the importance of a nexus of contracts, transactions and the formal ties connecting the various shareholders of a firm. Instead, the behavioral theories are more interested in the human side of the corporate governance, looking at the attitude, the commitment over the firm and the social capital existing within the different shareholders.

Depending on how the corporate ownership has been treated (as an independent, a dependent or a control variable), the following theories have considered the role of corporate ownership:

- Contingency theory
- Agency theory
- Transaction cost economics theory
- Stewardship theory
- Social capital theory
- Resource-dependence and resource-based view theories.

Contingency Theory

The contingency theory looks at the corporate ownership as a dependent variable. Accordingly, the design of corporate ownership and governance depends primarily on features at country, industry and firm level. For instance, at country level, cross-cultural differences (Aguilera and Jackson, 2003) reflect institutional differences in the corporate governance systems (La Porta et al., 1999). At industry level, the dominant technology, the competitive environment and the resource configuration shape the ownership structure of a firm (Huse, 2007; Zahra and Pearce, 1989). At firm level, different functions of ownership and governance may vary in importance depending upon the phase of a firm's lifecycle (Mayer, 2005; Mueller, 1972). For instance, there is a basic difference between a start-up and a company on the threshold of going public (Filatotchev and Wright, 2005).

Agency Theory

The agency theory framework is the most utilized skeleton to analyze how corporate ownership matters for a firm's performance. Based on the assumptions drawn from Jensen and Meckling (1976), Fama (1980) and Fama and Jensen (1983), the popularity of this theory is related to several pitfalls observed in the management of the large publicly-held corporations, particularly in the Anglo-American capitalistic system (Amihud and Lev, 1981; Baumol, 1967; Berle and Means, 1932; Fruhan, 1984; Tosi and Gomez-Mejia, 1989). Agency theory can also be applied to privately-held firms. Conflicts between the principal and the agent arise, respectively, at the level of the owners and the managers, due to the natural opportunism of the latter. However, conflicts may take place also at the level of the sole ownership, for instance between the controlling and the non-controlling shareholders, or even among various controlling shareholders. This is the case of family firms, where, even if not existing with the management, agency conflicts are very common among different family members, particularly when the family involvement over the company is extended to siblings, cousins, and so on. Agency conflicts may occur also at the level of managers, sometimes between the top and the middle-management, or between the top management team and the operating managers. This may be the case of large family-controlled firms, where the family appoints managers to run the company more efficiently. When the conflicts arise at different levels of the ownership and management (i.e. conflicts between the owners, the board representing the ownership, and the management), agency theory may be integrated by its most recent advancement: the double agency and the multiple agency perspectives (Child and Rodrigues, 2003). Arthurs et al. (2008) contribute to multiple agency theory by examining cases in which ventures making initial public offerings have managerial agents on their boards, whose goals conflict with those of the investment bank agents hired to underwrite the stock.

While it has been widely used, agency theory is not the most comprehensive and exhaustive framework to understand how ownership and governance matters in privately-held firms. Undeniably, this theory has virtually ignored the effects of good social relationships that may exist among owners and managers (Ghoshal and Moran, 1996).

Transaction Cost Economics

Another theory, drawn from economics, that has been used to analyze corporate ownership, specifically when it is considered a dependent variable is transaction cost economics (TCE), a theory that primarily relies on the vision of the firm as a nexus of contracts. One of the main domains of TCE when studying corporate ownership is the problem of allocating property rights among different classes of firms' patrons (Hansmann, 1996). As we mentioned in the introduction, owners are a class of firms' patrons. As pointed out by Hansmann, any patron "can control the firm's behavior only by seeking enforcement of his contract with the firm in favor of whatever other alternatives the market offers him. When the relationship is one of ownership, in contrast, the patron has the additional option of seeking to control the firm's behavior directly through the firm's mechanisms for internal governance" (Hansmann, 1996: 19–20). Transaction cost economics has been utilized to analyze when privately-held owner-ship (as a synonym of hierarchy) is more convenient than publicly-held (as a synonym of market). In this sense, for instance, the benefits of family ownership overcome the costs of retaining the firm's control within the same family unit. In fact, the family business works as an internal mana-gerial market of labor for unemployable family members as it internalizes the flow of wealth for the family, and family ownership gives a long-term orientation to the company. The TCE approach has been largely utilized to explain other forms of ownership; i.e. the non-investor forms of ownership. Why does the government prefer to exert a tight control over state-owned enterprises instead of selling them out to private inves-tors? State-owned enterprises in the Western world were mostly born in response to repeated market failure, particularly in the absence of market regulation. But, even when the market is regulated, the government can be interested in continuing to exert a control over its companies, due to the potential benefits of pursuing socio-political goals that, instead, are not of interest to private investors.

Stewardship Theory

The stewardship theory (Davis et al., 1997) is a theoretical framework, built upon the basic paradigm of Theory X and Theory Y (McGregor, 1960), that is used when analyzing privately-held firms (Uhlaner et al., 2007). Unlike the agent, the steward is a self actualizer, motivated to serve the collective good while fulfilling both social and higher needs of growth and achievement (Davis et al., 1997). The stewardship theory can be applied to both managers and owners. In privately-held firms, owners and managers are likely to focus on governance structures that facilitate and empower those below them. Some executives may pursue the inter-ests of the organization even though this may conflict with their own interests. This is the case of family firms, where founders are expected to behave like stewards; while in other privately-held firms non-founders are expected to act more like agents. In family firms, the presence of the founder serves as a moderator variable with respect to executive remu-neration (Wasserman, 2006). This situation, in turn, positively affects firms' performance.

Social Capital Theory

Social capital theory provides a further explanation for why steward-ship matters (Granovetter, 1985; Portes, 1998; Leana and Van Buren III, 1999). Two key components of the social capital have been singled out:

trust and associability. For instance, Uhlaner et al. (2007) argue that, under conditions of high associability, a firm is likely to perform better than under conditions of low organizational social capital. When studying family firms, the most common form of privately-held companies, social capital theory may be used to explain not only the importance of associability, but also how social relationships among the owner-family members and management are structured (Mustakallio et al., 2002). In fact, various forms of social capital do exist under structural, relational and cognitive dimensions (Nahapiet and Ghoshal, 1998). Within the social capital theory, other conceptual frameworks have been utilized to discuss the importance of corporate ownership. For instance, social exchange theory (Bishop et al., 2005; Shore and Wayne, 1993), social identity theory (Ellemers, 2001; Tajfel and Turner, 1993) and organization citizenship behavior have been used in a study of Uhlaner et al. (2007) on 233 directors of a random sample of privately-held Dutch firms. Even if a bit different from the other behavioral theories, the organizational justice perspective, together with the agency theory, was used to examine the differential effects of the controlling owner's self-control (i.e. the governance mechanisms they adopt and how they administer these mechanisms) on the justice perceptions of the family and non-family employees (Lubatkin et al., 2007).

Resource Dependence Theory and the Resource-based Theory

The use of the resource dependence theory and of the resource-based view within the studies of corporate ownership is very frequent. Such theories are mainly derived from strategy research as they emphasize the role and importance of corporate ownership as a source of valuable resources to a firm's competitive advantage. Accordingly, who is the owner does matter for firms, since he or she brings resources, capabilities and core competencies that are extremely valuable. For instance, within the literature on family business, family ownership is considered valuable for the firm's growth and its 'familiness' (Chrisman et al., 2005) – a notion that encompasses interactions between family members, the family and the business – has been included among resources and capabilities leading to a firm's competitive advantage. Consequently, when further modifications occur at the level of family ownership, i.e. when the firm is venture-backed, it is not surprising if the new owners continue to interact with the existing shareholders and give them power and some control over the decision-making process, because the 'familiness' is considered a source of competitive advantage that enhances, not destroys, the intervention of venture capitalists.

CORPORATE OWNERSHIP AND THE GOVERNANCE BOUNDARIES OF PRIVATELY-HELD FIRMS

When it is considered as a governance mechanism, firm ownership matters for both strategic and competitive processes. Particularly in privately-held firms, corporate ownership shapes the firm's governance boundaries in that it affects:

- the use of the other governance mechanisms – the board of directors and the executive compensation system;
- the implementation of unconventional governance devices, for instance family agreements in family-owned firms;
- the scope of the governance functions – the extent of the two traditional functions of monitoring and control;
- and the nature of the governance ties – contractual vs relational, depending on how shareholders are connected to each other.

We shall discuss each of these governance issues succinctly, moving from the statement that privately-held firms violate almost all the underlying assumptions of more traditional governance approaches (Mustakallio et al., 2002). This is due primarily to the emotional attachment that shareholders have to private firm ownership and that may divert the firm's focus from its economic goals and financial targets. For instance, in family-owned firms both the business and the family require additional governance to safeguard the owner's family long-term interests (Gersick et al., 1997; Lansberg, 1999; Neubauer and Lank, 1998). They may use informal family agreements to prevent the spin-off or the divestiture of the family firm, in case of a succession. In addition, they may not change the legal form of the company to avoid a re-allocation of shares among all the family members. They even use a family council instead of setting the board of directors.

Conventional Governance Mechanisms

While it has been largely used in large publicly-held corporations, when it applies to privately-held companies the market for corporate control is not a reliable governance device. The market for corporate control is in fact an external disciplinary device that, in addition to other external pressures shaped by the market's forces, is effective when the behavior of (opportunistic) managers is severely scrutinized (Hitt et al., 1996). Whereas according to an agency theory perspective, the market for corporate control is universally efficient (Demsetz, 1983; Demsetz and Lehn,

1983; Fama, 1983; Jensen and Meckling, 1976), the takeover threat does not function when the firm operates under the tight control of an identifiable ultimate owner. Even in public companies, when stockholdings are concentrated and information asymmetries are low, the ability of stockholders to remove a management team is high and managers are likely to feel constrained to pursue strategies that are in stockholders' interest (Hill and Snell, 1989). In the specific case of privately-held firms, the effectiveness of external governance pressure is restrained to the 'exit, voice or loyalty' strategies (Hirschman, 1971) implemented by institutional investors, but this occurs only when they have a (minority) stake within the targeted firms.

When you look at the publicly-held corporations an effective alignment between the interests of the managers and the owners is likely to occur under three governance conditions: (1) when there is a strong and independent board that monitors, evaluates and challenges executives; (2) when there is a major stockholder who monitors the strategic and resource allocation decisions made by executives; and (3) when executives own stock in their firms which gives them an incentive to pursue long-term value creation. All the governance conditions reported above generate agency costs. However, these mechanisms work in a different way within privately-held firms, particularly in family businesses where governance is likely to be an oxymoron (Martin, 2004).

Among the internal corporate governance devices, the board of directors continues to receive the most remarkable attention from scholars and practitioners. Consistent with organization theory's classification of control into behavior control and output control, Baysinger and Hoskisson (1990) propose two board-level controls: strategic control and financial control.

In privately-held firms, the board is the long arm of the corporate ownership (Huse, 2000; Huse and Landstrom, 2001; Huse et al., 2002). First, there is a board only when the firm is incorporated, and most of the small and medium-sized private firms have different legal forms. Second, how the board is constituted and formed, the board size and the board tenure, the ratio between outside and inside directors, its role in exerting a financial or a strategic control, and the provision of directors' share ownership are the immediate result of how corporate ownership has formed and how the different owners' attitudes and behaviors work. Due to the effect of both institutional settings at the country level and the greater attention devoted to the governance devices' effectiveness at the firm level, the board of directors is slowly becoming the most important internal governance mechanism. Particularly, during business ownership transitions, the board is the only mechanism protecting the goals of the different owners and investors. For instance, the growth of 'institutional capitalism' in privately-held firms increased the importance of the board of directors as the most reliable governance mechanism able to satisfy all the different owners' expectations. However, even in companies not dealing with transition, but firmly depending on the efforts of a sole ultimate owner (i.e. family firms), the BoD is an effective way of monitoring and controlling the firm in a different room than the rest of the company.

Executive compensation systems and ownership concentration are two additional governance devices very useful at firm level. According to agency theory prescriptions, both these internal governance mechanisms work effectively when companies have dispersed ownership structures. On one side, executive compensation systems, namely in forms of stock (option) plans, help align the interests of shareholders with those of managers, by giving the latter the same rights belonging to the former. Even if findings are sometimes contradictory, there is empirical evidence that managerial ownership, one of the most common forms of executive compensation, tends to increase the firm's competitiveness, long-term performance and corporate entrepreneurship (Zahra et al., 2000), because overall executives' commitment over the company results strengthened. On the other side, ownership concentration by means of large-block shareholders allows the owners to circumvent rights and rents expropriation from the managers.

The two mentioned mechanisms function in a different way when firms are privately-held. Stock option plans and other executive compensation systems are tools to involve the executives into the sphere of the ownership by enhancing their commitment toward the company. Due to high ownership concentration, the problem may be the opposite: how is it possible to de-concentrate the ownership structure in order to benefit from the contribution of additional shareholders? This is the case, for example, for family-owned firms where additional non-family members are invited by the owners to enter the company as shareholders. More specifically, when such additional shareholders are private equity or venture capital firms, their presence may contribute to revitalizing corporate governance, strategy and organization.

Unconventional Governance Mechanisms

In privately-held, as well as in government-held firms, a wide spectrum of unconventional governance mechanisms is introduced by the owners in order to protect their rights and rents. For instance, in the case of discrepancy between the ultimate ownership and control, various means of control – multiple classes of shares, pyramidal structures, holding through multiple control chains, and cross-holding – may enhance the likelihood of having control rights in excess of the cashflow rights (Faccio and Lang, 2002). Further, within family-owned firms the use of family holdings and trusts, family office, family councils, family agreements and constitutions is common (Neubauer and Lank, 1998), and such governance mechanisms serve as effective tools to protect the prerogatives of the owners, to perpetuate the family involvement over the company, to avoid expropriation from other non-family members, and to protect some family members from the high-demanding requests coming from other family members, and to enhance the right of the heir apparent to succeed in the management of the company (Gilding, 2005). In particular, trust (Bhattacharya et al., 1998) is used as a relational governance mechanism in family-owned firms, since it allows to share a firm's common vision among the family members, without the necessity of dealing with more formal and sophisticated devices. While Mustakallio et al. (2002) argue that family institutions (informal get-togethers, formal family meetings, family councils, and family plans) represent and integrate the needs and interests of the owner-family members and link the family and the company, Huse (2007) emphasizes the role of paternalism. In paternalisms the core issue is the welfare of the family. Decisions are made to protect nonfinancial welfare of the family (or of employees) normally at the expense of profit maximization or executive remuneration.

Governance Functions

In essence there are two governance functions of a firm. On one side, corporate governance is about holding management accountable, thus minimizing downside risks to shareholders (Keasey and Wright, 1993; Monks and Minow, 2008). On the other side, corporate governance is about enabling management to exercise enterprise in order to assure that shareholders benefit from the upside potential of firms (Filatotchev and Wright, 2005). How these two functions work in publicly-held versus privately-held firms is a topic of primary interest; their quality is almost shaped by the functioning of the corporate governance devices, both external and internal ones.

In most public corporations, the corporate governance function is that of accountability. This is a subset of governance that involves monitoring, evaluation and control of organizational agents to ensure that they are behaving in the interests of the shareholders and the other stakeholders (Keasey and Wright, 1993). Due to information asymmetries, owners may incur agency costs to hold managers more accountable (Jensen and

Meckling, 1976). In addition, as we have observed beforehand the market for corporate control may be an effective disciplinary device (Hitt et al., 1996).

Conversely, in privately-held firms, the function of enterprising is more important than the accountability function. In some countries (including Germany), these dual functions are formally separated in two distinct governance structures (the supervisory board and the management board) while in the majority of other countries, the two functions are exerted by the board of directors and its internal committees. In addition, ownership differences may change the need for accountability and, once again, business ownership transitions may matter, as occurs in the case of private equity or venture capital backed firms. For instance, a venture capitalist is more likely to require additional formal devices – such as a more sophisticated reporting system – to exert better the monitoring over the company.

Due to their strong commitment over the firm, owners are involved in several tasks, such as the building of organizational reputation, the formulation or ratification of strategy and networking for the firm (Uhlaner et al., 2007). In other words, what makes publicly- and privately-held firms different is the scope (or the latitude) and the quality of such primary functions as accountability and enterprising. For instance, when we look at family-owned businesses, where firms are exclusively operated by the founder and her or his family members, the function of accountability is less important, and it could be possible that even the board of directors doesn't exist. Indeed, to whom is the firm accountable, when it is the primary tool of the family's wealth?

However, when family-owned firms are targeted by private equity or venture capital firms, some structural entities designed for the accountability functions (such as the board of directors and the executive compensation systems) are considered of primary importance for such investors. Accordingly, the quality of governance functions is improved and the latitude of both the accountability and the enterprises is in such a way extended.

In addition to the two mentioned governance functions, privately-held firms need to develop governance structures that promote cohesion and shared vision within founding owners and reduce conflict. This is once more particularly true in the case of family firms. As Mustakallio et al. (2002) mention: "The first goal must be achieved by employing formal controls that minimize opportunism, mirroring the prescriptions of agency theory. The second goal calls for the implementation of social control that promotes social interaction and the formation of shared vision among the various stakeholders" (p. 205).

The Nature of Governance Ties

The boundaries of corporate governance also depend on the nature of the ties among the patrons, specifically the owners. In publicly-held corporations, the ties among the owners and between ownership and management are contractual and very formal. In fact, to enhance such ties firms incur agency costs that are, by definition, corporate governance costs to safeguard the owners' rights and to avoid disproportionate managerial opportunism. In privately-held firms, on the contrary, ties are very informal and relational. Relational governance is strictly related to the owner's attitudes, including the owner's commitment to the firm and her or his collective norms and goals (Uhlaner et al., 2007). For instance, in family businesses, social or relational governance mechanisms are generally solid and long lasting as they are based on tradition, bonding relationships, loyalty and altruism (Schulze et al., 2002 and 2003).

PRIVATELY-HELD OWNERSHIP AND THE FIRM'S COMPETITIVENESS

The relationship between corporate ownership and the firm's competitiveness is normally absorbed into the analysis of the firm ownership–firm performance correlation, to which studies in corporate finance have dedicated a great deal of attention. However, performance is only the ultimate dimension of a firm's competitiveness as it is a variable that can be measured along different indicators. In fact, competitiveness is a broad notion that includes several performance dimensions such as results, processes and potentials, and has several implications at the strategic, organizational, economic and financial levels. Accordingly, competitiveness is a multifaceted notion whereby analyzing how corporate ownership matters is more important than analyzing the simple association with the firm's performance. In the following paragraph, we briefly recall the notion of competitiveness at the firm level, then we attempt to categorize how different forms of privately-held ownership matter to firm competitiveness.

Competitiveness is a notion that can be referred to at the country, industry and firm levels. The notion of competitiveness at the country level has received wide attention in many disciplines as it is intertwined with that at the industry and the firm level. This occurs since a number of studies have demonstrated that all these different levels cannot be easily separated. The World Economic Forum and the Institute for Management Development have released overall measures of competitiveness that, even if applied at the country level, widely support this statement (Sala-i-Martin et al., 2003). Within strategic management, the notion of competitiveness at the industry level was developed by Porter (1985), reversing some of the main assumptions of industrial organization economics which posited that, particularly in a perfect market competition, firms' behavior and competitive dynamics do not matter in any way in determining the level of pricing.

While Porter (1986 and 1990) and Hamel and Prahalad (1994) have contributed to the advancement of competitiveness literature, at the firm level the conceptualization and measurement of competitiveness have vague and insufficient. Porter views competitiveness primarily as productivity growth, whereas Hamel and Prahalad define it in terms of 'core competence' and the bundle of skills and technologies that a company possesses. Both definitions are interesting, but they give an unsatisfactory depiction of what competitiveness means at the firm level.

As mentioned before, the concept of competitiveness is broader than the well-known notion of competitive advantage. In addition, the notion of competitive advantage is associated to only one of the three categories mentioned by scholars at a time: cost leadership, differentiation and focalization, and each of them typically excludes the others. Instead, a firm's competitiveness is to be assessed along several dimensions, in order to evaluate how it varies over time and to scrutinize whether the potential or the process dimensions may generate a sustainable competitive advantage over time. The firm's competitiveness is at the same time path- and time-dependent.

In this respect, the Aldington Report (1985) states that "a firm is competitive if it can produce products and services of superior quality and lower costs than its domestic and international competitors. Competitiveness is synonymous with a firm's long-run profit performance and its ability to compensate its employees and provide superior return to its owners" (p. 2). This definition, even if it is not fully inclusive, nonetheless suggests that there are various measures of competitiveness and they can be categorized into three main groups: competitive performance, competitive potential and management process (Buckley et al., 1988). More recently, in a similar way Ambastha and Momaya (2004) have clustered three different key dimensions of competitiveness: assets, processes and performance.

If the firm's competitiveness is the ultimate set of measures viable to assess how a firm is going on, looking at the drivers of such competitiveness is extremely important as well. One of the main drivers, even if not largely analyzed by management scholars, is certainly corporate ownership. Accordingly, who is the owner, how she or he behaves, and what is the emotional attachment to the firm are primary questions which cannot be neglected, particularly when studying privately-held firms.

In order to explore how corporate ownership matters for firms' competitiveness, we need to combine different types of privately-held firms with various meanings of competitiveness. Existing literature provides different findings. In a broad way, according to Dooley and Fryxell (1999) how the ownership and governance boundaries are intertwined with the firm's strategy and competitiveness is explained by the quality of strategic decision making since it determines the content of a firm's strategies and its commitment to their implementation. The strategic decision making is the management process (Buckley et al., 1988) or the processes dimension (Ambastha and Momaya, 2004) of the competitiveness notion.

Different types of ownership lead to different levels of firm competitiveness. For instance, managerial ownership empowers executives to initiate and champion 'corporate entrepreneurship' (Finkelstein and D'Aveni, 1994), such as innovation and venturing initiatives designed to increase the long-term value of the firm (Hitt et al., 1994).

Buckley et al. (1988) consider access to capital as a potential dimension of competitiveness at the firm level. In fact, Anglo-American firms suffer from the lack of 'patient money', and this happens because the stock exchange is expected to require rapid quarterly returns and the valuation of companies is suggested to be oversensitive to short-term performance (this view is called 'short-termism'). The accusation of short-termism in the Anglo-American corporate governance system is regarded as a competitive disadvantage (Porter, 1992). On the contrary, family firms benefit of more 'patient money' and of a bundle of resources that may become a source of potential competitive advantage (Habbershon and Williams, 2004). Accordingly, privately-held firms are supposed to be interested in the potential and management processes of the competitiveness dimension more than in that of the performance dimension. However, this statement is not always true, since Miller et al. (2004) provided extensive empirical evidence that family-owned firms perform better than non-family firms.

The dilemma of whether privately-held firms are more competitive than publicly-held ones cannot be easily resolved. It primarily depends on what we mean for firms' competitiveness and how we assess it. Competitiveness indicators are important not per se, but in regards of the expectations and interests of the different stakeholders, i.e. shareholders, banks and other financiers and employees. Consequently, privately-held firms are more likely to be assessed along various dimensions of competitiveness, i.e. the potential or the management process, since they do not have extensive obligations to other stakeholders, whereas public corporations have to match the needs of various categories of individuals within a shorter time-horizon.

CONCLUSIONS AND IMPLICATIONS FOR FUTURE RESEARCH

The aim of this chapter was to explore the 'black box' filled by the corporate ownership issues, governance boundaries, strategic management and competitiveness of privately-held firms. Accordingly, it has provided a preliminary discussion framework to understand how corporate ownership matters for firm competitiveness, looking primarily at a specific category of investor-owned firms: privately-held firms. Since there is little evidence and theory development is much needed in this important field of study, our intention was to fill this gap by providing a compass that may indicate the directions helpful for further research.

This study has drawn attention to the importance of incorporating the behavioral perspective into the corporate governance literature, particularly when studying the most important governance mechanism in privately-held firms: corporate ownership. As we have mentioned, within such categories of investor-owned companies, the firm ownership shapes the other governance and management themes and, in turn, affects the firm's management and competitiveness. Accordingly, who is the owner, which are her or his behaviors and attitudes are topics of primary importance.

The nature and the identity of the investors cannot be neglected. Their different attitudes and behaviors matter since they influence significantly both the organizational and the strategic processes of the firm. The behavioral perspective sheds new light on the topic of the corporate ownership, in that it goes behind the traditional theories based on the importance of contracts, transactions and formal relationships among different shareholders. Even if a bit heterodox compared to the traditional corporate governance theories, the behavioral perspective is useful also to strengthen the bridge between the organizational behavior and the strategic management within the managerial disciplines. On one side, recent studies on organizational behavior devote much attention to governance issues, in addition to the traditional pillars of the discipline represented by the individuals, groups and organizations. On the other side, research on strategic management is going back to the roots of the 'administrative behavior' by stimulating more interest in the psychological and sociological foundations of the strategy studies.

Despite these remarkable goal and specific angles, the frame of discussion provided presents a few limitations. First, it focuses only on a particular form of business ownership, i.e. privately-held firms vis-à-vis publicly-held corporations. Specifically, it places attention on investor-owned firms, while we acknowledge that other forms, largely falling into the broad spectrum of the non-investor-owned organizations, are becoming dominant in several industries and countries.

Second, our analysis does not control for different types of institutional settings that, instead, are very important since they can differently moderate the relationship between corporate ownership and firms' competitiveness.

Third, our analysis does not take into account the industry effect and the firm size effect. Such control variables are very important, since they may significantly moderate the relationship between corporate ownership and firms' competitiveness. On one side, Hansmann (1996) noted that, in certain industries, the prevalence of some ownership forms over others is closely related to the industry's characteristics and features. For instance, the ". . .employee-owned firms traditionally [are] so common among service professionals. . ." (Hansmann, 1996: 3), while ". . . consumer cooperatives [are] so common – far more so than is generally realized – among wholesale and supply firms but so rare among retail firms" (Ibidem: 3). On the other side, Wright and Filatotchev (2005) noted that the business lifecycle evolution shapes the nature of the corporate ownership and governance and, in turn, it affects also the strategic performance of the firm.

Fourth, a further limitation concerns the fact that we do not explore in detail the strategic issues related to corporate ownership. According to our discussion framework, whether a firm formulates and implements a strategy at both the corporate and the business levels ultimately depends on how that firm's governance boundaries are shaped by ownership. It means that the same corporate strategy (diversification or internationalization strategy) may have different meanings irrespective of the fact that the firm is owned by a sole individual, a family, another privately-held firm, or if it is a firm in transition due to the presence of outside temporary investors (as a private equity or venture capital firm). We do not explore such issues, which deserve more dedicated attention by strategy and entrepreneurship scholars.

Fifth, a final relevant challenge to our framework is how to turn all the concepts and assumptions about the 'black box' into an effective empirical study. As Uhlaner et al. (2007) noted, it is important to adopt alternative methodologies in addition to the most commonly used large sample statistical analysis. The advancement of knowledge in the area of corporate ownership passes through case histories, longitudinal analysis and triangular studies that enhance better the understanding of the complex relationship between corporate ownership and firms' competitiveness.

NOTE

1. Transition is a buzzword that has not univocal meaning. In this study, with the word transition we mean: (a) transition of a firm from the start-up phase to the next step of its lifecycle (Filatotchev and Wright, 2005); (b) transition from single to multiple ownership structure; (c) transition from the founder's control to the family's next generation in family firms (Lansberg, 1999); (d) transition of firms that are getting ready for IPOs; (e) transition to private ownership of a publicly listed corporation through MBO or LBO operations (Thompson and Wright, 1995); (f) transition of firms adjusting ownership and business portfolio structure via divestiture (Brauer, 2006); (g) transition from public corporations to privately-held firms through market delisting (this is a clear reverse pattern).

REFERENCES

Aguilera, R.V. and G. Jackson (2003), 'The cross-national diversity of corporate governance: dimensions and determinants', *Academy of Management Review*, **28**, 447–465.

Ambastha, A. and D.K. Momaya (2004), 'Competitiveness of firms: review of theory, framework and models', *Singapore Management Review*, **26** (1), 45–61.

Amihud, Y. and B. Lev (eds) (1981), 'Risk reduction as a managerial motive for merger', *Bell Journal of Economics*, **12**, 609–617.

Anderson, R.C. and D.M. Reeb (2003), 'Founding family ownership and firm performance: evidence from the S&P 500', *Journal of Finance*, **58** (3), 1301–1328.

Arthurs, J.D., R.E. Hoskisson, L.W. Busenitz and R.A. Johnson (2008), 'Managerial agents watching other agents: multiple agency conflicts regarding underpricing in IPO firms', *Academy of Management Journal*, **51** (2), 277–294.

Baumol, W.J. (ed.) (1967), *Business Behavior, Value, and Growth*, New York: Macmillan.

Baysinger, B. and R.E. Hoskisson (1990), 'The composition of board of directors and strategic control: effects on corporate strategy', *Academy of Management Review*, **15** (1), 72–87.

Berle, A.A. and G.C. Means Jr (eds) (1932), *The Modern Corporation and Private Property*, New York: Macmillan.

Bhattacharya, R., T.M. Devinney and M.M. Pillutla (1998), 'A formal model of trust based on outcomes', *Academy of Management Review*, **23** (3), 459–472.

Bishop, J.W., K.D. Scott, M.G. Goldsby and R. Cropanzano (2005), 'A construct validity study of commitment and perceived support variables group', *Organization Management*, **30** (2), 153–180.

Brauer, M. (2006), 'What have we acquired and what should we acquire in divestiture research? A review and research agenda', *Journal of Management*, **32** (6), 751–785.

Buckley, P.J., C.L. Pass and K. Prescott (1988), 'Measures of international competitiveness: a critical survey', *Journal of Marketing Management*, **4** (2), 175–200.

Child, J. and S.B. Rodrigues (2003), 'Corporate governance and new organizational forms: issues of double and multiple agency', *Journal of Management and Governance*, **7** (4), 337–360.

Chrisman, J.J., J.H. Chua and L. Steier (2005), 'Sources and consequences of distinctive familiness: an introduction', *Entrepreneurship Theory and Practice*, **29** (3), 237–247.

Claessens, S., S. Djankov and L.H.P. Lang (2000), 'The separation of ownership and control in East Asian corporations', *Journal of Financial Economics*, **58**, 81–112.

Davis, J., F.D. Schoorman and L. Donaldson (1997), 'Toward a stewardship theory of management', *Academy of Management Review*, **22** (1), 20–47.

Demsetz, H. (1983), 'The structure of ownership and the theory of the firm', *Journal of Law and Economics*, **26**, 375–390.

Demsetz, H. and K. Lehn (1985), 'The structure of corporate ownership: theory and consequences', *Journal of Political Economy*, **93**, 1155–1177.

Dooley, R.S. and G.E. Fryxell (1999), 'Attaining decision quality and commitment from dissent: the moderating effects of loyalty and competence in strategic decision-making teams', *Academy of Management Journal*, **42** (4), 389–402.

Ellemers, N. (2001), 'Social identity, commitment, and work behavior', in M.A. Hogg and D.J. Terry (eds), *Social Identity Processes in Organizational Contexts*, Philadelphia, PA: Psychology Press, Taylor and Francis Group, pp. 101–114.

Faccio, M. and L. Lang (2002), 'The ultimate ownership of Western European corporations', *Journal of Financial Economics*, **65**, 365–395.

Fama, E.F. (1980), 'Agency problems and the theory of the firm', *Journal of Political Economy*, **88**, 288–307.

Fama, E.F. (1983), 'Separation of ownership and control', *Journal of Law and Economics*, **26**, 301–325.

Fama, E.F. and M. Jensen (1983), 'Separation of ownership and control', *Journal of Law and Economics*, **26**, 301–325.

Filatotchev, I. and M. Wright (eds) (2005), *The Life-cycle of Corporate Governance*, Cheltenham: Edward Elgar.

Finkelstein, S. and R.A. D'Aveni (1994), 'CEO duality as double-edged sword: how boards of directors balance entrenchment avoidance and unity of command', *Academy of Management Journal*, **37**, 1079–1108.

Fruhan, W.E. (1984), 'How fast should your company grow?', *Harvard Business Review*, **62**, 84–93.

Galbraith, J.K. (ed.) (1967), *The New Industrial State*, New York: New American Library.

Gersick, K.E., J.A. Davis, M. McCollom Hampton and I. Lansberg (eds) (1997), *Generation to Generation: Life Cycles of the Family Business*, Boston: Harvard Business School Press.

Ghoshal, S. and P. Moran (1996), 'Bad for practice: a critique of the transaction cost theory', *Academy of Management Review*, **21** (1), 13–47.

Gilding, M. (2005), 'Families and fortunes', *Journal of Sociology*, **41** (1), 29–45.

Granovetter, M.S. (1985), 'Economic action and social structure: the problem of embeddedness', *American Journal of Sociology*, **91** (3), 481–510.

Habbershon, T.G. and M.L. Williams (2004), 'A resource-based framework for assessing the strategic advantages of family firms', *Family Business Review*, **12** (1), 1–25.

Hamel, G. and C.K. Prahalad (eds) (1994), *Competing for the Future*, Boston: Harvard Business School.

Hansmann, H. (ed.) (1996), *The Ownership of Enterprise*, Cambridge: The Belknap Press of Harvard University Press.

Hill, C.W.L. and S.A. Snell (1989), 'Effects of ownership structure and control on corporate productivity', *Academy of Management Journal*, **32** (1), 25–46.

Hirschman, A. (1971), *Exit, Voice, and Loyalty: Responses to Decline in Firms, Organizations, and States*, Cambridge, MA: Harvard.

Hitt, M.A., R.E. Hoskisson and D.R. Ireland (1994), 'A mid-range theory of the interactive effects of international and product diversification on innovation and performance', *Journal of Management*, **20**, 297–326.

Hitt, M.A., R.E. Hoskisson, R.A. Johnson and D.D. Moesel (1996), 'The market for corporate control and firm innovation', *Academy of Management Journal*, **39** (5), 1084–1119.

Huse, M. (2000), 'Relational norms as a supplement to neo-classical understanding of directorates: an empirical study of boards of directors', *Journal of Socio-Economics*, **22**, 219–240.

Huse, M. (2005), 'Corporate governance: understanding important contingencies', *Corporate Ownership and Control*, **2** (4), 41–50.

Huse, M. (ed.) (2007), *Boards, Governance and Value Creation: The Human Side of Corporate Governance*, New York: Cambridge University Press.

Huse, M. and H. Landstrom (eds) (2001), *Corporate Governance in SMEs*, Halmstad: SIRE.

Huse, M., H. Landstrom and G. Corbetta (eds) (2002), *Governance in SMEs*, Oslo: BI.

Jensen, M. (1989), 'The eclipse of public corporation', *Harvard Business Review*, Sept-Oct. Available at SSRN: http://ssrn.com/abstract=146149 or http://dx. doi.org/10.2139/ssrn.146149.

Jensen, M.C. and W.H. Meckling (1976), 'Theory of the firm: managerial behavior, agency costs and ownership structure', *Journal of Financial Economics*, **3**, 305–360.

Kroll, M., P. Wright, L. Toombs and H. Leavell (1997), 'Form of control: a critical determinant of acquisition performance and CEO rewards', *Strategic Management Journal*, **18** (2), 85–96.

La Porta, R., F. Lopez-de-Silanes and A. Shleifer (1999), 'Corporate ownership around the world', *Journal of Finance*, **54** (2), 471–517.

Lansberg, I. (ed.) (1999), *Succeeding Generation: Realizing the Dream of Families in Business*, Boston, MA: Harvard Business School Press.

Leana, C.R. and H.J. Van Buren III (1999), 'Organizational social capital and employment practices', *Academy of Management Review*, **24** (3), 538–555.

Lubatkin, M., Y. Ling and W. Schulze (2007), 'An organizational justice-based view of self-control and agency costs in family firms', *Journal of Management Studies*, **44** (6), 955–971 (September).

Marris, R. (ed.) (1964), *The Economic Theory of Managerial Capitalism*, London: Macmillan.

Martin, H.F. (2004), 'Is family governance an oxymoron?', *Family Business Review*, **14** (2), 91–96.

Mayer, C. (2005), 'Venture capital and the corporate governance life cycle', in I. Filatotchev and M. Wright (eds), *The Life-cycle of Corporate Governance*, Cheltenham: Edward Elgar.

Miller, D., I. Le Breton-Miller, R.H. Lester and A.A. Cannella (2007), 'Are family firms really superior performers?', *Journal of Corporate Finance*, **13**, 829–858.

Mueller, D.C. (1972), 'A life cycle theory of the firm', *Journal of Industrial Economics*, **20**, 199–219.

Mustakallio, M., E. Autio and S.A. Zahra (2002), 'Relational and contractual governance in family firms: effects on strategic decision making', *Family Business Review*, **15** (3), 205–222.

Nahapiet, J. and S. Ghoshal (1998), 'Social capital, intellectual capital, and the organizational advantage', *Academy of Management Review*, **23** (2), 242–266.

Neubauer, F. and A. Lank (eds) (1998), *The Family Business: Its Governance for Sustainability*, New York: Routledge.

Pfeffer, J. and G.R. Salancik (eds) (1978), *The External Control of Organization: A Resource Dependence Perspective*, New York: Harper and Row.

Porter, M.E. (1985), *Competitive Advantage: Creating and Sustaining Superior Performance*, New York: The Free Press.

Porter, M.E. (ed.) (1986), *Competition in the Global Industry*, Boston, MA: Harvard Business School.

Porter, M.E. (ed.) (1990), *The Competitive Advantage of Nations*, New York: The Free Press.

Porter, M.E. (1992), 'Capital disadvantage: America's failing capital investment system', *Harvard Business Review*, **70**, 65–82.

Portes, A. (1998), 'Social capital: its origins and applications in modern sociology', *Annual Review of Sociology*, **24**, 1–24.

Sala-i-Martin, X., J. Blanke and F. Paua (2003), 'The growth competitiveness index: analyzing key underpinnings of economic growth', Global Competitiveness Report of the World Economic Forum, Geneva.

Salancik, G.R. and J. Pfeffer (1980), 'The effects of ownership and performance on executive tenure in US corporations', *Academy of Management Journal*, **23** (4), 653–664.

Scholes, L., M. Wright, P. Westhead, A. Burrows and H. Bruning (2007), 'Information sharing, price negotiation, and management buy-outs of private family-owned firms', *Small Business Economics*, **29**, 329–349.

Schulze, W.G., M.H. Lubatkin and R.N. Dino (2002), 'Altruism, agency and the competitiveness of family firms', *Managerial and Decision Economics*, **23** (4/5), 247–259.

Schulze, W.G., M.H. Lubatkin and R.N. Dino (2003), 'Toward a theory of agency and altruism in family firms', *Journal of Business Venturing*, **18** (4), 473–490.

Sharma, P. (2004), 'An overview of the field of family business studies: current status and directions for the future', *Family Business Review*, **17** (1), 1–36.

Shore, L.M. and S.J. Wayne (1993), 'Commitment and employee behavior: comparison of affective commitment and continuance commitment with perceived organizational support', *Journal of Applied Psychology*, **78** (5), 774–780.

Tajfel, H. and J.C. Turner (1985), 'The social identity theory of intergroup behavior', in S. Worchel and W.G. Austin (eds), *Psychology and Intergroup Relations*, 2nd edition, Chicago: Nelson-Hall, pp. 7–24.

Thompson, S. and M. Wright (1995), 'Corporate governance: the role of restructuring transactions', *Economic Journal*, **105** (430), 690–703.

Thomsen, S. and T. Pedersen (2000), 'Ownership structure and economic performance in the largest European companies', *Strategic Management Journal*, **21**, 689–705.

Tosi, H.L. and L.R. Gomez-Mejia (1989), 'The decoupling of CEO pay and performance: an agency theory perspective', *Administrative Science Quarterly*, **34**, 169–189.

Uhlaner, L., R. Floren and J. Geerlings (2007), 'Ownership commitment and relational governance in the privately-held firms. An empirical study', *Small Business Economics*, **29**, 275–293.

Uhlaner, L., M. Wright and M. Huse (2007), 'Private firms and corporate governance: an integrated economic and management perspective', *Small Business Economics*, **29**, 225–241.

Useem, M. (ed.) (1996), *Investor Capitalism: How Money Managers Are Changing the Face of Corporate America*, New York: Basic Books.

Vilaseca, A. (2002), 'The shareholder role in the family business: conflict of interests and objectives between nonemployed shareholders and top management team', *Family Business Review*, **15** (4), 299–320.

Wasserman, N. (2006), 'Stewards, agents, and the founder discount: executive compensation in new ventures', *Academy of Management Journal*, **49** (5), 960–976.

Williamson, O.E. (ed.) (1964), *The Economics of Discretionary Behavior: Managerial Objectives in a Theory of the Firm*, New York, Englewood Cliffs: Prentice Hall.

Zahra, S.A. and J.A. Pearce (1989), 'Board of directors and corporate financial performance: a review and integrative model', *Journal of Management*, **15** (2), 291–334.

Zahra, S.A., D.O. Neubaum and M. Huse (2000), 'Entrepreneurship in medium-size companies: exploring the effects of ownership and governance systems', *Journal of Management*, **26** (5), 947–976.

Zahra, S.A., D.O. Neubaum and L. Naldi (2007), 'The effects of ownership and governance on SMEs' international knowledge-based resources', *Small Business Economics*, **29** (3), 309–327 (October).

26 Competitive strategy research's impact on practice
Constantinos Markides

INTRODUCTION

More books on strategy are written and more journals are now dedicated to strategy research than ever before. Yet, all this output seems to fall on deaf ears. In a survey of 220 senior executives from 28 countries carried out at London Business School in 2006, more than 55 percent told us that they "almost never" read articles published in major managerial journals such as *HBR* and more than 82 percent claimed to "rarely if ever" implement what they read in books or journals. More than 90 percent said that they do not understand the papers published in the main strategy journal (*SMJ*) and more than half suggested that they spend less than 20 minutes on any given (business) book.

Why is the diffusion of ideas so low in the strategy field? Several possible answers have been proposed to us, such as: (a) the diffusion of ideas in strategy does not take place through books or journal articles but through classroom teaching; (b) the recipients of this new knowledge (the managers) do not need this knowledge to make informed decisions; (c) new knowledge in strategy gets incorporated in how managers think about issues rather than as tools or practices that are visible to outside observers; and so on. Even though all these reasons make sense, we aim to explore another one in this chapter. Specifically, we will argue that the 'product' itself (that is, ideas and knowledge on strategy) is not of high enough quality for consumers (that is, managers) to purchase and use, either because the producers of new knowledge (the academics) and their research are of low quality or the product itself is not well defined. Along with presenting our logic for this, we will also be offering our thoughts on how to improve the perceived impact of strategy research on practice.

A LOW-QUALITY 'PRODUCT'

Consider a senior executive who has to develop a strategy for their organization. What issues should this executive address in thinking about a new strategy and how should they think about them?

Pity the executive who turns to the management literature for guidance on this question! Despite its apparent simplicity, it is one of the most controversial issues in management, particularly among business academics. Academics seem to disagree about almost everything contained in this question: they disagree about the relevant issues that need to be addressed in developing strategy; about the process that a manager can go through to develop strategy; and about the actual physical output that one should have at the end of a strategy process. They even disagree over whether we can actually 'think' about strategy or not.

Disagreement One: What is Strategy, Really?

There is no question that every company needs a strategy, either explicit or implicit. Yet, there is surprisingly little agreement as to what strategy really is. Within both business and academic circles, it would be quite surprising if you could identify two people who shared the same definition of strategy. For example, consider the numerous ways that academics have defined strategy over the years: as positioning the company in its industry environment (Porter, 1980); as a collection of a few simple rules (Eisenhardt and Sull, 2001); as hustle (Bhide, 1986); as stretch and leverage (Hamel and Prahalad, 1993); as the embodiment of a company's values (Collins and Porras, 1994); and so on. Add to these the plethora of other possible definitions currently making the rounds (definitions which might include such hot concepts as strategic intent, vision, core competences, breaking the rules, learning, systems thinking and so on) and you begin to understand why even the *Economist* has claimed that[1] "Nobody really knows what strategy is."

Similar confusion and disagreements also exist on the process by which good strategies are developed. According to Gary Hamel, we are all experts after the fact in identifying companies with superior strategies but we have little to say on how these superior strategies were created in the first place or how other companies could develop similarly innovative strategies (Hamel, 1996). Along similar lines, the big debate that ensued following the publication of Michael Porter's 1996 *Harvard Business Review* article, 'What is Strategy?', was whether a company can choose its strategy through a rational thinking process or whether the strategy really emerges through a process of experimentation (Porter, 1996).

Interesting as these debates might be, when one goes beyond the rhetoric, one could identify two main schools of thought on what strategy is: on the one hand, we find the more Porterian view of strategy which emphasizes the positioning elements of strategy. This school views strategy primarily as positioning the company in its industry environment, which is another way of saying that strategy is all about choosing a good game to play. On the other hand, we find a second school of thought which considers positioning as 'static' and old news. Proponents of this school are encouraging us to embrace the new and more dynamic view of strategy which emphasizes outplaying and outmaneuvering our competitors, no matter what game they are playing. This way of thinking proposes that strategy is all about how you play the game rather than choosing what game to play (D'Aveni, 1994).

It should be quite obvious to all that strategy is both of these things: strategy must decide what game we want to play and then determine how to play that game well. Both are important decisions and both belong to strategy. Deciding what game to play boils down to making choices on two dimensions: who to target as customers and what to offer them. Determining how to play this game requires us to decide what value-chain activities we will perform (and what not to). Put the two together and it becomes quite clear that strategy is all about finding answers to three inter-related questions (Markides, 2000): Who will be my targeted customers? What products and services should I be offering? And how should I offer these products and services to my targeted customers in an efficient and innovative way?

It is true that most managers are pre-occupied with the 'how' question. It is also true that most companies do not bother to actively think about the 'who' and the 'what' questions – either because they do not think they cover strategic choices which the company makes or because they think that once they've made these choices they should never revisit them. But it is also true that most breakthroughs in strategy occur not so much when the 'how' is questioned but when the 'who-what' choices are challenged. Innovations in strategy usually take place when companies question and challenge the answers they gave (a long time ago in their history) to the 'who-what' questions (Markides, 1997).

Disagreement Two: How do we Develop Strategy?

The discussion so far has focused on the question: 'what is strategy?' It is obvious that differences of opinion exist as to the answer to this question. Unfortunately, similar confusion and disagreements also exist on the process by which good strategies are developed. As argued by Gary Hamel

(1997): ". . .the *practice* of strategy must be reinvented. Sorry, did I say *re-invent*? Let's not pretend. There's little that's worth *re*-inventing. Surely we're not going to start with the traditional planning process in our quest to increase the value-added of strategy! No, we must start from scratch."

The big disagreements on the process of creating strategy revolve around two issues: first, can we plan for strategy or do good strategies emerge through experimentation and trial and error? This addresses the design versus emergent schools of thought (Ansoff, 1991; Grant, 2003; Mintzberg, 1990 and 1991; Pascale, 1984; Sinha, 1990). Second, in developing strategy do we start with an analysis of the market and then think what we need to do in this market or do we start with an analysis of our existing core competences and think how to build competitive advantage on the back of these competences? – The industrial organization school versus the resource-based view of the firm (Barney, 2006; Prahalad and Hamel, 1990; Porter, 1980).

CAN WE PLAN STRATEGY?

A marvelous articulation of the first debate (i.e. can we plan strategy?) is found in the exchange of letters between Porter on the one side and MacMillan and McGrath (1997) on the other, following Porter's article, 'What is Strategy?' Whereas Porter seems to imply that strategy can be a well-thought-out plan of action, MacMillan and McGrath argue that strategy is nothing more than the final outcome of a process of trial and error and learning by doing.

As before, the answer to this debate lies somewhere in the middle of these two extreme points of view: strategy must encompass both ends of this spectrum. On the one hand, it has to be thought out and planned at a general level; on the other hand, it must remain flexible and adaptable to new learning and changes in the market. Although analysis will not produce a full-fledged strategy ready to be implemented, it does help us narrow the options. Experimentation can then follow on a limited number of options so that the dead ends can be identified and the 'unexpected' opportunities uncovered. It would take a hopelessly romantic planner to argue that in-depth analysis alone is what creates masterful strategies. However, it would be equally silly to pretend that analysis or thinking are not necessary ingredients and that trial and error alone will give rise to a winning strategy. Both are essential elements of strategy: analysis sketches the skeleton of a possible strategy; experimentation allows us to refine, add or change altogether our original skeleton.

The process of developing superior strategies is part planning, part trial and error until you hit upon something that works. Sometimes you start with the planning part and then adjust what you have through trial and error. Other times you start with trial and error and then use planning to fine-tune the system.

Strategy-making must encompass both elements of this spectrum. This point must be emphasized because it has become popular lately for people to argue that in today's volatile environment, planning is useless – by the time you decide on a plan, the claim goes, the environment has changed so much that your plan is no longer valid. The best you can do is to develop an organizational environment that allows superior ideas and strategies to emerge through day to day experimentation by everybody in the organization.

Without denying the importance of developing such an organizational environment, I'd like to argue that this is not enough. A company that relies only on trial and error to develop its strategy is like a rudderless ship being torn apart in the middle of the ocean. The parameters within which the firm will operate must be developed before experimentation is allowed to take place; and these parameters can only be developed by top management – not by just anybody in the organization. Experimentation without clear boundaries will lead to chaos, confusion and ultimately a de-motivated workforce. Similarly, top managers that shy away from deciding the parameters within which their people can maneuver (in the name of democracy and flexibility), are abdicating one of the most crucial responsibilities of leadership.

Therefore, to repeat my main point, the ideas that make up a strategy (such as what customers to target or what products to sell) can emerge through careful planning or after experimentation. Anybody in the organization can come up with these ideas, but it is the responsibility of top management to decide what will be implemented and what will be discarded.

WHERE DO WE START OUR ANALYSIS?

The second debate on creating strategy stems not so much from disagreements as differences in emphasis: should we start our strategy process by analyzing the external market or should we start by building upon our existing competences? The first approach emphasizes an external orientation while the second approach stresses an internal one.

Needless to say, consideration of both the outside market and the inside competences must underpin any strategy development – after all, the goal is to discover a fit between the inside and the outside so consideration must be given to both. However, how we decide to start will ultimately determine how creative we are in thinking of strategic options.

This is because most companies have a dominant way of thinking about strategy – some start with the outside market and try to decide what to do while others start with their internal competences and try to leverage them. The problem is that, after following the dominant way of thinking a few times, people become comfortable in that way of thinking and passive thinking sets in. As a result, we don't really think about the issues in a creative way. For this to happen, people must become 'uncomfortable'.

Therefore, innovations in strategy take place when a company is able to switch from its dominant way of thinking to an alternative way. It is this continuous switching from one way of thinking to another and the continuous switching from one sequence of questions to another that 'wakes up' the mind and prompts active thinking. And it is active thinking that leads to strategic innovation. This implies that sometimes a company must start its strategy process with an external orientation and then switch to an internal orientation. At other times, it should start with an internal orientation and then switch to an external one. It is the continuous switching from one to the other which is crucial, not picking one of them as the 'right' one.

A 'PRODUCT' THAT IS NOT VERY WELL DEFINED

The second major problem with strategy today is that we often confuse tools and frameworks for the strategy itself while rational analysis of data has become the accepted way to develop strategy. Strategic thinking and strategic planning in the modern corporation have degenerated into a search for 'the formulae of success' where wishful thinking (stargazing), sexy slogans (vision statements) and/or non-thinking and logical analysis of data have replaced true strategic thinking. In many companies, strategic planning takes the form of mindless number crunching and endless projections whose ultimate purpose is to prepare huge reports that nobody will read.

Inevitably, there has been a backlash against such waste of company time and resources. One response has been to get rid of the strategic planning department and to abandon strategic planning altogether. Another response has been to emphasize the importance of emergent strategies over planned ones – that is, strategies that apparently emerge over time through experimentation and trial and error. Yet another response has been the recent rise of the democratic way to develop strategy – where everybody in the organization is expected to put on their army-general hats and contribute to the development of the company's strategy. My position is that all these reactions are unnecessary and the wrong medicine for the problem at hand.

Strategy should be a mixture of rational thinking and creativity; of analysis and experimentation; of planning and learning. Researchers who have examined how the eyes of chess masters move during a competitive game have found that once their opponent has made a move, the chess master's eyes will go straight to the best move possible 75 percent of the time. However, after this initial reaction, the chess master's eyes will evaluate other possible moves before eventually returning (75 percent of the time) to the original best move. This suggests that chess masters rise to the top on the basis of creativity and analysis. Strategy should not be any different.

To be effective, strategic thinking should be creative and intuitive (rather than just rational) and should be based on (but not substituted by) analysis. Effective strategic thinking is a process of continuously asking questions and thinking through the issues in a creative way. Thus, correctly formulating the questions is often more important than finding a 'solution'; thinking through an issue from a variety of angles is often more productive than collecting and analyzing unlimited data; and actually experimenting with new ideas is often more critical than scientific analysis and discussion.

Unfortunately, as Kenichi Ohmae has commented in *The Mind of the Strategist*, the culture of the modern corporation exalts logic and rationality; hence, it is analysts rather than innovators who tend to get ahead (Ohmae, 1982).

To be effective, strategic thinking should be a creative thinking process based on real facts and analysis which tries to combine the rational with the emotional. Thus, the essence of effective strategic thinking is (a) to think through the issues in a creative way; and (b) to not only come up with innovative new ideas but to generate the necessary emotional commitment on the part of the organization that will result in people actually changing their behaviors to effectively implement these new ideas. A good strategy must, therefore, balance:

- the emotional with the logical and rational;
- the thinking process with the application and implementation of ideas;
- creative jumps with the analysis of facts.

Most strategy books and most teaching on strategy tend to focus on the techniques and the analytical tools that people can use in developing strategy, forgetting that tools are not a substitute for thinking. Any manager entrusted with developing strategy must understand that the thinking process that they go through is more important than finding 'the answer'; and that strategy is based more on creativity than analysis.

A major reason for the current sad state of affairs is the way we teach strategy at business schools. When one looks at how companies develop strategy, the process that they use (either formally or in the CEO's head) is one of trying to find answers to specific questions, such as: who are my competitors and how can I position myself relative to them? Who are my customers and how can I satisfy their needs? What are the key success factors in this business and what can I do to develop a competitive advantage? What changes are taking place in my business and how should I react to them?

Yet, when one opens any strategy book (which supposedly aims to help managers develop a strategy), one very rarely finds the book devoted to helping managers to ask and answer these questions. What you find instead is a book with chapter titles such as 'Cost and differentiation strategies' or 'Analyzing the environment'. In other words, we do not structure our books in the way a manager thinks of strategy but in self-contained chunks of knowledge which we then expect the manager to assemble into a strategy.

This implies that the strategy field is in need of process reengineering. We never look at the issue of how to develop strategy from the customer's point of view. We are – like every other organization in this world – supply-driven. We therefore teach our MBA students a course on Marketing, a course on Finance and a course on Organizational Behavior (OB) and we then expect them to do the integration. Our strategy books provide the intellectual inputs that go into a strategy but we then leave it up to the customer to put it all together and develop the strategy.

However, our customers do not think like this. They have certain questions to answer, such as: 'Who are my competitors and what shall I do to gain competitive advantage over them?' In answering this question, they have to use some knowledge from marketing and some from OB. But they do not care if some of this knowledge we call marketing and some OB. Just like a customer who doesn't care if it is the front desk or the room service people who messed up his stay at the hotel, the customer of strategy is not interested in the labels we put on our different inputs. What they want is a total service from us. Thus, to be truly customer-driven, we need to identify all the relevant questions that a manager needs to address and then help this manager think through these questions.

The worst side-effect of our tendency to be supply-driven rather than customer-driven is the chasm that has been created between strategy formulation and implementation. We have very little to say to our customers about how to do anything. We have been preoccupied with telling them how to think about something and we left them to do it as they saw fit. It is only when we think in terms of the questions that they themselves think that it becomes impossible for us not to think of the implementation issues as well. It is only when we look at the issues as they (the customers) see them that formulation and implementation cease to be two separate entities and, as if by magic, fuse into one.

A 'PRODUCT' WHICH LACKS PERSPECTIVE

The third and final problem with strategy today is that it is ahistorical – that is, it does not place a company in its historical context. Yet, what a company needs to do and what strategy it needs to follow are often contingent on where in its evolution that company is. For example, whether a company should 'stick to its knitting' or diversify out of its core depends to a large extent on whether a technological innovation is about to destroy the company's core. Similarly, whether a company should try to be better than its competitors or try instead to be different by breaking the rules of the game depends primarily on where in its evolution that company's industry is located.

Failure to think of companies in such a dynamic way has resulted in two major problems. The first and more apparent problem is the conflicting and contradictory advice given to companies by academics or consultants. Examples abound: following the success of the book *In Search of Excellence* (Peters and Waterman, 1982) companies were advised to stick to their knitting. Yet, another consultant (Richard Foster) from the same firm (McKinsey) in his study of technological innovations (Foster, 1986) suggested that the last thing a company wants to do is stick to its knitting. Similarly, Ted Levitt (1960) argued in his influential article 'Marketing Myopia' that companies should define their business according to the underlying functionality of their products. Yet, Hermann Simon (1996), in his study of German success stories (*The Hidden Champions*) found that these German companies succeeded by defining their business narrowly, according to the product they were selling. Finally, a well-known dictum from marketing is that companies should stay close to and listen to their customers. Yet, the article that won the McKinsey award in the 1995 *HBR* argued that companies that pay too much attention to their existing customers at times of technological change will fail (Bower and Christensen, 1995). All these examples are meant to show that no advice – however sound and practical – will apply to all the firms all the time. What a firm should do depends on its own particular circumstances, which are in turn determined by where in its evolution that company is. Strategic advice that fails to put the company in its historical context runs the risk of being dangerous advice.

The second problem with being ahistorical is the failure of strategy to consider how a company's past as well as its future influence its strategic choices of today. What the company does today will determine what options the company has tomorrow. This should have an effect on what the company decides to do. Similarly, just because the future has not happened yet, it does not mean that a company cannot do anything about it today to prepare for things to come. For example, every company ought to know that its product will eventually mature and will most likely be replaced by another product made possible by a technological innovation. This will happen some time in the future but surely the company's strategy today ought to take this into consideration. It should therefore ask: 'What can I do today to make sure that, when the death of my product arrives, I am ready for it?' It should not wait for this to happen before doing anything.

A DYNAMIC VIEW OF STRATEGY

There is no question that success stems from the exploitation of a distinctive or unique strategy and that strategy is nothing more than the answers we have given to the 'who-what-how' questions. Unfortunately, no position will remain unique or attractive forever. Not only do attractive positions get imitated by aggressive competitors but also – and perhaps more importantly – new strategic positions are emerging all the time. A new strategic position is simply a new viable who-what-how combination – perhaps a new customer segment (a new who), or a new value proposition (a new what), or a new way of distributing or manufacturing the product (a new how). Over time, these new positions may grow to challenge the attractiveness of our own position.

This happens in industry after industry: once formidable companies that built their success on what seemed to be unassailable strategic positions find themselves humbled by relatively unknown companies which base their attacks on creating and exploiting new strategic positions in the industry.

New strategic positions – that is, new who-what-how combinations – emerge all around us all the time. As industries change, new strategic positions emerge to challenge existing positions for supremacy. Changing industry conditions, changing customer needs or preferences, countermoves by competitors and a company's own evolving competences give rise to new opportunities and the potential for new ways of playing the game. Unless a company continuously questions its accepted norms and behaviors, it will never discover what else has become available. It will miss these new combinations and other, more agile players will jump in and exploit the gaps left behind.

Therefore, a company must never settle for what it has. While fighting it out in its current position, it must continuously search for new positions to colonize and new opportunities to take advantage of. Simple as this may sound, it contrasts sharply with the way most competitors compete in their industries: most of them take the established rules of the game as given and spend all their time trying to become better than each other in their existing positions – usually through cost or differentiation strategies. Little or no emphasis is placed at becoming different from competitors. This is evidenced from the fact that the majority of companies which strategically innovate by breaking the rules of the game tend to be small niche players or new market entrants. It is indeed rare to find a strategic innovator who is also an established industry big player – a fact that hints at the difficulties of risking the sure thing for something uncertain.

There are many reasons why established companies find it hard to become strategic innovators. Compared to new entrants or niche players, leaders are weighed down by structural and cultural inertia, internal politics, complacency, fear of cannibalizing existing products, fear of destroying existing competences, satisfaction with the status quo, and a general absence of incentives to abandon a certain present for an uncertain future. In addition, since there are fewer industry leaders than potential new entrants, the chances that the innovator will emerge from the ranks of the leaders is unavoidably small.

Despite such obstacles, established companies cannot afford not to strategically innovate. As already pointed out, dramatic shifts in company fortunes can only take place if a company succeeds in not only playing its game better than its rivals but in also designing and playing a different game from its competitors. Strategic innovation has the potential to take third-rate companies and elevate them to industry leadership status; and it can take established industry leaders and destroy them in a short period of time. Even if the established players do not want to strategically innovate (for fear of destroying their existing profitable positions), somebody else will. Established players might as well pre-empt that before it happens.

The culture that established players must develop is that strategies are not cast in concrete. A company needs to remain flexible and ready to adjust its strategy if the feedback from the market is not favorable. More importantly, a company needs to continuously question the way it operates in its current position while still fighting it out in its current position against existing competitors.

Continuously questioning one's accepted strategic position serves two vital purposes: first, it allows a company to identify early enough whether its current position in the business is losing its attractiveness to others (and so decide what to do about it); second and more importantly, it gives the company the opportunity to proactively explore the emerging terrain and hopefully be the first to discover new and attractive strategic positions to take advantage of. This is no guarantee: questioning one's accepted answers will not automatically lead to new unexploited goldmines. But even a remote possibility of discovering something new will never come up if the questions are never asked.

HOW TO IMPROVE THE IMPACT OF STRATEGY RESEARCH ON PRACTICE

Can we, as academics, improve the state of affairs? Can we do anything that would ensure that our research has more impact on practice? I believe that for such an outcome to emerge, we need to do three things.

First, we need to stop hiding behind words and get precise with our definitions. Everybody talks about 'strategy' as if it's one thing and yet we all have different definitions in mind. This can only produce confusion and disagreements. Let me highlight this disease by talking a bit about another strategy topic that has also been abused by lack of precision and loose language: the topic of innovation.

We all agree that every company wants to achieve growth and profitability and what better way to do so than by creating totally new market space through innovation? Hence, innovation is a good thing! While this is pretty obvious and non-controversial, the devil is always in the detail. For example, what exactly does the phrase 'create new market space through innovation' mean?

New markets could be created in a variety of ways. For example, Apple, 3M and Nestlé created new market space by discovering the iPod, Post-It and Nespresso, respectively. This is what we traditionally call product innovation. On the other hand, Enterprise Rent-A-Car created the huge 'replacement' market in the car rental industry without even introducing a new product – they did it by being creative in how they segmented the market. Similarly, Schwab and Amazon created new market space by utilizing the internet to grow online brokerage and bookselling respectively: this is what we now call business-model innovation. And Canon, Honda and P&G did it by using innovative strategies to scale up existing product niches – the copier, motorcycle and disposable diaper markets respectively – and convert them into mass markets.

All these companies utilized innovation to create new market space but the type of innovation that Apple used is fundamentally different from the type of innovation that Enterprise used. The point is that 'innovation' is not one thing. There exist different types of innovation – such as product, technological, business-model and so on – all of which are capable of creating new market space. And it should come as no surprise to hear that what a company needs to do to achieve one type of innovation is totally different to what it must do to achieve another type of innovation. This implies that the question 'how can I make my company more innovative?' does not make sense! A useful prescription cannot be given unless we first specify what specific type of innovation we aspire to achieve.

The same could be said about strategy. How can we offer useful prescriptions to managers on how to develop and implement value-creating strategies if we cannot even agree on what strategy really is?

The second thing that we need to do is to change the way we do our research. Let's not forget that we are the ones advising companies to change their ways of operating and embrace 'open' innovation. Shouldn't we be willing to take some of our own medicine? At the organizational level, what open innovation implies for business schools is the need to go beyond the school boundaries for help. Either through alliances with external bodies (such as consulting firms) or by working closely with corporate universities, a business school could bring its academic faculty closer to the managerial world. At the individual level, open innovation implies that researchers need to begin working on research projects with non-academics – such as consultants and managers – or academics from other disciplines.

Finally, we need to appreciate that we can influence practice not only through publications but also through our teaching. This means that we should be willing to bring more of our own research findings into the classroom. If we truly believe this, perhaps we could develop incentives that reward people who utilize their research findings in their teaching. Or maybe business schools should forbid faculty from developing and teaching an elective course unless they bring their own research findings into their elective teaching. Whatever we choose to do, it should be obvious that talk is cheap: only a structural change to the academic system (our academic values and incentives) can bring a lasting change in our behaviors.

NOTE

1.   *The Economist*, March 20, 1993, p. 106.

REFERENCES

Ansoff, H.I. (1991), 'The design school: reconsidering the basic premises of strategic manage-
    ment', *Strategic Management Journal*, **12** (6), 449–451.
Barney, J. (ed.) (2006), *Gaining and Sustaining Competitive Advantage*, 3rd edition, Upper
    Saddle River, NJ: Prentice Hall.
Bhide, A. (1986), 'Hustle as strategy', *Harvard Business Review*, **64** (5), 59–65.
Bower, J. and C. Christensen (1995), 'Disruptive technologies: catching the wave', *Harvard
    Business Review*, January–February, 43–53.
Collins, J. and J. Porras (eds) (1994), *Built to Last: Successful Habits of Visionary Companies*,
    New York: HarperBusiness.
D'Aveni, R. (1994), *Hypercompetition: Managing the Dynamics of Strategic Maneuvering*,
    New York: The Free Press.
Eisenhardt, K.M. and D. Sull (2001), 'Strategy as simple rules', *Harvard Business Review*,
    79 (1), 107–116.
Foster, R. (ed.) (1986), *Innovation: The Attacker's Advantage*, New York: Summit Books.
Grant, R.M. (2003), 'Strategic planning in a turbulent environment: evidence from the oil
    majors', *Strategic Management Journal*, **24** (6), 491–517.
Hamel, G. (1996), 'Strategy as revolution', *Harvard Business Review*, July–August, 69–82.
Hamel, G. (1997), 'The search for strategy', unpublished working paper, London: Business
    School.
Hamel, G. and C.K. Prahalad (1993), 'Strategy as stretch and leverage', *Harvard Business
    Review*, **71** (2), 75–84.
Levitt, T. (1960), 'Marketing myopia', *Harvard Business Review*, July–August.
MacMillan, I. and R. Gunther McGrath (1997), letter published in *Harvard Business Review*,
    January–February, 154–156.
Markides, C. (1997), 'Strategic innovation', *Sloan Management Review*, **38** (3), 9–23.
Markides, C. (ed.) (2000), *All the Right Moves: A Guide to Crafting Breakthrough Strategy*,
    Boston, MA: Harvard Business School Press.
Mintzberg, H. (1990), 'The design school: reconsidering the basic premises of strategic man-
    agement', *Strategic Management Journal*, **11** (6), 171–195.
Mintzberg, H. (1991), 'Learning 1, planning 0', *Strategic Management Journal*, **12** (6),
    464–466.
Ohmae, K. (ed.) (1982), *The Mind of the Strategist*, New York: McGraw-Hill.
Pascale, R.T. (1984), 'Perspectives on strategy: the real story behind Honda's success',
    California Management Review, **26** (3), 47–72.
Peters, T. and R. Waterman (eds) (1982), *In Search of Excellence*, London: HarperCollins.
Porter, M.E. (ed.) (1980), *Competitive Strategy*, New York: The Free Press.
Porter, M.E. (1996), 'What is strategy?', *Harvard Business Review*, November–December,
    61–78.
Prahalad, C.K. and G. Hamel (1990), 'The core competence of the corporation', *Harvard
    Business Review*, May–June, 79–91.
Simon, H. (ed.) (1996), *Hidden Champions*, Boston, MA: HBS Press.
Sinha, K. and Deepak (1990), 'The contribution of formal planning to decisions', *Strategic
    Management Journal*, **11** (6), 479–492.

Index

internal development 283, 293
internal factors 28, 34–36
internal market competences 565–566
International Business (IB) 360,
    368–369
internationalization strategies 31–32,
    132
internet as data source 393
interorganizational field 171
interpretation 152–153
    of actions 158
    analysis 383
    of responses 160
    semiotic methods and annual
        reports 409, 412
    structures 154
interpretive analysis 383, 387, 388, 391,
    392, 395
interviews and field studies 386, 387,
    390
investment 229
    choices 523
    decisions 330–331
    exploratory 333–334
    relational specific 367
    see also financial structure of firms;
        ownership of firms, corporate
        governance and investment
investors 254
invisibility and supply inelasticity 127
Irizar 485, 488–491
Italy 498
iterations (computer simulation
    modeling) 416–417, 419

Jefferson, T. 489
Jensen-Meckling incentives 315
joint ventures 265, 267–270, 272,
    273–274, 275, 494–495
    duration 273–274
    dyadic 275
    instability 273–274
    multi-party 275
    ownership structure 273
    termination 272
Jomini, A.-H. de 49
judgment tasks 390, 391, 394

knowledge:
    -base 28, 169–170

-based improvement 36–37
-based resources in strategic alliance
    formation 266
-based theory 115
-based view of firm 52
entrepreneurship 336
external 294
flows and innovation and
    technology management 286
literature 60–61
multinational firms 366–367, 368
spillovers 94, 96–97
structure, preexisting 174–175
tacit 95, 301
transfer 95
trust 450

language games 158
leadership 92, 241, 484
leakage 291
learning 84–85, 86, 366–367, 368
    creative and imaginary 196–197
    entrepreneurship 328
    experiential 196
    maximization 332
    organizational 301
    -race perspective 266
    see also knowledge
legal infrastructure 96
legitimacy 156–157, 403–404, 405, 406,
    408–409
leverage 526–527, 529–530, 531
licenses 270
licensing policy 219, 226–227
linear regression techniques 383, 387,
    390, 392, 395
linkages creation 369
Linux 475, 481
liquidity 310
lock-in 194
longitudinal approach 257, 386–387,
    391, 393–394, 448
loyalty 445
    programs 228

M-form hypothesis 428
macro-conditions 182–184, 185–186,
    189–190, 191–197
management:
    board 551

realism 64
philosophical 66
reciprocal adaptation 160
Red Queen theory 99
reductionism 65–66, 67–68, 75
black boxes and structures 68
and methodological individualism
68–70
and scientific progress 66–67
regression techniques 387, 388, 391
regulations 30
reinforcement 470–471, 472–473, 474
relatedness and corporate governance
310
relational capital 308
relational embeddedness 275
relational governance 270
relational networks/ties 175
relational view in alliance formation
and dynamics 275
relationships, interfirm non formal 124
reliability 89, 404
rents:
appropriation 76, 138–139
distribution 269
Schumpeterian 328
see also economic rents
replicability 238
repositioning strategy 494
representative model of competitive
strategy 26–36
external factors 28–34
internal factors 34–36
reputation 148–149, 156–157, 173, 446
business models 472
family businesses 351, 353
multinational firms 366
research & development (R&D) 36–37,
281, 284–289, 293–294, 310
intensity 477
multinational firms 364
research directions in competitive
strategy 83–100
ecological processes 97–99
geographic location 94
group rivalry 93–94
groups 91–93
interfirm networks 88
multimarket rivalry 87–88
multimarket structure 86–87

multiunit rivalry 85–86
multiunit structure 84–85
network structure 88–91
spatial structure 94–97
research time frames trend 386
resignations and firings 404
resource/resources 93, 159
allocation 225
competitive positions 186
complementary 219, 227–229
and corporate strategy 132
definition 114–115
dependence theory 303, 316, 546
endowment 244
financial 338
and firm performance 131–132
identification and use of 360
intangible 115
integration 244
multinational firms 365
partitioning theory 98
-picking 126
quantity of 522
scarcity 140, 329, 340
slack 248–249
strategic 129, 134
and strategic alliances 132–133
and strategic networks (systems)
133–134
tangible 114–115
transfer/sharing/exploitation 256
see also resource-based theory
resource-based theory 51–53, 58–59,
64, 70, 73–74, 76–77, 109–141, 564
capabilities 115
causal ambiguity 112
clean state opportunity set situation
111
competitive advantage 114, 118
competitive positions 182–183
core competencies 115
corporate governance 301, 308
dynamic 7
economic rents (definition) 114
entrepreneurship 135, 327
factor market competition and
economic rents 117–118
family businesses 48–49, 346–347,
349, 355
heterogeneity 116–117, 118